Linda Konnerth
A Grammar of Karbi

Mouton Grammar Library

Edited by
Georg Bossong
Bernard Comrie
Patience L. Epps
Irina Nikolaeva

Volume 82

Linda Konnerth
A Grammar of Karbi

DE GRUYTER
MOUTON

ISBN 978-3-11-099207-6
ISSN 0933-7636

Library of Congress Control Number: 2020931427

Bibliographic information published by the Deutsche Nationalbibliothek
The Deutsche Nationalbibliothek lists this publication in the Deutsche Nationalbibliografie;
detailed bibliographic data are available on the Internet at http://dnb.dnb.de.

© 2022 Walter de Gruyter GmbH, Berlin/Boston
This volume is text- and page-identical with the hardback published in 2020.
Typesetting: Integra Software Services Pvt. Ltd.
Printing and binding: CPI books GmbH, Leck

www.degruyter.com

Acknowledgments

This grammar is a revised version of my doctoral dissertation, which I completed at the University of Oregon in 2014. I remain grateful to everybody I acknowledge in my dissertation. In addition, I am most grateful to my wonderful editor Pattie Epps, who had excellent comments and suggestions, which in many ways improved this grammar. The revisions I have carried out were also influenced by the feedback from the ALT's Panini award committee, headed by Nick Enfield, as well as by Scott DeLancey, whose research never ceases to inspire me. My colleague and partner Pavel Ozerov has supported my work for the publication of this grammar as well as all my other research in all possible ways. In the final stages of proof-reading and getting the manuscript ready for print, I was lucky to receive tremendous help from Raphael Kraut, and I am also very thankful to the professional and friendly de Gruyter Mouton team.

For the original research that led to the first version of this grammar and my dissertation, my deepest gratitude goes to my mentor Scott DeLancey. In addition to sharing his knowledge, Scott has always supported me, inspired me, and led me back to see the big picture when I was lost in details. The Karbi descriptive grammar project was born in 2007 when members of the *Karbi Lammet Amei* (Karbi Literary Association) contacted Scott. This was serendipitous, as Scott had just weeks earlier given me the late Karl-Heinz Grüßner's 1978 grammar of Karbi phonology and morphology to look at; I happily took on this exciting project. Before my first trip to India, I was able to get in touch with Karl-Heinz and visited him in Tübingen, Germany, where he let me into the magical realm of his attic. I spent hours perusing his notes, transcriptions, and other Karbi materials he had collected. Meeting and getting to know Karl-Heinz was a very special experience and I will always remember and be grateful for his generosity, encouragement, and the friendly welcome I received from him and his family, both in Tübingen and in Shillong. Karl-Heinz suddenly passed away in 2014 but he lives on in his invaluable work on the Karbi language, as well as in the memories we have of his warm and friendly personality and the jokes he was never short of.

During my first trip to India I met Sikari Tisso, who was to become my main language consultant and collaborator, and who made everything possible. His dedication and tireless efforts make him a true hero for all who value the wonderful language and culture of the Karbi people. While this project was ongoing, his son passed away much too young; this grammar is also dedicated to the memory of Sarpo Rongkhelan Tisso.

I am deeply grateful to UV Jose. His enormous knowledge of the languages in the area and of the people speaking them as well as his generosity and advice inspired and helped me during all this time. Many thanks also to Brother Benjamin Ingti Kathar, who shared his language and warm friendship with me.

This project would not have existed without the effort of the *Karbi Lammet Amei* to preserve their beautiful and rich language and inherent culture and knowledge for future generations. Khorsing Teron as well as Dharamsing Teron (not actually a KLA member) volunteered much time and effort to the project. Thanks also to Hokursing Rongpi, and to Budheswar Timung (Nowgong KLA). Due to space limitations, other Karbi speakers that have made this project possible are acknowledged in §2.3.1.

I would like to thank Amphu Rongpipi, Klirdap Teronpi, Serdihun Beypi, Larshika Tissopi, and Sarlomet Tisso, who all greatly contributed to the project by preparing transcriptions, struggling through translations, and helping with the analysis.

None of my research would have been possible without a place for me to stay. In Diphu, *Kro hem* always had their doors open for me: Sashikola Hansepi, Member Kro, Ruplin, Sintu, Rasinza, and Sampri. Jirsong Asong in Diphu also offered me a warm and friendly place to stay - many thanks to Fr. Vinod! In Umswai, I stayed with the wonderful Hanse family: Albina Teronpi, Holiwel Hanse, Hunmily, Basapi, John, and Platinum.

At the University of Oregon, my dissertation committee offered great feedback and plenty of food for thought: thank you to Spike Gildea, Doris Payne, and Zhuo Jing-Schmidt! More generally, I feel very fortunate and grateful about my time at the Linguistics Department at the University of Oregon, where I received support, friendship, and encouragement from many sides. Thanks in particular also to my then fellow grad students, Shahar Shirtz, Amos Teo, Krishna Boro, Danielle Barth, Anna Pucilowski, Dan Wood, and especially Gwen Hyslop.

I am grateful to a number of other linguists who have given me feedback on my work and have inspired me, in particular, Northeast Indianists Mark Post, Stephen Morey, and Jyotiprakash Tamuli; Tibeto-Burmanists David Bradley, Christina Willis, Dave Peterson, Stephen Watters, and Robert Schikowski; as well as Antoine Guillaume.

This research was funded in part by National Science Foundation Grant # BCS-0951749. At the UO, further support was provided by the Center for the Study of Women in Society; the Center for Asian and Pacific Studies; and the Oregon Humanities Center. I was working through the revisions while in residence at the Martin Buber Society of Fellows at the Hebrew University of Jerusalem, whose support and engaging research environment is also gratefully acknowledged.

Finally, I have always had incredible support from my family and friends, and none of my work would have been possible without them. I have received love, encouragement, and advice from Roswitha, Arthur, Arne, Sascha, Irmi, Juli, Franzi, and everybody else in my extended family and of my wonderful friends; they all sustained me when I was writing my dissertation, and they all sustained me when I, with new challenges and new priorities, worked through the revisions. The revisions were supposed to be finished before Yaniv arrived, but they did not – and consequently, with much less time on my hands for the best reason possible, they could not have been finished without Pasha, my partner in life in every sense.

Contents

Acknowledgments —— V

List of Figures —— XXIII

List of Tables —— XXV

1	Introduction —— 1	
1.1	Karbi people, language, and culture —— 1	
1.1.1	Names and ISO codes for the Karbi language —— 1	
1.1.2	Number of speakers and geographical spread of Karbi —— 2	
1.1.3	Aspects of Karbi culture —— 3	
1.1.3.1	Traditional culture and social organization —— 3	
1.1.3.2	Oral literature —— 5	
1.1.3.3	Song language —— 7	
1.1.4	The Karbi Lammet Amei (KLA) —— 8	
1.1.5	The Karbi Anglong and West Karbi Anglong districts —— 8	
1.2	Karbi in Tibeto-Burman —— 9	
1.2.1	Tibeto-Burman languages of Northeast India —— 9	
1.2.2	Karbi in Tibeto-Burman classification proposals —— 10	
1.3	On the role of contact in the development of Karbi —— 12	
1.3.1	Linguistic evidence for contact with Austroasiatic, Indo-Aryan, and other Tibeto-Burman languages —— 12	
1.3.2	Non-linguistic evidence for contact with populations speaking Austroasiatic and Indo-Aryan languages —— 14	
1.3.3	A creolization account for grammatical characteristics of Karbi —— 16	
1.3.3.1	Areal ethnolinguistic profile —— 17	
1.3.3.2	Aspects of a "creoloid" grammatical profile —— 18	
1.3.3.3	Non-obligatoriness of grammatical markers —— 19	
1.3.4	Summary —— 22	
1.4	Varieties of the Karbi language —— 23	
1.4.1	Plains Karbi ("Amri Karbi") and Hills Karbi —— 24	
1.4.2	Relationships between the Hills Karbi 'dialects' —— 25	
1.4.3	Hills Karbi: Differences between Rongkhang (Hills Karbi; Diphu) and Amri (Hills Karbi; West Karbi Anglong) dialects —— 26	
1.4.4	Variation in lexemes —— 27	
1.5	Sociolinguistic profile of language endangerment —— 28	
1.5.1	Setting factors —— 28	
1.5.2	Domains/vitality/attitudes —— 29	
1.5.3	Other factors —— 30	
1.5.4	Summary of degree of endangerment —— 30	

1.6	Previous study of Karbi grammar —— 31	
1.6.1	Early work on Karbi —— 31	
1.6.2	Karl-Heinz Grüßner's work —— 31	
1.6.3	Longkam Teron's work —— 32	
1.6.4	Other resources on Karbi grammar and lexicon —— 33	
1.7	Writing in Karbi and conventions followed in this grammar —— 33	
1.8	Organization of this grammar —— 35	
2	**Methodology and data —— 36**	
2.1	Approach and theoretical framework —— 36	
2.1.1	Functional-typological framework —— 36	
2.1.2	Collaboration with the language community —— 37	
2.1.3	Historical-comparative perspective —— 38	
2.2	Corpus —— 38	
2.2.1	Data types —— 38	
2.2.2	Access to the corpus —— 39	
2.3	Primary data collection —— 39	
2.3.1	Acknowledgment of Karbi speakers that facilitated data collection —— 40	
2.3.2	Data collecting team —— 41	
2.3.3	Recorded speakers: Ethical considerations —— 41	
2.3.4	Recorded genres —— 42	
2.3.5	Recording procedures and settings —— 43	
2.4	Data annotation and presentation —— 45	
3	**Phonology —— 48**	
3.1	Consonants —— 48	
3.1.1	Consonant onsets —— 48	
3.1.1.1	Stop onset minimal sets —— 51	
3.1.1.2	Fricative onset minimal set —— 52	
3.1.1.3	Sonorant onset minimal sets —— 52	
3.1.1.4	Marginal onset consonants and consonant clusters —— 52	
3.1.2	Consonant codas —— 53	
3.1.2.1	Stop coda minimal set —— 54	
3.1.2.2	Sonorant coda minimal set —— 54	
3.1.2.3	Marginal coda consonants —— 55	
3.2	Vowels —— 55	
3.2.1	Hills Amri Karbi sixth vowel —— 56	
3.2.2	Marginal vowels and phonetic variation —— 57	
3.3	Syllable —— 59	
3.4	Palatal glide coda versus diphthongs —— 60	
3.5	Tone —— 61	
3.5.1	Tone minimal sets: Monosyllabic roots —— 63	

3.5.2	Tone minimal sets: Disyllabic roots —— 65	
3.5.3	Phonological basis of the tone system —— 65	
3.5.4	Low functional load —— 67	
3.5.4.1	Native speakers' difficulty to identify tone categories —— 68	
3.5.4.2	Low contrastiveness —— 68	
3.5.4.3	Large amount of contextuality —— 68	
3.5.4.4	Speaker differences in realization of mid versus high tones —— 69	
3.5.4.5	Production-perception mismatch —— 70	
3.5.4.6	Prosodic tone changes and indeterminability —— 70	
3.5.5	Word-internal tone sandhi effects —— 72	
3.5.6	Tone and phonological and morphological units —— 73	
3.5.7	Tone (changes) in compounds —— 75	
3.5.8	Strategies used for identifying tones of roots and suffixes —— 76	
3.5.8.1	Syllable under investigation is the last syllable of the word and non-stopped —— 76	
3.5.8.2	Syllable under investigation followed by -lò 'realis' —— 76	
3.5.8.3	Syllable under investigation followed by -Cē 'negative' —— 77	
3.5.9	Representation of tone in this grammar —— 77	
3.5.10	Remarks on grammatical functions of tone —— 78	
3.6	Stress —— 80	
3.7	Characteristics of hypoarticulated speech —— 81	
3.7.1	/t/ → ∅ / ___ v, l —— 81	
3.7.2	Imperative onsets: /n/ → [α nasal] / [α nasal] ___ —— 81	
3.7.3	-jí 'IRR2?', -lò '?', -si '?' → a / ___ -lāng 'still', -nāng 'hortative' —— 82	
3.8	Phonological shapes of morpheme types —— 82	
3.8.1	Roots —— 82	
3.8.2	Suffixes —— 82	
3.8.3	Prefixes —— 82	
3.8.4	Clitics —— 83	
3.8.5	Interjections —— 85	
3.8.6	Reduplication —— 85	
3.8.6.1	Reduplication of stems (without vowel change) —— 85	
3.8.6.2	Reduplication of stems with vowel change —— 86	
3.8.6.3	Negation: Onset reduplication of last stem syllable —— 87	
3.9	Morphophonemics —— 88	
3.9.1	Tone changes —— 88	
3.9.1.1	Stem tone change induced by che- 'reflexive/reciprocal' and cho- 'auto-benefactive/malefactive' —— 88	
3.9.1.2	Stem tone change induced by possessive prefixes —— 89	
3.9.1.3	Derivational suffix tone change —— 90	
3.9.1.4	Idiosyncratic tone allomorphy —— 91	
3.9.2	Prefix allomorphs and prefix-induced stem vowel deletion —— 91	

3.9.2.1	Prefix vowels: *ke-* 'NMLZ', *pV-* 'CAUS', *che-* 'RR', *cho-* 'AUTO.BEN/MAL', *a-* 'POSS' —— 92	
3.9.2.2	*cho-* 'auto-benefactive/malefactive' and *che-* 'reflexive/reciprocal': Differences in phonological strength —— 95	
4	**The major word classes: Nouns and verbs and 'adjectival verbs'** —— **97**	
4.1	Nouns and verbs —— 97	
4.1.1	Morphosyntactic criteria for nouns and verbs at the root level —— 97	
4.1.2	Lack of word class distinctions with suffixal aspect, modality, and negation —— 99	
4.1.3	Summary: Nouns and verbs in Karbi —— 102	
4.2	Verbs and 'adjectival verbs': The status of property concept terms —— 102	
4.2.1	Basic property concept terms (PCTs) —— 104	
4.2.2	Possible property concept term (PCT) criteria: Gradability, intensification, adverb derivation —— 105	
4.2.3	Possible verbhood criteria: Aspectual and modal suffixes, directives —— 108	
4.2.4	Noun modification —— 110	
4.2.5	Summary: Basic property-concept terms (PCTs) —— 111	
4.2.6	Marginal types of property concept terms (PCTs) —— 111	
4.3	Summary: The clausal functions of nouns, verbs, and property concept terms (PCTs) —— 115	
5	**Subclasses of nouns** —— **117**	
5.1	Classifiers —— 117	
5.1.1	Sortal classifiers —— 119	
5.1.1.1	Typical classifiers —— 119	
5.1.1.2	Not fully grammaticalized classifier *bàng* 'CLF:HUM:PL' —— 121	
5.1.2	Mensural classifiers —— 122	
5.1.2.1	Typical classifiers —— 122	
5.1.2.2	Not fully grammaticalized classifiers —— 123	
5.1.3	Self-referential classifiers —— 124	
5.1.4	Human and animal classifiers and personification —— 125	
5.2	Nouns that are counted with numerals only (without classifiers) —— 127	
5.3	Human/personified vs. non-human/non-personified —— 129	
5.4	Relator nouns —— 129	
5.4.1	General relator noun *-lòng* 'locative' —— 133	
5.4.2	Locational relator nouns —— 135	
5.4.3	Locational/temporal relator nouns —— 139	
5.4.4	Temporal relator noun —— 141	
5.4.5	Causal relator nouns —— 141	

5.4.6	Relator nouns with other functions	142
5.4.7	Further grammaticalization of relator nouns	144
5.4.7.1	Subordinators	144
5.4.7.2	Adverbs	145
5.5	Bound noun roots	146
5.5.1	Body part terms	146
5.5.2	Kinship terms	147
5.5.3	Other inalienably possessed items	147
5.6	Other possible noun classes with frozen prefixes (Grüßner 1978: 44–6)	148
5.7	Collective noun roots	148
6	**Other word classes**	**149**
6.1	Pro-forms	149
6.1.1	Personal pronouns and personal possessive prefixes	149
6.1.2	Reflexive/reciprocal pronouns	151
6.1.3	Demonstratives	154
6.1.4	Interrogative pronouns and pro-adverbs, and positive polarity indefinite construction	156
6.1.4.1	Positive indefinite construction with -nē 'indefinite'	159
6.1.4.2	Interrogative pronouns in indirect questions	159
6.1.4.3	Co-relative construction	160
6.1.5	Parallelism between demonstrative and interrogative adverbs	160
6.1.6	Pronouns and pro-adverbs of universal quantification	161
6.2	Verb subclasses	163
6.2.1	Property concept terms	163
6.2.2	Copulas	163
6.2.2.1	Existential and locative copulas	163
6.2.2.1.1	Positive dō and negative avē	163
6.2.2.1.2	Quantifying copula óng 'exist much'	167
6.2.2.2	Negative equational copula kalī	167
6.3	Frozen prefixes in disyllabic verb and noun roots	168
6.3.1	Frozen prefix ing-	168
6.3.2	Frozen prefix ar-	170
6.3.3	Other possible frozen prefixes in disyllabic noun and verb roots	170
6.4	Minor word classes	170
6.4.1	Adverbs	170
6.4.1.1	Temporal adverbs	171
6.4.1.1.1	Day and year ordinals	171
6.4.1.1.2	Other underived temporal adverbs	173
6.4.1.1.3	Temporal adverbs with -váng 'every'	173
6.4.1.1.4	Intensifier reduplication construction	173

6.4.1.2	Locative adverbs —— 173
6.4.1.3	Other adverbs —— 174
6.4.2	Numerals —— 174
6.4.3	Subordinators and coordinators —— 176

7 Nominal morphology —— 179
7.1	Overview: Noun stems and noun words —— 179
7.2	Compounding —— 180
7.2.1	Simple root compounding —— 180
7.2.2	Higher level elaborate expression compounding —— 181
7.3	Nominal prefixes —— 181
7.3.1	General possessive or 'attributive' prefix *a-* 'POSS' —— 182
7.3.2	Personal possessive prefixes —— 184
7.3.3.	Verbalizer *pe-* ~ *pa-* —— 185
7.4	Nominal suffixes —— 186
7.4.1	Gender suffixes *-pī* and *-pō* —— 187
7.4.1.1	Female and augmentative *-pī* —— 187
7.4.1.2	Male (and non-productive modifier-deriving) *-pō* —— 188
7.4.1.3	Augmentative and modifier-deriving *-pī* and *-pō* —— 188
7.4.2	Diminutive *-sō* —— 189
7.4.3	Gender/augmentative and diminutive suffixes in names of animal (/plant) subspecies —— 190
7.4.4	Human plural *-mār* —— 191
7.4.5	Superlative *-si* —— 191
7.5	Reduplication —— 192
7.5.1	Dual —— 192
7.5.2	(Distributive) plural —— 193

8 Verbal morphology: Overview and pre-root slots —— 196
8.1	Compounding —— 196
8.2	Overview: Position classes in the Karbi verb —— 196
8.2.1	Derivational and inflectional affixes, and the verb stem —— 197
8.2.2	Overview of pre-root slots —— 198
8.3	Proclitic slot: Non-subject speech act participant cross-referencing and cislocative marking —— 200
8.3.1	Non-subject speech act participant marking —— 200
8.3.1.1	Introduction —— 201
8.3.1.2	Cross-referencing SAP primary objects —— 201
8.3.1.3	Cross-referencing SAP in non-core roles —— 204
8.3.1.4	Summary —— 205
8.3.2	Cislocative marking —— 206
8.3.2.1	Directional —— 206

8.3.2.2	Associated motion ('come and V') —— 208	
8.3.2.3	Semantic extensions —— 210	
8.3.2.4	Summary: Cislocative marking —— 211	
8.3.3	Summary —— 212	
8.4	Prefixal derivational morphology —— 213	
8.4.1	Nominalizer *ke-* —— 213	
8.4.2	Causative *pe- ~ pa-* —— 214	
8.4.3	Reflexive/reciprocal *che-* —— 215	
8.4.4	Auto-benefactive/malefactive *cho-* —— 219	
8.4.5	On the functional overlap between reflexive/reciprocal *che-* and auto-benefactive/malefactive *cho-* —— 220	
9	**Verbal morphology: Post-root slots —— 222**	
9.1	Overview of post-root slots —— 222	
9.1.1	Cooccurrence restriction between negative *-Cē* and irrealis *-jí* and *-pò* (slots 8 and 10) —— 223	
9.1.2	Slot 9 *-pín* 'experiential' —— 223	
9.1.3	Slot 10 *-làng* 'still' and *-jí-lāng* 'IRR2-still' —— 223	
9.2	Suffixal predicate derivations —— 224	
9.2.1	Overview —— 225	
9.2.1.1	Structural properties —— 225	
9.2.1.1.1	Scope of negation and reduplication —— 225	
9.2.1.1.2	Discontinuous predicate derivations —— 227	
9.2.1.1.3	Productivity —— 228	
9.2.1.2	Origins of predicate derivations —— 229	
9.2.1.3	Functional categories of predicate derivations —— 230	
9.2.2	Manner —— 230	
9.2.2.1	Non-ideophonic manner —— 230	
9.2.2.2	Ideophonic manner —— 231	
9.2.2.3	Degree or extent —— 231	
9.2.2.3.1	Quantification derivations —— 232	
9.2.2.3.2	Comparative *-mū~-mūchòt* and superlative *-néi~-nái* —— 233	
9.2.3	Result —— 233	
9.2.4	Direction, (associated) motion, path —— 234	
9.2.5	Argument and argument structure related functions —— 238	
9.2.5.1	Argument quantification —— 238	
9.2.5.2	Argument structure highlighting —— 239	
9.2.5.2.1	Benefactive/malefactive *-pī* —— 239	
9.2.5.2.2	Instrumental, comitative *-ī* —— 240	
9.2.5.3	Argument classification —— 241	
9.2.5.4	Argument structure changing —— 242	
9.2.6	Aspect/aktionsart and time —— 242	

9.2.6.1	Overview —— 242	
9.2.6.2	Perfect -ét —— 243	
9.2.6.3	Continuative -bòm~-bōm —— 243	
9.2.6.4	Perfective2 -tāng —— 244	
9.2.6.5	Completive -ròk —— 244	
9.2.6.6	Perfective3 -lèt —— 245	
9.2.6.7	Durative -klùng —— 246	
9.2.7	Other functions —— 246	
9.2.7.1	Involvement -dùn~-dūn 'JOIN' —— 246	
9.2.7.2	Formal -īk —— 248	
9.3	Reduplication —— 249	
9.3.1	Habitual —— 249	
9.3.2	Argument plurality and iterative —— 250	
9.3.3	Intensification —— 251	
9.4	Negative -Cē (onset reduplication) —— 251	
9.5	Post-stem aspect: Exhaustive perfective -dèt and experiential -pín —— 252	
9.5.1	Exhaustive perfective -dèt —— 252	
9.5.2	Experiential -pín —— 253	
9.6	Mood: Realis and irrealis —— 254	
9.6.1	Realis -lò —— 254	
9.6.1.1	Overview of verbal functions —— 254	
9.6.1.2	Action verbs: The argument against 'past tense' —— 255	
9.6.1.3	Copular and property concept term (PCT) verbs: Change of state —— 257	
9.6.1.4	Indicating a logical relationship: Cause and result —— 258	
9.6.1.5	Correcting a wrong assumption —— 260	
9.6.1.6	Summary —— 262	
9.6.1.7	Realis -lò on nominal predicates and focus =lo —— 262	
9.6.2	Irrealis marking: -pò and -jí —— 265	
9.6.2.1	Functions common to -pò and -ji —— 266	
9.6.2.1.1	Future marking —— 266	
9.6.2.1.2	Habitual marking in procedural texts —— 266	
9.6.2.1.3	Hypothetical and counterfactuals —— 267	
9.6.2.1.4	Epistemic reading —— 269	
9.6.2.1.5	Expressing necessity/obligation —— 270	
9.6.2.1.6	Expressing desiderative —— 270	
9.6.2.1.7	Subordinate purpose clause marking —— 271	
9.6.2.2	Past habitual marking via -pò —— 271	
9.6.2.3	Summary —— 271	
9.7	Subordinating verbal suffixes —— 272	
9.7.1	Non-final marker: Realis -si and irrealis -ra (clause-chaining) —— 272	
9.7.2	Non-final -pen —— 273	

9.7.3	Conditional -*te* —— 274	
9.7.4	Marker of complement clauses functioning as indirect questions: -*nē* 'indefinite' —— 275	
9.8	Aspect II: -*làng* 'still' —— 275	
9.9	Non-declarative speech act suffixes —— 276	

10	**The noun phrase —— 277**	
10.1	Elements of the Karbi noun phrase —— 277	
10.1.1	Overview: Karbi noun phrase structure —— 277	
10.1.2	Occurrence of other elements in head noun slot —— 278	
10.1.2.1	Conjunctive coordination constructions —— 278	
10.1.2.1.1	Juxtaposition —— 278	
10.1.2.1.2	With coordinator =*pen* or *lapèn* —— 279	
10.1.2.2	Quotative *pu* —— 280	
10.1.3	The noun phrase delimiter *abàng* —— 281	
10.2	Evidence for Karbi noun phrase structure —— 281	
10.3	Diachronic significance of the possessive construction —— 287	
10.4	Possessive *a*- marking of head nouns —— 288	
10.5	Preposed modifiers —— 291	
10.5.1	Demonstratives —— 292	
10.5.2	Possessives —— 292	
10.5.3	Other preposed modifiers —— 294	
10.5.3.1	Interrogative pronouns and derived indefinites —— 294	
10.5.3.2	Adverbials —— 296	
10.5.3.3	Clausal modifiers —— 297	
10.6	Postposed modifier: Plural marking noun -*tūm* —— 297	
10.7	Modifiers that occur preposed or postposed —— 298	
10.7.1	Deverbal modifiers: PCT-based modifiers and relative clauses —— 298	
10.7.1.1	Post-head PCT-based modifiers and pre-head relative clauses —— 299	
10.7.1.2	Pre-head PCT-based modifiers (and post-head relative clauses) —— 300	
10.7.2	Enumeration constructions —— 303	
10.7.2.1	Four basic enumeration constructions —— 304	
10.7.2.1.1	Typical classifier construction —— 304	
10.7.2.1.2	Self-referential classifier construction —— 305	
10.7.2.1.3	Not fully grammaticalized classifier construction —— 305	
10.7.2.1.4	Non-classifier (direct enumeration) construction —— 306	
10.7.2.2	Pre- vs. post-head order —— 307	
10.7.2.3	Anaphoric use of classifiers —— 308	
10.7.2.4	Juxtaposition of two numerals or classifier-numeral words to indicate indefiniteness or vagueness —— 308	
10.7.2.5	'Another' additive construction —— 310	
10.7.2.6	Constructions based on 'one' enumeration —— 310	

10.7.2.6.1	Preposed 'one' enumeration as an indefinite article construction —— 310	
10.7.2.6.2	Indefinite pronoun construction —— 311	
10.7.2.6.3	Postposed 'one' enumeration expressing 'whole' —— 311	
10.7.2.6.4	Postposed 'one' enumeration expressing 'same' —— 311	
10.8	Noun phrase clitics —— 312	
10.8.1	Comitative, instrumental, ablative =pen —— 313	
10.8.2	Nominal quantifier constructions based on =án 'this much; all' —— 315	
10.8.3	Additive, topic, and focus clitics —— 317	
10.8.3.1	Additive =tā —— 317	
10.8.3.1.1	Overview of functions —— 317	
10.8.3.1.2	Simple additive 'also' —— 317	
10.8.3.1.3	Bisyndetic coordination —— 318	
10.8.3.1.4	Scalar additive 'even' —— 318	
10.8.3.1.5	Universal quantification —— 319	
10.8.3.1.6	Intensifier verb construction —— 320	
10.8.3.1.7	Discourse (information structure) function —— 320	
10.8.3.2	Information and discourse structure clitics —— 320	

11 Monoclausal predicate constructions —— 321

11.1	Overview —— 321	
11.1.1	Non-verbal predicates —— 321	
11.1.2	Verbal and nominal predicate negation —— 322	
11.2	Modal and other markers at the monoclausal end of the complementation scale —— 324	
11.2.1	Overview —— 324	
11.2.2	Remarks on the complementation scale in Karbi —— 324	
11.2.3	Morphosyntactic tests for structural properties of modals —— 326	
11.2.3.1	Under scope of nominalization along with main verb root? —— 326	
11.2.3.2	Following adverbial construction [V]$_{\text{main verb}}$ [pa-V]$_{\text{adv}}$? —— 327	
11.2.3.3	Modified itself by a predicate derivation? —— 328	
11.2.4	Morphophonological evidence —— 329	
11.2.5	The modals —— 329	
11.2.5.1	Deontic (-)náng 'need, must' —— 329	
11.2.5.2	Non-control (-)lōng 'GET' —— 331	
11.2.5.2.1	Function —— 331	
11.2.5.2.2	Structure and distribution —— 333	
11.2.5.3	Skillful ability (-)thèk~(-)thēk 'know how' —— 334	
11.2.5.4	Physical ability (-)ùn~(-)ūn 'be able' —— 335	
11.2.5.5	Other markers —— 336	
11.3	Adverbial constructions —— 338	
11.3.1	Overview —— 338	
11.3.2	Causative adverbial construction [V]$_{\text{main verb}}$ [pa-V]$_{\text{adverbial}}$ —— 339	

11.3.3	Nominalization adverbial construction [ke-V]$_{\text{main verb}}$ [V]$_{\text{adverbial}}$ —— 340	
11.3.4	Non-final preposed adverbial constructions —— 341	
11.3.4.1	Non-final -pen construction [ke-V-pen]$_{\text{adverbial}}$ [V]$_{\text{main verb}}$ —— 341	
11.3.4.2	Non-PCT root construction [ke-V-si]$_{\text{adverbial}}$ [V]$_{\text{main verb}}$ —— 342	
11.4	Periphrastic constructions based on copulas —— 344	
11.4.1	Progressive construction with non-final suffix -si plus copula dō —— 344	
11.4.2	Copula argument quantification construction —— 345	
11.5	Complex motion construction —— 346	
11.6	'Noun plus verb' predicate constructions —— 347	
11.6.1	Non-possessed noun incorporation —— 347	
11.6.2	Psycho-collocations and possessed noun incorporation —— 349	
11.6.3	Light verb construction —— 352	
11.6.4	Cognate object construction —— 353	
11.6.5	Hybrid construction —— 355	
11.7	Other complex predicate constructions discussed elsewhere —— 355	
12	**Nominalization —— 356**	
12.1	Derivational nominalization —— 356	
12.2	Property concept term (PCT)-based noun modification —— 358	
12.3	Relativization —— 360	
12.3.1	Standard (externally-headed, pre-head) relativization —— 360	
12.3.1.1	Relativization on different clause participants —— 360	
12.3.1.2	Irrealis-marked relative clauses —— 364	
12.3.1.3	Head noun occurring with personal possessive prefix —— 365	
12.3.2	Internally-headed (or post-head) relativization —— 365	
12.4	Complementation —— 368	
12.4.1	Standard complementation —— 368	
12.4.2	Irrealis-marked complement clauses —— 371	
12.4.2.1	Irrealis-marked complement clauses with purpose marker aphān —— 371	
12.4.2.2	Irrealis-marked complement clause with noun phrase delimiter abàng —— 372	
12.4.3	Functional types of complement-taking verbs —— 373	
12.5	Adverbial subordination —— 373	
12.5.1	Nominalized adverbial subordination: Subordinators from relator nouns —— 373	
12.5.2	Semantic types —— 374	
12.5.3	Adverbial subordination constructions with additional marking —— 381	
12.6	Irrealis-marked nominalized subordinate clauses —— 381	
12.7	Main clause constructions —— 384	
12.7.1	Nominalization plus existential copula construction —— 384	
12.7.2	Adverbial constructions —— 388	

12.7.3	Diachronic nominalization constructions in main clause grammar —— 388	
12.7.3.1	Focus constructions —— 388	
12.7.3.1.1	Inconsistent occurrence of *ke-* —— 389	
12.7.3.1.2	General argument focus construction —— 389	
12.7.3.1.3	Content question focus construction —— 390	
12.7.3.1.4	Co-relative focus construction —— 391	
12.7.3.1.5	Historical development —— 392	
12.7.3.2	Imperfective construction —— 393	
12.7.3.3	Ambiguity between focus and imperfective interpretation —— 396	
12.8	Inconsistent occurrence of *ke-* 'nominalizer' in nominalization constructions —— 397	

13 Clause participants: Overview, participants, noun phrase delimiter —— 401

13.1	Preliminaries —— 401	
13.1.1	Terminology —— 401	
13.1.2	The argument-oblique continuum and the syntax, semantics, and pragmatics in role marking —— 402	
13.2	The predicate: Defining argument roles —— 403	
13.2.1	Argument roles in typical declarative clauses —— 403	
13.2.1.1	Monovalent predicate: Unmarked S argument —— 404	
13.2.1.2	Bivalent predicates: Marking of A and O arguments —— 405	
13.2.1.3	Trivalent predicates: Marking of A, R, and T arguments —— 406	
13.2.1.3.1	R-marked trivalent construction —— 406	
13.2.1.3.2	T-marked trivalent constructions —— 408	
13.2.1.3.3	Unmarked trivalent construction —— 411	
13.2.1.3.4	Summary: Trivalent constructions —— 412	
13.2.1.4	Alignment in typical declarative clauses —— 413	
13.2.2	Declarative clause constructions with non-typical role marking of arguments —— 414	
13.2.2.1	Motion constructions with unmarked and *-lòng* marked goals —— 414	
13.2.2.2	'Need' construction —— 416	
13.2.2.3	Existential copula constructions: Simple locative and possessive constructions —— 417	
13.2.2.3.1	Simple locative construction —— 417	
13.2.2.3.2	Predicational possession construction with unmarked A/possessor and possessive-marked O/possessed —— 418	
13.2.2.3.3	Predicational possession construction with locative-marked A and unmarked O argument —— 420	
13.2.2.4	Topical possessor construction —— 420	
13.2.2.5	Comparative constructions —— 422	
13.2.3	Predicates with derivationally changed argument structure —— 423	

13.2.3.1	Causative *pe-~pa-* —— 423	
13.2.3.2	Benefactive/malefactive (affective) *-pī* —— 425	
13.2.4	Non-subject speech act participant indexing on the verb —— 427	
13.2.5	Other grammatical relations constructions —— 428	
13.3	Overview: Clause participant marking —— 429	
13.4	Lexical noun phrase versus pronoun versus zero anaphora —— 429	
13.4.1	Lexical noun phrase —— 430	
13.4.2	Pronoun —— 431	
13.4.3	Zero anaphora —— 432	
13.5	Noun phrase delimiter *abàng* —— 433	
13.5.1	Distribution of noun phrase delimiter *abàng* —— 435	
13.5.2	Diachronic source construction: Human classifier as syntactic head noun —— 437	
13.5.3	Coocurrence of *abàng* with role markers —— 438	
13.5.4	Co-occurrence of *abàng* with core information/discourse structure clitics —— 440	
13.5.5	Differences between speakers, texts, genres —— 441	
14	**Role marking and core information/discourse structure marking —— 444**	
14.1	Role marking —— 444	
14.1.1	Unmarked noun phrases —— 445	
14.1.1.1	S argument —— 445	
14.1.1.2	A argument —— 446	
14.1.1.3	O-low argument —— 446	
14.1.1.4	T argument —— 447	
14.1.1.5	R argument (T-marked trivalent construction) —— 447	
14.1.1.6	Goal/locative argument/participant of motion verbs —— 448	
14.1.1.7	Other types of participants —— 448	
14.1.2	Functions of 'non-subject' *-phān* —— 450	
14.1.2.1	O-high argument —— 450	
14.1.2.2	R argument (R-marked trivalent construction) —— 451	
14.1.2.3	T argument (T-marked trivalent construction) —— 452	
14.1.2.4	Semantic marking with *náng* 'need' —— 452	
14.1.2.5	Marking the standard of comparison —— 452	
14.1.2.6	Other types of participants —— 453	
14.1.3	Functions of 'locative' *-lòng* —— 455	
14.1.3.1	Locative/goal R argument (T-marked/unmarked trivalent constructions) —— 455	
14.1.3.2	Locative O-like argument —— 456	
14.1.3.3	Motion verb locative/goal —— 457	
14.1.3.4	Semantic marking with possessor construction —— 458	
14.1.4	Semantically marked participants —— 458	

14.1.4.1	Semantically specific marking of functionally core roles —— 458
14.1.4.1.1	Comitative, instrumental, ablative =pen —— 459
14.1.4.1.2	Goal arguments marked with semantically specific relator nouns —— 460
14.1.4.2	Semantically specific relator noun marking of obliques —— 461
14.1.5	Differential marking —— 461
14.1.6	Marking variation —— 462
14.1.6.1	che-tòng 'RR-meet' —— 462
14.1.6.2	arjū-dām 'ask-GO' —— 463
14.2	Core information/discourse structure marking —— 464
14.2.1	Topic =ke —— 465
14.2.2	Additive =tā —— 468
14.2.3	Realis focus =si —— 471
14.2.4	Irrealis focus =le —— 474
14.2.5	Relationships between core information/discourse structure clitics —— 476
14.2.6	Other information/discourse status constructions —— 479
14.2.6.1	Constituent order —— 479
14.2.6.2	New participant marking —— 482
14.2.6.3	Restrictive focus markers —— 482

15	**Clause types and clause combining —— 486**
15.1	Non-declarative main clause types —— 486
15.1.1	Interrogatives —— 486
15.1.1.1	Question particle =ma —— 487
15.1.1.2	Content questions with interrogative pronouns and adverbs —— 487
15.1.1.2.1	Verb occurring without =ma —— 487
15.1.1.2.2	Verb occurring with =ma —— 488
15.1.1.3	Polar interrogatives and disjunctive interrogatives —— 489
15.1.1.4	Polar interrogatives —— 489
15.1.1.4.1	Polar interrogatives with =ma —— 489
15.1.1.4.2	Polar interrogatives with prosody only —— 491
15.1.1.5	Disjunctive interrogatives —— 493
15.1.1.5.1	Type 1: A=ma A-NEG —— 493
15.1.1.5.2	Type 2: A=ma B —— 493
15.1.1.5.3	Type 3: A=ma B=ma —— 494
15.1.1.5.4	Type 4: A=ma ma B=ma —— 494
15.1.1.6	Interrogative assumption =bo —— 495
15.1.1.7	Tag question dī —— 496
15.1.1.8	Feedback request with déi —— 496
15.1.2	Imperatives and prohibitives —— 497
15.1.2.1	Bare stem imperative —— 497

15.1.2.2	Informal conditioned imperative *-nōi* —— 498	
15.1.2.3	Conditioned imperative *-nōn* —— 499	
15.1.2.4	Conative imperative *-thā* —— 499	
15.1.2.5	Unconditioned imperative *-tū* —— 500	
15.1.2.6	Imperatives *-nōn*, *-thā*, and *-tū* and Grüßner's (1978) account of politeness differences —— 501	
15.1.2.7	Prohibitive *-rī* —— 501	
15.1.2.8	Prohibitive construction via combination of prohibitive and imperative suffix —— 501	
15.1.3	Hortatives —— 502	
15.1.3.1	General hortative *-nāng* —— 502	
15.1.3.2	Jussive construction with causative *pa-* and hortative *-nāng* —— 504	
15.1.3.3	Extended forms: Emphatic hortative *-lonāng* and conative hortative *-sināng* —— 505	
15.2	Non-nominalized subordinate clause types —— 507	
15.2.1	Non-final clauses in clause chains —— 507	
15.2.1.1	Morphologically marked clauses: *-si* 'non-final:realis', *-ra* 'non-final:irrealis', *-pen* 'non-final:with' —— 507	
15.2.1.2	Prosodically marked clauses —— 510	
15.2.2	Complement clauses —— 512	
15.2.2.1	Verb juxtaposition —— 512	
15.2.2.2	Indirect questions —— 513	
15.2.2.3	Topic *=ke* marked complement clauses —— 514	
15.2.2.4	Quotative *pu* and *pusi* complementizers —— 514	
15.2.3	Adverbial clauses —— 516	
15.2.3.1	Conditional *-te* —— 516	
15.2.3.2	Purpose clauses with quotative complementizers —— 517	
15.2.3.3	Concessive *sitā~setā* —— 517	
15.3	Irrealis clause types: Irrealis-sensitivity in non-final and focus markers —— 518	
15.3.1	Overview —— 518	
15.3.2	Non-declarative speech acts —— 519	
15.3.3	Negation —— 521	
15.3.4	Deontic clauses (expressing necessity/obligation; with *náng* 'need, must') —— 522	
15.3.5	Conditional subordinate clauses —— 523	
15.4	Non-nominalized insubordination (formally non-finite declarative main clause types) —— 523	
15.4.1	Main clauses marked with *=ke* 'topic': Background information construction —— 523	
15.4.2	Main clauses marked with *pu* 'quotative': Desiderative construction —— 524	

15.4.3	Stand-alone indirect questions —— 526	
15.5	Clause coordination —— 527	
15.5.1	Conjunctive coordination —— 527	
15.5.1.1	Conjunctive coordinator *lapèn* 'and' —— 527	
15.5.1.2	Additive particle clause/VP coordination constructions —— 527	
15.5.1.3	Clausal NP coordination —— 528	
15.5.2	Disjunctive coordination —— 529	
15.5.3	Adversative coordination —— 530	
15.6	Lack of a syntactic pivot —— 531	

16 Discourse constructions —— 532

16.1	Discourse structuring constructions —— 532
16.1.1	Clause parallelism —— 532
16.1.2	Tail-head linkage —— 534
16.1.3	Discourse connectors —— 536
16.1.4	Discourse structuring markers e and '*mh* —— 537
16.2	Rhetorical constructions —— 539
16.2.1	General extender constructions —— 539
16.2.2	Elaborate expression constructions —— 543
16.2.2.1	Forms of elaborate expressions —— 543
16.2.2.2	Embedding into parallelism or compound construction —— 547
16.2.2.3	Functions of elaborate expressions —— 549
16.2.3	Copy verb constructions —— 550
16.2.3.1	Assertive (with =*ke* 'topic') —— 551
16.2.3.2	Intensifier declarative (with =*tā* 'additive') —— 553
16.2.3.3	Intensifier non-declarative (with =*le* 'focus:irrealis') —— 554
16.2.3.4	Perseverance construction (with =*ma* 'question particle') —— 555
16.2.4	Constructions with negative equational copula *kalī* —— 556
16.2.4.1	Disagreement construction based on quasi-reduplication and negative equational copula —— 556
16.2.4.2	Nominalization-based intensifier construction *ke*-V-*sō kalī* —— 557
16.2.5	Prosodic emphasis —— 558
16.3	Particles —— 558
16.3.1	Quotative *pu* —— 560
16.3.1.1	Reportative function of *pu* —— 560
16.3.1.2	Desiderative function of *pu* —— 561
16.3.2	Reportative *tànghò* —— 562
16.3.3	Dubitatives *bón, tahái, menē* —— 564
16.3.4	Always *titī* —— 565
16.3.5	Emphatic *ti* —— 566
16.3.6	Interactive emphatic *ho* —— 569

16.3.7	Vocative ó —— 570	
16.3.8	Exclamative function of irrealis focus =le —— 571	
16.3.9	Afterthought =he —— 572	
16.3.10	Background information: =ke 'topic' marked main clauses —— 574	
16.3.11	Common ground marker =mati —— 577	
16.3.12	Narrative style hedī —— 578	
16.4	Honorific and formality marking —— 579	
16.4.1	Honorific -lī on pronouns and addressing words —— 580	
16.4.2	Formal -īk on predicates —— 580	
16.4.3	Honorific -héi ~ -hái on kinship terms —— 582	
16.5	Interjections —— 582	
16.6	Hesitation and correction words —— 584	
16.6.1	Hesitation words kenē and mane (<Assamese) —— 584	
16.6.2	Correction words chē and bá (<Assamese) —— 586	

Appendix A
    Abbreviations —— 589

Appendix B
    Folk story: Chonghokaloso lapen Misorongpo (RBT, ChM) —— 591

Appendix C
    Stimuli-based narrative: Pear Story (SiT, PS) —— 610

Appendix D
    Metadata —— 622

Appendix E
    Glossary —— 626

Bibliography —— 647

Index Karbi grammar —— 657

Author Index —— 665

List of Figures

Figure 1	Northeast India (taken from openstreetmap.org, "Myanmar" and "Karbi Anglong" labels added, accessed February 28, 2020) —— 3
Figure 2	Approximate outline of the Karbi-speaking area (based on a map taken from openstreetmap.org, accessed on February 28, 2020; outline and names for countries as well as Indian states added) —— 5
Figure 3	Priest performing a duck sacrifice —— 6
Figure 4	Jambili athon —— 6
Figure 5	Classification of Tibeto-Burman according to Bradley (2002) —— 10
Figure 6	Burling's (2003: 184) 'Relationships among the languages of the Eastern Border' —— 10
Figure 7	Pnar, Khasi, War, and Lyngam speaking areas (Daladier 2014) —— 15
Figure 8	Standard Karbi vowel monophthongs —— 55
Figure 9	Amri Karbi vowels —— 57
Figure 10	Semantic map of basic clausal functions of Karbi parts of speech (following Croft's (2001: 99) model) —— 116
Figure 11	Position classes in the Karbi verb —— 197
Figure 12	Overview of cislocative functions of nang= —— 211
Figure 13	Post-root slots of the Karbi verb —— 223
Figure 14	Karbi noun phrase structure —— 277
Figure 15	Noun phrase clitic slots —— 312
Figure 16	Grammaticalization scenario for =si 'focus' (starting as copula) —— 392
Figure 17	Possible grammaticalization pathway for the imperfective construction —— 396
Figure 18	Schematic overview of argument expression in Karbi —— 430
Figure 19	Role marking possibilities —— 444
Figure 20	Waveform and spectrogram of interrogative and subsequent declarative *enutvetlo* 'he was alone' (HK, TR 005-6) —— 492
Figure 21	F_0 contour of interrogative and subsequent declarative *enutvetlo* 'he was alone' (HK, TR 005-6) —— 492
Figure 22	Prosodic emphasis in full predicate reduplication of *baithekthe* (KK, CC 012) —— 559

List of Tables

Table 1	Locations of Karbi-speaking villages outside Karbi Anglong —— 4	
Table 2	Vowel alternations —— 27	
Table 3	Subcorpora of Karbi data —— 38	
Table 4	Text genres —— 42	
Table 5	Syllable-initial consonants —— 49	
Table 6	Minimal set for bilabial stop onsets —— 51	
Table 7	Minimal set for alveolar stop onsets —— 51	
Table 8	Minimal set for palatal stop onsets —— 51	
Table 9	Minimal set for velar stop onsets —— 52	
Table 10	Minimal set for fricative onsets —— 52	
Table 11	Minimal set for nasal onsets —— 52	
Table 12	Minimal set for liquid and glide onsets —— 52	
Table 13	Syllable-final consonants —— 54	
Table 14	Minimal sets for stop codas —— 54	
Table 15	Minimal sets for sonorant codas —— 54	
Table 16	Minimal sets for vowels in open syllables —— 56	
Table 17	Minimal sets /ei/, /ai/, /oi/, /ui/ —— 56	
Table 18	Set of items with /ɪ/ in Amri Karbi —— 57	
Table 19	Marginal vowels —— 58	
Table 20	Syllable types —— 59	
Table 21	Onset cluster types —— 60	
Table 22	Minimal sets for tones after voiceless onsets —— 63	
Table 23	Minimal sets for tones after voiced onsets —— 63	
Table 24	Additional stopped syllable tone minimal triplet —— 64	
Table 25	Stopped syllable tone minimal pairs for M-H, L-H, and L-M —— 64	
Table 26	Minimal triplets of disyllabic roots —— 65	
Table 27	Minimal pairs of disyllabic roots —— 66	
Table 28	Tone sandhi effects on low tone suffix after mid tone stem —— 72	
Table 29	Internal sandhi effects on stem induced by prefix *cho-* 'AUTO.BEN/MAL' —— 73	
Table 30	Grüßner's (1978) account of tone assignment to toneless syllables —— 74	
Table 31	Compound tones —— 75	
Table 32	Tone representation on unstressed syllables in disyllabic morphemes (default and non-default) —— 78	
Table 33	Verb-Noun tone minimal pairs (G = Grüßner 1978) —— 79	
Table 34	Tone minimal pairs in semantically related verbs according to Grüßner (1978: 91) —— 79	
Table 35	Karbi prefixes —— 83	
Table 36	Karbi clitics —— 84	
Table 37	Full reduplication of roots or suffixes without vowel change —— 85	
Table 38	Vowel change patterns in quasi-reduplicative constructions —— 86	
Table 39	Forms of quasi-reduplicative *-Cē* 'NEG' with different stems —— 87	
Table 40	Monosyllabic stem tone changes after *che-* 'RR' and *cho-* 'AUTO.BEN/MAL' —— 88	
Table 41	Disyllabic stem tone changes following possessive prefixation —— 89	
Table 42	Tone change patterns for derivational suffixes —— 90	
Table 43	List of derivational suffixes that participate in tone change —— 90	
Table 44	Idiosyncratic tone allomorphy of *-vèt ~ -vét* 'only' —— 92	
Table 45	Forms of prefix *ke-* 'NMLZ' —— 93	

Table 46	Forms of prefix *pV-* 'causative'	93
Table 47	Forms of prefix *che-* 'reflexive/reciprocal'	94
Table 48	Initial vowel deletion in *ing-* stems after prefixes *ke-*, *pV-*, *cho-*	94
Table 49	Vowel deletion between *ar-* stems and prefixes *ke-*, *pV-*, *che-*, *a-*	95
Table 50	Morphosyntactic criteria for the attempt to identify a class of 'adjectives'	103
Table 51	Basic property concept terms: Karbi sample roots	104
Table 52	Sample complex stems expressing concepts of HUMAN PROPENSITY	105
Table 53	Possible morphosyntactic criteria for 'adjectives'	111
Table 54	Marginal types of property concept term	112
Table 55	Classifier types	118
Table 56	List of sortal classifiers that occur in typical classifier construction (G = Grüßner (1978: 68–70))	119
Table 57	Not fully grammaticalized classifier *bàng* 'CLF:HUM:PL'	121
Table 58	List of mensural classifiers (G = Grüßner (1978: 68–70))	123
Table 59	Not fully grammaticalized mensural classifiers	124
Table 60	Self-referential classifiers	124
Table 61	Nouns counted with numeral only (without classifier)	128
Table 62	Relator nouns	130
Table 63	Overview of locational relator nouns	136
Table 64	Locational/temporal relator nouns	139
Table 65	Relator nouns with other functions	142
Table 66	Personal pronouns and personal possessive prefixes	150
Table 67	Morphological structure of independent pronouns and pronominal possessive prefixes	151
Table 68	Demonstratives	154
Table 69	Words with demonstrative roots	156
Table 70	Interrogative pronouns and adverbs	157
Table 71	Corresponding demonstratives and interrogatives	161
Table 72	Pronouns of universal quantification	161
Table 73	Day ordinals	171
Table 74	Year and day ordinals	171
Table 75	Numerals from 'one' to 'ten'	174
Table 76	Numerals over 'ten'	175
Table 77	Subordinators grammaticalized from relator nouns	176
Table 78	Coordinators	177
Table 79	Noun-noun and noun-verb compounds	180
Table 80	Personal possessive prefixes	185
Table 81	Proper nouns with *-pī*, *-pō*, or *-sō* suffix	190
Table 82	Cross-referencing 'paradigm' of *nang=*	201
Table 83	Proclitic cross-referencing 'paradigm'	206
Table 84	Discontinuous predicate derivations	227
Table 85	Sample highly productive PDs	228
Table 86	Sample PDs that mean 'quite' (productive and non-productive PDs)	228
Table 87	Non-productive intensifier PDs	229
Table 88	Some predicate derivations and related lexical items	229
Table 89	Sample non-ideophonic manner predicate derivations	230
Table 90	Sample ideophonic manner derivations	231
Table 91	Sample PDs that indicate a considerable degree ('quite') (productive and non-productive PDs)	231

Table 92	Non-productive intensifier PDs	232
Table 93	PDs indicating argument quantification and degree or extent	232
Table 94	Sample result derivations	233
Table 95	Direction, motion, and path derivations	234
Table 96	Argument quantification derivations	238
Table 97	Sample predicate derivations that function as argument classifiers	241
Table 98	Aspect/aktionsart and time derivations	243
Table 99	Non-declarative speech act suffixes	276
Table 100	NP structure	282
Table 101	Enumeration constructions	304
Table 102	Examples of enumeration constructions	304
Table 103	Proper adverbial constructions (ADVCs)	338
Table 104	Non-final adverbial constructions (NF-ADVCs)	338
Table 105	Noun incorporation	348
Table 106	Sample psycho-collocations	350
Table 107	Possessed noun incorporation expressions (non-psycho-collocations)	351
Table 108	Semantic types of nominalized adverbial subordinate clauses	374
Table 109	Object marking in trivalent constructions	406
Table 110	Co-occurrence of *abàng* with core information/discourse structure clitics	440
Table 111	Occurrence of *abàng* across texts	441
Table 112	Frequencies of occurrence of core information/discourse structure clitics	465
Table 113	Distribution of restrictive focus markers	482
Table 114	Functions of restrictive focus markers	483
Table 115	Disjunctive interrogative types	493
Table 116	Irrealis contexts for *-ra* 'NF:IRR' and *=le* 'FOC:IRR'	519
Table 117	Discourse connectors	536
Table 118	Formal patterns in elaborate expressions	545
Table 119	Interjections	582
Table 120	Metadata of texts representing the main corpus for this grammar	622
Table 121	Brief descriptions of texts that have formed the main corpus for this grammar	623
Table 122	Metadata of speakers of texts that have formed the main corpus for this grammar	625
Table 123	Word classes and grammatical morpheme types indicated in the glossary	626

1 Introduction

This is a grammar of Karbi as spoken in the hills of the Karbi Anglong district in Assam, Northeast India. It expands on research findings reported in Grüßner's (1978) grammar of the phonology and morphology of the language, but also offers a more comprehensive treatment of issues in Karbi syntax, semantics, and pragmatics.

This chapter is organized as follows. In §1.1, the Karbi people and their language and culture are introduced. Next, an overview of the linguistic context of Karbi is offered, i.e., the relationships between Karbi and surrounding languages, as that context helps understand why modern Karbi grammar is the way it is. On the one hand, that involves the relationship to other Tibeto-Burman languages, as discussed in §1.2. On the other hand, and importantly, it also involves the contact relationship specifically with the Austroasiatic Khasi languages, and possibly other Tibeto-Burman languages, as discussed in §1.3.

In §1.4, an overview of what is known on different varieties of Karbi is provided, including the major dialectal divide between Hills and Plains (or, Amri) Karbi, and some notes on variation within Hills Karbi, the major dialect group that this grammar is based on. A sociolinguistic profile of language endangerment (mostly based on Hills Karbi) is included in §1.5. In §1.6, an overview of the linguistic literature and linguistic resources on Karbi is provided.

Finally, §1.7 discusses Karbi orthography and ongoing issues in standardization efforts as well as an outline of conventions followed in this grammar. The organization of this grammar is outlined in §1.8.

1.1 Karbi people, language, and culture

1.1.1 Names and ISO codes for the Karbi language

In the last few decades, there has been a movement among the Karbis to push for the autonym *Karbi* or the elaborate form *Karbi Karbak* (see §16.2.2 on elaborate expressions). While this name has long been in use, it is a recent development that *Karbi* is favored over the logonym *Arleng* (i.e., *arlēng* 'man, person').[1] This might be due to the existence of *arlēng* as a simple noun root for 'man, person'.[2]

---

[1] In one of the recorded texts collected for the corpus of this grammar, the storyteller finds himself saying *Arlengpi* for 'Karbi woman' (using the female *-pī* suffix) and corrects himself and says *Karbipi*.
[2] Note, however, that there also is another general noun *monit* 'person, man', which is a borrowing from Asamese.

Mikir is a formerly commonly used exonym, which has become pejorative within the last few decades in particular. Now most Karbis have strong objections against it, which has to do with a number of offensive hypotheses for the etymology of this name. *Bhoi Mynri* is mentioned by Grüßner (1978: 6) as an exonym used by the neighboring Khasis of Meghalaya, to the immediate west of Karbi Anglong. According to my language consultants, this term *Bhoi Mynri* may also specifically refer to the variety of Plains Karbi spoken across the western border of Assam in Meghalaya (§ 1.4.1).

The Hills Karbi variety has the ISO 639-3 code 'mjw', whereas the Plains Karbi variety has the ISO code 'ajz' (for dialect differences, see § 1.4.1).

1.1.2 Number of speakers and geographical spread of Karbi

The Census of India from 2001 reports a total of 419,534 native speakers of Karbi, which is also the figure cited in the Ethnologue (Simons and Fennig 2017). The *Karbi Lammet Amei* (§ 1.1.4) estimates a higher number of speakers, at over half a million. Karbi is the third-largest minority language in the state of Assam in terms of number of speakers, following Boro and Mising.

Karbi is spoken in Assam and adjacent areas in neighboring states in Northeast India. For a map of the Eastern Himalayan region, including Northeast India and surrounding countries, see Figure 1.

Today most Karbi speakers live in the Karbi Anglong and West Karbi Anglong districts of Assam, which until 2015 formed a single Karbi Anglong district (see § 1.1.5). However, the geographic spread of Karbi speaking villages is much larger. Table 1 provides the locations of Karbi speaking villages outside the Karbi Anglong district.

Based on the locations given in Table 1, we can plot the approximate outline of the Karbi speaking area as done in Figure 2.

As the topographical map in Figure 2 shows, the Karbi speaking area extends from the valley of the river banks of the Brahmaputra southwards across plains and low to moderate hills into the Barak Valley around Silchar.

The present-day core region of the Karbi speaking area are the Karbi Anglong and West Karbi Anglong districts. These districts are located in the lower hills that mark the transition between the Brahmaputra valley area and the hill range that extends to the south and the southeast.[3]

---

[3] This is part of the hill range that extends all the way into Southeast Asia and represents something of a cultural area, with similar histories of the people inhabiting them, see Scott (2009).

Figure 1: Northeast India (taken from openstreetmap.org, "Myanmar" and "Karbi Anglong" labels added, accessed February 28, 2020).

1.1.3 Aspects of Karbi culture

1.1.3.1 Traditional culture and social organization

Changes in the lifestyle of the Karbis are occurring at an exponentially increasing pace in recent years. Due to urbanization and increased physical and virtual infrastructure, elements of the traditional culture are becoming both more endangered as well as newly embraced and cherished. Traditional village life involving *jhum* cultivation and collecting wild vegetables and fruit in the jungles and forests is becoming more and more confined to remote places that are not connected with physical infrastructure.

While a substantial number of Karbis have nowadays converted to Hinduism or Christianity, the traditional religion of the Karbis is still practiced by a considerable portion of the population. It involves different gods and goddesses, but also has a strong animist element. In cases of major life events such as weddings or deaths, as

Table 1: Locations of Karbi-speaking villages outside Karbi Anglong.

State	District	# of villages
Assam	Golaghat	?
	Marigaon	?
	Biswanath	19
	Lakhimpur	5
	Nagaon	18
	Hojai	18
	Kamrup (mostly Dispur LAC, but also Guwahati East LAC and Guwahati West LAC)	180
	NC Hills	64
	Kachar Plains	?
Meghalaya	Ri-Bhoi and West Jaintia Hills	58
Arunachal Pradesh	Papum Pare	5

For the information in this table, I am indebted to Ajit Kathar, who provided a list of villages in Kamrup; to Manik Rongpi, a student at Tezpur University, who contributed lists of Karbi speaking villages in the Biswanath and Lakhimpur districts of Assam as well as in Arunachal Pradesh; to Keson Klein of Marmein in Meghalaya for a list of villages in Meghalaya; and to Joysing Ronghi of Umrongso, Dima Hasao, for a list of villages in the NC Hills. And, most importantly, many thanks to Sikari Tisso for contacting them and others and collecting all this information.

well as other crucial times such as sickness or before going on a long trip, priests perform rituals that typically involve sacrifice of animals (such as chickens or ducks) in conjunction with chants that are orally transmitted from generation to generation, typically using the Karbi song language (§ 1.1.3.3), see Figure 3.

An important cultural symbol is the Jambili athon (Figure 4). The bird on top represents values such as wisdom, intellectuality, and leadership. The lower four birds in the four directions are the followers.

There are five major clans in Karbi society: Terang, Teron, Inghi (also spelled Enghi or Enghee), Ingti (also spelled Engti), and Timung.[4] These five major clans are further divided into subclans. This division into clans and subclans has important societal consequences such as marriage restrictions.

An excellent resource on Karbi cultural studies are the two volumes 'Karbi Studies'. The first volume is edited by Dharamsing Teron, with contributions both from Karbi

---

[4] These are the clan names in the Hills Karbi variety; in Plains Karbi, some names are slightly different, e.g., *Timung* is *Tumung* (see § 1.4.1 on dialect differences between what I refer to as Plains and Hills Karbi).

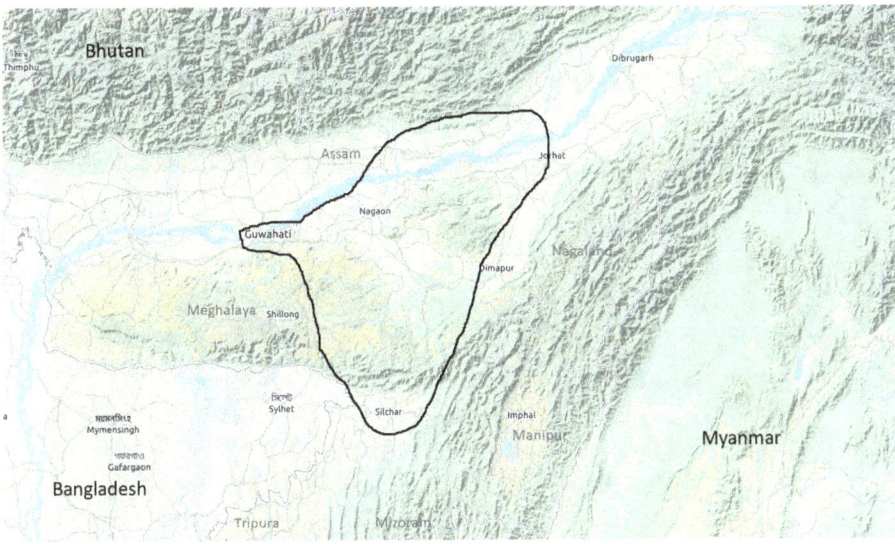

Figure 2: Approximate outline of the Karbi-speaking area (based on a map taken from openstreetmap.org, accessed on February 28, 2020; outline and names for countries as well as Indian states added).

and international scholars (Teron 2012), while the second volume is entirely authored by Teron (Teron 2011). Further information can also be obtained from a blog originally created by Morningkeey Phangcho although no new posts have appeared since 2009 (http://karbi.wordpress.com/).

1.1.3.2 Oral literature

The orally transmitted traditional literature of the Karbis is a fundamental part of Karbi culture. As part of data collection for this grammar, a number of folk stories were recorded that tap into this rich treasure of Karbi oral literature. While the stories are always narrated in the ordinary language, there are a lot of songs (mostly ballads that tell a particular story) as well as (religious) chants which are sung using the song language (see § 1.1.3.3 below). However, also the ordinary language used to tell folk stories has elements specific to the genre, see § 16.1.4 on the discourse structuring markers *e* and *'mh*, as well as § 16.3.12 on the 'narrative style marker' *hedī*, in particular.

Karbi oral literature shares many types of folk stories with other ethnic groups in Northeast India. A typical genre is folk stories about the origins of subclans, such as the story about the three Bey brothers (Konnerth and Tisso 2018: 334–48). Typically, these stories offer a (mythological) explanation of how the division into subclans among members of a particular clan or subclan came about, and they often also contain societal rules such as restrictions on (everyday life) interactions between members of particular subclans.

Figure 3: Priest performing a duck sacrifice.

Figure 4: Jambili athon.

Second, an apparently common story in the context of Northeast India that exists in Karbi oral literature as well is the story *Miso-rongpo lapen Chongho-kaloso* (see Appendix B). This folk story starts with a fight between a frog and an ant (although it might involve other animals in the traditions of other language communities), resulting in a chain reaction of events, in which one animal suffers from being disturbed or hurt by another animal, and as a consequence accidentally disturbs or hurts another animal, and so on. Examples from what appears to be the same basic story in Khumi (South-Central or 'Kuki-Chin'[5], spoken in the Bangladesh/Burma border area) are used in a discussion of elaborate expressions in Khumi by Peterson (2010: 96–7), and I have come across stories with the same basic structure in other South-Central languages as well, such as Monsang, Lamkang, and Thadou.

Another narrative that is characteristic of the region (specifically the hill region stretching from Northeast India across Southeast Asia) concerns the loss of an allegedly previously existing script. This narrative is analyzed by Scott (2009) as a literary-mythological account of an intentional decision by these peoples for an oral literary tradition and against a written tradition. He makes this argument in the context of his larger hypothesis that the hills peoples of Southeast Asia[6] have a history of intentionally fleeing the developing civilizations in the valleys (which were heavily built on slavery in their early beginnings) in order to maintain (cultural and political) independence and societal equality. In Karbi, similar to other languages of the region, the lost script narrative tells that the only record of the script was on a deer hide, which in a time of starvation had to be eaten in order to survive, and was therefore lost.

1.1.3.3 Song language

The Karbi song language is used for oral literature that is sung or chanted (hence the name) rather than narrated. It is also referred to as the poetical language. According to my language consultants, between the two major dialects of Hills and Plains Karbi, there is an interesting relationship between song language and ordinary language such that Hills Karbi song language words are ordinary language words in Plains Karbi and vice versa.[7]

---

5 'Kuki-Chin' is referred to here in single quotes since this label is offensive to speakers of some of the languages included within it, such as Monsang, Moyon, Lamkang, Anal from the state of Manipur in Northeast India. I am also using the name "South-Central" here, following the considerations mentioned in Konnerth (2018: 19).
6 That is, the peoples inhabiting the hill range that stretches across Southeast Asia, which Scott (2009) refers to as *Zomia*, with the claim that that is not only a geographic label but also needs to be understood as an area of a shared cultural-political history.
7 Note that it is not common for members of the Karbi language community to understand all the song language words. They typically know a few individual words, but no more than that.

Many lexical items that occur in the Hills Karbi song language represent borrowings from Khasi languages (with which there exists a history of contact, §1.3). For example, the word *um* is used for 'water' in the song language, which is a common component of toponyms in West Karbi Anglong in names such as Umswai, Umlapher, Umkachi (or Amkachi), etc. The song language is thus an important object for further study in order to trace Khasi borrowings in Karbi. A first move in this direction is the book *Karbi lamlir achili* (lit., 'the seeds of the Karbi poetical language'), a collection of Hills Karbi song language words (some of which with context in songs and chants in which they are used) edited by eminent Karbi language and literature scholar Longkam Teron (Teron 2008). It is furthermore a topic for future study to investigate the grammatical structure of song language texts.

Note that an interesting aspect in the transition from traditional to modern culture is that the song language is also used in modern (Indic, Bollywood-style) Karbi pop songs. However, Christian songs do not make use of the song language but of the ordinary language.[8]

1.1.4 The Karbi Lammet Amei (KLA)

This grammar is the result of close collaboration with members of the Karbi Lammet Amei, who in fact initiated the project in 2007: most notably Mr. Sikari Tisso, as well as Mr. Khor Sing Teron. The Karbi Lammet Amei (KLA; from *Karbì lám-mét a-méi* 'Karbi word-artful POSS-assembly') is a language and literature organization based in the Karbi Anglong district capital Diphu, but with branches in larger villages and towns. The KLA was founded on March 27, 1966, with the goal of preserving and promoting the Karbi language so it could be taught in schools and other institutions of higher education, while also engaging in the promotion of Karbi literature (Khor Sing Teron, p.c.).

1.1.5 The Karbi Anglong and West Karbi Anglong districts

The Karbis have had their own autonomous Karbi Anglong district (i.e., *Karbi a-inglóng* 'Karbi POSS-hill' > 'Karbi hills') for a number of decades. The district was first formed in 1951, although at that time, the North Cachar Hills region to the south still belonged to the district (then called 'United Mikir and North Cachar Hills District'). In 1970, the two parts were separated, and the 'Mikir Hills' district was renamed as Karbi

---

8 There might be several reasons for this. For once, it might be because most Karbi speakers do not understand song language words. Another reason could be that the song language is closely linked to the traditional religious belief and rituals.

Anglong in 1976, with Diphu as the capital.⁹ Until 2015, the Karbi Anglong district comprised of an eastern and a western part, with the capital Diphu in the eastern part. In 2015, the western part split off and is now a separate district of Assam, called West Karbi Anglong. The term Karbi Anglong now refers only to the eastern part.

The Karbi Anglong and West Karbi Anglong districts are located at the southern edge of the Brahmaputra Valley (the Brahmaputra being the river to the north) and most of it in the lower hills that mark the transition between the river valley area and the hill range that extends to the south and the southeast as hinted at in Figure 1 above.¹⁰

The district capital of Karbi Anglong is Diphu and is located in the southern portion of the district. West Karbi Anglong is generally considered to be home to the traditional-cultural center of the Karbis. Specifically, the village of Ronghang Rongbong near Hamren, the district capital of West Karbi Anglong is considered to be the major traditional-cultural center of the Karbis as it is home to the Karbi kings, i.e., *lindókpō*.

1.2 Karbi in Tibeto-Burman

While there has never been any doubt that Karbi is a Tibeto-Burman language, the exact phylogenetic status inside Tibeto-Burman has not been possible to determine. This is despite the fact that information on Karbi has been available early on (§ 1.6.1), and that it has been considered in the early large-scale Tibeto-Burman classification proposals as well as in the modern, detailed comparative work. The difficulties of working out the exact phylogenetic status of Karbi are likely in large part due to a history of language contact and grammatical reorganization as a result of it (§ 1.3).

1.2.1 Tibeto-Burman languages of Northeast India

Northeast India is home to the greatest diversity of Tibeto-Burman languages, including languages from several different branches, such as Bradley's (2002) Western, Sal, and Central branches, see Figure 5.

The Sal branch in Bradley's proposal is a more inclusive version of this branch whose name was coined by Burling (1983), but renamed later more transparently as the 'Bodo-Konyak-Jinghpaw' branch (Burling 2003). Besides this Bodo-Konyak-Jinghpaw subbranch, Burling's (2003) proposal to classify the Tibeto-Burman languages

---

9 This information comes from http://www.karbianglong.nic.in/, which is the official website of the Karbi Anglong District Administration, accessed on February 3, 2014.
10 This is part of the hill range that extends all the way into Southeast Asia and represents something of a cultural area, with similar histories of the people inhabiting them, see Scott (2009).

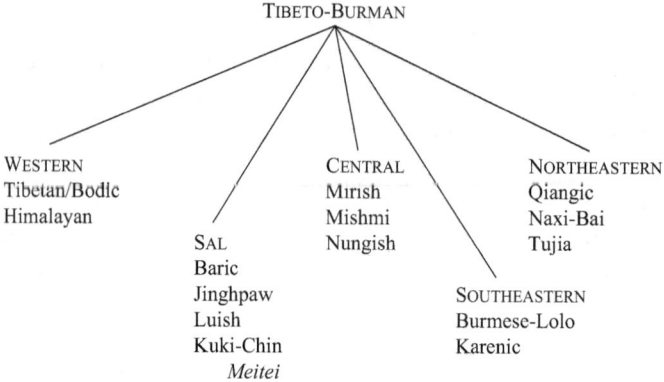

Figure 5: Classification of Tibeto-Burman according to Bradley (2002).

of Northeast India includes a substantial number of other low-level branches, whose higher-level groupings remain far from clear. As seen in the classification of the languages of the 'Eastern Border' in Figure 6, Karbi has in this context always been one of two languages (the other being Meitei, the state language of Manipur) that have been particularly difficult to associate with one of the other low-level branches.

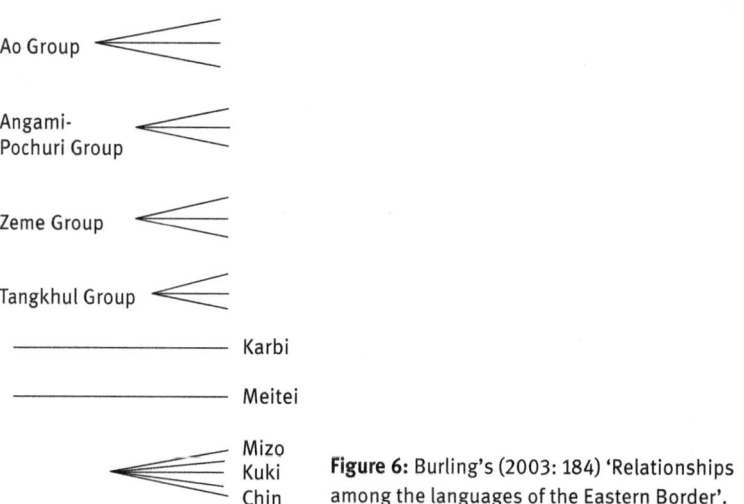

Figure 6: Burling's (2003: 184) 'Relationships among the languages of the Eastern Border'.

1.2.2 Karbi in Tibeto-Burman classification proposals

Karbi (then referred to as 'Mikir') was included in the Linguistic Survey of India (LSI) by Grierson and Konow in the early 20th century (Grierson 1903), which represents the first attempt at classifying Tibeto-Burman languages. Already at that time, there was a fair amount of information available on the language. In the LSI, it is noted that Karbi "has received some attention from the missionaries who work among them", and "we have a vocabulary and some short pamphlets written in it and an admirable grammar with selected texts from the pen of the late Sir Charles Lyall" (Grierson 1903: 69). Still it was unclear where in the classification Karbi belongs:

> In Volume III, Part ii of the Survey I have classed Mikir as falling within the Nāgā-Bodo Sub-Group. The language has affinities with Bodo, but subsequent investigation has shown that it is much more closely connected with Kuki, and that it should be classed [...] as belonging to the Nāgā-Kuki Sub-Group, in which it occupies a somewhat independent position. (Grierson 1903: 69)

While the absence of a closer link between Karbi and Bodo-Garo[11] has not been controversial since, there are three groups in particular that have been linked to Karbi in proposals in the literature: Meitei, 'Naga', and 'Kuki-Chin' (the latter two of which were put into one group, going back to the LSI, see above).[12]

However, the evidence that underlies the grouping of Karbi with Meitei might better be analyzed as borrowings (§ 1.3). The putative grouping with 'Naga' is complicated due to the fact that it is not currently clear at all what 'Naga' actually is, as there is a long-standing confusion of ethnic and linguistic labels surrounding the term 'Naga' (Burling 2003) (i.e., using ethnic labels as linguistic labels, see also § 1.4.2 for a similar problem within Karbi 'dialects'). A possible link to South-Central or 'Kuki-Chin' currently appears promising. As pointed out in various places throughout this grammar, particular links to 'Kuki-Chin' exist, for example with respect to: the negative equational copula (§ 6.2.2.2); the cislocative as well as speech act participant non-subject marking (§ 8.3.1.4); the reflexive/reciprocal prefix (§ 8.4.3); and the realis focus marker =si (§ 12.7.3.1.5), among other constructions. However, working out the exact details as well as implications of these similarities and apparent cognates is a matter of future research. This will likely include the difficult work of carefully disentangling areally from genetically shared features.

In sum, it has remained difficult to come up with a classification proposal that places Karbi in a closer relationship with one of the (geographically) neighboring branches. This is despite early availability of information on Karbi grammar and lexicon (§ 1.6.1), but certainly has to be seen in the context of the remaining lack of information on some of the 'Kuki-Chin' and so-called 'Naga' languages. What appears quite obvious, however, is that a major factor in obscuring the relationships between Karbi and other Tibeto-Burman languages has been language contact and contact-

---

[11] Bodo-Garo languages form a "compact, low-level branch of Tibeto-Burman" (DeLancey 2012). The few similarities that exist between Karbi and Bodo-Garo, such as the Karbi *ke-* nominalizer that is a cognate of a Bodo-Garo adjectival prefix (Konnerth 2009, 2012), stem from a very high node, possibly Proto-Tibeto-Burman.

[12] There also was a proposal by Bauman (1976) to consider Karbi the missing link in a connection between 'Kuki-Chin' and Lepcha.

induced changes in Karbi grammar and lexicon. In particular, it has been known since the Linguistic Survey of India that Karbi has been in close contact (and, in fact, the closest contact of all TB languages) with the Austroasiatic Khasi languages to the west in Meghalaya.

1.3 On the role of contact in the development of Karbi

1.3.1 Linguistic evidence for contact with Austroasiatic, Indo-Aryan, and other Tibeto-Burman languages

A proper investigation of lexical and grammatical/constructional borrowings in Karbi has not yet been conducted. In what follows, I will describe the evidence that I have encountered in the course of preparing this grammar.

As far as lexical borrowings are concerned, a very preliminary picture can be obtained from the glossary appended to this grammar. Of a total of about 1,600 entries, there are 88 lexical items identified as apparently coming from Assamese or Indo-Aryan more broadly (e.g., Bengali); 11 as Khasi; 5 as English; and 2 as Pnar. A few caveats limit the informative value of these numbers, however. First, these items were only identified in an opportunistic way, rather than systematically. Therefore, given closer examination, we would expect to find more borrowings. This is particularly true for borrowings from Khasi and Pnar, as the language consultants I have mostly worked with do not know these languages well. Further, although I have tried to eliminate from the glossary all those words in particular from Assamese and English that seemed to be instances of spontaneous code-switching rather than being widely used borrowings, there may still be some code-switching items from Assamese listed in the glossary that I did not identify as such. Also, it needs to be kept in mind that some borrowings might have passed through another language before entering Karbi (see also the discussion in Joseph and Konnerth 2015). Thus, the numbers from the glossary represent merely a rough picture of the amount of borrowing in the Karbi lexicon. Nonetheless, it is interesting to note that the Karbi lexicon apparently only contains a rather small amount of borrowed vocabulary.

Another set of lexical borrowings was identified by Grüßner (1978): a number of lexical items referring to social organization as well as the kingdom system are borrowings from Khasi or Pnar, obviously suggesting that the concept was borrowed along with the word. Examples include the Karbi *lindók-pō* 'king' (with the male suffix *-pō*) from Khasi *lyngdoh* 'priest' (or Pnar *lŋdɔʔ* (see Ring 2015)), and the word *kúr* for 'clan'.

With respect to closed class borrowings, we find a small number of borrowings from Assamese, such as the reflexive pronoun *anijé* 'REFL' or *-lokòt* 'along with', which is used as a relator noun in Karbi. Also borrowed from Assamese, we find interjections, such as the exclamation *ekdóm*, the correction word *bá*, and the hesitation word *mane* (§ 16.5, § 16.6). As far as closed class borrowings from other languages are concerned, one example is the Karbi singular human classifier *-nūt*, which Joseph (2009) argues to derive either from Standard Khasi (there reconstructed as **shi-ngut*) or Pnar (reconstructed form **chi-ngut*).

No clear cases of borrowings have been identified in the domain of grammatical constructions.[13] However, the causative prefix *pe-~pa-* may represent a borrowing from Austroasiatic (cf. § 8.4.2).

Otherwise, one case of possible contact with the Tibeto-Burman language Meitei are the peculiar, corresponding numeral systems in both languages. As discussed in § 6.4.2, the numerals 'eight' and 'nine' are morphologically complex forms that translate as 'ten minus two' and 'ten minus one' in both languages. This subtractive construction for 'eight' and 'nine' is not attested so far in any other language in the region. The corresponding constructions in Karbi and Meitei look calqued, since the individual morphemes do not correspond.

Another form that connects Karbi to Meitei, although also to 'Kuki-Chin', is the suffix *-pī* 'female; augmentative' (§ 7.4.1.1). The Meitei suffix has the segmentally identical form *-pi* 'female'. Likewise, in 'Kuki-Chin', we find an augmentative form reconstructed by VanBik (2009: 84) as **puy*, which in most of the languages takes the form *-pi*. This is noteworthy because it is not a typical Tibeto-Burman form and to my knowledge not attested anywhere else in the family. It is not clear yet what to make of this apparent correspondence.

In addition to the evidence from numerals and the female suffix, there are several other correspondences that could potentially contribute to a model of Karbi-Meitei contact, but without being strong evidence. For example, the Karbi word *ōk* 'meat' is peculiar because the more common Tibeto-Burman root for a word 'flesh' is something like Matisoff's (2003) reconstructed **sya*. The Meitei word for 'pig' is *ók* (Chelliah 1997), and considering that pork is the major and favorite type of meat eaten by the Karbis, *ōk* might be a borrowing from this Meitei word for 'pig'. At the same time, the Meitei *ók* is similar to roots for the word 'pig' in other Tibeto-Burman languages. Mat-

---

[13] Note that one intruigingly parallel construction between Karbi and 'Kuki-Chin' is the marking of non-subject, or object, speech act participants on the verb. In Karbi, the marker is *nang=*, derived from a second person form (§ 8.3.1). The exact same construction, with a slightly different second person possessive form *nə-* is also found in Purum (Sharma and Singh 2008; see Konnerth 2015) and a vowel-harmonic form *nV-* in Chiru (Chiru 2019), both languages from the Northwestern subbranch of 'Kuki-Chin'. In addition, Aimol (Northwestern 'Kuki-Chin') also has a marker *na-* for indexing first person O arguments (personal fieldwork). Other 'Kuki-Chin' languages have innovated first person or first/second person O argument marking from different source constructions, but the prevalence of this kind of construction is very typical for 'Kuki-Chin'. But despite the near-identity of the construction in Karbi on the one hand and Purum and Chiru on the other hand in terms of synchronic function and diachronic source, it is unclear whether to propose that language contact plays a role here. There are other similarities between Karbi and 'Kuki-Chin', but they may be due to a phylogenetic link rather than contact.

isoff (2003) here reconstructs *p^wak (the Karbi word is *phāk*). Therefore, this does not represent strong evidence for a borrowing from Meitei into Karbi.[14]

Finally, suggestive evidence for contact between Karbi and Austroasiatic populations comes from the set of common female Karbi names that start with *ka-*, which is the female article in Khasi and Pnar, for example, *Kare, Kasang, Kahan, Kache*, as insightfully observed by U.V. Joseph (personal communication).

1.3.2 Non-linguistic evidence for contact with populations speaking Austroasiatic and Indo-Aryan languages

The current state of research presented in the previous section, while being only a preliminary survey, suggests that there is not much linguistic evidence for contact between Karbi and other languages. However, there is also some non-linguistic evidence to complement the linguistic evidence. This non-linguistic evidence so far includes just several pieces of the much larger puzzle regarding the history of language contact between Karbi and Austroasiatic languages on the one hand and Indo-Aryan languages on the other hand. The limited facts presented here do not allow yet to model the contact scenarios. But they do bear witness to the existence of considerable contact between Karbi and languages of these two language families. Note that I remain purposefully vague about the exact languages involved. Among the Austroasiatic languages, the two most likely candidates for contact with Karbi appear to be Pnar and Khasi; among Indo-Aryan languages, it would be Assamese and Bengali. All four languages (and perhaps others) have probably been in contact with Karbi at some time, and it is difficult and in many cases probably impossible to tell a Pnar origin from a Khasi origin, and an Assamese origin from a Bengali origin.

As a first piece of evidence, consider the present-day geographic distribution of languages. Figure 7 provides the locations of Pnar, Khasi, War, and Lyngam speaking populations. The West Karbi Anglong district is located at the northeastern border of these areas. This map shows that the geographic spread of populations speaking the Austroasiatic Pnar and Khasi languages overlaps with the Karbi speaking area. It is in particular Pnar that is in close contact with Karbi as it is spoken in pockets inside the West Karbi Anglong district and borders the Karbi speaking area to the south. Khasi is spoken along the western border of the Karbi speaking area but not inside it.

A history of close contact with Pnar and Khasi in the western part of the Karbi speaking area is also evidenced by the names of Karbi villages whose etymologies go back to Pnar or Khasi. For example, a number of village names in West Karbi Anglong

---

[14] In addition, there is also a demonstrative *si* in Meitei (Chelliah 1997) that represents an alternative (or possibly ultimately the same) cognate for the focus marker =*si* in Karbi (which is suggested to be connected to an equational copula *si(i)* in Central 'Kuki-Chin' in § 12.7.3.1.5).

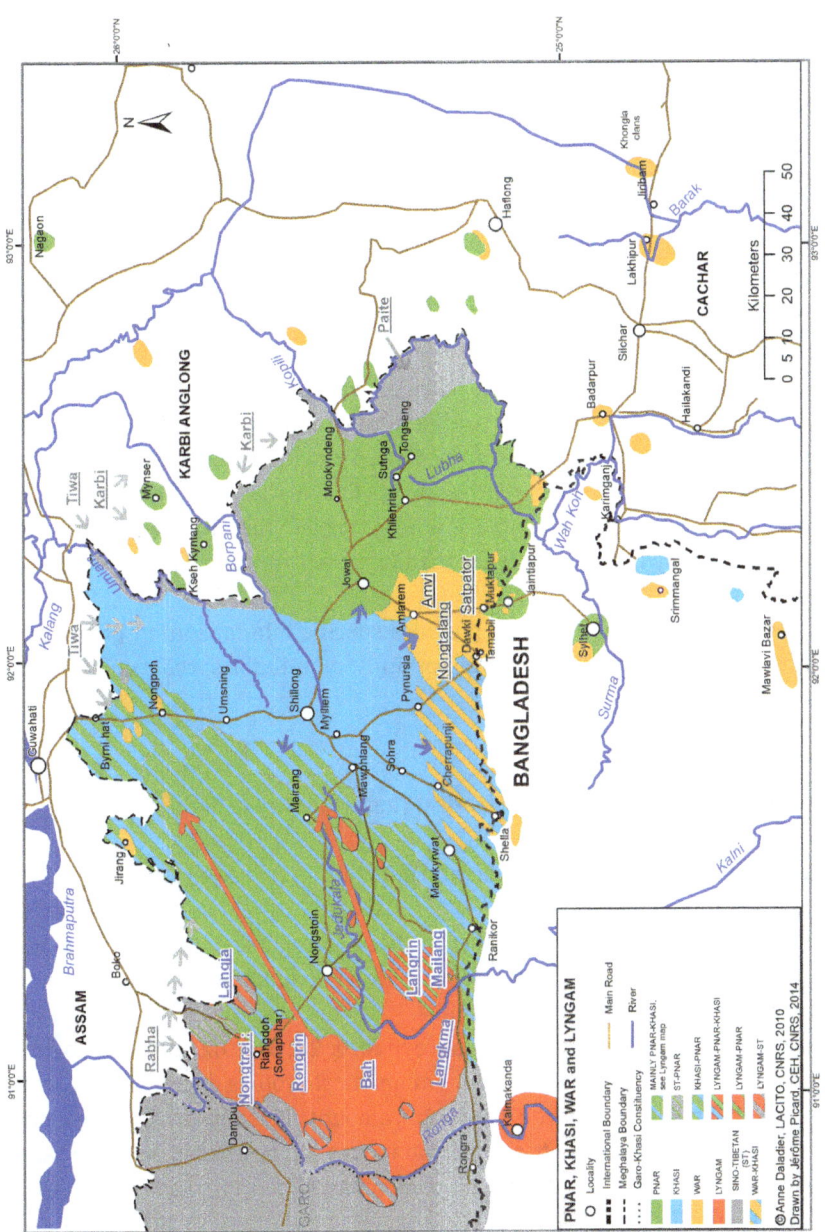

Figure 7: Pnar, Khasi, War, and Lyngam speaking areas (Daladier 2014).

contain a syllable *um*, which is the word for 'water' in both Pnar and Khasi. Examples are *Umswai, Umpanai, Umlaper*, as well as probably village names with *am*, such as *Amkachi* or *Amtereng*. This evidence suggests that these villages used to be Khasi or Pnar territory and at some point were resettled by Karbis.

Another piece of non-linguistic evidence for contact between Karbi and Austroasiatic and Indo-Aryan comes from the ethnographic-historical work by Stack and Lyall (1908). Without citing a source, they claim that, "during the Burmese wars in the early part of the last century [...] many Assamese are reported to have taken refuge with [the Karbis], and to have become [Karbis]" (Stack and Lyall 1908: 22). They even provide further detail with respect to how people from other communities were able to become Karbis: "[...] in North Cachar outsiders are admitted into the tribe and are enrolled as members of one of the *kurs*, after purification by one of the Bē-kuru *kur*" (Stack and Lyall 1908: 23; italics original). They also provide a remarkable photograph with the caption "Group of Mikirs [=Karbis] (North Cachar)", where five men of widely varying physical appearance are seen. The authors explain that "[i]n the group [...] the short man is evidently a Khasi, while the man to his left appears to be an Assamese" (Stack and Lyall 1908: 23).

This ethnographic evidence thus provides specific information on practices of accepting non-Karbis, and therefore importantly, non-Karbi speakers, into Karbi society.

1.3.3 A creolization account for grammatical characteristics of Karbi

Many aspects of Karbi grammar can be understood in terms of a more general type of grammatical profile that DeLancey (2010, 2011b, 2012, 2013) has called "creoloid". This section is dedicated to a discussion of these grammatical characteristics as a way of connecting facts about Karbi grammar. It is argued that we find the "creoloid" signature across many grammatical domains.

In a number of recent articles, DeLancey (2010, 2011b, 2012, 2013) has offered an explanatory account for the divergent grammatical profiles that are found in the Tibeto-Burman family: Some have a substantial amount of fusional morphology; have verbs with rigid syntagmatic slots and person indexation systems of, in some cases, extremely high synchronic and diachronic complexity. Others may have the opposite: agglutinating, transparent morphology; verbal systems with grammatical markers in flexible position and hence semanto-pragmatic rather than morphosyntactic organization, and no verbal person indexation.

DeLancey argues that the latter type of grammatical profile is innovative. It is correlated with what we may refer to as a particular 'ethnolinguistic profile', which includes several factors that are related to language contact. Particular case studies of this grammar type, characterized by transparent morphology and the absence of verbal person indexation, among other features, include the ancestral languages of the Bodo-Garo branch (DeLancey 2012) and of Sinitic (DeLancey 2011b).

While Bodo-Garo is argued to have an origin in a lingua franca in DeLancey's proposal,[15] such an extreme case of contact influence does not need to be assumed in the case of Karbi. However, a considerable impact from contact has to be part of the history of Karbi as well. As I argue in this section, DeLancey's framework provides a useful approach to understanding Karbi grammar in a holistic way. It allows us to see parallels across different grammatical domains. The following sections will provide an overview of the areal ethnolinguistic profile of Karbi (§ 1.3.3.1); aspects of its overall grammatical profile (§ 1.3.3.2); as well as one brief case study that illustrates a more general characteristic of the grammatical make-up of the language. It shows what we may refer to as the non-obligatoriness of grammatical markers: they are found lacking in morphosyntactic contexts that should require their presence (§ 1.3.3.3).

1.3.3.1 Areal ethnolinguistic profile

DeLancey (2013) provides case studies in which languages with a "creoloid" grammatical profile (§ 1.3.3.2) are argued to have become that way due to a situation of intense language contact. The type of language contact that is required in order to reshape the grammatical make-up of a language involves one or several events of a substantial number of adult second language learners entering into the community. The idea is that these adult non-native speakers cannot learn the language perfectly and thus speak a 'decomplexified' version of it, which becomes the way the language is spoken in the community at large.

Within the local context, the (pre)historical events of adult non-native speaker influxes would have naturally been common in the valley areas of the Eastern Himalayan region where the expansions of kingdoms and new conquests happened on a regular basis. Certain hilly areas also underwent similar events, in particular those near the large valley areas where there has always been a lot of back and forth between valley and hills.

If the historical scenario for the reshaping of grammar towards a "creoloid" profile has to do with one or several periods of adult non-native speaker influxes, then we will also expect that we are dealing with a community of a substantial size to accept the incoming strangers into the society. This kind of account is thus more plausible if the community is large both in terms of number of speakers and in terms of the size of the area where the language is spoken.

To sum up, the ethnolinguistic profile that lends itself naturally to correlate with "creoloid" grammar involves variables such as (a) number of speakers; (b) size of area covered by the language; and (c) location of the area covered by the language in terms of topography.

---

15 This proposal goes back to Burling (2007).

As for (a), the estimate of the total number of speakers is somewhere around a half million (§ 1.1.2). This makes Karbi the third largest tribal language in terms of number of speakers in Assam. The language with the highest number of speakers is Boro, which is one of DeLancey's (2013) case studies for his argument.

In terms of (b), the size of area covered by the language, we find that Karbi speakers are spread across a very large area. The approximate outline of today's Karbi speaking area is shown in Figure 2 in § 1.1.2. It extends across all of the central districts of Assam as well as into eastern Meghalaya and southern Arunachal Pradesh.

Karbi has also historically been recognized as a particularly large community and language in the local context. In the preface to his Karbi dictionary, Walker (1925) says, "[...] the Mikirs [=Karbis] are among the more numerous of the Assam frontier races, and [...] they are scattered over a wide area, from Golaghat to Kamrup and the Khasi Hills beyond Gauhati, and from the Cachar plains near Silchar to the forests north of Bishnath in Darrang [...]." A similar remark about the wide geographic spread of the Karbi community stems from the Linguistic Survey of India, where it is noted that "it cannot be doubted that in former times the Mikirs occupied a comparatively large tract of country in the lower hills and adjoining lowlands of the central portion of the range stretching from the Garo Hills to the Patkoi" (Grierson 1903: 69). According to this account, the historical spread of the Karbi speaking area extended even further east than today as there do not appear to be villages found nowadays in the Patkoi hill range, i.e., in any of the far eastern districts of Assam or in Nagaland, Manipur, or Mizoram.

This last quote also mentions the topographic location "in the lower hills and adjoining lowlands", which is an accurate characterization for the modern extension of the Karbi speaking area as well. Therefore Karbi does not exactly align with either the "Valley" or the "Hills" type of languages and cultures that have repeatedly been found to exhibit very different characteristics (cf. Scott 2009; DeLancey 2013 and references therein). However, the immediate adjacency of the Karbi speaking lowlands area to the Brahmaputra Valley clearly represents another factor in favor of reconstructing the kind of high contact scenario that has shaped the evolution of Karbi grammar.

In sum, Karbi has an ethnolinguistic profile very similar to that of other languages argued to have "creoloid" grammar by DeLancey (2012; 2013): large community size, large area covered, and location in the lower hills adjacent to the Brahmaputra Valley.

1.3.3.2 Aspects of a "creoloid" grammatical profile

DeLancey's "creoloid" grammatical profile revolves around the notion of morphosyntactic transparency. As DeLancey puts it, "A characteristically creoloid morpheme has a unitary, coherent meaning, which is inherent to the morpheme itself, not dependent on paradigmatic or syntagmatic relations to other morphemes" (2013: 45). This notion of transparency can be broken down into a number of characteristics, which Karbi shares with languages of DeLancey's "creoloid" type.

First, Karbi has consistently agglutinating morphology. The amount of morphophonemics is minimal, and is restricted to a small number of tone changes and allomorphy in the limited prefixation processes (§ 3.9). There are no irregular forms (such as, for example, verb stem alternations in the 'Kuki-Chin' languages (King 2009)).

There is also a considerable amount of evidence that Karbi is not concerned with transitivity as a morphosyntactic notion. Although on the one hand, it is the case that several predicate derivation suffixes can be argued to change the argument structure, as shown in § 9.2.5.4. On the other hand, however, other, including more typical derivational categories do not always affect the argument structure in a consistent way. First, the causative prefix *pe-~pa-* is shown to produce different argument structures in § 13.2.3.1 without any additional marking. The examples show that the same transitive verb *chetòng* 'meet' can occur with two different argument structures when the causative prefix is added to derive the meaning 'make somebody meet somebody'. Also, the reflexive/reciprocal marker *che-* can be used on a transitive verb without resulting in an intransitive verb with a single argument. As § 8.4.3 shows, there are a number of examples where a *che-* marked, reflexive verb still has what we would analyze as an A and an O argument. In those cases, the reflexive meaning lies in the identity of the A with the possessor of the O argument. Furthermore, as discussed in § 9.2.5.2, there are two applicative-like verbal suffixes *-pī* 'benefactive/malefactive' and *-ī* 'instrumental, comitative', which cannot be considered true applicatives precisely because they do not lead to a consistent change in argument structure (see also § 13.2.3.2). Also more generally, Chapter 13 argues that there is no direct morphosyntactic assignment of clausal participants to either argument or oblique roles. The lack of a clear distinction further speaks to the fact that transitivity is not an important notion in Karbi (see specifically § 13.1.2).

There are also no person indexation paradigms in Karbi as found in the conservative Tibeto-Burman languages. There is the phenomenon of indexing non-subject speech-act participants, as well as the cislocative, via *nang=* as discussed in § 8.3, but this is strikingly different from the rich and archaic person marking systems found elsewhere in the family. More generally, Karbi has shed much of the archaic morphology that we can still find in other Tibeto-Burman languages. While there are reflexes of the Proto-TB nominal prefixes **a-* '3SG' (§ 7.3.1), **m-* 'intransitive, durative, reflexive' (§ 6.3.1), and **r-* with an unclear function (§ 6.3.2), as well as the verbal prefix **gV-* 'nominalizer' (Chapter 12), the language is predominantly suffixing. A particularly rich suffixal category are predicate derivations, among which a number of recent grammaticalizations can be found (§ 9.2).

1.3.3.3 Non-obligatoriness of grammatical markers

Another characteristic of Karbi grammar that is arguably a direct outcome of its "creoloid" nature surfaces in many different grammatical domains. It can be described as a general non-obligatoriness of grammatical markers. It is another way in which Karbi has apparently replaced rigid morphosyntax with pragmatics.

As discussed in Chapter 12, the nominalizer *ke-* not only has synchronically productive functions but also has grammaticalized, within particular constructions, to verbal markers of imperfective aspect and focus. However, the focus construction is difficult to analyze because the occurrence of *ke-* is not consistent. Possibly, this has to do with the grammaticalization of the construction, which has resulted in the reanalysis of one component of the construction as a dedicated focus particle, as argued in § 12.7.3.1.1, which would have left the *ke-* without a synchronic function. Perhaps it is a result of not serving a synchronic function that *ke-* is often left out in this construction. However, even in those cases where *ke-* does serve a synchronically nominalizing function, it turns out that its occurrence is not consistent in all cases where its presence is expected to be required. These cases are discussed in § 12.8. One example is (616), which is repeated below as (1).

(1) Lack of *ke-* 'NMLZ' on relative clause verb
[...] "he matsi", hala apiso abang pulo,
he komāt=si hála a-pisò abàng pù-lò
hey! who=FOC:RL that POSS-wife NPDL say-RL

"he therak thekthe apinso"
he [[therāk thèk-Cē] a-pinsò]
hey! **be.ashamed know.how-NEG** POSS-married.man
'[...] "Hey, who is that!", the wife said, "hey, (you are) a man who doesn't feel any shame".' [SeT, MTN 034]

Another highly frequent grammatical marker of Karbi is *a-* 'possessive'. It attaches to a head noun that is modified by a preceding modifier of any kind, be it a relative clause, a derived property concept term modifier, or a demonstrative (§ 10.4). However, also *a-* is occasionally found lacking, for example in (381), repeated as (2).

(2) Preposed demonstrative *lasō* 'this' without *a-* on head noun
[...] amat laso sarpita ajo mek janglo [...]
[amāt **[lasō sarpī=tā]** a-jó mēk jáng-lò]
and.then **this old.woman=ADD** POSS-night eye fall-RL
'[...] [A]nd then also that old woman slept at night. [...]' [KK, BMS 118]

In addition to what we have just seen with *ke-* and *a-*, we also find "non-obligatoriness" of marking in the clausal domain, more specifically with respect to noun phrases that express additional, "non-core" roles.[16] Typically, noun phrases that express these additional participants are found inside a relator noun construction or with the

---

[16] See, however, Chapter 13 for argumentation that Karbi does not strictly distinguish between core and oblique participants in its morphosyntax.

comitative/instrumental/ablative clitic =*pen*. However, even these oblique NP's may remain unmarked as discussed in § 14.1.1.7. An example is (708), which is repeated as (3). In this example, the second clause *nangtumke mandule cho* has an unmarked locative NP *mandule* 'in the *mandu* (field hut)'.

(3) Unmarked (non-salient) locative NP with *chō* 'eat', but marked salient locative NP (*angsóng* 'high up')
 *[...] nangpole **hemtap angsong** chote, nangtumke mandule*
 [[nang-pō=le **[hēmtāp a-ngsóng]** chō-tē] nang-tūm=ke
 2-father=FOC:IRR **tree.house POSS-high.up** eat-if 2-PL=TOP
       cho
 [mandú=le] chō]
 field.hut=FOC:IRR eat
 '[...] "[I]f your father takes his meal in the *hemtap*, you eat in the *mandu*".' [CST, RO 017]

We also find "non-obligatoriness" in subordinate clause markers. The marker -*ī* 'with' on a relative clause verb, which regularly indicates that an instrumental clause participant is being relativized on, is not obligatory (§ 12.3.1.1). This is illustrated by (550), repeated as (4), where the relative clause verb *tòk* 'pound' is only nominalized by *ke-* rather than additionally being marked with -*ī* as would be expected.

(4) Instrument relativization without -*ī*
 lasi la thap ketok alengpumta
 lasì [là **[thàp ke-tòk]**_{RC} a-lengpūm=tā]_{HN}
 therefore this **cake.for.rice.beer NMLZ-pound POSS-pestle**=ADD
 otdunno, [...]
 ót-dùn-nō
 touch-JOIN-be.bad
 'The pestle with which the rice beer cake is ground is bad to touch. [...]'
 [WR, BCS 037]

Relative clauses with a future sense are also expected to be explicitly marked as such by carrying the irrealis2 marker -*jí* (§ 12.3.1.2). Nonetheless, -*jí* also turns out to occasionally be lacking where it should be required. An instance of this is discussed in (553), (partially) repeated as (5).

(5) Future relative clause without -*jí*
 ta ne kethan atomo abangke [...]
 tā [[nè **ke-thán**] a-tomó abàng=ke]
 but 1EXCL **NMLZ-tell** POSS-story NPDL=TOP
 'the story I'll be telling now, [...]' [KK, CC 008]

Finally, the proclitic *nang=*, which highlights the involvement of non-subject speech-act participants, may be left out. While *nang=* regularly occurs on the verb to cross-reference first or second person O arguments, this is only the case in one of two instances in (210), repeated as (6) (§ 8.3.1.2). There are two parallel sentences in this example, with parallel relative clauses in which A and O are the same and only the relative clause verb changes. Despite the parallel structure, or more likely because of it, the second instance of the same second person O argument is not cross-referenced with *nang=* while the first one was.

(6) Third person acting on second person (3→2)
*athema nangphan **nangkelang** inut donangji*
athēma **[[[nàng-phān nang**=ke-làng] e-nūt] dō-náng-jí]
because **you**-NSUBJ 1/2:NSUBJ=NMLZ-see one-CLF:HUM:SG exist-need-IRR2

kevan kepon inut donangji [...]
[[[ke-vàn ke-pòn] e-nūt] dō-náng-jí]
NMLZ-bring NMLZ-take.away one-CLF:HUM:SG exist-need-IRR2
'Because there needs to be somebody to look after you, there needs to be somebody to bring you and to take you. [...]' [SH, CSM 066]

This section has surveyed a number of different grammatical markers, across a variety of grammatical domains, which all share the property that they are not syntactically obligatory. What all these cases arguably have in common then is that rather than exhibiting the expected one-to-one mapping between form and function, these grammatical morphemes indicate a function that can also be left unmarked, letting the context disambiguate what the utterance is about. Bringing this back to the proposed "creoloid" profile of the language, it is argued that such a pragmatically oriented morphosyntax, which leaves a considerable amount of disambiguation to the (non-linguistic) context, is likely to have its origin in a high contact situation where the influx of adult second language learners "interrupts" the language transmission process to the new generation (McWhorter 2007).

1.3.4 Summary

The current state of research suggests that there is not much linguistic evidence for contact between Karbi and languages from other language families, specifically Austroasiatic or Indo-Aryan, that would help explain the creoloid aspects of Karbi grammatical structure as argued above. Nonetheless, there is non-linguistic evidence for contact that strongly suggests that there were second language learners of Karbi joining the community. The hypothesis at this point can thus be that there may have been native speakers of different languages joining Karbi society. If it was not a single group that joined then it makes sense that we do not see large amounts of borrowings from a single language but rather the kind of systematic grammatical restructuring that has resulted in present day Karbi grammar.

As discussed in the next section, apart from a single major dialect divide, there is little dialectal variation in Karbi. This may reflect a rather shallow time depth of the modern Karbi language that has been emerging as a consequence of the assumed restructuring.

1.4 Varieties of the Karbi language

While the details of the Karbi dialect situation are outside the scope of this grammar, it appears that there is a high degree of homogeneity – perhaps surprisingly so, given the large geographic spread of the language. This was also noted by Walker (1925) as he writes in the preface to his dictionary that "in spite of the fact [...] that [the Karbis] are scattered over a wide area, [...], the language is practically one and the same throughout."

The simplified 'big picture' of the dialect situation, is that there is a major dividing line (political as much as linguistic in nature) between the Hills Karbis (Karbis from *Karbi Anglong* and *West Karbi Anglong* ((W)KA)) and the Plains Karbis (Karbis mostly living in the plains of Assam largely north of (W)KA), as discussed in § 1.4.1.

Within each of these major two varieties, there is relatively little dialectal variation. However, investigating the nature of dialectal variation is complicated due to the application of dialect labels by Karbi native speakers, which are grounded in historical ethnic/familial and/or geographical affiliation, as outlined in § 1.4.2.

Following this discussion, § 1.4.3 further discusses two of these dialect labels from the Hills Karbi variety: the Rongkhang or Ronghang dialect, which (with apparently wide-spread acceptance) is being used as the basis for standardization; and the Hills (not Plains) Amri Karbi dialect, which is spoken in West Karbi Anglong, where the traditional-cultural center of the Karbis lies.

Finally, § 1.4.4 offers a list of some lexemes that have been found to exhibit (mostly, vowel) alternations in the speech of different native speakers, without, however, actually appearing to represent dialect isoglosses.

Note that besides these geographical and historical/ethnic dialect groups, there appears to be some evidence for a Christian sociolect (possibly specifically in the Tika region), with some slight differences in lexicon and grammar from the non-Christian sociolect (see § 1.6.2 on Grüßner's work, which was based on a variety with some such features). All of these issues pertaining to linguistic varieties of Karbi require further research.

In the discussion of varieties of the Karbi language, in the following subsections as well as in the entire grammar, I want to emphasize that not a single word is written with a political motive behind it. My goal has always been to describe the linguistic landscape in a scientific way and to be as neutral as possible when it comes to the politics that are, of course, tied to it in real life. I truly hope that no part of the discussion of the different varieties of the Karbi language is offensive to anybody.

1.4.1 Plains Karbi ("Amri Karbi") and Hills Karbi

The Plains Karbi variety spoken in the Kamrup and Marigaon districts of Assam as well as partly in the Ri-Bhoi district of Meghalaya is commonly referred to as 'Amri Karbi' in the linguistic literature and in the Ethnologue (Lewis, Simons, and Fennig 2013). However, it should be noted right away that Karbis identifying with the western subvariety of Hills Karbi use the same name for themselves, possibly because of an ultimately shared geographical origin and/or common ancestors (§ 1.4.3).

Members of the Karbi Lammet Amei (§ 1.1.4) have expressed their concern to me over the use of the name Amri for the Plains Karbi variety, while this name is embraced by many speakers of this variety. The term 'Dumra' or 'Dumrali' is also used to refer to this variety of the Karbi language and the people that speak it.

In the following discussion, I will use the geographically based terms 'Plains Karbi' and 'Hills Karbi' to refer to the two major linguistic varieties of the Karbi language, which, again, include further 'sub'-varieties based on linguistic features, which are, however, not as different from one another as are the two major varieties. Although these geographic terms are not ideal either since there are Karbis living in the plains who do not speak the 'Plains Karbi' variety, I follow Teron and Tumung (2007) in using 'Plains Karbi' and 'Hills Karbi' in these ways, as the terminological debate is currently still ongoing and there simply is no ideal set of terms to use at this point. Note that the name Amri refers to a historical administrative unit in the Karbi kingdom, and, as mentioned above, in addition to Plains Karbis, the group of Hills Karbis living in the West Karbi Anglong district also identify with this name, see § 1.4.2 and § 1.4.3 below.

There is a strong political movement on part of the Plains Karbis to consider their variety of Karbi a different language rather than just a different dialect from the variety of Karbi that is spoken in the Hills. This likely has to do with the unequal power relations between the two groups. While there are close to half a million native speakers of Hills Karbi that have autonomy in the Karbi Anglong and West Karbi Anglong districts, the Plains Karbi speaking population is scattered across a number of districts, and a 2003 figure reported by the Ethnologue estimates the number of speakers at a total of 125,000 (Simons and Fennig 2017).[17]

---

[17] It is not clear what the basis is for this figure provided by the Ethnologue. The Census data of close to a half a million native speakers of Karbi do not specify whether a distinction was made between Hills and Plains Karbi (and hence it likely was not).

According to my Hills Karbi language consultants, there is a high degree of mutual intelligibility between the Hills and Plains Karbi.[18] This is especially true for Hills Karbi speakers that are fluent in Assamese (which most people living in the urban areas are), as the Plains Karbi variety has a large number of Assamese loans due to closer contact with Assamese in the plains. It is also noted in the Ethnologue that "some Amri Karbi villages shifted completely to Assamese due to intermarriage and the perception that Assamese is preferred for children to do well in school."

In addition to the larger number of Assamese loans, some of the more noticeable ways in which Plains Karbi is different from Hills Karbi are the following. First, there are differences between the song language (§ 1.1.3.3) and the ordinary language. Specifically, Plains Karbi uses lexemes in ordinary, colloquial speech, which are only used in the song language of Hills Karbi, and vice versa.

A phonological difference is that Plains Karbi has preserved coda /l/, which in Hills Karbi has changed to a glide codas (see § 3.4).

In the domain of morphology, there are two salient differences. First, the unusual onset-reduplicative negative suffix -Cē in Hills Karbi (§ 3.8.6.3) corresponds to just -e without the onset reduplication in Plains Karbi. Second, the Hills Karbi negative existential copula is avē, while Plains Karbi instead uses the form ingjong (§ 6.2.2.1.1).

With respect to syntax, there are two frequently occurring Plains Karbi constructions that are not used in Hills Karbi. On the one hand, the positive existential copula dō is often used following a bare stem. It is not clear to my Hills Karbi language consultants what the function of this construction is, but it is very striking to them. On the other hand, habitual aspect is marked by the suffix -man in Plains Karbi, where in Hills Karbi simply the bare stem is used.

Within the Plains Karbi variety, there is also some amount of dialectal variation. For example, in the Ri-Bhoi district of Meghalaya, the Bhoi Mynri variant is spoken.

A good resource on the Plains Karbi variety is the trilingual dictionary edited by Teron and Tumung (2007), which includes both Plains and Hills Karbi forms of each lexical item, as well as translations into Assamese and English.

1.4.2 Relationships between the Hills Karbi 'dialects'

There are four 'dialect' labels that are used by Hills Karbi native speakers to identify their own and other people's speech: Amri, Rongkhang (or Ronghang), Chinthong, and Killing. Originally, however, these labels are connected to historical administrative units of the Karbi kingdom and the people that lived in these administrative units. Therefore, while there certainly is a historical connection between an individual's

---

18 I myself have not carried out any research on the differences between the two dialect groups. Almost everything I report here is second-hand information from my Hills Karbi language consultants.

affiliation to one of these groups and the variety s/he speaks, this is not always the case anymore today.

Since this discussion of these different groups is only for the purpose of sketching out the linguistic landscape, everything said here comes through the lens of linguistic variation and is considered in its relevance to linguistic varieties. I would like to acknowledge that it is shorthand to speak of 'Amri Karbi' or 'Rongkhang Karbi' and that the more accurate way of referring to the people that identify with these names is to say *Amri aso* 'children / inhabitants of Amri' and *Rongkhang aso* 'children / inhabitants of Rongkhang.'

According to Dharamsing Teron (p.c.), the following can be said about these 'dialect' groups:

The three major groups are Amri, Rongkhang, and Chinthong. The Killing group appears to be a part of the Rongkhang group. The Amri group was the first to migrate into the present-day Karbi Anglong area. They split up and some of them went to present-day West Karbi Anglong (i.e., the group discussed in § 1.4.3), while others moved into the plains (i.e., the Plains Karbis, discussed above in § 1.4.1).

The Rongkhang group is mostly located in the southern portion of (eastern) Karbi Anglong, where the district capital Diphu is located. This group became the most dominant and influential group, which is why the Rongkhang 'dialect' is currently considered the standard dialect. Note, however, that linguistically, it is not possible for my language consultants to pinpoint defining differences between Rongkhang and the 'dialects' of (eastern) Karbi Anglong and the area to the south, i.e., Chinthong, and Killing. (The Killing group is geographically centered in places such as Kheroni, Jyrikyndeng, and further into the North Cachar Hills area.)

1.4.3 Hills Karbi: Differences between Rongkhang (Hills Karbi; Diphu) and Amri (Hills Karbi; West Karbi Anglong) dialects

While any particular differences between the Rongkhang dialect and other dialects to the north and the south are not easy to discern for my language consultants (although among themselves, they may identify with different dialect groups, see § 1.4.2 above), there are a number of differences between, on the one hand, Rongkhang and the other putative dialects, and, on the other hand, the Amri dialect in West Karbi Anglong. These differences are not only lexical in nature, but also include two systematic phonological differences. First, the Amri dialect has a sixth phonemic vowel, which is a high to mid-high, front, centralized /ɪ/ (§ 3.2.1). Second, the Amri dialect has preserved both the /ei/ and the /ai/ rhymes, while the Rongkhang dialect has merged them to /ai/ (§ 3.2).

In addition, there are a number of differences in other grammatical domains as well. For example, the *pe-~pa-* 'causative' prefix is seemingly only ever produced as *pa-* in the Amri dialect, i.e. without any allomorphy (see § 3.9.2.1). Another difference

1.4.4 Variation in lexemes

is that the 'afterthought' particle =*he* (§ 16.3.9) is more frequently used in Amri speech, and that the particle *hedī* is prominently used as a marker of narrative style specifically in this dialect (§ 16.3.12).

1.4.4 Variation in lexemes

Table 2 provides sample lexemes of which there are two (or more) variants based on vowel alternations. No study has been conducted yet to see whether these alternation patterns somehow align in the speech of individual native speakers or whether the variants are tied to particular dialects. My consultants do not consider any forms more correct than others but just report that all variants are used, and that they have not noticed any sociolinguistic patterning of this variation.

Table 2: Vowel alternations.

Alternation	Gloss	/i/	/e/	/a/	/o/	/u/
i~e~u	'banana'	phinū	phenū			phunū
i~e	'trade'	bihá	behá			
	'match'	chináng	chenáng			
	'eggplant'	hipī	hepī			
	'main people in charge'	khitirí	khetirí			
	'king(<Ind)'	richó	rechó			
i~u	'yam'	phirùi				phurùi
	'snake'	phirūi				phurūi
	'rat'	phijū				phujū
e~a	'field hut'		mendu	mandu		
	'dried fish'		menthu	manthu		
	'when'		(ko)mentu, (ko)nemtu	(ko)mantu, (ko)namtu		
e~o	'cotton'		pheló		pholó	
	'alkaline'		phelō		pholō	
	'story'		temó		tomó	
a~o	'girl'			okarjāng	okorjāng	
a~u	'carry on back'			bā		bū

While Table 2 shows that many different vowel alternation patterns exist, it should be noted that in almost all cases, the vowel alternation occurs in the first syllable of a disyllabic word. The only two exceptions are the two words listed last: *okarjāng~okorjāng* 'girl' and *bā~bū* 'carry on back'.

In addition to the simple vowel alternations in lexemes listed in Table 2, there also exists lexical variation in other words, such as *mensopi* or *nemsopi* for 'papaya'.

1.5 Sociolinguistic profile of language endangerment

The UNESCO Atlas of the World's Languages in Danger lists Karbi as a 'vulnerable' language (Moseley 2010). This section contains a brief sociolinguistic evaluation of the current status of endangerment of the Karbi language.[19] It includes a discussion of setting factors; the impact of language contact; issues relating to domains, vitality, and attitudes; and the official policy concerning the language. Along with a summary of the degree of endangerment of Karbi, the last section reports on current, and proposes future, remedial actions to strengthen the status of the language.

1.5.1 Setting factors

A number of setting factors have an impact on the degree of language endangerment. First, the number of speakers is a relevant factor, and Karbi has a relatively large community of native speakers at approximately half a million people (for more information, see §1.1.2). In addition, this section will discuss the following factors: (a) languages represented in education; (b) virtual and physical infrastructure in the community; (c) the relationship between government and language (policy); and (d), how Karbi is represented in mass media.

As far as the **languages representend in education** are concerned, even within the Karbi Anglong and West Karbi Anglong districts, most schools have either Assamese or English as the medium of instruction, depending on whether they are government or Christian schools. Within the last twenty years or so, a few Christian primary schools started to teach in Karbi (and other local minority languages), spearheaded by Frs. U.V. Joseph and Joseph Teron, and textbooks have been developed (along with Br. Benjamin Kathar). However, by now these schools have mostly reverted back to English. There are a few private schools that teach in Karbi, and there has been an effort to translate existing textbooks from Assamese into Karbi. By and large, however, children go to Assamese or English medium schools. At the same

---

[19] This profile was put together as part of a seminar on 'The Sociolinguistics of Language Endangerment' offered by David and Maya Bradley at the 2011 LSA Institute in Boulder, CO. I would like to thank them for the feedback they provided me and for engaging me in thinking about these issues.

time, as of the year 2019, there are now official plans to devise a full curriculum for Karbi language classes from primary to high school.

With respect to **infrastructure**, a very sudden increase in virtual infrastructure in recent years (which was very noticeable even just between 2008–2012), i.e., availability of electricity, TVs, cell phones, and the internet, will likely affect the community. Increase in physical infrastructure has recently improved mobility, and will almost certainly affect the community as well. A lot is currently changing, and the endangerment situation ten years ago was likely substantially different from what the situation will be like in five to ten years from now.

Language shift to Assamese is a lot more common among those Karbis who live in the plains, compared to *Karbi Anglong* Karbis, who live in the hills. This has likely been the case historically (in the last several centuries or so) as well, since there are a lot more Assamese loans in the Plains Karbi variety (§ 1.4.1).

In terms of the **relationship between government and language (policy)**, the Karbis live in their autonomous *Karbi Anglong* and *West Karbi Anglong* districts. *Karbi Anglong* has the *Karbi Anglong Autonomous Council* (and that is also its official name, i.e. it is in English rather than Karbi) (see § 1.1.5). This political autonomy strengthens the status of the language.

As far as **mass media** are concerned, there are a few newspapers in Karbi. The *Arleng Daily* and the *Thekar*[20] are written in Roman script, while there are also newspapers that use the Assamese script. The KLA publishes quite a lot of books in Karbi. There is a local film industry that produces movies and comedy shows (and some documentaries) in Karbi. There also is a Karbi language TV program.

There has been a recent increase in availability of Karbi media on the internet. In particular, there are Karbi blogs and there are a number of songs sung in Karbi (but following the 'mainland' Indian *Bollywood* style) on Youtube.

1.5.2 Domains/vitality/attitudes

This section discusses the domains in which Karbi is used, the overall vitality, and the attitudes that native speakers have towards the language.

With respect to the **domains of language use**, there are two situations of language use within the Karbi community that I have experienced first hand and can comment on. One is life in the *Karbi Anglong* district capital Diphu, the other is life in a Christian village in rural *West Karbi Anglong*. Both sets of experiences stem from the time between 2009–2012. As would be expected, the differences are very noticeable.

In Diphu, especially among the middle class, it is typical for Karbis under the age of 35 to 40 years or so, to be quadrilingual. While Karbi is the native language that is

---

[20] The *Thekar* now also has an online edition: http://thekararnivang.com/.

spoken in the home, it is also common for them to use Assamese, English, and Hindi (probably in that order of frequency) on a regular basis. It is therefore no problem for them to switch to whatever language is shared with their interlocutor(s). If several languages are shared, it is typically with first priority Karbi and then Assamese that are used, but that is not always the case, and people enjoy switching between languages. For example, I have heard Karbi native speakers in their late twenties talk to each other using Karbi, but suddenly switch to Assamese or English words or entire sentences.

In the villages that I have visited, this multilingual situation does not exist to that extent. While it is common for Karbis except for the older generation to speak Assamese to varying degrees, they may only ever use Assamese when they go to the weekly or biweekly market where many sellers only speak Assamese and no Karbi. There is a trend for the younger generation, especially with increases in physical and virtual infrastructure, to be exposed to English and Hindi and to know how to say a few things in these languages. In addition, in the villages in *West Karbi Anglong* with Tiwa-speaking[21] villages nearby, it is also common for Karbis to know Tiwa to varying degrees (and vice versa).

The overall **vitality** is currently good for Hills Karbi. Most commonly, Karbi is transmitted to the younger generation and used in the homes.

The **attitudes** of the Karbi community towards their language are generally positive. I have not met Karbis who did not consider their language important to them. The fact that the KLA (§ 1.1.4) exists also speaks to that: The KLA is a non-governmental organization that survives on private donations; its members volunteer, with no monetary compensation for their work.

1.5.3 Other factors

The major dominant language in the area that many Karbi speakers shift to is Assamese. Shifting to Assamese occurs among all of Assam's minority languages, since it is the main lingua franca for speakers of different minority languages. While English functions as a lingua franca to some degree as well (especially in the Christianized areas), Assamese is more widespread.

1.5.4 Summary of degree of endangerment

The Karbi language currently looks healthy. However, especially the increase in infrastructure is changing so dramatically that consequences will likely become more and more noticeable in the near future. Although the facts are that (a) there are a large

---

21 Tiwa is a Bodo-Garo language spoken mostly inside the *West Karbi Anglong* district.

number of speakers; (b) the language is almost always transmitted to the children; and (c) the community is politically protected by having their own autonomous district, the dominant Assamese language creates a lot of pressure that many in the community feel. The KLA's largest current concern is the standardization of the writing system. This will serve both the purpose of doing language maintenance as well as result in added prestige.

In accordance with the KLA's concerns, the standardization of the orthography could be a large step to strengthen the language, as it would likely represent a prerequisite for the large-scale development of school materials in Karbi and the use of Karbi in higher education. In fact, as of 2019, there are official plans to create a comprehensive curriculum to teach Karbi language classes in schools.

1.6 Previous study of Karbi grammar

There are a small handful of important names in Karbi linguistics, which should be mentioned at the outset of this section. The chronologically first mention should be made to George D. Walker, who published a fairly comprehensive dictionary in 1925. In the mid 1960s, the late French missionary Father Balawan put together a word list with parts of a grammatical description (published as Balawan (1978)). Not much later, Karl-Heinz Grüßner worked on Karbi grammar. Around the same time, Karbi scholar Professor Rongbong Terang published a Karbi dictionary (Terang 1974). Within the last decade or so, substantial contributions have also been made by another important Karbi scholar, Longkam Teron.

1.6.1 Early work on Karbi

Early resources on Karbi include word lists by Robinson (1849), Stewart (1855), and Kay (1904), as well as information provided in sections on Karbi in the Linguistic Survey of India (Grierson 1904). A historical ethnographic description with some references to Karbi grammar as well as several texts with translation was "edited, arranged and supplemented" by Sir Charles Lyall based on notes by the Indian Civil Service officer Edward Stack (Stack and Lyall 1908). Several other early resources on Karbi linguistics are listed by Grüßner (1978: 218–21).

1.6.2 Karl-Heinz Grüßner's work

Karl-Heinz Grüßner worked on Karbi in the early 1970s. Based in Shillong, he collaborated with Karbi native speakers Harrison Langne and Clement Singnar and took a number of trips to villages in West Karbi Anglong to record texts and work with other native speakers. Grüßner wrote a grammar of Karbi as his PhD dissertation at the University of Heidelberg in Germany, published as Grüßner (1978). The grammar is an excellent resource especially on Karbi phonology and morphology, which is all the more impressive considering the relative non-availability of technical equipment at the time. Grüßner made reel-to-reel audio tape recordings, which he subsequently transcribed for use as examples in his grammar.[22] Grüßner was the first to investigate the tone system of Karbi and he systematically indicated tones in his work. While he was working on Karbi grammar he also began compiling words for what became a 241-page dictionary manuscript, which he never published.

Grüßner's work was mostly based on the speech of Christianized Karbi native speakers from around Tika in West Karbi Anglong. According to some of my language consultants, there are some subtle aspects of the variety Grüßner worked on that partially overlap and are partially different from their own varieties:

For example, Grüßner reports the systematic use of *pe-* 'causative' before monosyllabic roots but the allomorph *pa-* before disyllabic roots (corresponding to parallel allomorphy in the nominalizer *ke-~ka-(~ki-)*), which is a pattern found in Rongkhang speech; however, Grüßner also reports the use of /ei/ instead of only /ai/, which is typical of (Hills Karbi) Amri speech (§ 1.4.3). There also are some lexical differences according to my language consultants. For example, while one of the bamboo parts used to make fire via friction is referred to as *theng-dang* in my consultants' speech (with the first element in the compound being *thēng* 'wood'), Grüßner reports the word to be *me-dang* (with the first element being *mē* 'fire'). These subtle differences are suspected to be part of an (again, subtly) distinct sociolect typical of the Christian villages in the area. While the issue of Karbi varieties cannot be treated here in a comprehensive way (see also § 1.4), it should be noted that certain discrepancies in grammatical description between Grüßner's work and the present work might be due to dialectal/sociolectal differences.

The lasting contribution of Grüßner's work cannot be underestimated. The level of detail and carefully researched description, especially given the historical context when much less was known about the Tibeto-Burman language family, is truly remarkable.[23]

1.6.3 Longkam Teron's work

Longkam Teron's perhaps most well-known contribution is a grammar with the Karbi name *Karbi lamtasam* (Teron 2005a). Significant other contributions include his collections of proverbs (Teron 2005b), and idioms and phrases (Teron 2006). Particularly

---

[22] Grüßner has since digitized his old audio recordings.
[23] I also want to take this opportunity to again thank Karl-Heinz for all his support, his enthusiasm, and for freely and fully sharing everything and anything he had that could possibly help me in my endeavours to work on Karbi grammar.

important for further study of the origins of Karbi and the historical contact situation is the collection of words used as part of the (Hills Karbi) song language, *Karbi lamlir achili* (lit., 'the seeds of the Karbi poetical language') (Teron 2008) (see § 1.1.3.3 above).

1.6.4 Other resources on Karbi grammar and lexicon

In 1966, besides Father Michael Balawan, Father John Mariae also produced work on Karbi grammar and lexicon, which was only later published and is now available as a booklet called 'Karbi Self-taught' (Mariae 2007). An overview of the history of research on Karbi grammar is offered by Teron (2011: 148–57).

In addition to the resources on Karbi grammar mentioned above, important contributions are also a number of dictionaries. The first comprehensive dictionary (Karbi to English and English to Karbi) was published by Walker (1925).

The Karbi scholar Bidorsing Kro produced a Karbi to Karbi dictionary with explanations in Assamese and English that was first published in 2002, with a second edition that has been published since (Kro 2009). Another dictionary emerging from scholarship from within the Karbi community is Taro (2010). A comparative dictionary of Plains and Hills Karbi by Teron and Tumung (2007) represents an important resource on the differences between the two major dialects of the language.

1.7 Writing in Karbi and conventions followed in this grammar

The Karbi orthography based on Roman script was developed by missionaries in the 19th century. Currently there also exists a Karbi orthography using the devanagari-based Assamese script. However, the *Karbi Lammet Amei* advocates for the use of the Roman script. Although there is a standardized set of letters in the Roman script that adequately represent Karbi phonemes, the orthography is to date not standardized, which is a matter of concern for many in the community, especially, of course, for the members of the *Karbi Lammet Amei*.

The controversial issues arise with respect to (a) word boundaries; (b) capitalization after adding prefixes; (c) syllable boundaries; and, most importantly, (d) the representation of tone.

Regarding (a) word boundaries, the status of clitics is controversial. For example, it is not clear whether the very frequently occurring topic marker =*ke* (§ 14.2.1) should be attached to the last word of the noun phrase that it is phonologically bound to, or not.

With respect to (b) capitalization after adding prefixes, the most frequent issue is the occurrence of the possessive prefix *a-* (§ 7.3.1) on proper names. For example, in the simple noun phrase 'this Karbi woman', the word 'Karbi woman', i.e., *Karbipi*, needs to have the *a-* prefix on it. That is, one could write this noun phrase as *laso aKarbipi*, with *a-* in lower case and *Karbipi* capitalized, but that looks odd to some members of the community.

The issue of (c) representing syllable boundaries is often (but not exclusively)[24] encountered when a vowel-initial syllable occurs in the middle of a word. This represents a problem because vowel onsets are accompanied by glottalization, which is not represented in the writing system, but is noticeable in this context since it prevents resyllabification (see § 3.3). For example, adding the predicate derivation suffix -*ò* 'much' (§ 9.2.5.1) to the existential copula *dō* results in a pronunciation of [dō?ò]. As a result, many members in the community dislike a representation as *doo*, resorting to either using a dash (i.e., *do-o*) or an apostrophe (i.e., *do'o*).

Finally, (d) the representation of tone has typically been avoided. Neither the Roman script nor the Assamese devanagari-based script has been successfully modified to represent tone. Different proposals have been put forth to do so, but none has been systematic; either only one tone (usually the most salient mid tone that features glottalization) is represented and/or only certain rhymes are marked for tones (and not actually consistently). For example, tone in open syllables that lack a coda consonant has been represented with an <h> coda by some Karbis – however, it is sometimes the low tone that is represented by this orthographic <h> coda (e.g., *neh* '1EXCL'), and sometimes the mid tone (e.g., *meh* 'fire'). Another proposal specifically aiming at the representation of the mid tone in nasal coda syllables was to write an orthographic homorganic stop, e.g., *(a-)tump* for the plural word with a bilabial nasal coda, *(a-)phant* for the non-subject marker with an alveolar nasal coda, or *langk* for 'water' for a velar nasal coda.

Except for where the representation is not systematic or phonological (i.e., the attempts so far at representing tone), all of these issues are mostly political in nature and there is no right or wrong in linguistic terms. In this grammar, I follow the orthography Grüßner (1978) used. This has the following implications for the four orthography problems outlined above:

For (a) word boundaries, clitics are written as one word with the element that they are phonologically bound to. For (b) capitalization after adding prefixes, the above representation is used, i.e., lower case prefix with capitalized proper noun stem (i.e., *aKarbipi*). With respect to (c) syllable boundaries, the apostrophe is used, i.e., *do'o* for the example word from above. Finally, for (d), the representation of tone, Grüßner's approach with diacritical marks is used: the grave for low tone (e.g., low tone *thì* 'die'); the acute for high tone (e.g., *thí* 'snatch, grab'); and the macron[25] for mid tone (e.g., *thī* 'be short').

---

[24] The other situation where this issue arises is when a multisyllabic word contains a consonant combination of /pl/, /pr/, /kl/, or /kr/ between two vowels, where the two consonants could be split up as coda plus initial or an open syllable followed by a consonant cluster.

[25] Note that in his dictionary manuscript, Grüßner also sometimes used the circumflex for the mid tone, e.g., representing 'be short' as *thî*.

In this grammar, examples are offered with both a word line and a morpheme line, where tone is only indicated in the morpheme line but not in the word line. The details of the representation of tone is further discussed in § 3.5.9; the details of the representation of data in general in this grammar (including different types of brackets) is further discussed in § 2.4.

1.8 Organization of this grammar

This grammar is organized as follows. Chapter 2 discusses the theoretical framework and methodological approach employed in this grammar, as well as the data that were collected and produced as part of this research, and that are used as a basis for the grammatical description.

Chapter 3 is dedicated to Karbi phonology, a large portion of which concerns the Karbi tone system, which poses difficulties for thorough description due to its low functional load.

Karbi word classes are the topic of Chapters 4–6. Chapter 4 deals with the major word classes of nouns, verbs, and discusses the status of property concept terms. Chapter 5 goes over the subclasses of nouns, while Chapter 6 provides an overview of other word (sub)classes, including pro-forms, verb subclasses, and minor word classes, such as adverbs and numerals.

This leads into the morphologies of the two large word classes of nouns and verbs. While nominal morphology is treated in Chapter 7, the discussion of verbal morphology is divided up into Chapter 8 with a general overview and the presentation of pre-root morphology, and Chapter 9, which deals with post-root morphology.

In Chapters 10 and 11, syntactic issues concerning the noun phrase and predicate constructions are discussed.

Chapter 12 is solely dedicated to nominalization and nominalization-based constructions, as nominalization represents a major structural device with functional application in a number of different domains of grammar (including simple derivation of nouns from verbs, noun phrase modification, monoclausal predicate constructions, as well as clause combining).

The status of clausal participants and the ways in which they may be marked is the topic of Chapters 13 and 14.

A discussion of clause types and clause combining, including non-declarative speech acts, is offered in Chapter 15.

Finally, Chapter 16 provides an overview of the major constructions that have functions on the level of the larger discourse.

2 Methodology and data

This chapter deals with the methodology and general approach to grammar writing that underlies this grammar, as well as some relevant points about the collection and organization of the data that this grammar is based on.

Most of the existing literature on linguistic data management has been published within the fields of language documentation (Himmelmann 1998; Gippert, Himmelmann, and Mosel 2006; Himmelmann 2006a; Woodbury 2011) and the description of (especially endangered) languages (Austin and Sallabank 2011). While this grammar of Karbi is primarily aimed to be a descriptive resource, attempts were made to incorporate the insights from the recently emerged (or, as some would argue, revived) field of 'language documentation' (or 'documentary linguistics').

This chapter begins with a discussion of the general approach and theoretical framework underlying this grammar (§2.1). In §2.2, an overview of the corpus is offered. Aspects of primary data collection are discussed in §2.3, while §2.4 covers the ways in which the data have been annotated and are presented in this grammar.

2.1 Approach and theoretical framework

The approach taken in this grammar contains three major components. First, it is firmly rooted in a functional-typological framework. Second, it embraces collaboration with the language community as the best approach for data collection and analysis. Third, the analysis presented in this descriptive grammar gains explanatory force through a historical-comparative perspective on the grammatical constructions that are discussed.

2.1.1 Functional-typological framework

First and most importantly, this grammar is based on a functional-typological framework. This approach permeates all aspects in the design, data collection, and analysis and write-up.

For the design and data collection aspects, this framework puts an overarching emphasis on a data-driven and inductive, as well as data-rich approach to document how Karbi is actually spoken in a wide variety of natural uses of the language. As a result, the vast majority of examples that are offered in this grammar to illustrate a particular point come from naturally produced speech rather than elicitation via translation from English. Elicitation serves an important purpose in supplementing information that did not happen to be provided in data from natural speech, but it should always be treated with the necessary caution.

The implications of using this framework for the analysis and argumentation consist of the understanding that there most typically are functional motivations for patterns and that there are also functional motivations for exceptions to patterns.

For example, Karbi classifiers generally do not mark a distinction between singular and plural: the same classifier is used when counting one or many items of a particular kind. This is functionally motivated because classifiers only ever occur with numerals to form classifier-numeral words in Karbi (§ 5.1). Therefore, having different classifier forms to distinguish singular from plural would be redundant.

However, there is one case in which there actually are two forms that are used for classifying the same entity: humans (or personified animals or objects in folk stories, § 5.1.4). For humans, there are two classifiers, the singular classifier *nūt* and the plural classifier *bàng*. On a first level of explanation, there are two forms for the human classifier, because *nūt* actually is a borrowing from Khasi (Joseph 2009). On a deeper level of explanation, however, it is functionally motivated that the classifier (set) for humans is more special than most if not all other classifiers and is also the most frequently used classifier (set) in the corpus.

The functional-typological approach takes function and use seriously. From there, as this approach considers language a tool for a language community, the typological component is relevant: It motivates why some aspects of language are shaped similarly cross-linguistically, which is due to the shared aspects of human life everywhere in the world. But it also motivates why other aspects of language are shaped differently cross-linguistically, which is due the aspects of human life that are different in different parts of the world, just as there exist different cultures.

2.1.2 Collaboration with the language community

This grammar project was initiated by the Karbi community through the *Karbi Lammet Amei* (KLA; § 1.1.4), and was therefore collaborative in nature from the beginning. Due to this close collaboration with the KLA, numerous aspects of data collection and processing were enhanced.

For example, the KLA (and specifically my closest collaborator Sikari Tisso) identified speakers that were able to tell particular stories and provide particular information. Due to the KLA's own interest in the success of the project, they (and again, most importantly Sikari Tisso) also greatly helped with all aspects of the practical realization and facilitation of the project, which always represents a major and time-consuming task in fieldwork (which at times is even impossible for an outsider linguist without collaborators from within the community).

2.1.3 Historical-comparative perspective

The historical-comparative approach to linguistic explanation understands grammatical constructions as being shaped by their historical origins, which can often be investigated by conducting comparative research.

For example, there are main clause constructions in Karbi that feature the *ke-* prefix that functions as the main nominalizer in the language, without having an inflected element to render the clause finite (§ 12.7.3). The historical perspective taken in that section aims to explain how that the *ke-* prefix in those constructions can still be diachronically analyzed as the nominalizer, even though it has to be analyzed as a different element synchronically. A specifically comparative component to explanation is part of the analysis for the diachronic nominalization construction to indicate focus. This construction can be accounted for with recourse to a copular form that does not exist in Karbi but does exist in the related "Kuki-Chin" branch of Tibeto-Burman.

2.2 Corpus

2.2.1 Data types

The data that were collected and generated for this grammar can be grouped into three subcorpora, as laid out in Table 3. They are (1) data based on individual recording sessions; (2) context-free elicitation data; and (3) the lexical database. All of these data are – or are based on – spoken data. Additionally, three other types of data were available: (4) data from Grüßner's (1978) work and specifically his transcriptions and translations of audio data he had collected, which, therefore, are also spoken data, (5) an extensive dictionary manuscript that Grüßner provided me, containing 240 pages of morphemes with indication of tone, and (6) data extracted from written texts, mostly school textbooks.

Table 3: Subcorpora of Karbi data.

Subcorpus	Content
1. Texts / Recording session data	Audio/Video recordings (and images) along with their transcriptions, translations, and analyses
2. Elicitation data	Elicitation based on grammatical, phonological, or lexical topics
3. Lexical database	Database including all morphemes occurring in recordings
(4. Grüßner's (1978) data)	Transcriptions / translations of audio recordings; individual examples
(5. Grüßner's dictionary manuscript)	Manuscript of a dictionary of 240 pages with tones represented
(6. Written text data)	Mostly from school textbooks, but also from other published sources

The most important data type are the **data from recording sessions,** as they represent the most natural use of the language (§ 2.1.1). Most of the time and effort spent on this grammar research were devoted to the transcription, translation and analysis of the speech recordings. As detailed in Appendix D, which shows the metadata for those texts that were fully transcribed, translated, analyzed and further annotated, the primary data that these texts are based on consist of a total of 01:21:36 (hh:mm:ss) of media files that include video, and a total of 00:40:02 of audio-only recordings, for a total of two hours. As for the data derived from these media data, the two hours of spoken language are represented by a total of approximately 12,500 transcribed Karbi words.

Context-free elicitation data were collected on phonological and grammatical topics, although grammatical topics were mostly investigated through textual examples and elicitation based on those. An example of context-free elicitation used for this grammar were elicited clauses that included comparative constructions or clauses that included indefinite quantifiers in order to learn more about these particular grammatical constructions. Phonological elicitation was mostly aimed at the Karbi tone system, e.g., eliciting roots that undergo morphophonemic changes due to adding certain prefixes, or elicitation of words with similar tone patterns.

The **lexical database** has been built up parallel to the text database of recording session based data due to the way the software Toolbox, which was used for grammatical annotations, works. Therefore, the lexical database includes all morphemes that occur in the recorded texts with some additional opportunistic data entries. It is a basic lexical database, which will require further work to be usable as a dictionary. As of now, entries generally only consist of the Karbi morpheme, an English gloss, a part of speech label, and in some cases additional grammatical, lexical, or cultural notes.

2.2.2 Access to the corpus

The core text database of all 18 texts (for metadata see Appendix D) which this grammar is primarily based on is freely accessible online in the *Himalayan Linguistics Archive* (Konnerth and Tisso 2018). This document provides the full transcription, translation, and morpheme-by-morpheme glosses of all of these texts.

In addition, all media files are available in the Endangered Languages Archive (ELAR) (Konnerth and Tisso 2019).

2.3 Primary data collection

Data collection was carried out over a total of 15 months consisting of five phases: January–March 2009 (phase 1); February–May 2010 (phase 2); January–March 2011 (phase 3); September–December 2011 (phase 4); September–December 2012 (phase 5).

Specifically, phase 1 mostly consisted of word elicitation aimed at Karbi phonology and simple sentence elicitation without recording much. During phase 2 a festival to celebrate Karbi culture took place in the local capital Diphu. This festival brought a number of village elders to Diphu, about ten of who agreed to be recorded, performing a variety of genres. We were able to record them in a recording studio in Diphu and collected a lot of primary data in the form of recording sessions involving both audio and video data. These data are mostly folk stories as well as some procedural texts. A lot of song data were also recorded during phase 2, which, however, have not been analyzed yet since Karbi song language is entirely different from the ordinary language and requires further research (§ 1.1.3.3).

During phase 3 some additional phonological data were collected. As part of phase 4, a one-week recording trip was carried out in November 2011, which resulted in a number of recorded interviews, conversations, narrations of local histories and folk stories, most of them pertaining to a research project dedicated to investigating the status of women in Karbi society. During the final stage of phase 5, a few other texts were collected, including an on-line narration of the Pear Story (Chafe 1980).

2.3.1 Acknowledgment of Karbi speakers that facilitated data collection

I would like to acknowledge the participation and support from the following people: Maloti Rongpharpi, Kache Rongpharpi, the Assistant Teachers at Lorulangso LP School: Punyalata Ingtipi and Rani Teronpi, Maggie Katharpi, Chandra Kanta Terang, Puspa Engtipi, Kahan Terangpi, and Dr. Janta Pator (Diphu); Burnesh Milikpi, Keshop Terang, Jugal Timung, Rajen Kro, Dim Teron, and Hemari Rongpi (Jyrikyndeng); Aren Ingti, Pretty Ingtipi, and Kamal Chandra Kro (Dongkamokam); Chandra Sing Tisso (Podumsarpo); Harsing Ronghang, Ronghang Lindok and his assistants (Ronghang Rongbong); Longsing Tokbi (Amtereng); Bidyaram Rongpi (Hamren); Dhansing Terang, Kare Rongpipi, and Harsing Kro (Boythalangso); Anjan Teron and Dhaniram Ingleng (Bhoksong); Modon Kro (Rambangla); Sarthe Phangcho (Putsari Hindu arong); Mahin Phangcho (Umpanai); Hem'ari Ingjai (Pharkong Abi); Sika Hansepi (Men Terang); Kache Kropi (Balijuri); Chandra Sing Teron; Kasang Teronpi (Dingso Terang); Rongbang Teron and Seng Tisso (Ujandongka); Welisbon Ronghipi (Umswai Model); Longsing Bey (Murap, Umlaper); Joysing Tokbi (Laru aum, Umlaper); the people of Sohliya (Meghalaya); Owen Terang and the people of Marmein (Meghalaya); Dhiren Ingti and Dhiren Ronghang (Kamrup); Khayasing Hanse (Bokoli); Sarhon Ronghang, KLA; Sangvai Teronpi and Hangmiji Hanse (Hongkram); Dr. Mansing Rongpi, MLA, Dispur; and Father Joseph Teron, Don Bosco. Kardom.

2.3.2 Data collecting team

The data collecting team consists first and foremost of Mr. Sikari Tisso, who represents the Karbi Lammet Amei (§ 1.1.4). As my main collaborator on this project, he was involved in and/or facilitated almost every recording session. He also interviewed various Karbi speakers for this project.

Mr. Tisso was born in 1955 and grew up in West Karbi Anglong but moved to Diphu in his late twenties. He says of himself that he now speaks an idiolect where he mostly speaks the main Diphu dialect of Karbi interspersed with several features of the West Karbi Anglong Amri dialect that he grew up speaking.

Furthermore partially involved in the primary data collection efforts were especially Mr. Bhudeswar Timung, as well as Ms. Amphu Rongpipi, and the Kro and Hanse families in Diphu and Umswai, respectively. Mr. Bhudeswar Timung played an important role in the data collection trip of November 2011, where he interviewed speakers and also facilitated data collection otherwise. He currently lives and is originally from Socheng in (eastern) Karbi Anglong. He speaks the standard (*Rongkhang*) dialect of Karbi. Ms. Amphu Rongpipi facilitated the collection of recordings from her mother, Puspa Ingtipi, and her grandmother, Kahan Terangpi. She and her family are from Diphu and speak the standard dialect. The Kro family has been my main host family. I stayed with them and enjoyed their generous hospitality for large periods of my time in Karbi Anglong. I was able to record Mrs. Sashikola Hansepi and Ms. Rasinza Kropi of the Kro family. The Hanse family was my host family in Umswai, West Karbi Anglong for a few weeks in fall 2011 and fall 2012. They also facilitated the recording of native Karbi speakers of Umswai.

2.3.3 Recorded speakers: Ethical considerations

Metadata information about the fifteen speakers of the fully annotated texts that represent the main corpus for this grammar is provided in Appendix D. Before recording sessions, the data collection team made sure to obtain informed consent from the speaker(s) that we were going to record following standard practice (see for example Dwyer 2006: 43–5) as well as fulfilling requirements imposed by the University of Oregon's Institutional Research Board (IRB). To that end, consent forms were created in English and translated into Karbi. The consent forms gave speakers the following explicit options:
1) Do you want to be acknowledged or remain anonymous?
2) Is it okay for us to video record you? (a) no, (b) yes, but only if the video is used for linguistic analysis but not for public access, (c) yes and public access is fine
3) For each one of the following three types of data individually: (1) video data, (2) audio data, (3) transcriptions of video/audio data; what type of access do you agree to? (a) no access, (b) access restricted, to be determined by Karbi Lammet Amei, (c) public

The speakers were asked to check the appropriate and sign and date. Although Dwyer (2006: 44) reports that in certain cultural settings "written forms may breed mistrust" and that they "may wisely be viewed with suspicion", my experience was that the written consent forms were actually viewed as carrying prestige, and one of my host families asked for another copy to keep and told other people about it in my presence.

2.3.4 Recorded genres

Both from a documentary and descriptive linguistics perspective it is desirable to collect texts from as many different types of genres as practically feasible (which, however, does impose a very real limit) since certain aspects of grammar and certain constructions may only be used in particular speech genres. Since speech genres vary according to a number of different parameters, one of the goals of documentary linguistics is to discover what parameters may be crucially involved in defining significantly different speech genres. One parameter suggested to play an important role by Himmelmann (1998: 176ff.) is spontaneity. The list of genres collected for this corpus is provided in Table 4 organized according to this parameter of spontaneity (see also Appendix D, where the genre of each fully annotated recording is listed).

Table 4: Text genres.

Spontaneity	Category	Genre
Less spontaneous	Monologue	Folk tale
↕		Procedural text
		Personal narrative
		Pear story
More spontaneous	Dialogue	Interview/Conversation

The folk tales are the least spontaneously produced genre, as they follow a given plot line and to some degree probably also particular structural patterns. Despite this (in some sense, undesirably) low level of spontaneity, this genre was recorded the most: Not only was it very important for the *Karbi Lammet Amei* (§1.1.4) to record as many folk tales as possible, but this genre also has a high priority from a documentary viewpoint as it represents the major component of the Karbi oral literature (§1.1.3.2). As such, it is important for academic disciplines besides linguistics, such as anthropology, ethnography, or folklore studies, and, it can also provide information on the cultural-linguistic history of the Karbis, thus relating back to being of immediate concern to linguistics.

Procedural texts may or may not be as spontaneous as folk tales. Some of the procedural texts in the main corpus narrate traditional cultural practices that are likely to be retold and transmitted, and therefore not spontaneous. An example is the text about the alkaline food *kangmoi ahan* that involves burning *jhum* fields and picking up the ashes as an ingredient ('SiH, KH'). Other procedural texts, however, such as the recipe for pork with fermented bamboo shoots ('PI, BPR'), are clearly spontaneously produced.

Personal narratives are intermediate with respect to spontaneity. The two personal narratives in the main corpus, 'SH, CSM' and 'SiT, HF', both represent retellings of trips to festivals the day before. In both cases, the speakers retell the events from their memories without much planning or outlining, but due to the nature of them being monologues, less spontaneity is involved.

The Pear Story (Chafe 1980) was recorded as an on-line narration: The speaker was telling what was happening as he was watching the video clip. Therefore, this was all spontaneous.

Finally, the core corpus also includes (about two thirds of) an interview/conversation between two speakers. While the interviewer had an outline with questions he wanted to ask, everything produced on part of the interviewee was fully spontaneous.

2.3.5 Recording procedures and settings

To ensure highest quality, audio recordings were created in .wav format with a sampling rate of 48 kHz with a bit depth of 16 or 24 following best practices that recommend at least 44.1 kHz and 16 bits (Johnson 2004: 147; Austin 2006: 107), while anticipating that 48 kHz and 24 bits will be the future archival standard for audio files (Nathan 2011: 260). During all recording sessions, the actually recorded audio was monitored by using headphones (Austin 2006: 90).

Another aspect involved in the attempt to collect high quality audio data has to do with the recording setting. A notorious difficulty in collecting high quality audio data in the fieldwork context is the level of background noise. This was certainly the case for this project, where it often seemed impossible to escape the constant background noise.[26] However, early on in the project, Sikari Tisso was able to identify a sound studio in Diphu, owned privately by Mr. Chandra Kanta Terang, who made it available for recordings for this grammar research. As a consequence, a number of recordings were made in the sound studio in order to get audio data of better quality by eliminating most of the background noise.

---

[26] Specifically, background noise such as animal sounds, people chatting or singing, children crying, people physically working on some project, echo inside rooms, noisy electricity or generators, fans, etc.

However, a new issue (of unclear ramifications) that arose as a result of solving the background noise problem, was that this recording studio would get hot and stuffy after some time since it did not have any direct opening to the outside. Due to the stuffiness, other native Karbi speakers were not very motivated to join the recording sessions, resulting in several sessions that were recorded with speakers one-on-one, which is not ideal considering the goal of obtaining data in natural settings. Nonetheless, it is not clear what type of impact (if any) this procedure had on the speech or grammar used in the recordings obtained that way. It might be the case that some speakers were actually more comfortable being in a dark room by themselves without other people gathering around them and watching them.

The recording equipment that was used included a high definition video camera, two different digital audio recorders, and various microphones for use in different recording contexts (for details, see metadata spread sheet in Appendix D). More often than not, a session was recorded both with the video camera and with the audio recorder to ensure high quality audio data.[27]

A variety of microphones were used, including a cardioid condenser hand-held microphone, an omni-directional condenser hand-held microphone, 2 lavalier clip-on omni-directional condenser microphones, one head-mounted unidirectional dynamic microphone, and one omni-directional dynamic hand-held microphone (see metadata spread sheet in Appendix D for exact models).

The most versatile and most often used microphone was the hand-held condenser microphone, which was used in various settings. Depending on the model used on a given the trip, the hand-held condenser microphone picked up sound either in a cardioid or an omni-directional pattern, both of which were used to record several speakers.

The condenser omni-directional microphone (which has enhanced capabilities of picking up sound due to additional battery / phantom power) proved a lot more useful than the dynamic omni-directional microphone (which in fact turned out useless). The two omni-directional lavalier microphones were used in recording interviews and other conversations, especially those involving just two speakers. Lastly, the head-mounted unidirectional microphone was used for phonetic recordings, as well as in the monologue narration of the Pear Story. The head-mounted type was considered somewhat uncomfortable by speakers, and thus was not used much.

---

27 This practice proved useful since the special cable connecting external microphones to the video camera (female XLR to 3.5mm mini plug) turned out – after several recordings – to be of inconsistent quality during the 2010 trip.

2.4 Data annotation and presentation

In what follows, I discuss the various annotation components, including segmentation, transcription, translation, morphological analysis, and notes. The discussion is roughly ordered according to the typical workflow, although in practice, preparing annotations of course often requires a back-and-forth between these types: (a) the segmentation of the audio or video file into intonation units; (b) the transcription; (c) the analysis including parsing, glossing; (d) the translation; and (e) adding ethnographic and grammatical notes.

Segmentation of audio files of spoken texts was carried out based on a combination of auditory impressions and identification of morphemes that indicate the end of a grammatical unit. The goal of the segmentation was practical in nature, namely to obtain grammatical units that we (language consultants and myself) could easily work with for the morphosyntactic analysis and general understanding of what was said. As such, segmentation yielded grammatical units, often – but certainly not always – akin to sentences. Typically, I myself did the segmentation, mostly due to the fact that this was something I could do relatively quickly compared to research assistants who did not use computers on a regular basis.

The **transcription** of texts was carried out by native Karbi speaking research assistants Amphu Rongpipi, Klirdap Langne Teronpi, Serdihun Beypi, and Larshika Tissopi. All of them read and write English and Karbi.

All texts were transcribed using a Karbi orthography that follows Grüßner's (1978) work (§1.7); phonetic transcriptions were not prepared. Within the orthographical transcription, however, certain very basic non-linguistic and paralinguistic aspects were transcribed as suggested by Schultze-Berndt (2006: 229): whispering, laughing, the existence of short pauses, and hesitation markers are indicated. Furthermore, false starts were transcribed, as also advised by Himmelmann (2006b: 269), as they "may prove crucial for various interpretative and analytical tasks".

An issue was the accurate transcription of minor dialect or idiolect differences such as using a different vowel. For example, some speakers use *richo* for 'king', whereas most speakers would use *recho* (see §1.4.4). Research assistants transcribing texts would understandably often slip into transcribing how they would say a word instead of how the recorded speaker said it. While we tried to carefully go over transcriptions with this issue in mind, there may still be occasional mis-transcriptions of this kind. Overall, we tried to do text transcription as closely as possible to what was uttered in the recording. False starts and other types of misspoken words were indicated by angular brackets < >.

The way Toolbox works, every project typically involves a text database and a lexical database. Because of that, **morphological parsing and glossing** becomes semi-automated with a growing lexical database. In choosing glosses for grammatical morphemes, the conventions of the February 2008 version of the Leipzig Glossing Rules were followed.

Translations from Karbi into English were typically added while analyzing a text, intonation unit by intonation unit, although a few texts were translated in the process of being transcribed. The type of translation provided for most texts was rather close to the original Karbi structure, so a more literal than free translation. This decision was based on the wish to highlight Karbi idiomatic expressions or constructions. Where the actual meaning became obscure, a brief explanation was added in the free translation or in the ethnographic notes. As advised by Schultze-Berndt (2006: 236), anything that had to be added in the translation in order to render the particular English clause grammatical, most typically noun phrases or pronouns, was put in parentheses to indicate that the corresponding form was absent in the Karbi original text.

Ethnographic notes were added, for example, for customs that were perhaps referred or alluded to in a particular clause in a text. **Linguistic notes** were added if, for example, (a) a language consultant told me that the use of a particular morpheme was unacceptable in her/his dialect or odd; or (b) if there was something peculiar about a phonological issue, such as a much lengthened vowel; or (c) when doing minor text-based elicitation, such as asking whether a particular information/discourse structure marker could be replaced by a different one with roughly the same meaning. The ethnographic and linguistic notes have remained in the original Toolbox files and are not included in the text collection published as Konnerth and Tisso (2018).

Following these annotation principles, the **presentation of text examples** in this grammar include four lines, as illustrated in (7), (a) through (d).

(7) Representation of text examples in this grammar
   (a) *[...] alamthe neli lapu'ansi non*
   (b) [a-lamthē   nè-lì   lapù=án=si   nón
   (c) POSS-matter   1EXCL-HON   like.this=that.much=FOC:RL   now

   (a) *ephonglokke atomo kethan*
   (b) e-phóng-lók=ke]   [a-tomó   ke-thán
   (c) one-CLF:time-only=TOP   POSS-story   NMLZ-tell

   (a) *kangton'iklo; kardom'iklo ho*
   (b) ke-ingtòn-īk-lò]   kardóm-īk-lò   ho]
   (c) NMLZ-conclude-FRML-RL   GREETING-FRML-RL   EMPH:INTERACT
   (d) '[...] this matter I'm telling, just this one thing (i.e., I don't want to tell any other stories), I'm finished telling the story, thank you'
   [SeT, MTN 052]

In (a), the word line, tone is not marked (see §3.5.9), except in some cases where prosodic extra high pitch occurs, typically serving as non-final marking, as in (8) below (see §15.2.1.2). The spelling conventions for Karbi that are used in the word line (and elsewhere) are outlined in § 1.7. Square brackets with three dots [...] are included whenever either the beginning or the end of an intonation unit, or both, are left out (because they are irrelevant to the point being made). In order to indicate words or parts of words that the speaker apparently did not intend to say (where s/he "misspoke"), <angle brackets> are used. If these are full words, then they are also listed in the morpheme and gloss lines (and translated in the translation line). Finally, {curly brackets} are used for utterances (usually questions, affirmative interjections, or repeated parts of previous sentences) by a Karbi native speaker who was mostly *listening* to the primary storyteller for a more natural storytelling situation.

In the morpheme and gloss lines, (b) and (c), there are three symbols that may indicate a morpheme boundary: the dash ('-') as the default, which includes the morpheme boundary between affixes, and between roots in compounds; furthermore, the equal sign ('=') for clitics; and finally, the tilde ('~') for reduplication.

Moreover, in the morpheme line (b), tone is marked following the conventions discussed in § 3.5.9. This line may also include square brackets that indicate constituency. In the gloss line (c), abbreviations follow the Leipzig Glossing Rules where possible. Borrowings are indicated where known, e.g., *monît* 'person(<Asm)' is identified as being a borrowing from Assamese. The period ('.') is used when more than one English word or abbreviation is needed as a gloss for the Karbi morpheme. The colon (':') is used to indicate a subtype: for example, 'CLF:round' stands for the classifier that classifies round entities. Here, the first component of the gloss, 'CLF', represents the general type or category of element, while the second component, 'round', indicates the particular subtype of classifier, i.e., the classifier for round entities.

Finally, the translation line (d) corresponds with the word line in indicating (with square brackets and dots inbetween) when the beginning or end of the intonation unit are not included. Parentheses are used when additional words are needed in the translation to render the English sentence grammatical, or when context is needed that is pragmatically understood in Karbi but not in English, e.g., the fact that *há* in (8) refers to the wife's parents' place.

(8) Data presentation: Additional information
amat la apiso abangke akhalun
amāt [là a-pisò abàng=ke] a-khalùn
and.then this POSS-wife NPDL=TOP POSS-kd.big.basket

chinghortangló *ha kedamlo amāt*
che-inghór-tāng-lò há ke-dàm-lò amāt
RR-carry.load-finish-RL over.there NMLZ-go-RL and.then
'And then, the wife put the basket rope around her head and was just leaving to go over there (to her parents' place), and then [...].' [SeT, MTN 041]

3 Phonology

This chapter begins with a description of Karbi segmental phonology including consonant phonemes and allophones (§3.1), vowel phonemes and allophones (§3.2), and syllable structure including permissible onset clusters (§3.3). Syllables with (orthographic) rhymes <ei>, <ai>, <oi>, or <ui> are phonologically better described as rhymes with a monophthong nucleus and a glide coda. Sections §3.2 and §3.3 follow this analysis. The alternative analysis of considering these rhymes diphthongs is discussed in §3.4.

Moving on to suprasegmental elements of Karbi phonology, §3.5 discusses the tone system, which is peculiar due to its low functional load, and §3.6 offers a few remarks on stress. In §3.7, several characteristics of hypoarticulated speech are presented, and §3.8 offers a brief overview over the characteristic phonological shapes of different morpheme types including a discussion of the exceptional phonological features of interjections (§3.8.5) and patterns of reduplication (§3.8.6).

Finally, §3.9 discusses morphophonemics. Morphophonological tone changes are discussed (§3.9.1), as well as the allomorphy of and/or resulting from the prefixes *ke-* 'nominalizer', *pV-* 'causative', *che-* 'reflexive/reciprocal', and *cho-* 'auto-benefactive/malefactive' (§3.9.2).

For a thorough discussion of phonological strategies involved in the nativization of especially older (rather than more recent) borrowed lexical items, see Grüßner (1978: 28–33). Grüßner points out what happens with onset voiced aspirated stops from Indic, onset clusters such as /sm/, /skh/, and /sy/ from Khasi, and documents vowel changes and tone assignment.

3.1 Consonants

There are a total of 18 consonant phonemes in Karbi that contrast with each other in minimal sets. All but one of the 18 phonemes, which is the velar nasal /ŋ/, occur at the beginning of syllables (see §3.1.1 and Table 5), whereas the syllable coda position is limited to a much more restricted set of consonants (see §3.1.2 and Table 13).

3.1.1 Consonant onsets

In the class of syllable onset consonants (see Table 5), stops are the only manner of articulation that exists at all places of articulation except for the glottal stop. Phonetically, there is a glottal stop in the language, which, however, only surfaces as part of the mid tone and occurs in conjunction with glottalization across the whole syllable (see §3.5), as well as with syllable-initial vowels (§3.3). Note that Table 5 shows one phoneme in two different cells: the palatal /ɟ~j/ has allophonic variation in its manner of articulation, and is therefore given as both a stop and a glide. Details will be discussed below.

Table 5: Syllable-initial consonants.

	Bilabial		Alveolar			Palatal		Velar		Glottal
Stops	b p	pʰ~ɸ <ph>	d t		tʰ <th>	ɟ~j <j>	c <ch>	k	kʰ <kh>	
Fricatives	β~w <v>		s							h
Nasals	m		n							
Lateral			l							
Rhotic			r~ɾ							
Glide						ɟ~j <j>				

Representation in <angle brackets> indicate the orthographic representation of the respective phoneme followed in this grammar.

The bilabial voiceless aspirated stop /pʰ/ is in free variation with a bilabial voiceless fricative /ɸ/. It seems as though the younger generation, and particularly speakers of the Christian sociolect, tend to use /ɸ/ more. It should also be noted that the name of the capital *Diphu* as a specific lexical item is most commonly pronounced with /ɸ/. Grüßner (1978: 12) also noted the use of the fricative /ɸ/ in the then younger generation and ascribes it to contact with the dominant language Assamese, where the fricative production is the standard realization of orthographic, or perhaps 'original', <ph> according to him. Scott DeLancey (p.c.) notes that this allophonic alternation between /pʰ~ɸ/ also occurs in Boro (Boro-Garo, Tibeto-Burman; Assam, Northeast India), and may be an areal feature. Indeed, the alternation between /pʰ~ɸ/ geographically extends into Northeastern Bhutan, where it is found in at least Kurtöp (but presumably other languages as well) (Hyslop 2011: 106).

The alveolar stop series /d/, /t/, /tʰ/ is complete, while the palatal and velar series each lack one member: the palatal series /ɟ/, /c/ (<ch>) lacks the voiceless aspirated stop, while the velar series /k/, /kʰ/ lacks the voiced stop. Lacking specifically the velar voiced stop is common across phonological systems of languages of the world for a phonetic reason: it is more difficult to produce a negative voice onset time (VOT) for the velar place of articulation because there is less room in the vocal tract for voicing to build up (Ohala 2010: 667).

The palatal voiced stop [ɟ] is in free variation with the palatal glide [j]. The choice of which allophone should be considered primary largely depends on whether one wants to focus more on synchrony or more on diachrony. The stop articulation [ɟ] is more common in the dialects now considered standard. Perhaps related to the orthographic representation as <j>, there is a prescriptive tendency in favor of the stop [ɟ], while rejecting the glide pronunciation. However, especially in word-medial position, most native speakers at least sometimes produce a glide instead of the stop. The glide [j] pronunciation appears quite frequent in the more conservative varieties in West Karbi Anglong, and perhaps also more so among older people. It also seems that sometimes an intermediate, fricative-like version is produced such that it almost seems to be more of an allophonic continuum of manner of articulation that spans from a more stop-like across a more fricative-like to a more glide-like production.

Grüßner (1978: 12) also reports a voiced "fricative" production of /ɟ~j/,[28] which he says he especially noticed among older people and particularly in the context of singing and reciting traditional texts. He also cites data from Robinson (1849), which show transcriptions of this phoneme sometimes as <j> and sometimes as <y>. Grüßner (1978: 12) suspects that there was and is an ongoing sound change from the "fricative" to the stop citing Shafer (1966) for the claim that "*/y/" is historically earlier. More recent research by Matisoff (2003) suggests that the Karbi /ɟ~j/ phoneme does indeed reconstruct to Proto-Tibeto-Burman as the glide */j/.[29] To summarize, then, the stop pronunciation [ɟ] is primary synchronically in the now considered standard dialects in that it is most frequent. The glide pronunciation [j], however, is primary diachronically, because it appears to be reconstructible and is quite frequent in the more conservative dialects and especially among older speakers. See also §3.1.1.4 for more evidence that this phoneme is not a straightforward member of the voiced stop series.

The fricative series is restricted to /s/ and /h/ as well as a bilabial voiced fricative /β/ (rather than a bilabial glide [w] as reported by Grüßner (1978: 12) or a labiodental voiced fricative [v] as suggested by the spelling). By describing this as a bilabial voiced fricative /β/, we can explain two salient facts. First, it can be observed that speakers produce this consonant more like a bilabial rather than a labiodental. Second, especially preceding unrounded vowels, it sounds a lot more like a fricative (and, indeed, closer to [v]) than a glide. The exact production of this phoneme also seems to be variable between a more fricative-like and a more glide-like articulation when comparing different dialects. While the subdialects of Hills Karbi tend more towards a fricative-like articulation, a more glide-like articulation is found in the Ri-Bhoi variety spoken in the border area between Assam and Meghalaya.

---

28 Grüßner (1978: 12) writes that it is a fricative using [j] as a phonetic symbol for it; it appears that he has the glide in mind instead.
29 Evidence includes the following forms: *arjàp* 'to stand' from Proto-Tibeto-Burman *r(y)ap; *hijap* 'fan' from *ya:p; *phijū* 'rat' from *b-yəw; *jòng* 'to point' from *yuŋ 'finger'; *jó* 'night' from *ya; *jòr* 'to sell' from *ywar; *thijōk* 'deer' from *d-yuk; and *arjāng* 'to be lightweight' from *r-ya:ŋ.

In onset position, nasals are limited to bilabial /m/ and alveolar /n/. Other sonorants include the lateral /l/ and rhotic /r~ɾ/, the latter of which is usually produced as the flap /ɾ/ in onset position rather than the trill /r/.[30]

The onset position allows clusters of two consonants. These are exclusively combinations of stops with the lateral or the rhotic. Permissible onset clusters are discussed in §3.3.

3.1.1.1 Stop onset minimal sets

A minimal triplet for the bilabial stop series (voiced, voiceless, aspirated) in onset position with an open, mid tone rhyme is presented in Table 6.

Table 6: Minimal set for bilabial stop onsets.

b__	bī	'to be small'
p__	pī	'to give'
ph__	phī	'to roast'

Table 7 offers a minimal triplet for the alveolar stop series (voiced, voiceless, aspirated) in onset position with an open, low tone rhyme.

Table 7: Minimal set for alveolar stop onsets.

d__	dè	'tongue'
t__	tè	'older sister', 'to spread out in sun'
th__	thè	'to be big'

Table 8 gives a minimal pair for the two palatal stops: voiced /ɟ~j/ (<j>) (also listed in a minimal set with liquid onsets in Table 12) and voiceless unaspirated /c/ (<ch>), with a low tone, velar nasal coda rhyme.

Table 8: Minimal set for palatal stop onsets.

j__	jèng	'to spin (thread)'
ch__	chèng	'to begin'

---

[30] The rhotic occurs in an onset cluster with the voiceless aspirated alveolar stop in two lexical items, *thrōk* 'six' and *thrōksí* 'seven'. In this case, the rhotic is produced like the approximant /ɹ/ (see §3.3 and Table 21), which is a production also found in coda position (see §3.1.2).

Table 9 offers a minimal pair for the aspirate-nonaspirate contrast among voiceless velar stops. The voiced velar stop is not a native phoneme of Karbi (but see §3.1.1.4 for the voiced velar onset in borrowings).

Table 9: Minimal set for velar stop onsets.

k__	kán	'to dance'
kh__	khán	'to be in a hurry'

3.1.1.2 Fricative onset minimal set

In Table 10, monosyllabic roots with the same, stopped low tone rhyme but different fricative onsets, voiced /β~w/ (<v>), voiceless /s/, and voiceless /h/, are contrasted.

Table 10: Minimal set for fricative onsets.

v__	vèk	'to swim; to steer'
s__	sèk	'to put, to attach'
h__	hèk	'to open up'

3.1.1.3 Sonorant onset minimal sets

Tables 11 and 12 give minimal pairs for the two nasal onset phonemes /m/ and /n/, and for the liquids /l/ and /r/ and the palatal glide (/stop) /ɟ~j/, respectively.

Table 11: Minimal set for nasal onsets.

m__	mò	'strip of field'
n__	nò	'ear'

Table 12: Minimal set for liquid and glide onsets.

l__	ló	'to send'
r__	ró	'to praise'
j__	jó	'night'

3.1.1.4 Marginal onset consonants and consonant clusters

Through prolonged contact and (more modern) multilingualism with Indic languages, the majority of Karbi speakers nowadays produce voiced aspirated onsets in borrowed lexical items that have them. In the past, a typical strategy to avoid the voiced aspirate used to consist of breaking it up with a vowel, resulting in the sequence voiced stop –vowel–/h/, i.e., CʰV → CVhV, where C may be /b,d,g/ and where the epenthetic vowel V generally copies the following vowel.

In texts from the main corpus that were recorded a decade ago, we can observe that two different speakers used the word /bhari/ 'big (<Asm)'. Although both are fluent in Assamese, one person produced the voiced aspirate and pronounced it as /bhari/, while the other person pronounced it as /bahari/, inserting the vowel. Therefore vowel insertion is not entirely gone but it is becoming less and less common as many of the older borrowings are being reborrowed by modern multilingual speakers, who then easily pronounce the voiced aspirate stops.

Other commonly used Assamese borrowings with voiced stops are *dhani* 'rich' (previously also *dohoni*); *dhorom* 'religion' (previously also *dohorom*); *ghati* 'brass pot used as jug' (previously also *kohoti* and later *gohoti*); *ghatana* 'incident' (previously also *kotona* and later *gahatana*). The voiced stop series that has been borrowed into Karbi from Assamese includes /bh/, /dh/, and /gh/. The palatal voiced stop /jh/ [ɟʰ] was not borrowed, however. Thus, Assamese *jhamela* 'crisis, jolt' is borrowed into Karbi as *jamela*. This is interesting as it provides evidence that Karbi /j/ with its allophonic variation between [ɟ]~[j] (§3.1.1) is not phonemically part of the voiced stop series.

Historical onset cluster simplification can also be found in borrowings from English. For example, the onset cluster in the word 'school' used to be broken up by an inserted vowel by borrowing the word as /sikur/ (also replacing word-final /l/ by /r/). In modern times, this word has been reborrowed as /skul/.

Another marginal onset consonant is /g/, which, for example, is produced in *garí* 'car (<Asm)' or in the reborrowed form *gakhír* 'milk (<Asm)', which in an older borrowed version is *kakhír*.

3.1.2 Consonant codas

Table 13 shows all consonants found in syllable-final position. Compared to the 17 phonemes found in onset position, only 8 contrastive phonemes occur in coda position.

In syllable-final position, there is only a single series of unreleased voiceless stops, as well as three nasals, the rhotic, and the glide, which in orthography looks like a diphthong. The velar nasal is the only syllable-final consonant that does not also occur as a syllable onset. The glide coda does not display allophony with a fricative pronunciation as in onset position. The rhotic /r~ɾ/ varies between a more flap-like production and a more trill-like production, as in onset position. Word-finally, it often is a trill. Word-medially before a syllable starting in an alveolar consonant, the rhotic is often produced like an approximant in alveolar position, [ɹ], or in retroflex position, [ɻ]. In fact, it appears that speakers of the younger generation in general tend towards an approximant production of rhotic codas. Grüßner (1978: 15) also notes that some

Table 13: Syllable-final consonants.

	Bilabial	Alveolar	Palatal	Velar	Glottal
Stops	p̚ (<p>)	t̚ (<t>)		k̚ (<k>)	
Fricatives					
Nasals	m	n		ŋ (<ng>)	
Lateral					
Rhotic		r~ɾ~ɹ			
Glide			j (<i>)		

speakers produce what he calls a retroflex (and uses the symbol of the retroflex flap [ɽ] for) for the rhotic, in free variation with [r].

Note that Plains Karbi has preserved coda /l/ in words such as *phirul* 'snake', *mol* 'back', or *ingkol* 'twenty', which in Hills Karbi has turned into a glide coda: *phirūi* 'snake', *mòi* 'back', and *ingkòi* 'twenty' (see §3.4).

3.1.2.1 Stop coda minimal set

Table 14 shows two sets of three monosyllabic verb roots that are minimally contrasted by their coda stops.

Table 14: Minimal sets for stop codas.

_p	thàp	'to put inside'	ráp	'to help'
_t	thàt	'to slaughter, to kill'	rát	'public (<Asm)'
_k	thàk	'to weave', 'to answer'	rák	'to tear'

3.1.2.2 Sonorant coda minimal set

Table 15 offers two near-minimal sets contrasting sonorant codas. Fully minimal sets with the same tone throughout could not be identified. The /d/-initial set has the

Table 15: Minimal sets for sonorant codas.

_m	vám	'waist'	dám	'to oust'	bām	'to embrace'
_n	ván	'share'	dán	'to trap'	bán	'slave'
_ng	vàng	'to come'	dáng	'to put on stove'	bàng	'somebody'
_r	vár	'to throw'	dār	'to break'	bár	'to start'
_i (/j/)	ingvài	'to choose'			bài	'to console'

same tone for nasals at all three places of articulation. Although the rhotic and glide codas in these examples have the same tone distinctions (high tone for rhotic coda and low tone for glide coda), this is just a coincidence. An example where the root tones are difference is *chòr* 'to cut' and *chói* 'shirt'.

3.1.2.3 Marginal coda consonants

Hills Karbi speakers of especially the young to middle-aged generations and especially those living in the towns rather than the villages may keep the lateral /l/ in coda position in modern borrowings (or, reborrow the words with /l/ coda), such as *skúl* 'school' from English, or *narikol* 'coconut' from Assamese. Coda /l/ used to be (and still is in the speech of some speakers) changed to either coda /r/ or /j/. Thus, the older borrowed version of English 'school' is *sikúr*, while the older borrowed version of Assamese 'coconut' is *narikói*.

Another and even more marginal coda consonant is /h/. The typical pronunciation of the interjections *dah!* 'let's go!' and *dih!* 'leave me!', as well as *boh*, an interjection borrowed from Assamese to express surprise, is with coda /h/ (§16.5).

3.2 Vowels

Karbi has a five vowel monophthong system with /i/, /e/, /a/, /o/, and /u/, see Figure 8 (though also note §3.2.1). There are no diphthongs (but see §3.4). In open syllables, the vowels are articulated as more maximally dispersed from each other, while in closed syllables, they are more centralized. While /i/, /e/, /a/, and /o/ are produced in a manner very similar to the basic phonetic values of [i], [e], [a], and [o], the /u/ vowel is often produced without much lip rounding. In syllable-initial position, vowels are always preceded by a glottal stop (also see §3.3).

Figure 8: Standard Karbi vowel monophthongs.

Table 16 offers minimal sets for vowels in open syllable roots. The data are organized into three sets according to tone: the first set involves low tone roots, the second set involves mid tone roots, and the third set involves high tone roots.

Karbi rhymes /ei/, /ai/, /oi/, and /ui/ are analyzed as monophthongs with glide codas (see §3.4). Table 17 provides a minimal set of these rhymes. Note that the /ei/ rhyme only occurs in the Amri dialect of Hills Karbi spoken primarily in West Karbi Anglong. The Amri dialect has both the /ei/ and the /ai/ rhymes, while the standard Rongkhang dialect has merged them to /ai/ (see §1.4.3 on Hills Karbi dialects).

Table 16: Minimal sets for vowels in open syllables.

/i/			bī	'to be small', 'goat'	bí	'to keep'
/e/	bè	'handle', 'to chase away'	bē	'CLAN'	bé	'to sieve'
/a/	bà	'paddy disease'	bā	'to carry (child) on back'		
/o/	bò	'to apply fish poison'	bō	'inner part of fruit'	bó	'to sacrifice'
/u/			bū	'to carry (child) on back', 'small bamboo basket'	bú	'to plait', 'bundle'

Table 17: Minimal sets /ei/, /ai/, /oi/, /ui/.

[/ei/	bèi	'to console'	théi	'EE:méi' ('assembly')]
/ai/	bái	'older sister (<Asm)',	thāi	'arrow'
/oi/	bói	'to be miserable, to die (poet.) (<Asm)'	thói	'plains (<Asm)'
/ui/	bùi	'to accumulate, pile up'	thùi	'to wrap'

Although both examples with the /oi/ rhyme in Table 17 are borrowings from Assamese, there are lexical items with /oi/ in Karbi that are not borrowed from Assamese as well, such as *krōi* 'to agree' or *mòi* 'back'.

3.2.1 Hills Amri Karbi sixth vowel

As mentioned above, the Hills Amri Karbi variety is interesting in that it has the /ei/ diphthong that does not exist in the standard Hills Karbi (Rongkhang) variety. The Amri Karbi variety is also very interesting for its vowel monophthong system. While the five monophthong vowel system shown in Figure 8 above is the accepted standard vowel inventory of Karbi, the Amri Karbi variety from West Karbi Anglong has an additional vowel.[31] This sixth vowel is a high to mid-high, front, centralized vowel /ɪ/ (see Figure 9).

A full study of this vowel still needs to be conducted to examine any co-occurrence or positional restrictions in detail. It seems clear, however, that wherever /ɪ/ occurs in Amri Karbi, the standard Karbi varieties have the high front vowel /i/. A few items where /ɪ/ occurs are given in Table 18. Note that the standard Karbi variety has the

---

[31] Note that there may be a difference between the Christian and non-Christian sociolects of the Amri Karbi variety. While the non-Christian sociolect definitely has the sixth vowel, it appears that the Christian sociolect does not. This would also explain why Grüßner (1978), who had worked with speakers of the Christian sociolect of the Amri Karbi variety, does not report this vowel.

Figure 9: Amri Karbi vowels.

same items except for using /i/ instead of /ɪ/. The minimal pairs that contrast /i/ and /ɪ/ in Amri Karbi are therefore homophonous in the standard Karbi varieties.

Table 18: Set of items with /ɪ/ in Amri Karbi.

	Item with /ɪ/	Gloss	Minimal pairs
1	ɪ̀	'to sleep'	ì 'to defecate', è 'to plant'
2	thɪ́	'to snatch'	
3	thìnɪ̀	'to almost die'ᵃ	
4	rɪ̄	'base of a tree'	rī 'rope'
5	rɪ́	'hand'	
6	sɪ'ɪ̄	'leprosy'	
7	Inghɪ̀	'CLAN'	
8	pɪsàr	'mother's younger sister'	
9	thèngpɪ̄	'tree'	thèng-pī 'beat-BEN', 'to beat for somebody'
10	mēkkrɪ̄	'beautiful eyes (poetic)', 'NAME'	mēkkrī 'tear'

ᵃThe verb *thìnì* is a lexicalized item, where *thì* 'to die' is clearly recognizable, but *nì* does not appear to synchronically be a suffix.

The ten examples given in Table 18 have /ɪ/ in different positions in the word and with different tones. The existence of minimal pairs between /i/ and /ɪ/ suggests that /ɪ/ historically was a phoneme of pre-modern Karbi that was later on merged in the standard dialects, while the more conservative Amri Karbi variety has preserved the /ɪ/.

Basic five vowel systems with a less stable sixth vowel are also found in the Boro-Garo branch. Burling (2013) gives an interesting comparative description of the 'sixth' vowel in these languages, which in Boro-Garo, however, are all back and not front as in Karbi (though also high to mid-high). In the modern Boro-Garo languages, the basic five vowels have not changed and can be easily reconstructed, while the 'sixth' vowel is different in the different languages, and has merged with either /u/ or /o/ in one of them, Dimasa.

3.2.2 Marginal vowels and phonetic variation

There are three marginal monophthong vowels that occur in a very limited set of morphemes. These are the open [ɛ], the open [ɔ], and the [oʷ] off-glide version of /o/.

Table 19 shows all three with examples. Note that all of the examples in Table 19 are phrase-final or phrase-'independent' markers with highly pragmatic functions.[32] It seems that the open [ɛ] and the open [ɔ] are better analyzed as part of prosody (perhaps with the function of marking the end or boundary of a phrase).[33] This will need to be addressed in future research.

The off-glide [oʷ] is not so much associated with morphemes that occur in regular discourse. Seemingly the most frequent morpheme where this off-glide occurs is *ho* 'here.you.go', which is an interjection that accompanies an act of offering an object, usually when the intended recipient of that object has their attention focused elsewhere. This *ho* 'here.you.go' and a separate discourse particle *ho* form a very clear minimal pair for /oʷ/ versus /ɔ/. Otherwise, /oʷ/ also occurs in the expression used to call dogs when they are fed, in *dododo* (multiple repetitions of *do* with /oʷ/, not just exactly three). Finally, the off-glide [oʷ] also occurs as a variant of [o], seemingly for stylistic reasons, whose exact effects are unclear. For example, I have heard people sometimes say *avelo* 'not exist anymore' articulated more as [aβeloʷ] than [aβelo].
For a discussion of the functions of the interjections and hesitation words listed in Table 19, see Chapter 16.

Table 19: Marginal vowels.

Vowel	Example items	Meaning / Function
[ɛ]	-te	'if'
	=ke	'TOP'
	=le	'FOC:IRR'
	he	'AFTERTHOUGHT'
	mane	'HESIT'
/ɔ/	to	'okay'
	ho	'EMPH.INTERACT'
	ko	addressing word among men
/oʷ/	ho	'here.you.go'
	dododo	'[calling dogs to feed them]'

---

[32] Their highly pragmatic function in phrase-final position is also the reason why these are unmarked for tone. It has been impossible to determine the tone given that the pitch on these markers is heavily influenced by prosodic patterns (§3.5.9).
[33] Another phenomenon I have observed is that in Y/N-questions without the question particle *ma* at the end, if the verb has the suffix *-lò* 'RL' (for example in common questions like *àn chō-ét-lò?* 'have you eaten?'), the *-lò* is typically produced with a very open /ɔ/ as compared to the parallel answer or statement *àn chō-ét-lò* '(I) have eaten'.

Besides these marginal monophthong vowels, there also is one lexical item borrowed from Assamese, which has a unique two vowel sequence: *diá* 'forgive(<Asm)'. There is no glottal stop between the two vowels, but instead a glide transition. Some speakers produce a more nativized version of this verb root by inserting a palatal voiced stop (which anyway alternates with the glide in onset position), resulting in *dijá*.

3.3 Syllable

Table 20 gives an overview of all syllable types of Karbi, and provides a sample monosyllabic root for each.

Table 20: Syllable types.

Description		Schematic	Example	Gloss
Onset	Coda			
None	None	V	*ì*	'to sleep'
	Yes	VC	*ìk*	'older brother', 'to be black'
Simple	None	CV	*ló*	'to send'
	Yes	CVC	*lám*	'language', 'word', 'matter'
Cluster	None	CCV	*kló*	'to fall'
	Yes	CCVC	*pláng*	'to become'

Both open and closed syllables can have either no consonant onset, a single consonant onset, or a consonant cluster onset. If there is no consonant onset, the vowel is realized with a preceding glottal stop. This glottal stop surfaces strongly in word-medial syllables, where it prevents resyllabification. If there is a single consonant onset, that consonant belongs to the set provided in Table 5. All possible coda consonants are shown in Table 13. The set of consonant clusters that occur in onset position is given in Table 21. This table shows that only voiceless stops occur as the first consonant in onset clusters, and only the rhotic or the lateral occur as the second consonant in onset clusters. The bilabial stops feature most productively in clusters: both voiceless stops, the unaspirated /p/ and the aspirated /ph/, occur with both the rhotic and the lateral.[34]

As for alveolar stops, only the aspirated stop occurs with the rhotic, and only in two words, and really just in one morpheme: *thrōk* 'six' and *thrōksí* 'seven' (which is

---

[34] There appears to be some amount of dialectal variation such that /phr/ (as in the western Amri, Rongkhang, and Chinthong dialects) may be produced without aspiration as [pr] in the eastern dialects. For example, the word *samphrì* 'sun (poetic); NAME' may be pronounced as *samprì*, *aphráng* 'front' may be pronounced as *apráng*, and *nemphrù* 'have sweet smell' may be pronounced as *nemprù*.

Table 21: Onset cluster types.

Stop	Liquid	Cluster	Example	Gloss
/p/	/l/	/pl/	pláng	'to become'
	/r/	/pr/	prāp	'to be fast'
/ph/	/l/	/phl/	phlòng	'to burn'
	/r/	/phr/	phráng	'front'
/th/	/r/	[/thr/]	thrōk	'six'
/k/	/l/	/kl/	klém	'to do'
	/r/	/kr/	Krō	'CLAN'
/kh/	/r/	[/khr/]	khràng	'tree sp.'[a]

[a]Grüßner (1978: 13) mentions that the botanical name for khràng is "Amora Rehituka".

derived from thrōk 'six' plus isī 'one'). I have heard Karbi speakers[35] say that thrōk 'six' comes from a longer form therok without the onset cluster, and this longer form is also recorded by Matisoff (2003: 145). That means then, that the alveolar stops essentially do not participate in onset clusters with the lateral and the rhotic, which also makes sense from an articulatory point of view. It presumably is also because of this reason that in thrōk 'six' and thrōksi 'seven', the rhotic is produced as an approximant, which it is not otherwise in onset position. The velar voiceless unaspirated stop /k/ productively occurs in clusters with both the lateral and the rhotic, while the voiceless aspirated stop /kh/ only occurs with the rhotic and only in a limited number of morphemes, mostly in suffixes. The example given in Table 21, khràng 'tree sp.' might be the only actual root that has this onset cluster.

Finally, it should be noted that the syllable is a very salient unit in Karbi. It appears that the majority of roots and certainly the great majority of affixes are monosyllabic. To my knowledge, resyllabification does not occur across morpheme boundaries.

3.4 Palatal glide coda versus diphthongs

For syllables such as bai, bei, boi, or bui, it is possible to treat them as CVC syllables where the coda is a palatal glide /j/, or as CVV syllables with a diphthong nucleus. In what follows, I argue for an analysis of this rhyme as representing glide codas, unlike in Konnerth (2014).[36]

---

[35] I particularly noted that Mr. Sikari Tisso mentioned this longer form therok. Mr. Tisso is originally from Boksong in West Karbi Anglong and identifies himself as an Amri dialect speaker, specifically of the non-Christian sociolect.
[36] I would like to thank my editor Pattie Epps for suggesting this.

The diphthong analysis would introduce more complexity at the level of possible syllable types. Instead of having a constant monophthong nucleus with either no, one, or two consonants in onset position and with either no or one consonant coda, we now would have monophthong or diphthong nuclei in open syllables, but only monophthong nuclei in closed syllables. Both the introduction of a new type (i.e., the possibility of a diphthong nucleus) and of the resulting asymmetry (i.e., the occurrence of diphthong nuclei only in open syllables) are disadvantages to this analysis.

The palatal glide analysis only requires us to characterize the palatal glide with a minor asymmetry, that is allophony in onset position but no allophony in the coda position. This restriction in the coda position aligns with the more general restriction on phonemic distinctions among coda consonants compared to the onset.

The historical perspective can be considered to provide further support for the glide coda analysis. While these Karbi rhymes are generally not reflexes of the Proto-Tibeto-Burman rhymes conceptualized by Matisoff (2003) as "palatal diphthongs",[37] there are a number of instances in which Karbi /ei/, /ai/, /oi/, and /ui/ reconstruct back to a monophthong plus coda */-l/ in PTB.[38] This reconstruction also explains the dialectal difference, where Plains Karbi has the forms *phirul* 'snake', *mol* 'back', or *ingkol* 'twenty'. Hence a palatal glide analysis preserves the originally "consonant-coda character" of these rhymes.

Despite the preferential phonological analysis of these rhymes as representing palatal glide codas rather than diphthongs, for practical purposes this grammar follows the current orthographic standard and writes "orthographic diphthongs" /ei/, /ai/, /oi/, and /ui/.

3.5 Tone

Karbi has three tones, which I will refer to as low, mid and high, following Grüßner (1978). However, while low and high would seem to be fitting labels, the "mid" tone is not consistently in the mid-pitch range and is more generally the odd one out of the three tone categories. When contrasting monosyllabic roots in a minimal triplet of tone, the auditory characteristics of the three tones are as follows.

---

[37] I only found one item where PTB *-ay may be reflected by Karbi -ai, which is *chài* from PTB *dzay 'cattle' (Matisoff 2003). In my own corpus I only have *chainōng* 'cow', which is clearly a compound with the second root coming from *nōng* 'to cultivate, loosen soil'. In a dictionary manuscript that Grüßner was working on in the 1970s, he also lists *chài* as an individual root meaning 'mithun, Gaxaeus Ganrus'.

[38] Evidence includes Hills Karbi words *ingvùi* 'to mix, stir' from PTB *ŋwal; *phurūi* 'snake' from *s-brul; *thùi* 'to wrap (something large)' from *r-tul; *herēi* 'hail' from *ryal; *ingkòi*, 'twenty' from *m-kul; and, *thāi* 'arrow' from *tal.

The low tone seems to be produced at about the normal pitch level of a given speaker. It is usually realized with a slightly falling contour.

The high tone is produced at a significantly higher pitch level, and sometimes has a slightly rising contour associated with it when followed by at least one other syllable within the same word. When the high tone is on a word- or phrase-final syllable, for example in the case of eliciting a monosyllabic stem as its own word, then the high tone is produced with a steep falling contour as part of an additional layer of phrase-final prosody.

Lastly, the mid tone sometimes has an intermediate pitch level between the low and the high tone, but not always, as will be discussed below in more detail below. It is different from the low and the high tone in that it has glottalization associated with it. This glottalization surfaces most clearly in open and sonorant-final syllables when they occur as the last (or only) syllable of a word.

A significant finding of this grammar is that stopped or checked syllables, i.e., those ending in a stop /p/, /t/, or /k/, may be mid tone. The previous description of the tone system by Grüßner (1978) had stopped syllables be exclusively low or high, while reserving the mid tone for non-stopped syllables only, i.e., open or sonorant-final syllables.

The three tones can be contrasted in minimal sets as shown in §3.5.1 and §3.5.2. These minimal sets were discovered both in an early stage of the research for this grammar that was dedicated to phonological issues, as well as later on and throughout the project when encountering new roots in the process of analyzing texts. In the early stages of the research project, some time was spent going through the list of phonotactically possible monosyllables and eliciting which possible syllables were indeed morphemes of Karbi and which were not. That way, a few minimal pairs were discovered. However, identifying the tone even just of monosyllabic roots, but even more so of disyllabic or polysyllabic roots or of suffixes or clitics has remained a challenge throughout the course of research for this grammar. It is my goal for this section to both justify why what we have in Karbi should indeed be analyzed as a tone system, and to then lay out why it has been so challenging to describe this tone system, and to apply the tonal analysis to the task of accurately representing spoken Karbi in the transcription of texts recorded for the main corpus of this grammar. Note that this grammar only indicates tone at the morpheme but not the word level, and only on roots and suffixes, but not on prefixes, the one proclitic, or enclitics (see §3.5.6 and §3.5.9).

In §3.5.3, I describe how the minimal sets and at least two other kinds of evidence form the basis of the claim that Karbi does indeed have tone. With this in mind, §3.5.4 then lays out why this tone system is weak and carries a low functional load.

The next section §3.5.5 discusses two tone sandhi effects that occur across stems and suffixes. In §3.5.6, the interactions between tone and different phonological and morphological levels are discussed. This includes a discussion of the tone-bearing unit and tone at the word level, which is not marked in this grammar. In §3.5.7, remarks on some of the tone patterns and tone changes that occur in compounds are offered. A discussion of practical strategies that can be and have been used to identify the tones of individual morphemes is given in §3.5.8. This is followed by a section that describes the conventions for marking tones that are followed in this grammar in §3.5.9. Finally, §3.5.10 provides some remarks on a few tone minimal pairs across nouns and verbs that may suggest a historically derivational function of tone in Karbi, which is, however, synchronically not productive.

3.5.1 Tone minimal sets: Monosyllabic roots

There are two tables below that offer tone minimal sets for monosyllabic roots that have either a voiceless onset (Table 22), or a voiced onset (Table 23). Since the voicing status of the onset is known to give rise to tonogenesis cross-linguistically, it is important to note that all three tones occur after voiced and voiceless onsets in Karbi.

Table 22: Minimal sets for tones after voiceless onsets.

Tone	Open syllable		Sonorant coda		Stop coda	
L	phì	'grandmother'	sàng	'to spread'	hùt	'to dig (a large hole)'
M	phī	'to roast'	sāng	'raw rice'	hūt	'time' (*ahūt* 'during')
H	phí	'to give birth'	sáng	'to take rest'	hút	'to question/examine a wrongdoer'

Table 23: Minimal sets for tones after voiced onsets.

Tone	Open syllable		Sonorant coda		Stop coda	
L	lò	'male animal'	ròng	'village'	rèt	'to cut off small pieces'
M	lō	'banana leaf'	rōng	'plant'	lūt	'to enter'
H	ló	'to send, let loose'	róng	'to borrow'	rét	'to stalk prey'

Both Tables 22 and 23 also give minimal triplets across coda type. No 'perfect' minimal triplet in which all roots belong to the same word class could be found. This is telling of the low functional load of this tone system (see §3.5.4.2). As mentioned above, this study has found stop coda syllables carrying the mid tone, contrary to Grüßner (1978). However, stopped mid tone syllables are still a bit different from non-stopped mid tone syllables: stopped mid tone syllables appear to participate in phonological contrast a lot less frequently than non-stopped mid tone syllables. In fact, when I first came across stopped mid tone syllables, I thought they were mid tone **because** they did not participate in tone contrast. These were roots such as *tūk* 'to dig (a small hole)', *ūp* 'to boil', and *e-nūt* 'one-CLF:HUM:SG', which do not have segmentally identical counterparts with a low or high tone. Further research has revealed, however, that there are some minimal pair contrasts that mid tone stopped syllables participate in (see below). Regarding a three-way tone contrast, I only have found one single fairly good minimal triplet for stopped monosyllabic roots, the one given in Table 22: *hùt*, *hūt*, and *hút*. Even this minimal triplet is a bit problematic, because *hūt* may only ever be used as a relator noun with a dependent noun, or a subordinator with a dependent clause, in both of which cases it occurs with the *a-* 'possessive' prefix. Non-stopped monosyllabic roots, on the other hand, display the three-way tone contrast clearer with a number of true minimal triplets (presumably around a dozen to perhaps a couple of dozen). Tables 22 and 23 provide minimal triplets following a voiceless onset and following a voiced onset.

There is one other minimal triplet for stopped syllables that I have come across, which is given in Table 24. Note, however, that the high tone item is a type of exclamative expression that is usually accompanied with a gesture that indicates the amount or size of a given entity.

Table 24: Additional stopped syllable tone minimal triplet.

Stop coda	
thèk	'to know'
thēk	'to move wood in fire'
(là) thék	'this much!'

Table 25 offers minimal pairs of stopped syllables displaying all three pairwise contrasts: the mid tone versus the high tone, the low tone versus the high tone, and the low tone versus the mid tone. While especially for the low versus high but also the low versus mid oppositions of stopped syllables, there are a few other minimal pairs

Table 25: Stopped syllable tone minimal pairs for M-H, L-H, and L-M.

Minimal pair	L tone		M tone		H tone	
M vs. H			dūk	'dust'	dúk	'hardship(<Asm)', 'be poor(<Asm)'
			hōk	'truth'	hók	'to approve'
L vs. H	ràp	'to stick'			ráp	'to help'
	chòk	'to beat'			chók	'to be okay'
L vs. M	mèk	'wound'	mēk	'eye'		
	sòk	'to get water'	sōk	'paddy'		

besides the ones listed in Table 25, the two minimal pairs of the mid versus high opposition given in this table are the only ones I have come across.

Note also that *dúk* 'hardship; be poor' is a borrowing from Assamese. Borrowings from the non-tonal surrounding languages that have been strong donor languages in the history of contact with Karbi, i.e., Indic languages (Assamese, Hindi, Bengali), English, and Khasi, typically receive the high tone (see also Grüßner (1978: 31–32)).

3.5.2 Tone minimal sets: Disyllabic roots

Table 26 offers two minimal triplets of disyllabic roots, where only the ultimate, i.e., prominent, syllable (cf. §3.6) carries contrastive tone. These were the only tone minimal triplets of disyllabic roots I was able to identify, although there might be additional ones, especially with one of the frequent first syllables and frozen prefixes *ing* or *ar* (cf. §6.3).[39]

Table 26: Minimal triplets of disyllabic roots.

Tone	Triplet 1		Triplet 2	
L	ingthì	'to kill a louse'	inglè	'wild fig tree'
M	ingthī	'to wash, rinse (an object)'; 'comb'	Inglē	'FEM.NAME'
H	ingthí	'to wash, clean (head, hair)'	inglé	'to offer'

See § 3.5.9 for explanations of how tone is marked in morphemes with more than one syllable. Note that in this grammar, tone is only marked at the morpheme level but not at the word level (§ 3.5.6).

Table 27 complements Table 26 with more contrastive sets of disyllabic roots. For the minimal pair *ingrī* 'sp.grass' versus *ingrí* 'be intoxicated', Grüßner, in his dictionary manuscript, also lists a low tone counterpart, actually making it a minimal triplet. However, *ingrì* 'to have equal portions, be equal' seems to only occur with the *pV*- 'CAUS' prefix as *pangrì* 'to make equal', which is why it is not listed here.

3.5.3 Phonological basis of the tone system

There are at least three different pieces of evidence for the phonological basis of the Karbi tone system that also serve to justify analyzing it as a tone system. First and

---

[39] The phonological study of disyllabic roots with initial *ing* and *ar* would have been impossible for me without the thorough compilation of those forms by Grüßner in his dictionary manuscript.

Table 27: Minimal pairs of disyllabic roots.

Minimal pair	L tone		M tone		H tone	
M vs. H			inghōr	'carrying load'	inghór	'to carry a load'
			ingrī	'sp.grass'	ingrí	'be intoxicated'
L vs. H	chitìm	'half'			chitím	'mosquito'
	ingjìr	'sister'			ingjír	'to dissolve'
L vs. M	phelò	'cotton'	phelō	'potash'		
	phurùi	'yam'	phurūi	'snake'		
	inglìt	'be slippery'	inglīt	'water leech'		

foremost, of course, we need to consider the evidence of minimal pairs and triplets that contrast monosyllabic and also a couple of disyllabic roots for tone, presented in the previous sections §3.5.1 and §3.5.2. The fact that there is a large number of monosyllabic roots, and still a considerable number of disyllabic roots that are segmentally identical and are only distinguished by pitch height or a combination of pitch height and glottalization should lead us to believe that tone is as phonological as are the consonant and vowel phonemes.

Second, there is a certain level of awareness of tones among native speakers. For example, my consultant Sikari Tisso pointed out a small number of cases where in the recordings that we collected for this project and then analyzed, the speaker in a particular recording made a speech error that consisted of using the wrong tone.[40] The fact that he was able to tell me he heard the wrong tone speaks to the phonological basis of tones. Furthermore, many different people have mentioned to me the tone minimal pairs of *phurùi* 'yam' versus *phurūi* 'snake', and *làng* 'to see, look' versus *lāng* 'water', after I say that I am studying Karbi. What is interesting, however, is that it tended to be exactly these two minimal pairs that people point out to me, as if they were the conventionalized prototypes of tone minimal pairs. Another example of the awareness of tones among native speakers is the tongue twister given in (9), which also is something several different people have pointed out to me, and Grüßner (1978: 26) also recorded it.

(9) Tone tongue twister
lang langlanglanglang
lāng làng-langláng-làng
water see-try-still
'still trying to see the water'

---

[40] Examples are the use of a high tone in *a-phí instead of low tone *a-phì* 'POSS-grandmother' in KK, BMS 093, and a low tone pronunciation of high tone *nón* 'now' in *nón-pu-án-tā* 'up until now' in SiH, CW 017.

Native speaker awareness of tones is also evidenced in attempts to incorporate some tone marking in the orthography. There is a movement to represent the salient glottalized mid tone in sonorant-final syllables by adding a homorganic stop at the end, such as <atump> for *a-tūm* 'POSS-PL', <ront> for *rōn* 'custom, or <langk> for *lāng* 'water'. However, the proposal does not include marking the mid tone on open or stopped syllables, and does not at all include marking the low or the high tone (see also the discussion in §1.7). Thus, despite these different signs of native speaker awareness of tones, it is not clear how truly systematic or phonological this awareness is.

A last type of evidence for the phonological basis of tone comes from morphophonological patterns that change the tonal category of a root or a suffix depending on the morphological environment (see §3.9.1). Since there are a number of different such patterns where the tone category affiliation of a syllable changes to another tone category, this logically then is evidence that there are, in fact, tone categories.

3.5.4 Low functional load

The idea that different phonemic contrasts may have different degrees of functional load in the overall phonemic system goes back to the Prague School (*inter alia* Mathesius 1929; Jakobson 1931). There have also been approaches to quantify the functional load of phonemic contrasts (e.g. Hockett 1967; Surendran and Niyogi 2006). The goal of this section is, however, to argue in a qualitative way for why tones in Karbi only carry a low functional load.

In the following subsections, I present six different types of evidence that the Karbi tone system does indeed carry a low functional load within Karbi phonology. While each piece of evidence by itself would not be conclusive, the various types of evidence together form the argument for the low functional load of tones in Karbi.

The first type of evidence comes from native speakers' difficulty in identifying tone categories. The next two types of evidence come from what we can refer to as the paradigmatic and syntagmatic dimensions of the functional load of tone. The paradigmatic dimension consists of the contrastiveness of the tone system or the existence of tone minimal sets. The syntagmatic dimension consists of the context of a tonal morpheme, both within the same word and at the phrasal or clausal level, which may greatly contribute to the identification of that morpheme. The fourth type of evidence presented here is the occurrence of categorical tone changes and cases of indeterminability of the tones of certain morphemes due to over-layering prosody. The fifth type of evidence comes from a phonetic study that looked at both acoustic measurements of tones and at the performance of native speakers as they tried to identify lexical items in a perception study (Konnerth and Teo 2014). Lastly, evidence for the low functional load of the tone system also comes from the fact that only roots and suffixes bear tone (see §3.5.6).

3.5.4.1 Native speakers' difficulty to identify tone categories

My Karbi language consultants experience a lot of difficulty in identifying the tone category of a morpheme, especially when there is no tone minimal counterpart. The method of humming or whistling the tone as a way to get rid of the disturbance introduced by the segmental structure, a method often used in fieldwork to identify the tone of a syllable, was not successful. Instead, what we would do to determine the tone of a morpheme was try and find a near minimal counterpart that would have the same rhyme or at least close to the same rhyme, and/or follow the strategies outlined in §3.5.8.

Even those native speakers heavily invested in the project, i.e., members of the *Karbi Lammet Amei* (see §1.1.4), who also work on a dictionary that is supposed to indicate tone, have a hard time trying to learn to determine the tone category of a root or a suffix, which, I believe, is already suggestive of the low functional load of this tone system.

3.5.4.2 Low contrastiveness

By 'low contrastiveness' I refer to the overall small number of tone minimal triplets (see §3.5.1 and §3.5.2), and to the virtual absence of tone minimal triplets where all three members belong to the same basic morphosyntactic word class (the only example I have come across is the all-verbal triplet *ingthì* vs. *ingthī* vs. *ingthí* in Table 26). Since roots generally do pattern quite differently in discourse depending on whether they are nominal (being able to take the *a-* 'POSS' prefix) or verbal (being able to take the *ke-* 'NMLZ' prefix) (see §4.1.1), a minimal triplet, where one member is verbal while the other two are nominal, or vice versa, practically only counts as minimal **pair** at the discourse level. Of course, minimal pairs also matter, and there still are a lot of minimal pairs, where both members belong to the same word class.

Furthermore, it appears that minimal sets only exist within monosyllabic roots and perhaps a handful of monosyllabic suffixes, as well as within disyllabic roots. Also, the kind of disyllabic roots that occur in minimal sets are mostly those that have the common first syllable *ing* or *ar* (see §3.5.2). Other than those, there are only very few minimal sets of disyllabic roots.

3.5.4.3 Large amount of contextuality

If the morphological (or phrasal/clausal) context of a tonal morpheme frequently helps identify its meaning or function, then that reduces the functional load of that tonal morpheme. In Karbi, there is a large class of predicate derivation suffixes, some of which combine more productively with different kinds of roots, but some of which also have very specific semantics and only combine with a very limited number of verbs, sometimes even just one (§9.2.1.1.3). This latter type of predicate derivation suffixes with narrow semantics is of interest here, because it provides a morphological context that helps identify stems that are part of tone minimal sets.

Furthermore, even if a particular predicate derivation suffix may occur with a small number of different stems, there are certain stem-suffix collocations that seem remarkably frequent, such that they seem (a) semantically close to the prototypical meaning of the stem without the suffix, and (b) to some degree lexicalized as a unit of their own. As a result of that, native speakers have quite frequently used predicate derivations to differentiate between members of minimal sets in the course of research on tone for this project. Examples are *thī-hèk* 'be.short-small' and *thí-jòk* 'snatch-quickly' (§9.2.1.1.3). Thus the existence of predicate derivations with narrow semantics and especially the cases of frequently collocating stem-suffix combinations are another factor that reduces the functional load of tone in Karbi.

Another, quite curious piece of evidence that suggests that the context of a root matters is that for recordings made for the phonetic analysis of tone, where stems were recorded once in isolation followed by three times in a carrier phrase ("*Neli ___ pusi kepu.*"), one particular speaker merged mid and high tone items produced in isolation to the low tone such that the phonetic recordings of the items *thī* 'be short' and *thí* 'snatch' would be (and sound to other native speaker) as follows:

"**Thì**. *Neli thī pusi kepu. Neli thī pusi kepu. Neli thī pusi kepu.*" (for *thī* 'be short')

"**Thì**. *Neli thí pusi kepu. Neli thí pusi kepu. Neli thí pusi kepu.*" (for *thí* 'snatch')

Note that other native speakers thought this speaker was first saying the verb 'die' and then switched to 'be short' or 'snatch', respectively.

It is perhaps not clear whether this should count as evidence that the context matters so much that an item without a context, i.e. if produced in isolation, does not receive tonal specification by this speaker. However, it does represent more evidence for the low functional load of tone.

3.5.4.4 Speaker differences in realization of mid versus high tones

An acoustic study of Karbi tone has shown that there are differences between speakers in whether they realize the mid versus high tone distinction in pitch (Konnerth and Teo 2014). This study examines two native Karbi speakers, one female and one male, in their respective realizations of the three tones in the following three contexts: (1) monosyllabic bare stems, (2) monosyllabic stems with the suffix *-jī* 'IRR2', and (3) monosyllabic stems with the suffix *-pò* 'IRR1'. Although both speakers originally come from different areas of Karbi Anglong, they have both lived in Diphu for a long time.

Averaged F0 values of the three tones show that the male speaker consistently differentiated the mid and the high tone through F0 in all three contexts, while the female speaker merged the mid and the high tone. For both speakers, the low tone was consistently lower than the mid or the high tone in a statistically significant way.

It is not quite clear what the reason behind this difference between the two speakers in the realization of the mid versus the high tone is, but to evaluate the phonological basis of the mid versus high tone distinction produced by the male speaker, a follow-up perception study was conducted, discussed in the next section.

3.5.4.5 Production-perception mismatch

A perception study to investigate the phonological basis of the differential realizations of the mid versus high tones of two native Karbi speakers (§3.5.4.4) is described in Konnerth and Teo (2014). It turns out that the statistically significant F0 differentiation between the mid and the high tone produced by the male speaker did not help listeners correctly identify the target member of tone minimal sets. Both the female and the male speaker's stimuli of mid and high tone members of tone minimal sets elicited error rates of 50% or higher in the case of stems either with the suffix -jí 'IRR2' or with the suffix -pò 'IRR1'.[41] Since listeners essentially guessed the target stem at chance level, there is an interesting mismatch between production and perception in the case of the male speaker: Although he produced a statistically significant F0 difference between the mid and the high tone in these two contexts, listeners were not able to pick up on it. Strikingly, the male speaker himself participated in the perception study and listening to his own stimuli, he still had an error rate of 20% for stems with the suffix -jí 'IRR2' and an error rate of 50% for stems with the suffix -pò 'IRR1'. These results of the acoustic and follow-up perception study underscore the low functional load of tone in Karbi.

3.5.4.6 Prosodic tone changes and indeterminability

There are at least two types of instances in the corpus of recorded texts where a morpheme that we know to have a particular tone in a pragmatically unmarked context occurs with a different tone in a particular pragmatic or prosodic context. This is different from morphophonemic tone changes, discussed in §3.9.1, which are explained purely by the morphological environment of a tonal morpheme without reference to prosody.

In (10), *kopù* 'how' in *kopuloma* is originally low tone, as indicated in the morpheme line. However, in the emphatic context in this example (i.e., with a sense of 'how only', as the speaker is desperate) *kopù* is actually produced with a high tone, as indicated in the word line.[42]

This prosodic tone change is even more striking considering that *kopú* with the high tone exists separately and means 'where'.[43]

---

[41] Listeners could listen to the stimuli as much as they wanted. The stimuli were the target item once in isolation and three times in the carrier phrase *Neli ___ pusi kepu.* 'I said ___'.
[42] This tone change appears to not be restricted to this speaker or text. My language consultants recognize the change to high tone as something natural in a context such as this one.
[43] The two items *kopù* and *kopú* are parallel to *lapù* 'like this' and *lapú* 'this side, here', although with the demonstrative *la*, this prosodically-driven tone change does not happen to my knowledge.

(10) Prosodic tone category change *kopù* 'how'
*mh bojarta **kopú**loma chetongji?*
mh   bojár=tā   **kopù**=lo=ma   chetòng-jí
INTERJ   market(<Asm)=ADD   how=FOC=Q   meet-IRR2
'In the market, how only will I possibly meet her?' [KK, BMS 067][44]

The suffix *-dèt* 'PFV' also consistently becomes high tone *-dét* when followed by *-pen* 'NF:with' as in (11), or when followed by a relator noun derived subordinator such as *aphī* 'after' in (12) (see also §15.2.1.2).

(11) Prosodic tone category change *-dèt* 'PFV' preceding *-pen* 'NF:with'
*lole**dét**pen pini bamhetsi mh diho*
ló-Cē-**dèt**-pen   pini   bām-hèt-si   mh   [diho
let.loose-NEG-PFV-NF:with   HESIT   embrace-firmly-NF:RL   DSM   leave.me!

puta kroikredetlo ansi
pù=tā]   krōi-Cē-dèt-lò   ánsi
QUOT=ADD:although   agree-NEG-PFV-RL   and.then
'He didn't let her go, he was embracing her tightly, although she said "leave me (alone)!", he didn't agree.' [KK, BMS 080][45]

(12) Prosodic tone category change *-dèt* 'PFV' preceding *aphī* 'after'
*garipen vang**dét** aphisi netum dakpen Hongkram*
garí=pen   vàng-**dèt**   aphī=si   ne-tūm   dāk=pen   Hongkrām
car(<Asm)=with   come-PFV   after=FOC:RL   1EXCL-PL   here=from   PLACE

kedam kechenglo
ke-dàm   ke-chèng-lò
NMLZ-go   NMLZ-begin-RL
'After the car came, we started going from here to Hongkram.' [SH, CSM 008][46]

As a related phenomenon, there are two interjections, where an additional pitch level contrast appears to exist on top of glottalization that typically uniquely identifies the mid tone. The two items are *ōi* with a lower pitch level, which is a frequent affirmative interjection 'yes', and *ōi* with a higher pitch level, which is used as an addressing word among Karbi women. This 'pseudo pitch contrast' most certainly only exists

---

[44] The audio file for KK, BMS 067 is available at https://scholarsbank.uoregon.edu/xmlui/handle/1794/13657.
[45] The audio file for KK, BMS 080 is available at https://scholarsbank.uoregon.edu/xmlui/handle/1794/13657.
[46] The audio file for SH, CSM 008 is available at https://scholarsbank.uoregon.edu/xmlui/handle/1794/13657.

due to the inherent functional difference between an affirmative interjection and an addressing word used to get somebody's attention, but it should perhaps still be noted, because it is consistent and salient to native speakers.

Finally, the tone categories of enclitics as well as of suffixes such as *-te* 'COND' and *-si* 'NF:RL' seem almost impossible to determine due to the high prominence of prosodic contours over those morphemes (see §3.8.2 and §3.8.4). The same is true for discourse markers such as *te* 'so then' or *mati* 'common ground (CG)' (cf. *vàng-lò=ke=mati* 'come-RL=TOP=CG' with low tone on *mati*, versus *dō=mati ho* 'exist=CG EMPH:INTERACT', with high tone on *matí*).⁴⁷

3.5.5 Word-internal tone sandhi effects

A consistent word-internal tone sandhi effect is found on low tone suffixes after mid tone stems. Specifically, low tone suffixes following mid tone stems share characteristics with mid tone suffixes. Table 28 gives examples of a low tone suffix, *-ò* 'much:S/O' and a mid tone suffix, *-thū* 'again', as they follow the mid tone stem *chō* 'eat'. In the stem plus suffix forms in the second column, i.e., *chō-ò* and *chō-thū*, the low tone suffix *-ò* 'much:S/O' is still clearly different from *-thū* 'again': the latter carries the salient word-final glottalization associated with the mid tone, while the former does not.

Table 28: Tone sandhi effects on low tone suffix after mid tone stem.

Suffix	*chō* 'to eat' with suffix	+ *-lò* 'RL'	+ *-Cē* 'NEG'
-ò 'much:S/O'	*chō-ò*	*chō-ò-lò*	*chō-ò-ē*
-thū 'again'	*chō-thū*	*chō-thū-lò*	*chō-thū-thē*

The low tone suffix does, however, behave like a mid tone suffix in the third and fourth columns, after *-lò* 'RL' or *-Cē* 'NEG' are added. This is diagnosed with the help of these two suffixes, which can be used to identify the tone of a stem (see §3.5.8.2 and §3.5.8.3), and particularly attaching *-lò* 'RL' makes the mid tone very salient.

This internal sandhi effect, whereby a low tone suffix shares contour characteristics with mid tone suffixes, only occurs after mid tone stems. After a low tone stem such as *dàm* 'go' (or after a high tone stem), this internal sandhi effect does not occur, and *dàm-ò-lò* and *dàm-thū-lò* have clearly distinct pitch contours.

Another internal sandhi effect occurs on the tone of a stem that follows the prefix *cho-* 'auto-benefactive/malefactive' ('AUTO.BEN/MAL'). While both prefixes *che-* 'reflexive/reciprocal' ('RR') and *cho-* 'AUTO.BEN/MAL' change the tone on monosyllabic stems

---

47 See HK, TR 023 and 092.

such that a low tone turns into a mid tone and a mid tone into a high tone (see §3.9.2.2), the *cho-* 'AUTO.BEN/MAL' prefix induces additional tone sandhi (see also §3.9.2.2 for a discussion of the differences between *che-* and *cho-*). The internal sandhi surfaces as a higher pitch level compared to either the *che-* 'RR' prefixed counterpart or a *ke-* 'NMLZ' prefixed stem that matches the stem tone derived by *che-* and *cho-*. Table 29 contrasts the same stems with *cho-* 'auto-benefactive/malefactive' and *che-* 'reflexive/reciprocal'. The internal tone sandhi is indicated by **bold** print. The internal sandhi effect also persists on high tone stems, although no category tone change occurs. The example in Table 29 is *thán* 'to tell'. Here, *chethán* with the *che-* 'RR' prefix and *kethán* with the *ke-* 'NMLZ' prefix are identical in pitch contour, whereas *chothán* with the *cho-* 'AUTO.BEN/MAL' prefix displays the higher pitch internal sandhi.

Table 29: Internal sandhi effects on stem induced by prefix *cho-* 'AUTO.BEN/MAL'.

Stem	Gloss	*cho-* 'AUTO.BEN/MAL'	*che-* 'RR'	*ke-* 'NMLZ'
thàn	'to cut'	[cho-**thān**]	[che-thān]	
hūm	'to pick up'	[cho-**húm**]	[che-húm]	
thán	'to tell'	[cho-**thán**]	[che-thán	ke-thán]

See §3.5.6 and §3.5.9 on how tone is marked in this grammar (specifically, only on roots and suffixes but not on prefixes, for reasons outlined in those sections).

The internal sandhi effects discussed in this section thus represent changes in the expression of a tone category but not changes from one tone category to another one. We could refer to this type of change as morphophonetics or morphotonetics. In contrast, morphophonemic or morphotonemic processes of one tone category changing to another tone category are discussed in §3.9.1.

3.5.6 Tone and phonological and morphological units

Due to the low functional load of the tone system argued for in §3.5.4, it has not been possible to describe tone patterns at the word level. While certain word tone patterns at a phonetic, non-contrastive level could be observed, they have continually proven to not be strong, consistent, or categorical enough to allow for a phonological description. Future research with a more narrow focus on these issues will hopefully shed more light on them.

For the purposes of this grammar, tone is considered a property of syllables in tonal morphemes, i.e., in roots and suffixes. Tonal morphemes can be regularly contrasted with other tonal morphemes and their tone can thus be identified. The one (verbal) proclitic slot, the half a dozen prefixes, and the roughly same number of enclitics (see §3.8) – which are all monosyllabic – are considered toneless morphemes. Likewise, non-final syllables of multisyllabic morphemes are also typically toneless. Most probably, an analysis of tone at the word level and the difference between tone-bearing syllables and toneless syllables requires a phonetic in-depth study of stress. In the current work, stress is only discussed briefly in §3.6.

While the accuracy of tone assignment on monosyllabic tonal morphemes is near-perfect, some difficulty is encountered in disyllabic and, much more so, in polysyllabic tonal morphemes, when a syllable other than the last syllable may carry an inherent tone. This is especially the case in borrowings and in compound nouns (for the latter see §3.5.7). While borrowings generally carry the high tone (Grüßner 1978: 31–32), it is not always clear whether in disyllabic borrowings, the first, unstressed syllable tends to also be high tone or toneless. To my knowledge, most instances of disyllabic borrowings do not have a tonally specified first syllable, such as *tarík* 'date (<Asm)', *biskút* 'baked.snack (<Eng)', or *semé* 'vow (<Pnr)'. Grüßner, in his dictionary manuscript, however, also lists *tárí* 'knife (<Asm)', *dáktár* 'doctor (<Eng)', and *tásám* 'stress, wear and tear (<Khs)', all with a high tone first syllable.

While the present work does not describe tone at the word-level, Grüßner (1978: 19) does offer a description of how tone is realized on toneless syllables. This description suggests that toneless syllables alternate between low and high surface realizations, see Table 30, which needs to be read from right to left. If the tone-inherent, stressed syllable (right-most column in the table) is low, then the preceding toneless syllable (middle column in the table) is realized as ('realized as' is indicated by the arrow in the table) high. If the tone-inherent syllable is mid or high, then the preceding toneless syllable is realized as low. If there is another toneless syllable (left-most column) preceding a first toneless syllable, then this syllable is realized as low tone if followed by a high tone syllable, and is realized as a high tone if followed by a low tone syllable. According to Grüßner, sequences of toneless syllable follow this alternating pattern.

Table 30: Grüßner's (1978) account of tone assignment to toneless syllables.

Preceding toneless, unstressed syllable	Preceding toneless, unstressed syllable	Tone-inherent, stressed syllable
→ low	→ high	LOW
→ high	→ low	MID
→ high	→ low	HIGH

While auditory observations confirm Grüßner's basic idea that the first toneless syllable of a sesqui- or disyllabic word appears to build up a pitch contrast to the following tonal syllable, the alternating pattern in multisyllabic words described by Grüßner (1978: 19) has not been found. My own impression is that instead, the pitch contrast builds up across the sequence of toneless syllables, followed by the fully realized tone of the tone-inherent syllable.

3.5.7 Tone (changes) in compounds

There are certain tendencies for the tone patterns in disyllabic compounds. Table 31 gives an overview of those. The tone patterns low-mid (LM), mid-mid (MM), and high-low (HL) are underlined, because they appear to be robust patterns, which occur on many items. The patterns mid-low (ML) and mid-high (MH) are in [square brackets] to indicate their marginal status: Only *vōtèk* as ML, and *thrōksí* and *thēngphráng* as MH were found in the corpus. The LL and LH patterns do not appear as marginal as ML and MH, but also not as robust as LM, MM, and HL. Those compounds that have changed one or both tones compared to the respective tone of each part that they appear to be derived from are in **bold**.

Table 31: Compound tones.

Tone pattern	Compound	Gloss	First Root	Gloss	Second Root	Gloss
LL	tàrkòng	'bamboo mat to sit on'	tàr	'bamboo mat'	?	?
LM	ànsām	'cold rice'	àn	'rice'	ingsām	'be cold'
	mèthān	'dog'	armē	'tail'	thàn	'to cut'
	pìbā	'cloth to carry baby on back'	pé	'cloth'	bā	'to carry baby on back'
	nòklāng	'molasses'	nók	'sugarcane'	lāng	'water'
LH	làmmét	'literature'	lám	'language'	?	?
[ML]	vōtèk	'wild bird'	vō	'bird'	?	?
MM	lōthē	'banana (fruit)'	lō	'banana leaf'	thē	'fruit'
	chōjūn	'feast, celebration (kd)'	ʔchō	'to eat'	ʔjùn	'to drink'
[MH]	**thrōksí**	'seven'	thrōk	'six'	isī	'one'
	thēngphráng	'EE: thengpī ('tree')'	thēng	'wood'	?	?
HL	hánthàr	'sp.vegetable'	hán	'vegetable'	?	?

The only two tone patterns that are not listed in Table 31 are high-mid (HM) and high-high (HH). The HH pattern does appear to exist outside of borrowings (for which there are a number of attested items, see §3.5.6) in compounds recorded by Grüßner (1978: 36): *tím-kráng* 'sp.mosquito' (first part from *chitím* 'mosquito'), or *krák-sái* 'opening' (first part from *ingkrák* 'hole'). Grüßner (1978: 36) also offers one item with what he transcribes as a HM pattern: *ták-sū* 'wood chip' (from *ingták* 'splinter' and *ingsū* 'thorn'). However, the first part *ták* might actually be mid tone,[48] which then would

---

[48] According to Grüßner, stopped syllables are only low or high but never mid.

match the word *jintāk* 'bamboo strap', which occurs in the corpus of this grammar. The HM pattern might then not actually occur in compounds. Evidence in favor of this hypothesis is that in Table 31, the first part of *nòk-lāng* 'molasses' is *nók* 'sugarcane', and the first part of *pì-bā* 'cloth to carry baby on back' is *pé* 'cloth', so that HM patterns changed into LM patterns. While the HM pattern perhaps does not occur in compounds, it does, however, occur in words formed by a high tone stem with the diminutive suffix *-sō*, such as *lám-sō* 'a small matter' or *lún-sō* 'a little song'. Among them, there is also *chérsō* 'splinter', which is (historically) composed of *chēr* 'to chip off' and *-sō* but has arguably undergone lexicalization.

It appears then that there are no clear restrictions on tone patterns in disyllabic bimorphemic stems, but there are tendencies for more common patterns.

3.5.8 Strategies used for identifying tones of roots and suffixes

There are several strategies that have greatly facilitated the daunting task of marking tone in the texts that represent the corpus for this grammar. In what follows, I describe these strategies. The two strategies described in §3.5.8.2 and §3.5.8.3 use suffixes to help identify root tones and are largely based on differences in the distribution of perceived prominence among the target tonal morpheme and the added suffix.

3.5.8.1 Syllable under investigation is the last syllable of the word and non-stopped

If the syllable whose tone needs to be determined is an open or sonorant-final syllable, i.e., does not end in /p/, /t/, or /k/, and if it is either a monosyllabic root or suffix, or the last syllable of a multisyllabic root (or suffix, although there are very few multisyllabic suffixes), then it helps to listen out for the word-final glottalization that occurs with the mid tone. The word-final mid-tone glottalization is quite salient. The difference between the low tone and the high tone is not as easy to perceive, because a single word out of context always receives a phrase-final falling intonation. What our research team has done to identify low versus high tones is compare near-minimal pairs (if minimal pairs do not exist). This has sometimes been a difficult task as well, because the slightly different segmental shape of a near-minimal pair was at times distracting to the task of determining category membership. The method of humming tones to get rid of the distraction from segmental differences did not work for our research team.

3.5.8.2 Syllable under investigation followed by *-lò* 'realis'

Adding *-lò* 'realis' (§9.6.1) to stems has proven the best way to perceive tone categories of roots or derivational suffixes. Compared to determining the tone category of a word-final tonal morpheme (§3.5.8.1), this strategy eliminates the problem of phrase-final intonation, because the target syllable is not the last syllable of the word. This helps distinguish low from high tone on the target syllable. However, in comparison to that same strategy, we are also left without the salient glottalization associated with the mid tone. It turns out, however, that even in the absence of glottalization, the mid tone leaves a very salient auditory trace when -*lò* 'realis' is added. Specifically, a prominence shift happens with mid tone stems, whereby mid tone stem plus -*lò* 'RL' has a perceived prominence on the suffix, while with low or high tone stems plus -*lò* 'RL', the perceived prominence remains on the stem. Phonetically underlying this perceived prominence shift from mid tone stem to suffix appears to be a delay in the falling pitch contour of low tone -*lò* 'realis'. While after low and high tone stems, the falling pitch contour over -*lò* 'realis' is more or less linear, after mid tone stems it is delayed across the /l/ and only falls at the beginning of the vowel /o/.

Since this strategy helps identify the mid tone without relying on glottalization, it led to the discovery of the mid tone on stopped syllables, which due to their segmental nature with unreleased coda stops are already perceived as glottalized.

3.5.8.3 Syllable under investigation followed by -*Cē* 'negative'

An additional strategy that facilitates distinguishing between the mid and the high tone (which often is a difficult task, see §3.5.4.4 and §3.5.4.5) consists of adding the mid tone negative suffix -*Cē*. Here again (as with -*lò* 'realis', see the previous section §3.5.8.2), the emerging tone patterns between the three different target syllable tones and the suffix tone are different in the distribution of perceived prominence. While the emerging tone pattern of a low or mid tone target syllable and -*Cē* 'NEG' has the -*Cē* 'NEG' suffix more prominent, while the emerging tone pattern of a high tone target syllable and -*Cē* 'NEG' has the high tone target syllable more prominent. This strategy then helps distinguish between a high tone versus a mid tone (or low tone) target syllable, while it does not help distinguish between a low tone and a mid tone target syllable.

3.5.9 Representation of tone in this grammar

In the text examples in this grammar, tone is only marked on morphemes but not on words. In particular, it is only marked on roots and suffixes, not on the items in the verbal proclitic slot or on prefixes. On enclitics, it is generally not marked, although the additive particle =*tā* is realized with a clear and consistent glottalization that identifies it as mid tone. The other enclitics are not marked for tone due to their susceptibility to assimilate to pitch contours of prosody (§3.8.4).

If a tone changes due to morphophonemics (see §3.9.1), the new tone (and not the underlying tone) is indicated. For example, the prefix *che-* 'reflexive/reciprocal' changes the low tone of *dàm* 'go' to a mid tone, and so the in-text example will indicate the tone of the stem in *che-dām* 'RR-go' as mid.

In disyllabic or sesquisyllabic morphemes (or prefix-stem combinations, for that matter), the default realization of the preceding, unstressed, toneless syllable is to build up a contrast to the tone of the tone-inherent, stressed, final syllable such that a toneless syllable preceding a final low tone syllable is realized as high tone, and a toneless syllable preceding a final mid or high tone syllable is realized as low tone (see §3.5.6). If the unstressed syllables in a particular multisyllabic morpheme follow that default pattern of realization, their tone is not marked. If they deviate from this pattern, then their tone is marked. Table 32 gives examples of how tone is represented on the unstressed syllable of disyllabic roots in this grammar.

Table 32: Tone representation on unstressed syllables in disyllabic morphemes (default and non-default).

Default pattern	Example (tone unmarked)	Gloss	Non-default pattern	Example (tone marked)	Gloss
H-L	han̲thàr	'sp.vegetable'	L-L	tàrkòng	'bamboo mat to sit on'
	nang=lè	'CIS=reach'	M-L	vōtèk	'wild bird'
L-M	in̲ghōn	'to love'	M-M	phūlē	'pot'
	nang-pō	'2:POSS-father'	H-M	chérsō	'splinter'
L-H	in̲glóng	'hill'	M-H	thēngphráng	'EE: thengpī ('tree')'
	a-hán	'POSS-cooked.vegetable'	H-H	bírík	'chili'

The first three columns show the default patterns H-L, L-M, and L-H, for which the unstressed first syllable remains unmarked. One example of a disyllabic stem and one example of a prefix plus monosyllabic stem each are given. The second three columns show the non-default patterns L-L, M-L, M-M, M-H, and H-H, for which the unstressed first syllable is marked for tone. An example for each is given; note, however, that the examples of M-L and M-H are the only ones there are in the corpus (see also §3.5.7). Furthermore, the H-M example *chérsō* 'splinter' is (historically) composed of *chēr* 'to chip off' and the diminutive suffix *-sō* but has arguably lexicalized so that it is listed here as a disyllabic stem.

Note that there are some individual roots and suffixes that are not marked for tone in this grammar. These represent instances where I have not yet been able to confirm the correct tones.

3.5.10 Remarks on grammatical functions of tone

There are some hints towards the possibility of historical grammatical functions of tone in Karbi since there are corresponding noun and verb stems that form tone minimal pairs as first noted by Grüßner (1978: 47; 53). I repeat some of his examples along with my own examples (Table 33).

It can be noted that nouns tend to take the mid tone, and may correspond to (and perhaps be derived from) low or high tone verbs, although there is also one example each of a high tone noun corresponding to a low tone verb and of a low tone noun corresponding to a high tone verb. In addition, there are also homophonous verb-noun pairs such as *ing'òm* 'cheek; to carry in mouth'.

There is another pattern among tone minimal pairs that Grüßner (1978: 91) mentions. This is between verbs that Grüßner suggests are semantically related. However, the semantic relationships between the seven minimal pairs he lists (copied into Table 34) are not always obvious. There is one potentially compelling example, which is *chàm* 'wash' and *chām* 'be wet'. In absence of further minimal pairs with an action-result type of relationship, however, this may just be a coincidence.

Table 33: Verb-Noun tone minimal pairs (G = Grüßner 1978).

Tone pattern (Verb-Noun)	Verb		Noun	
L-M	ingkrùng	'to sieve' (G)	ingkrūng	'strainer' (G)
	thàn	'to cut' (G)	thān	'piece' (G)
	bùi	'to compile'	būi	'pile'
	ingsìr	'to filter'	ingsīr	'filter'
	kàm	'to step'	kām	'step (classifier)'
H-M	béng	'to chop off' (G)	bēng	'chip, piece' (G)
	arpán	'be wide' (G)	arpān	'width' (G)
	bú	'to plait'	bū	'bamboo container'
	inghór	'to carry a load'	inghōr	'carrying load'
L-H	ingnìm	'to smell' (G)	ingním	'smell' (G)
H-L	lún	'to sing' (G)	lùn	'song' (G)

Table 34: Tone minimal pairs in semantically related verbs according to Grüßner (1978: 91).

L tone		H tone (or M tone)	
àp	'shoot, hit'	áp	'fit, be correct'
chàk	'receive'	chák	'put down a deposit, provide collateral'
chòk	'beat'	chók	'be okay, be fine'
chàm	'wash, clean'	chām	'be wet'
plèng	'be full'	pléng	'be finished'
làng	'see'	láng	'refund, return (collateral)'
ràp	'stick'	ráp	'help'

In addition to these possible traces of grammatical tone in changing word classes, it is also interesting to note that there are two arguable cases of iconic occurrence of the mid tone with its characteristic glottalization feature. One is in vocative forms (see §16.3.7). The other is in the whole list of hortative and imperative/prohibitive suffixes (§9.9, §§15.1.2, 15.1.3).

3.6 Stress

Stress arguably is not part of Karbi phonology proper, because it never creates a lexical contrast between two morphemes. A detailed phonetic study of stress is outside the scope of this grammar. That said, however, a few remarks on stress are in order. Stress does play a major role in the surface realizations of word-level tone, and the study of stress would also complement the (diachronic and synchronic) understanding of word and morpheme structure.

There is an interaction between stress and tone. Grüßner (1978: 23; my translation) remarks that "in syllables with main stress and medium stress, tones are pronounced clearly. In syllables with weak stress, tones become indistinguishable and approximately converge towards Tone 1 [i.e., the low tone]". He continues to link the strength of stress to morpheme type: "the main stress usually resides on the stem syllable, [i.e.] the syllable with the semantically most important function. It [i.e., that syllable] is usually the syllable of a free morpheme. If this [morpheme] is multisyllabic, then the main stress resides on the last syllable".

My own observations match Grüßner's. There exists an iambic stress pattern in Karbi multisyllabic morphemes such that the sequence of syllables is unstressed-stressed. There are a large number of disyllabic roots that almost exceptionlessly follow this iambic pattern, and the same stress pattern exists on combinations of prefixes with monosyllabic stems such as *a-lám* 'poss-language' or *ke-chō* 'NMLZ-eat'. In fact, this iambic pattern is typical in many branches of Tibeto-Burman (though note that Tibetan and Kiranti, for example, are trochaic), and exists both across the modern languages and has diachronically shaped cognates all across the family. Matisoff (2003: 153–4) in his Handbook of Proto-Tibeto-Burman remarks on this as follows.

> Compounding has been a pervasive morphological process for at least the past two millennia of the history of the ST [Sino-Tibetan] family, as part of the languages' response to the ever-present danger of homophony among their monosyllabic morphemes. [...] The unstressed vowel of the first syllable in such a compound is typically schwa; the tone loses its original contour and becomes "neutral"; if there is a final consonant it tends to drop; and eventually its semantic identity is likely to become obscured. This is the process of "prefixization", whereby a fully meaningful morpheme is reduced to a prefix, in such a way that the original disyllable becomes a sesquisyllabic unit.

While there is a tendency in Karbi for unstressed syllables (and especially pre-stem ones and non-ultimate ones inside the stem) to be toneless (see §3.5.6), future research needs to investigate this in detail. In particular, the unstressed (because more inflection-like, see §8.2.1) modal suffixes -lò 'realis', -pò 'IRR1', and -jí 'IRR2' are certainly tonal: -lò and -pò are low tone, while -jí is high tone.

The derivational suffixes, on the other hand, are part of the stem, and as such, a derivational suffix added to a simple stem may receive the main stress. Take, for example, lè-lē 'reach-NEG', where the stress is on the suffix and indicated by underlining (though see §3.5.8.3 for a description of the prominence shift that happens with high tone simple stems), or dàm-bōm 'go-CONT', where it is also the suffix that is more prominent. This can be contrasted with nè=tā '1EXCL=ADD', where the first person exclusive pronoun is stressed and not the additive enclitic.

There is a single exception to the iambic stress pattern that I have come across, which is the distal demonstrative hála. It has a very prominent first syllable, although the vowel is actually quite short as if the onset /l/ of the second syllable also closed the first syllable. The second syllable is unstressed and reduced.

3.7 Characteristics of hypoarticulated speech

This section describes several characteristics of hypoarticulated speech observed across different native speakers.

3.7.1 /t/ → Ø / ___ v, l

The change described by the rule [/t/ → Ø / ___ v, l] is not specific to particular morphemes but happens generally. Examples of this hypoarticulation pattern are konát=lo 'where=FOC', which ends up pronounced as konálo or, showing the same pattern twice: e-nūt-vèt-lò 'one-CLF:HUM:SG-only-RL', which ends up pronounced as enuvelo.

3.7.2 Imperative onsets: /n/ → [α nasal] / [α nasal] ___

In hypoarticulated speech, the two imperative suffixes -nōi 'informal conditioned imperative (INFRML.COND.IMP)' (§15.1.2.2) and -nōn 'conditioned imperative (COND. IMP)' (§15.1.2.3) assimilate their alveolar nasal onset to the place of articulation of a nasal in coda position of the preceding syllable. This has been observed in forms such as vàng-nōn 'come-COND.IMP' or dàm-nōi 'go-INFRML.COND.IMP', which, in hypoarticulated speech, are produced as vàng-ngōn and dàm-mōi, or, perhaps more accurately, và.ngōn and dà.mōi, since gemination is not audible in hypoarticulated imperatives. The rapid speech in these hypoarticulated imperatives is also underscored by the mid tone on the suffixes, which actually appears quite iconic for the imperative semantics, also because all other imperative suffixes also have the mid tone (see §15.1.2).

3.7.3 -jí 'IRR2?', -lò '?', -si '?' → a / ___ -lāng 'still', -nāng 'hortative'

This rule aims to represent the changes from *vàng-jí-lāng* 'come-IRR2?-still' and *dàm-lonāng* 'go-HORT:EMPH' or *dàm-sināng* 'go-HORT:CON' to *vàngalāng* and *dàmanāng*, respectively, in hypoarticulated speech. This hypoarticulated production has been observed in the speech of several speakers and confirmed as a natural pattern. Since it is specifically these two constructions where this hyperarticulation reduction happens, it likely indicates ongoing grammaticalization / lexicalization (see also §9.1.3). In fact, *-jí-lāng* may better be analyzed as a single lexicalized suffix, the same way as *-lonāng* and *-sināng* should probably be considered single lexicalized suffixes (and not sequences of *-lò* 'RL' or *-si* 'non-final:realis' and *-nāng* 'hortative', see §15.1.3.3).

3.8 Phonological shapes of morpheme types

This section presents an overview of the characteristics of the different morpheme types with respect to their phonological shape.

3.8.1 Roots

Roots carry tone, and probably the majority of roots are monosyllabic. There are, however, also a large number of disyllabic roots and sesquisyllabic roots (i.e., with a reduced first syllable), while very few roots have more than two syllables. There are two very prominent, synchronically non-morphemic first syllables that occur in many of the disyllabic roots: /ing/ and /ar/, which are discussed in §6.3.

3.8.2 Suffixes

Suffixes are minimally syllabic, and mostly monosyllabic, although there are a few disyllabic ones. Besides roots, suffixes are the only morpheme type that carries tone. However, the tones of subordinating suffixes that have clausal scope and therefore are highly susceptible to prosodic pitch contours have been impossible to determine, such as *-te* 'conditional' and *-si* 'non-final:realis', and are therefore not marked for tone.

3.8.3 Prefixes

Prefixes are toneless, and there are only a small number of them, which are exhaustively listed in Table 35. With the exception of personal possessive prefixes, the category

3.8 Phonological shapes of morpheme types

Table 35: Karbi prefixes.

Word class of host stem	Prefix	Gloss
Nominal (Classifier)	e-	'one'
Nominal	a-	'POSS'
	ne(lì)-	'1EXCL.POSS(.HON)'
	e(lì)-	'1INCL.POSS(.HON)'
	nang(lì)-	'2.POSS(.HON)'
	alang(lì)-	'3.POSS(.HON)'
Verbal	pV-	'VBLZ', 'CAUS'
	ke-	'NMLZ'
	che- ~ ch-	'RR'
	cho-	'AUTO.BEN/MAL'

of prefixes in Karbi is characterized by a highly reduced phonological shape. When added to monosyllabic stems, they form sesquisyllables (Matisoff 2003: 153ff.) such as *a-lám* 'POSS-language' or *ke-chō* 'NMLZ-eat' (see also §3.6).

Only the second and third person possessive prefixes have a coda consonant, and only the personal possessive prefixes as a group can be extended with the honorific *-lì* (§16.4.1).

3.8.4 Clitics

All attested clitics are listed in Table 36. They are generally unmarked for tone, since they occur at phrasal boundaries, where prosodic pitch contours are so prominent that the underlying tone labels such as 'low tone' or 'high tone' do not appear to apply. There are three exceptions: *=tā* 'additive' and *=tamē* 'any', which consistently occur with mid tone glottalization and are therefore marked as such, and *=ân* 'this much' (in a few instances, a longer form *=ánsèt* is found), which consistently occurs with high tone.

Clitics are generally reduced monosyllables without a coda consonant. The exception is *nang=* and the longer pronominal forms with the *-lì* 'honorific' in the proclitic category, as well as *=pen* 'with; from' and 'non-final' among the enclitics, as well as disyllabic discourse markers that appear synchronically lexicalized, i.e., *=mati* and *=tamē*.

In this grammatical description, the status of a morpheme as a clitic is mostly identified by its higher degree of grammatical independence from the element it is

Table 36: Karbi clitics.

Clitic position	Functional domain	Form	Gloss
Proclitic	Path	nang=	'CIS' (§8.3.2)
	Person marking	ne(li)=	'1EXCL.NSUBJ' (§8.3.1.4)
		e(li)=	'1INCL.NSUBJ'(§8.3.1.4)
		nang(li)=	'1/2.NSUBJ'(§8.3.1.4)
Enclitic	Information/ discourse structure	=ke	'TOP' (§14.2.1)
		=si	'FOC:RL'(§14.2.3)
		=le	'FOC:IRR' (§14.2.4)
		=lo	'FOC' (§9.6.1.7)
		=tā	'ADD'(§14.2.2)
		=he	'AFTERTHOUGHT' (§16.3.9)
		=mati	'CG' (§16.3.11)
		=lok	'only' (§14.2.6.3)
		=nat	
	Interrogative	=ma	'Q' (§15.1.1.1)
		=bo	'ITROG.ASSUM' (§15.1.1.6)
	Other	=pen	'with; from' (§10.8.1)
		=tamē	'any' (§10.8.3.1.5)
		=án(sèt)	'this.much; all'(§10.8.2)

phonologically bound to compared to affixes. This is not a strict criterion and as a result, there are more prototypical and less prototypical examples of clitics.

Generally, the higher degree of grammatical independence is identified based on the following characteristics. First, clitics generally have grammatical scope over a larger phrase rather than just the particular word that it is phonologically bound to. For example, the topic marker =ke in *laso alam abang***ke** 'these stories' (CST, HM 070) has scope over the entire noun phrase rather than just the noun phrase delimiter *abang*. Second, clitics may not be restricted to occur bound to elements of a single word class or the same syntactic units. For example, the same topic marker =ke may occur on clauses as well as noun phrases (§15.2.2.3, §15.4.1).

The decision to identify the proclitics in Table 36 as clitics is debatable as it is based only on their diachrony. Their etymological origin in the possessive person indexes shows their diachronic flexibility to occur with different syntactic units (i.e., nouns and predicates). However, from a synchronic point of view, these "proclitics" have grammaticalized enough to be considered separate morphemes from the possessive markers, and as such, are actually better considered affixes than clitics.

3.8.5 Interjections

It is cross-linguistically typical for phonological shapes of interjections to push the phonological and phonetic boundaries of the sound system of a language. In Karbi, this is also documented in various sections of this chapter on phonology.

For example, addressing words may participate in an otherwise non-phonemic vowel contrast (cf. *ko* [kɔ] in §3.2.2), or in an otherwise non-phonemic tone contrast (cf. *ōi* in §3.5.4.6). Moreover, the expressions *dah* 'let's go!,' *dih* 'leave me!,' and *boh* to express surprise are typically said with final aspiration, which is otherwise not a phonemic category of Karbi (see §3.1.2.3).

3.8.6 Reduplication

Karbi makes use of several productive patterns of reduplication and quasi-reduplication at the morphological level as discussed in this section. Syntactic reduplication of full verbs also occurs, but is discussed in §16.2.3. In the sections below, the phonological properties of reduplication of noun and verb stems is discussed. The typical pattern is that the last syllable of the stem represents the portion that is reduplicated, while the semantic or syntactic scope is over the whole stem. For the various grammatical functions of reduplication, see §7.5 for reduplication in nouns, and §9.3 for reduplication in verbs.

Reduplication patterns are as follows. There is reduplication without a vowel change, as discussed in §3.8.6.1, reduplication with a change in vowel in the reduplicated form, as shown in §3.8.6.2, and finally we find a peculiar quasi-reduplicative construction of repeating just the onset in the verbal negative construction discussed in §3.8.6.3. Note that the different phonological patterns with respect to involving a vowel change or not involving a vowel change do not align with functional differences.

3.8.6.1 Reduplication of stems (without vowel change)

Table 37 lists some of the examples of reduplication found in the corpus. Note that the tone patterns recorded here should be considered preliminary and require further research.

Table 37: Full reduplication of roots or suffixes without vowel change.

Example	Gloss	Source
thè-ò~ò	big-much~DIST.PL	HK, TR 177
thakthāk	same	RBT, ChM 053
serhè~serhé	fast~INTENS	HK, TR 093

Table 37 (continued)

Example	Gloss	Source
ke-chō-dūn~dūn	NMLZ-eat-JOIN~HAB	KK, BMS 060
hín-hìn	side~DL	HI, BPh 006
kengkèng	all the way	SiT, PS 010
nang=pa-kló-rùi~rùi-lò	CIS=CAUS-fall-many:S/O~DIST.PL-RL	KTo, PS 004
thēp-hòi~hōi-lò	dry.up-little.bit~INTENS-RL	PI, BPR 013

The reduplicated form *kéngkèng* is apparently derived from *kèng* 'be straight' (ultimately from *kèng* 'foot').

As we can see, reduplication without vowel change occurs with all vowels. While it is typically only the last syllable of the stem that is reduplicated (which is the suffix in the cases of *thè-ò~ò* and *ke-chō-dūn~dūn*), we also find disyllabic reduplication, as in *serhè~serhé*.

3.8.6.2 Reduplication of stems with vowel change

Table 38 offers different examples of stem reduplication in which the vowel in the reduplicated portion changes. The pattern we can observe is that every vowel changes to /a/, while /a/ changes to /u/.

Table 38: Vowel change patterns in quasi-reduplicative constructions.

Vowels	Example	Gloss	Source
i ~ a	siksāk	be.difficult	RBT, ChM 017
	arlèng-pìk~pāk	be.steep-very~DIST.PL	SiT, HF 020
u ~ a	ingjòng-lùn~làn-lò	move-big~DIST.PL-RL	HK, TR 180
e ~ a	bī-hèk~hāk-làng	be.small-small~DL-still	CST, RO 006
	pòn-pē pon-pā	carry-NEG carry-EE:NEG	KK, BMS 109
	pí-nē~pina-nē-dèt-jí	what-INDEF~EE:pínē-NEG-PFV-IRR2	HK, TR 140
ei ~ ai	hei~hai	these~DIST.PL	SiT, HF 018
o ~ a	kedō kedā	NMLZ-exist NMLZ-EE:dō	HK, TR 058
	thè-ò~á	be.big-very~DIST.PL	SiT, HF 050
a ~ u	kàr-hàng~hùng-lò	burn-quite~DIST.PL-RL	HK, TR 180
ai/ei ~ ui	hai~hui	these~DIST.PL	SH, CSM 014
	hei~hui		SiH, CW 008

This quasi-reduplication strategy that involves a change in vowel is employed in several domains of grammar. It is found in nominal morphology, see §7.5; in verbal morphology, see §9.3; in elaborate expressions, see §16.2.2.1; and in the disagreement construction, see §16.2.4.1.

3.8.6.3 Negation: Onset reduplication of last stem syllable

Verbal negation is indicated by the onset reduplicating suffix -Cē, which repeats the full onset of the last syllable of the verb stem. Table 39 offers a number of sample monosyllabic and disyllabic stems with their respective forms of the negative suffix. The sample forms in Table 39 show that the rhyme of the suffix is invariably /ē/, while the onset of the suffix repeats the simple onset of onset cluster (as in **krōi-krē**) of the last syllable of the stem. If the last syllable of the stem does not have an onset consonant, i.e., if it is vowel-initial, in which case the syllable starts with a glottal stop, then the suffix repeats that (as in *ar'ī'ē*).

Table 39: Forms of quasi-reduplicative -Cē 'NEG' with different stems.

Type	Stem	Gloss	Stem with -Cē 'NEG'
Monosyllabic	lè	'to reach'	lè-lē
	krōi	'to agree'	krōi-krē
	kán	'to dance'	kán-kē
	thàk	'to answer', 'to weave'	thàk-thē
Disyllabic	ar'ì	'to crave'	ar'ì-ē
	teròi	'to do'	teròi-rē
	ingtòn	'to conclude'	ingtòn-tē
	hijūk	'to laugh'	hijūk-jē

Example (13) gives an text example of the verbal negation of the complex stem *chesik-mek'et* that has one prefix and two suffixes. It shows that only the last syllable /èt/ is relevant to determine the form of the negative suffix, which consequently is simply -ē.

(13) Text example of verbal negation of a complex stem
adappen, hadakpen nangchesikmek'et'edetlo
adàp=pen   hádak=pen   nang=che-sík-mék-èt-**Cē**-dèt-lò
morning=from there=from CIS=RR-prepare-in.advance-all:S/O-**NEG**-PFV-RL
'From the morning, from there we hadn't prepared everything at all in advance.'
[SH, CSM 062]

3.9 Morphophonemics

This section discusses phonological changes that occur as a result of morphological processes. This includes tone changes in stems and suffixes (§3.9.1), and prefix allomorphs and prefix-induced stem vowel deletion (§3.9.2).

3.9.1 Tone changes

There are several robust patterns of tone change whereby the tone of a stem or a suffix changes from one category to another. These tone category changes represent evidence for the phonological basis of the Karbi tone system.

Note that there are also morphological contexts in Karbi where just the expression (or articulation) of a particular tone category changes although the tone category itself does not shift. Such changes are discussed in §3.5.5.

3.9.1.1 Stem tone change induced by *che-* 'reflexive/reciprocal' and *cho-* 'auto-benefactive/malefactive'

Grüßner's (1978: 37) excellent work on Karbi phonology was the first to note that the *che-* 'reflexive/reciprocal' and *cho-* 'auto-benefactive/malefactive' prefixes change the tone of immediately following monosyllabic stems according to the pattern shown in Table 40: low tone stems become mid, mid tone stems become high, and high tone stems do not change (though see §3.5.5 for additional phonetic sandhi effects that occur as a result of prefixing *cho-* 'auto-benefactive/malefactive').

Table 40: Monosyllabic stem tone changes after *che-* 'RR' and *cho-* 'AUTO.BEN/MAL'.

Underlying stem tone	New stem tone	Sample stem	With *che-* 'RR'		With *cho-* 'AUTO.BEN/MAL'	
LOW →	MID	rì	che-rī	'find (one's own)'	cho-rī	'find (for oneself)'
MID →	HIGH	kūp/tūk	che-kúp	'cover (one's own, oneself)'	cho-túk	'dig (for oneself)'
HIGH →	HIGH	thán	che-thán	'teach (one's own children)'	cho-thán	'teach (for a living)'

In addition to this pattern, *cho-* 'auto-benefactive/malefactive' also has the same morphophonemic effect on at least low tone disyllabic verb stems such as *ingvài* 'choose', which turns into mid tone, *cho-ngvāi*. This is not true for *che-* 'reflexive/reciprocal', and so *ch-ingvài* remains low tone (see also a discussion of other differences between *che-* and *cho-* in §3.9.2.2). There are several stems that do not change their tone after *che-* is added: *ch-arjū* 'RR-ask', *che-tòng* 'RR-meet', *cherùi* 'return' (*rùi* by itself does not occur), *che-ràp* 'RR-stay.together', *ch-ingkī* 'RR-chat'.

Contrary to Grüßner's (1978: 37) account, however, our research team did not find a tone change, whereby a mid tone stem that turned into a high tone stem after *che-*, such as *che-én* from *ēn* 'take', subsequently turned into a low tone stem if followed by the negative suffix: **che-èn-ē*; instead, the stem remained high tone, *che-én-ē*.

3.9.1.2 Stem tone change induced by possessive prefixes

As first pointed out by Grüßner (1978: 21; 39), disyllabic nominal stems may change their tones as well when a prefix is added. Grüßner described this change primarily as a stress shift and the tone change as epiphenomenal, which is certainly an interesting idea worth investigating further. The reliable pattern is that mid-mid disyllabic stems change to high-low after *a-* 'possessive' or *ne-* '1EXCL:POSS' (or presumably a different personal possessive prefix, although the other prefixes were not specifically checked) is attached. This is illustrated in Table 41.

Table 41: Disyllabic stem tone changes following possessive prefixation.

Underlying tones	New tones	Sample stem	With *a-* 'possessive' and *ne-* '1EXCL.POSS'	
MID-MID →		*sōpī*	*a-sopì*	'daughter'
			ne-sopì	'my daughter'
	HIGH-LOW	*hēmtāp*	*a-hemtàp*	'house on stilts'
LOW-HIGH →		*biskút*	*a-biskùt*	'baked.snack(<Eng)'
		kulát	*a-kulàt*	'shop(<Asm)'

The mid-mid to high-low tone change is almost exceptionless[49] but there also seems to be a pattern for low-high stems to change to high-low as well, such as *biskút* and *kulát* in Table 41. At this point, it is not clear how productive this pattern is and whether it might be limited to borrowings. Note that no change was found to occur in LL stems such as *kòngsìn* 'kind of shovel' and *a-kòngsìn*, LM stems such as *korpī* 'sister-in-law' and *a-korpī* or *lamthē* 'matter' and *a-lamthē*, HL stems such as *kortè* 'same gender siblings' and *a-kortè*, but also other LH stems such as *lammét* 'literature', which remains *a-lammét* and does not undergo the tone change compared to other LH stems given in Table 41.

---

[49] The only exception I have encountered is in compounds with the clan name *Krō* (although the clan name *Bēy*, pronounced as /bē/, is regular). Here, if *hēm* 'house, family' is added, then *Krō-hēm* does not change to **a-Kro-hèm*, but remains *a-Krō-hēm*. With the clan name *Bēy*, the pattern is regular and *Bēy-hēm* changes into *a-Bey-hèm*. The same is true for the difference between *Krō-pī* 'CLAN-female', which remains mid-tone *a-Krō-pī*, while *Bēy-pī* regularly turns into *a-Bey-pì*, curiously enough.

3.9.1.3 Derivational suffix tone change

There are a number of derivational suffixes that have low and mid tone allomorphs where the mid tone allomorph occurs after low or mid tone stems, while the low tone allomorph occurs after high tone stems. Table 42 illustrates this pattern with the suffix *-dùn ~ -dūn* 'JOIN' following sample low, mid, and high tone verb stems.

Table 42: Tone change patterns for derivational suffixes.

Stem tone	Suffix tone	Sample stem	With *-dùn ~ -dūn* 'JOIN'	
LOW	→ MID	thàk	thàk-*dūn*	'answer-JOIN'
MID	→ MID	pī	pī-*dūn*	'give-JOIN'
HIGH	→ LOW	lóng	lóng-*dùn*	'get-JOIN'

Table 43 offers an exhaustive list of all derivational suffixes that have so far been found to participate in the tone change exemplified in Table 42.[50] It also lists the lexical source of the suffix where synchronically found in the language. It may not be a coincidence that all of the lexical source verbs are low tone, i.e., that the original low tone leads to this allomorphy.

Table 43: List of derivational suffixes that participate in tone change.

Derivational suffix	Gloss	Lexical source
-dàm ~ -dām	'GO'	<*dàm* 'go'
-dùn ~ -dūn	'JOIN'	<*dùn* 'join'
-bòm ~ -bōm	'CONT' ('continue')	–
-thù ~ -thū	'again'	–
-pòn ~ -pōn	'take.away'	<*pòn* 'carry, take'
-hài ~ -hāi	'dare'	<*hài* 'dare; win'
-ùn ~ -ūn	'be.able'	<*ùn* 'win, conquer'
-thèk ~ -thēk	'know.how'	<*thèk* 'know (how)'

In addition to the derivational suffixes in Table 43, the bound forms *-thòm ~ -thōm* of the numeral *kethòm* 'three', which occur suffixed to classifiers, undergo the same tone allomorphy. Examples of low, mid, and high tone classifiers used with *-thòm ~ -thōm*

---

50 Grüßner (1978: 37) mentions some of these as well.

are: *hòng-thōm* 'CLF:long.cylindrical-three', *jōn-thōm* 'CLF:animal-three', and *phóng-thòm* 'CLF:times-three'.[51]

3.9.1.4 Idiosyncratic tone allomorphy

There also are cases of more idiosyncratic tone changes. There is one example in the corpus, where *pV-* 'causative' changes mid tone *mē* 'be good' into a high tone, *pamé*, see (14). Since *pV-* 'causative' occurs with a very low frequency, it is not clear whether this is a robust pattern or not.

(14) Stem tone change *pa-mé* from *mē* 'be good'
 ok paka paka han paka paka
 ōk paká paká hán paká paká
 meat very.good very.good curry very.good very.good

 lopen thuidun pame pamepo
 lō=pen thùi-dūn pa-**mé** pa-**mé**-pò
 banana.leaf=with wrap-JOIN CAUS-be.good CAUS-be.good-IRR1
 'She would wrap very good meat and very good curry very nicely for him to take along (to the field).' [CST, RO 014]

A highly idiosyncratic instance of tone allomorphy occurs in the suffix *-vèt* ~ *-vét* 'only'. Table 44 shows different numerals that this suffix may attach to (though it also attaches to other nominal stems). The numerals are sorted into three columns: the one that only low tone *-vèt* attaches to, those that only high tone *-vét* attaches to, and, lastly, those for which both low tone *-vèt* and high tone *-vét* were deemed acceptable. I do not see any kind of pattern to the different judgments of acceptable allomorphs of this suffix depending on the stem.

3.9.2 Prefix allomorphs and prefix-induced stem vowel deletion

Prefixes are generally reduced monosyllables (although the personal possessive prefixes form an exception, see §3.8.3). Due to their reduced structure, prefixes also tend to have allomorphs, which are described in this section. There also is a sense, however, that certain prefixes have more 'phonological strength' than others and may cause vowel deletion on the stem. The difference in 'phonological strength' is par-

---

[51] Grüßner (1978: 65) also mentions the alternation in *-thòm* ~ *-thōm*, and claims that mid tone classifiers become low tone in this construction, e.g. *jōn-thōm* were to become *jòn-thōm*. I don't have any evidence, however, that this particular construction results in any idiosyncratic tone change of that kind; I rather assume Grüßner here describes a general pattern of tonal unspecificity on unstressed syllables.

Table 44: Idiosyncratic tone allomorphy of -vèt ~ -vét 'only'.

Only -vèt acceptable		Only -vét acceptable		Both -vèt and -vét acceptable	
sirkēp	'nine'	isī	'one'	hiní	'two'
		kethòm	'three'	phlī	'four'
		kēp	'ten'	phō	'five'
		pharó isī	'one hundred'	thrōk	'six'
				thrōksí	'seven'
				nerkēp	'eight'
				pharó kethòm	'three hundred'

ticularly striking between the two similar prefixes *che-* 'reciprocal/reflexive' and *cho-* 'auto-benefactive/malefactive', which is discussed in §3.9.2.2.

An important caveat to keep in mind here is that the following discussion is based on transcriptions of these prefixes in the text corpus. However, as mentioned above, these prefixes are very reduced. Their vowel may be reduced to just two to three periodic voicing cycles. Although our research team double-checked transcriptions to achieve a high level of accuracy, there are still a number of instances in the corpus where it remains unclear whether the vowel should be transcribed as /e/ or /a/.

3.9.2.1 Prefix vowels: *ke-* 'NMLZ', *pV-* 'CAUS', *che-* 'RR', *cho-* 'AUTO.BEN/MAL', *a-* 'POSS'

Grüßner (1978: 93) describes a pattern of allomorphy between *ke-* and *ka-* of the nominalizer as well as *pe-* and *pa-* of the causative, whereby *ke-* and *pe-* occur before monosyllabic stems, while *ka-* and *pa-* occur otherwise; "suffixes do not count in determining monosyllabicity, prefixes, however, make the verb multisyllabic". This regular pattern is not found in the corpus of this grammar. Instead a much messier pattern emerges as shown in Tables 45 and 46.

As shown in Table 45, monosyllabic stems always take *ke-*, and there appears to only be one exception: *ka-prék* 'NMLZ-be.different'. As pointed out by UV Jose (personal communication), however, *prék* is likely to be an early borrowing from Assamese *belek* (which has now been reborrowed as *belek*). If that is indeed the history of Karbi *prék*, then the *ka-* is a neat piece of evidence because it tells the disyllabic origin of *prék*.

In every context other than pure monosyllabic stems, there seems to be free allomorphic variation between *ke-* and *ka-*. Although some tendencies may turn out to align with dialectal areas, there is some amount of variation within the same speaker, which shows that it is not just a matter of different dialects.

Table 45: Forms of prefix *ke-* 'NMLZ'.

Form of stem	Form	Example	Gloss	Example source
Monosyllabic	ke-	ke-dàm	'NMLZ-go'	CST, RO 026
Disyllabic (due to another prefix)		ka-pa-lì	'NMLZ-CAUS-flow'	ST, HF 021
		ke-pa-sáng	'NMLZ-CAUS-rest'	ST, HF 026
		ke-pe-thì	'NMLZ-CAUS-die'	RBT, ChM 028
Disyllabic starting with consonant	ke- ~ ka-	ka-tikí	'NMLZ-loosen.soil'	CST, RO 007
		ke-laná	'NMLZ-take.care'	KK, BMS 105
Disyllabic starting with /ing/ or /ar/		ka-ngtòn	'NMLZ-conclude' (< *ingtòn*)	CST, RO 056
Disyllabic starting with other vowel		ke-ora	'NMLZ-take.care'	CST, HM 063
		ka-ora		KK, BMS 105

Table 46 gives examples of the two allomorphs of *pV-* 'causative'. Unlike the allomorphy of *ke-* 'nominalizer', *pe-* appears to only ever occur before monosyllabic stems, although *pa-* is used in that context as well, seemingly especially in the non-Christian variety of the Hills Amri dialect in West Karbi Anglong.

Table 46: Forms of prefix *pV-* 'causative'.

Form of stem	Form	Example	Gloss	Example source
Monosyllabic	pe- ~ pa-	pe-kló	'CAUS-fall'	RBT, ChM 021
		pa-klàng	'CAUS-appear'	HK, TR 090
Disyllabic (due to another prefix)		pa-che-ūn	'CAUS-RR-be.able'	WR, BCS 023
Disyllabic starting with consonant	pa-	pa-the'āng	'CAUS-dawn'	KK, BMS 062
Disyllabic starting with /ing/ or /ar/		pa-rtìng	'CAUS-spin' (<*artìng*)	KK, BMS 103
Disyllabic starting with other vowel		pa-ora	'CAUS-take.care	KK, BMS 110

The reflexive/reciprocal prefix *che-* alternates with *ch-*, which only occurs before disyllabic stems that begin with /ar/ or /ing/, as shown in Table 47. In the corpus of this grammar, *che-* followed by /ar/ always results in /char/. However, discussions within our research team suggest that the resulting first syllable can often be pronounced either as /char/ or as /cher/ (as in *chermát* in Table 47, but also, e.g., *charlì* ~ *cherlì* 'to learn, study'). Forms with /cher/ are also recorded by Grüßner in his dictionary manuscript.

Another morphophonemic change that occurs in conjunction with prefixes is vowel deletion in disyllabic roots starting with *ing-* and *ar-* (see §6.3 on these frozen prefixes in disyllabic roots). Table 48 shows that the initial vowel of disyllabic stems

Table 47: Forms of prefix *che-* 'reflexive/reciprocal'.

Form of stem	Form	Example	Gloss	Example source
Monosyllabic	che-	che-thāk	'RR-weave'	KST, PSu 007
Disyllabic (due to another prefix)		che pe thì	'RR CAUS die'	RBT, ChM 023
Disyllabic starting with consonant		che-mathá	'RR-think'	CST, HM 067
Disyllabic starting with other vowel		che-erí	'RR-let.loose (<Asm)'	KK, BMS 122
Disyllabic starting with *ing-* or *ar-*	ch- (~che-)	ch-arkòk	'RR-clean'	KK, BMS 113
		charmát (~chermát)	'test if taste is good'	SiH, KA 009
		ch-ingthùm	'RR-go.and.bring'	RBT, ChM 027

Table 48: Initial vowel deletion in *ing-* stems after prefixes *ke-*, *pV-*, *cho-*.

Prefix	Stem	Vowel deletion
ke-		ka-ngnì
pV-	ingnì 'to sit'	pa-ngnì
cho-		cho-ngnī
a-	ingtòng 'type of bamboo basket'	a-ngtòng

beginning with *ing-* is deleted after the prefixes *ke-* 'nominalizer, *pV-* 'causative', *cho-* 'auto-benefactive/malefactive', and the possessive prefix *a-*.

Examples of the vowel deletion that occurs between prefixes *ke-* 'nominalizer', *pV-* 'causative', and, less robustly, *che-* 'reflexive/reciprocal' and *a-* 'possessive/ modified' and disyllabic stems that start in *ar-* is given in Table 49 (see discussion of Table 47 above for the case of *che-* 'RR'). Note that in the case of the *a-* prefix, there is typically no morphophonemic change if the *ar-* disyllabic root is a lexical noun (e.g., *arnàm* 'god'). If instead the *ar-* disyllabic root is, however, a noun that almost always occurs with the *a-* prefix (like relator noun *arlō*, or presumably any other noun that requires a possessive prefix, see §5.5), one of the two /a/ vowels typically is deleted.[52]

---

[52] More research is required to understand under exactly which circumstances the *a-* prefix is not used or pronounced on nouns that begin with *ar-*, or, rather, under which circumstances it actually is used, as there are only two instances in the corpus, where that is the case (*a-arnàm* 'POSS-god' in HK, TR 111 and *a-arlēng* 'POSS-person' in SH, CSM 039).

Table 49: Vowel deletion between *ar-* stems and prefixes *ke-*, *pV-*, *che-*, *a-*.

Prefix	Stem	Vowel deletion
ke-	arjū 'to ask'	karjū
pV-	artìng 'to spin'	partìng
[che-	(armát)	che-rmát, ch-armát]
a-	arnàm 'god'	[a'arnam]
	arlō 'inside (relator noun)'	arlo

Lastly, one question regarding prefix vowel allomorphy concerns the difference between *ke-* and *pV-* as they occur before monosyllabic stems with either a high or a non-high vowel. Due to the perception of vowel harmony that assimilates *ke-* to *ki-* and *pe-* to *pi-* before high vowels, the Karbi Lammet Amei (§1.1.4) has issued the spelling rule to write *ki-* and *pi-* (or *pa-* depending on the dialect, see discussion above) in those instances.[53] However, the first person exclusive possessive prefix *ne-* is not perceived to change to *ni-* before high vowels. A brief phonetic study to evaluate whether *ke-* and *ne-* behave the same before monosyllabic stems with high vowels or not is described in Konnerth (2014). The result of this study indicates that there is indeed a difference between the vowels or vowel variability in *ke-* compared to *ne-*, and choosing different spelling conventions for the two can in fact be argued for.

3.9.2.2 *cho-* 'auto-benefactive/malefactive' and *che-* 'reflexive/reciprocal': Differences in phonological strength

This section considers three differences between the similar prefixes *cho-* 'auto-benefactive/malefactive' and *che-* 'reflexive/reciprocal' with regard to what may be understood as phonological strength. The similarity between the prefixes is not only their shared onset palatal stop, but also the tone change both prefixes cause in monosyllabic stems, see §3.9.1.1.

The first difference consists of *cho-* changing low tones into mid tones in disyllabic stems in addition to monosyllabic stems such that low tone *ingvài* 'choose' turns into mid tone *cho-ngvāi* due to prefixation of *cho-*, while prefixation of *che-* does not result in a tone change, so *ch-ingvài* remains low tone (§3.9.1.1). The tone change from mid tone to high tone in disyllabic stems, however, does not seem to occur. Instead, mid tone disyllabic stems remain mid tone after prefixation of *cho-*. Examples are *cho-ngdī* from *ingdī* 'break a long object'; *cho-nghū* from *inghū* 'steal'; and *cho-ngmōi* from *ingmōi* 'cook with alkaline'.

---

[53] Note that the same vowel assimilation applies in the case of the bound numeral *e-* (§6.4.2), as the vowel is raised to /i/ when the following classifier contains a high vowel, e.g. *inut* 'one (person)' from *e-nūt* 'one-CLF:HUM:SG'.

The second difference can be seen in the same example: *cho-* keeps its /o/ vowel when attaching to disyllabic stems that start with /ing/, while *che-* looses its vowel.

The third difference is described in §3.5.5: While *che-* and *cho-* both change the tone category of low and mid tone monosyllabic stems (as described in §3.9.1.1), *cho-* additionally induces an internal sandhi effect that is absent in the prefixation and resulting tone change caused by *che-*. Therefore, while *che-dām* and *cho-dām* both change low tone *dàm* 'to go' to mid tone, the resulting *che-dām* has the same pitch contour as *ke-bān* 'NMLZ-be.old', a non-derived sesquisyllabic mid tone stem, while *cho-dām* has a higher pitch contour.

These three differences thus provide converging evidence that *che-* is phonologically/phonetically "weaker" than *cho-*. Due to the related semantics of *che-* and *cho-* in that both function to detransitivize, i.e., *che-* as a reflexive/reciprocal marker and *cho-* as a auto-benefactive/malefactive marker, the following historical scenario can be hypothesized: The origin of *cho-* could be a bimorphemic sequence of *che-* plus another prefix, which was fused while leaving behind these traces of being more than just a typical, sesquisyllabically patterning prefix like *che-*. It is not clear at this point, however, what the second morpheme in that assumed historical morpheme sequence could have been.

4 The major word classes: Nouns and verbs and 'adjectival verbs'

Chapters 4 to 6 deal with Karbi word classes. The present chapter starts with the two major word classes of nouns and verbs (§4.1), and then tackles the question of what the status of property concept terms or 'adjectives' is in Karbi in §4.2. Specifically, it is argued that property concept terms are a subclass of verbs, which is substantiated with a number of morphosyntactic tests. The next section §4.3 then offers a summary of the previous two sections by discussing the clausal functions of nouns, verbs, and property concept terms.

4.1 Nouns and verbs

There are two cross-linguistically basic elements of the clause: the predicate and its argument(s). In Karbi, we have distinct verbal and nominal roots, and there is a statistical correlation such that verbal roots more frequently occur in the element that fulfills the function of predication, and nominal roots more frequently occur in the element that fulfills the function of reference (i.e., expressing the argument(s)). However, as discussed in the following sections, there is an asymmetry such that an element of any word class can function as the predicate of the clause (without the need of derivational morphology that makes it a verb stem), while nominalization is necessary for a verbal root to function as a noun stem.

Below I will argue that Karbi has old prefixal morphology that distinguishes between nominal and verbal roots, but that the (perhaps younger) suffixal morphology that usually occurs on verbs is much less restrictive.

4.1.1 Morphosyntactic criteria for nouns and verbs at the root level

The two most frequent prefixes in Karbi are *a-* 'possessive (POSS)' (see §7.3.1) and *ke-* 'nominalizer (NMLZ)' (see §8.4.1). Using these two prefixes, it is possible to divide the Karbi lexicon into three categories: (a) those roots that only take *a-* 'POSS' but not *ke-* 'NMLZ'; (b) those roots that only take *ke-* 'NMLZ' but not *a-* 'POSS'; and (c) those roots that take neither. While this last category of items that take neither is a residual category that needs to be further investigated with the help of other morphosyntactic tests, the first two categories are Karbi noun roots and Karbi verb roots. At the root level, all and only Karbi verbs can take the *ke-* 'NMLZ' prefix, e.g., *chō* 'eat' in (15), and all and only Karbi nouns can take the *a-* 'POSS' prefix, e.g., *àn* 'cooked rice' in (16).

(15) Morphological behavior of a verb root
    (a) *ke-chō*   (b) **ka-chō*
       NMLZ-eat   POSS-eat
       'eating'

(16) Morphological behavior of a noun root
    (a) **ke-àn*   (b) *a-àn*
       NMLZ-cooked.rice   POSS-cooked.rice'
                         '(particular) rice'

Since *ke-* is a nominalizer, however, the derived stem that carries *ke-* becomes a member of the word class of nouns, and is then eligible to take *a-* 'POSS', as in (17), where the verb root *kú* 'crow (of a rooster)' is nominalized via *ke-* and then takes the possessive *a-*.

(17) Nominalization of a verb root
    a-ki-kú[...]
    POSS-NMLZ-crow
    'his crowing (of a rooster) [...]' [SeT, MTN 010]

There is thus an asymmetry between these two word-class diagnostic prefixes: the nominalizer *ke-* attaches to roots, while the possessive *a-* attaches to stems.

As for syntactic criteria that distinguish between nouns and verbs, the largely cross-linguistically valid ones apply. For example, nouns head noun phrases in which they may be modified by a range of different elements including demonstratives, numerals (in classifier constructions), or relative clauses (see Chapter 9). Verbs typically form the predicate and occur clause-finally (although nominal predicates do occur in Karbi), and have different restrictions as to what types of predicate constructions they may occur in. There are certain predicate constructions that only verbs occur in, but never nouns (see Chapter 10). In addition, unmarked nouns (but not unmarked verbs) may function as modifiers, as in (18).

(18) Unmarked *richó* 'king' as a modifier (possessor) of *sōpī* 'daughter'
    richo *asopi abang ha langhe lang kachinglu...*
    [**richó** a-oso-pì]   abàng há   lānghē   lāng   ke-chinglú]
    king   POSS-child-FEM NPDL over.there washing.place water NMLZ-take.bath
    '[...] [T]he daughter of the king was taking a bath there at the washing place [...].'
    [RBT, ChM 026]

4.1.2 Lack of word class distinctions with suffixal aspect, modality, and negation

It is cross-linguistically common that only verb stems may carry morphology dedicated to the marking of tense, aspect, and modality. In Karbi, it is certainly the case that more frequently verbal hosts have aspectual and modal suffixes attached to them. But aspectual and modal suffixes on nouns, adverbs, or interjections are not unacceptable to Karbi native speakers, when those stems function as non-verbal predicates.

Take as examples the irrealis suffixes *-pò* 'IRR1' and *-jí* 'IRR2' (§9.6.2), which typically go on verb stems, and cover a wide range of irrealis functions, including future, epistemic uncertainty, and past habituals, among others. However, (19) shows that irrealis *-pò* may also attach to content question words such as *kosón* 'how.' In this case, *kosón* functions as a nominal predicate, which translates as 'how will it be?' due to the future reading of the irrealis marker after a preceding conditional clause marked by *-te* 'conditional, if'.

(19) Irrealis *-pò* on content question word *kosón* 'how'
"*o neta dak dokokte kosonpo?*"
[o   nè=tā   dāk   dō-kòk-te]   **kosón-pò**
INTERJ 1EXCL=ADD here stay-firmly-COND how-IRR1
'[...] "Oh, if I stay back here, how will it be?" [...]' [SH, CSM 062]

Moreover, irrealis *-pò* may attach to other types of nominal stems. In (20), it attaches to the extended classifier stem *e-nūt-vét* 'one person only, alone', which functions as a noun phrase in this example, and specifically a nominal predicate. Again, the irrealis suggests a future interpretation, translating as '(she) will be alone.'

(20) Irrealis *-pò* on numeral plus classifier *e-nūt* functioning as a nominal stem
anke komat aphansi kipitekangpo,
[ánke   [komāt aphān=si]   ke-pī-tekáng-pò]
and.then who   NSUBJ=FOC:RL NMLZ-give-leave-IRR1

enutvetpo
e-nūt-vét-pò
one-CLF:human:SG-only-IRR1
'But who will (we) give (her) to, (she) will be alone' [SH, CSM 063]

What holds for irrealis *-pò* also holds for irrealis *-jí*. In (21), *-jí* attaches to *hōk* 'truth', which is clearly recognized as a noun by the possessive prefix *a-*. Here the irrealis has an epistemic reading of expressing uncertainty, 'might (they) be the truth?".

(21) Irrealis *-jí* on nominal *a-hōk* 'POSS-truth'
ai! laso alam abangke ahokjima laho?
ai   [lasō   a-lám   abàng=ke]   **[a-hōk-jí=ma**   laho]
how.strange! this   POSS-word   NPDL=TOP   POSS-truth-IRR2=Q   EMPH
'Oh, might these stories (that the children are telling) be true (lit., the truth)?'
[CST, HM 070]

The morphologically interesting word *pinepinanedetjima* in (22) shows quite clearly the range of verbal suffixes that a nominal stem may take, even in natural discourse. Following the derived indefinite stem *pí-nē* 'something' and a reduplicative suffix *~pinā*, which indicates distributive plurality ('any kinds'), we find the negative suffix *-Cē*, the perfective suffix *-dèt*, and the irrealis suffix *-jí*, lastly followed by the question particle *=ma*.

(22) Negative, perfective *-dèt*, and irrealis *-jí* on derived indefinite stem *pí-nē* 'something'
te mo pinepinanedetjima ko jirpo pu
te   mò   **pí-nē~pinā-Cē-dèt-jí=ma**   ko   jīrpō   pu
therefore future   what-INDEF~DIST.PL-NEG-PFV-IRR2=Q   buddy:VOC   friend   QUOT
'"And there won't be any (difficulties/problems/dangers), my friend?"' [HK, TR 140]

In addition to irrealis *-pò* and *-jí*, which attach to different kinds of nominal stems without any prior requirement of verbalization (though there is a verbalizing prefix *pa-*, see §7.3.3), realis *-lò* also commonly occurs on non-verbal stems, as discussed in §9.6.1.7.

Other verbal suffixes include continuative *-bōm~-bòm*, emphatic *-vèk* 'definitely', and the verbal honorific *-īk*. The typical use of continuative *-bōm~-bòm* on verb stems is shown with *vàng* 'come' in (23) (also see §9.2.6.3), whereas (24) shows that it also occurs on the adverb *lasón* 'like this, this way' for a predicate reading of 'this way / like this it would go on and on.'

(23) Continuative *-bōm~-bòm* on verb stem *vàng* 'come'
vangbomlo vangbomlo
vàng-bōm-lò   **vàng-bōm-lò**
come-CONT-RL   come-CONT-RL
'(One after the other, i.e. the tigers) keep coming.' [HK, TR 182]

(24) Continuative *-bōm~-bòm* on adverb stem *lasón* 'like this'
lasonbomlo, haita haipik
lasón-bòm-lò   [hài=tā   hài-pìk]
that.way-CONT-RL   have.bad.character=ADD   have.bad.character-very
'This way it would go on and on, as far as bad characters go, she really had a very bad character [...].' [CST, RO 016]

In (25), the certainty marking suffix -vék 'definitely' occurs on a verb stem, which is where it usually occurs (although more typically with one of the irrealis suffixes -pò or -jí). But in (26), we find -vék 'definitely' on the interjection kalàng 'yes' with the purpose of showing that the speaker emphatically agrees.

(25) -vék 'definitely' on verb stem lóng-dùn 'get-JOIN'
tangka atibuk longdunvekpo ili
tángká   a-tibùk   **lóng-dùn-vék-pò**   ì-lì
money   POSS-earthen.pot   get-JOIN-definitely-IRR1   1PL:INCL-HON
'Together (we will) surely get the earthen pots with money, we (will).' [HK, TR 136]

(26) -vék 'definitely' on interjection kalàng 'yes'
kalangveklo, la abangke; lapulo di
[**kalàng-vék-lò**   là   abàng=ke]   [lapù-lò   dī]
yes-definitely-RL   this   NPDL=TOP   like.this-RL   Q.tag
'It's very true, this (is), it's like this, isn't it?' [KaR, SWI 057]

Lastly, (27) and (28) provide another example of a typically verbal suffix used on a noun stem: the formality marker -īk (see §16.4.2). In (27), it attaches to the verb stems chetòng 'meet' and thán 'tell'. Note also that the pronoun ilitum carries a separate -lì 'honorific' marker, which acts as a nominal honorific/formal counterpart to the verbal -īk marker.

(27) Formality marker -īk on verb stems
pini chetong'ikloklo, ilitum temole
pinì   **chetòng-īk-lòk-lò**   e-li-tūm   temó=le
today   meet-FRML-happen.to-RL   1PL.INCL-HON-PL   story=FOC:IRR

chethan'ikronglonang
che-thán-īk-ròng-lonāng
RR-tell-FRML-instead-HORT:EMPH
'"[...] (T)oday we happened to meet, let's tell a story instead (of doing other things)!"' [CST, HM 002]

In (28), the formality marker -īk occurs on the head noun a-lám of the noun phrase non ethe alam 'another issue', which functions as a nominal predicate in this example.

(28) Formality marker -īk on nominal predicate
non ethe alam'iklo
nón   e-thē   **a-lám-īk-lò**
now   one-CLF:word/matter   POSS-matter-FRML-RL
'(Let's talk about /) there is another issue.' [KaR, SWI 176]

4.1.3 Summary: Nouns and verbs in Karbi

The evidence presented in §4.1.1 and §4.1.2 shows that there are inherently nominal roots and inherently verbal roots. A pair of diagnostic affixes are the *a-* 'possessive' prefix, which attaches to nominal but not verbal roots, and the *ke-* 'nominalizer' prefix, which attaches to verbal but not nominal roots. As is the case cross-linguistically, knowing that a particular root belongs to the Karbi word class of verbs predicts that it will most frequently function as the predicate of a clause. Knowing that a particular root belongs to the Karbi word class of nouns predicts that it will relatively rarely function as the predicate of a clause, and instead regularly heads a noun phrase in order to indicate reference to an entity.

The evidence presented above has further demonstrated that noun roots/stems do not need to be modified in any way to function as predicates. Nominal predicates may contain a range of prototypically verbal suffixes including the irrealis modal *-pò* and *-jí* suffixes, aspectual suffixes such as *-dèt* 'perfective', *-bōm~-bòm* 'continuative', the certainty expressing suffix *-vék* 'definitely', the formality marker *-īk*, and even the quasi-reduplicative negative suffix, which perhaps is the most surprising given its tight morphophonological integration with the stem it attaches to as well as considering that there is a negative equational copula *kalī*, which could easily (and does usually) serve to negate nominal predicates (see §6.2.2.2 and §11.1.2).[54] Overall, the ease with which nominal roots or stems function as predicates in Karbi has likely functioned as a catalyst for the grammaticalization of nominalization-based constructions such as nominalized main clause constructions (see §12.7.3), or the development of subordinators from relator nouns (§6.4.3).

As for the other direction, for verbal roots to function as noun stems, nominalization via *ke-* is required (see Chapter 12).

4.2 Verbs and 'adjectival verbs': The status of property concept terms

The previous section has shown that we can sort roots into the large categories of nouns and verbs. A third major word class in languages of the world are 'adjectives'. I use quotation marks because the term 'adjectives' inherently implies that there is a structural class of adjectives with the semantics of referring to property concepts. The existence of such a class is however not universal across languages of the world, which has been widely shown ever since the publication of Dixon's (1977) 'Where

---

54 As another example of negating a nominal predicate by means of the quasi-reduplicative suffix, consider *tekè* 'tiger' and *tekè-kē* 'it's not a tiger', which was deemed acceptable. However, *tekè kalī* with the syntactic expression of nominal predicate negation via the equational negative copula *kalī* would be the more normal way of saying 'it's not a tiger.'

4.2 Verbs and 'adjectival verbs': The status of property concept terms

have all the adjectives gone?' In order to talk about the semantic class of 'adjectives' without the implication that they form a lexical category, I will use the expression 'property concept term' (PCT) (Thompson 1988).

In what follows, I show that there is a tremendous overlap in the kinds of morphosyntactic constructions that simple (i.e., underived) prototypical verb stems and simple stems with the semantics of property concept terms occur in. One such construction was already discussed above: the prefixation of the nominalizer *ke-*, which occurs on PCT roots just as productively as it occurs on prototypically verbal roots. Similarly, the sequence of *a-* 'possessive' and *ke-* 'nominalizer' derives a full noun from both prototypical verb roots (see §4.1.1) as well as PCT roots, see (29).

(29) *helō* 'be far' marked nominalized and possessed in reference function
akehelopen <nang> kevang apot
a-ke-helō=pen   <nang=>   ke-vàng   apōt
POSS-NMLZ-be.far=from nang=   NMLZ-come   because
'[...] since she has come from (a) far away (place) [...]' [SH, CSM 048]

Table 50 gives an overview of the morphosyntactic constructions that are discussed in the following sections in an attempt to identify criteria to distinguish between the semantic category of actions or events (i.e., 'verbs') and the semantic category of PCTs (i.e., 'adjectives').

Table 50: Morphosyntactic criteria for the attempt to identify a class of 'adjectives'.

Possible PCT class criteria
May take *-mū(-chòt)* 'comparative'
May take *-néi* 'superlative'
"V=tā V-suffixes" intensifier construction
"V pa-V" adverb construction
Possible verbhood criteria
May take aspectual and modal suffixes (May function as the predicate of a clause)
May take an imperative / hortative suffix
Noun modification
May modify nouns (*ke-* 'NMLZ' required)

The following subsections are organized as follows. Before discussing the criteria in Table 50, I provide a list of roots that belong in different semantic types of property concept terms in §4.2.1. Then I discuss the 'possible PCT class criteria' (as listed in

Table 50) in §4.2.2, and 'possible verbhood criteria' in §4.2.3, and move on to whether there are differences in 'noun modification' constructions in §4.2.4. The discussion of the various criteria is summarized in §4.2.5, and §4.2.6 surveys some marginal types of PCTs with different morphosyntactic properties.

4.2.1 Basic property concept terms (PCTs)

According to Dixon (1977, 2004), the most basic property concept terms fall under the semantic domains of AGE, DIMENSION, VALUE, and COLOR. Dixon predicts that even languages with very small, closed adjective classes have adjectives that belong in these four semantic domains. According to him, if languages have larger adjective categories, their members will also cover the semantic domains of SPEED, PHYSICAL PROPERTY, and HUMAN PROPENSITY. In Karbi, roots that belong in six of Dixon's seven domains share the properties discussed in the following sections. All domains except for that of HUMAN PROPENSITY are expressed by roots; some basic ones are given as examples in Table 51.

Table 51: Basic Property Concept Terms: Karbi sample roots.

Type	Sample roots	Gloss
AGE	bī	'be young, small'
	sàr	'be old (person)'
DIMENSION	thī	'be short'
	thè	'be big'
VALUE	mē	'be good'
	henō	'be bad'
COLOR	lòk	'be white'
	èt	'be yellow, fair, brown'
	lìr	'be grue (green, blue)'
	lù	'be grue (green, blue)'
	èr	'be red'
	ìk	'be black'
SPEED	pràp	'be fast'
	inglèn	'be slow'
PHYSICAL PROPERTY	ingtāng	'be strong, tough'
	ingdūk	'be soft, immature'
	sò	'be hot'
HUMAN PROPENSITY	n/a	n/a

The domain of HUMAN PROPENSITY is the only one for which simple roots are not readily found; no such root occurs in the corpus.[55] Instead what we find is that derived stems and complex predication constructions are used to express concepts of HUMAN PROPENSITY. Table 52 offers examples of derived stems and of so-called 'psycho-collocations' (Matisoff 1986), i.e., predicate constructions that involve an obligatory noun like -*nīng* 'heart/mind' along with a property concept term root (for further discussion, see §11.6.2).

Table 52: Sample complex stems expressing concepts of HUMAN PROPENSITY.

Type	Stem structure	Gloss	Translation
Derived stem	*ch-ingkī-mē*	'RR-talk-GOOD'	'nice to talk to, kind, generous'
	làng-nō	'see-BAD'	'be bad, evil'
Psycho-collocation	*(a-)nīng ingsām*	'(POSS-)heart/mind be.cold'	'be glad, happy, be grateful'
	(a-)nīng aróng	'(POSS-)heart/mind be.happy'	'be happy'

4.2.2 Possible property concept term (PCT) criteria: Gradability, intensification, adverb derivation

What is perhaps most commonly cited as a prototypical semantic characteristic unique to property concept terms is gradability (see, e.g., Croft 2001: 87). That is, the prototypical morphosyntactic property of adjectives is a dedicated construction to indicate the comparative ('more X') and superlative ('the most X') degrees. In Karbi, this criterion fails to isolate property concept terms from the larger verb category. First consider (30) and (31), where the comparative suffix -*mūchòt* and the superlative suffix -*néi* attach to the PCT root *thè* 'be big'.

(30) Comparative -*mūchòt* on *thè* 'be big'
 *anke ejon nangtetphlut <a...> nang**themuchot***
 ánke e-jōn nang=tèt-phlùt <a> nang=**thè-mūchòt**
 and.then one-CLF:animal CIS=exit-suddenly.big.A/O <a.> CIS=**be.big-COMPAR**
 'And then, one (tiger) came out (of the jungle or some area in the *Rongker* ground) and he was bigger (than expected and than the previous one).' [HK, TR 172]

---

[55] Exceptions are metaphorically extended roots, such as *rè* 'be sharp (like, e.g., a blade)', which, just like English, has a metaphoric sense 'be smart, clever' (see, e.g., HK, TR 064).

(31) Superlative *-néi* on *thè* 'be big'
 ake*thenei* *akehoineilo tangho [...]*
 a-ke-**thè-néi** akehòi-néi-lò tànghò
 POSS-NMLZ-**be.big**-SPLT powerful.person-SPLT-RL REP
 'He was the biggest and the most powerful one (so they say) [...].' [HK, TR 033]

Compare this to (32), where the same comparative and superlative suffixes attach to the underived, propotypical (i.e., non-PCT) verbal stems *chō* 'eat' and *kán* 'dance'.

(32) Comparative and superlative forms of non-PCT verb stems
 chō-mūchòt 'eat-COMPAR' *kán-mūchòt* 'dance-COMPAR'
 chō-néi 'eat-SPLT' *kán-néi* 'dance-SPLT'
 [SiT 130827, elicitation]

The resulting meaning is 'eat more', 'eat the most', and 'dance more' and 'dance the most', i.e., quantification of the action or event ('dancing more'), or, in a sense, quantification of the object in transitive events ('eating more'). The comparative and superlative constructions are fully productive among roots that may take *ke-* 'nominalizer', i.e., both PCT roots and prototypical verb roots (see also §9.2.5.1). Grüßner (1978: 107) even provides the example shown in (33), where the superlative *-néi* attaches to a classifier marked diminutive by *-sō*, in order to get a reading of 'the smallest [of the given cylindrical items]'.

(33) Superlative marking of a classifier
 a-plàng-sō-néi
 POSS-CLF:cylindrical-DIM-SPLT
 'the smallest (loaf of bread)' (Grüßner 1978: 107)

I was able to confirm the construction in (33) as a productive pattern, but only with classifiers. In order to use this construction with a common noun, a noun phrase as in (34) needs to be formed so the superlative still occurs on a diminutive marked classifier. Using a noun root in this construction such as **hēm-sō-néi* 'house-DIM-SPLT' is unacceptable.

(34) Superlative marking of a classifier
 modifying a noun
 hēm a-hūm-sō-néi
 house POSS-CLF:container-DIM-SPLT
 'the smallest house'

Lastly, also note that there is another superlative construction, which consists of the suffix *-sí* attaching to nominal PCTs, as in (35) (see §7.4.5).

(35) Superlative construction with -sí
 ne-ìk a-klèng-sí
 1EXCL:POSS-older.brother POSS-old.one-SPLT
 'my oldest brother'

It turns out then that gradability is not a useful criterion for defining a word class of property concept terms (PCTs) in Karbi. Comparative and especially superlative constructions by no means exclusively take PCT roots.

Another construction semantically related to gradability is the "V=tā V-suffixes" copy verb construction (see §16.2.3.2). It has an intensifying function, which may (*a priori*) be more prototypically related to property concept terms rather than actions or events. However, (36) and (37) show that not only PCT roots like *mē* 'be good', but also prototypical verb roots like *lè* 'reach' participate in this construction.

(36) "V=tā V-suffixes" construction with PCT root *mē* 'be.good'
 "*nang vangchitlo!* **meta melo**" *pu tangho* (both laughing)
 [nàng vàng-chìt-lò] **[mē=tā mē-lò]** pu tànghò
 you come-just.right-RL be.good=ADD be.good-RL QUOT REP
 '"You came just right, it's excellent!" (he) said (*both laughing*).' [HK, TR 082]

(37) "V=tā V-suffixes" construction with verb root *lè* 'reach'
 [...] **leta ledappranglo** *Bokolia'an*
 lè=tā lè-dàppràng-lò Bokoliá-án
 reach=ADD reach-early-RL PN-till
 '[...] [W]e reached Bokolia early.' [SH, CSM 012]

An example of the copy verb construction of a non-PCT verb root without any derivational suffixes is (38).

(38) "V=tā V-suffixes" construction with verb root *pòn* 'take away'
 ponta ponnoi [...]
 [pòn=tā pòn-nōi]
 take.away=ADD.INT take.away-INF.COND.IMP
 '"Do take them!" [...]' [KK, BMS 112]

Lastly, let us turn to a derivational adverb construction. It consists of the main verb stem followed by a modifying root that carries the causative prefix *pe-* (§11.3.2). An example is (39), where *tòk* 'pound' is modified by *pe-mé* 'CAUS-be.good' to mean 'pound well'.

(39) Derivational adverb construction
lapente menthuta ekdom langpong tok peme
lapènte   menthū=tā   ékdóm   langpōng   [tòk
after.this dried.fish=ADD EXCM(<Asm) small.bamboo.container pound
pe-mé]
CAUS-be.good
'after that, you need to pound the dried fish in the Langpong well' [SiH, KH 011]

It appears that prototypically verbal roots do not participate in this construction. For example, it is not possible to say **dàm pa-vèk* 'go CAUS-steer/drive' to mean 'go by driving' or **ch-ingkī paháng* 'RR-talk CAUS-shout' to mean 'talk to one another by shouting'.

However, this construction is not entirely productive with (basic) PCTs either. For example, *tún pa-mé* 'cook CAUS-be.good' to mean 'cook well' is acceptable, but *tún pa-henō* 'cook CAUS-be.bad' to mean 'cook poorly, badly' is not acceptable.[56] For further discussion, see §4.2.5.

4.2.3 Possible verbhood criteria: Aspectual and modal suffixes, directives

Among morphosyntactic constructions that are prototypically verbal, predication is not a useful one in Karbi because different types of nominal and pronominal stems quite easily function as predicates (§4.1.2). It comes as no surprise then that PCT roots also easily function as predicates and take a range of aspectual and modal suffixes. Examples are (40) and (41), in which *mén* 'be ready to eat' and *mē* 'be good' function as predicates and take the perfect suffix *-ét* 'already' with realis *-lò* in (40), and the negative quasi-reduplicative, the perfective suffix *-dèt* and realis *-lò* in (41), respectively.

(40) PCT root/stem with aspectual/modal suffixes
  [...] han an men'etló [...]
  hán   àn   **mèn-ét-lò**
  curry rice be.ready.to.eat-PRF-RL
  '[...] [T]he food is ready [...].' [KK, CC 036]

---

56 However, it is possible to say *tún pa-lang-nō* 'cook CAUS-look-BAD' with that meaning.

4.2 Verbs and 'adjectival verbs': The status of property concept terms

(41) PCT root/stem with aspectual/modal suffixes
[...] tovar mesen nangji apotlo, bonseta tovarta'an memedetlo
továr	mē-sén	náng-jí	apōtlo	bónsetā	továr=tā=án
road	be.good-INTENS	need-IRR2	should	but	road=ADD=all

mē-Cē-dèt-lò
be.good-NEG-PFV-RL
'[...] [T]he road should be good, but the road is not good at all.' [SH, CSM 022]

Even though a range of declarative verbal suffixes occur with simple stems consisting of PCT roots in the corpus, there is no instance of a PCT root occurring with directive suffixes such as conative imperative *-thā*, conditioned imperatives *-nōn* and *-nōi*, prohibitive *-rī*, and hortative *-nāng* and conative hortative *-nàng* (§15.1.2 and §15.1.3). Instead, where PCT roots occur with directive suffixes, they also take the causative prefix *pe-~pa-* as in (42). In this example, *pa-* is obligatory.

(42) PCT root with *pe-~pa-* 'causative' and directive suffix
paprapnang ho {mm}
pe-pràp-nàng	ho	{mm}
CAUS-be.quick-HORT:CON	EMPH:INTERACT	AFF

'Let's try to be quick (i.e., with our Rongker)!' [HK, TR 155]

This apparently is not a general characteristic of non-volitional events, as shown in (43), where the lexicalized collocations *nīng vàng* 'mind come' and *phú sò* 'head be hot' have the meaning of 'throw up' and 'have a fever', and can occur with the prohibitive suffix *-rī*.

(43)
nang-nīng	vàng-rī	nang-phú	sò-rī	
2POSS-mind	come-PROH	2POSS-head	be.hot-PROH	
'Don't throw up!'		'Don't have a fever!'		[SiT 130825]

Besides *sò* 'be hot' in the expression for 'have a fever', the PCT *thè* 'be big' also takes a directive suffix, as in *thè-thā* 'be.big-CON.IMP', which may be said to children with the meaning 'Grow up (well)!'. It is not clear whether *thè* in this case is the PCT 'be big' or a case of polysemy, where it is actually a verb with the meaning 'grow up'.

All in all then, evidence from directive suffixes does point towards a distinction between 'proper' verbs and PCTs. Being more of a semantic rather than a structural issue, however, this is not the kind of evidence we might want to strongly rely on to talk about a separate word class of adjectives.

4.2.4 Noun modification

The last morphosyntactic construction that deserves mention here is evidence from noun modification. It was previously assumed (see Grüßner (1978) and Konnerth (2011), which was based on data in Grüßner (1978)) that the noun modification constructions of PCT roots and prototypical verb roots show a clear syntactic difference. While both are marked morphologically the same, i.e., nominalization via *ke-*, the order of head noun and modifier appeared to mark a clear difference: PCT-based modifiers are post-head, whereas prototypical verb-based relative clauses are pre-head. Elicited PCT-based modifiers and prototypical verb-based relative clauses have shown the same pattern.

It turns out, however, that this clear distinction does not hold up against a large body of natural data. There are instances in the corpus of pre-head PCT-based modifiers and there is one potential instance of a post-head relative clause (although it is impossible to distinguish in purely structural terms a simple (i.e., verb-only) post-head relative clause from a simple internally-headed relative clause in a verb-final language such as Karbi).

Noun modification nominalization constructions are discussed in detail in §10.7.1, but relevant examples are repeated here: (44) shows a 'standard' post-head PCT-based modifier, (45) a 'standard' pre-head prototypical verb-based relative clauses, while (46) shows a pre-head PCT-based modifier, and (47) what can be interpreted as a post-head, but also as an internally-headed, relative clause.

(44) PCT root following the head noun it modifies
 [...] kasu keme harlung kemepen [...]
 [[kasú]_{HN} **[ke-mē]**_{PCT} **[harlūng]**_{HN} **[ke-mē]**_{PCT}**=pen]**
 plate   NMLZ-be.good bowl   NMLZ-be.good=with
 '[...] from brass (lit. good) plates and bowls [...]' [KK, BMS 056]

(45) Relative clause verb preceding the head noun it modifies
 Lily, la nelitum aphan nangkejapon aosopi
 Lilý **[là [ne-li-tūm   aphān nang=ke-já-pòn]**_{RC}
 NAME this 1EXCL-HON-PL NSUBJ 1/2:NSUBJ=NMLZ-lead-take.away
 [a-osopì]_{HN}**]**
 POSS-lady
 '[...] Lily, the lady who took us there [...]' [SiT, HF 034]

(46) Pre-head PCT-based modifier *dúk* 'be poor'
 halata kidukthektik amonitlo
 hála=tā   **[[ke-dúk-thektík]**   **a-monít-lò]**
 that=ADD NMLZ-be.poor-as.much.v.as.it.can.be POSS-man-RL
 'That one also is an unimaginably poor man.' [HK, TR 128]

(47) Possibly post-head relative clause
 nangso kithike enutnat [...]
 [[nang-os ō]ₕₙ [ke-thì=ke]ᵣ𝒸] e-nūt-nàt
 2:POSS-child NMLZ-die=TOP one-CLF:HUM:SG-only
 'Only one of your children has died (lit. as for your children that have died, it is just a single one) [...].' [RBT, ChM 043]

4.2.5 Summary: Basic property-concept terms (PCTs)

To summarize the discussion above, consider Table 53, which is based on Table 50 above, but has added columns that show the participation of prototypical verb roots and PCT roots in each construction.

Table 53: Possible morphosyntactic criteria for 'adjectives'.

Possible adjective class criteria	Prototypical Verbs	PCTs
May take -mū(-chòt) 'comparative'	YES	YES
May take -néi 'superlative'	YES	YES
"V=tā V-inflection" intensifier construction	YES	YES
"V pa-V" adverb construction	**NO**	**SOME**
Possible verbhood criteria		
May take aspectual and modal suffixes (May function as the predicate of a clause)	YES	YES
May take an imperative / hortative suffix	**YES**	**Mostly NO**
Noun modification		
May modify nouns (*ke-* 'NMLZ' required)	**YES, pre-head or post-/internal-head**	**YES, post-head or pre-head**

Printed in **bold** in this table are those three constructions that do show a difference between prototypical verb roots and PCT roots, whereas all the other constructions do not. Out of the three constructions, there is not a single one that shows the kind of clear evidence that one would comfortably use to argue in favor of a really distinct adjective class. I conclude that 'adjectives', or basic PCT roots, are a subclass of verbs in Karbi.

4.2.6 Marginal types of property concept terms (PCTs)

The majority of PCTs share the properties laid out in the previous sections. But there are a few other, marginal types of PCTs that occur in the corpus and should be mentioned. They are generally more complex: phonologically, all of them are at least disyllabic; morphologically, most contain more than just a root morpheme, at least diachronically. The list of all of these PCTs encountered so far is given in Table 54, which also references relevant examples given below. Note that a majority of these PCTs have semantics related to SIZE. However, since there are so few of them, it it not possible to generalize over the semantics.

Table 54: Marginal types of property concept terms.

	Form	Gloss	Pre- or Post-head	Example
Nominal, non-reduplicated	ajahák	'some'	pre-head	(48)
	aklèng	'old one'	post-head	(49),(51)
	adakvám	'second-born one'	post-head	(50),(51)
Nominal, reduplicated	achitchit	'tiny'	pre-head	(52)
	ajerjer	'small'	post-head	(53)
PCT.root-*pō/-pī* derived	thè-pō	'big-modif'	post-head	(54)
	thè-pī	'big-augment'	post-head	(56)
	díng-pō	'long-modif'	post-head	(55)
Borrowed	paká	'very good'	pre-head	(58)
			post-head	(59)
	bharí	'very big'	pre-head	(55),(56)
			post-head	(57)
Other	penáng	'a lot'	post-head	(60)

So far we have identified a small handful of PCTs that begin with what must be the *a-* 'possessive' prefix and therefore can be called 'nominal'. There are three items that are non-reduplicated (see (48), (49), (50), (51)) and two that are reduplicated, see (52) and (53). The reduplicated ones are apparently somewhat synonymous while among the non-reduplicated ones, two refer to human age and one to quantity.

(48) *Ajahák* as nominal modifier
ajahak atheke longle athak klobom lapusonta do
[[**ajahák a-thē=ke]** [longlē a-thàk] kló-bòm] [làpusón=tā dō]
some POSS-fruit=TOP earth POSS-on.top fall-CONT like.this=also exist
'Some (pieces of) fruit keep falling on the ground, that's also (something that is) happening.' [SiT, PS 005]

(49) *Aklèng* as nominal modifier
nangong akleng ahemke, nangong
[nang-ōng **aklèng** a-hēm=ke] [nang-ōng
2:POSS-maternal.uncle old.one POSS-house=TOP 2:POSS-maternal.uncle

4.2 Verbs and 'adjectival verbs': The status of property concept terms — 113

    ahemripo ahemke
    a-hēm'rī-pō   a-hēm=ke]
    POSS-oldest.son-male POSS-house=TOP
    'the family of your older maternal uncle, the family of your uncle who is the eldest son of the family [...]' [WR, BCS 014]

(50) *Adakvám* as nominal modifier
    [...] nangong adakvam ahemsi [...]
    [nang-ōng   **adakvám**   a-hēm=si]
    2:POSS-maternal.uncle second.born POSS-house=FOC:RL
    '[...] (it's) (to) the house of your second-born maternal uncle [...]' [WR, BCS 013]

(51) *Aklèng* and *adakvám* as nouns
    Bey atum korte bangkethom do; **aklengsi** *abangke*
    [Bēy   a-tūm   kortè   bàng-kethòm   dō]   **[aklèng-sí**   abàng=ke
    CLAN POSS-PL brother CLF:HUM:PL-three exist old.one-SPLT NPDL=TOP

    Bey Ki'ik, adakvam abangke Bey Ke'et,
    Bēy   ke-ìk]   **[adakvám**   abàng=ke Bēy   ke-èt
    CLAN NMLZ-be.black second.child NPDL=TOP CLAN NMLZ-be.yellow

    akibi abangke Bey Ronghang
    [a-ke-bī   abàng=ke Bēy   Ronghāng]
    POSS-NMLZ-be.small NPDL=TOP CLAN CLAN
    'There were three Bey brothers, the oldest one was Bey the Black, the second one was Bey the Fair, and the young/small one was Bey Ronghang.' [WR, BCS 002]

(52) *Achitchit* preceding its head
    [...] isi hini achitchit arong [...]
    [isī   hiní   **achítchít**   a-ròng]
    one two tiny   POSS-village
    '[...] one or two tiny villages [...]' [SiT, HF 017]

(53) *Ajerjer* following its head noun
    atema ajerjer do mati ho
    [a-temá   **ajerjēr]**   dō   matí   hò
    POSS-tobacco.container(<Asm) **small**   exist CG   EMPH:INTERACT
    'He had a small tobacco container, OK?' [HK, TR 018]

Next we find instances of PCT roots with the suffix *-pō* that function as nominal modifiers. This is not productive derivation. Modifiers such as *the-pō* 'be.big-modifier' in (54) or *ding-pō* 'be.long-modifier' in (55) are only used in particular idiomatic contexts.

(54) *thè-pō* 'big (< *thè* 'be big' and *-pō* 'MODIF') following its head noun
anke ha langso asiluka thepota pulelo
ánke   há   [langsō a-síluká   **the-pō=tā**]   pù-lè-lò
and.then over.there this   POSS-sp.tree(<Asm) be.big-MODIF=ADD say-again-RL
'And then, there, this big siluka tree replied (said again).' [KK, BMS 107]

(55) *díng-pō* 'long (< *ding* 'be long' and *-pō* 'MODIF') following its head noun and *bharí* 'very big (<Ind)' preceding its head noun[64]
*bhari arleng **dingpo** arluló*
[bharí   arlèng **dīng-pō**]   arlū-lò
very.big(<Ind) slope **be.long**-MODIF climb-RL
'She climbed a very big slope.' [SeT, MTN 046]

Instead of *-pō*, the suffix *-pī* can also be used to derive a nominal modifier although it further provides carries an augmentative connotation, see (56). This likewise is not a productive derivation. The fact that *-pō* and *-pī* occur in a paradigm with the same (unproductive) derivational function suggests that these suffixes are etymologically identical to the gender suffixes of the same form. See also §7.4.1.3.

(56) *thè-pī* 'big (< *thè* 'be big' and *-pī* 'AUGMENT') following its head noun and *bharí* 'very big (<Ind)' preceding its head noun
*la bhari talo **thepi** nangkekapji kopuloma*
là   [bharí   taló   **the-pī**]   nang=ke-káp-jí
this very.big(<Ind) sea **be.big**-AUGMENT CIS=NMLZ-cross.water-IRR2
kopú=lo=ma
how=FOC=Q
'How will we be able to cross the huge sea?' [KK, BMS 100]

There are at least two borrowings from Indic that are also regularly used as PCTs: *bharí* 'very big' and *paká* 'very good'. They have evidently been borrowed as more emphatic versions of existing Karbi 'equivalents'. Due to their borrowed origins, they are syntactically free and can occur before their head noun (see *bharí* in (55) and (54), and *paká* in (58)) or after their head noun (see (57) and (59)).

---

57 Note that there is another occurrence of *-pō* 'big(?)' in the corpus, where it is less clear whether it's a productive use of *-pō*, or an idiosyncratic, lexicalized instance. This is *ingnar nothongpo* 'deaf elephant', a character in a folk story (note also the use of *-pō* and *-pī* in animal species names in §7.4.1):

[...] ***ingnar nothongpo*** *aphan arjudamlo*
[ingnàr   **nothōng-pō** aphān] arjū-dām-lò]
elephant deaf-male   NSUBJ   ask-GO-RL
'[...] he went to ask the deaf elephant' [RBT, ChM 032]

(57) *bharî* 'very big (<Ind)' following its head noun
　　[...] *langso atalo bhari*
　　langsō　[a-taló　**bharí**]
　　this　　POSS-sea　very.big(<Ind)
　　'[...] this huge sea' [KK, BMS 044]

(58) *paká* 'very good(<Ind)' preceding its head noun
　　paka angplum khaipiklo
　　[**paká**　　　　a-ingplùm]　khái-pìk-lò
　　very.good(<Ind)　POSS-sprouts　grow-very-RL
　　'[...] it is sprouting very nicely [...]' [HK, TR 149]

(59) *paká* 'very good(<Ind)' following its head noun
　　[...] *an kelok angthip pura pura ekdom*
　　àn　　ke-lòk　　　　angthíp　　　　purá　　　purá　　　ékdóm
　　rice　NMLZ-be.white　unbroken.rice　all(<Asm)　all(<Asm)　EXCM(<Asm)

　　han paka
　　[hán　**paká**]
　　curry　very.good(<Ind)
　　'[...] all of it only the white unbroken (=the best) rice, oh so good, very good curry' [CST, RO 035]

Finally, a PCT of unclear (morphological) etymology that acts as a nominal modifier and is rather commonly used, especially in the colloquial language, is *penáng*, see (60).

(60) *penáng* 'a lot' following its head noun
　　[...] *photo **penang** endunlo*
　　[photó　　**penáng**]　ēn-dūn-lò
　　photo(<Eng)　a.lot　　take-JOIN-RL
　　' [...] ([W]e) took many photos.' [SiT, HF 035]

4.3 Summary: The clausal functions of nouns, verbs, and property concept terms (PCTs)

Croft (2001: 99) presents a figure that shows a semantic map of English parts of speech constructions, mapping particular constructions that English nouns, adjectives, and verbs occur in onto the three basic clausal functions of reference, modification, and predication. In Figure 10, I have copied Croft's visual representation for mapping parts of speech constructions onto clausal functions for Karbi without, however, providing details of different constructions. Instead I have limited this figure to a very basic, and in that sense simplified, picture of the clausal functions of noun, PCT, and verb roots in Karbi.

What is striking about Figure 10 is that nouns can assume any clausal function without overt marking, and that noun, PCT, and verb roots all can function as the predicate of a clause without overt marking. Furthermore, basic PCT and prototypical verb roots basically pattern the same, although I indicate the different syntactic tendencies in noun modification by the narrowly dotted line.

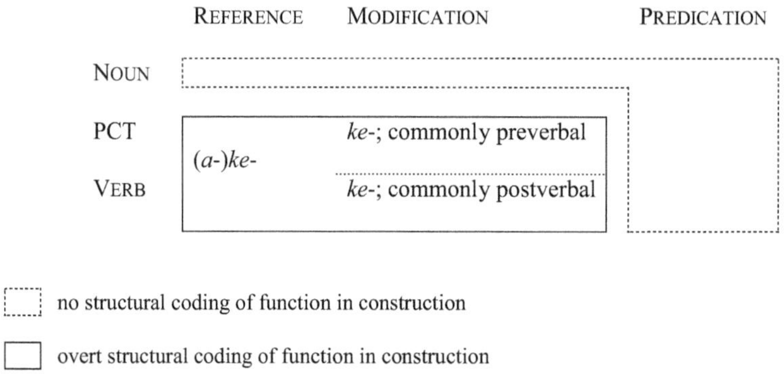

	REFERENCE	MODIFICATION	PREDICATION
NOUN			
PCT	(a-)ke-	ke-; commonly preverbal	
VERB		ke-; commonly postverbal	

▫ no structural coding of function in construction

▫ overt structural coding of function in construction

Figure 10: Semantic map of basic clausal functions of Karbi parts of speech (following Croft's (2001: 99) model).

I have shown nouns (§4.1.2) and PCTs (§4.2.3) in predicate function, as well as PCTs and prototypical verbs marked by *ke-* 'nominalizer' in modification function (§4.2.4), and when marked by *a-ke-* 'POSS-NMLZ-' in reference function (§4.1.1, §4.2). For an unmarked noun functioning as a modifier, see §4.1.1.

5 Subclasses of nouns

Proper nouns represent the largest word class that we can consider a subclass of nouns but they are not discussed further here; see §4.1 and §4.3 for a general discussion of the morphosyntactic properties of nouns. The second-largest subclass of nouns are classifiers, which are discussed in §5.1. In turn, classifiers create subclasses of nouns by virtue of being classifiers. That is, we can consider all nouns that are enumerated with the use of one particular classifier as representing a subclass of nouns. Some nouns are not enumerated in classifier constructions, however, but instead are directly modified by numerals; information on this is found in §5.2. Section §5.3 briefly discusses how nouns with human/personified referents are treated differently from nouns with non-human/non-personified referents in Karbi grammar. Section §5.4 examines relator nouns, i.e., those words that function the same way adpositions do in other languages. In §5.5, the subclass of those nouns that need to carry a possessive prefix is investigated, including body part and kinship terms. Note that relator nouns as well as body part and kinship terms all need to be considered bound roots since they require a possessive prefix in order to occur in an utterance. Nevertheless, the different clausal function of relator nouns compared to body part and kinship terms advocates for their discussion in separate sections. Lastly, §5.6 offers a brief discussion of frozen nominal prefixes given by Grüßner (1978).

5.1 Classifiers

Numerals typically require classifiers in order to form a classifier-numeral word that can then be used in noun modification (for an exception to this general principle, see §5.2 and §10.7.2.1.4 for the 'non-classifier' or 'direct enumeration' construction). Classifiers can be categorized into groups depending on which of three different constructions they occur in: (a) the typical classifier construction (see §10.7.2.1.1); (b) the self-referential classifier construction (see §10.7.2.1.2); and (c) the 'not fully grammaticalized' construction (see §10.7.2.1.3). In addition, in the case of typical classifiers and not fully grammaticalized classifiers, we can distinguish whether classifiers are 'true', i.e., sortal classifiers, or mensural classifiers; this distinction does not occur within the class of self-referential classifiers, as they classify themselves. The five different types of classifiers that emerge from this categorization are shown in Table 55.

In the sections that follow, §5.1.1 gives an overview of sortal classifiers (including 'typical' and 'not fully grammaticalized' ones), §5.1.2 an overview of mensural classifiers (likewise including 'typical' and 'not fully grammaticalized' ones), and §5.1.3 shows self-referential classifiers.

Table 55: Classifier types.

Sortal	Mensural
Typical classifiers	Typical classifiers
Not fully grammaticalized classifiers	Not fully grammaticalized classifiers
Self-referential classifiers	

Classifiers represent a subclass of nouns in that they may take the possessive/ modified *a-* prefix (§4.1.1). In (61), the speaker uses the classifier *-púm* for round objects to refer to a 'tube-shaped' object, here specifically the long iron bar of a bicycle that connects the seat and the handle bar. In this example, the classifier functions just like a noun, evidenced not only by prefixing *a-* 'possessive', but also by being modified by *ingchìn* 'iron', and occurring in the relator noun construction with *-lòng* 'LOC'.

(61) Classifier for round objects *-púm* functioning as a head noun 'tube'
lapenke hala kangni adim along ingnithekthesi <a>
lapèn=ke   [hála ke-ingnì a-dím   a-lòng] ingnì-thēk-Cē-si
and.then=TOP that NMLZ-sit POSS-place POSS-LOC sit-see-NEG-NF:RL

*si ingchin **apum** along ingnisi... saikel*
sì   [[ingchìn **a-púm]**   a-lòng] ingnì-si... saikél
therefore iron   **POSS-CLF:round** POSS-LOC sit-NF:RL   bicycle(<Eng)

kevekponlo
ke-vèk-pōn-lò
NMLZ-steer-take.away-RL
'And then, he doesn't know how to sit down on that sitting place (seat), and then on the iron bar he is sitting and steering the bicycle away.' [SiT, PS 024]

Some classifiers appear to only occur with *a-* 'possessive' in a universal quantification construction that additionally requires suffixation of *-tín* 'each', as in (62); further research is required to confirm this.

(62) Human singular classifier *nūt* with *a-* 'possessive' and *-tín* 'each'
*anke osomar atumta **anuttinta***
ánke   osō-mār a-tūm=tā   **a-nūt-tín**=tā
and.then child-PL POSS-PL=ADD POSS-CLF:HUM:SG(<Khs)-each=ADD

arep amoi kesolo
a-rēp   a-mòi   ke-sò-lò
POSS-side POSS-back NMLZ-hurt-RL
'And then, even the children as well, each of them, had their waist and back hurting [...].' [SH, CSM 070]

Of course many classifiers have their origins in and still synchronically exist side-by-side with true nouns, in which case they have a regular noun counterpart. One could consequently argue that whenever *a-* occurs on a 'classifier', that instance actually represents the noun and not the classifier. However, *nūt* in (62) is a good test case because it is a classifier borrowed from Khasi, as Joseph (2009) has convincingly argued, and thus does not originate in a native Karbi noun. Still *nūt* may occur with *a-* 'possessive' and *-tīn* 'each', which provides evidence for arguing that classifiers are a subgroup of nouns.

5.1.1 Sortal classifiers

Sortal classifiers are 'true' classifiers in the sense that they actually 'classify' or 'sort' nouns into categories, in Karbi specifically only when they are counted (although see §10.7.2.6.1 for the grammaticalization of an indefinite article from a classifier-numeral word counting 'one' item). The great majority of sortal classifiers are fully grammaticalized classifiers (§5.1.1.1), but there is one, perhaps the most frequently used classifier, that is not fully grammaticalized, which is the human plural classifier *bàng*, discussed in §5.1.1.2.

5.1.1.1 Typical classifiers

Table 56 offers a list of grammaticalized sortal classifiers. The 'source' column specifies whether a particular classifier is recorded in my corpus ('C') and/or by Grüßner

Table 56: List of sortal classifiers that occur in typical classifier construction (G = Grüßner (1978: 68–70)).

Category	Classifier	Gloss / Description	Classified items	Source
Animate	nūt[a]	'CLF:HUM:SG(<Khs)'	one human being (only used for singular reference)	C/G
	dón	'CLF:family'	families/houses (in a village)	C/G
	jōn[b]	'CLF:animal'	animals: dogs, tigers, birds	C/G
	rōng	'CLF:plant'	referring to the plant as a whole (e.g., trees)	C/G
Physical properties	hòng	'CLF:long.cylindrical'	long, cylindrical items: arms, legs, table legs, jambili athons (Karbi totem, see Figure 4 in §1.1.3), matches (G)	C/G
	pàk[c]	'CLF:flat'	medium- to large-sized flat items: knives, shovels, books, shirts, bamboo mats	C/G
	plàng	'CLF:small.flat'	small flat items: baked items,	C/G

Table 56 (continued)

Category	Classifier	Gloss / Description	Classified items	Source
	púm	'CLF:round'	round items: e.g. round fruits like oranges, apples, eggs	C/G
	jèng[d]	long/thin[e]	hair	G
	krì	'CLF:line'	long, flat items: strips of meat	C/G
	rī	long/thick	ropes	G
Functional properties	hùm	'CLF:house'	houses, busses (G), packs of cigarettes (G)	C/G
	pòng	bigger containers	water containers made from bamboo	G
	bòng	smaller containers	cups/bowls	G
	thē	fruit and animal calls[f]	oranges, animal calls	G
	bè[g]	tools with handles	brooms	G
Nature and environment	kròng	'CLF:road'	roads, paths	C/G
	jài[h]	fields	paddy fields	G
	ròi	water areas, moving waters	rivers	G
	mū	grains, seeds	rice grains	G
	pháng[i]	bush, shrub	bamboo bush	G
Generics/ Abstract items	sòn	'CLF:thing'	"things" (hormú 'thing'), words, songs, matters, news; also: for kinds/ types of items (e.g. drums),	C/G
	thē	'CLF:word'	words, matters, issues	C/G
	lòng[j]	'CLF:place'	markets (G),	C/G
Time	jōn[k]	'CLF:month'	months	C/G

[a] From Standard Khasi reconstructed form *shi-ngut or Pnar reconstructed form *chi-ngut (Joseph 2009).
[b] Perhaps from arjōn 'length of an animal from head to tail' (Grüßner 1978: 66).
[c] This may be cognate with Meitei pak 'be broad, be wide' (Chelliah 1997: 335).
[d] Presumably from jèng 'thread' (Grüßner 1978: 66).
[e] See footnote 65.
[f] As with jōn (see below), Grüßner (1978: 68) suggests there is only one classifier thē, although we may want to pose two homophonous classifiers based on the highly diverging semantics.
[g] Presumably from bè 'handle (n.)'.
[h] Presumably from jāi 'EE:rīt (field)'.
[i] The same form *phaŋ is reconstructed for Proto-Bodo-Garo as a "classifier for plants" (Joseph and Burling 2006: 120).
[j] Presumably related to the relator noun -lòng 'LOC'.
[k] Grüßner (1978: 67) suggests there is only one classifier jōn that is used to enumerate both animals and months (as well as moons and, according to him, eyes). I have kept the two separate here.

(1978) ('G').[58] The classifiers are sorted by semantic category for presentational purposes. Potentially related Karbi lexical or grammatical items and/or Tibeto-Burman cognates are given in footnotes.

5.1.1.2 Not fully grammaticalized classifier *bàng* 'CLF:HUM:PL'

The plural human classifier *bàng* (Table 57) is the only sortal classifier attested so far that is not fully grammaticalized. This is evidenced by the fact that independent instead of bound numerals are used for 'two' and 'three' (but not 'one', since only *nūt* is used to count 'one person').

Table 57: Not fully grammaticalized classifier *bàng* 'CLF:HUM:PL'.

Form	Gloss	Classifies	Source	Lexical origin
bàng	'CLF:HUM:PL'	humans (plural only)	C/G	bàng 'body'

This is shown in (63), where *bàng* takes the independent numeral *hiní* 'two' instead of the bound numeral *-ní*, which in the same example occurs in the first line on the typical classifier *púm*. In (64), *bàng* occurs with the independent numeral *kethòm* 'three' instead of bound *-thòm ~ -thōm*.

(63) Classifier *bàng* with full form of numeral *hiní* 'two'
 an laso a'oso abang thesere pumni hala
 án [lasō a-osō abàng] [theseré púm-ní] [[hála
 and.then this POSS-child NPDL fruits CLF:round-two that

 ajirpo banghini aphan chepaklangdamlo
 a-jirpò **bàng-hiní**] aphān] che-pa-klàng-dām-lò
 POSS-friend **CLF:HUM:PL-two** NSUBJ RR-CAUS-appear-go-RL
 'And then, this boy went to show the two pieces of fruit to those two friends.'
 [SiT, PS 040]

(64) Classifier *bàng* with full form of numeral *kethòm* 'three'
 hako ahut hedi, Bey atum korte bangkethom do tangho
 [hakó ahūt hedī] [Bēy a-tūm] [kortè **bàng-kethòm**] dō tànghò
 that.time during EMPH TITLE POSS-PL brother CLF:HUM:PL-three exist REP
 'In the old days, you know, right?, there were three Bey brothers, they say.'
 [WR, BCS 001]

---

[58] For the items recorded by Grüßner only but not in the present corpus, a characterization of what is classified is provided instead of a full gloss.

The classifier *bàng* must have grammaticalized from the noun *bàng* 'body', which must also be the origin of the indefinite *bàng* 'somebody'. Presumably the classifier has then also given rise to what I call here the 'noun phrase delimiter' *abàng* (see §13.5). The noun *bàng* 'body' also occurs in a grammaticalized construction, in which it is used with a personal possessive pronoun instead of just the personal pronoun by itself, seemingly in order to specifically refer to a person's physical presence, as in (65).

(65) *Nang-bàng* '2:POSS-body' used instead of *nàng* 'you'
"*O vo'arbipi, nangbang doma?*", *pulo*, "*Do.*"
[[o võarbí-pī **nang-bàng** dō=ma] pù-lò] [dō]
VOC sp.bird-female 2:POSS-body stay=Q say-RL stay
'"O Voarbipi, are you there?", (the king and his people) said, "(I) am (here)".'
[RBT, ChM 039]

5.1.2 Mensural classifiers

Unlike sortal classifiers, mensural classifiers are not 'true' classifiers in the sense that they do not 'classify' items but only 'measure' them. Some mensural classifiers are grammaticalized and occur in the 'typical classifier' construction that sortal classifiers in Table 56 in §5.1.1.1 occur in as well (which is a good reason to call both types 'classifiers'). They are listed in §5.1.2.1. Others are not fully grammaticalized, and may even be created *ad hoc*; these are discussed in §5.1.2.2.

5.1.2.1 Typical classifiers

Table 58 offers a list of mensural classifiers that appear in the 'typical' classifier construction, i.e., including a head noun and a numeral-classifier word which in turn consists of a classifier and a bound numeral. The classifiers are sorted into semantic categories for presentational purposes.

As an example of a mensural classifier, see *bēng* 'CLF:half' in (66).

(66) Classifier for 'half' *bēng*
hala arleng ebeng'an amatsi akhalun
hála arlèng **e-bēng-án** amātsi a-khalùn
that slope one-CLF:half-up.to and.then POSS-kd.big.basket

ingpuvakló [...]
ingpú-vàk-lò
open-RES:open-RL
'She (had climbed) half of the slope and then she opened her *khalun* basket [...].'
[SeT, MTN 050]

Table 58: List of mensural classifiers (G = Grüßner (1978: 68–70)).

Category	Form	Gloss / Description	Measured items	Source	Possible lexical origin
Animate	jàk	group[a]	people, animals	G	
	hùr	group	people, animals	G	
Food and drink	óm	'CLF:mouthful'	mouthfuls	C/G	ing'òm 'cheek', 'to carry in mouth'
	jói	sip, drink	liquor	G	
	ván	share, portion	rice, curry	G	ván 'id. (n.)'
	bō	pieces of naturally partitioned fruit	pieces of orange, jackfruit	G	bō 'inside of fruit (n.)'
	chèt	piece	meat, bread	G	chèt 'small piece'
Bundles	pèng	bundle of chopped wood	bundle of chopped bamboo	G	
	thìk	bundle	(10–15) bananas	G	
	làp	bundle	grass, thatch	G	? -làp 'completely'
Part of whole	sēk	'CLF:section'	bamboo sections, periods of time	C	
	bēng[b]	'CLF:half'		C, G	
	thān[c]	piece	stone	G	thàn 'cut (v.)'
	phán	pieces of a whole	–	G	
	mò	strip of field	fields	G	mò 'id. (n.)'
Specific number	chór	'CLF:pair'	drums, cows, earrings	C, G	chór 'spouse'
Other	phār	layers	cloth	G	
	dú	windings	windings of rivers	G	

[a]See footnote 58.
[b]Grüßner (1978: 65-66) reports the form engbèng instead of bēng for 'half'.
[c]Note that in the case of thān '(CLF:)piece', we see a pattern of corresponding low tone verbs and mid tone classifiers/nominals. For more information on this tone correspondence, see § 3.5.10.

Note that Grüßner (1978: 70–1) lists additional measuring units including ones for weight, volume, length, area, money, traditional items, and time; he provides some traditional units and units borrowed from Assamese/Indic and English.

5.1.2.2 Not fully grammaticalized classifiers
In his list of classifiers, Grüßner (1978) offers the three that I provide below in Table 59, which occur in the not fully grammaticalized construction involving the head noun, the classifier, and the independent numeral, e.g., sabí betùng isī 'one set of keys'

Table 59: Not fully grammaticalized mensural classifiers.

Form	Gloss	Measured items	Source
betùng	bundle	grape-type fruit, keys	G
phār	layers	cloth	G
mokhá	a few	books	G

(Grüßner 1978: 69). In addition to these, any noun that denotes a container of some sort can be used *ad hoc* as a mensural classifier in this construction, e.g., *harlūng* 'cup' to measure cups of tea, for example, or *bórtín* 'bucket' to measure buckets of water (Grüßner 1978: 70).

5.1.3 Self-referential classifiers

A list of all self-referential classifiers attested so far is offered in Table 60. The term 'self-referential classifier' is taken from DeLancey and Boro (in preparation). It refers to those classifiers that count themselves instead of counting (and being morphosyntactically dependent on) a head noun (see §10.7.2.1.2).

Table 60: Self-referential classifiers.

	Form	Gloss	Measured items	Source	Possible lexical origin
Time	arnì ~ nì [a]	'CLF:day'	days	C/G	arnì 'day (noun)'
	jó	'CLF:night'	nights	C/G	jó 'night (noun)'
	rūi	'CLF:week'	weeks	C/G	
	phói	'CLF:times'	once, twice, etc.	C	
	phòng			C/G	
	bói			C/G	
	[pùr			G]	
Other	kām[b]	'CLF:step'	steps	C	kàm 'step (v.)'

[a]The enumeration with 'one' is irregular: it is *arnì-sī* 'day-one' for 'one day', rather than **e-nì*.
[b]Note that in the case of *kām* 'CLF:step', we see a pattern of corresponding low tone verbs and mid tone classifiers/nominals. For more information on this tone correspondence, see § 3.5.10.

Almost all self-referential classifiers are time units as has also been noted for self-referential classifiers in Boro (DeLancey and Boro in preparation). However, in Karbi there is additionally *kām* counting steps, which also acts as a self-referential classifiers as seen in (67). For *jó* 'night' and *nì* 'day' acting as self-referential classifiers, see (68). Note the irregular form for 'one day' as *arnì-sī* – there is no other classifier found so far that follows this pattern.

(67) Self-referential classifier *kām* 'CLF:step'
amat hala hi'ipi abangke ekam anta kamkelang
amāt	[hála	hī'ipī	abàng=ke]	**[e-kām**	**án=tā]**	kàm-Cē-làng
and.then	that	witch	NPDL=TOP	one-CLF:step	that.much=ADD	step-NEG-still

'And then, the witch, didn't even (wasn't even able to) take just one step.'
[CST, HM 105]

(68) Self-referential classifiers *jó* 'CLF:night' and *arnì* 'CLF:day'
aphi atum ejo arnisi dokokta
a-phì	a-tūm	e-**jó**	**arnì**-sī	dō-kòk=tā
POSS-grandmother	POSS-PL	one-CLF:night	CLF:day-one	stay-back=ADD

"ehem chedamnang erit chedamnang [...]"
e-hēm	chV-dām-nāng	e-rīt	chV-dām-nāng
1PL.INCL-house	RR-go-HORT	1PL.INCL-field	RR-go-HORT

'The grandmother and grandfather stayed just one night and one day, and then (the old man) said, "Let's go home, let's go to our property! [...]".'
[KK, BMS 093]

5.1.4 Human and animal classifiers and personification

In folk stories, animals frequently act as rational beings. This has ramifications on the classifier-marked distinction between humans and animals, as the human classifiers *-nūt* (for singular) and *bàng-* (for plural) are typically used for animals as well in these contexts. Although in (69), the dog *methān-sibóngpō* is counted via the animal classifier *jōn*, as the storyteller summarizes that between the one dog and the two people, there were three of them, she uses the plural human classifier in the classifier-numeral word *bàng-kethòm*.

(69) Dog (*methān-sibóngpō*) included in count with human classifier *bàng*
"dah!" pu'ansi, methan-sibongpo ejon,
dáh	pu-ánsi	**methān-sibóngpō**	e-**jōn**
go!	QUOT-after.that	dog-SPECIES	one-CLF:animal

aphipen aphu, mh, bangkethom
a-phì=pen	a-phù	mh	**bàng-kethòm**
POSS-grandmother=with	POSS-grandfather	DSM	CLF:HUM:PL-three

vangchomchomchomchomchom
vàng-chóm~chóm~chóm~chóm~chòm
come-a.little~DIST.PL~DIST.PL~DIST.PL~DIST.PL

"'Let's go!", and then one dog, his grandmother and his grandfather, all three, went step by step by step.' [KK, BMS 099]

An even clearer example is (70), where the human plural classifier *bàng* is used to count ants, which represent protagonists in this folk story.

(70) Human classifier *bàng* used to count animals in folk story
      <chongh..> *miso-rongpo atum korte **banghini***
      <chongh..> **[misò-rongpō** a-tūm]   [kortè   **bàng**-hiní]
      <fro(g)>   **ant.sp**   POSS-PL   brother CLF:HUM:PL-two
      'There were two <fro(g)>, ant brothers.' [RBT, ChM 008]

The lines in (71) and (72) give the context for the converse use of the animal classifier to refer to a human in (73). In this folk story, tigers celebrate the same ceremony as humans/Karbis, which requires sacrificing chickens and/or goats, as explained in (71) (which represents an utterance not by the primary storyteller but by a native Karbi speaking listener, as indicated by the curly brackets).

(71) Context for (73)
      {la monitsi kenangpohe, halatum aphanke,
      [là   monít=si   ke-náng-pò=he]   [hála-tum aphān=ke]
      this man=FOC:RL NMLZ-need-IRR1=AFTERTHOUGHT that-PL   NSUBJ=TOP

      halatum aphanke bi vosi ketheklo}
      hála-tūm aphān=ke bī   vō=si   ke-thèk-lò
      that-PL   NSUBJ=TOP goat chicken=FOC:RL NMLZ-see-RL
      '{[...] They will need human beings, right? They consider them goats and chickens (i.e. what is sacrificed).}' [HK, TR 042]

The line in (72) immediately precedes (73) and mentions the 'village head tiger' (where the use of this terminology further underscores the personification), who collects the humans that are caught by the other tiger as sacrifice for the ceremony.

(72) Context for (73)
      huladak ateke akangbura ahemsi
      húladāk a-tekè   a-kangburá   a-hēm=si
      there   POSS-tiger POSS-village.head.man(<Asm) POSS-house=FOC:RL

      bidamlo tangho {mm}
      bí-dàm-lò   tànghò   mm
      keep-go-RL REP   AFF
      '[...] That tiger had gone and put them in the house of the village head tiger.' [HK, TR 045]

The line in (73) clearly refers to the tigers requiring one more human being as sacrifice. The animal classifier *jōn* anaphorically refers to humans used as sacrifice.

(73) *e-jōn* 'one-CLF:animal' used to refer to human in folk story
bidamlo... te, ejon nangalang
bí-dàm-lò   te   **e-jōn**   náng-jí-lāng
keep-go-RL   and.then/therefore   one-CLF:animal   need-IRR2-still
'He had gone and put them there, and then, one more is needed [...].' [HK, TR 046]

What these examples show is that classifier use may be dynamically shifting according to the perspective of the speaker rather than strictly reflecting referential properties of, e.g., human vs. animal.

5.2 Nouns that are counted with numerals only (without classifiers)

Besides self-referential classifiers (§5.1.3), there is also a class of nouns that occur in enumeration constructions with independent numerals only, rather than with bound numerals as self-referential classifiers do (§10.7.2.1.4). Examples (74) and (75) show the difference between *ningkán* 'year', which is counted with the independent numerals *isī* 'one' and *hiní*, as opposed to *arnì ~ nì* 'CLF:day', which is a self-referential classifier that occurs with bound numerals *-ní* 'two' and *-thōm* 'three'.

(74) *Ningkán* 'year' counted with independent numerals
[...] ningkan isi hini dolo
[ningkán   **isī**   **hiní**]   dō-lò
year   one   two   stay-RL
'[...] [T]hey stayed (like this) for a few years.' [KTa, TCS 078]

(75) *Arnì ~ nì* 'day' as a self-referential classifier
anke ninibak do nithombak do [...]
ánke   nì-**ní**-bāk   dō   nì-**thōm**-bāk   dō
and.then   CLF:day-two-about   stay   CLF:day-three-about   stay
'And then, they stayed a few days [...].' [KTa, TCS 018]

Table 61 offers a list of these nouns that are counted with independent numerals (instead of classifier-numeral words), sorted into 'monosyllabic', 'disyllabic', and 'borrowed'. Note that some of the 'monosyllabic' and 'disyllabic' nouns may in fact be borrowed as well, which is, however, yet to be investigated.

The reason a distinction is drawn between monosyllabic and disyllabic stems is that Grüßner (1978: 64–5) suggests that this might be a criterion: he suggests that multisyllabic stems occur with independent numerals, whereas monosyllabic stems occur with bound numerals. As Table 61 shows, this is not true without exceptions, but it does seem to be the tendency.

Table 61: Nouns counted with numeral only (without classifier).

Category	Form	Gloss
Monosyllabic	hák	'finely woven bamboo basket'
	ròng[a]	'village'
	khái	'tribe, community'
Disyllabic	phatáng	'kind of bamboo basket'
	ningkań	'year'
	batái	'time' (as in 'once', 'twice', etc.)
	arlōng	'stone, rock'
	hamphāng	'society'
	róng'ajé	'festival'
	jamboróng	'bag'
Borrowed	hoptá	'week(<Asm)'
	khontá	'hour(<Asm)'
	pór	'time(<Asm)'
	bahák	'share, portion(<Asm)'
	joiné	'reason(<Ind)'

[a]Grüßner (1978: 67) reports that *ròng* occurs as a self-referential classifier the same way as *jó* 'night' (§ 5.1.3).

Words borrowed from Assamese/Indic or English (as, e.g., 'computer') occur in this direct enumeration construction and not with classifiers. An example is (76), where the Assamese derived *hoptá* 'week' is counted with the independent numerals *isī* and *hiní* without an additional classifer.

(76) Assamese derived *hoptá* 'week' in direct enumeration construction
 lasi dak hopta isi hini angbong dolo [...]
 [lasì dāk **[[hoptá isī hiní]** angbòng] dō-lò]
 therefore here week(<Asm) one two middle stay-RL
 'And like this it was for up to one or two weeks [...].' [KK, BMS 117]

While certain nouns only occur in the direct enumeration construction, other nouns may either occur in the direct enumeration construction or in a classifier construction. An example is (77), in which *lám* 'matter' is counted with *isī* 'one' instead of the more common use of the classifier *e-sòn* 'one-CLF:thing'.

(77) *Lám* 'matter' in direct enumeration instead of classifier construction
 *sita non **isi alam** abangke*
 setā nón **[isī a-lám]** abàng=ke
 but now **one** POSS-**matter** NPDL=TOP
 'But on another matter [...].' [KaR, SWK 097]

This option to occur in the direct enumeration construction may in fact be true of all nouns even if they more typically (still?) occur in classifier constructions. According to Grüßner (1978: 67), it is true of all nouns with inanimate referents; while those that refer to humans or animals still have to be counted with the classifiers *nūt* 'CLF:HUM:SG', *bàng* 'CLF:HUM:PL', or *jōn* 'CLF:animal'. Nonetheless, (78) shows that perhaps at least mistakenly,[59] even nouns with animate referents may occur in the direct enumeration construction in natural texts, here *básápī* 'wife of headman'.

(78) Noun with human referent in direct enumeration construction
 *ako langmemedet setame **isi basapi**lo*
 akó làng-mē-Cē-dèt setāmē [isī básápī-lò]
 then see-GOOD-NEG-PFV nevertheless **one wife.of.headman**-RL
 'And then, even though I may not be perfect (in it) (lit., look good/fit for it), I'm a *Basapi* (wife of headman).' [KK, CC 006]

Although the extent of the interchangeability between direction enumeration and classifier use requires more research, my general impression is that younger speakers use direct enumeration more frequently than older speakers do. In addition, the younger generation of native Karbi speakers have been observed to switch to Assamese numbers in enumeration constructions, which is an expected type of contact influence given that markets are typically Assamese-speaking places.

5.3 Human/personified vs. non-human/non-personified

It may be fairly universal that languages have some grammatical domains where human/personified referents are distinguished from non-human/non-personified ones, for example in English interrogative pronouns 'who' versus 'what'. In Karbi, this distinction additionally exists in classifiers (though see the discussion in §5.1.4), as well as in 'differential' plural marking via *-tūm* (§10.6) and primary object marking via *-phān* (§14.1.5). While this suggests that Karbi grammatically distinguishes between human vs. non-human nouns, it is important that this distinction is pragmatically dependent on the construal of the speaker (therefore also "personified" vs. "non-personified").

5.4 Relator nouns

Relator nouns exhibit structural properties of nouns while functioning the same way adpositions do in languages that have them as a distinct category (Starosta 1985; DeLancey 1997). The reason why they structurally overlap with nouns is because they

---

[59] It was suggested to me that the speaker in (78) mistakenly said *isī* instead of *e-nūt*.

grammaticalize from lexical nouns. In Karbi, the possessive construction that relator nouns most typically occur in involves a possessor noun followed by an *a-* 'possessive/modified' marked possessed noun, schematically: [N]$_{posr}$ [a-N]$_{posd}$ (see also §10.3 and §10.4); the *a-* marked possessed noun is the relator noun. In (79) *a-rài* is the relator noun, and the expression *langrōi a-rài* 'at the side of the river' functions like an adpositional phrase in English, here specifically as a locational oblique.

(79) Relator noun *a-rài*
 anke dak langroi arai chingki chethan
 ánke dāk [langrōi **a-rài**] chingkī che-thán
 and.then here river POSS-side talk RR-tell
 'And then, here, at the side of the river, they discussed everything among themselves.' [KK, BMS 104]

Relator nouns are bound roots. Although they most frequently occur with the *a-* 'possessive, modified' prefix in the corpus, they may also occur with personal possessive prefixes. An example is (80).

(80) *-thàk* 'on.top' with personal possessive prefix *e-* '1PL:INCL'
 [...] pholong jonni hu ethakpen barithe aso
 [pholòng jōn-ní] hú **e-thàk=pen** [barithè
 grasshopper CLF:animal-two over.there 1PL.INCL-on.top=from god
 a-osō]
 POSS-child

 nangklochomlo dei
 nang=kló-chòm-lò déi
 CIS=fall-together.few.close-RL OK?
 '[...] [T]wo grasshoppers, over there, from above us, children of god, fell down, okay?' [KTa, TCS 009]

A list of so far attested relator nouns is given in Table 62. They are grouped by semantic domain in this table. Instances of the common pathway of metaphorical shift of

Table 62: Relator nouns.

Semantic domain	Form	Gloss	Lexical source or related item	Gloss
Locational (§5.4.2)	-thàk	'on.top'		
	-ingsóng	'high.up'		
	-ingnò	'in.front'	ingnò	'front'
	-rúm	'below'		

5.4 Relator nouns — 131

Table 62 (continued)

Semantic domain	Form	Gloss	Lexical source or related item	Gloss
	-rèi ~ -ràia	'at.side.of'	-rèi~-ràib	'sideways'
	-kùng			
	-dūngc	'near'		
	-lìng	'at.bottom.of'		
	-arlō	'inside'		
	-nát(thū)d	'towards'		
	-ingdéne	'towards' (general direction)f		
	-jō	'amidst'		
	[-dàk	'road.inbetween']		
Locational/	-ingbòng	'in.middle.of'g		
Temporal	-phràng	'before'	a-phràng	'front'
(§5.4.3)	-phī	'after'	a-phī	'backside'
Temporalh (§5.4.4)	-hūt	'during'		
Causal	-pōt	'because'		
(§5.4.5)	-joiné			
	-jōk			
Otheri	-lòng	'LOC'	lòng	'classifier:place'
(§5.4.6)	-phān	'for; NSUBJ; GOAL'		
	-lokòt ~ -logòt	'with(<Asm)'	logot (<Asm)	'id.'
	-pár	'beyond'		
	-tèng	'according.to'		
	-hín	'associated.with'	hín	'side'

[a] Grüßner (1978: 77) reports this item with high tone as *réy*.
[b] A text example of this suffix is in the verb *che-lāng-rài-lò* 'RR-see-sideways-RL' meaning 'looked sideways' (HK, TR 053).
[c] Grüßner (1978: 77) reports this item with high tone as *dúng*.
[d] Grüßner (1978: 77) reports this item with high tone on *-thú*.
[e] Grüßner (1978: 77) reports this item with low tone as *ingdèn*.
[f] Grüßner (1978: 77) reports the meaning 'opposite from' for *ingdèn*. I have put "general direction" in brackets to indicate that this item has a more general sense than the more specific *anát(thū)*.
[g] The difference in meaning between *angbòng* 'in.middle.of' and *ajō* 'amidst' is that *angbòng* locates a person or thing right in the middle or center of something, whereas *ajō* more generally locates a person or thing within a defined area.
[h] Grüßner (1978: 77) also lists *akó* 'as long as, until' as a relator noun. Since this marker only occurs as a subordinator in the corpus, I discuss it in § 5.4.7.1.
[i] Grüßner (1978: 77) also records the Assamese loan *abîrudhé* 'against, opposed to' as a relator noun. This form does not occur in the present corpus.

'locational > temporal > causal' are *-ingbòng*, *-phràng*, and *-phī*, of which at least the latter two have corresponding lexical nouns with locational semantics that undoubtedly represent their origins. In Table 62, apparent lexical sources or related lexical/grammatical items are provided where known. Some of the relator nouns given here are recorded with different tones by Grüßner (1978), which is mentioned in footnotes.

Relator nouns may occur with *=pen* 'with, from' to add an ablative dimension to the meaning of the relator noun. Examples are (81) and (82).

(81) Relator noun *-ngsóng* 'high.up' with *=pen* meaning 'from high up'
thengpi angsongpen nangkeklosi {mm} thinilo {mm} [...]
thengpī **angsóng=pen** nang=ke-kló-si mm thìnì-lò mm
tree/wood high.up=from CIS=NMLZ-fall-NF:RL AFF be.almost.dead-RL AFF
'(He) had fallen down from up high in the tree and hurt himself badly (lit. almost died) [...].' [HK, TR 196]

(82) Relator noun *-nát* 'towards' with *=pen* meaning 'from the direction of'
anung anatpen ketheklong <ma> kosonma angno
[[anùng **a-nát=pen**] ke-theklōng <ma> kosón=ma] [[angnò
back POSS-direction=from NMLZ-see Q how=Q in.front

anatpen ketheklong kosonma
a-nát=pen] ke-theklōng kosón=ma]
POSS-direction=from NMLZ-see how=Q
'From the backside, how (the houses) look, from the front, how they look, (we went to see) [...].' [SiT, HF 048]

Finally, a frequent use of relator nouns in discourse is that of discourse connectors at the beginning of an intonation unit. This construction involves an anaphoric use of the proximal or distal demonstrative followed by a relator noun, as in (83) and (84).

(83) RN discourse connector construction with *-hūt* 'during'
halaso ahut documentaryta paklangbom [...]
[**hálasō ahūt**] documentary=tā pa-klàng-bōm
that during doc.=ADD CAUS-appear-CONT
'At that time they also were showing a documentary, [...].' [SiT, HF 057]

(84) RN discourse connector construction with *-phī* 'after'
laso aphi laso aHingchong musoso hala habit
[**lasō aphī**] lasō a-Hingchòng musosō hála habít
this after this POSS-CONSTELLATION siblings:DL that jungle

kethondamti ahut mok ingchirlo
ke-thòn-dām-tí ahūt mōk ingchìr-lò
NMLZ-drop-go-get.rid.off during breast be.hungry-RL
'After that, the Hingchong sisters, as they were dropped in that jungle, they were hungry.' [CST, HM 025]

5.4.1 General relator noun *-lòng* 'locative'

The general relator noun *-lòng* 'LOC' is the most frequent relator noun in the corpus, due to its bleached semantic content. It can be used instead of a relator noun with a more specific semantic content. Examples below show the functional range covered by *-lòng* 'LOC'. First, (85) shows two instances of *-lòng* 'LOC' in its locative function.

(85) Relator noun *-lòng* with basic locative function
"*[...] richoke ha pharla alongsi*
[richó=ke há **[pharlá a-lòng=si]**
king=TOP over.there outside.part.Karbi.house POSS-LOC=FOC:RL

pohui moidai along doji [...]"
[pohùi mòidāi a-lòng] dō-jì
pillow backrest POSS-LOC exist-IRR2
'"[...] [T]he king will be over there in his *pharla*, on his comfortable bed (lit., on his pillows and back cushions) [...].'" [CST, HM 044]

Examples of other locational uses of *-lòng* are given below. In (86), *-lòng* has an allative function of 'motion towards' a place, or location of a person or entity. In (87), *-lòng* indicates a relationship where one item is attached to another item. Example (88) shows that *-lòng* may be used even when there is a more specific relator noun that could be used, in this case *arlō* 'inside'.

(86) Relator noun *-lòng* with allative function
voarbipi along richo atum damlilo
[vōarbípī a-lòng] [richó a-tūm] dàm-lì-lò
bird.sp POSS-LOC king POSS-PL go-again-RL
'The people of the king in turn (lit. 'again') went to the Voarbipi bird.' [RBT, ChM 038]

(87) Relator noun *-lòng* marking attachment
anke laso athongkup along lujisi
ánke **[lasō a-thongkūp a-lòng]** lují=si
and.then this POSS-tobacco.container POSS-LOC mirror=FOC:RL

kapabon
ke-pa-bōn
NMLZ-CAUS-be.attached
'And then, on this tobacco container, there was a mirror attached.' [HK, TR 026]

(88) Relator noun *-lòng* meaning 'inside'
anke hala jamborong alongke... dak laso aduma
ánke   **[hála   jamboróng   a-lòng=ke...]**   dāk   [lasō   a-dumá
and.then that   bag   POSS-LOC=TOP   here   this   POSS-tobacco

thongkup dolo {dolo}
thongkūp]   dō-lò   {dō-lò}
tobacco.container exist-RL   exist-RL
'And then, inside this bag..., here he had this tobacco container.' [HK, TR 073]

In (89), the metaphorical use of *-lòng* is shown, as the context here is 'working *for* a particular project'. Furthermore, (90) shows that for certain verbs, such as *dùn* 'follow', *-lòng* marks the object, i.e., the person being followed.

(89) Relator noun *-lòng* meaning 'for'
Hydro-Electric-Project alongsi kam klem'ikbom
[Hydro-Electric-Project   a-lòng=si]   kám   klém-īk-bōm
NAME   POSS-LOC=FOC:RL   work   do-FRML-CONT
'I work for the Hydro-Electric Project.' [KaR, SWK 010]

(90) Relator noun *-lòng* marking O argument of *dùn* 'follow'
apiso along chidunkri [...]
[a-pisò   a-lòng]   chV-dūn-krì
POSS-wife   POSS-LOC   RR-follow-follow.closely
'He followed his wife closely [...].' [KK, BMS 082]

Finally, there are instances where *-lòng* heads clauses and *alòng* with the frozen *a-* prefix functions as a subordinator. In (91), *-lòng* functions as the head noun of the locative relative clause 'where the birds don't chirp'. In (92) and (93), *alòng* marks subordinate clauses that indicate simultaneity in (92) and perhaps causality in (93) (where the elaborate expression *boché charí* 'rule, be in charge of' occurs in a parallelism construction, see §16.1.1).

(91) Relator noun *-lòng* functioning as locative relative clause head noun
*[...] hi'ipi abangke etum aphan ha **votek ingrengre***
[hī'ipī   abàng=ke]   [e-tūm   aphan]   há   **[[vōtèk**
witch   NPDL=TOP   1PL.INCL-PL   NSUBJ   over.there   wild.bird

ingrèng-Cē]
call(small.animals)-NEG

voso ingrengre along ekethondamti
[vōsō   ingrèng-Cē]   a-lòng]
EE:vōtèk call(small.animals)-NEG **POSS-LOC**
e=ke-thòn-dām-tí
1PL.INCL=NMLZ-drop-GO-get.rid.off
'[...] [T]hat witch took and abandoned us over there where the birds don't chirp.'
[CST, HM 062]

(92) Relator noun *alòng* with subordinating function
ingparke bhari arleng dingpo karlu alongke,
ingpár=ke   [bharí   arlèng dīng-pō   ke-arlū   alòng=ke]
besides=TOP   very.big(<Ind) slope   be.long-big NMLZ-climb   LOC=TOP

la apenan abangke barso kedo kangtung
là   a-penàn   abàng=ke barsō ke-dō   ke-ingtúng
this POSS-husband NPDL=TOP urine NMLZ-exist NMLZ-desire
'And then, when she was climbing up on the long slope, the husband felt the need to go to the bathroom.' [SeT, MTN 048]

(93) Relator noun *alòng* with subordinating function
si la hemtun isi kaboche along kachari along
sì   là   hēmtūn   isī [[ke-boché   alòng] [ke-charí   alòng]]
therefore   this good.family one   NMLZ-create   LOC   NMLZ-rule   LOC

<*so'arlosomar atum*> *arlosomar atum arpu ko'an do?*
<sō'arlosō-mār a-tūm>   árlosō-mār a-tūm   arpū   ko'án   dō
women-PL   POSS-PL woman-PL   POSS-PL responsibility how.much exist
'So with running a family and being in charge, how much responsibility do women have?' [KaR, SWK 026]

5.4.2 Locational relator nouns

Examples of locational relator nouns are given below in (94)–(106). They are given in the order of Table 62 as repeated in Table 63 for easier reference.

(94) Relator noun *-thàk* 'on.top'
[...] *ok an hor setame longle athaksi pichomchomlo*
[ōk   àn   hōr   setāmē]]   [longlē a-thàk=si]
meat   rice liquor   nevertheless   earth   POSS-on.top=FOC:RL

pī-chòm~chòm-lò]
give-a.little~DIST.PL-RL
'[...] [T]hey gave him a little bit of meat and rice and liquor each, on the ground.'
[KK, BMS 055]

(95) Relator noun -*ingsóng* 'high.up'
ha thengpi angsongsi dolo banghinita {mm}
há   **[thengpī   a-ingsóng=si]**   dō-lò
over.there tree/wood   POSS-high.up=FOC:RL   exist-RL
bàng-hiní=tā   mm
CLF:HUM:PL-two=ADD   AFF
'High up there in the tree they are, both of them.' [HK, TR 152]

(96) Relator noun -*ingnò* 'in.front'
korte banghini <angno> angno nangklolo
[kortè   bàng-hiní   <a-ingnò>   a-ingnò]
same.gender.siblings   CLF:HUM:PL-two   POSS-in.front   POSS-in.front
nang=kló-lò
CIS=fall-RL
'[...] [I]n front of the two brothers they fell.' [KTa, TCS 010]

(97) Relator noun -*rúm* 'below'
thengpi arum nanglelo [...]
[thengpī   a-rúm]   nang=lè-lò
tree/wood   POSS-below   CIS=reach-RL
'He arrived (at the place) right below the tree [...].' [SiT, PS 017]

Table 63: Overview of locational relator nouns.

Form	Gloss
-*thàk*	'on.top'
-*ingsóng*	'high.up'
-*ingnò*	'in.front'
-*rúm*	'below'
-*rèi* ~ -*rài*	'at.side.of'
-*kùng*	
-*dūng*	'near'
-*lìng*	'at.bottom.of'
-*arlō*	'inside'
-*nát(thū)*	'towards'
-*ingdén*	'towards' (general direction)
-*jō*	'amidst'
[-*dàk*	'road.inbetween']

(98) Relator noun -*rài* 'at.side.of'
anke dak langroi arai chingki chethan
ánke   dāk   **[langrōi   a-rài]**   chingkī   che-thán
and.then here   river   POSS-at.side.of   talk   RR-tell
'And then, here, at the side of the river, they discussed everything among themselves.' [KK, BMS 104]

(99) Relator noun -*kùng* 'at.side.of'
tovar akungkung laso kejorta penang'an do
[[továr   **a-kùng~kūng]**   [lasō]   [ke-jòr-tā]]   penáng-án   dō
road   POSS-at.side.of~DIST.PL   this   NMLZ-sell-if   a.lot-that.much exist
'At the sides of the road, there are a lot of (places where they) sell (pineapple).' [SiT, HF 016]

(100) Relator noun -*dūng* 'near'
laso <la> thesere kelik amonit adung'an nanglelo
[lasō   <là>   theseré   ke-lík   a-monít]   a-dūng-án]   nang=lè-lò
this   this   fruits   NMLZ-pluck   POSS-man   POSS-near-up.to   CIS=reach-RL
'He arrived near this fruit picking man.' [SiT, PS 010]

(101) Relator noun -*lìng* 'at.bottom.of'
ha Hajong aling abojar pulo tangho
há   **[Hajōng   a-lìng]**   a-bojár   pù-lò
over.there(<Pnr)   HILL   POSS-at.bottom.of   POSS-market(<Asm)   say-RL
tànghò]
REP
'"There (to) the market at the foot of the *Hajong* it is said that (she will come) […]."' [KK, BMS 064]

(102) Relator noun -*arlō* 'inside'
"konatlo?" pu, "ha, longku arlo"
konát=lo?   pu   há   **[longkū   a-arlō]**[60]
where=FOC   QUOT   over.there   cave   POSS-IN
'"Where (are they)?", (the king asked), "Over there, inside the cave.", (the girls said).' [CST, HM 111]

---

[60] Note that when *a-* 'possessive, modified' attaches to disyllabic roots that start in *ar-*, one of the two /a/ vowels that end up occurring in a row is often deleted, especially in grammaticalized constructions such as the relator noun construction (see §3.9.2.1).

(103) Relator noun -nát 'towards'
pen pasi'idunvotsi phutup humra aphi
pèn   pasi'í-dùn-vòt-si   phutūp hūm-rà   **[a-phī**
and.then whistle-JOIN-fast.sound-NF:RL hat   pick.up-NF:IRR POSS-backside

anat chevangthulo
a-nát]   che-vàng-thū-lò
POSS-towards RR-come-again-RL
'And then, he whistled for him, picked up the hat and came back (to return it).' [SiT, PS 036]

(104) Relator noun -jō 'amidst'
ha nampi namdur ajo<pen>] pathite
há   **[[nāmpī   nāmdūr a-jō]**   <=pen>] pa-thì-tē
over.there(<Pnr) big.forest EE:nampī **POSS-AMIDST** <=from> CAUS-die-if

pathikhangjanganang pu amat
[pa-thì-khangjáng-lonāng   pu   amāt]
CAUS-die-do.irreversibly-HORT:EMPH   QUOT   and.then
'"[...] [I]n the middle of the jungle, if this causes them to die, then let it happen!"' [CST, RO 049]

The status of -*dàk* 'road inbetween' is less clear. In (105), it appears to assume the function of a relator noun as it occurs with the locational expression *Dobokapen Hojai* 'from/between Doboka and Hojai'. However, in half of the instances of -*dàk* in the corpus, it occurs with the demonstrative *lasō*, as in (106). In this case, it does not actually function as a relator noun. This fact about the actual usage of this noun suggests that it is not as grammaticalized as the other relator nouns shown in this section.

(105) -*dàk* 'road.inbetween' as relator noun
bonseta Dobokapen <Hojai> Hojai adak
bónsetā **[[[Doboká=pen** <hojai> **Hojái] a-dàk]**
but   PN=**from**   PN   PN   POSS-**road.inbetween**

abangke tovar henopik
abàng=ke]   továr   henō-pìk
NPDL=TOP   road   bad-very
'But between Doboka and Hojai the road is very bad' [SH, CSM 017]

(106) -*dàk* 'road.inbetween' as relator noun or lexical noun
lasi laso adakke tovarta mesen apot
lasì   **[[[lasō   a-dàk=ke]**   továr=tā
therefore this   POSS-road.inbetween=TOP   road=ADD

mē-sén]   apōt]
be.good-INTENS because

leta ledappranglo Bokolia'an
lè=tā   lè-dàppràng-lò Bokoliá-án
reach=ADD reach-early-RL PN-till
'So (on/as for) this stretch, the road was good, and so we reached Bokolia early.' [SH, CSM 012]

The corpus of this grammar does not contain an example of *angdén* 'towards'.

5.4.3 Locational/temporal relator nouns

Relator nouns that encode both locational and temporal concepts are expected to originate in locational lexical nouns. As part of a typical shift from locational to temporal concepts, they then end up encoding temporal relations as well. Table 64 lists three locational/temporal relator nouns. Below examples are given that show the locational use of *angbòng* 'amidst' in (107) and its temporal use in (108).

Table 64: Locational/temporal relator nouns.

Form	Gloss
-ingbòng	'in.middle.of'
-phráng	'before'
-phī	'after'

(107) Locational use of *-ingbòng* 'amidst'
amatsi etum aphanke dak habit angbongsi
amātsi   e-tūm   aphān=ke   dāk   [habît a-ingbòng=si]
and.then 1PL.INCL-PL NSUBJ=TOP here jungle POSS-in.middle.of=FOC:RL

nangkethonti
nang=ke-thòn-tí
CIS=NMLZ-drop-get.rid.off
'And then, she took us here in the middle of the jungle and abandoned us.' [CST, HM 052]'

(108) Temporal use of *-ingbòng* 'amidst'
lasi dak hopta isi hini angbong dolo [...]
lasì   dāk   [[hoptá   isī   hiní] a-ingbòng] dō-lò
therefore here week(<Asm) whole two   POSS-amidst   stay-RL
'And thus they stayed for (within) one or two weeks [...].' [KK, BMS 117]

The uses of *-phī* 'backside' and of *-phráng* 'front' as lexical nouns are shown in (109) and (110). Although the corpus does not contain occurrences of *aphī* and *aphráng* as relator nouns, the acceptability of expressions like *rūi-ní aphī/aphráng* 'after/before two weeks' and *chiklō e-jōn aphī/aphráng* 'after/before one month' was confirmed in elicitation.

(109) *-phī* used as lexical noun 'backside'
    *pen pasi'idunvotsi phutup humra **aphi***
    pèn   pasi'í-dùn-vòt-si   phutūp hūm-rà
    and.then whistle-JOIN-fast.sound-NF:RL hat   pick.up-NF:IRR
    [a-phī
    POSS-backside

    ***anat** chevangthulo*
    a-nát]   che-vàng-thū-lò
    POSS-towards RR-come-again-RL
    'And then, he whistled for him, picked up the hat and came back (to return it).' [SiT, PS 036]

(110) *-phráng* used as lexical noun 'front'
    *lapenke saikel along **aphrang anatsi** kethap*
    lapèn=ke   [saikél   alòng] **[a-phráng** a-nát=si]
    and.then=TOP bicycle(<Eng) LOC   POSS-front POSS-towards=FOC:RL
    ke-thàp
    NMLZ-put.inside
    'And then he put them on the bicycle in the front.' [SiT, PS 023]

Synonyms of *-phī* and *-phráng* used as lexical nouns for 'back(side)' and 'front' are *-nùng* and *-ingnò*, see (111).

(111) *-nùng* 'back' and *-ingnò* 'front'
    anung anatpen ketheklong <ma> kosonma angno
    [[**a-nùng** a-nát=pen]   ke-theklōng <ma> kosón=ma]
    POSS-back POSS-direction=from NMLZ-see Q   how=Q
    [[**a-ngnò**
    POSS-in.front

    anatpen ketheklong kosonma
    a-nát=pen]   ke-theklōng kosón=ma]
    POSS-direction=from NMLZ-see how=Q
    'From the backside, how (the houses) look, from the front, how they look, (we went to see) [...].' [SiT, HF 048]

5.4.4 Temporal relator noun

So far only one relator noun is attested that is used to express a temporal relationship without also expressing location: *-hūt* 'during'. An example is given below. Note that other temporal relator nouns have further grammaticalized to subordinators (see §5.4.7.1 and §12.5.2).

(112) Relator noun *-hūt* 'during'
<aphrang> hako adin ahut so'arlosomar
<a-phráng>   [hakó   a-dín   **a-hūt**]   [sō'arlosō-mār
POSS-first   that.time POSS-day(<Asm) POSS-during   women-PL

atumpen non adin ahut non akai
a-tūm=pen]   [[nón   a-dín   **a-hūt**]   [nón   a-kái
POSS-PL=with now   POSS-day(<Asm)   POSS-during   now   POSS-time(<Asm)

ahut so'arlosomar atum la kangdat
a-hūt]]   [sō'arlosō-mār a-tūm]   [là   ke-ingdát
POSS-during   women-PL   POSS-PL   this   NMLZ-make.a.living

katelopen lahai kadokave along hedi o
ke-teló-pen]   [lahái kadókavē alòng]   hedí   o
NMLZ-EE:ingdát-NF   these   all   LOC   okay?   AFF(<Asm)
'(Besides) working to make a living in the case of both the women from the old days and the women nowadays (lit., the women of today and the women of now), in all of these cases, right?' [KaR, SWK 061]

5.4.5 Causal relator nouns

There are three causal relator nouns: *-pōt*, *-jōk*, and *-joiné*. They all occur much more frequently as subordinators (see §5.4.7.1 and §12.5.2) than as relator nouns. In fact, *-jōk* does not occur as a relator noun in the corpus, but *-pōt* and *-joiné* do, as in (113) and (114).

(113) Relator noun *-pōt* 'because'
amatsi penang kedamta eduk dolo
amātsi   penáng   ke-dàm=tā   e-dúk   dō-lò
and.then   a.lot   NMLZ-go=ADD 1PL.INCL-hardship(<Asm)   exist-RL

<arlong>   la inglong arlok apot
<arlōng>   là   [[inglóng   arlòk]   a-pōt]
stone   this   hill   foot.of.hill   POSS-because
'And then, as we go we have to suffer a lot because of all the up and down.' [SH, CSM 023]

(114) Relator noun *-joiné* 'reason'
laso akenemphru ajoinesi han

[lasō	a-ke-nemprù	**a-joiné=si**
this	POSS-NMLZ-have.sweet.smell	POSS-reason=FOC:RL

hán
prepared.vegetables

akechome [...]
a-ke-chō-mē]
POSS-NMLZ-eat-GOOD
'This fragrant smell is the reason why the curry is tasty [...].' [SiH, KH 015]

5.4.6 Relator nouns with other functions

Relator nouns that express functions other than locational, temporal, and causal notions are given in Table 65.

Table 65: Relator nouns with other functions.

Form	Gloss
-lòng	'LOC'
-phān	'for; NSUBJ; PURP'
-lokòt ~ -logòt	'along.with(<Asm)'
-pár	'beyond, besides'
-tèng	'according.to'
-hín	'associated.with'

The general relator noun *-lòng* was already discussed in §5.4.1, and the functions of *-phān* are illustrated in §14.1.2. Examples of the other four relator nouns in this list are given below.

(115) Relator noun *-lokòt* 'along.with(<Asm)'
[...] anke laso asarpiburita laso alokot dun

[ánke	lasō	a-sarpīburì=tā	[lasō	a-lokòt]	dùn]
and.then	this	POSS-old.woman=ADD	this	POSS-along.with(<Asm)	join

'[...] And then this old woman went along with that one.' [KK, BMS 121]

(116) Relator noun -pár 'besides'
nephanke aker apar nangkethanke
ne-phān=ke   **[a-kēr   a-pár]**   nang=ke-thán=ke
1EXCL-NSUBJ=TOP POSS-bad.omen POSS-besides 1/2:NSUBJ=NMLZ-tell=TOP

avelo
avē-lò
not.exist-RL
'To me, this is nothing but a bad omen.' [KK, BMS 021]

(117) Relator noun -tèng 'according.to'
"orapondetnang!", pulo amat thik laso
orá-pòn-dèt-nāng   pù-lò   amātsi   thík   **[[lasō**
take.care-take.away-PFV-HORT say-RL   because right.then this

api alam ateng amat laso a'osomar
a-pī   a-lám]   a-tèng]   amāt [[lasō
POSS-female.animal POSS-matter POSS-according.to then this
a-osō-mār]
POSS-child-PL

Hingchong musoso aphan laso ateke jonni
[Hingchòng   musosō]   aphān]] lasō a-tekè   jōn-ní
CONSTELLATION   siblings:DL NSUBJ   this POSS-tiger CLF:animal-two

abangphu inut ing'omponkreilo [...]
a-bangphú   e-nūt   ing'òm-pōn-krèi-lò
POSS-each.one one-CLF:HUM:SG keep.in.mouth-in.passing-DISTR.PL-RL
'"Let's take them away and take care of them!", (she) said, and then, right then, according to the female's words, the two tigers took these children each one in their mouths and carried them away [...]' [CST, HM 034]

(118) Relator noun -hín 'associated.with'
nelitum Karbi Lammet Amei ahinpen lamthe
ne-li-tūm   [[Karbì   lammét   a-méi]   **a-hín=pen]**
1EXCL-HON-PL   PN   literature POSS-assembly POSS-associated.with=from

lamthe kimi kiri
[lamthē ke-mī]   ke-rì
word   NMLZ-be.new NMLZ-search
'On behalf of the Karbi Lammet Amei, we are looking for new (i.e., special or rare) words and expressions [...].' [KaR, SWK 001]

5.4.7 Further grammaticalization of relator nouns

5.4.7.1 Subordinators

The grammaticalization of relator nouns to subordinators is a common phenomenon in Tibeto-Burman languages (Genetti 1986, 1991). Since nominalization is so pervasive, relator nouns are readily available for use as subordinators of nominalized clauses. The temporal relator nouns *aphī* 'after', *aphráng* 'before', and *ahūt* 'while' (with the possessive/modified *a-* prefix frozen onto them) frequently function as subordinators, as shown in (119), (120), and (121).

(119) Subordinator *aphī* 'after' (grammaticalized from relator noun)
[...] laso hem nangkachiri aphi, apenan abang sunjoi [...]
[[lasō hēm nang=ke-che-rī] **aphī]** a-penàn abàng sūn-jòi
this house CIS=NMLZ-RR-search after POSS-husband NPDL descend-quietly
'[...] After she went back to search for it in the house, the husband quietly came down [...].' [SeT, MTN 042]

(120) Subordinator *aphráng* 'before' (grammaticalized from relator noun)
laso kethap aphrang aphrang, <la> longle
[lasō ke-thàp aphráng~aphráng] <là> [[longlē
this NMLZ-put.inside before~INTENS this earth

keklo alongpen humsi, laso aketer
ke-kló alòng=pen] hūm-si] [lasō a-ke-tèr
NMLZ-fall LOC=from pick.up-NF:RL this POSS-NMLZ-be.dirty

athesere <la> longle kero'anke halaso apepensi venlo
a-theserē <là> longlē ke-rō-án=ke] [hálasō a-pé=pen=si]
POSS-fruits this earth NMLZ-hit-all=TOP that POSS-cloth=with=FOC:RL
vēn-lò
wipe-RL
'Just before putting them into (the basket), he picks them up from having fallen onto the ground, and these dirty fruits, all the ones that were dirty with (had hit the) earth, with this cloth, he wiped them.' [SiT, PS 008]

(121) Subordinator *ahūt* 'while' (grammaticalized from relator noun)
elitum hako pirthe kangduk ahut inglong kedo
[e-li-tūm **[[hakó pirthé ke-ingdūk] ahūt]** [[inglóng ke-dō]
1PL.INCL-HON-PL that.time world NMLZ-immature during hill NMLZ-stay

ahutke sabun tangho kopine tangho la konane
ahūt=ke] [sabún tànghò kopí-nē tànghò là konát-nē
during=TOP soap(<Asm) REP what-INDEF REP this where-INDEF

asempu non'alom ke'enthapvaret,[...]
a-sempuĺ] nón-alōm ke-ēn-tháp-varèt]
POSS-shampoo(<Eng) now-while NMLZ-take-mindlessly-for.long.time
'Long ago, when the world was immature, when we lived in the hills, (it was just like today) soap, they say, and whatever, shampoo from wherever, now (people) use (them without knowing the origins or anything of it) [...].' [SiH, CW 003]

Furthermore, some subordinators clearly look like relator nouns (i.e., they carry the *a-* prefix), while they do not require the subordinate clause to be nominalized. They thus represent an advanced stage of grammaticalization. An example is *akó* 'before, when', which occurs in a construction with a negated, non-nominalized verb to convey the meaning 'before', as in (122). For more information on subordinators, see §6.4.3 and §12.5.

(122) Subordinator *akó* 'before, when'
bang vangve ako eli damnangji {mm}
[bàng **vàng-Cē akò]** è-lì dàm-náng-jí mm
CLF:HUM:PL come-NEG before 1PL.INCL-HON go-must-IRR2 AFF
'[...] [W]e need to go before anybody gets there.' [HK, TR 142]

5.4.7.2 Adverbs
In addition to grammaticalizing to subordinators, relator nouns also productively occur as adverbs in Karbi. In that function, they always carry the *a-* like a frozen prefix, and do not form a syntactic unit with any other item but occur alone. Examples are (123) and (124).

(123) Relator noun *adūng* 'near' functioning as an adverb
adung nopak epak do {mm}
adūng nopàk e-pàk dō mm
near dao one-CLF.flat exist AFF
'Nearby he had a dao.' [HK, TR 072]

(124) Relator noun *arúm* 'below, down' functioning as an adverb
dondon chedonsi... anke amonit abang
[dondón che-dón-si...] [ánke [a-monít abàng]
ladder RR-place.ladder/bridge-NF:RL and.then POSS-man NPDL

<a> pe akelokpen keroi isi ajamborong
[[pé a-ke-lòk=pen ke-ròi isī a-jamboróng
cloth POSS-NMLZ-be.white=with NMLZ-sew one POSS-bag

arlosi lahai kethap lapen arum kevan
arlō=si]   [lahái]   ke-thàp]]   lapèn   **[arúm   ke-vàn]]**
inside=FOC:RL these   NMLZ-put.inside   and   down   NMLZ-bring
'He has placed himself a ladder… and then, the man, into one bag sown from white cloth he puts these (fruits), and then brings them down.' [SiT, PS 003]

5.5 Bound noun roots

Body part and kinship terms, and inalienably possessed nouns have in common that they are bound noun roots, i.e., they do not (typically) occur without a possessive prefix (but see below for exceptions). This may be either the general possessive/modified prefix *a-* (§7.3.1) or one of the personal possessive prefixes (§6.1.1).

These roots may occur with a personal possessive prefix even in the case of an indefinite referent, as in (125).

(125) Possessive-marked bound noun root representing indefinite referent
"*ne nahokpen setame… e ne nechor*
nè   nahōk=pen   setāmē   e   nè   **ne-chór**
1EXCL anywhere=from nevertheless DSM 1EXCL **1EXCL:POSS-spouse**

chirithupo" pu […]
che-rī-thū-pò   pu
RR-search-again-IRR1   QUOT
'"No matter from where but I will find another wife!" (he thought by himself) […].' [CST, RO 009]

5.5.1 Body part terms

A lot of body part terms are monosyllabic and have clear Tibeto-Burman origins, e.g., *-mēk* 'eye', *-nò* 'ear', *-dè* 'tongue', *-só* 'tooth', *-rí* 'hand, arm', *-kèng* 'foot'. Some, however, are disyllabic, such as *-maháng* 'face' and *-nokan* 'nose'. A subset is disyllabic and has the *ing-* prefix (see §6.3.1), for example, *-ing'òm* 'cheek', *-inghò* 'mouth', *-ingphór* 'lungs', and *-ingmūm* 'beard'.

A frequently used root that should also be listed here is *-nīng* 'mind', which commonly occurs in the psycho-collocation construction (§11.6.2). Within this construction, there are several text examples where *-nīng* occurs without any possessive prefix and is therefore used as a *de facto* free root.

5.5.2 Kinship terms

A comprehensive list of kinship terminology is provided by Grüßner (1978: 73 ff.), who reports a total of 70 different forms including forms of reference and forms of address (some of which are, however, formed via productive suffixes such as *-pī* 'female' and *-pō* 'masculine'). Another resource is Phangcho (2012), where 34 different forms are reported. Besides the fact that kinship terms are bound roots (or stems) that generally require a possessive prefix (but see below for exceptions), one other morphological characteristic is that certain kinship terms may take the suffix *-héi~-hái* for more formal address and reference (§16.4.3).

Note that kinship terms actually do not always have to carry a possessive prefix. Evidence is provided in (126), where *pīsō* 'wife' occurs in a non-referential, idiomatic construction: *piso (some) ke'en* 'to get married (lit. take a wife)', where *a-* is not used. Whether this phenomenon relates only to this particular construction, or has to do with the pragmatics of spouses as kin, requires further research.

(126) *pīsō* 'wife' without possessive prefix
 anke latum thelo dinglo piso some enlo tangho
 ánke [la-tūm thè-lò dīng-lò] [[pīsō sōmē] ēn-lò] tànghò
 and.then this-PL be.big-RL be.long-RL wife EE:pīsō take-RL REP
 'And then, they grew up and they got married, so they say.' [WR, BCS 003]

Also, kinship terms in vocative forms with the mid tone (§3.5.10) occur without the possessive prefix, as in (127).

(127) Vocative *phū* 'grandfather' without possessive prefix
 jumepik phu [...]
 arjū-mē-pìk phū
 listen-be.good-very grandfather:VOC
 'Very nice to hear, grandfather [...]!' [HK, TR 200]

5.5.3 Other inalienably possessed items

In addition to relator nouns, and body part and kinship terms, a few other nouns carry a frozen possessive prefix and can be analyzed as being historically bound roots. Synchronically, fused with the frozen *a-* prefix, these are free roots. In this group we find the following items: *angdēng* 'border, mark', *angkāng* 'circumference', *angpìp* 'foam', *angthíp* 'unbroken rice', *angthòr* 'hole (inhabited by an animal such as a rat)', *apāi* 'somebody's turn (in a particular procedural order)', *aphái* 'number', *asáp* 'a little bit'. This presumably has to do with these nouns only ever being used in a relational sense, i.e., as they relate to another concept.

5.6 Other possible noun classes with frozen prefixes (Grüßner 1978: 44–6)

Grüßner (1978: 44–6) has sorted disyllabic lexical roots by shared first syllables. The two by far most frequent ones, *ing-* and *ar-*, are discussed below (§6.3). In addition to those two, Grüßner also offers lists of only disyllabic nouns (i.e., no verbs) that share the first syllable *kar-* (seven roots in total), those that share *ke-* as their first syllable (seven roots in total), those that share *che-* as their first syllable (fifteen roots in total), and those that share *me-* or *ma-* as their first syllable (five roots in total). Grüßner suggests that the respective first syllables are frozen prefixes, whose meaning is no longer recoverable. In addition to these 'frozen prefixes' that according to Grüßner only occur with nouns, there are other ones that occur with both nominal and verbal disyllabic roots (see §6.3.3).

5.7 Collective noun roots

There are collective noun roots that indicate reference to a general group of people, such as *so'arlō* 'the women' (compare *árlosō* 'woman, girl') and *sopinsō* 'the men' (compare to *pinsō* 'married man').

6 Other word classes

This last chapter on word classes begins with an overview of pro-forms that include personal pronouns, demonstratives, interrogative pronouns and pro-adverbs, and pronouns and pro-adverbs of universal quantification (§6.1). Section §6.2 briefly reviews verb subclasses, although the discussion of the large verbal subclass of property concept terms is found in §4.2. In §6.3, frozen prefixes on Karbi nouns and verbs are surveyed. Some of these have long been known and used in the reconstruction of Proto-Tibeto-Burman morphology. Finally, §6.4 goes over the remaining minor word classes, including adverbs, numerals, as well as subordinators and coordinators.

6.1 Pro-forms

The pro-forms listed below have the same distribution as noun phrases. In addition, demonstratives and interrogative pronouns have limited distributional properties of nouns as well (note that nouns may function as noun phrases), but this is not the case for personal pronouns. Evidence for this difference comes from the possessive/modification construction, in which both demonstratives and interrogative pronouns may function as pre-head modifiers with the head marked *a-* 'possessive' (and therefore behave like other nouns), while personal pronouns have their own possessive prefixes, thus functioning differently from nouns.

6.1.1 Personal pronouns and personal possessive prefixes

Table 66 shows the forms of personal pronouns. Karbi distinguishes between first person exclusive (the speaker and possibly also non-speech act participants, excluding the addressee) and inclusive (the speaker and the addressee and possibly also non-speech act participants). The inclusive form requires pluralization via *tūm* (see below) for use as an independent pronoun, but not for use as a possessive prefix. The exclusive form is the same as the first person singular form, which is a cross-linguistically common syncretism called "only-inclusive" by Cysouw (2003). In this grammar, *nè* and *ne-* are always glossed as '1EXCL' even if the context makes it clear that there is a singular rather than a plural reference.

For honorific forms (see §16.4.1) *-lī* is added. Possessive forms are prefixes, which do not have a tonal specification. Honorific possessive prefixes have the same *-lī*, but are probably best analyzed as disyllabic prefixes rather than a sequence of two prefixes, which would require us to posit the existence of both a suffix *-lī* and a prefix *lī-* in the Karbi lexicon, when it is clearly the same affix.

Table 66: Personal pronouns and personal possessive prefixes.

Personal pronoun (honorific)	Gloss	Possessive prefixes (honorific)
nè(lì)	'1EXCL'	ne(li)-
e(li)-tūm (only plural)	'1INCL'	e(li)-
nàng(lì)	'2'	nang(li)-
alàng(lì)	'3'	[alang(li)-; a-]

In Table 66, the third person possessive forms *alang(li)-* and *a-* appear in square brackets. This is meant to indicate that there is not actually a dedicated productive third person possessive prefix in Karbi. Sometimes, *alang(li)-* is used as a third person possessive prefix, for example, *alanglimen Basapi* 'her name is Basapi' (with *mén* 'name'). However, *alang(li)-* is not commonly used, and instead the *a-* 'possessive / modified' prefix is used, which receives a third person possessive interpretation from context (and is, in fact reconstructible to a Proto-Tibeto-Burman third person possessive **a-* prefix, see §7.3.1). For example, consider the possessive clause construction in (128). The possessive clause construction requires a possessor, a possessed item, and the existential copula (see §6.2.2.1.1). In (128), only the general possessive prefix *a-* is acceptable to index the third person possessor *ne'ik akleng* on the possessed item *osomar* 'children'.

(128) Possessive clause construction showing third person possessive marked by *a-*
[ne-ìk   aklèng]   **a**-so-màr   bang-kethōm   dō
1EXCL:POSS-older.brother old.one   POSS-child-PL   CLF:HUM:PL-three   exist
'My older brother has three children (lit., (as for) my older brother, **his** three children exist).' [elicited SiT 090220]

Plural forms of personal pronouns involve the (bound) plural noun *-tūm* (see §10.6).[61] Table 67 gives the example of the first person exclusive independent pronoun *nè* and its possessive prefix counterpart *ne-* in honorific, plural, and other possessive constructions.

---

[61] It is impossible to tease apart whether the plural pronoun forms should be phonologically analyzed as a prefixal or compound construction since all of the pronouns are low tone. Thus, both the phonological compound interpretation leads to a low-mid tone pattern, e.g., on *nè-tūm*, as does the prefix interpretation where the toneless prefix *ne-* would be realized with a low tone before a mid tone syllable (see §3.5.6).

Table 67: Morphological structure of independent pronouns and pronominal possessive prefixes.

[Pron.	(HON)	(PL / N)]	[a-N]	Gloss	Translation
nè				'1EXCL'	'I'
nè	-lī			'1EXCL-HON'	'I' (honorific)
ne-li-		tūm		'1EXCL-HON-PL'	'we' (honorific, exclusive)
[ne-li-		tūm]	[a-hēm]	['1EXCL-HON-PL'] [POSS-house]	'our house' (honorific, exclusive)
ne-		hēm		'1EXCL-house'	'my house'
ne-li-		hēm		'1EXCL-HON-house'	'my house (honorific)'

(Possessive) pronouns combine with the plural noun *-tūm* the same way they combine with the 'differential primary object' marker *-phān* (§14.1.2) and the locative *-lòng* (§14.1.3). Here, third person pronoun forms involve either *alàng(-lì)* or the demonstratives, onto which the grammatical markers attach directly, as in *alangli-tūm*, *alangli-phān*, or *(ha)la-tūm* and *(ha)la-phān* for the proximate *là* and distal *hála*.

6.1.2 Reflexive/reciprocal pronouns

Reflexive pronouns are formed by adding personal possessive prefixes to the reflexive nouns *-metháng* or, less commonly, *-mená* 'self'. Commonly, in clauses that have a reflexive pronoun, the verb is marked reflexive/reciprocal by *che-* (§8.4.3).

Co-reference between the subject and the (reflexive) possessor of another (oblique) clause participant is illustrated in (129) and (130). Note that the *a-* prefix on *monít* 'man' in (129) indicates the modification by the preceding classifier-numerals word *inut* as well as the minimal relative clause *chotiki chonghoi*. The *a-* prefix on the reflexive pronoun *metháng* represents the regular third person inflection to indicate 'himself' or 'his (own)'.

(129) Co-reference between subject and possessor of clause participant
[...] *inut chotiki chonghoi amonit amethang*
[e-nūt   [cho-tikī   cho-inghói]   **a-monít]**ᵢ **[[a-metháng]**ᵢ
one-CLF:HUM:SG AUTO.BEN-cultivate AUTO.BEN-do POSS-man POSS-self

abiri arlopen eson <athe...> thesere] kelik
a-birī]   arlō=pen]   e-sòn   <a-thē...>   theseré   ke-lík
POSS-garden   inside=from   one-CLF:thing   POSS-fruit   fruits   IPFV-pluck
'[...] **[[O]ne farmer (lit., one man who is doing cultivation)]**ᵢ from (inside) **his**ᵢ (own) garden is picking a kind of fruit.' [SiT, PS 002]

(130) Co-reference between subject and possessor of clause participant
latum bangkethomke amethang atovar chedamlo [...]
[là-tūm bàng-kethòm=ke]ᵢ   [[a-metháng]ᵢ [a-továr]]   che-dām-lò
this-PL CLF:HUM:PL -three=TOP POSS-self   POSS-road RR-go-RL
'[The three of them]ᵢ went theirᵢ (own) way [...].' [SiT, PS 034]

Elicited examples that show coreference between A and O are (131) and (132). In (132), the A argument occurs as a zero anaphora.

(131) Coreference between A and O (third person)
[Ruplin]ᵢ [a-methán (a-phān)]ᵢ   che-theklōng-lò
NAME   POSS-self POSS-NSUBJ   RR-see-RL
'Ruplinᵢ saw herselfᵢ.' [BIK 110205]

(132) Coreference between A and O (second person)
[nang-methán (a-phān)]   che-theklōng=ma?
2:POSS-self   POSS-NSUBJ   RR-see=Q
'Do (you) see yourself?' [BIK 110205]

Reflexive pronouns are also used to emphatically refer to the subject in Karbi. In (133), the reflexive pronoun *nemethang* 'I myself' is used with the verb *thurdappranglo* 'got up early' to signal the contrast to the following clause, which states that the subject also 'woke up the children'. This contrast is further marked by the use of the additive particle =*tā* on the corresponding NPs: the subject in the first clause and the object in the second clause.[62]

(133) Reflexive pronouns used for emphatic/contrastive subject reference
lasi nemethangta thurdappranglo lang
lasì   **ne-metháng**=tā thùr-dàppràng-lò   lāng
therefore **1EXCL-self**=ADD wake.up-very.early-RL water

chinglu'et ajat'etlo osomar aphanta ingthurlo
chinglú-ét   aját-ét-lò   [osō-mār aphān=tā] ingthùr-lò
take.bath-PRF GENEX-PRF-RL   child-PL NSUBJ=ADD   wake.up-RL
'So I **myself** got up early in the morning and took a bath and everything and also woke up the children.' [SH, CSM 003]

---

62 Note that *nemethang* in (133) is indeed an S argument here and not an O argument, as *thùr* 'wake up' is intransitive, compared to transitive *ingthùr* 'wake up' (which, actually, goes against the hypothesis that *ing-* has a detransitivizing function, see §6.3.1).

To add yet greater emphasis to the referent of the subject (in contrast to other referents), the reflexive pronouns *-metháng* or *-mená* may be combined with a third reflexive form *-māt* using a possessive construction, i.e., [REFL.PRO] [a-māt] (following the possessive construction: [N_{POSR}] [**a**-N_{POSD}], see §10.3), as in (134) and (135).

(134) Reflexive pronouns used for emphatic/contrastive subject reference, with added
 a-māt 'POSS-self'
 lapen laso kabor'i ajokpen non inut
 lapèn   [lasō ke-bor'í   ajōk=pen]   [nón e-nūt
 and.then this NMLZ-w.great.effort because=with now one-CLF:HUM:SG

 banghini atum... o nelimena amatta...
 bàng-hiní   a-tūm]   o   **ne-li-mená**
 CLF:HUM:PL-two   POSS-PL   AFF(<Asm) **1EXCL:POSS-HON-self**
 a-māt=tā
 POSS-SELF=ALSO
 'And then, because of this effort (they make), another few people (are able to go out to make money)..., I myself also...' [KaR, SWK 065]

(135) Reflexive pronouns used for emphatic/contrastive subject reference, with added *a-māt* 'POSS-self'
 bisar alamke nangliphan amatta jong nangkokpo
 [bisár   a-lám=ke]   [**nang-li-phān   a-māt=tā**]   jòng
 case(<Asm)   POSS-matter=TOP **2-HON-NSUBJ   POSS-SELF=EVEN**   point
 náng-kòk-pò
 need-firmly-IRR1
 'We can even see (it in your case), you yourself..., right, for this case, we also need to point at you yourself.' [KaR, SWK 066]

Furthermore note that just like the verb prefix *che-* (§8.4.3), *-metháng* not only allows a reflexive but also a reciprocal interpretation. In (136), the sense is clearly reciprocal rather than reflexive, because the people no doubt know their own languages, they just don't know each other's languages.

(136) Reciprocity expressed by *-metháng*
 penke ongdung aNaka akhei hala alangtum
 pèn=ke   [óng-dùng   a-Naká   a-khéi]   [hála
 and.then=TOP   exist.much-exceedingly   POSS-TRIBE   POSS-community that
 alàng-tūm
 3-PL

angbong amethang alam chethekvangve pusitame halatum
angbòng] [[a-mettháng a-lám] che-thēk-vàng-Cē pùsitāmē]
middle **POSS-self** **POSS-language** RR-see-PL-NEG even.though
[hála-tūm
that-PL

Nagamesesi kaningje common languageke Nagamese [...]
Nagamese=si ke-ningjé [common language=ke Nagamese]
LANGUAGE=FOC:RL NMLZ-speak common language=TOP LANGUAGE
'And then, all the many Naga communities, even though among each other they don't understand each other's languages, they speak Nagamese, the common language is Nagamese [...].' [SiT, HF 041]

The etymology of *-metháng* or *-méná* 'self' is not known. However, there may exist a link between Karbi *-metháng* and Meitei *məthən* 'himself' (or just *thən* 'self') (Chelliah 1997: 329). The fom *-māt* is likely related to *komāt* 'who' (§6.1.4).

6.1.3 Demonstratives

Table 68 gives an overview of demonstrative forms. Note that there is only a single true demonstrative root: *là*. By itself it functions as the proximal demonstrative, and in combination with *há* as the distal demonstrative. The forms followed by a tilde in brackets are contracted forms that occur in spoken Karbi as attested in the corpus.

Table 68: Demonstratives.

Semantics	Form of demonstrative	May function as NP?	May function as modifier?
Proximal	*là*	YES	YES
	lasō (~ sō)	sometimes	YES
	labangsō (~ langsō)	sometimes	YES
Distal	*hála*	YES	YES
	hálasō (~ hásō)	?	YES
	hálabangsō	?	YES

The deictic *há* also occurs individually as a distal adverb 'over there' and almost always precedes a more specific locational expression. A typical example is (137), where *há* is followed by the relator noun construction *longku arlo* 'inside the cave'. This element *há* may be a borrowing from Jaintia Khasi (Pnar) according to several of my language consultants.

(137) Distal locative *há* 'over there'
"*konatlo?*" *pu*, "*ha longku arlo*"
konát=lo? pu **há** longkū arlō
where=FOC QUOT over.there cave inside
'"Where (are they)?", "Over there inside the cave."' [CST, HM 111]

All demonstrative forms in Table 68 productively function as modifiers. The forms ending in -*sō*, however, occur much less frequently as pro-NPs. Grüßner (1978: 84) does not report forms in -*sō* functioning as pro-NPs at all, but (138) shows the NP clitic =*ke* 'TOP' attaching to *lasō*, which therefore clearly is a pro-NP here.

(138) Demonstrative *lasō* functioning as pro-NP
[...] *isi a-rong'aje do; lasoke, alanglitum kipuke, areng*
isī a-róng'ajé dō] **[lasō=ke** [alang-li-tūm ke-pù=ke] [a-rèng
one POSS-festival exist **this=TOP** 3-HON-PL NMLZ-say=TOP POSS-skin

kelok alampen Hornbill-Festival, la langdunnang
ke-lòk a-lám=pen] Hornbill.Festival là làng-dūn-nāng
NMLZ-be.white POSS-word=with Hornbill.Festival this see-JOIN-HORT
'[...] [T]here is one festival; this one (i.e. the festival), they call it 'Hornbill Festival' in English (lit, the language of the white skins), this (festival) let's go and watch!' [SiT, HF 002]

According to Grüßner, the -*sō* in the forms that are apparently used more frequently as modifiers is the diminutive suffix -*sō* (§7.4.2). However, it is clear that there is no synchronic diminutive function associated with the use of *lasō* as opposed to *là*. I do not know what the -*sō* is or what it could be derived from.

The basic forms *lá* and *hála* frequently occur in place of the third person pronoun *alàng*. They follow the personal pronoun pattern of having the plural marker -*tūm* and the primary object marker -*phān* attach directly, as in *la-tūm* and *hála-tūm*, and *la-phān* and *hála-phān*. In addition, *là* occurs in *lahéi~laháí* for third person plural inanimate pro-NP function.

Finally, *là-bàng*, the combination of the demonstrative with the noun phrase delimiter *abàng* (§13.5), is used as a pro-form in a co-relative construction (§12.7.3.1.4) in (139), while Grüßner (1978: 84) also reports this form being used in modifier function. Grüßner furthermore reports that this form is used with the gender suffixes -*pī* and -*pō* (§7.4.1) to mean 'this woman' and 'this man'.

(139) Demonstrative pro-NP *labàng*
lasi laso ahonjeng komatma keteroiun
lasì lasō a-honjèng komāt=ma ke-teròi-ùn
therefore this POSS-thread who=Q NMLZ-walk.cautiously-be.able

labangke ahoklo
là-abàng=ke   a-hōk-lò
this-NPDL=TOP POSS-truth-RL
'Therefore, whoever can walk over this thread, that one is true.' [CST, HM 096]

Table 69 offers a list of words that contain proximal *là* and/or distal locational *há*. The rightmost column lists the combining morpheme(s) where known. Some of the inherently deictic forms that the demonstratives combine with in this table also occur along with interrogatives (see §6.1.5).

Table 69: Words with demonstrative roots.

Function		Form	Gloss	Other morpheme
Deictic	Manner	*lasón, lapù, lapusón*	'this way, like this'	*asón* 'like', ? *pù* 'say / quotative'
	Time	*hakó*	'(in) the old days'	*kó* 'time'
	Place	*lapú*	'this side'	?*pú*
		hapú	'that side'	
		ladāk	'here'	*dāk* 'here'
		háladāk ~ hádāk	'there'	
		lapúnatthū (<*lapú anatthū*)	'over there'	*natthu* 'direction, towards'
	Amount	*la'án*	'this much'	*án* 'this much; all'
Discourse connector / coordinator		*lasì*	'therefore, then'	?*si* 'focus'
		lapèn	'and'	=*pen* 'with'

6.1.4 Interrogative pronouns and pro-adverbs, and positive polarity indefinite construction

Table 70 gives an overview of interrogative pronouns and pro-adverbs. All forms generally consist of the bound interrogative morpheme *ko-* plus an additional element. Where this additional element is still recognizable, I provide form and meaning in the rightmost column. In *(ko)pí* 'what', the interrogative *ko-* is often left out, which also sometimes happens with other interrogative words especially in colloquial speech.[63]

---

[63] An often asked question when meeting a familiar person on the road is *Konatlo kedam(po)?* 'Where are (you) going?', which often gets reduced to simply *Na(t)lo?*, with the /t/ typically left unpronounced (§3.7.1).

Table 70: Interrogative pronouns and adverbs.

Semantic field	Form	Gloss	Combination of ko + ...
TYPE	kolo(-sō)	'which'	?lo
	kolobang		
PERSON	komāt	'who'	(a-)māt 'self'[a]
THING	(ko)pí	'what'	?pi
PLACE	konát	'where'	nát 'direction'
	kodāk		dāk 'here'
	kohín	'where.to'	hín 'side'
REASON	kopīsi	'why'	?pí 'what' + =si 'FOC'
	(pí) (ka)chonghói(si)		inghói 'do (v.)'
	pí apōt		apōt 'reason'
TIME	komantú	'when'	
MANNER	kosón~ kolosón	'how'	asón 'like'
	kopu		pù 'say, quotative'
AMOUNT	ko'án	'how much'	-án 'this much; all' (§10.8.2)

[a] For a discussion of the reflexive function of -māt, see §6.1.2. Also note that Daai Chin has *mat* for 'one' (So-Hartmann 2009: 128), which might be related.

The TYPE interrogative forms *kolo(-sō)*, *kolobàng* usually occur as modifiers rather than pro-NPs. An exception is (140), in which *kolo* is used as a pro-NP.

(140) *Kolo* 'which' used nominally
"*ante kolo nangkeneptang [...]*"
ánte   **kolo**   nang=ke-nèp-tāng
OK.then which   CIS=NMLZ-catch-finish
'"If so, which one have you already caught?" [...]' [HK, TR 090]

Examples of the other interrogative pronouns and adverbs in the corpus are given below, in the order of Table 70.

(141) Person interrogative *komāt* as O argument, with differential primary object marker *aphān*
anke komat aphansi kepitekangpo
ánke   **komāt** aphān=si   ke-pī-tekáng-pò
and.then who   NSUBJ =FOC:RL NMLZ-give-leave-IRR1
'And then, who will we give her to? [...]' [SH, CSM 063]

158 —— 6 Other word classes

(142) Thing interrogative *kopí* as O argument
ne kopilo kevipo laho <m>
nè **kopí**=lo ke-vì-pò là-ho
1EXCL what=FOC NMLZ-do-IRR1 this-EMPH:INTERACT
'What should I do?' [CST, HM 013]

(143) Place interrogative *konát*
"*konatlo?*" *pu*, "*ha longku arlo*"
konát=lo pu há longkū arlō
where=FOC QUOT over.there cave inside
'"Where (are they)?", "Over there inside the cave."' [CST, HM 111]

(144) Reason interrogative *kopīsi*
[…] "kopisi nang nesopi aphan kipithima?" […]
[**kopīsi** nàng [ne-oso-pì aphān] ke-pV-thì=ma]
why 2 1EXCL:POSS-child-female NSUBJ NMLZ-CAUS-die=Q
'[…] "For what possible reason did you kill my daughter?" […]' [RBT, ChM 028]

(145) Time interrogative *komantú*
komantupo aRongkerjike {mm}
komantú-pò a-Ròngkèr-jí=ke mm
when-IRR1 POSS-festival(kd)-IRR2=TOP AFF
'When will it be, the Rongker?' [HK, TR 103]

(146) Manner interrogative *kosón*
nesomar pule kosonsi thengpi abeng
ne-oso-màr pu=le **kosón**=si thengpī a-bēng
1EXCL:POSS-child-PL QUOT=FOC:IRR how=FOC:RL tree/wood POSS-piece

nangketetroiroidetlo
nang=ke-tèt-ròi~rói-dèt-lò
CIS=NMLZ-exit-PL.solid.obj~DIST.PL-PFV-RL
'If they are my children, how did they come out as pieces of wood?' [CST, HM 023]

(147) Amount interrogative *ko'án*
si la hemtun isi kaboche along kachari along
sì là hēmtūn isī [ke-boché alòng] [ke-charí alòng]
therefore this good.family one NMLZ-create LOC NMLZ-rule LOC

<so'arlosomar atum> arlosomar atum arpu ko'an do?
<sō'arlosō-mār a-tūm> árlosō-mār a-tūm arpū   **ko'án**
women-PL   POSS-PL woman-PL POSS-PL responsibility how.much
dō
exist
'So with running a family and being in charge, how much responsibility do women have?' [KaR, SWK 026]

Interrogative pronouns and adverbs equally function as noun modifiers, see §10.5.3.1. Further discussion of content questions in the context of other interrogative constructions is presented in §15.1.1.2.

6.1.4.1 Positive indefinite construction with -*nē* 'indefinite'
In positive clauses, interrogative pronouns and adverbs occur with -*nē* 'indefinite (INDEF)' as indefinite pronouns and adverbs: *komāt-nē* 'somebody, anybody', *(ko) pí-nē* 'something, anything', *konát-nē* 'somewhere, anywhere', etc. An example of *komāt-nē* 'somebody, anybody' in a positive clause is (148).

(148) *komāt-nē* 'somebody, anybody'
komatneke... *la ser kapali'et asonsi*
[**komāt-nē=ke** là   sér   ke-pa-lì-èt   asón=si]
who-INDEF=TOP this gold NMLZ-CAUS-flow-RES:yellow like=FOC:RL

acharpen ketheklong langmepik
[[a-chár=pen   ke-theklōng] [làng-mē-pīk]]
POSS-far.away=from NMLZ-see   see-be.good-very
'As if **somebody** had colored it with gold to make it look yellow and shiny, from far away it's very nice to see [...].' [SiT, HF 021]

Indefinite -*nē* also occurs on clauses as it marks complement clauses that represent indirect questions, see §9.7.4 and §15.2.2.2. Based on that construction, -*nē* also marks main clauses in an insubordination construction (§15.4.3).

The negative indefinite construction makes use of a different set of pronominal and adverbial forms, see §6.1.6.

6.1.4.2 Interrogative pronouns in indirect questions
In complement clauses functioning as indirect questions (§9.7.4 and §15.2.2.2), interrogative pronouns are often marked by -*tōng* 'indirect interrogative pronoun (INDIR.ITROG)', as in (149).

(149) Interrogative pronoun marked with -tōng 'INDIR.ITRG'
[komāt-**tōng** ke-vàng-nē] nè chiní-nē
who-**INDIR.ITROG** NMLZ-come-INDEF 1EXCL know-NEG
'I don't know who came.' [SiT 090224]

6.1.4.3 Co-relative construction

A co-relative construction consists of two clauses with corresponding elements, which in Karbi are an interrogative and a corresponding demonstrative pronoun. Interrogative pronouns carry the question clitic =ma (see §15.1.1.4.1) to participate in the co-relative construction (§12.7.3.1.4), as shown in (150) and (151). In (150), the =ma marked interrogative pronoun functions as a simple relative pronoun, whereas in (151), it functions as an indefinite or universal relative pronoun 'whoever'.

(150) Relative pronoun construction with konát 'where' + =ma
la kedambom ahut Patkai-College **konatma** kedo
là ke-dàm-bōm ahūt Pátkái-College **konát=mà** ke-dō
this NMLZ-go-CONT during PN **where=Q** NMLZ-stay

lata nangpaklanglo
là=tā nang=pa-klàng-lò
this=ADD 1/2:NSUBJ=CAUS-appear-RL
'While we were going, they also showed us where Patkai College is (lit., where Patkai College is, that they also showed us).' [SiT, HF 011]

(151) Indefinite relative pronoun construction with komāt 'who' + =ma
lasi laso ahonjeng **komatma** keteroiun
lasì lasō a-honjèng **komāt=ma** ke-teròi-ùn
therefore this POSS-thread **who=Q** NMLZ-walk.cautiously-be.able

labangke ahoklo
labàng=ke a-hōk-lò
this=TOP POSS-truth-RL
'Therefore, whoever can walk over this thread, that one is true.' [CST, HM 096]

6.1.5 Parallelism between demonstrative and interrogative adverbs

Table 71 gives an overview of words with corresponding demonstrative (lá / há(la)) and interrogative (ko) roots (see also Grüßner (1978: 87)).

Table 71: Corresponding demonstratives and interrogatives.

Function	Demonstrative	Interrogative	Other morpheme
Manner	*lasón, lapù, lapusón*	*kosón, kolosón, kopù*	*asón* 'like', *?pù* 'say / quotative"
Place	*ladāk*	*kodāk*	*dāk* 'here'
	háladāk ~ hádāk		
	lapúnatthū (<lapú anatthū)[a]	*konát*	*natthu* 'direction, towards'
Amount	*la'án*	*ko'án*	*án* 'this much; all'

[a] Grüßner (1978: 87) also reports *là-nát* 'over here' and *há-nát* 'over there'.

6.1.6 Pronouns and pro-adverbs of universal quantification

The pronouns and adverbs of universal quantification, which are all used in the negative indefinite construction ('nobody', 'nothing', etc.), are listed in Table 72 (for information on the positive indefinite construction, see §6.1.4.1). Some forms may also occur in positive clauses (i.e., as 'all', 'everything', etc.) as indicated in the table.

Table 72: Pronouns of universal quantification.

Semantic field	Form of pronoun	Gloss	Origin	Positive / negative polarity
PERSON	*badu=tā*	'anybody'		negative only
	majok=tā			
	bangpak=tā		*bàng* 'somebody' + *?pak*	
	kadokavē=tā	'everybody'	*?ke-dō k-avē* 'NMLZ-exist NMLZ-not.exist'	positive/ negative
THING	*aját=tā*	'anything'	*ját* 'type(<Ind)'	
	tháng=tā			
PLACE	*nahók=ta*	'anywhere'		
TIME	*kái(ke)=ta*	'always'	*kái* 'time(<Ind)'	

Unlike many Tibeto-Burman languages, Karbi does not use interrogative pronouns in negative indefinite constructions. Karbi is a typical Tibeto-Burman language though in employing the additive particle to indicate universal quantification (see §10.8.3.1.5). The negative indefinite construction thus consists of a pronoun or adverb of universal quantification marked by additive =tā, followed by a negated verb, as in (152) and (153).[64]

(152) *aját=tā* 'anything' in negative polarity clause
*[...] halake **ajatta** van'un'elo, ajirpo abangke [...]*
hála=ke   **a-ját=tā**   vàn-ūn-**Cē**-lò   [a-jirpò   abàng=ke]
that=TOP **POSS-TYPE=ADD** bring-be.able-**NEG**-RL POSS-friend NPDL=TOP
'[...] [T]hat one didn't manage to carry anything, his friend [...].' [HK, TR 196]

(153) *tháng=tā* 'anything' in negative polarity clause
***thangta** kali [...]*
[**tháng=tā**   kalī]
anything=ADD NEG.EQU.COP
'It's nothing [...].' [SeT, MTN 016]

Examples of the positive indefinite construction are (154) and (155). Note that in (154), it is not directly the additive particle that attaches to *nahōk(=pen)*, but the longer form *setāmē*.

(154) *nahōk* 'anywhere' in positive polarity clause
*"ne **nahokpen** setame... e ne nechor*
nè   [**nahōk**=pen   setāmē]   e   nè   ne-chór
1EXCL   **anywhere**=from nevertheless DSM   1EXCL   1EXCL:POSS-spouse

chirithupo" pu anke [...]
che-rī-thū-pò   pu   ánke
RR-search-again-IRR1   QUOT   and.then
'"From anywhere, I will find a wife again" (he thought), and then [...].' [CST, RO 009]

(155) *kadókavē* 'anybody' in positive polarity clause
*[...] ilitum abangke **kadokave'anta** laso ahan a'an*
[e-li-tūm   abàng=ke   **kadókavē**-án=tā] [lasō   a-hán   a-àn]
1INCL-HON-PL   NPDL=TOP   **anybody**-all=ADD this   POSS-curry   POSS-rice

ilitum chohorpensi ilitum cholongji
e-li-tūm   cho-hōr-pen-si   e-li-tūm   chō-lōng-jí
1INCL-HON-PL   AUTO.BEN/MAL-serve.food-NF-NF:RL   1INCL-HON-PL   eat-GET-IRR2
'[...] [W]e all get to serve for ourselves and eat.' [SiH, CW 015]

---

64 Post (2007: 618) calls the analogous construction in Galo the "Dismissive" construction.

6.2 Verb subclasses

Besides the main subclass of verbs denoting actions, states, processes, etc., the second-largest subclass of verbs are property concept terms (§4.2). While verbs can be roughly divided into intransitives, transitives, and ditransitives, these are not salient emic categories of Karbi verbs. One way to group verbs into subclasses is to compile lists of all those that may occur with a particular predicate derivation suffix (§9.2), since many predicate derivations tend to not be fully productive. An example is the predicate derivation -chèk 'firmly', which occurs with the following verbs: kòk 'tie', nèp 'catch', ót 'touch, hold', and thít 'tie'. In a sense then, semantically rich predicate derivations classify verbs the same way classifiers classify nouns. There is also a sense in which less semantically rich verb morphology classifies verbs. For example, cho- 'auto-benefactive/malefactive' only occurs with certain verbs (while, for example, che- 'reflexive/reciprocal' appears to occur with any verb). While these are all possible ways of subdividing the large class of verbs, there do not appear to be several different morphosyntactic tests that would converge on a particular subclassification of verbs. I therefore limit myself here to only one subsection on copulas.

6.2.1 Property concept terms

The argument for considering property concept terms a subclass of verbs is presented in §4.2 above.

6.2.2 Copulas

Sections §6.2.2.1 and §6.2.2.2 discuss existential/locative copular forms and the negative equational copula, respectively. Copulas are verbs in Karbi as they can take the nominalizer ke- (§4.1.1).

6.2.2.1 Existential and locative copulas
In addition to a basic existential and locative copula (§6.2.2.1.1), Karbi also has an additional copula óng with a quantifying function (§6.2.2.1.2).

6.2.2.1.1 Positive dō and negative avē
The positive form of the basic existential/locative copula dō occurs in existential constructions, as typically found at the beginning of stories, for example in (156).

(156)　Existential function of *dō* for introduction of characters in stories
　　　hako ahut hedi, Bey atum korte bangkethom do tangho
　　　[hakó　　　ahūt　　hedī]　[Bēy　a-tūm]　[kortè　bàng-kethòm]　　**dō**
　　　that.time　during　EMPH　CLAN　POSS-PL　brother　CLF:HUM:PL-three　exist
　　　tànghò
　　　REP
　　　'In the old days, you know, there were three Bey brothers, they say.' [WR, BCS 001]

An example of the locative function of *dō* is (157). It is taken from a real-time narration of the pear story, where 'that man' is the same man that the video clip starts with, i.e., this use of *dō* does not have an existential sense ('there is a man high up in the tree'), but clearly a locational sense ('that man is located high up (in the tree)').

(157)　Locative function of *dō*
　　　amonit abangke angsongsi do
　　　a-monít　　abàng=ke　angsóng=si　　**dō**
　　　POSS-man　NPDL=TOP　high.up=FOC:RL　exist
　　　'[...] [T]hat man (who is picking the fruit) is up high (in the tree).' [SiT, PS 017]

The existential/locative copula *dō* is also the verb used in the possessive construction (see §13.2.2.3.2 and §13.2.2.4), which typically contains a topic =*ke* marked possessor, a possessed noun as S argument, and the copula, as in (158).

(158)　*dō* in possessive construction
　　　[...] nangke nangdin dolang
　　　nàng=ke　nang-dín　　　　　　**dō-làng**
　　　you=TOP　2:POSS-day(<Asm)　exist-still
　　　'[...] "You still have your life (to live)."' [KK, BMS 084]

Surprisingly, there are some data that suggest that *dō* may additionally function as an equational copula. One type of data is a construction that nominalizes the main verb and adds *dō* 'exist', as shown in (159) (see §12.7.1).

(159)　*dō* 'exist' in nominalization construction
　　　[...] kechungkreng dolo, marjeng dolo, lok'hu dolo, lokphlep dolo;
　　　[ke-chungkrèng　**dō-lò]**　　[marjèng　**dō-lò]**　　[lòk'hù　**dō-lò]**　　[lòkphlèp
　　　NMLZ-be.thin　　exist-RL　　be.thin　　exist-RL　　be.pale　exist-RL　be.pale
　　　dō-lò]
　　　exist-RL

kithita kedothupo, kejangta
[ke-thì=tā   ke-**dō**-thū-pò]   [ke-jāng=tā
NMLZ-die=ADD   NMLZ-**exist**-again-IRR1   NMLZ-hang.down= ADD

kedothupo
ke-**dō**-thū-pò]
NMLZ-**exist**-again-IRR1
'[...] [T]hey became thin, they became pale, and they were about to die.' [CST, RO 022]

A different example is (160), where it seems virtually impossible to analyze *dō* as anything but an equational copula that links two arguments: *so'arlo atumsi* 'the women' and *keklem abang* 'the working ones'.

(160) *dō* 'exist' apparently functioning as an equational copula
so'arlo atumsi keklem abang dopo
[[sō'arlō   a-tūm=si]   [ke-klém a-bàng]   dō-pò]
women:COLL   POSS-PL=FOC:RL   NMLZ-DO POSS-CLF:HUM:PL   exist-IRR1

pinso atum abangke osomarpen chelemrong
[[pinsō   a-tūm   abàng=ke] osō-mār=pen   che-lém-ròng
married.man   POSS-PL   NPDL=TOP   child-PL=with   RR-play.with.toys-instead

titi; lason arjulonghe
titī]   [lasón   arjū-lōng=he]
always   that.way   hear-GET=AFTERTHOUGHT
'[...] [T]he women would be the working ones, the men would always play with the children instead, this is actually what I've heard.' [KaR, SWK 071]

It is very unexpected to find *dō* apparently functioning as an equational copula. Combining the functions of an existential and a locative copula is very typical in Tibeto-Burman languages, but equational clauses usually have a very different structure. Often, they just consist of simple juxtaposition of the two NPs, as is the case in Karbi in most instances as well.

The lexical origin of the copula, i.e., *dō* 'stay, reside', is homophonous with the copula, although the grammatical difference between the lexical verb and the copula surfaces in negated forms. Whereas the lexical verb takes the regular verbal quasi-reduplicative negative suffix (i.e., *dō-dē*), the copula has a suppletive negative form, *avē*.[65] Examples (161) and (162) show *avē* in the locative function and in the possessive construction.

---

[65] There may be other formal/phonological differences that exist despite the surface homophony. For example, it appears that there is a stress/prominence difference between *dō-làng* meaning either

(161) *avē* with locative function
thondamtilo anke halaso aKarbipi ahem
[thòn-dām-tí-lò   ánke]   [[hálasō   a-Karbì-pī]   a-hēm
drop-go-get.rid.off-RL   and.then that   POSS-PN-fem   POSS-house

nangchevanglo ja'e along nangchelanglo asomar ave
nang=che-vāng-lò]   ja'ē   alòng   nang=che-lāng-lò]   [a-oso-màr   **avē**]
CIS=RR-come-RL   cradle LOC   1/2:NSUBJ=RR-see-RL POSS-child-PL not.exist
'(The witch) abandoned (the children there), and then the Karbi woman came home, she looked in the cradle, her children were not there.' [CST, HM 015]

(162) *avē* 'not.exist' in possessive construction
[...] amat neta neri ave nekeng ave [...]
amāt   nè=tā   ne-rí   **avē**   ne-kèng   **avē**
and.then   1EXCL=ADD   1EXCL:POSS-hand not.exist   1EXCL:POSS-foot   not.exist
'[...] [A]nd then also, I don't have hands or feet [...].' [RBT, ChM 030]

Note that *dō* as an existential copula has apparent cognates in other Tibeto-Burman languages, such as *doŋ* in Boro (DeLancey and Boro in preparation), or presumably Proto-Tani **doŋ* 'lie down; exist' (Sun 1993; Post 2007). The negative form *avē* is interesting because it contains another widespread copular form in Tibeto-Burman, *ve* (a reflex of what Matisoff (2003: 221–2) reconstructs as PTB **way*), presumably with a negative *a-* prefix. There are both "Kuki-Chin" and "Naga" languages that have apparent reflexes of PTB **way*. Among "Naga" languages, Tenyidie (Angami) has a verbal suffix *-wē*, which "every verbal form that contains a direct statement usually ends with", and which appears to have a clear copula use in the example *mā-po-wē* '(I) am a man (of such and such a village)' where *mā po* means 'man' (Hutton 1921: 305–6).[66] Matisoff (2003: 221) also suggests that a genitive particle *wui* in Tangkhul is a reflex of **way*. Among "Kuki-Chin" languages, there is a *ve* existential copula in Daai Chin; interestingly, Daai Chin also has a preverbal *am* negative marker (So-Hartmann 2009: 213). Negative /a-/ prefixes are also found elsewhere in Tibeto-Burman (DeLancey 2014: 26), such as the Northern Naga language Chang (Coupe 2014) or in Tamangic although the prefixes there reconstruct to **ha-* in Proto-Tamangic (Noonan 2011).

In the Plains (Amri) Karbi dialect, instead of the negated form *avē*, a different form *ingjong* is used, while the positive form *dō* is the same. It is unclear what the

---

'there still is (more of something)' or 'still staying/living (somewhere)'. For the copula, the stress appears to be shifted to the suffix, whereas for the lexical verb, there is more prominence on the root, as is the case with other lexical roots when they take *-làng* 'still'. This looks like ongoing grammaticalization of the copula, but more research is required to provide clear evidence.

66 Surprisingly, no such suffix is reported in the recent grammatical description of Tenyidie by Kuolie (2006).

etymology of the root, i.e., the second syllable of *ingjong* could be. What is interesting, however, is that the first syllable is the frozen *ing-* prefix, which in the Karbi song language typically is replaced by *ma-* (see §6.3.1), and *ma* is in fact a very widespread Tibeto-Burman negative marker that has also been reconstructed to Proto-Tibeto-Burman.

6.2.2.1.2 Quantifying copula *óng* 'exist much'

Karbi also has a quantifying existential copula *óng*, as shown in (163) and (164). It is not clear whether *óng* also participates in locative or possessive constructions the way *dō* and *avē* do.

(163) Quantifying existential copula *óng* 'exist much'
 *ha nangkelelesi **ke'onglang** {mm}*
 há nang=ke-lè-Cē=si ke-**óng**-làng mm
 over.there CIS=NMLZ-reach-NEG=FOC:RL NMLZ-**exist.much**-still AFF
 'Over there still many of them haven't reached.' [HK, TR 183]

(164) Quantifying existential copula *óng* 'exist much'
 *parok-jangphongke penang'an **ong***
 parókjàngphòng=ke penáng-án **óng**
 pineapple=TOP a.lot-that.much **exist.much**
 'There were many pineapples.' [SiT, HF 015]

The *óng* copula has also grammaticalized to a verbal suffix *-óng* (9.2.5.1) with the meaning 'too much, many'. An apparent cognate of *óng* is Daai Chin *to:ng* 'too much' (So-Hartmann 2009: 157).

6.2.2.2 Negative equational copula *kalī*

The negative equational copula is *kalī*. It is most frequently used when predicate nominals are negated, as in (165), or when negating nominalized verbs (although the verbal negation strategy, i.e., the onset reduplicating suffix *-Cē*, may also be used).

(165) Negative equational copula *kalī*
 ai nesomarlole laho theng beng
 ái [ne-oso-màr-lò=le laho] [thēng bēng
 how.strange! 1EXCL:POSS-child-PL-RL=FOC:IRR EXCLM firewood piece

kalilo nesomarlole laho
kalī-lò]   [ne-oso-màr-lò=le   laho]
NEG.EQU.COP-RL   1EXCL:POSS-child-PL-RL=FOC:IRR   EXCLAM
'How strange, they are my children! They are not pieces of wood anymore, they are my children!' [CST, HM 082]

Etymologically, *kalī* likely consists of a negation morpheme represented by the first, velar-initial syllable, and a copular element represented by the second, lateral-initial syllable. Evidence for this analysis comes from a number of apparent cognates of both historical morphemes. Velar-initial negatives occur in the reconstructed Bodo-Garo negative existential copula (Wood 2008: 92) and in the Daai Chin ("Kuki-Chin") prohibitive (So-Hartmann 2009: 306). The lateral-initial copular element is likely cognate with the Meitei progressive suffix -*li* (Chelliah 1997: 239).

There is no positive equational copula. Instead, nouns typically act as predicates by themselves (see §4.3). However, what sometimes appears to act as an assertive counterpart to *kalī* is the realis marker -*lò*, as in (166).

(166) Realis -*lò* as assertive counterpart to negative equational copula
       kalī netumke arlengpi asolone kaline
       ne-tūm=ke   arlēng-pī   **a-sō-lò-nē**   **kalī-nē**
       1EXCL:POSS-PL=TOP person-female   POSS-child-RL-INDEF   NEG.EQU.COP-INDEF
       'Whether we are the children of the Karbi woman or not (we don't know).' [CST, HM 087]

6.3 Frozen prefixes in disyllabic verb and noun roots

Karbi has a large number of disyllabic roots with either *ing*- or *ar*- as their first syllable. Among them, there are both verb and noun roots. In compounds, *ing*- or *ar*- are dropped (see §7.2.1).

6.3.1 Frozen prefix *ing*-

The frozen prefix *ing*- is quite clearly a reflex of a Proto-Tibeto-Burman nasal prefix *m- (Benedict 1972; Matisoff 2003: 117ff.). There is an abundance of cognates that show the regular correspondence between the *ing*- prefix and descendants of *m- in other Tibeto-Burman languages. A neat piece of evidence appears to come from the Karbi song language (§1.1.3.3), which in a considerable number of cases has *ma-* instead of *ing-* (Grüßner 1978: 43).[67, 68]

On verbs, *ing-* has been suggested to have an intransitive or medial function (Grüßner 1978: 42), which is also the proposal for the function of PTB **m-* (also including related functions such as "durative" and "reflexive") (Benedict 1972: 117ff.; Matisoff 2003: 117ff.).[69] Benedict furthermore suggests that **m-* on verbs is the same element as the **m-* that occurs on nouns (p. 118), where the function on nouns has to do with inalienable possession, as evidenced by their occurrence on body part or kinship terms.

In modern Karbi, a number of verb and noun roots with *ing-* fit this account: there are a number of *ing-* verb roots with intransitive[70] or medial function, and there are a number of *ing-* noun roots which represent body part and kinship terms. These are recorded in the above mentioned sources, and Grüßner additionally lists nine *ing-* roots with corresponding *ing-*less monosyllabic counterparts. Examples of *ing-* in intransitive and medial verbs include *inglàng* 'to float' (perhaps related to *làng* 'water'), *inglók* 'to break (intransitive)' (compared to *lók* 'to break (transitive)'), and *ingplòng* 'to run (animals), gallop'. Other examples that could be added in support of the hypothesis that /ing/ in Karbi still retains a semantic association with middle voice and intransitivity are *ingthàng* 'to dawn', *ingrí* 'to get intoxicated', *ingjír* 'to dissolve', *ingjàr* 'to fly', *ingjàng* 'to look proper, well prepared', *ingchìr* 'be hungry', or *inghōn* 'to love', among others.

There are, however, plenty of other *ing-* roots that do not obviously fit in, or even have opposite functions. Nouns that are not body/kinship terms or otherwise understandable as a part of a whole include, for example, *inghàn* 'mud', *ingkī* 'silkworm', *ingkòi* 'twenty', *inglóng* 'hill', *ingnām* 'forest', *ingnàr* 'elephant', *ingrī* 'species of grass', *ingthēk* 'sign', *ingtí* 'salt', or *ingtòng* 'big bamboo basket'. Sample *ing-* verbs that are problematic for a synchronic intransitivity account include *ingdōi* 'push', *inghór* 'carry a load', *ingpú* 'open (something)', *ingsìr* 'separate', *ingthùm* 'go and bring', or *ingthùr* 'wake (somebody) up'. This last root *ingthùr* is particularly problematic, because it has a monosyllabic counterpart *thùr*, which has the intransitive sense of 'wake up', and thus is opposite to the suggested pattern.

---

67 According to Grüßner, this is only the case in verb roots. The examples he gives are *ingrèng ~ marèng* 'call (small animals)', *ingtìng ~ matìng* 'be dark', and *ingnìm ~ manìm* 'smell'.
68 Although I assume that the *ma-* is inherited, the possibility that the *ma-* is borrowed should not be entirely ruled out. I am grateful to Pattie Epps (p.c.) for pointing this out.
69 Matisoff (2003: 117) further assumes that the semantics of this prefix as it goes on verbs have to do with signaling "inner-directed states or actions, including 'middle voice' notions like stativity, intransitivity, durativity, reflexivity".
70 Note that Daai Chin (Southern 'Kuki-Chin') still has a productive intransitive velar nasal *ng-* prefix with reciprocal and reflexive functions (So-Hartmann 2009: 202ff.).

6.3.2 Frozen prefix *ar-*

The frozen prefix *ar-* is the other highly frequent element besides *ing-* in Karbi. It is a reflex of a Proto-Tibeto-Burman *r-* prefix (Wolfenden 1929: 43–4; Benedict 1972: 109; Matisoff 2003: 127). Although Wolfenden suggests *r-* is a "directive" prefix, Benedict and Matisoff remain agnostic about its function. Likewise in Karbi it appears impossible to find anything all the noun and verb roots with *ar-* have in common.

Note that as with *ing-*, the *ar-* prefix has a different form in the Karbi song language, where it changes to *ra-* or *ru-*, as in the pairs *arnàm ~ rinàm* 'god' and *arvè ~ ruvè* 'rain' (Grüßner 1978: 43).

6.3.3 Other possible frozen prefixes in disyllabic noun and verb roots

In addition to *ing-* and *ar-*, Grüßner (1978: 43) reports *tV-*, *the-*, *pi-*, *phe-*, *se-*, and *he-* as possible frozen prefixes that occur as the first syllable in disyllabic noun and verb roots.

6.4 Minor word classes

Minor word classes discussed here include adverbs, numerals, as well as subordinators and coordinators. Discourse-based minor word classes such as particles, discourse connectors, and interjections are discussed in Chapter 14.

6.4.1 Adverbs

While there is not a morphosyntactically coherent word class of adverbs in Karbi, the subsections below discuss some of the common lexical items that function as adverbs.

Adverbs provide extra information to a unit of utterance. The Karbi adverbs presented in the subsections below all have clausal scope. Adverbial modification of verbs rather than clauses is expressed either via suffixes (predicate derivations; see §9.2), or in adverb predication constructions (§11.3).

The framing function of adverbs with clausal scope may be made more salient by using the topicalization construction, which adds the topic enclitic =*ke* while the respective element occurs clause-initially (although several elements can occur in the topicalization construction, as a consequence of which they are stacked at the beginning of the clause), see §14.2.1.

6.4.1.1 Temporal adverbs

6.4.1.1.1 Day and year ordinals

A list of day ordinals with respective forms for the day as a whole, only the morning, and only the evening/night are given in Table 73.

Table 73: Day ordinals.

	Whole day	Morning	Evening/Night
<3 days before today	tumidik isī	tumidik isi adap	tumidik isi arni aningve(thu)
<2 days before today	tumidik	tumidik adap	tumidik aningve(thu)
<Yesterday	(pa)tumì	timidap	tovē, tumi (a)ningve(thu)
Today	pinì	padàp, todap	peningve, moningve
>Tomorrow	penàp	penapdap, moning adap	penap (a)ningve(thu)
>2 days after today	penapdik	penapdik adap	penapdik (a)ningve(thu)
>3 days after today	penapdik isī	penapdik isi adap	penapdik isi (a)ningve(thu)

Note that unique expressions for 'whole day' terms are limited to today, tomorrow, and yesterday. For two days into the future or past, the suffix *-dik* is added, while further days into the future or past just add the independent numerals that count how many more days are added (*isī* for 'one'). The 'morning' terms all have the word *dáp* 'morning' in them: as compounds in terms for 'tomorrow' and 'yesterday', in a syntactic possessive construction for further days into the future or past, and only the word for 'this morning' has just a prefix along with *dáp* 'morning'. The 'evening/night' terms pattern the same as the 'morning' terms except for *tovē* 'last night', which also has a simple disyllabic stem that consists of a prefix along with the second syllable of *ningvē* 'evening/night' (in fact, this form is even more reduced than the forms for 'tonight': *peningve, moningve*).

In order to compare the prefixes, consider Table 74, which also includes terms for year ordinals.

Table 74: Year and day ordinals.

	Year	Day	Morning	Evening/Night
<1 before	**chu**-ning	(**pa**-)**tu**-mì	**ti**-mi-dap	**to**-vē, tu-mi (a)ningve(thu)
Present	**pe**-ning	**pi**-nì	**pa**-dàp, **to**-dap	**pe**-ningve, **mo**-ningve
>1 after	**mo**-ning	**pe**-nàp	**pe**-nap-dap, **mo**-ning adap	**pe**-nap (a)ningve(thu)

What is quite striking is that although we get three basic prefixes: *pV-*, *tV-*, and *mo-* (ignoring *chu-*, which only occurs in the form for 'last year'), they do not align the way we might have expected. The form *pV-*[71] occurs in all 'present' ordinals, but it additionally occurs in the elongated expression *patumi* 'yesterday' as well as in *penàp* 'tomorrow'. The form *tV-* occurs in all '1 before' ordinals (except for 'last year'), but additionally also in *todap* 'this morning'. Finally, *mo-* occurs in '1 after' forms as well as in *mo-ningvē* 'tonight'. A reasonable hypothesis to explain two of the unexpected forms, *todap* 'this morning' and *mo-ningvē* 'tonight', is that they are typically used around midday, when 'this morning' is in the past and 'tonight' in the future, which would explain the *tV-* and the *mo-* prefix if we assume they originally mark past and future, respectively. However, this turns out to be not correct. For 'this morning', either *to-dap* or *pa-dap* may be used interchangeably, no matter whether it is 4:00AM and somebody talks about plans to do at 7:00AM, or if it is already 4:00PM, and they talk about something that happened at 7:00AM. The same is apparently true for *pe-ningvē* and *mo-ningvē* for 'tonight', which are used irrespectively of whether the reference is to the past or the future. Nevertheless, it seems likely that this is how the forms originated. We do not know the etymology of *tV-* and therefore do not have independent evidence that it has a past association. But there is further evidence for a 'future' meaning of the *mo-* prefix as we can link it with the temporal deictic *mò*, which has the meaning 'in the future' or 'later on', as in (167).

(167) *mò* 'in the future'
"*te mo pine**pinane**detjima,*
te   mò   pí-nē~**pinā-Cē**-dèt-jí=ma
and.then/therefore future   what-INDEF~**DIST.PL-NEG**-PFV-IRR2=Q

ko jirpo?" pu {mm}
ko   jīrpō   pu   Mm
buddy:VOC friend   QUOT AFF
"'And there won't be anything (any difficulties, problems, dangers) in the future, my friend?'" [HK, TR 140]

The other unexpected forms in Table 74 are the forms for 'today', 'tomorrow', and 'yesterday', in that all three of them contain *pV-*. Here, it looks as if *pV-* was reinterpreted as an element that means 'day' rather than indicating present, past, or future, and that that is the reason why it got extended to the words 'tomorrow' and 'yester-

---

[71] Apparently the same prefix is also found in a spatial context of location near the speaker in the form *parái* 'this side of the river' which apparently historically contrasts with *harái* 'that side of the river' (cf. *há* 'over there', §6.1.3), see the elaborate expression *parái harái* in §16.2.2.1.

day'. I do not know, however, of any comparative evidence for such a root for 'day' in other languages of the region.

6.4.1.1.2 Other underived temporal adverbs
In addition to day and year ordinals, there are a few other temporal adverbs, such as *nón* 'now', *thík* 'right then', or relator nouns that are used as adverbs, such as *aphráng* 'before, earlier' or *aphī* 'later, afterwards' (see §5.4.7.2). Deictic, interrogative, and universal quantifier temporal adverbs are listed in §6.1.3, §6.1.4, and §6.1.6, respectively.

6.4.1.1.3 Temporal adverbs with *-váng* 'every'
There is a subclass of adverbial temporal nouns that take the suffix *-váng* 'every': e.g., *aningkán-váng* 'each year' and *arnì-váng* 'each day'. It is likely that this *-váng* suffix is related to the verb *vàng* 'come', considering functionally similar expressions in, for example, English such as 'in the coming years' to mean 'in future years'. Also note the possibly related verb suffix *-vàng* 'plural:S/A' (§9.2.5.1).

6.4.1.1.4 Intensifier reduplication construction
Example (168) shows that the deictic temporal adverb *hákó* '(at) that time' may be reduplicated as *hákó~kò* for the purpose of intensification.

(168) Reduplication
[...] hakokota so'arlo atumke hem
[hákó~kò=tā   [sō'arlō   a-tūm=ke]   [hēm
that.time~INTENS=ADD   women:COLL   POSS-PL=TOP   house

akam kachoklem ajoine [...]
a-kám]   ke-cho-klém]   a-joiné
POSS-work   NMLZ-AUTO.BEN/MAL-do   POSS-reason
'In the old, old days, because the women had to do the house work [...].'
[KK, CC 009]

6.4.1.2 Locative adverbs
Locative adverbs include *dāk* 'here' (used with interrogative *ko-* and demonstratives *(ha)la-*, see §6.1.5), *arvī* 'left' and *ar'ē* 'right', *hín* 'this side' (also used with interrogative *ko-*), *pú* 'this side'. Locative relator nouns such as *arúm* 'down' or *angsóng* 'high up' also function as locative adverbs (see §5.4.7.2).

6.4.1.3 Other adverbs

Other adverbs, i.e., those with neither temporal nor locative meaning, include *ajátnōn* 'anyway' (with the components *a-* 'POSS', *ját* 'type(<Asm)', *?nón* 'now'); *akelé* 'more' (perhaps from *a-* 'POSS', *ke-* 'NMLZ', *?lè* 'reach'); *abesí* 'more(<Asm)', and furthermore reduplicated forms such as *ménmèn* 'suddenly' and *serhéserhé* 'in.a.hurry'. There are also several words for 'like this', such as *lasón, lapú*, etc. (see §6.1.5).

6.4.2 Numerals

Numerals from 'one' to 'ten' are listed in Table 75. For numerals 'one', 'two', and 'three', there exist bound forms that occur with classifiers (see §5.1). While the bound forms of numerals 'two' and 'three' are suffixes that represent the second syllable of the respective independent forms, the bound form of 'one' is a prefix, and similarly represents the first syllable of the independent form (displaying vowel allophony between /e/~/i/).[72] The forms for 'seven', 'eight', and 'nine' are morphologically complex and are based on addition (in the case of 'seven') or subtraction ('eight' and 'nine').

Table 75: Numerals from 'one' to 'ten'.

Independent form	Gloss	Bound form (if different)	Internal structure
isī	'one'	e- (~ i-)	
hiní	'two'	-ní	
kethòm	'three'	-thōm ~ -thòm	
phlī	'four'		
phō	'five'		
thrōk	'six'		
thrōksí	'seven'		thrōk-sí 'six-one' (addition)
nerkēp	'eight'		ne-r-kēp 'two-R-ten' (subtraction)
sirkēp	'nine'		si-r-kēp 'one-R-ten' (subtraction)
kēp	'ten'		

Particularly the forms of 'eight' and 'nine' are interesting in the Tibeto-Burman context, as this unusual subtractive pattern also exists in Meitei. There the form for 'eight' is

---

[72] Specifically, the underlying form of this prefix is *e-*. The vowel is raised to /i/ if the vowel of the following syllable is a high vowel, e.g. *inut* 'one (person)' from *e-nūt* 'one-CLF:HUM:SG'. This vowel allophony also occurs in other prefixes, see §3.9.2.1.

nipan and has the internal structure *ni* 'two (< *əni*)' + *pan* 'subtract', and similarly the form for 'nine' is *məpan*, which is *mə* 'one (< *əmə*)' + *pan* 'subtract' (Chelliah 1997: 85). Since this is a highly unusual pattern that so far has not been attested in other TB languages, neither genetic inheritance nor parallel innovation are likely explanations, but instead contact is the probable source. How exactly a contact scenario between Karbi and Meitei has to be modeled is, however, currently not clear (§1.3.1).

Table 76 gives a list of numerals over 'ten'. The interesting ones, again (and perhaps unsurprisingly so), are *throknerkep* 'eighty' and *throksirkep* 'ninety'. Their respective internal structures may be interpreted in two different ways, as done by Grüßner and Joseph. According to Grüßner (1978: 64), *throk* "has taken over the function of indicating the 'ten'", as a result of which the words would be parsed as *throk-nerkep* and *throk-sirkep*. This seems a bit bizarre given that *thrōk* is the word for 'six'.

Joseph (2009: 156) offers a different account that tries to hold on to *thrōk* meaning 'six'. In order for that to be the case, he parses *throkne-r-kep* so that the *-ni* 'two' goes with *thrōk*, yielding 'six' plus 'two' times 'ten'. While this is very sensical, for *throksirkep* 'ninety', he has to pose a non-surfacing *-ni* 'two' so that things add up correctly: 'six' plus 'one' plus 'two' times 'ten'. This seems a bit speculative; an alternative is to propose that *throksirkep* was formed in analogy to *throknerkep*.

For the numerals in the teens, *kré-* is prefixed onto independent numerals, i.e., *kré-isī* 'eleven', *kré-hinī* 'twelve', etc. For other double-digit forms (or for counting to

Table 76: Numerals over 'ten'.

In steps of ten	Gloss	Internal structure
kré-	'-teen'	possibly a contraction of *kēp=ra* 'ten-NUM.CONN' (also suggested by Joseph (2009: 156))
ingkói	'twenty'	(< PTB **m-kul*)
thomkēp	'thirty'	*thòm* 'three' + *kēp* 'ten'
phlīkēp	'fourty'	*phlī* 'four' + *kēp* 'ten'
phōkēp	'fifty'	*phō* 'five' + *kēp* 'ten'
thrōkkēp	'sixty'	*thrōk* 'six' + *kēp* 'ten'
throksikep	'seventy'	*thrōksí* 'seven' + *kēp* 'ten'
throknerkep	'eighty'	*thrōk* 'ten(<'six'?)' + *nerkēp* 'eight' (Grüßner 1978: 64) (*thrōk* 'six' + *-ni* 'two') + R + *kēp* 'ten' (Joseph 2009: 156)
throksirkep	'ninety'	*thrōk* 'ten(<'six'?)' + *sirkēp* 'nine' (Grüßner 1978: 64) *thrōk* 'six' + *-si* 'one' [+ *-ni* 'two'] + R + *kēp* 'ten' (Joseph 2009: 156)
pharó	'hundred'	
surí	'thousand'	

even higher numbers with more than two digits), =ra is used as a connecting element, e.g., *ingkoi=ra isī* 'twenty-one', *ingkoi=ra hiní* 'twenty-two', etc. An example of a more complex form is given in (169).

(169) Complex numeral word
[[[*pharó   kré-sirkēp=ra]   phlī-kēp=ra]   phlī]   *a-ningkǎn*
  hundred teen-nine=NUM.CONN four-ten=NUM.CONN four   POSS-year
'the year 1944' [SiT, HF 194]

6.4.3 Subordinators and coordinators

Most subordinators have grammaticalized from relator nouns, which is the case for all shown in Table 77; an exception is *sitā~setā* 'although'.[73]

Table 77: Subordinators grammaticalized from relator nouns.

Semantic domain	Form	Gloss
Temporal	*ahūt*	'while, when'
	akó	'when'; 'before' (with NEG)
	aphī	'after'
	aphráng	'before'
Causal	*apōt*	'because'
	ajōk	

A list of coordinators that are currently attested is given in Table 78, along with an indication of whether a particular form coordinates NPs or predicates/clauses. Note that Grüßner (1978: 128) additionally lists as coordinators: *(ko-)pí-má* 'for (causal), therefore', *tháng-bák-má* 'for (causal), therefore', and *jóng(-sí)* 'if(<Asm)'.

Examples of the coordinators listed in Table 78 are given below.

---

[73] *Sitā~setā* 'although' almost certainly is a combination of *-si* 'NF:RL' and *=tā* 'ADD'. See §10.8.3.1.4.

Table 78: Coordinators.

Coordination type	Form	Meaning	Syntactic unit
Conjunctive	=pen	'with'	NP
	lapen	'and'	NP, predicates/clauses
Disjunctive	bá	'or(<Asm)'	NP
	bón(si/se)tā	'but'	predicates /clauses
	màtè	'otherwise, or'	predicates /clauses

(170) =pen 'with' used as an NP coordinator
Rengsopen Onso atemo chethannang pulo [...]
[Réngsō=**pen** Ōnsō] a-temó che-thán-nāng pù-lò
NAME=with NAME POSS-story RR-tell-HORT say-RL
'"Let's tell each other the story of Rengso and Onso!"' [...]' [CST, RO 002]

(171) *lapèn* 'and' coordinating clauses
dondon chedonsi... anke amonit abang
[dondón che-dón-si...] [ánke [a-monít abàng]
ladder RR-place.ladder/bridge-NF:RL and.then POSS-man NPDL

<a> pe akelokpen keroi isi ajamborong
[[pé a-ke-lòk=pen ke-ròi isī a-jamboróng
cloth POSS-NMLZ-be.white=with NMLZ-sew one POSS-bag

*arlosi lahai kethap **lapen** arum kevan*
arlō=si] [lahái] ke-thàp]] **lapèn** [arúm ke-vàn]]
inside=FOC:RL these NMLZ-put.inside and down NMLZ-bring
'He has placed himself a ladder... and then, the man, into one bag sown from white cloth he puts these (fruits), and then brings them down.' [SiT, PS 003]

(172) *bá* 'or(<Asm)' coordinating NPs
ako ingti tharmit ba birik jokjite, jokpo
akó ingtí tharmìt **bá** bírík jòk-jí-tē, jòk-pò
then salt turmeric or(<Asm) chili add-IRR2-if add-IRR1
'Then if you want to add salt, turmeric, or chili, you should add those.' [PI, BPR 005]

(173) *bóntā* 'but' coordinating clauses inside same intonation unit
lapenke... phatang along thesere thaplelo... **bonta** *isi*
lapèn=ke... phatáng alòng theseré thàp-lè-lò... **bóntā**
and.then=TOP kd.basket LOC fruits put.inside-again-RL **but**
isī
one

aphatang along thesere chetheklongledetlo
a-phatáng alòng theseré che-thēklōng-Cē-dèt-lò
POSS-kd.basket LOC fruits RR-see-NEG-PFT-RL
'And then, he again put (more) fruit in the baskets, but in one basket he didn't see any fruit.' [SiT, PS 044]

(174) *màtè* 'otherwise, or' coordinating clauses
lapen latum haladak... la botor bokan areng
lapèn là-tūm háladāk [la botór bokán a-rèng
and.then this-PL there this climate(<Asm) EE:botór POSS-skin

kelok alampenke climate pulo laso
ke-lòk a-lám=pen=ke climate pù-lò lasō
NMLZ-be.white POSS-language=with=TOP climate(<Eng) say-RL this

kemesen apotlone mate la Naka
ke-mē-sén a-pōt-lò-nē] **màtè** [là Naká
NMLZ-be.good-INTENS POSS-reason-RL-INDEF **otherwise** this TRIBE

atum aphan ketheklongpen akele aning
a-tūm aphān ke-thēklōng-pèn] [akelé a-nīng
POSS-PL NSUBJ NMLZ-see-NF more.than.expected POSS-mind

kangsampik apotlone
ke-ingsām-pīk] a-pōt-lò-nē
NMLZ-be.cold-very POSS-reason-RL-INDEF
'And then, they... maybe the reason was that the *botor bokan*, 'climate' in English (lit., the white skins' language), was good or the reason was seeing the Nagas, (but) everybody was exceedingly happy.' [SiT, HF 036]

7 Nominal morphology

This chapter discusses nominal word formation. There are very few morphological constructions that Karbi nouns may occur in. Cross-linguistically common categories of productive nominal morphology such as role (or case) marking and plural do not exist as such: While there are two role markers (i.e., -phān, §14.1.2, and -lòng, §14.1.3), as well as a plural marker (i.e., -tūm, see §10.6), these are syntactic and not morphological constructions. They represent transparent grammaticalizations of the possessive construction, as evidenced by their initial a- (i.e., the possessive/modified a- prefix, see §7.3.1 below as well as §10.3).

Although this chapter only lists a handful of prefixes and a handful of suffixes, there are some additional elements that may modify noun stems (e.g., =pen 'with, from' or =tā 'additive'), which are, however, best considered clitics and therefore discussed in Chapter 9.

This chapter begins with an overview of the morphology of noun stems and noun words (§7.1). Next, two types of compounding are discussed in §7.2. In §7.3 and §7.4, an overview of nominal prefixes and nominal suffixes, respectively, is offered. Lastly, §7.5 briefly discusses functions of noun stem reduplicative morphology.

7.1 Overview: Noun stems and noun words

Nouns are morphologically not very complex in Karbi. There are only two derivational suffix slots and one inflectional prefix slot.

Generally, a root can function as a stem without being modified and can function as a word without being modified. However, a noun stem can also be complex: it can be a compound (§7.2) or it can carry a derivational suffix. Nominal derivational suffixes are not frequent in the corpus, but the gender/size suffixes -pī and -pō (§7.4.1) may occur in a first suffix slot, and either the human plural suffix -mār (§7.4.4) or a reduplicative suffix (§7.5) may occur in a second suffix slot, as illustrated in (175).[74]

(175) Nominal derivational suffixation
    (a) *sar-pī-mār*   (b) *jīr-pō~pō*
        adult-female-PL   friend-male~DUAL
        'women'   '(two) male friends'

---

[74] It is also possible to add the honorific suffix -lī to nouns that have the human plural suffix -mār, apparently to create vocative forms, see §16.4.1.

Noun stems can function as noun words without additional morphology, but can also occur with one of two prefixes to function as noun words: with the general possessive/modified prefix *a-* (§7.3.1) or with one of the personal possessive prefixes (§7.3.2).

7.2 Compounding

The sections below discuss two types of compounds in Karbi. The first falls under the traditional notion of compounds, where one noun root is combined with either another noun root or a verb root into a new noun stem. The second type is more specific to the South/Southeast Asian context and is a type of 'elaborate expression' construction.

7.2.1 Simple root compounding

New noun stems may be formed by compounding a noun root with another root. Examples of noun-noun and noun-verb compounds are given in Table 79. For further examples of compounds, see Grüßner (1978: 54–5).

Table 79: Noun-noun and noun-verb compounds.

Type	Compound	Meaning	Root 1	Gloss	Root 2	Gloss
N-N	noklāng	'molasses'	nók	'sugarcane'	lāng	'water'
	lōthē	'banana (fruit)'	lō	'banana leaf'	thē	'fruit'
	hēmphū	'house owner'	hēm	'house'	phù	'grandfather'
N-V	mūmdīng	'long-bearded ones, muslims'	ingmūm	'beard'	dīng	'be long'
	phumèn	'elder'	phú	'head'	mèn	'be ripe'
	phulòk	'elder'	phú	'head'	lòk	'be white'
	ànsām	'cold rice'	àn	'rice'	ingsām	'be cold'
	mèthān	'dog'	armē	'tail'	thàn	'to cut'
	pìbā	'cloth to carry baby on back'	pé	'cloth'	bā	'carry baby on back'
	chainōng	'cow'	chài	'mithun' (Grüßner not dated)	nōng	'plow'

Compounds provide evidence for the fact that frozen prefixes such as *ing-* and *ar-* are peripheral to the core semantic part of disyllabic roots, as they get dropped in compounds like *mūm-dīng* (*mūm* < *ingmūm*), *an-sām* (*sām* < *ingsām*), and *me-thān* (*mè* < *armē*). For further examples of this productive process that drops frozen prefixes in compounding (as well as the first syllables of disyllabic roots in other cases), see Grüßner (1978: 35–6).

7.2.2 Higher level elaborate expression compounding

Elaborate expression constructions are characteristic of Karbi discourse. This is generally discussed in §16.2.2; for the same compounding construction in verb stem formation, see §8.1.

Example (176) shows how two compound noun stems *[[àn-bòr] [hán-bòr]]* can be treated as a yet higher-level compound. The evidence consists of the *a-* 'possessive' prefix attaching only once at the beginning of the complex compound.

(176) *àn-bòr hán-bòr* as elaborate expression compound
anbor chipurlo, amethang la apo abang
àn-bòr   che-pūr-lò   a-metháng   [là   a-pō   abàng]
rice-wrapped.bundle RR-open.unfold-RL POSS-self   this   POSS-father NPDL

***a'anbor hanbor** tangte an kelok,*
[[a-àn-bòr]   [hán-bòr]]   tángtē   [àn
POSS-rice-wrapped.bundle   curry-wrapped.bundle   TOP   rice
ke-lòk]
NMLZ-be.white

angthip pura pura ekdom han paka
angthíp   purá   purá   ékdóm   hán   paká
unbroken.rice   all(<Asm)   all(<Asm)   EXCM(<Asm)   curry   very.good(<Ind)
'They opened their rice bundles, and then when the father opened his own rice and curry bundles, all of it was only the white unbroken (=the best) rice, oh so good, very good curry.' [CST, RO 035]

7.3 Nominal prefixes

The following subsections discuss the nominal prefixes of Karbi: the general possessive or 'attributive' prefix *a-*, the set of four personal possessive prefixes (including their systematically derived honorific forms), and the verbalizer *pe-* ~ *pa-*.

7.3.1 General possessive or 'attributive' prefix *a-* 'POSS'

The general possessive or 'attributive' prefix *a-* is the most frequent morpheme in the Karbi corpus. It occurs on nouns that are modified by pre-head elements (but not if modified by post-head elements). As such, it occurs on a head noun if that head noun is modified by a pre-head demonstrative, content question word, possessor noun, or adverbial (§10.5), by a pre-head deverbal modifier (§10.7.1), or by a pre-head classifier or numeral (§10.7.2). The *a-* prefix furthermore marks third person possession (along with *alang(li)-*, see §6.1.1). For a discussion of the diachronic significance of the possessive construction (and, hence, the *a-* prefix) in acting as a source construction for the grammaticalization of new elements, see §10.3.

An example of an *a-* marked noun modified by a preceding demonstrative is *lasō a-jangrēngsō=ke* in (177). Note that in this example, *halaso arni* does not have the *a-* on *arnì* 'day', which, however, is due to the fact that nouns beginning with *ar-* (typically) do not occur with the *a-* prefix for morphophonemic reasons (§3.9.2.1). Another instance of *a-* in this example is on *pōk* 'stomach', where it marks third person possession (in a noun incorporation-type construction, see §11.6.1).

(177)   Possessive *a-* indicating preceding demonstrative
anke halaso arni.... **laso ajangrengsoke**.... apok
ankè   hálasō   arnì   [lasō   **a**-jangrēngsō=ke...].   a-pōk
and.then   that   day   this   **POSS**-orphan=TOP   POSS-stomach

ingchirdukke mati di {mm}
ingchìr-dùk=ke   matì   dī   mm
be.hungry-INTENS=TOP   CG   Q.tag   AFF
'On that day, this orphan was suffering from hunger, wouldn't he have been?'
[HK, TR 010]

Examples (178) and (179) show that a classifier-numeral modifier only triggers the *a-* prefix on its head noun if it precedes its head noun, as in *a-tekè* 'POSS-tiger' in (178), but not if it follows it, as in *vōpī* 'hen' in (179).

(178)   *a-* marked head noun: modified by preceding classifier-numeral word
hu arni kangsam apor abangke {mm}
hú   arnì   ke-ingsām   a-pór   abàng=ke   {mm}
then.later   sun   NMLZ-be.cold   POSS-time   NPDL=TOP   AFF

***ejon ateke** konatpenlone vanglo tangho {mm}*
[**e-jōn**   **a-tekè**]   konát=pen=lo-nē   vàng-lò   tànghò   mm
one-CLF:animal   POSS-tiger   where=from=FOC-INDEF   come-RL   REP   AFF
'Then, at the time when the sun was becoming cold (i.e. just before sunset)... one tiger appeared out of nowhere.' [HK, TR 030]

(179) Unmarked head noun: modified by following classifier-numeral word
[...] *ningveke elitumta e vopi ejon*
ningvē=ke   e-li-tūm=tā   e   **[vō-pī   e-jōn]**
evening=TOP 1PL.INCL-HON- PL=ADD DSM   chicken-female one-CLF:animal

chothatnang pulo [...]
cho-thāt-nāng]   pù-lò]
AUTO.BEN/MAL-slaughter-HORT   say-RL
'"[...] [L]et's kill ourselves one hen tonight", he said [...].' [SeT, MTN 007]

Karbi *a-* is generally considered a reflex of Proto-Tibeto-Burman **a-* (Wolfenden 1929; Benedict 1972; Matisoff 2003). Note that the Karbi possessive construction [N$_{POSR}$] [**a-**N$_{POSD}$], which marks the possessed item while leaving the possessor unmarked, has parallels in Bahing (Kiranti), Lepcha, Aimol (Kuki-Chin), and in Burmese and Lahu (both Lolo-Burmese), where the identical construction [N$_{POSR}$] [**a-**N$_{POSD}$] is found (Benedict 1972: 121; Matisoff 2003: 106).[75] In addition to these languages, Meitei also has a cognate *ə-* prefix, which Chelliah (1997: 86) calls the "attributive derivational prefix"; it attaches to "verbal nouns" to derive adjectives.

Besides the possessive/attributive and third person possessive marking functions shown above, there are other occurrences of *a-* that require a different explanation. One set of occurrences is exemplified by (180), where *ingnàr* 'elephant' is marked with *a-* without there being a modifier and without *a-* indicating third person possession. The reason why *a-* is used here is that this is a reduction of *lasō a-ngnàr* 'this POSS-elephant' according to my consultants, who explain that this kind of reduction occurs as part of regular colloquial speech. Remember that a noun is regularly marked possessive via *a-* if modified by a demonstrative.

(180) *a-* in *angnar* from *laso angnar*
angnarta kangrong ajat <ku> turthap turphrulo [...]
a-ingnàr=tā   ke-ingròng   aját   túr-tháp   túr-phrú-lò
POSS-elephant=ADD   NMLZ-roar   GENEX kick-mindlessly kick-EE:tháp-RL
'This elephant was roaring and everything and kicked around mindlessly [...].'
[RBT, ChM 025]

Another set of occurrences of *a-* is represented by *akibisi* 'the youngest one' in (181). I follow Grüßner (1978: 52) in hypothesizing that *a-* is used here in order to mark this deverbal form more clearly as a referent (i.e., noun) as opposed to a modifier (which

---

[75] Benedict gives the Aimol example *rul ə-rmai* 'snake POSS-tail', which is cognate in all three elements with the same NP in Karbi: *phurūi **a-armē*** 'snake POSS-tail', and the Bahing examples "*biŋ əta-mi* 'calf' (cow its-child), *byar əpwaku* 'sugar-cane' (cane its-juice)."

is also marked by the nominalizer *ke-*, see §4.3). In Grüßner's terms, "due to the generally referring function [of *a*-], this prefix is used to form abstract nouns from gerunds [i.e., nominalizations via *ke*-]" (my translation).

(181)   *a-* in *akibisi* to perhaps indicate referentiality
   latumke **akibisi** *atumlo [...]*
   [la-tūm=ke   **a**-ke-bī-sí   a-tūm-lò]
   this-PL=TOP **POSS**-NMLZ-be.small-SPLT   POSS-PL-RL
   'They were (the children/descendants of) the youngest [...].' [WR, BCS 027]

Possibly the same type of occurrence of *a-* on property concept terms (PCTs) is also frequently found when the PCT acts as a preposed modifier, as in (182) (for a discussion of preposed PCT modifiers, see §10.7.1.2). The reason why this may be the same type of occurrence of *a-* is because in this case of preposed PCT modification, the underlying construction may be a possessive construction (§10.5.2), in which the preposed PCT modifier is nominalized in order to act as the (nominal) possessor or modifier.

(182)   Pre-head PCT-based modifier *mī* 'be new', marked with *a-ke-* 'POSS-NMLZ-'
   lasonthotsi Lindata ketheklongpen aning kerong,
   [lasón-thót=si   Líndá=tā ke-theklōng-pèn] [a-nīng   ke-aróng]]
   that.way-exactly=FOC:RL PN=ADD   NMLZ-see-NF   POSS-mind NMLZ-be.happy

   akimi ahormulo, *amonit atum aphanta theklonglo*
   [a-ke-mī   **a-hormú-lò**]   a-monít   a-tūm   aphān=tā
   POSS-NMLZ-be.new   **POSS-thing-RL**   POSS-man   POSS-PL   NSUBJ=ADD
   theklōng-lòk-lò
   see-happen.to-RL
   'Seeing exactly this, Linda was happy, it was a new thing, she also got to see the people.' [SH, CSM 035]

7.3.2 Personal possessive prefixes

Personal possessive prefixes are discussed along with the independent pronouns they derive from in §6.1.1; Table 80 repeats the forms (with the optional honorific marker *-lì* in parentheses). Note that first person exclusive *ne(li)-* is also used for first person singular reference.

Table 80: Personal possessive prefixes.

Possessive prefixes (honorific)	Gloss
ne(li)-	'1EXCL'
e(li)-	'1INCL'
nang(li)-	'2'
[alang(li)-; a-]	'3'

7.3.3. Verbalizer *pe-* ~ *pa-*

The verbalizer *pe-* ~ *pa-* (for the allomorphy, see §3.9.2.1) is related to (or arguably the same morpheme as) the causative *pe-* ~ *pa-* prefix (§8.4.2). Since nouns can function as predicates without additional marking (§4.3), the use of *pe-* ~ *pa-* typically has a causative, or perhaps change-of-state, implication 'make X (be) [N]'. In (183), for example, the literal meaning is 'make the backside (be) the front', i.e., 'turn around'.

(183) Verbalizer *pe-* ~ *pa-* on noun root *ingnò* 'front'
   [...] *aphi anatsi* **chepangnophit**
   a-phī   a-nát=si   che-**pa**-ingnò-phìt
   POSS-backside POSS-direction=FOC:RL   RR-**VBLZ**-front-right.away
   '[...] ([H]e) turned around right away.' [HI, BPh 006]

Grüßner (1978: 93) provides similar examples, such as *chór* 'pair, couple' and *pa-chór* 'marry off', or *dūk* 'dust' (recorded as low tone by Grüßner) and *pa-dūk* 'pulverize'. In addition, Grüßner offers examples of the prefix on a classifier-numeral word (*pa-khéi-ní* 'VBLZ-CLF:group-two > divide into two groups', and on onomatopoeia (*pa-ók'ók* 'to make the sound *ok-ok*, to grunt (of pigs)'.

However, there are also examples of *pe-* ~ *pa-* on nouns such as in (184), where the opposite of a 'change of state' is indicated in *nangpa'okorjangdunlonglang* 'still getting to remain / still be (and participate in society as) a girl' and the equivalent *nangparisomardunlonglang*. It appears that in this example, *pa-* only functions as a verbalizer, and not a causative. We may hypothesize that some speakers prefer to use *pe-* ~ *pa-* as an overt verbalizer in longer, more complex predicates.

(184) Verbalizer *pe- ~ pa-* on noun roots *okorjāng* 'unmarried.girl' and *risō* 'unmarried.boy'
la'an akemesen atovar kedamtheksi
[la-án   a-ke-mēsén   a-továr   ke-dàm-thēk-si]
this-that.much POSS-NMLZ-be.good POSS-road NMLZ-go-know.how-NF:RL

hako amonit atumke nonpu'anta
[[hakó   a-monít   a-tūm=ke]   nón-pu-án=tā
that.time POSS-man POSS-PL=TOP now-QUOT-all=ADD

*ilitum a'ansose **nangpa'okorjangdunlonglang***
e-li-tūm   a-án-sosē
1PL.INCL-HON-PL POSS-that.much-more
nang=**pa**-okorjāng-dūn-lōng-làng
CIS=**VBLZ**-unmarried.girl-JOIN-GET-still

nangparisomardunlonglang
nang=**pa**-risō-mār-dūn-lōng-làng]
CIS=**VBLZ**-unmarried.boy-PL-JOIN-GET-still
'They know how to go on a good road up to a high degree (i.e., know how to do things properly, how to keep everything clean, etc.), and, because they know how to keep everything clean and nice, those people back then up until today, get to stay even more like girls and boys (i.e., young) than we do.' [SiH, CW 017]

In (185), *pa-* occurs on *thē* 'fruit' to mean 'to bear fruit', and Grüßner also records *pa-tì* 'VBLZ-egg > to lay eggs'. These examples suggest that *pe- ~ pa-* may also function to express 'cause [N] to exist'. Further research will need to investigate whether there are any factors that determine the function of *pe- ~ pa-* on a particular noun stem.

(185) Verbalizer *pe- ~ pa-* on noun root *thē* 'fruit'
[...] *pholo epen, **pathepo**, ingdakpo*
[pholó   è-pen]   [**pa**-thē-pò]   [ingdàk-pò]
cotton plant-NF **VBLZ**-fruit-IRR1 burst.open-IRR1
'[...] [A]fter having planted the cotton, (the cotton tree) carries fruit, then (the seeds) will burst open.' [KST, PSu 003]

7.4 Nominal suffixes

The discussion of nominal suffixes starts with the gender suffixes *-pī* and *-pō*, which have further functions as augmentative and modifier-deriving markers (§7.4.1). In §7.4.2, information on the diminutive *-sō* is offered, and §7.4.3 discusses the occurrence of the diminutive and the two gender and augmentative/modifier-deriving suffixes in names of animal/plant subspecies. In §7.4.4, the plural suffix *-mār*, which occurs on nouns with human referents, is presented, and §7.4.5 offers an account of the nominal superlative suffix -sí.

7.4.1 Gender suffixes -pī and -pō

Karbi has two gender suffixes, -pī 'female' and -pō 'male'. There are a number of nouns with human referents that may be specified for gender via one of the two suffixes, for example sō-pī 'daughter' and sō-pō 'son', jīr-pī 'female friend' and jīr-pō 'male friend', or sàr-pī 'married woman' and sàr-pō 'married man'.[76] 'Female' -pī also occurs productively with animal referents, whereas 'male' -pō is often replaced by -lò (which is commonly used as a noun rather than a suffix, e.g., in vō a-lò 'chicken POSS-male > rooster'). Below I discuss each suffix separately.

7.4.1.1 Female and augmentative -pī

The 'female' suffix -pī occurs in several places, where -pō is not or not typically used for the male counterpart. One example is clan names. Children carry the clan name of their father, for example Krō or Tīssō. But while the clan names of sons (or men) do not require the 'male' suffix, the clan names of the daughters (or women) do, so the daughter would be called Krōpī or Tīssōpī, but the son would be Krō or Tīssō, just like his father.

'Female' -pī is also used on nouns with animal referents, for example vō-pī 'chicken-female > hen'. The lexical noun -pī still exists, so it is also possible to say vō a-pī 'chicken POSS-female > hen' or bī a-pī 'goat POSS-female > female goat'. The noun -pī 'female (person/animal)' apparently derives from pēi ~ pāi 'mother'.

While a form -pō for male referents, or grammaticalized as a nominalizer, exists all across Tibeto-Burman, 'female' -pī is not very common. Interestingly, however, Meitei also has a 'female' -pi suffix as in nu-pi 'female human' or hənu-bi 'old woman' (Chelliah 1997: 244), and so does 'Kuki-Chin' (§1.3.1).

Polysemically related to the 'female' marking function, and presumably more specifically related to the meaning of 'mother', -pī also has an augmentative function. This is common in Tibeto-Burman as well cross-linguistically (Matisoff 1992). Examples of Karbi 'female' -pī as an augmentative are thói-pī 'vast plains', inglóng-pī 'large mountain', or the name of a river, Lāngpī (lit. 'water-AUGMENT').

The 'female, augmentative' -pī occurs on PCT roots, arguably in its augmentative function; this is discussed below in §7.4.1.3.

---

[76] Note that sàr-pō is often replaced by the word sàr-burá in colloquial speech, where the second part burá is a borrowing from Assamese. There is no directly analogous female form, but instead a form with both suffixes, i.e., sàr-pī-burí, is used in addition to sàr-pī. The male form sàr-pō is still used in ceremonial speech.

7.4.1.2 Male (and non-productive modifier-deriving) -pō

The male suffix -pō is related to the lexical noun -pō 'father', a common root in Tibeto-Burman with the same semantics of 'male' or 'father'. Examples are *bamón-pō* 'wise old man (borrowed from Indic *Brahmin*)' (which also has a female counterpart, *bamón-pī*), or *bokolá-pō*, a character in folk stories whose stupidity results in entertaining, funny stories.

'Male' -pō alternates with 'female' -pī as augmentatives in the noun stem 'thumb', which may be either *mùn-pī* or *mùn-pō*. This appears to be an exception, however; generally, only -pī is used as an augmentative suffix on noun stems.

There are several occurrences that suggest that -pō has historically derived modifiers from PCT roots in a synchronically no longer productive way. This is interesting considering that -pa/-po nominalizers are found in a large number of Tibeto-Burman languages from different branches of the family (LaPolla 2008: 52). Examples are (186) and (187), which come from folk stories. Example (186) shows that the elephant in the story is characterized as *nothōng-pō* 'deaf', where *nothōng* is a compound of -nò 'ear' and *ingthòng* 'deaf'.

(186)   -pō in modifier *nothōng-pō* 'deaf'
        ingnar **nothongpo** ano lutchok arkevaret
        [[ingnàr   nothōng-**pō**]   a-nò]   lūt-chòk   arkè-varèt
        elephant   deaf-**MODIF**   POSS-ear   enter-disappearing   scratch-INTENS
        '(The bird) got into the ears of a deaf elephant, and scratched around.' [RBT, ChM 024]

It is not clear what word class affiliation *nothōng* has. There is a productive compounding process that derives noun stems from a combination of a noun root and a verb root (§7.2.1), so *nothōng* could be a noun stem, but since it doesn't occur by itself, it is impossible to know for sure. With -pō, however, it clearly acts as a modifier, and -pō does not indicate that this is a male elephant.

Additional examples are *[vō ìk-pō] [vō thè-pō]* 'big black bird' in (187). Here, -pō occurs on straightforward PCT roots and derives modifiers of the head noun *vō* 'bird'.

(187)   -pō in modifiers *ìk-pō* 'black' and *thè-pō* 'big'
        [...] vo **ikpo** vo **thepo** do
        [vō   ìk-**pō**]   [vō   thè-**pō**]   dō
        bird be.black-**MODIF**   bird be.big-**MODIF**   exist
        '[...] [T]here is a big black bird.' [SeT, MTN 018]

7.4.1.3 Augmentative and modifier-deriving -pī and -pō

Examples (188) and (189) demonstrate the equivalent uses of -pī and -pō, as they occur on the PCT root *thè* 'be big' to form a modifier of the preceding head noun (see also §4.2.6).

(188) *thè-pō* 'big (< *thè* 'be big' and *-pō* 'big')'
 *anke ha langso asiluka **thepota** pulelo*
 ánke   há   [langsō a-sílukā   thè-**pō**=tā]
 and.then over.there this   POSS-sp.tree(<Asm)   be.big-MODIF=ADD
 pù-lè-lò
 say-again-RL
 'And then, there, this big siluka tree replied (lit., said again).' [KK, BMS 107]

(189) *thè-pī* 'big (< *thè* 'be big' and *-pī* 'AUGMENT')'
 *la bhari talo **thepi** nangkekapji kopuloma*
 là   [bharí   taló thè-**pī**]   nang=ke-káp-jí
 this very.big(<Ind)   sea   be.big-**AUGMENT** CIS=NMLZ-cross.water-IRR2
 kopú=lo=ma
 how=FOC=Q
 'How will we be able to cross the huge sea?' [KK, BMS 100]

The fact that *-pī* also appears to derive a modifier from the PCT root *thè* 'be big' in (189) – just like *-pō* does in (188) – is surprising. It is the only instance in the corpus of *-pī* occurring on a PCT root rather than on a noun. One possibility is to consider *taló-thè* 'big sea' a compound noun stem (parallel to, for example, *mūm-dīng* 'long bearded (person)', from *ingmūm* 'beard' and *dīng* 'be long'). However, *taló-thè* does not occur without *-pī*, so this is not an appealing explanation. A perhaps better interpretation is that *-pī*, possibly in analogy with *-pō*, may also function to derive modifiers from PCT roots, with additional augmentative semantics.

7.4.2 Diminutive *-sō*

There is only one occurrence of the diminutive suffix *-sō* in the corpus, which is given in (190).

(190) Diminutive *-sō* on *phu'īk* 'earthen pot'
 ansi lang dungpo, anke lasi <ka> ingsir'etlo tangte
 ánsi   [lāng   dúng-pò]   ánke   [lasì   <ka>   ingsīr-ét-lò   tángtē
 then   water   pour-IRR1   and.then then   <...> filter-PRF-RL   if

 pacharmatpo; chenangchitpen, phu'iksopen
 pacharmát-pò]   [chenáng-chìt-pèn   phu'īk-**sō**=pen
 test.if.taste.is.good-IRR1 match-finally-NF   earthen.pot-**DIM**=with

ilitum han tun'ikpo
e-li-tūm hán tún-īk-pò]
1PL.INCL-HON-PL vegetables cook-FRML-IRR1
'And then, we pour water and then when (the funnel) has filtered (the ashes), we test the taste, and after finding it matching, we cook the curry in a small *phu-ik* pot.' [SiH, KH 007]

Grüßner (1978: 55) also records other occurrences of the diminutive, such as *arvó-sō* 'little leaf' or *bí-sō* 'small pond'. Another example is (191), where *-sō* occurs on a classifier. It appears that *-sō* is used productively to derive diminutive stems of nominal elements (i.e., nouns and classifiers).

(191) Diminutive *-sō* on classifier root
a-plàng-sō-néi
POSS-CLF:cylindrical-DIM-SPLT
'the smallest (loaf of bread)' (Grüßner 1978: 107)

7.4.3 Gender/augmentative and diminutive suffixes in names of animal(/plant) subspecies

A number of proper nouns that refer to animal (and some plant) subspecies end in the gender/augmentative suffixes *-pī* or *-pō*, or the diminutive suffix *-sō*. Table 81 offers a list of examples attested in the corpus (and Grüßner (not dated) provides more examples in his dictionary manuscript).

Table 81: Proper nouns with *-pī*, *-pō*, or *-sō* suffix.

Proper nouns with *-pī*		Proper nouns with *-pō*		Proper nouns with *-sō*	
phàk-beléngpī	'pig-SPECIES'	misò-rongpō	'ant-SPECIES'	chonghō- kalósō	'frog-SPECIES'
vō-arbípī	'bird-SPECIES'	methān-sibóngpō	'dog-SPECIES'		
		karlē-sibóngpō	'squirrel-SPECIES'		
		vō-arkókpō	'plant-SPECIES'		

The *-pī* and *-pō* suffixes here do not mark gender/sex. Instead, *-pī* is probably the augmentative counterpart to *-sō* 'diminutive' to indicate that a particular subspecies is relatively large or small. The *-pō* suffix then is likely to be a purely structural element that derives the modifier that characterizes the particular subspecies.

7.4.4 Human plural -mār

The plural suffix -mār only occurs on nouns with human referents, e.g., riso-mār 'unmarried boys', osō-mār 'children', sarpī-mār 'married women', sarpō-mār 'married men'.

The more general plural marking strategy is a possessive construction involving the 'plural noun' -tūm (§10.6). As seen in (192), nouns that already carry -mār in addition often occur in the -tūm plural construction.

(192) Pleonastic plural marking via -mār and atūm
      anke laso a'osomar atum nangke'otkrei atheseresi
      ánke   [lasō **a-osō-mār**   **a-tūm**] nang=ke-ót-krèi
      and.then this **POSS-child-PL** **POSS-PL** CIS=NMLZ-touch-DISTR.PL
      a-theseré=si
      POSS-fruits=FOC:RL

      langdunveretlo... [...]
      làng-dūn-verèt-lò...
      see-JOIN-INTENS-RL
      'And then, he (the old man) keeps watching the fruit that these children are each holding [...].' [SiT, PS 045]

Interestingly, (193) suggests that -mār functions as a derivational (rather than an inflectional) suffix, as it forms an extended noun stem risō-mār, which then is verbalized with pa-.

(193) Plural -mār
      [...] *nangparisomardunlonglang*
      nang=pa-risō-**mār**-dūn-lōng-làng]
      CIS=VBLZ-unmarried.boy-**PL**-JOIN-GET-still
      '[...] ([T]hey) get to stay even more like [girls and] boys (i.e., young) than we do.' [SiH, CW 017]

Note that the honorific suffix -lì may occur on -mār pluralized nouns. Honorific -lì otherwise only occurs on pronouns (and personal possessive prefixes), see §6.1.1 on pronoun forms, and §16.4.1 on honorific -lì.

7.4.5 Superlative -sí

The suffix -sí occurs on nominal stems with property concept semantics to indicate a superlative degree. In (194), the suffix attaches to a-ki-bī 'POSS-NMLZ-be.small > young one'. While -sí may ultimately bear a relationship with the realis focus marker =si (§14.2.3), they are synchronically different elements: superlative *-sí* is a suffix that occurs on the noun stem as seen in (194), whereas focus *=si* is a clitic that attaches to an entire phrase.

(194) Superlative *-sí* on nominalized *akibī*
*latumke **akibisi** atumlo, latumta*
[la-tūm=ke   a-ke-bī-**sí**   a-tūm-lò]   la-tūm=tā
this-PL=TOP POSS-NMLZ-be.small-**SPLT** POSS-PL-RL this-PL=ADD

piso some enlo potsi ahem arit dolo
pīsō sōmē ēn-lò] [pōt=si   a-hēm   a-rīt   dō-lò]
wife EE:pīsō take-RL reason=FOC:RL POSS-house POSS-field exist-RL
'They were (the children/descendants of) the youngest, they also had gotten married and so they had their house and property.' [WR, BCS 027]

Example (195) shows that *-sí* may also occur on adverbs – here, an adverb derived from a relator noun.[77]

(195) Superlative *-sí* on *aphī* 'after, last'
*[...] si aphi abangke **aphisi** vanglo, mh*
sì   a-phì   abàng=ke aphī-**sí**   vàng-lò mh
and.then POSS-grandmother NPDL=TOP afterwards-**SPLT** come-RL DSM
'[...] [A]nd then, the grandmother was the last one who came.' [KK, BMS 074]

7.5 Reduplication

Reduplication of verb stems occurs more frequently and has more different functions (§9.3) compared to reduplication of noun stems. Nevertheless, there are some cases where reduplication of noun stems occurs. So far dual and (distributive) plural functions of reduplicated noun stems have been attested. Note that reduplication of noun and verb stems consists of the reduplication of the last syllable of the stem, with scope typically over the whole stem, but see §9.2.1.1.1 with scope differences in verbs.

7.5.1 Dual

Reduplication of the last syllable of a noun stem may indicate duality, as shown in (196), where *jīrpō~pō* refers to 'two friends'. A plural interpretation (in a different context) is not acceptable.

---

[77] It needs to be double-checked that *aphī* here cannot instead be interpreted as a noun with the meaning 'the later/last one'.

(196) Reduplication with dual marking function
anke damlo adapprang halatum damlo tangho, jirpopo {mm}
ánke   dàm-lò a-dappráng hála-tūm dàm-lò tànghò   jīr-pō~pō
and.then go-RL POSS-dawn   that-PL   go-RL REP   friend-male~DUAL
'and then, they went, early in the morning they went, the two friends'
[HK, TR 146]

Also note (197) from an on-line narration of the pear story (i.e., the speaker is describing what is going on as he is watching the video clip). Here, the reduplicative dual form *arlososo* from the noun *arloso* 'woman/girl' does not mean that there are two girls, but instead refers to the dual number of the boy on the bike colliding with the girl on the bike, i.e., the dual number of the girl and the boy.

(197) Reduplication with dual marking function: associative dual
<la> <saikel…> <a> <la> arlososo abangpen
<là> <saikél…>   <là> **[árlosō~sō**   abàng=pen]
this bicycle(<Eng) this **woman~DUAL**   NPDL=with

chetongder amat aphutup klophit
che-tōng-dèr   amāt   a-phutūp kló-phìt
RR-collide-IDEOPHONE   and.then POSS-hat fall-right.away
'The bicycle…, with the girl he collided and then his hat fell down.' [SiT, PS 028]

Further examples of specific lexicalized instances of this dual marking reduplication pattern are, for example, *pēi-pō~pō* 'mother-father~DL' > 'mother and father', *sō-pī~pī* 'child-female~DL' > 'daughter and son', *pō-sō~sō* 'father-child~DL' > 'father and son' (Grüßner 1978: 57).

7.5.2 (Distributive) plural

As discussed in §9.3.2, one of the functions of reduplication of verb stems is to indicate the (sometimes distributive) plurality of an argument, typically the S or the O argument. Similarly, the inanimate plural demonstrative *(la)héi* or *(la)hái* has a reduplicated form *(la)héi~hái* (or *(la)héi~húi*, or *(la)hái~húi*), which indicates not only plurality (which is already part of the meaning of *(la)héi*), but a 'plurality of types' or distributive plurality in the sense of 'these different ones'. This is the intended meaning in (198), for example, where *laheihui* anaphorically refers to two types of plants used as soap in traditional times.

(198) Reduplication with distributive plural marking function
lapente ephu kechingthike vo'arkokpo tangho,
[lapènte e-phú ke-chingthí=ke] [vō'arkókpō tànghò]
and.then 1PL.INCL-head NMLZ-clean.thoroughly=TOP sp.plant REP

lapente plimplam abo tangho, laheihui helo
[lapènte plimplām a-bō tànghò] lahéi~**húi**-heló
and.then sp.sour.fruit POSS-fruit.inside REP these~DIST.PL-RL:EMPH
'And then, to wash our head, the things (we use) are *voarkokpo* and then the inside of the *plimplam* fruit, it is those different ones.' [SiH, CW 008]

In (199), *heihai* with its sense of 'different ones' occurs in a general extender construction (see §16.2.1).

(199) *heihai* in general extender construction
Europe lapen kaprek kaprek adet
Europe lapèn ke-prék ke-prék a-dét
Europe(<Eng) and NMLZ-be.different NMLZ-be.different POSS-country

America heihaipen phorena atum dopik hadak
America **héihái**=pen phorená a-tūm
America(<Eng) different.kinds.of=from foreigner(<Eng) POSS-PL
dō-pīk hádāk
exist-very there
'From Europe and from many different countries, (such as) from America etc., there were many foreigners there.' [SiT, HF 037]

Other examples of reduplication in nominal elements that indicate plurality are offered in (200) and (201).

(200) Reduplication in *pí-nē~nē* indicating plurality
hala kopinene adum pinene
[hála **[kopí-nē~nē** a-dùm] **[pí-nē~nē**
that what-INDEF~DIST.PL POSS-plains.fishermen what-INDEF~DIST.PL

amumding atum aphan {mm} daksi arklipo
a-ingmūm-dīng] a-tūm aphān] mm dāk=si arklì-pò
POSS-beard-be.long POSS-PL NSUBJ AFF here=FOC:RL bewail-IRR1
'Here, they will sacrifice those different people from the fishermen community that live in the plain, [and] those long-bearded ones.' [HK, TR 112]

(201) Reduplication in *e-nūt~nū*t indicating plurality
{la monit akaprek kaprek
là	monít	a-ke-prék	ke-prék
this	man	POSS-NMLZ-be.different	NMLZ-be.different

akhei inutnut} mm mm {oi}
a-khēi	**e-nūt~nūt}**	mm	mm	{ōi}
POSS-community	one-CLF:HUM:SG~DIST.PL	AFF	AFF	yes

'{these people from all the different communities?!}' [HK, TR 113]

8 Verbal morphology: Overview and pre-root slots

The verbal morphology of Karbi is discussed in two chapters. This chapter presents the overview and goes over all morphological elements that precede the verb root. The next Chapter 9 deals with the more extensive inventory of morphology that follows the verb root.

This chapter begins with a short note on compound verbs in §8.1. In §8.2, an overview of approximate position classes in the Karbi verb is provided. The remainder of this chapter as well as the following Chapter 9 follow the order of position classes in the verb in discussing the respective morphemes involved in verbal word formation. For more details, see §8.2 for the organization of this chapter.

8.1 Compounding

Just as in nominal word formation (§7.2.2), compound verb stems can be formed based on elaborate expression root pairs (§16.2.2.2). For example, the two roots *tún* 'cook' and *dàng* 'put on stove' form an elaborate expression meaning 'cook' in (202).

(202) Verbal elaborate expression in compound construction
 [...] hem kedo atum aphanta
 [[hēm ke-dō a-tūm] a-phān=tā]
 house NMLZ-stay POSS-PL POSS-NSUBJ=ADD

 tun-dangpikang'et nangjilang
 tún-dàng-pī-káng-ét náng-jí-lāng
 cook-put.on.stove-BEN/MAL-leaving-PRF need-IRR2-still
 '[...] [A]lso for those who stay at home, (the women) have to cook (the food).'
 [KaR, SWK 074]

8.2 Overview: Position classes in the Karbi verb

Figure 11 lays out approximate position classes in the Karbi verb. There are four pre-root slots, and six post-root slots. Slot 6 consists of predicate derivations, more than one of which can occur in a given verb. Note that all pre- and post-root slots are entirely optional: the bare stem (consisting of just the root) may function as the predicate all by itself.

The discussion of Karbi verbal morphology in this chapter and Chapter 9 follows the order of morphological slots shown in Figure 11. This chapter goes over all pre-root slots. Section §8.3 deals with the proclitics. This is followed by the prefixal derivational morphology of slot 2 (i.e., the nominalizer *ke-*) as well as of the scope-sensitive

8.2 Overview: Position classes in the Karbi verb — 197

1	2	3+4	5	6	7	8	9	10
nang=	ke-	che- pa-	ROOT	DERIV*	RDPL	-Cē	-dèt	-jī
ne=		pa- che-					-pín	-pò
e=		cho- pa-						-lò
		(pa- cho-)						-si
		cho-						-ra
		che-						-pen
		pa-						-làng
								-nāng
								...

1: proclitic slot
2: nominalization
3+4: argument structure influencing
5: root (/stem)
6: predicate derivations, including modals
7: reduplication
8: negation
9: aspect
10: mood, aspect, subordinate, non-declarative speech act marking

Figure 11: Position classes in the Karbi verb.

slots 3 and 4 in §8.4. Chapter 9 goes over the much richer verbal morphology that occurs in post-root slots.

The remainder of this section discusses the issue of derivational versus inflectional verbal affixes (§8.2.1), and then introduces the pre-root slots and discusses ordering possibilities among them (§8.2.2).

8.2.1 Derivational and inflectional affixes, and the verb stem

We can draw a distinction between derivational and inflectional affixes in the following way. In Figure 11, slots 2 up to and including slot 8 with the negative suffix are derivational, and slots 9, 10, and 11 are inflectional. This division does a fairly good job of recognizing typically derivational categories that are semantically rich, and typically inflectional categories that grammatically specify a verb for use in a particular context. The result also aligns with our typological understanding that derivational categories are closer to the root or stem, and inflectional categories are further removed from the root or stem.

Derivational prefixes then include the nominalizer (changing the part of speech) and the argument structure influencing prefixes: the causative, the auto-benefactive/malefactive, and the reflexive/reciprocal. Derivational suffixes include the large class of predicate derivations as well as reduplication and the negative suffix. Inflection is only carried out by suffixes and includes categories of aspect, mood, subordination, and speech act marking.

As we would expect, some *prima facie* issues remain. For example, the nominalizer *ke-* has been reanalyzed as an imperfective marker in the language (see §12.7). As a result the new inflectional *ke-* 'imperfective' prefix also goes in slot 2, making slot 2 a derivational-inflectional hybrid slot. Another analytical issue is that suffixes of functionally related aspectual categories go in three different positions, i.e., slots 6, 9, and 10. Of course these are not actual problems – they are just evidence of typical diachronic change.

8.2.2 Overview of pre-root slots

The elements that may occur in pre-root slots are limited to the ones listed in Figure 11 above, which include three proclitics (cross-referencing non-subject speech act participants and marking the cislocative), the nominalizer *ke-* (and imperfective *ke-*), and two slots for argument structure influencing prefixes with scope-sensitive ordering options: *pV-* 'causative', *che-* 'reflexive/reciprocal', and *cho-* 'auto-benefactive/malefactive'. Below I provide examples for the ordering possibilities between the causative prefix on the one hand, and the reflexive/reciprocal and auto-benefactive/malefactive prefixes on the other hand. The reflexive/reciprocal and auto-benefactive/malefactive prefixes cannot co-occur on the same verb.

First, (203) offers a verb form with all prefix slots and the proclitic slot filled: *nang=* cross-referencing the first person causee (or the first/second person possessor, see §8.3.1.3), the nominalizer *ke-*, the causative *pV-*, and the reflexive/reciprocal *che-*. In this verb, the causative precedes the reflexive/reciprocal. This results in the causative having scope over the stem consisting of the reflexive/reciprocal-marked root, i.e., *pa-[che-tòng]* 'cause (somebody) [to meet (somebody)]'.

(203) Verb form with all pre-root slots filled (causative preceding reflexive/reciprocal)
[...] "*nephi aphan* **nangkapachetongji** *pule,*
[ne-phì   aphān   **[nang=]₁ [ke-]₂ [pV-]₃ [che-]₄** tòng-jí
1EXCL-grandmother NSUBJ   1/2:NSUBJ=NMLZ-CAUS-RR-meet-IRR2
pu=le
QUOT=FOC:IRR

nangpachetongte" [...]
nang=pa-che-tòng-Cē
1/2:NSUBJ=CAUS-RR-meet-NEG
'[...] "([Y]ou) said (you) would make/help me meet my (should be 'your') grandmother, but (you) didn't help me meet her", (said *bamonpo*) [...].'
[KK, BMS 073]

Note, however, that in this particular case, *che-tòng* 'RR-meet' has actually lexicalized and is only diachronically analyzable into a reflexive/reciprocal prefix and a root. This is evidenced by the fact that only *chetòng* is ever used, and never just *tòng*.

An example that shows that the causative prefix may also synchronically precede the reflexive/reciprocal prefix is (204).

(204) Verb form with causative preceding reflexive/reciprocal
lasi pinso arlo ba apai apota
lasì   [[pinsō   arlò]   bá   [a-pāi   a-pō=tā]]
therefore married.man woman or(<Asm) POSS-mother POSS-father=ADD

pachehoman osomar aphan, [...]
pV-che-homán   osō-mār   a-phān
CAUS-RR-be.equal(<Asm) child-PL POSS-NSUBJ
'So the men and women, or the mothers and fathers, if they **make themselves equal** for the children [...].' [KaR, SWK 052]

In (205), the scope is reversed: the reflexive/reciprocal prefix precedes, and therefore has scope over, the causativized stem *che-[pa-ngthìr]*.

(205) Verb form with reflexive/reciprocal preceding causative
lapente monit atum kedo kethak
lapènte   [monít a-tūm]   [ke-dō   ke-thák
and.then   man   POSS-PL NMLZ-stay   NMLZ-EE:dō(<Asm)

kachepangthir *nangji]*
ke-**che-pa-**ingthìr   náng-jí
NMLZ-**RR-CAUS-**be.clean   must-IRR2
'And then, people need to stay and live in a clean way.' [SiH, CW 001]

Note that in (205), the reflexive/reciprocal has middle-like and specifically auto-benefactive semantics (i.e., 'be clean for themselves') (§8.4.3), while the causative is part of an adverbial construction here (§11.3.2).[78]

Finally, let us consider the ordering options between the causative prefix and the auto-benefactive/malefactive prefix. In the verb *kachopethepen* in (206), the auto-benefactive/malefactive precedes the causative, as *pe-thè* 'CAUS-be.big' means 'raise', and *cho-* adds a (weak) auto-benefactive/malefactive sense to it.

---

78 This adverbial construction in its simplest form consists of a lexical verb that is followed by a causative-marked (typically PCT) verb: $[V]_{\text{main verb}} [pa\text{-}V]_{\text{adverbial}}$. Here *kedo kethak* 'stay (and live)' is the main verb, modified by *kachepangthir* 'in a clean way'.

(206) Verb form with auto-benefactive/malefactive preceding causative
hako ahutke so'arlo atumke la hem arlo
[hakó   a-hūt=ke]   [sō'arlō   a-tūm=ke]   [là   [hēm   arlō]
that.time POSS-during=TOP women:COLL POSS-PL=TOP this house inside

ketun kedang asomar
[kV-tún   kV-dàng]   [a-oso-màr
NMLZ-cook NMLZ-put.on.stove POSS-child-PL

kachopethepen <abahere> angparke [...]
kV-**cho-pe**-thē-pen]   <a-baheré>
NMLZ-**AUTO.BEN/MAL-CAUS**-be.big-NF:with   POSS-beyond(<Asm)
anpár=ke]
besides=TOP
'in the old days, the women, beyond doing household works and **raising children** [...]' [KaR, SWK 063]

The order of the causative preceding the auto-benefactive/malefactive does not appear to occur synchronically. There are examples such as *nangkapachobeima* in (207), which look like they contain *pa-cho-*, but *chobēi* here really has to be treated as a lexicalized root with the meaning 'lie (not telling the truth)', as *bèi* without *cho-* means 'console'.

(207) Verb form with causative preceding fossilized auto-benefactive/malefactive
[...] *nephan nangpakolikma {oi} **nangkapachobeima***
ne-phān   nang=pakolík=ma   ōi
1EXCL-NSUBJ 1/2:NSUBJ=lie=Q   yes
nang=ke-**pa-cho(-)**bēi=ma
1/2:NSUBJ=NMLZ-**CAUS-(AUTO.BEN/MAL-)**lie=Q
'[...] "Are you lying to me? Are you telling me a lie?" (said the tiger).' [HK, TR 087]

8.3 Proclitic slot: Non-subject speech act participant cross-referencing and cislocative marking

The proclitic slot on the verb consists of *nang=* indexing speech act participants in non-subject roles (as well as, in some dialects, *ne=* < *nè* '1EXCL' and *e=* < *e-* '1INCL'), and cislocative *nang=* (defined as a marker of motion towards a reference point). Based on the different functions, we may synchronically consider the person cross-referencing *nang=* a different morpheme from the cislocative marking *nang=*. Historically, however, all the evidence suggests that there is just one *nang=* proclitic, which goes back to the second person pronoun *nàng*. This is further discussed in the summary §8.3.3.

8.3.1 Non-subject speech act participant marking

This section discusses the function of *nang=* (and *ne=* and *e=*) to cross-reference non-subject speech act participants (SAPs). In §8.3.1.2, an overview is provided of the frequent cross-referencing of SAPs that function as primary objects, and §8.3.1.3 offers examples of instances where SAPs in other, non-core, roles are cross-referenced; §8.3.1.4 summarizes this section.

8.3.1.1 Introduction

The proclitic *nang=* is used to index or cross-reference speech-act participants that are not subjects in the clause, independent of the person of the subject, as shown in Table 82.

Table 82: Cross-referencing 'paradigm' of *nang=*.

'non-A' A	1	2	3
1	–	+	–
2	+	–	–
3	+	+	–

While I interchangeably use the terms 'indexing' or 'cross-referencing', what we find is non-obligatory but very common marking of speech-act participants that are not subjects in the clause. An independent pronoun referring to the same participant may or may not be present.

All of these properties of *nang=* are illustrated with examples in the following subsections.

8.3.1.2 Cross-referencing SAP primary objects

In (208) and (209), *nang=* occurs on verbs that mark events in which a first person A argument acts on a second person O argument, which may be both singular as in (208), or plural as in (209). The second person O argument may occur as an independent pronoun in addition to the preverbal clitic, as in *nangphanke* in (208), or only in the form of the preverbal clitic (i.e., with no independent pronoun present), as in (209).

(208) First person acting on second person (1→2)
 [...] nangphanke nangkeponpo
 nang-phān=ke   **nang**=ke-pòn-pò
 you-NSUBJ=TOP   1/2:NSUBJ=NMLZ-take.away-IRR1
 '[...] (I) will carry you away.' [HK, TR 059]

(209) First person acting on second person (1→2)
   [...] nangkecharjulo, peipen po
   nang=ke-che-arjū-lò   pēi=pen   pō
   1/2:NSUBJ=NMLZ-RR-ask-RL   mother=with father
   '[...] [W]e are asking you, mother and father.' [CST, HM 117]

Example (210) shows that *nang=* also occurs when there is a third person acting on a second person. The second part of this example also shows, however, that this cross-referencing via *nang=* is not obligatory. Although the two clauses (*[[nangphan nangkelang] inut] donangji* 'there needs to be somebody to look after you' and *[[kevan kepon] inut] donangji* 'there needs to be somebody to bring you and to take you') are parallel in their structure and in their reference to the second person, *nang=* is only used on the verb in the first clause and not the second.

(210) Third person acting on second person (3→2)
   *athema nangphan **nangkelang** inut donangji*
   athēma **[nàng**-phān **nang**=ke-làng   e-nūt   dō-náng-jí]
   because **you**-NSUBJ 1/2:NSUBJ=NMLZ-see one-CLF:HUM:SG exist-need-IRR2

   kevan kepon inut donangji [...]
   [ke-vàn   ke-pòn   e-nūt   dō-náng-jí]
   NMLZ-bring NMLZ-take.away one-CLF:HUM:SG exist-need-IRR2
   'because there needs to be somebody to look after you, (because) there needs to be somebody to bring you and to take you, [...]' [SH, CSM 066]

In addition to second person arguments, *nang=* also cross-references first person arguments, i.e., SAPs generally, in non-subject roles. This is shown in (211) and (212), which have a third person and a second person acting on a first person, respectively. In both examples, the first person primary object is indicated by the independent pronoun marked as primary object in the form *ne-phān*, and is cross-referenced by *nang=*.

(211) Third person acting on first person (3→1)
   amat Bokolapo abang "Are! Ladak nephan matsi
   amāt   Bokolā-pō abàng áré   ladāk **ne-phān**
   and.then   NAME-male NPDL   SURPRISE(<Asm)   here   **1EXCL-NSUBJ**
   māt=si
   who=FOC:RL

   *po pu **nangkehang** abang kedolo?" pu*
   pō   pu   **nang**=ke-háng   a-bàng   ke-dō-lò   pu
   father QUOT 1/2:NSUBJ=NMLZ-call POSS-CLF:HUM:PL   NMLZ-exist-RL QUOT
   'And then Bokolapo (said), "How strange! Who is here to call me 'father'?"'
   [HI, BPh 012]

(212) Second person acting on first person (2→1)
nephan nangpakolikma {oi} **nang**kapachobeima {oi}
ne-phān   **nang**=pakolík=ma   ōi   **nang**=ke-pa-chobēi=ma   ōi
1EXCL-NSUBJ   1/2:NSUBJ=lie=Q   yes   1/2:NSUBJ=NMLZ-CAUS-lie=Q   yes
'[...] "[A]re you lying to me? Are you telling me a lie?" (said the tiger).' [HK, TR 087]

Example (213) shows that *nang=* also cross-references the standard of comparison in the comparative construction, which is also indicated by the *-phān* 'non-subject' marked independent first person exclusive pronoun, *ne-phān*.

(213) Cross-referencing the standard of comparison in comparative construction
opeija **nephanta** *halasi* **nang**sarlang (both laughing)
opeija   **ne-phān**=tā   hála=si   **nang**=sàr-làng
my.goodness!   1EXCL-NSUBJ=ADD   that=FOC:RL   1/2:NSUBJ=be.old-still
'Oh my goodness! This one is even older than me! (*both laughing*)' [HK, TR 098]

Although *nang=* may be used to cross-reference speech act participants in general, some speakers use the forms of the first person inclusive and exclusive pronouns as proclitics to specifically cross-reference non-subject inclusive and exclusive first person arguments, as in (214) and (215).

(214) First person inclusive primary object (3→1INCL) marked with *e=* '1INCL:NSUBJ'
[...] **itum** *aphanke ha nampi namdur alongsi*
e-tūm   aphān=ke   há   nāmpī   nāmdūr   alòng=si
1INCL-PL   NSUBJ=TOP   over.there   big.forest   EE:nampī   LOC=FOC:RL

ekethondamlo
e=ke-thòn-dām-lò
1INCL:NSUBJ =NMLZ-drop-GO-RL
'[...] (The witch) abandoned us over there in the deep forest.' [CST, HM 076]

(215) First person exclusive primary object (2→1EXCL) marked with *ne=* '1EXCL:NSUBJ'
mh **nephan ne***chiriphetnoi*
mh   **ne-phān**   **ne**=che-ríp-hèt-nōi
DSM   1EXCL-NSUBJ   1EXCL:NSUBJ=RR-hold.firmly-firmly-INFRML.COND.IMP
'"Hold (yourself) firmly onto me!"' [KK, BMS 046]

Although it may be dialectal variation that underlies the preference to use *ne=* or *e=* to cross-reference first person non-subjects instead of *nang=*, there is an even more interesting sociolinguistic dimension to this, as even the same speaker, in the same text, and even in the same utterance, may switch between using *e=* or *nang=* for a first person inclusive O argument. This is shown in (216), where the beginning of the utterance, *ethapkangdetpen aphi*, is part of a tail-head linking construction (§16.1.2), which repeats the verb from the previous utterance, which in fact was *itum aphanke [...] ethapkanglo*, i.e., marked with *e=* to cross-reference the argument also indicated by the primary object marked first person inclusive pronoun *itum aphanke*. After this beginning in (216), even though the O argument remains constant (while the A argument changes), the speaker switches to *itum aphan nangkelangun'e*, using *nang=* to cross-reference the first person inclusive argument.

(216) First person inclusive primary object (3→1INCL) marked with *e=* '1INCL:NSUBJ' and *nang=* '1/2:NSUBJ' in the same utterance
ethapkangdetpen aphi, hi'ipi abangke
[e=thàp-káng-dét-pèn   aphī]   hī'ipī   abàng=ke
1INCL:NSUBJ=put.inside-leaving-PFV-from   after   witch   NPDL=TOP

itum aphan nangkelangun'e epei
e-tūm   aphān   nang=ke-làng-ùn-Cē   e-pēi
1PL.INCL-PL   NSUBJ   1/2:NSUBJ=NMLZ-see-be.able-NEG   1PL.INCL-mother

aphan kelangun'e
aphān   ke-làng-ùn-Cē
NSUBJ   NMLZ-see-be.able-NEG
'After (our mother) put us in the cradle, the witch could not (stand) see(ing) us, she also couldn't (stand) see(ing) our mother.' [CST, HM 051]

My hypothesis is that the invariable use of *nang=* to cross-reference both second and first person arguments is original, and using *ne=* and *e=* is an innovation based on a 'logical insight' that *ne=* and *e=* better correspond to *nephan* and *itum aphan*. There are both Karbi-internal and comparative-TB reasons to believe this is actually the case. As for the Karbi-internal reasons, there is a prescriptive movement claiming that *ne=* and *e=* are more correct than *nang=*. Also, I was told that the invariable use of *nang=* is typical in the more remote villages (which will need to actually be investigated). On comparative grounds, the invariable use of *nang=* fully conforms with the SAP/cislocative syncretism in Kuki-Chin languages (see summary in §8.3.3).

8.3.1.3 Cross-referencing SAP in non-core roles

Proclitic *nang=* may also cross-reference SAPs in non-core roles. In (217) and (218), first and second person possessors are cross-referenced by *nang=*.

(217) Cross-referencing the possessor (1→2)
*[...] **nang**jat **nang**khong **nang**pavir'etji, sala!", therdamlo.*
nang-ját **nang**-khóng **nang**=pa-vír-èt-jí   sala
2-type   2-tribe   1/2:NSUBJ=CAUS-lose-all:S/O-IRR2 damn.you!
thér-dàm-lò
threaten-GO-RL
'"[...] (I) will destroy your tribe and your species, damn you!", (he) threatened (the plantain).' [RBT, ChM 046]

(218) Cross-referencing the possessor (2→1)
*"Ai richo, **ne**pran **nang**enri nemui*
ái   richó **ne**-prán   **nang**=ēn-rī   **ne**-múi
how.bad! king   1EXCL-life   1/2:NSUBJ=take-PROH   1EXCL-EE:prán(<Ind)

nangenri"
nang=ēn-rī
1/2:NSUBJ=take-PROH
'"Oh no, king, don't take my life!"' [RBT, ChM 041]

We may label examples such as (218)(217) and (217) instances of 'possessor raising', i.e., 'promoting' the possessor to a core role. However, (219) provides evidence that the use of *nang=* cannot be generalized in syntactic terms, but that semantic/pragmatic principles determine whether a SAP is indexed on the verb. That is why *nang=* in (219) can cross-reference the second person argument, which, syntactically, is the subject of a relative clause that modifies the O argument of the main verb. (Note that *nàng* is indeed the subject of the relative clause rather than a possessor of the nominalized verb.)

(219) Cross-referencing a relative clause subject (1→2)
*{**nang** kedo adim ne **nang**chinike}*
{[[**nàng** ke-dō]REL a-dím]   nè   **nang**=chiní=ke}
you   NMLZ-stay POSS-place 1EXCL 1/2:NSUBJ=know=TOP
'{I know the place where you are staying.}' [HK, TR 105]

8.3.1.4 Summary

Procliticized *nang=* (and, via dialectal variation, also *ne=* and *e=*) cross-references SAP in non-subject roles depending on pragmatic as well as syntactic factors. If this were a strictly syntactic construction, we would expect that we could define, and predict, which syntactic role is cross-referenced in this way, and that that particular syntactic role is cross-referenced every time it occurs in a clause. Example (210) above, however, shows that *nang=*, (perhaps) the same as independent pronouns, may be left out as a zero anaphor. And (219) above shows that it is not just a particular syntactic role that is cross-referenced, but that it instead appears to be a non-agentive, affected SAP that is pragmatically cross-referenced via *nang=*.

Table 83 gives an overview of the person interactions that allow (but not automatically trigger) cross-referencing via *nang=* (or *ne=/e=*). Instead of the typical A→O format of such tables, I used the notation A→'non-A' to highlight that it is not just first and second person O arguments that are cross-referenced in this construction.

Table 83: Proclitic cross-referencing 'paradigm'.

'non-A' A	1	2	3
1	----	[nang=]	----
2	[nang=] ~ [ne= / e=]	----	----
3	[nang=] ~ [ne= / e=]	[nang=]	----

8.3.2 Cislocative marking

This section gives examples of the different cislocative-related functions of *nang=*, i.e., functions related to the marking of motion towards a reference point. This includes purely directional marking (§8.3.2.1); associated motion in the sense of 'come and V' (§8.3.2.2); and metaphorical extensions of the cislocative function (§8.3.2.3). A summary is offered in §8.3.2.4.

8.3.2.1 Directional

The directional cislocative function occurs on motion verbs and indicates that this motion is directed towards a reference point or deictic center. An example of a manner motion verb is in (220), where *ardòn* 'ride, straddle' occurs with *nang=* to express 'ride (a bicycle) towards (the reference point)'. This is further (i.e., redundantly) indicated here through the construction that *nangardon* occurs in. This verb is marked non-final via *-si*, and the sentence ends with the lexical cislocative verb *vàng* 'come'.

(220) 'Standard' cislocative indicating motion towards reference point
laso ahut amat inut akaprek amonit
lasō a-hūt   amāt   e-nūt   a-ke-prék
this POSS-during and.then   one-CLF:HUM:SG   POSS-NMLZ-be.different
a-monít
POSS-man

> abangke saikel **nangardonsi** vanglo... [...]
> abàng=ke saikél **nang**=ardòn-si vàng-lò...
> NPDL=TOP bicycle(<Eng) CIS=ride-NF:RL come-RL
> 'In this moment, another person riding on a bicycle came [...].' [SiT, PS 015]

The occurrence of *nang=* on path-encoding motion verbs is frequent in the corpus. In (221) and (222), *nang=* occurs on *sūn* 'descend' and *kló* 'fall' to indicate vertical motion towards a reference point.

(221) Cislocative *nang=* on *sūn* 'descend'
> *[...] amat laso arni abangke hala osomar atum mandu*
> amāt [[lasō arnì abàng=ke [hála osō-mār a-tūm mandú
> and.then this day NPDL=TOP that child-PL POSS-PL field.hut

> *kecho apo abangta **nang**suntuklo [...]*
> ke-chō] [a-pō abàng=tā **nang**=sūn-tùk-lò]]
> NMLZ-eat POSS-father NPDL=ADD CIS=descend-sd.of.stepping-RL
> '[...] [A]nd then that day, in order for those children to eat in the *mandu* (i.e., the hut in the field), the father came down (from the tree house) [...].' [CST, RO 030]

(222) Cislocative *nang=* on *kló* 'fall'
> *bang hantharsi nemoi*
> [bàng hanthàr=si ne-mòi
> CLF:HUM:PL vegetable.sp=FOC:RL 1EXCL-back

> ***nang**klodup, neta keso*
> **nang**=kló-dùp] [nè=tā ke-sò
> CIS=fall-falling.sound.from.high.solid.obj 1EXCL=ADD NMLZ-hurt

> *kasiksaksi*
> ke-siksāk-si]
> NMLZ-be.difficult-NF:RL
> 'A *hanthar* fruit fell on my back, so I was hurt and disturbed.' [RBT, ChM 057]

In (223) and (224), *nang=* occurs with its cislocative function on *chi-rùi* 'RR-return' and *che-lē* 'RR-reach'. Both stems carry the reflexive/reciprocal prefix *che-*, which here additionally emphasizes that the motion is directed back towards the starting point (also serving as the reference point). In (225), *nang=* is used with *tèt* 'exit' for the motion out of the womb, into the world (which acts as the reference point).

(223) Cislocative *nang=* on *chi-rùi* 'RR-return'
 netum ako nangchiruithulo
 ne-tūm akó   **nang**=che-rùi-thū-lò
 1EXCL-PL DC(<Asm) CIS=RR-return-again-RL
 'After we had tea, then we again returned to Diphu.' [SH, CSM 068]

(224) Cislocative *nang=* on *che-lē* 'RR-reach'
 vangsi ajo baji nerkep aporsi
 vàng-si   a-jó   bají   nerkēp   a-pór=si
 come-NF:RL POSS-night o'clock(<Asm) eight   POSS-time=FOC:RL

 netum hem nangchelelo
 ne-tūm hēm   **nang**=che-lē-lò
 1EXCL-PL house CIS=RR-reach-RL
 'We were coming back and at eight o'clock at night we arrived at home.'
 [SH, CSM 071]

(225) Cislocative *nang=* on *tèt* 'exit'
 nesomar pule kosonsi thengpi abeng
 ne-oso-màr   pu=le   kosón=si   thengpī   a-bēng
 1EXCL:POSS-child-PL QUOT=FOC:IRR   how=FOC:RL   tree/wood POSS-piece

 ***nang**ketetroiroidetlo*
 nang=ke-tèt-ròi~rōi-dèt-lò
 CIS=NMLZ-exit-PL.solid.obj~DIST.PL-PFV-RL
 'If they are my children, how did they come out as pieces of wood?' [CST, HM 023]

8.3.2.2 Associated motion ('come and V')

Cislocative *nang=* also occurs on non-motion verbs marking associated motion, i.e., indicating that the event denoted by the verb occurs against the background of a motion event (Guillaume 2013). Specifically, in the case of *nang=*, motion towards a reference point has occurred prior to the event denoted by the verb, in the sense of 'come and V.' In (226) and (227), a cislocative-marked motion verb precedes a cislocative-marked non-motion verb, i.e. *nangbi* 'come and put' and *nangjun* 'come and drink'.

(226) Associated motion 'come and keep/put'
 hala ejon ateketa vangpo laso angchin
 hála e-jōn   a-tekè=tā   vàng-pò   lasō a-ingchìn
 that one-CLF:animal POSS-tiger=ADD come-IRR1   this POSS-iron

    *a'umsi **nang**ing'omnaipo anke **nang**bikok...*
    a-úm=si   **nang**=ing'òm-nài-pò   ánke
    POSS-cage=FOC:RL   CIS=carry.in.mouth-big.solid:O-IRR1   and.then
    nang=bí-kòk
    CIS=keep-firmly
    'This one tiger will also come, this iron cage he will keep in his mouth and he will put it in a fixed place...' [HK, TR 167]

(227) Associated motion 'come and drink'
       *[...] alanglike latum ahemsi **nang**vursi sa*
       alàng-lì=ke   là-tūm   a-hēm=si   **nang**=vùr-si   sá
       3-HON=TOP   this-PL POSS-house=FOC:RL CIS=drop.in-NF:RL tea(<Ind)

       *ajat **nang**junlo*
       aját   **nang**=jùn-lò
       GENEX CIS=drink-RL
       '[...] [I]t was him, at their house we stopped by and had tea and everything.' [SH, CSM 067]

Examples (228) and (229) further illustrate the use of *nang=* on non-motion verbs with an implied preceding motion towards a reference point. In (228), the preceding motion is indicated by ablative *=pen* 'from'. Example (229) is given to demonstrate that even *dō* 'stay' may occur with cislocative *nang=* in this sense of 'come and stay'.

(228) Associated motion 'come and see'
       *det arlo angbongpen laso **nang**kelangdunta*
       [dét   arlō   angbòng=pen] lasō **nang**=ke-làng-dūn=tā
       country inside middle=from   this   CIS=NMLZ-see-along=ADD
       'From within the country they came to watch this (i.e., there were domestic tourists).' [SiT, HF 039]

(229) Associated motion 'come and stay'
       amatsi apenan abang pulo, "Ai sarpi!
       [amātsi   a-penān   abàng pù-lò] ai   sarpī
       and.then POSS-husband NPDL   say-RL how.strange! old.woman

       *Etumta dak ritlo **nang**kedo jailo **nang**kedo!"*
       e-tūm=tā   dāk   rītlō   **nang**=ke-dō   jàilò
       1PL.INCL-PL=ADD here inhabited.field CIS=NMLZ-stay EE:rītlō
       nang=ke-dō
       CIS=NMLZ-stay
       'And then, the husband said, "How bad, woman! We (have come here and) are staying here in the field (but should be staying in the village)."' [SeT, MTN 006]

8.3.2.3 Semantic extensions

In a number of occurrences in the corpus, *nang=* 'cislocative' has to be interpreted as having undergone semantic change. This includes a type of semantic narrowing such that instead of 'motion towards a reference point', *nang=* merely indicates 'orientation towards a reference point'. In the elicited example (230) (asking for a translation from English) and the corpus example (231), the orientation of a fan hanging down from the ceiling as well as long hair worn down are both expressed with cislocative *nang=* on the respective verbs, even though no motion is involved. They both represent the default reference point for vertical orientation towards the ground (or perhaps the default direction downwards, following gravity).

(230) Cislocative *nang=* marking orientation only, without movement involved
 *angsóng=pen=si phén **nang**=jāng-lìng*
 up.high=from=FOC:RL fan(<Eng) CIS=hang-small:S
 'The fan is hanging down from up high (from the ceiling)'. [Elicitation SiT 100515]

(231) Cislocative *nang=* marking orientation only, without movement involved
 achu nangjirhamsi aning ke'oi e
 [a-chū **nang**=jìr-hàm-si] [a-nīng ke-ói]
 POSS-hair CIS=climb.like.creeper-large:S/O-NF:RL POSS-mind NMLZ-be.sad
 e
 DSM
 '(Her appearance was that) she had her hair down and she was sad.' [KK, BMS 075]

In some occurrences of *nang=*, the cislocative function rooted in space has been metaphorically extended to the domain of time. The result of this is a perfect-like interpretation of events that occurred over time up until a (temporal) reference point. In (232), *nang=* thus indicates that the 'times changing' is a process that occurred until the moment of utterance. Similarly, the verbs at the end of (233) encode duration up until the moment of utterance, as also indicated by the suffix *-làng* 'still'.

(232) Metaphorical extension of cislocative *nang=* from space to time
 *non ahut abangke akai **nang**kekirlaló*
 [nón ahūt abàng=ke] a-kái **nang**=ke-kirlá-lò
 now during NPDL=TOP POSS-time(<Asm) CIS=NMLZ-turn.over-RL
 'Now, the time has changed.' [KST, PSu 013]

(233) Metaphorical extension of cislocative *nang=* from space to time
 la'an akemesen atovar kedamtheksi
 [la-án a-ke-mēsén a-továr ke-dàm-thēk-si]
 this-that.much POSS-NMLZ-be.good POSS-road NMLZ-go-know.how-NF:RL

hako amonit atumke nonpu'anta
[[hakó   a-monít   a-tūm=ke]   nón-pu-án=tā
that.time POSS-man   POSS-PL=TOP   now-QUOT-all=ADD

*ilitum a'ansose **nang**pa'okorjangdunlonglang*
e-li-tūm   a-án-sosē
1PL.INCL-HON-PL POSS-that.much-more
nang=pa-okorjāng-dūn-lōng-làng
CIS=VBLZ-unmarried.girl-JOIN-GET-still

***nang**parisomardunlonglang*
nang=pa-risō-mār-dūn-lōng-làng]
CIS=VBLZ-unmarried.boy-PL-JOIN-GET-still
'They know how to go on a good road up to a high degree (i.e., know how to do things properly, how to keep everything clean, etc.), and, because they know how to keep everything clean and nice, those people back then up until today, get to stay even more like girls and boys (i.e., young) than we do.' [SiH, CW 017]

8.3.2.4 Summary: Cislocative marking

Figure 12 summarizes what are described above as the basic and semantically extended functions of cislocative *nang=*. In the upper portion of the figure, we have the two functions of the prototypical directional and associated motion.

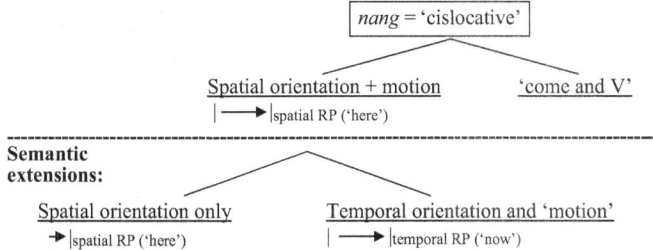

Figure 12: Overview of cislocative functions of *nang=*.

In the lower portion of Figure 12, the two metaphorically extended functions are included. They are represented as being extensions off of the directional cislocative function, which is defined as motion in the direction of a spatial orientation. This representation allows for the simplest analysis since only one semantic change has to have occurred in both cases. In the case of marking 'Spatial orientation only' (examples (230) and (231) above), the original motion component has disappeared. In the case of 'Temporal orientation and "motion"' (examples (232) and (233) above), the commonplace metaphorical extension from space to time has occurred such that the new reference point is temporal in nature ('now' rather than 'here'), and the 'motion' is time passing on, a common metaphor as well.

8.3.3 Summary

The two functions of non-subject speech act participant marking and cislocative marking are synchronically differentiated in Karbi: The person-marking *nang=* has the variants *ne=* and *e=* for first person non-subject marking, whereas the cislocative *nang=* does not have any variants. While this evidence bears the *caveat* that only some speakers use the variants, the fact that the variants were able to develop (assuming that they are indeed a later development) demonstrates that the person and the cislocative marking functions are functionally individuated enough that they enable structural differentiation.

Independent of the synchronic difference of the two functions of *nang=*, however, there are a number of occurrences of *nang=* in which elements from both functions can be recognized, thus representing possible bridging contexts of the type that would have given rise to the initial polysemy. Perhaps the most obvious bridging context is a clause with a motion verb whose goal or endpoint is a speech act participant. For example, in (222) above, repeated for convenience as (234), *nang=* occurs on the motion verb *kló* 'fall'. The vertical motion is thus marked as being oriented towards a reference point, which is a body part of a first person participant, *nemoi* 'my back'.

(234)   *nang=* marked motion verb with speech act participant body part goal
         bang hantharsi nemoi nangklodup,
         [bàng   hanthàr=si   ne-mòi
         CLF:HUM:PL   vegetable.sp=FOC:RL   my-back
         nang=kló-dùp]
         CIS=fall-falling.sound.from.high.solid.obj

   neta keso kasiksaksi
   [nè=tā   ke-sò   ke-siksāk-si]
   1EXCL=ADD   NMLZ-hurt   NMLZ-be.difficult-NF:RL
   'A *hanthar* fruit fell on my back, so I was hurt and disturbed.' [RBT, ChM 057]

Similarly, the motion verb *dùn* 'follow' takes a *-lòng* 'locative' marked 'O' argument. In (235), it is a second person argument, and the verb occurs with *nang=*.

(235)   *nang=* marked motion verb with speech act participant goal
         kevang akoke ne nanglong nangdunjuilo
         [ke-vàng   akó=ke]   [nè   **nang-lòng**   **nang**=dùn-jùi-lò]
         NMLZ-come   when=TOP   1EXCL   **2POSS-LOC**   CIS=follow-away-RL

   ne non chedamji abang thekthedetpo
   [nè   nón   che-dām-jí   abàng   thèk-Cē-dèt-pò]
   1EXCL   now   RR-go-IRR2   NPDL   know.how-NEG-PFV-IRR1

nangthondunnoi pulo tangho
nang=thòn-dūn-nōi pù-lò] tànghò
1/2:NSUBJ=drop-JOIN-SUGG.IMP2 say-RL REP
'"When we came, I followed you along far away [...], I now won't find my way back, (so) come along and drop us!", (the *bamonpo*) said.' [KK, BMS 097]

Note that in both (234) and (235), *nang=* is glossed as cislocative, because it cannot be replaced with *e=* or *ne=* for a first person goal interpretation.

The bridging context of motion verbs with SAP goals links the two functions together historically. Further evidence that we are in fact dealing with related functions that are best considered as having a common historical origin comes from typological parallels.

Cross-linguistic parallels for the syncretism between non-subject SAP and cislocative marking exist in several entirely unrelated languages. For example, in the (unrelated) North American West Coast languages Nez Perce and Shasta, cislocative markers have taken on the function of indicating speech act participant objects (Mithun 1996). Likewise, in Old Babylonian, the cislocative marker is used for speech act participant objects (Kouwenberg 2009). As Mithun (1996: 418) notes, "it would be a short semantic step to reanalyze a verb like 'Pass it here' to 'Pass it to me'." Now, in Karbi, the form *nang=* suggests that the (second) person function, rather than the cislocative function, is primary, as *naŋ* is a second person form all across the Tibeto-Burman family.[79]

There also are interesting parallels to Karbi *nang=* inside TB, and specifically in the 'Kuki-Chin' branch. In Sizang (or Siyin) Chin (Northern 'Kuki-Chin'), there is a preverbal cislocative *(h)ong*, which, in fact, parallel to Karbi, also marks non-subject speech act participants (Stern 1984; DeLancey 2001: 132–3).

Furthermore, in Purum (Northern 'Kuki-Chin'), a second person prefix also marks speech act participant objects in general.

For a more detailed discussion of *nang=* in a typological context, see Konnerth (2015).

8.4 Prefixal derivational morphology

8.4.1 Nominalizer *ke-*

The nominalizer *ke-* (with allomorphs *ki-* and *ka-*; see §3.9.2.1) is discussed in Chapter 11.

---

[79] A second person form *nang* is found in 'Kuki-Chin' languages such as Hakha Lai (Peterson 2003: 411), in the Bodo-Garo language Garo (Burling 2004: 215), and in Bodic languages such as Baram and Thangmi up in Nepal (Kansakar et al. 2011: 59). Matisoff (2003: 639) reconstructs it for Proto-Tibeto-Burman as one of two second person forms, the other one being the also very similar form *na*.

8.4.2 Causative *pe-* ~ *pa-*

The causative prefix *pe-* ~ *pa-* occurs on all verb stems including those based on prototypical verb roots and those based on property concept term (PCT) roots, and arguably the same prefix occurs as a verbalizer on nominal stems (§7.3.3). As it attaches to PCT-based stems, it may be part of an adverb construction (§11.3.2). For the morphophonological properties of this prefix, see §3.9.1.4 and §3.9.2.1.

An example of *pe-* ~ *pa-* is (236), where *pe-kló* 'CAUS-fall' means 'cause (the fruit) to fall (down)'.

(236) Causative *pe-* ~ *pa-*
phakbelengpi amoi peklodup
phàkbeléngpī a-mòi **pe**-kló-dùp
pig.sp POSS-back **CAUS**-fall-falling.sound.from.high.solid.obj
'It made it (the fruit) fall down onto the back of a pig.' [RBT, ChM 021]

Causative *pe-* ~ *pa-* is also used with a permissive function (i.e., 'let somebody do something'), as shown in (237).

(237) Causative *pe-* ~ *pa-* with permissive function
[...] lapenke inut oso abangke, la aphrang
lapèn=ke [[e-nūt osō abàng=ke] [là a-phráng
and.then=TOP one-CLF:HUM:SG child NPDL=TOP this POSS-front

along kedo, <a> arlong terekpiphitlo... penke
a-lòng ke-dō]] arlōng terék-pī-phìt-lò... pèn=ke
POSS-LOC NMLZ-exist stone move-BEN/MAL-away-RL and.then=TOP

padamlo
pa-dàm-lò
CAUS-go-RL
'[...] [A]nd then one child, the one who was in front, he moved the stone away for him, and then they (the children) **let him** (the bicycle boy) **go away** (i.e., the cleared the way for him).' [SiT, PS 033]

Note that Grüßner (1978: 93–4) reports the acceptability of a double causative, as in *pa-pe-mē* 'CAUS-CAUS-be.good > make somebody improve something', *pa-pe-thì* 'CAUS-CAUS-die > make somebody kill somebody'.

Matisoff (2003: 132) suggests that in Karbi (and in other Northeast Indian languages with similar forms, such as Dimasa (Bodo-Garo), Tenyidie (Angami Naga), as well as 'Kuki-Chin' languages such as Khumi and Maraa (Lakher)), causative *pe-* ~ *pa-* has grammaticalized from the verb 'give' *pī*. While this could be the case, it would have to be a fairly old instance of grammaticalization, because more recent grammaticalizations generally end up in suffix slots on the verb, such as the grammaticalization of *pī* 'give' to *-pī* 'benefactive' (§9.2.5.2.1). Another possibility is that this represents a borrowing from Austroasiatic (Shafer 1952; Diffloth 2008). A third possibility, recently advocated by Jacques (2019), is that this prefix represents an inherited marker from Proto-Tibeto-Burman (or Proto-Trans-Himalayan).

8.4.3 Reflexive/reciprocal *che-*

Besides marking the reflexive (in a broader than typologically expected way) and the reciprocal, *che-* also occupies part of the functional territory of a middle as defined by Kemmer (1993), and to some degree overlaps with *cho-* 'auto-benefactive/malefactive' (§8.4.4). For the morphophonological properties of this prefix, see §3.9.1.1 and §3.9.2.

First, for the reflexive function, see (238), where *che-* indicates the 'standard' reflexive where the A and O argument of a transitive verb refer to the same participant, here *che-thǎp* 'RR-put.inside' > 'put oneself inside (a hole in the tree)'. Note that while there are reflexive/reciprocal pronouns (§6.1.2), their presence is not obligatory, and *che-* may be the only indicator of reflexivity/reciprocity.

(238) (Typical) reflexive marking function of *che-* (A=O)
amat la apenan abangke the'angtanglo tangte
[amāt   [là   a-penàn   abàng=ke] [the'āng   táng-lò   tángtē]
and.then this POSS-husband NPDL=TOP   be.bright start-RL if

*ha **che**thapdamlutpo anke anbor*
há   **che-**thāp-dām-lùt-pò]   ánke   [àn-bòr
over.there **RR-**put.inside-GO-enter-IRR1 and.then rice-wrapped.bundle

pu ha peklobuppo bangke
pù   há   pe-kló-bùp-pò]   bàng=ke
like.this over.there CAUS-fall-IDEOPHONE-IRR1   CLF:HUM:PL=TOP

chotanglo juntangló
chō-táng-lò   jùn-táng-lò
eat-finish-RL drink-finish-RL

'And then, the husband, when it had gotten bright, over there he would **put himself** there in (the hole in the tree trunk), and then she dropped the rice bundle there (into the hole), and he ate and drank (everything).' [SeT, MTN 023]

A clause with a *che-* marked verb may, however, also have an O argument that is a different participant but is possessed by the A argument. This reflexive-marked coreferentiality between the A and the possessor of the O can be considered a form of possessor raising. Nevertheless, since an O argument may be present, reflexive *che-* does not change the valence of a verb (but see Chapter 13 and specifically §13.1.2 on why valence as a strictly syntactic concept is generally problematic in Karbi).

In (239), the same reflexive-marked verb as above, *che-thāp* 'RR-put.inside', has to be interpreted as 'put one's (own; here: tobacco container) inside (here: a bag)'

(239) Reflexive *che-*: A = possessor of O
anke.... duma alangpong
ánke   dumá   a-langpóng
and.then   tobacco   POSS-small.bamboo.container

che*thapponthotlo*
che-thāp-pōn-thòt-lò
RR-put.inside-away-into.opening-RL
'And then... he put the tobacco container inside (the bag) to carry it along.' [HK, TR 021]

In (240), (241), and (242), reflexive *che-* is used with human O arguments that are possessed by the A argument. The relationships are either kinship (children or wife in the examples) or friendship.

(240) Reflexive *che-*: possessive relationship = kinship
asomar aphan chititekangroklo
[a-oso-màr   aphān]   che-tí-tekáng-ròk-lò
POSS-CHILD-PL   NSUBJ   RR-get.rid.off-leave-completed-RL

chevarkangchorlo
che-vár-káng-chòr-lò
RR-throw.away-just-RES:away-RL
'He got rid of his children.' [CST, RO 050]

(241) Reflexive *che-*: possessive relationship = kinship
apiso along **chi***dunkri [...]*
[a-pisò   alòng]   **che-**dūn-krì
POSS-wife   LOC   **RR-**follow-follow.closely
'He followed his wife closely [...].' [KK, BMS 082]

(242) Reflexive *che-*: possessive relationship = friendship
ajirpo chehanglo tangho {mm}
a-jirpò   **che-**háng-lò   tànghò   mm
POSS-friend   **RR-**call-RL   REP   AFF
'He called his friend.' [HK, TR 126]

In the ditransitive clause in (243), *che-* indicates the friendship between the referents of the R argument and the A argument.

(243) Reflexive *che-*: possessive relationship = friendship
an laso a'oso abang thesere pumni hala
án	[lasō	a-osō	abàng]	[theseré	púm-ní]	[hála
and.then	this	POSS-child	NPDL	fruits	CLF:round-two	that

ajirpo banghini aphan chepaklangdamlo
a-jirpò	bàng-hiní	a-phān]	**che**-pa-klàng-dām-lò
POSS-friend	CLF:HUM:PL-two	POSS-NSUBJ	**RR**-CAUS-appear-GO-RL

'And then, this child went to show the two pieces of fruit to those two friends of his.' [SiT, PS 040]

As illustrated in (244), *che-* can also occur on motion verbs, here *dàm* 'go'. In this example, the reflexive marking on the verb cross-references *amethang atovar* 'their own road'. Similarly, *che-dām* 'RR-go' also occurs in clauses that contain *hēm* 'house, home' as the goal of the motion, as in (245).

(244) Reflexive *che-* on motion verb, cross-referencing path
latum bangkethomke amethang atovar chedamlo,
[[là-tūm	bàng-kethòm=ke]	a-methàng	a-továr	**che**-dām-lò]
this-PL	CLF:HUM:PL-three=TOP	POSS-self	POSS-road	**RR**-go-RL

lapenke saikel ingdoiponbomsi,
[lapèn=ke	saikél	ingdōi-pōn-bōm-si
and.then=TOP	bicycle(<Eng)	push-take.away-CONT-NF:RL

la aphrang kevang abang, dambomlo
[là	a-aphráng	ke-vàng	abàng]	dàm-bōm-lò]
this	POSS-first	NMLZ-come	NPDL	go-CONT-RL

'The three of them went their own way, and then pushing the bicycle, the one who first came (i.e. the one with the bicycle), he kept going.' [SiT, PS 034]

(245) Reflexive *che-* on motion verb, cross-referencing goal
"neke nepeipén nepo ahem chedampo"
nè=ke	[[ne-pēi=pen	ne-pō]	a-hēm]	**che**-dām-pò
1EXCL=TOP	1EXCL-mother=with	1EXCL-father	POSS-house	**RR**-go-IRR1

'"I will go to my mother and father's house."' [SeT, MTN 038]

In (246), *che-* functions as a reciprocal marker: *-nīng ói* means 'be sad', and *-nīng che'ói* means 'be upset with one another'.

(246) *che-* with reciprocal function
pangri pangdonrongló anke ha aphike la Bey
pangrí   pangdòn-ròng-lò   ánke   há   aphī=ke   [[là   Bēy
reconcile even.out-instead-RL and.then over.there after=TOP   this CLAN

Ke'etpen Bey Ki'ik abangke aning
ke-èt=pen]   [Bēy   ke-ìk   abàng=ke]]   a-nīng
NMLZ-be.yellow/fair=with CLAN NMLZ-be.black NPDL=TOP   POSS-mind

***che**'oitanglo*
che-ói-táng-lò
RR-be.sad-finish-RL
'They got married, and then quite some time later, Bey the Fair and Bey the Black got upset with each other.' [WR, BCS 017]

Reflexive/reciprocal *che-* occurs in a lot of middle contexts as defined by Kemmer (1993). Specifically, it is used with verbs of 'putting on/wearing', such as *ch-ingchói* 'put on (e.g., a shirt)' and *che-kūp* 'wear (a hat or something else that covers the head)'. It also occurs in verbs of 'grooming', such as *(lāng) ch-inglú* '(water) bathe'. Another example of the middle function of *che-* is in (247), where it occurs on *lūt* 'enter' in the context of the sun setting, i.e., entering into the horizon.

(247) 'Middle' function of *che-* 'reflexive/reciprocal'
anpenlole pulotangte adap ingthangvakpen
ánpen-lò=le   pùlotángtē a-dàp   ingthàng-vàk-pen
and.then-RL=FOC:IRR if   POSS-morning be.dawn-RES:open-NF

*arni ka**che**lut an ajo'an*
arnì   ke-**che**-lút   ánke   a-jó=án
sun   NMLZ-**RR**-enter   and.then POSS-night=up.to
'And then, according to what you have said so far, from morning until the sun enters (into the horizon), until night...' [KaR, SWK 056]

There are several pieces of evidence that *che-* is an old morpheme. First, there are phonological reasons. It is a prefix, and like other prefixes in Karbi, it is phonologically small, i.e., it only has an onset (but no coda) consonant and a weak vowel that is sometimes deleted. It also has morphophonological effects on the following root tone (§3.9.1.1). Second, there are a few verb roots whose first syllable is clearly the *che-* prefix because the semantics fit perfectly, but the portion without the *che-* is no longer used as a root independently, for example *chetòng* 'meet, run into', as shown in (248), where *tòng* by itself is not a root.

(248) *che-* in lexicalized roots: *chetòng* 'meet, run into'
       jangrengso aphan chetongloklo {mm}
       jangrēngsō   aphān   chetòng-lòk-lò   mm
       orphan   NSUBJ   meet-happen.to-RL   AFF
       'He ran into that orphan.' [HK, TR 049]

Since *che-* is relatively old, there are likely to be (apparent) cognates in other Tibeto-Burman languages. In fact, in Northern 'Kuki-Chin', a number of languages have a *ki-* reflexive/reciprocal prefix (Henderson 1965; Krishan 1980; Stern 1984; see Konnerth (2009: 120–123) and So-Hartmann (2013)).[80]

8.4.4 Auto-benefactive/malefactive *cho-*

Called the 'middle' by Grüßner (1978: 94),[81] *cho-* is more specifically a marker of an auto-benefactive and, in certain contexts, an auto-malefactive. In (249), *cho-jōr* 'AUTO.BEN/MAL-sell' means that the selling of the bananas was supposed to result in a benefit/profit for the seller.

(249) Auto-benefactive function of *cho-*
       *phinu **cho**jordamji aphan hu kulat*
       [phinū **cho-**jōr-dām-jí   a-phān]   [hú   kulát
       banana **AUTO.BEN/MAL-**sell-GO-IRR2   POSS-PURP   over.there shop(<Asm)

       anat damlo
       a-nát]   dàm-lò
       POSS-direction   go-RL
       'In order to go and sell bananas there he went towards the shop.' [HI, BPh 005]

The much rarer case of expressing a negative effect on the subject, i.e., the auto-malefactive, is represented in (250), where *sè cho-lóng* means 'get sick'.

---

[80] There also is a *kê-* prefix in Tenyidie (formerly known as Angami; belonging to the Angami-Pochuri group of Central Tibeto-Burman), which, however, combines reciprocal marking and verbalization (Kuolie 2006), so it may or may not be related to the 'Kuki-Chin' and Karbi prefixes.
[81] Grüßner suggests the function of *cho-* is to indicate that "the doer himself carries out the action" ("dass der Täter selbst die Handlung ausführt").

(250) Auto-malefactive function of *cho-*
sok sang hem chevan'etke Bamonpo abang
[sōk   sāng   hēm   che-vān-ét=ke]   [[Bamónpō   abàng
paddy   raw.rice house   RR-bring-PRF=TOP   PN   NPDL

*apiso abangke se **cho**long aphu kesolo*
a-pisò   abàng=ke]   sè   **cho**-lóng   a-phú   ke-sò-lò]
POSS-wife   NPDL=TOP   disease **AUTO.BEN/MAL**-get POSS-head   NMLZ-hurt-RL
'After they brought home the paddy, Bamonpo's wife got sick, and had a fever.'
[KK, BMS 013]

The auto-benefactive/malefactive *cho-* may co-occur with the general benefactive/malefactive *-pī* (§9.2.5.2.1). The only examples of this come from elicitation, where only either the auto-malefactive and a (non-subject) benefactive go together, as in (251), or the auto-benefactive and a (non-subject) malefactive, as in (252).

(251) Auto-malefactive marked by *cho-* and (general) benefactive marked by *-pī*
Kungri   a-phān   àn   **cho**-tún-**pī**-lò
NAME   POSS-NSUBJ   rice   **AUTO.MAL**-cook-**BEN**-RL
'(I) cooked for Kungri (but shouldn't have because Kungri turned out to be ungrateful in some way).' [SiT, KT]

(252) Auto-benefactive marked by *cho-* and (general) malefactive marked by *-pī*
phurùi   **cho**-phī-**pī**-dèt
yam   **AUTO.BEN**-roast-**MAL**-PFV
'I roasted yam for myself (though it belonged to somebody else, so my roasting the yam had a negative effect on the respective other person).' [SiT, KT]

8.4.5 On the functional overlap between reflexive/reciprocal *che-* and auto-benefactive/malefactive *cho-*

There is a certain degree of functional overlap between reflexive/reciprocal *che-* and auto-benefactive/malefactive *cho-*. For example, taking a minimal pair from Grüßner's (1978: 95) work, my language consultants report the meaning is actually the same, because using *che-* here also suggests an autobenefactive reading, see (253).

(253) Minimal pair between *che-* and *cho-*
    (a) *kolóm   nè   **che**-nám-jí*
        pen   1EXCL   **RR**-buy-IRR2
        'I will buy myself a pen'

    (b) *kolóm   nè   **cho**-nám-jí*
        pen   1EXCL   **AUTO.BEN/MAL**-buy-IRR2
        'id.'

In (254) 'teaching children', however, the minimal pair between *che-* and *cho-* yields different meanings: With *che-* the implication is that this is about one's own children, whereas *cho-* has the autobenefactive reading of teaching children for one's own benefit/profit, i.e., being a teacher professionally.

(254) Minimal pair between *che-* and *cho-*
    (a) *osō-mār   a-phān   lō   ka-**che**-thán*
        child-PL   POSS-NSUBJ   book   NMLZ-**RR**-tell
        'I teach my own children.'

    (b) *osō-mār   a-phān   lō   ka-**cho**-thán*
        child-PL   POSS-NSUBJ   book   NMLZ-**AUTO.BEN/MAL**-tell
        'I teach children (for a living).' (SiT, KT)

9 Verbal morphology: Post-root slots

This chapter continues the discussion of verbal morphology and deals with elements that occur after the root. After an overview (§9.1), the order of presentation follows the order in which the elements occur. Therefore the large class of suffixal predicate derivations is covered first in §9.2. This is followed by functions of reduplication (§9.3). Next comes the onset-reduplicative negative suffix -Cē (§9.4). Finally, the more inflectional suffixes are presented in the remaining four sections. This begins with an aspect category (§9.5), followed by a slot where four different types of suffixes may occur: mood marking suffixes (§9.6); subordinate marking suffixes (§9.7); one suffix marking aspect (§9.8); as well as non-declarative speech act suffixes (§9.9).

9.1 Overview of post-root slots

The structure of post-root slots is more complex than that of pre-root slots. This is already obvious from the fact that there are a hugely greater number of suffixes than prefixes in Karbi. But there are also several ways in which post-root verbal morphology defies the linguist's attempt to sort morphemes into a neat linear order. Let us return to the post-root portion of the position class diagram in Figure 13 (cf. Figure 11 in §8.2). While this figure looks fairly neat, there actually are co-occurrence restrictions between slots 8 and 10 that cannot be represented in such a position class diagram. They are discussed in §9.1.1. Further complications exist with respect to -*pín* in slot 9 (§9.1.2), as well as within slot 10, as -*jí* and -*làng* appear to co-occur. This is discussed in §9.1.3.

Moreover, another problematic slot is 7 'reduplication'. This is because reduplication does not frequently occur with other suffixes in the corpus. Examples (255) and (256) show, however, that reduplication (whose functions are discussed in §9.3) may occur before the quasi/onset-reduplicative negative suffix, which is why the position class diagram presented above has the two slots ordered that way.

(255) Reduplication suffix indicating (distributive) plural occurring before negative suffix
"te mo pine**pinane**detjima,
te mò pí-nē~**pinā-Cē**-dèt-jí=ma
and.then/therefore future what-INDEF~**DIST.PL-NEG**-PFV-IRR2=Q

ko jirpo?" pu {mm}
ko jīrpō pu mm
buddy:VOC friend QUOT AFF
"'And there won't be anything (any difficulties, problems, dangers) in the future, my friend?'" [HK, TR 140]

(256) Reduplication suffix occurring before negative suffix
 *chón-rai~**rai-rē***
 jump-RES:break~DIST.PL-NEG
 '(S/he) didn't repeatedly jump and break (something).' Or: '(S/he) repeatedly jumped on things without breaking them.' [KT 111208]

5	6	7	8	9	10
ROOT	DERIV*	RDPL	-Cē	-dèt	-jí
				-pín	-lò
					-sì
					-làng
					-nāng
					...

5: root (/stem)
6: predicate derivations, including modals
7: reduplication
8: negation
9: aspect
10: mood, aspect, subordinate, non-declarative speech act marking

Figure 13: Post-root slots of the Karbi verb.

9.1.1 Cooccurrence restriction between negative -Cē and irrealis -jí and -pò (slots 8 and 10)

The negative suffix -Cē may only co-occur with the irrealis suffixes -jí and -pò if perfective -dèt intervenes. Therefore, *lūt-lē-dèt-jí=ma* 'enter-NEG-PFV-IRR2=Q' (RBT, ChM 042) and *chók-chē-dèt-pò* 'be.fine-NEG-PFV-IRR1' (SH, CSM 049) are perfectly acceptable. However, **dàm-dē-jí* '*go-NEG-IRR2' and **dàm-dē-pò* '*go-NEG-IRR1' are unacceptable.

9.1.2 Slot 9 -pín 'experiential'

The experiential suffix -pín only occurs with -lò 'realis' of slot 10, but no other slot 10 suffixes. It also has mostly been found to occur in conjunction with negative -Cē in the sense of 'have never V-ed'. For more details, see §9.5.2.

9.1.3 Slot 10 -làng 'still' and -jí-lāng 'IRR2-still'

A problem for a position-class analysis is posed by -làng 'still'. It appears to be able to co-occur with one and only one suffix from the same slot 10: the suffix -jí 'irrealis2'. Specifically, it is acceptable to say *chō-jí-lāng* 'eat-IRR2-still' meaning '(s/he) is still eating (and will continue eating for awhile)'. However, **chō-pò-làng* or **chō-lò-làng* are both unacceptable. These acceptability data can be analyzed in two ways. One can either pose a slot 11 for *-làng* (and only *-làng*), or can argue that *-làng* should go in slot 10. I argue for the latter analysis. Specifically, I argue that *-jī-lāng* is undergoing grammaticalization/lexicalization, or mono-morphemization. There are phonological, morphological, and semantic reasons in favor of this analysis.

On a phonological level, note that low tone *-làng* turns into mid tone in *-jī-lāng*, and note that in hypo-articulated speech, a contraction to *-alàng* occurs (§3.7.3). That is, there is phonological evidence of *-jī-lāng* forming a close unit.

On a morphological level, note that it is possible to add *-jī-lāng* to a negated stem. It is acceptable to say *mèn-mē-jī-lāng* 'be.ripe-NEG-IRR2-still' meaning '(the fruit) won't be ripe yet', which 'violates' the principle that the irrealis suffixes cannot immediately follow the negative suffix without *-dèt* 'perfective' intervening (see above §9.1.1). The fact that *-jī-lāng* can immediately follow the negative suffix when *-jī* and *-pò* cannot represents morphological evidence of *-jī-lāng* being more than just a sequence of *-jī* 'irrealis2' and *-làng* 'still'.

On a semantic level, there is no obvious reason why *-jī-lāng* is acceptable but not *-pò-làng* (or *-pò-lāng*). The two irrealis suffixes *-jī* and *-pò* overlap in their semantic range to a large degree (§9.6.2.1). Again, this semantic fact only makes sense if *-jī-lāng* somehow already is a unit.

Now, *-jī-lāng* semantically still appears compositional: it means both 'future irrealis' and 'still'. Furthermore, in a language in which most morphemes are monosyllabic (with the only substantive exceptions of disyllables in *ing-* and *ar-*, §6.3), one may be less inclined to analyze a form with two very transparent parts as one morpheme. So the best analysis may be that *-jī-lāng* is neither one morpheme nor two morphemes, but that it is caught in-between, as a result of grammatical change.

9.2 Suffixal predicate derivations

Predicate derivations represent a very large class of suffixes in Karbi. This is a category common to many Tibeto-Burman languages of Northeast India. It has also been referred to as adverbial suffixes (Burling 2004) or modifying suffixes (Grüßner 1978), and there are a number of other labels that have been applied to this type of category (see Post 2009). I follow Post (2009) in calling them predicate derivations.

In his grammar of Karbi, Grüßner (1978: 105–22) lists a total of 164 suffixes, but his dictionary manuscript includes an even much larger number.[82]

---

[82] Note also that Bey (2010: 29–42), in a booklet on suggestions for how to standardize Karbi orthography, offers a list of predicate derivations with sample host roots for the particular suffixes.

9.2.1 Overview

By way of introducing suffixal predicate derivations, it is worth to consider structural properties on the one hand and functional categories of predicate derivations in Karbi on the other hand. In addition, a note on what little is known about the origins of these suffixes is in order.

9.2.1.1 Structural properties
While all predicate derivations are suffixes that occur in the same (repeatable) slot within the verbal template, particular properties along several structural dimensions are not shared between predicate derivations. In particular, predicate derivations differ in the scope of negation and reduplication; a small handful of predicate derivations are discontinuous while all others are not; and predicate derivations vary dramatically in how productive they are, i.e., how flexible they are to occur with different verb roots.

9.2.1.1.1 Scope of negation and reduplication
In a complex verb stem that consists of a root and a predicate derivation followed by the negative suffix, i.e. schematically: 'V.ROOT-P.DER-NEG', there are two options for the scope of negation. It could be either '[[V.ROOT-P.DER]-NEG]' or '[V.ROOT-[P.DER-NEG]]', that is, the scope of negation could be over the complex stem as a whole, or specifically just over the predicate derivation. While the result is often ambiguity between the two scope possibilities, it appears possible to sort a subset of predicate derivations into those that attract the scope of negation such that only the predicate derivation ends up negated, and those that form such a tight bond with the verb root or stem they attach to that negation can only ever have scope over the entire complex stem.

Predicate derivations that attract the scope of negation include certain highly productive derivations that quantify over the event or the O argument, such as -ò 'much' in (257).

(257) Scope of negation over predication derivation (quantifying derivation)
 chō-ò-ē
 eat-much-NEG
 '(S/he) ate but not much.'

Predicate derivations that are not able to be singled out under the scope of negation include some low productivity (§9.2.1.1.3) degree or extent derivation ones. An example is -jìr, which occurs with *ingthìr* 'be clean' to indicate a higher degree of cleanliness, 'very clean' or 'thoroughly clean'. However, if the negative suffix is added, the whole word as in (258) can only ever mean 'be not clean (at all)', and not 'be clean but not very clean'. That is, the scope of negation can only be over the whole verb stem, but not specifically over the suffix.

(258) Scope of negation over verb stem (degree/extent derivation)
ingthir-jìr-jē
be.clean-INTENS-NEG
'(It) is not clean (at all).' [KT 111103]

Result derivation are ambiguous when the negative suffix is added. In (259) and (260), the scope of negation may be specifically over the result derivation, such that the action denoted by the verb root occurred but without the result denoted by the suffix. Or the scope of negation may be over the verb stem as a whole such that neither the action denoted by the root occurred nor, consequently, the result denoted by the suffix.

(259) Scope of negation ambiguous (result derivation)
túr-pùr-pē
kick-RES:fall.over-NEG
'(S/he) kicked (it) but (it) didn't fall over.' Or: '(S/he) didn't kick it (and it didn't fall over).' [KT 111208]

(260) *ingnì-dūn-prèt-prē*
sit-JOIN-RES:affecting.inflated.object-NEG
'(S/he) sat down without affecting an inflated object.' Or: '(S/he) didn't sit down (and didn't affect an inflated object).' [KT 111103]

In addition, (261) shows that more scope issues arise when both a reduplication suffix and the negative suffix are added. The reduplication suffix, which here indicates plurality, in combination with the negative suffix, could have scope over the entire verb stem, i.e., over the action plus the result, with both being negated; or it could similarly have scope over the entire verb stem, but with only the result negated, which then leads to the interpretation of 'repeated jumping without breaking anything'.

(261) Scope of negation ambiguous (result derivation)
chón-rai~rai-rē
jump-RES:break~DIST.PL-NEG
'(S/he) didn't repeatedly jump and break (something).' Or: '(S/he) repeatedly jumped on things without breaking them.' [KT 111208]

Finally, note that reduplication in some instances may also only have scope over the suffix, as in (262), where the reduplication functions as an intensifier for *-hòi* 'a little bit'.

(262) *thèk-hòi~hōi*
know.how-little.bit~INTENS
'know just a tiny little bit'

9.2.1.1.2 Discontinuous predicate derivations

So far we have encountered two predicate derivations that are expressed via a suffix pair that occurs on two subsequent repetitions of the verb stem. These suffixes do not occur individually and do not have independent meanings. The meaning only arises as they co-occur in the particular pair. The two so far attested discontinuous predicate derivations are listed in Table 84, a text example of *-nèk ... -nòk* 'doing bad unnecessarily' is (263).

Table 84: Discontinuous predicate derivations.

Suffix1	Suffix2	Meaning
-chò	-hàp	everything (negative evaluation)
-nèk	-nòk	doing bad unnecessarily

(263) Discontinuous predicate derivation
  "pi chonghoisi nang harlongle <nang>
  [pí   chonghói=si   nàng   harlōng=le   <nang>
  what   reason=FOC:RL   you   stone=FOC:IRR   you

  kiturnek kiturnok?
  ke-túr-nèk   **ke-túr-nòk**]
  NMLZ-kick-doing.bad.unnecessarily.1   NMLZ-kick-doing.bad.unnecessarily.2

  Neso apran damjuilo [...]
  [ne-osō   a-prán   dàm-jùi-lò]
  1EXCL:POSS-child   POSS-life   go-away-RL
  '"What did you kick the rock for? The life of my daughter is gone [...]."' [RBT, ChM 033]

Although the suffix pair *-tháp ... -phrú* in (264) looks like an analogous case, here the first suffix *-tháp* 'mindlessly' may also occur by itself, which is why this particular suffix pair is instead treated as an elaborate expression, see §16.2.2.

(264) Verb suffix elaborate expression
  *amat chonghota **chonthap chonphrulo***
  amāt   chonghō=tā   chón-**tháp**   chón-**phrú-lò**
  and.then   frog=ADD   jump-**mindlessly**   jump-**EE:tháp-RL**

  kesolo... karlesibongpo adon chonrai
  ke-sò-lò   karlēsibóngpō   a-dón   chón-rài
  NMLZ-hurt-RL   sp.squirrel   POSS-bridge   jump-RES:solid.object.breaking
  'And then, the frog was jumping everywhere, (because) he was hurt, and he jumped on the ladder of the squirrel and it broke.' [RBT, ChM 018]

9.2.1.1.3 Productivity

Predicate derivations (PDs) vary with respect to their productivity, i.e., their flexibility to occur with different verb roots. Another way to look at this is to consider the various suffixes located on a grammatical-to-lexical continuum. While some predicate derivations have a purely grammatical function and can seemingly occur with any verb root, others are closer to the lexical end of the spectrum, and only occur with verb roots from a particular semantic field, or a subset of those, or even just a single one.

Sample PDs that are highly productive are given in Table 85. Functional categories include certain quantifying (or degree or extent indicating) ones such as *-ò* 'much'; argument structure modifying ones such as *-pī* 'benefactive/malefactive'; or aspectual ones such as *-ét* 'perfect'.

Table 85: Sample highly productive PDs.

Highly productive PDs	
-ò	'much'
-pī	'BEN/MAL'
-ét	'PRF'

Table 86 shows the productive degree/extent derivation *-hòi* 'quite' vis-à-vis some other suffixes that have essentially the same meaning but are not productive: they each only occur with a particular verb root. Note that for native speakers, the different suffixes in Table 86 clearly correspond with respect to their functions. Karbi speakers report that *-klùi* in *ardīkklùi* needs to change to *-tàng* if the verb root is *arjāng*.

Table 86: Sample PDs that mean 'quite' (productive and non-productive PDs).

PD	Host verb root
-hòi	[productive]
-hùi	làk 'be tired, exhausted'
-klùi	ardīk 'be heavy'
-tàng	arjāng 'be light'

Similarly, Table 87 offers a list of sample predicate derivations that act as intensifiers for a very small set of verb roots (in some case, a single one). As discussed in §3.5.4.3, the high-frequency collocation of non-productive (particularly, intensifier) predicate derivations can be exploited to differentiate tone minimal pairs. Note that the last three rows of Table 87 show PDs that uniquely identify members of the tone minimal triplet roots *thì* 'die', *thī* 'be short', and *thí* 'snatch'.

Table 87: Non-productive intensifier PDs.

PD	Host verb root(s)
-sén	mē 'be good'
-jìr	ingthìr 'be clean'
-krùng	sùng 'be difficult'
-sót	náng 'need, must'
-bor	klar 'shine'
-klìng	tōk 'pound, grind'
-lòt	thì 'die', mēk jáng 'sleep'
-jòk	thí 'snatch'
-hèk	thī 'be short', bī 'be small', chungkrèng 'be thin'

9.2.1.2 Origins of predicate derivations

The origins of predicate derivations (perhaps with the exception of the ideophonic ones) lie in lexical items that in some cases still co-exist in the language along with the suffixes. In the majority of cases, however, no corresponding lexical items can be found (anymore). Table 88 shows some sample predicate derivations with their apparent lexical origins.

Table 88: Some predicate derivations and related lexical items.

Predicate derivation	Gloss	Related lexical item
-pī	'BEN/MAL'	pī 'give' (V)
-lùt	'enter'	lūt 'enter' (V)
-lōng	'get.to'	lóng 'get' (V)
-chēng	'for.first.time'	chéng 'begin' (V)
-dùn~-dūn	'JOIN'	dùn 'join, follow' (V)
-mék	'in.advance'	mēk 'eye' (N)
-rèi~-rài	'sideways'	-rèi~-rài 'at.side.of' (RN)

While the tone may correspond between suffix and root, as in *-pī* 'benefactive/malefactive', it does not in other instances, such as *-chēng* 'for first time'. Furthermore, in some instances, the suffix has developed allomorphy, presumably as part of phonological reduction in the course of grammaticalization; an example is *-dùn~-dūn* 'JOIN'. While most of the traceable lexical origins of predicate derivations are verb roots, there are some cases, in which a noun root appears to be the source, e.g., *-mék* 'in advance', or *-rài~-rèi* 'sideways' (as in *làng-rèi* 'look briefly to the side'), which has to be related to what is synchronically a relator noun: *-rài~-rèi* 'at side of' (§5.4.2).

The historical development of verbal suffixes from verb roots has likely arisen through serial verb constructions, a common construction in (Southeast) Asia. The source construction for noun roots would likely be a noun incorporation construction.

9.2.1.3 Functional categories of predicate derivations

The main functional categories of Karbi predicate derivations include manner derivations (§9.2.2), result derivations (§9.2.3), direction, (associated) motion, and path derivations (§9.2.4), derivations that modify or highlight arguments and/or argument structure (§9.2.5), and aspect/aktionsart and time derivations (§9.2.6). Several other derivations that do not sort neatly into one of these categories are discussed in §9.2.7.

9.2.2 Manner

9.2.2.1 Non-ideophonic manner

The majority of non-ideophonic manner derivations have relatively rich semantics and are not very productive (§9.2.1.1.3). Comprehensively documenting them requires extended lexical entries that offer sample sentences as well as unacceptable collocations. Several such suffixes are given in Table 89 as examples. There is a very large number of non-ideophonic manner derivations in Karbi; of the functional categories presented in this grammar, the non-ideophonic manner category has the most member suffixes.

Table 89: Sample non-ideophonic manner predicate derivations.

Form	Gloss	Examples / Sample host verbs	Translation
-bòng	'nicely arranged'	*sōk a-rōng vàng-bòng* paddy POSS-plant come-*bòng*	'the paddy plants are growing beautifully'
		a-kèng dàm-bòng POSS-foot go-*bòng*	'(a baby) is walking nicely on its feet'
		ingthān-bòng~bòng cut-*bòng*~DIST.PL	'cutting (meat) neatly into pieces'

Table 89 (continued)

Form	Gloss	Examples / Sample host verbs
-bùp	'suddenly'	chingkói 'fall (humans)', kló 'fall', tekáng 'leave (behind)', ó 'put down', tengnè 'forget'; [*chō 'eat'; *dàm 'go']
-chèk	'firmly'	nèp 'catch', kòk 'tie', ót 'touch', thít 'tie'

9.2.2.2 Ideophonic manner

Table 90 shows several sample ideophonic manner derivations, whose phonological form corresponds to the perceived sound or to an auditory association of the event.

Table 90: Sample ideophonic manner derivations.

Form	Gloss	Sound of …	Sample host root
-sir	'sd.spinning'	spinning	artìng 'spin'
-dùp	'falling.sd.from.high.solid.obj'	falling (small, heavy object)	kló 'fall'
-chón	'sd.very.quickly'	running very quickly	kát 'run'

9.2.2.3 Degree or extent

There are both productive (general, grammatical) and non-productive (specific or idiosyncratic, lexical) suffixes that indicate the degree or extent of an event. Table 91 and Table 92, repeated from §9.2.1.1.3, offer some sample suffixes that vary in productivity.

Table 91: Sample PDs that indicate a considerable degree ('quite') (productive and non-productive PDs).

PD	Sample host root
-hòi	[productive]
-hùi	làk 'be tired, exhausted'
-klùi	ardīk 'be heavy'
-tàng	arjāng 'be light'

In addition to the non-productive intensifier derivations in Table 92, there also exists a productive, general intensifier -(v)arèt, which occurs with both adjectival as well as action verbs, see (265) and (266).

Table 92: Non-productive intensifier PDs.

PD	Host verb root	PD	Host verb root
-sén	mē̃ 'be good'	-lòt	thī 'die', mēk jáng 'sleep'
-jìr	ingthìr 'be clean'	-jòk	thí 'snatch'
-bòr	klàr 'shine'	-hèk	thī 'be short', bī 'be small', chungkrèng 'be thin'
-klìng	tōk 'pound, grind'		

(265) Intensifier -(v)arèt with adjectival verb ('very')
anke dak chevangpó, pi apotsi nang nangbang
ánke   [dāk che-vāng-pò]   [pí   a-pōt=si]   nàng   nang-bàng
and.then here RR-come-IRR1   what POSS-reason=FOC:RL you   2:POSS-body

lengvaretmati, sarbura" pu
léng-varèt=mati,   sàrburá   pu
be.fat.HUM-INTENS=CG   old.man   QUOT
'And then he would return, "Why are you so fat/healthy, man? (That's very strange!)"' [SeT, MTN 025]

(266) Intensifier -(v)arèt with action verb ('keep V-ing')
mathalo amatsi adappen chokang arsovaret
mathà-lò   amātsi   a-dàp-pèn   chòkàng   arsō-varèt
think-RL   and.then POSS-morning-from   axe   sharpen-INTENS

arsovaret arsovaretlo apiso abang arjulo...
arsō-varèt   arsō-varèt-lò   a-pisò   abàng   arjū-lò
sharpen-INTENS   sharpen-INTENS-RL   POSS-wife   NPDL   ask-RL
'He was thinking, and then since early in the morning, he was sharpening his axe for a long time, and his wife asked...' [SeT, MTN 014]

9.2.2.3.1 Quantification derivations

There are several highly productive suffixes shown in Table 93 that function as argument quantifiers (§9.2.5.1) with transitive and ditransitive verbs, but indicate the degree or extent on intransitive verbs.

Table 93: PDs indicating argument quantification and degree or extent.

Form	Gloss
-ò	'much'
-òng	'(too.)much'
-pìk	'a.lot'

For example, *chō* 'eat' with *-ò* 'much' becomes 'eat much', where *-ò* quantifies the O argument, but *mē* 'be good' with *-ò* 'much' becomes 'very good'. Non-adjectival intransitive verbs also occur with *-ò*, for example, *dàm-ò* 'go-much', in which case the scale is one of frequency: 'go a lot, go often'.

9.2.2.3.2 Comparative *-mū~-mūchòt* and superlative *-néi~-nái*

Comparative *-mū~-mūchòt* and superlative *-néi~-nái* are used with adjectival as well as non-adjectival verbs, as discussed in §4.2.2. Examples of both suffixes are repeated below. (See also §13.2.2.5 on comparative constructions.)

(267) Comparative *-mū~-mūchòt*
 anke ejon nangtetphlut <a> nangthemuchot
 ánke   e-jōn   nang=tèt-phlùt   nang=thè-**mūchòt**
 and.then   one-CLF:animal   CIS=exit-suddenly.big.A/O CIS=be.big-COMPAR
 'And then, one (tiger) came out (of the jungle or some area in the Rongker ground) and he was bigger (than expected and than the previous one).' [HK, TR 172]

(268) Superlative *-néi~-nái*
 akethenei akehoineilo tangho [...]
 a-ke-thè-**néi**   akehoì-**néi**-lò   tànghò
 POSS-NMLZ-be.big-SPLT   powerful.person-SPLT-RL   REP
 '(He) was the biggest and the most powerful one (so they say) [...].' [HK, TR 033]

9.2.3 Result

Table 94 offers some sample result derivations along with verb roots the suffixes may occur with. A corpus example with *-ràk* 'RES:little.wound' is provided in (269).

Table 94: Sample result derivations.

Form	Gloss	Sample host verbs
-bòp	'RES:death'	*ap* 'shoot', *thèng* 'beat', *pheré* 'fear'
-ràk	'RES:little.wound'	*arkè* 'scratch', *kòr* 'bite',
-dàk	'RES:split'	*phlàk* 'split'
-prèt	'RES:burst'	*ingnì* 'sit', *dòng* 'step'

(269) Result derivations
[...] *"o bang voarbipi akam kechomathale*
[o   bàng   vōarbípī   a-kám
VOC   CLF:HUM:PL   bird.sp   POSS-work
ke-chomathā=le
NMLZ-think.with.bad.intentions=FOC:IRR

neno nanglutchok nangarkerakrakdetkema?"
ne-nò   nang=lūt-chòk
my-ear   CIS=enter-disappearing
nang=arkè-**ràk**~ràk-dèt=ke=ma]
CIS=scratch-**RES:little.wound**~DISTR.PL-PFV=TOP=Q
'[...] "O Voarbipi, what were you thinking, coming into my ears and scratching and wounding me?!"' [RBT, ChM 034]

9.2.4 Direction, (associated) motion, path

Table 95 lists direction, motion, and path derivations.

Table 95: Direction, motion, and path derivations.

Form	Gloss	Sample host verbs
-dùn~-dūn	'JOIN'	[productive]
-pòn~-pōn	'on.the.way'	[productive]
-dàm~-dām	'GO'	[productive]
-tekáng~-káng	'leave.behind'	[productive]
-thòt	'into.opening'	*kló* 'fall'
-lùt	'enter'	*kòr* 'bite'
-jùi	'away:S'	*dàm* 'go', *dùn* 'follow',
-chòk	'disappearing'	*var* 'throw', *lūt* 'enter', **dàm* 'go'
-chòr	'away'	*var* 'throw', *tur* 'kick', *ingjar* 'fly',

An example of *-jùi* 'away' is (270).

(270) Predicate derivation *-jùi* 'away'
[...] *misorongpoke a'ik atum atipi atum*
misòrongpō=ke a-ìk   a-tūm   a-tepī   a-tūm
ant.sp=TOP   POSS-older.brother   POSS-PL   POSS-elder.brother's.wife   POSS-PL

adappen rit damjuilo
a-dàp=pen   rīt   dàm-**jùi**-lò
POSS-morning=from field   go-**away**-RL
'[...] [T]he ant's older brother and his wife had gone to the *jhum* field in the morning.' [RBT, ChM 009]

The two suffixes *-pòn~-pōn* 'on.the.way' and *-dùn~-dūn* 'JOIN' to some degree function in a complementary, or converse, way. First, consider *-dùn~-dūn* 'JOIN'. This suffix is used in situations where an event occurs against the background of something that is in motion (see also §9.2.7.1). For example, if runners are racing each other, people watching and giving the runners water can be said to *lāng pī-dūn* 'water give-JOIN' > 'give water (to the runners as they are moving along)'. If we switch perspective from the bystanders to the runners, we can say about the runners that they *lāng ēn-pōn* 'water take-on.the.way' > 'take water (as they are moving along)', here using *-pōn* indicating that the event occurs while the subject is in motion.

Other examples of *-dùn~-dūn* 'JOIN' and *-pòn~-pōn* 'on.the.way' can further clarify their functions. In (271), *-dùn~-dūn* 'JOIN' indicates that the food items are being wrapped in order to be taken to the field. This occurrence resembles the marking of 'associated motion' (cf. §8.3.2.2) in that the motion is associated with the event but will only occur after the event actually denoted by the verb has finished. (Note that *-dùn~-dūn* 'JOIN' also occurs in contexts that do not directly involve motion events, see §9.2.7.1.)

(271) Acting in the context of expected motion: *-dùn~-dūn* 'JOIN'
       [...] ok paka paka han paka paka lopen
       [ōk   paká   paká   hán   paká   paká   lō=pen
       meat   very.good   very.good   curry   very.good   very.good   banana.leaf=with

       thuidun pame pamepo
       thùi-**dūn**   pa-mé   pa-mé-pò]
       wrap-**JOIN**   CAUS-be.good   CAUS-be.good-IRR1
       '[...] [S]he wrapped very good meat and very good curry very nicely for him to take along (to the field).' [CST, RO 014]

Two more examples of *-pòn~-pōn* 'on.the.way' are offered in (272) and (273). First, (272) is parallel to the example of the runners: in this personal narrative, the speaker says that they stopped in a town on the way and bought some snacks and water for the trip.

(272) Acting while moving: *-pòn~-pōn* 'on.the.way'
       anke thesere haihuita namponlo <kecho> tovar
       ánke   theseré   háihúi=tā   nàm-pōn-lò   <ke-cho>   továr
       and.then   fruits   different.kinds.of=also buy-on.the.way-RL   NMLZ-eat   road

kecho aphan lang haihui namponlo
ke-chō   a-phān   lāng   háihúi   nàm-pōn-lò
NMLZ-eat   POSS-PURP water different.kinds.of buy-on.the.way -RL
'And then, we also bought some fruit (to carry along), to eat on the road, and we bought some water (to carry along).' [SH, CSM 014]

The next example (273) features the suffix twice. As *-pòn~-pōn* occurs on *kló* 'fall', the idea again is that the falling is happening during ongoing motion away from the deictic center. In the first occurrence of *-pòn~-pōn* on the manner motion verb *vèk* 'steer', however, the suffix simply highlights the translocative or andative, i.e., motion away from a point of reference.

(273) Motion away or occurring during ongoing motion away: *-pòn~-pōn* 'on.the.way'
saikel vekponbom dambomlo
[saikél   vèk-pòn-bōm   dàm-bōm-lò]
bicycle(<Eng)   steer-take.away-CONT   go-CONT-RL

atheta kloponpresi tovar soding kloponbomlo
a-thē=tā   kló-pòn-prè-si   továr   sodíng
POSS-fruit=also   fall-take.away-scattered-NF:RL   road   all.along
kló-pòn-bōm-lò
fall-take.away-CONT-RL
'He is steering the bicycle away and going away, and the fruit is falling down here and there and all along the road it keeps falling down.' [SiT, PS 025]

Another suffix that also indicates the translocative is *-dàm~-dām* 'GO', see (274).

(274) Translocative marking with *-dàm~-dām* 'GO'
latum achitimsi klodamduplo [...]
là-tūm   a-chitìm=si   kló-**dàm**-dùp-lò
this-PL   POSS-half=FOC:RL   fall-**GO**-falling.sound.from.high.solid.obj-RL
'He fell down right (and landed right) in the middle of them [...].' [HK, TR 189]

While in (274) the action of falling down (specifically, off a tree) is involuntary, *-dàm~-dām* 'GO' also and more commonly marks associated motion[83] with purposive semantics that translates as 'go and V', as in (275).

---

[83] Associated motion categories indicate that the event denoted by the verb occurs against the background of a motion event (Guillaume 2013).

(275) Associated motion 'go and V' marking with *-dàm~-dām* 'GO'
si hala bamonpopen bamonpike
[sì   [hála   bamón-pō=pen   bamón-pī=ke]
therefore that wise.person(<Ind)-male=with   wise.person(<Ind)-female=TOP

ha rit chotiki chonghoidam, <rit> inglong aritsi
há   rīt   cho-tikī   cho-inghói-**dàm**] <rīt>   [inglóng
over.there field AUTO.BEN-cultivate   AUTO.BEN-do-GO   field   hill
a-rīt=si
POSS-field=FOC:RL

kenongdam kisimdam sai chotikidamlo
ke-nōng-**dām**   ke-sìm-**dām**]   [sái   cho-tikī-**dām**-lò
NMLZ-loosen.soil-GO   NMLZ-hold-GO   labor   AUTO.BEN-cultivate-GO-RL
'Therefore, that *bamonpo* and *bamonpi* went there to the *jhum* field to cultivate it, to the hill field they went to loosen the soil and to work, to work they went.' [KK, BMS 009]

Finally, *-tekáng~-káng* 'leave behind' indicates another associated motion category, which signals in a sense the opposite of *-dùn~-dūn* 'JOIN'. While *-dùn~-dūn* 'JOIN' is about the involvement in another event (see also §9.2.7.1), *-tekáng~-káng* 'leave behind' is about the lack of involvement in another event. The difference, however, lies in where motion comes in. In verbs marked by *-dùn~-dūn* 'JOIN', the motion is associated with the 'other' event and not with the subject's event (i.e., in the example above, giving water to the runners, the runners are in motion but not the giver). In verbs marked by *-tekáng~-káng* 'leave behind', it is the subject that moves and leaves the location of the event, thus signaling the lack of involvement (i.e., due to moving on). An example is (276).

(276) Associated motion derivation *-tekáng~-káng* 'leave behind'
anke komat aphansi kepitekangpo,
ánke   komāt   a-phān=si   ke-pī-tekáng-pò,
and.then   who   POSS-NSUBJ=FOC:RL   NMLZ-give-leave.behind-IRR1

inutvetpo
e-nūt-vét-pò
one-CLF:HUM:SG -only-IRR1
'And then, who would we have given her to, she would have been alone (after we would have left her there).' [SH, CSM 063]

9.2.5 Argument and argument structure related functions

9.2.5.1 Argument quantification

Argument quantification derivations indicate the quantity of one of the arguments. In most cases, the suffixes indicate universal quantification, i.e., 'all', 'everything', 'everybody'. Table 96 lists all quantification derivations attested in the corpus and gives examples for the low frequency ones.

Table 96: Argument quantification derivations.

Form	Gloss	Examples
-ò	'much'	
-òng	'(too.)much'	
-pìk	'a.lot'	
-èt	'all:s/o'	
-rèp	'each:s/A'	dorep 'exist-each:s/a' (SH, CSM 064)
-théi~-thái	'all'	ne'enpithai 'have taken all (from me)' (KTa, TCS 082)
-làp	'all:s'	damlaplo 'everybody went' (KK, BMS 074) klolaplo 'everything fell out' (SiT, PS 030)
-chó ... -hàp[a]	'all.neg'	rikcho rikhaplo 'everything is scattered' (KK, BMS 093)
-phròng	'PL:S/A'	langphronglo 'everybody saw him' (HK, TR 190)
-rùi	'many:s'	thuruilo 'many have rotten' (WR, BCS 016)
-vàng	'PL:S/A'	chethekvangve 'they don't know' (SiT, HF 041)

[a]See §9.2.1.1.2.

Generally it appears possible to determine which syntactic role a given predicate derivation quantifies over, although further study is required to confirm that this is indeed syntactically fixed and not pragmatically flexible.

Examples of both -théi~-thái 'all' and -rùi 'many:s' occur in (277). Note that -théi in this example occurs after a separate construction to indicate universal quantification, which is the use of án 'all' in kesiktang'anta (§10.8.2).

(277) Instances of -théi~-thái 'all' and -rùi 'many:s'
[...] anke hala Bey Ki'ik ahemke piso hangdam'et jat'et,
ánke   [hála Bēy   ke-ìk   a-hēm=ke   pīsō
and.then that CLAN NMLZ-be.black POSS-house=TOP wife
hàng-dām-ét ját-ét]
call-GO-PFT GENEX-PFT

lo han sik'et jat'et kachepangri
[lō   hán   sík-ét   ját-ét]   [[[ke-che-pangrí
banana.leaf curry prepare-PFT type-PFT NMLZ-RR-reconcile

pangdon nangji aphan kesiktang'anta siktheilo,
pangdòn   náng-jí   aphān] ke-sík-táng-án=tā]   sík-**théi**-lò]
even.out need-IRR2 NSUBJ   NMLZ-prepare-finish-all=ADD prepare-**all:S/O**-RL

an hadak abangke lo han thuruilo [...]
[án   hádāk abàng=ke lō   hán   thū-**rùi**-lò]
and.then there NPDL=TOP banana.leaf curry rot-**many:S**-RL
'[...] [A]nd so he went to Bey the Black's house to ask for a wife and do all the formalities, and prepare the banana leaves and the curry (for the wedding) and everything, they prepared all of the necessary things for the wedding, and then there all the food got rotten [...].' [WR, BCS 016]

In (278), an instance of *-vàng* 'plural:S/A' is shown. This suffix is a negative polarity item and only occurs in combination with negative *-Cē*.

(278) Instance of negated *-vàng* 'plural:S/A' (negative polarity)
pisi kithurvangvedetma {mm}
pīsi ke-thùr-vàng-Cē-dèt=ma   mm
why   NMLZ-get.up-PL:S/A-NEG-PFV=Q   AFF
'Why didn't you all get up?' [HK, TR 154]

Note also the the likely relationship of *-vàng* 'plural:S/A' with *-váng*, which occurs on temporal adverbs and means 'each, every', as in *arnì-váng* 'each day' (§6.4.1.1.3), as well as the homophony and possible relationship with *vàng* 'come'.

9.2.5.2 Argument structure highlighting

The two suffixes *-pī* 'benefactive/malefactive' and *-ī* 'instrumental/comitative' are referred to as 'argument structure highlighting' rather than 'argument structure changing' or 'applicatives' because there is no evidence that they actually change the argument structure.

9.2.5.2.1 Benefactive/malefactive *-pī*

Benefactive/malefactive *-pī* highlights that the event is conceptualized as having a beneficiary or a maleficiary. This affected argument is marked by the non-subject marker *-phān*, such as *asitin akhei aphanta* in (279).

(279) Benefactive/malefactive *-pī*
lasō aphike asitin akhei aphanta
lasō aphī=ke [a-isī-tín a-khéi a-phān=tā]
this after=TOP POSS-one-each POSS-community POSS-NSUBJ=ADD

Isīsī ahem kikimpi do haduk governmentpen
isī~sī a-hēm ke-kìm-pī dō hádāk government=pen
one~DIST.PL POSS-house NMLZ-build-BEN exist there government=with
'And then, there was one house for every tribe, built by the government.' [SiT, HF 045]

Although *-phān* acts as a differential O marker (§13.2.1.2), which could be taken as evidence that *-pī* is an applicative that 'promotes' an oblique beneficiary to argument status, there is evidence presented in §13.2.3.2 which suggests that this 'promotion' is not marked by *-pī* but only 'highlighted' by *-pī*: The evidence consists of a sentence with a beneficiary participant marked by *-phān*, without *-pī* occurring on the verb.

9.2.5.2.2 Instrumental, comitative *-ī*

Unlike beneficiary and maleficiary participants, which can be marked by *-phān* 'non-subject' (see section above as well as §13.2.3.2, §14.1.2.6), there is no way to mark an instrumental or comitative participant with *-phān* 'non-subject'. Instrumental and comitative participants are only ever marked by *=pen* 'with' (§10.8.1). Nevertheless, the predicate derivation *-ī* may be used on the verb to 'highlight' that an instrumental or comitative participant is included in the conceptualization of the event. Consider (280) and (281).

(280) Instrumental *-ī*
nè motorsaikel=**pen**=si hethí ke-dàm-**ī**
1EXCL motorcycle=**with**=FOC:RL market(<Asm) NMLZ-go-**with**
'I went to the market on a motorcycle.' [SiT 090223]

(281) Comitative *-ī*
[...] mandu dopo, rit along sitame pinsomar
[mandú dō-pò] [rīt a-lòng setamē] [pinsō-mār
field.hut stay-IRR1 field POSS-LOC nevertheless married.man-PL

atum abangke hala osomarpen jui'irongpo [...]
a-tūm abàng=ke] hála osō-mār=**pen** jùi-**ī**-ròng-pò
POSS-PL NPDL=TOP that child-PL=**with** play-**with**-instead-IRR1
'[...] [T]hey would stay in the field hut, in the field or wherever (i.e., is true for other instances), the men, they would play with the children instead (of working in the field) [...].' [KaR, SWK 071]

Instrumental/comitative -*ī* can generally be used to 'highlight' a =*pen* marked participant, even in metaphorically extended contexts as in *amenpen* 'in the name of' in (282).

(282) Instrumental, comitative -*ī* corresponding with =*pen* 'with'
[...] lapenke lammet lamchong kaboche amenpen ketok
[lapèn=ke   [[[lammét lamchōng ke-boché]   a-mén=**pen**]
and.then=TOP   literature EE:lammét NMLZ-create POSS-name=with
ke-tòk
NMLZ-write

kacharli'icheng along [...]
ke-charlì-**i**-chéng   alòng]
NMLZ-study-INSTR-for.first.time   LOC
'[...] [A]nd then, when (I) first started writing in the name of creating Karbi literature [...].' [SiT, HF 030]

9.2.5.3 Argument classification

A set of predicate derivations classify arguments along physical dimensions relating to size and amount, among others. Table 97 offers some examples.

Table 97: Sample predicate derivations that function as argument classifiers.

Form	Gloss	Sample host roots	Use/meaning
-*bòr*	'appearing.small:S'	*tòt* 'squat', *(mek) kàr* 'burn (fire)'	appearing small but distinct and alone
-*lùn*	'appearing.big'	*tòt* 'squat', *ingnì* 'sit'	
-*tàn*	'appearing.very.big'	*tòt* 'squat', *ingnì* 'sit'	
-*chòm*	'together.few.close.people'	*ingnì* 'sit'	
-*kìng*	'some.weight:O'	*inghór* 'carry', *bū* 'carry on back', *arbàk* 'hold on lap', *parphang* 'put on shoulder', *rùng* 'lift'	e.g., an infant

Many argument-classifying predicate derivations are not productive, but are restricted to occurring with verbs from a particular semantic field. For example, -*bòr* 'appearing.small:S' in Table 97 occurs with *tòt* 'squat', as do -*lùn* and -*tàn*, which classify larger items. However, if we change the verb root to *ót* 'hold, touch', we can still use -*lùn* and -*tàn* for larger items, but for smaller items instead of -*bòr* we need to use -*dòng*. In order to speak about holding a flat object (e.g., paper), another classifying predicate derivation used with *ót* 'hold, touch' is -*hàm*.

9.2.5.4 Argument structure changing

A small number of predicate derivations change the argument structure. This includes -mē 'good.to', -nō 'bad.to', -movē 'nothing.to', and -memè 'inducing'.

In the case of -mē 'good.to' and -nō 'bad.to', the O argument of transitive verbs turns into an S argument, e.g., chō-mē 'eat-good.to' > 'be tasty; edible' (cf. Post (2007: 491) for a discussion of the same phenomenon in Galo, which he also refers to as adjectivalization).

In the case of -movē 'nothing.to', detransitivization also happens, but with the former A argument turning into an S argument of a verb meaning 'have nothing to V', e.g., 'have nothing to eat or drink' in (283).

(283) Predicate derivation -movē 'nothing.to'
       chomove junmove {mm}
       chō-**movē**   jùn-**movē**   mm
       eat-nothing.to   drink-nothing.to   AFF
       '(He) had nothing to eat, nothing to drink.' [HK, TR 009]

Finally, -memè 'inducing' turns a hypothetical causer into an S argument, e.g., ingnēk-memè 'laugh-inducing' > 'laughable, ridiculous'.

Note also that using the directional predicate derivation -dàm~-dām 'GO' with a two-argument verb makes it possible to use a motion verb argument structure. That is, the argument structure may reflect the predicate derivation rather than the lexical verb. See §14.1.6.2.

9.2.6 Aspect/aktionsart and time

9.2.6.1 Overview

Table 98 gives an overview of aspect/aktionsart and time derivations. I understand the label 'aktionsart' to refer to lexicalized aspect and hence the aktionsart/aspect continuum to correspond to a lexical-grammatical continuum. Thus, there are certain PDs that are more productive and grammatical (specifically, -ét 'perfect', -bòm~-bōm 'continuative', and -táng 'perfective2'[84]), and hence more like 'aspect'. On the other hand, -ròk 'completive' and -lèt 'perfective3' are less productive and collocate only with certain verb roots, and are hence more like 'aktionsart'.

---

[84] The aspect derivations -táng and -lèt are labeled 'perfective2' and 'perfective3', leaving the simple label 'perfective' for the much more frequent -dèt, which goes in a verb position class following the negative suffix (see §9.5.1).

9.2 Suffixal predicate derivations

Table 98: Aspect/aktionsart and time derivations.

Type	Form	Gloss		Productivity
Aspect / aktionsart	-ét	'perfect (PRF)'	§9.2.6.2	[productive]
	-bòm~-bōm	'continuative (CONT)'	§9.2.6.3	[productive]
	-táng	'perfective2 (PFV2)'[a]	§9.2.6.4	[productive]
	-ròk	'completive (COMPL)'	§9.2.6.5	[limited]
	-lèt	'perfective3 (PFV3)'	§9.2.6.6	[limited]
	-klùng	'durative (DUR)'	§9.2.6.7	[limited]
Temporal	-chéng	'for.first.time'		[productive]
	-thū	'again'		[productive]
	-lè~-lī	'again'		[productive]

[a] What could be glossed as 'perfective1' is -dèt (§9.5.1), which is, however, glossed as simply 'perfective' because it is very frequent as well as in a different slot in the verbal position-class.

9.2.6.2 Perfect -ét

The perfect -ét is very frequently used. For example, it occurs in the common Karbi greeting question shown in (284).

(284) Perfect -ét
 àn chō-ét-lò=ma
 rice/food eat-PRF-RL=Q
 'Have you eaten?'

9.2.6.3 Continuative -bòm~-bōm

The continuative -bòm~-bōm is quite frequent. An example is (285), where the continuative aspect is additionally iconically indicated by three repetitions of the verb stem.

(285) Continuative -bòm~-bōm
 lasonsi juibom juibom juibomlo
 lasón=si jùi-bōm jùi-bōm jùi-bōm-lò
 that.way=FOC:RL play-CONT play-CONT play-CONT-RL
 'This way, they played and played and played.' [CST, HM 058]

Continuative -bòm~-bōm is likely a reflex of a form reconstructed to Proto-Tibeto-Burman as *bam~*pam by Benedict (1972: 125), based on, among others, Meitei *pham* 'sit' and Lepcha *bam* 'remain'. In Lepcha, *bam* has further grammaticalized to become a progressive marker (Plaisier 2007: 119).

9.2.6.4 Perfective2 *-tāng*

Perfective2 *-tāng* is productively used with any verb root, but it is not as frequent as *-dèt* 'perfective' (§9.5.1). An example of *-tāng* is (286), where it is used on a nominalized verb, which is a common type of occurrence. (On the other hand, it appears that *-dèt* 'perfective' only occurs on predicates, which makes sense considering that *-tāng* can be analyzed as being derivational and *-dèt* as inflectional (§8.2.1).)

(286) Perfective2 *-tāng*
ante kolo nangkeneptang, nangpaklangtha
ánte ko=lo nang=ke-nèp-tāng
OK.then ITROG=FOC CIS=NMLZ-catch-finish
nang=pe-klàng-thā
1/2:NSUBJ=CAUS-appear-CON.IMP
'If so, which one have you already caught? You have to show me! [...]' [HK, TR 090]

Note that perfective2 *-tāng* may, however, co-occur with *-dèt* 'perfective' as on the predicate in (287).

(287) Perfective2 *-tāng* in combination with *-dèt* 'perfective'
"[...] an arni kethetangdetle!"
án arnì ke-thè-tāng-dèt=lē
that.much sun NMLZ-be.big-PFV2-PFV=EXCLAM
'"[...] (And) the sun has become so big already!"' [KK, CC 026]

The perfective2 suffix *-tāng* originates in an independent verb root *tāng* 'finish' that may function as a complement-taking verb, as in (288).

(288) Complement-taking *tāng* 'finish'
[...] amat lang kachinglu ketangpen kevang
[amāt lāng ke-chinglú **ke-tāng-pen** ke-vàng
and.then water NMLZ-take.bath **NMLZ-finish-NF:with** NMLZ-come

amat richo asopi aphan baplam
amāt richó a-oso-pì a-phān báp-làm]
and.then king POSS-child-female POSS-NSUBJ press.down-RES:paste.like
'[...] [A]nd then after having finished taking her bath, she was coming (home), and then (the rock) rolled over the king's daughter.' [RBT, ChM 026]

9.2.6.5 Completive *-ròk*

Completive *-ròk* occurs just nine times in the corpus. There are six occurrences with *lè* 'reach' and three occurrences with *tí* 'get rid off'. One of the occurrences with *tí* 'get rid of' is offered in (289).

(289) Completive *-ròk*
Rengsopen Onso aphanke tidamroklo
Réngsō=pen   Ónsō   a-phān=ke   tí-dàm-**ròk**-lò
NAME=with   NAME   POSS-NSUBJ=TOP   get.rid.of-GO-**COMPL**-RL

chevanvedetlo
che-vān-Cē̄-dèt-lò
RR-bring-NEG-PFV-RL
'[...] (He) had gotten rid of Rengso and Onso, (he) didn't bring them back anymore.' [CST, RO 054]

One of the occurrences with *lè* 'reach' is shown in (290), where in addition to *-ròk*, the perfective2 suffix *-tāng* is used. This is probably because the context is about reaching *Chom arong* (here: *Chom Rongme Chom Rongso*) which is the mythological place of the dead for the Karbis, so reaching there is definite, with no possibility of returning.[85]

(290) Perfective2 *-tāng* in combination with completive *-ròk*
[...] bangke Chom Rongme Chom Rongso [...]
[bàng=ke   Chóm   ròng-mē   Chóm   ròng-sō
CLF:HUM:PL=TOP   PLACE village-be.good   PLACE village-small

letangrok
lè-**tāng-ròk**]
reach-**PFV2-COMPL**
'[...] [A]nd she had already reached *Chom Rongme Chom Rongso* [...].' [KK, BMS 115]

9.2.6.6 Perfective3 *-lèt*
Perfective3 *-lèt* only occurs once in the corpus, with *jūt* 'finish', as shown in (291).

(291) Perfective *-lèt*
amat jutletlo
amāt   jūt-lèt-lò
and.then   finish-PFV3-RL
'And then, it (the story) is finished.' [SiT, PS 047]

---

[85] This particular story that (290) is taken from is actually about the impossibility of returning from the place of the dead. It resembles the Greek story of Orpheus and Eurydice as the wife dies and the husband (the *bamonpo*) in the story travels to *Chom arong* to try and get his wife to come back to the world of the living with him. But even though the *bamonpo* does not make a particular mistake like Orpheus, his wife still ends up having to go back to *Chom arong*.

Other verbs that come to mind to native speakers that *-lèt* may occur with are *chók* 'be okay, fit' and *ík* 'use up'. In the latter case, *ík-lèt* apparently has virtually the same meaning as *ík-làp* (for *-làp*, see §9.2.5.1), namely an exhaustive sense of 'used up all/ entirely'.

9.2.6.7 Durative *-klùng*

Like perfective3 *-lèt*, durative *-klùng* also only occurs once in the corpus, see (292).

(292)   Durative *-klùng*
      [....] mendu chikimra <sok nang arlu> hadak doklungnang [...]
      [mendú che-kīm-ra]   <sōk nàng arlù> [hádāk dō-klùng-nāng]
      field.hut RR-build-NF:IRR paddy you weed there stay-DUR-HORT
      '"[...] [L]et's build us a field hut, and stay there for a long time [...].' [KTa, TCS 007]

9.2.7 Other functions

9.2.7.1 Involvement *-dùn~-dūn* 'JOIN'

The involvement derivation *-dùn~-dūn* 'JOIN' (grammaticalized from the lexical verb *dùn* 'join, follow') is mentioned as an associated motion suffix in §9.2.4, due to examples such as (293), where *-dùn~-dūn* 'JOIN' indicates that the event is conceptualized against the background of a motion event. Here, in an example from a folk story, a frog tells an ant to pass through between his legs (as the frog is sitting in a way such that the road is blocked). As the ant is passing through, however, which is the backgrounded motion event, the frog sits down, on the ant.

(293)   Involvement *-dùn~-dūn* 'JOIN': acting on an object in motion
      [...] akengdak arum kilut ahut amat...
      [a-kèng-dàk]   arúm ke-lūt   ahūt   amāt
      POSS-foot-road.inbetween down NMLZ-enter during and.then

      anborpenpen chongho abang ingnidunpret
      àn-bòr=pén~pén   chonghō abàng
      rice-wrapped.bundle=with~DISTR.PL frog   NPDL
      ingnì-dūn-prèt
      sit-JOIN-acting.on.inflated.object
      '[...] [A]nd as (the ant) was passing through between the frog's legs with all its rice bundles, the frog sat down (pressing down the rice bundles).' [RBT, ChM 016]

The next two examples (294) and (295) show, however, that *-dùn~-dūn* 'JOIN' can also be used in contexts that do not necessarily involve motion. The larger and more abstract function of *-dùn~-dūn* 'JOIN' thus has to do with indicating that the event is conceptualized as occurring in the context of (or intervening in) an already established event, which may be a motion event, but does not have to be one.

In (294), a procedural text about traditional Karbi cooking with alkaline foods by using ashes, the speaker explains that after the fire has burned down the field, it is necessary to pick up the ashes quickly. The idea is that quickly picking up the ashes intervenes in a process, which is culturally known to occur otherwise, which is that the ashes that need to be collected will become wet in the morning dew or will be blown away by the wind, or will in some other way become unavailable.

(294) Involvement -dùn~-dūn 'JOIN': acting against the background of an ongoing (natural) process
ansi laso anglong arit kepan alongsi me
ánsi   [lasō a-inglóng a-rīt   ke-pān   alòng=si]   [mē
after.that this POSS-hill POSS-field NMLZ-clear.vegetation LOC=FOC:RL fire

kaipo lasi laso arjang aphelosi
kài-pò]   lasì   [[lasō arjàng   a-phelō=si]
set.fire-IRR1 therefore this   immature.bamboo POSS-alkaline=FOC:RL

elitum humdunji
e-li-tūm   hūm-**dūn**-jí]
1PL.INCL-HON-PL   pick.up-JOIN-IRR2
'After that, on the hill fields where we have cleared the vegetation, we have to set a fire and then these ashes from the immature bamboo we have to pick up together.' [SiH, KH 003]

In (295), the context of a war between England and Japan is already established. The use of -dùn~-dūn 'JOIN' on verbs such as *thì* 'die' or *dán* 'fight' indicates that these events are supposed to be understood in the already established context of this war.[86]

(295) Involvement -dùn~-dūn 'JOIN': event seen in context of another event
halaso ahut kithidun Britainpen ke'ongdung
[hálasō   ahūt   ke-thì-**dūn**   Britain=pen   ke-óng-dùng
that   during NMLZ-die-**JOIN** Britain=from NMLZ-exist.much-INTENS

aregiment do'ó laso aregiment kololo
a-regiment   dō-ò]   [lasō a-regiment   kòlò~lō
POSS-regiment   exist-much   this   POSS-regiment   which~DIST.PL

---

86 Note that although -dùn~-dūn 'JOIN' can have an additive function as in (296), the suffix here does not have an additive function in the sense of 'Japanese soldiers died and British soldiers died, too'. It would be perfectly acceptable to say 'in this war, not a single British soldier died' and use *thì-dūn-dē* 'die-JOIN-NEG' as the verb.

> amonitpenloma, koloso aregimentpensi, ladak
> a-monít=pen-lò=ma]   [kòlò-sō   a-regiment=pen=si]   ladāk
> POSS-man=with-RL=Q   which-DEM   POSS-regiment=with=FOC:RL   here
>
> kachedandunra <kithipen> kithidunma]
> ke-che-dán-**dùn**-rà   <ke-thì-pèn>   ke-thì-**dūn**=ma
> NMLZ-RR-fight-**JOIN**-NF:IRR   NMLZ-die-NF:with   NMLZ-die-**JOIN**=Q
> 'At the time, too many of the British died, many regiments died, from which different regiments are the people (that have died), from which regiment they are, did they fight together here, and did they die together (their names have been written here on the epitaphs).' [SiT, HF 028]

Finally, (296) shows that the involvement suffix -*dùn~-dūn* 'JOIN' can also be used with an additive function. Here the use of -*dùn~-dūn* 'JOIN' corresponds to the occurrence of the additive particle on *kadokave akheita* '(everybody from) every tribe' although the use of the additive particle is not obligatory.

> (296)   Involvement -*dùn~-dūn* 'JOIN' with additive function
> laso ahormu abangke kadokave akheita
> [[lasō   a-hormú   abàng=ke   kadókavē   a-khéi=**tā**
> this   POSS-thing   NPDL=TOP   all   POSS-community=ADD
>
> kacharlidunke mesen pusi neli matha
> ke-charlì-**dūn**=ke   mē-sén]   pusi]   nè-lì   mathà
> NMLZ-study-**JOIN**=TOP   be.good-INTENS   QUOT.COMP   1EXCL-HON   think
> 'I think for this thing, it would be good for (everybody from) every tribe (i.e. everybody in the world) to also learn it.' [SiT, HF 044]

There are also other contexts in which the suffix -*dùn~-dūn* indicates additivity (i.e., as a Karbi-specific category otherwise marked by the enclitic =*tā*, see §10.8.3.1). Evidence comes from its idiomatic use with certain verbs such as *thàk* 'answer', *arjū* 'listen', and *dèng* 'accept'. The semantics of these verbs inherently imply that there is a context in which these actions are performed: answering requires prior asking, listening requires prior talking or any other existence of sound, and accepting requires prior giving.

9.2.7.2 Formal -*īk*

The suffix -*īk* is used as a marker of a formal register or style (§16.4.2). As seen in (297) and (298), -*īk* is placed closest to the root, even breaking up near-lexicalized root-suffix sequences such as *mē-sén* 'be.good-INTENS' and *arjū-lōng* 'listen-GET'. (Note that -*sén* is on the far lexical end of the lexical-grammatical continuum of predicate derivations; to my knowledge, it does not occur with any root other than *mē* 'be good'.) This very salient placement of -*īk* may be reflective of its social importance.

(297) Formal -īk
si aphrangsi nanglimen chethan asonte <e>
sì   a-phráng-sí   nang-li-mén   che-thán   asón-tē
therefore   POSS-first-SPLT   2POSS-HON-name   RR-tell   like-COND

me'iksenji
mē-īk-sén-jí
be.good-FRML-INTENS-IRR2
'So first, if you could tell us your name, that would be wonderful.' [KaR, SWK 004]

(298) Formal -īk
nangli aphrangphrang, hakoko alam sitame
nàng-lì   aphráng~phràng   hakó~kò   a-lám   sitāmē
you-HON   first~DIST.PL   that.time~DIST.PL   POSS-matter   although

arju'iklong tahailo
arjū-īk-lōng   tahài-lò
listen-FRML-GET   DUBIT-RL
'You most probably have heard the different matters about the old days.' [KaR, SWK 059]

9.3 Reduplication

Full reduplication of the last syllable of the verb stem (either with or without vowel change, see §3.8.6.1 and §3.8.6.2) indicates a habitual reading, plurality of an argument or the iterative, or intensification, as shown in the respective sections below.

9.3.1 Habitual

In (299), reduplication of the last syllable of the verb stem *chō-dūn*, i.e., *chō-dūn~dūn* indicates the habitual.

(299) Reduplication of last syllable of verb stem indicating habitual
netumta nangtum nangpipo longle thak
[ne-tūm=tā   nang-tūm   nang=pī-pò   longlē   athàk
1EXCL-PL=ADD   2-PL   1/2:NSUBJ=give-IRR1   earth   on.top

nangbokchom titisi neta
nang=bók-chòm   titī-si]   [nè=tā
1/2:NSUBJ=serve.small.items-a.little   habitually-NF:RL   1EXCL=ADD

nangkechodundun
nang=ke-chō-dūn~**dūn**]
CIS=NMLZ-eat-JOIN~**HAB**
'You all would also give us (our food that way), you would always serve us (food) on the ground, I also **used to** eat like that.' [KK, BMS 060]

9.3.2 Argument plurality and iterative

In (300), the reduplication of *thè-ò* 'be.big-much' indicates the plurality of the S argument.

(300) Reduplication indicating plural of S argument
latum phelangpenta kali tinpenta
[là-tūm [[phelāng=pen=tā kalī]   [tín=pen=tā
this-PL thatch=with=ADD NEG.EQU.COP tin(<Eng)=with=ADD

kali arlong achetpensi kidip aphlak
kalī]]   [arlōng a-chèt=pen=si]   ke-dìp]   a-phlàk
NEG.EQU.COP stone POSS-piece=with=FOC:RL NMLZ-cover POSS-split.off.pieces

the'o'a la theklonglo
thè-ò~**á**   là   theklōng-lò
be.big-very~**PL:S** this see-RL
'Neither with thatch nor with tin, but with slabs of stone they cover (their roofs), the slabs of stone are very big, those also we got to see.' [SiT, HF 050]

In (301), reduplication of the stem can be interpreted as either iterative ('kept hearing') or as plurality of the people from whom the speaker was hearing about the issue ('heard from different people/sources'), which are semantically equivalent interpretations.

(301) Reduplication indicating iterative
[...] laso abang arjulonglong hedi <a> ingnekmeme alam asonlo [...]
[[lasō a-bàng]   arjū-lōng~lōng hedī] [[ingnēk-mémè
this POSS-CLF:HUM:PL   hear-GET~ITER   okay? laugh-inducing
a-lám]   asón-lò]
POSS-matter like-RL
'[...] [T]his I got to hear from different sources, it's like a laughable (funny) matter [...].' [KaR, SWK 070]

In (302), the reduplication of *-phrát* indicates a repeated, iterative event of beating.

(302) Reduplication indicating iterative
chongho aphan jamir abupen sapphratphratdet
chonghō aphān [jamír a-bú=pen]
frog NSUBJ grain.sp POSS-bundle=with
sáp-phrát~phrát-dèt
beat.w/sth.flexible-sd.beating~ITER-PFV

amat abang pevangphrok
amāt [a-bàng pe-vàng-phròk]
and.then POSS-CLF:HUM:PL CAUS-come-bulging.out
'And with a bundle of *jamir* they kept beating the frog so his skin got swollen.'
[RBT, ChM 079]

9.3.3 Intensification

Finally, reduplication of verb stems, in particular those including a predicate derivation, may also indicate intensification, as in (303), where *-jòi~jòi* can be translated as 'very quietly or secretly'.

(303) Reduplication indicating intensification
anungpen damjoijoisi berdamphlutlo tangho [...]
[anùng-pèn dàm-jòi~**jòi**-si] bér-dàm-phlùt-lò
back-from go-quietly~INTENS-NF:RL press.down-GO-miss/fail-RL
tànghò
REP
'From behind he was **very** secretly approaching and tried to jump on him, but failed [...].' [HK, TR 052]

9.4 Negative *-Cē* (onset reduplication)

The onset reduplicative negative suffix represents the main verbal negation construction (for nominal negation, the negative equational copula *kalī* is used, see §6.2.2.2 and §11.1.1). For (morpho-)phonological details, see §3.8.6.3. Morphosyntactically, the negative suffix forms the 'right edge' of the derivational verbal complex or verb stem (§8.2.1). An example of the negative suffix in a complex verb is (304).

(304) Onset reduplicative negative suffix -*Cē*
[...] *adappen hadakpen nangchesikmek'et'edetlo*
a-dàp=pen   hádāk=pen
POSS-morning=from   there=from

nang=che-sík-mék-èt-**Cē**-dèt-lò
CIS=RR-prepare-in.advance-all:S/O-**NEG**-PFV-RL
'[...] [F]rom the morning from there we hadn't prepared it (well).' [SH, CSM 062]

9.5 Post-stem aspect: Exhaustive perfective -*dèt* and experiential -*pín*

9.5.1 Exhaustive perfective -*dèt*

Perfective -*dèt* occurs with high frequency in the corpus (at a total of 134 occurrences). There are three semantic components to it: perfectivity, exhaustiveness, and, though much less prominently and less consistently, a stance component of a negative evaluation of the event by the speaker (in the sense of 'did X but should not have').

The perfective component is the most consistent semantic component of -*dèt*. It is particularly clear in examples such as (305), where a negated past event is expressed, i.e., something that did not happen.[87] Keep in mind that -*lò* 'realis' (which on non-negated stems typically has past implications) results in a future reading if directly attached to a negated stem (e.g., *dàm-dē-lò* 'go-NEG-RL' > 'won't go', see §9.6.1.2). Therefore, in order to express a negated past event, perfective -*dèt* is required, following which -*lò* 'realis' again has past implications even on negated stems.

(305) Exhaustive perfective -*dèt* between negative -*Cē* and realis -*lò*
[...] *adappen hadakpen nangchesikmek'et'edetlo*
a-dàp=pen   hádāk=pen
POSS-morning=from   there=from
nang=che-sík-mék-èt-**Cē-dèt-lò**
CIS=RR-prepare-in.advance-all:S/O-**NEG-PFV-RL**
'[...] [F]rom the morning from there we hadn't prepared it (well).' [SH, CSM 062]

---

[87] Another morphosyntactic type of occurrence of -*dèt* that especially highlights its perfectivity is in subordinate clauses with subordinator *aphī* 'after'. An example is *làng-dèt aphī* 'after watching' (SH, CSM 060).

Perhaps ultimately related to this perfective function, the presence of -*dèt* also allows the irrealis suffixes -*pò* and -*jí* to occur in conjunction with a negated stem, as in (306), which is otherwise not possible (§9.1.1).[88]

(306) Exhaustive perfective -*dèt* between negative -*Cē* and irrealis suffix
"*Chokjima?*" *pu nephan arjulo amatsi neta*
chók-jí=ma   pu   ne-phān   arjū-lò   amātsi   nè=tā
be.fine-IRR2=Q QUOT 1EXCL-NSUBJ ask-RL and.then 1EXCL=ADD

pulo "Chok. Pisi chokchedetpo? Mesenloke,
pù-lò   chók   pīsi   **chók-Cē-dèt-pò**   mē-sén-lò=ke
say-RL be.fine why   be.fine-NEG-PFV-IRR1   be.good-INTENS-RL=TOP

ennoi!" pu
ēn-nōi   pu
take-INFRML.COND.IMP   QUOT

"'Is it fine?', they asked me, and I replied, "It's fine, why would it not be fine? It's okay, take (the interviews)!'" [SH, CSM 049]

The exhaustive semantic component of -*dèt* surfaces in examples such as *chō-dèt* 'ate up'. In fact, this particular verb form was used frequently by six different Karbi native speakers that participated in a pilot study using the Fish Film experimental protocol (Tomlin 1995), in which speakers repeatedly describe events of fish swallowing up entire other fish.

Finally, there also appears to be a stance component associated with -*dèt* that at times surfaced in elicitation (although it remained difficult to pin down), such that the use of -*dèt* suggested that the speaker evaluated the occurrence of the -*dèt* marked event in a negative way, implying that it would have been better for the event not to actually have occurred.

9.5.2 Experiential -*pín*

In the corpus and in most elicitation data, -*pín* only occurs on negated verb stems and thus appears to be a negative polarity experiential marker 'never'. An example is *keningjejepinpi* in (307), which occurs inside a relative clause that marks exclamative force here.

---

[88] The function of the irrealis suffixes in (306) is to indicate counterfactuality. See §9.6.2.1.3 for more details.

(307) -pín 'never'
mh "an akai adin ne nangkapangreng
mh   [án   a-kái   a-dín   nè
DSM that.much POSS-time(<Asm)   POSS-day(<Asm)   1EXCL
nang=ke-pangrèng
1/2:NSUBJ=NMLZ-rear

ningke, nang keningjejepinpi amethan-sibongpole!"
nīngke] [nàng **[ke-ningjé-Cē-pín-pī**   a-methān-sibóngpō=le]]
even   you   NMLZ-speak-NEG-never-truly   POSS-dog-SPECIES=FOC:IRR
"'Even though all this time I have had you, you have been the dog who never talked before at all!'" [KK, BMS 019]

Some further elicitation on *-pín* suggests, however, that there may be a non-polarity counterpart (but possibly with a low tone) that occurs on non-negated stems in examples such as *àn chō-dèt, birík chō-pìn* 'after eating rice, eating chili (i.e., eating chili at the improper time)'.

9.6 Mood: Realis and irrealis

9.6.1 Realis *-lò*

Realis *-lò* mostly on verbal predicates, in various aspectual-pragmatic contexts, as argued below; an overview of these contexts is provided in §9.6.1.1. The suffix may also occur on nominal predicates, and there is a presumably related focus marker *=lo*, as discussed in §9.6.1.7. Realis *-lò* occurs with a very high frequency in the corpus, especially in narrative texts.[89] The etymology of *-lò* is not known.[90]

9.6.1.1 Overview of verbal functions

Previous research has ascribed some notion of past tense to *-lò*. Jeyapaul (1987: 113) calls it a past tense marker which becomes optional in the presence of an explicit time adverbial. In other contexts, he ascribes the function of perfect aspect to it claiming that it occurs if an action starts in the past but continues up to the present (p.114). Grüßner (1978: 99) calls the category marked by this suffix the "narrative past". He states that *-lò* marks a completed action, therefore setting the stage for a new action,

---

[89] In fact, because my main, fully annotated corpus (with a total of approximately 13,000 words) mostly contains narrative texts, there are over 1,000 occurrences of *-lò* 'realis' in it.
[90] An intriguing hypothesis is that Karbi *-lò* might possibly be related to the Daai Chin (Southern 'Kuki-Chin') 'inceptive aspect' and change of state marking *lo* (So-Hartmann 2009: 110–111).

and thus giving rise to a clear sequence of events expressed by verbs that carry this suffix.

In the present account of the verbal suffix -lò, I will argue that -lò is not a tense marker. Certain verb forms with -lò clearly refer to the future. Instead, I will argue that the frequent past reference of verb forms marked with -lò is a consequence of the aspectual-pragmatic functions of this marker.

The most obvious interpretation for many uses of Karbi -lò is perfective,[91] and, to a more limited extent, perfect aspect. There are several examples in which -lò resembles a perfective in languages that employ systematic marking of this category. Likewise, the concept of perfect marking plays a role, but in a broader sense than typically associated with this notion. However, -lò is used in other contexts as well.

Considering the morphosyntactic context of Karbi -lò, as it occurs in close paradigmatic opposition with the two irrealis suffixes -pò and -jí (§9.6.2), I gloss -lò as 'realis'. Clearly, a vague label such as 'realis' cannot explain the functional range of such a highly frequent grammatical element. The following subsections aim to break down this functional range into particular semantic and pragmatic contexts in which -lò is used. These are:

1) Event sequences in a narrative (§9.6.1.2)
2) A (temporal) change of state (either a stative verb or a negated action verb) (§9.6.1.3)
3) A (logical) cause-and-result situation (§9.6.1.4)
4) Correcting a wrong assumption (§9.6.1.5)

Examples in the following subsections are mostly taken from two stories, a personal narrative (SH, CSM) and a traditional story (HK, TK). The former was told by Sashikola Hansepi, a middle-aged woman from Diphu, and is about a trip to the Chomangkan Festival, a celebration to honor a family's relatives that have passed away. The traditional story was told by famous singer Harsing Kro, a middle-aged man from West Karbi Anglong, and is about an orphan and a tiger (hence referred to later as the Orphan and Tiger Story).

9.6.1.2 Action verbs: The argument against 'past tense'

In perhaps its most frequent usage, -lò appears on action verbs in the narration of past event sequences.[92] For example, (308) is the beginning of a simple personal narrative.

---

[91] A standard definition of perfectivity is "the view of a situation as a single whole, without distinction of the various separate phases that make up that situation" (Comrie 1976: 16).

[92] This function is also the most salient one to native speakers in the sense that everybody I have talked to will say that -lò marks past tense – which, however, likely reflects the attempt to impose English categories on Karbi.

(308) Realis *-lò* on action verbs
adapprang netum thurlo Hongkram Chomangkan dunji pu
a-dappráng   ne-tūm   thùr-lò   Hongkrām   Chomangkán
POSS-dawn   1EXCL:POSS-PL   get.up-RL   PN   PN
dùn-jí   pu
join-IRR2   QUOT
'We got up early in the morning to join the Chomangkan (Festival) in Hongkram.'
[SH, CSM 001]

Almost all predicates that appear as the sequence of events in narrative texts contain *-lò*, and just hearing the sequence of verbs with *-lò* would give the listener a fairly complete picture of what happened. This is similar to the use of perfective marking for completed events, and has probably given rise to interpreting it as a past tense marker in the literature.

As we will see below, stative or adjectival verbs in narratives often occur without *-lò*, which represents evidence that *-lò* does not mark past tense as it occurs on event sequences in narratives. But also in the case of action verbs, *-lò* does not always correspond to past tense. In (309), a negated bare stem without *-lò* in (a) is contrasted with the same form with *-lò* in (b) yielding a future sense. Likewise, the statement in (310) refers to the future.

(309) Realis *-lò* on negated action verb indicating future
   (a) *phàk-ōk   chō-chē*
       pig-meat   eat-NEG
       '(I) don't/didn't eat pork.'

   (b) *phàk-ōk   chō-chē-**lò***
       pig-meat   eat-NEG-**RL**
       '(I) **won't** eat pork anymore.'

(310) Realis *-lò* on negated action verb indicating future
   *alàng   vàng-thū-thē-**lò***
   3SG   come-again-NEG-**RL**
   'S/he won't come again.' [SiT 090220]

Both (309) and (310) show that *-lò* does not mark past tense. Here again, *-lò* is similar to a perfective marker, in that perfectives typically yield a future sense in combination with a present (or non-past) tense verb. Karbi *-lò* is different, however, as this is only the case with negated stems. Because Karbi does not mark tense at all, the interaction of *-lò* with tense is clearly different from traditional aspect languages such as Russian, which has different forms for past and non-past verbs.

One way we can interpret the function of *-lò* in these two examples is to consider it marking a change of state – which links it back to a perfective function, but from a different perspective. Of course, 'eat' and 'come' are action verbs, but since they are negated in these two examples, they resemble states more than actions. In (309), the (implied) previous state of actually eating meat or usually eating meat changes to the state of not eating meat at the time of utterance. Likewise, the state of 'him/her not coming again' in (310) begins at the moment of utterance, and so applies to the immediate or distant future, again implying that before the moment of utterance, this statement was not true.

In both examples, we can interpret *-lò* as marking the beginning of the state of the negated action statement. This could be seen as a purely temporal relationship, in which case 'currently or usually doing something' temporally precedes 'not doing something anymore right now or in the immediate or more distant future'. However, probably more often than not, there is an (implicit or explicit) logical relationship that explains the temporal relationship. In other words, usually, 'now, (I) won't eat pork anymore' implies some reason why this statement has become true, such as 'I have eaten so much pork already' or 'I have converted to Islam'. Even more so in the case of (310), 'not coming again', we probably automatically interpret that this 'now' – the beginning of the negated action state – refers to a reason that rules out the possibility of 'him/her coming again'. Given the other contexts in which *-lò* is used (especially the ones discussed in §9.6.1.4), it makes sense to consider this implied logical relationship an important component of the function of *-lò*.

9.6.1.3 Copular and property concept term (PCT) verbs: Change of state

We also find *-lò* on copular and property concept term (PCT) verbs, where we could motivate its occurrence as signaling a more typical type of change of state than the negated action change of state discussed in the previous section. Example (311) contrasts two ways of expressing the fact that 'there is no meat'.

(311) Realis *-lò* on negated copula indicating change of state
    (a) ōk   avē
        meat not.exist
        'There is no meat.'

    (b) ōk   *avē-lò*
        meat not.exist-**RL**
        'There is no meat left/anymore.'

In (a), the bare stem of the negative existential copula is used. This sentence would be used when, for example, a seller in the market does not sell meat, or a particular meal was vegetarian. The statement in (b), however, implies that meat is sold out, or the particular meal included meat, but all the meat is already eaten up. Therefore, this function marked by -*lò* in (311) is to denote a change of state.[93]

This change-of-state sense of *avē-lò* also explains (312), which is from the very beginning of the Orphan and Tiger Story, and is part of introducing the protagonist. The implication is that large families with a number of children are the rule in a village setting. Therefore, being all alone and not having any close relatives is likely to mean that this orphan lost not only his parents, but also brothers and sisters – as opposed to never having had any siblings.

(312) Change of state function of -*lò* 'realis'

apei avelo apo avelo....
a-pēi **avē-lò** a-pō **avē-lò....**
POSS-mother **not.exist-RL** POSS-father **not.exist-RL**

a'ik avelo ate avelo
a-ìk **avē-lò** a-tè **avē-lò**
POSS-older.brother **not.exist-RL** POSS-elder.sister **not.exist-RL**
'He didn't have a mother (anymore), he didn't have a father (anymore).... he didn't have any brothers or sisters (anymore).' [HK, TR 004]

Change of state is a typical function marked by perfectives, as perfectives typically focus on the completion of an event or the results of it.

9.6.1.4 Indicating a logical relationship: Cause and result

However, it is not always a focus on a change of state that is indicated by -*lò* as it occurs on stative verbs. We already noted above that a change of state situation can often be understood as an (implied) cause and result situation. In the excerpt in (313), there are two statements about the condition of a road, *henopik* 'be very bad' and *longle adukta dopiklo* 'be very dusty (< have much dust)'. The first predicate remains without -*lò*, whereas the second one obligatorily occurs with it in this sentence.

(313) Indicating a logical relationship: Cause and result
bonseta Dobokapen <Hojai> Hojai adak abangke
bónsetā [Doboká=pen <Hojai> Hojái a-dàk abàng=ke]
but PN=with PN PN POSS-road.inbetween NPDL=TOP

---

[93] Note that (311)(b) is vague with respect to tense. In the appropriate context, this utterance may also refer to the future, thus matching the examples in the previous section.

tovar henopik
továr   henō-pìk
road   bad-very
'But between Doboka and Hojai the road is very bad.' [SH, CSM 017]

anke <tovar> tovar longle adukta dopiklo
ánke   <továr>   továr   [lòngle̅   a-du̅k=tā]   dō-pìk-**lò**
and.then   road   road   earth   POSS-dust=ADD   exist-very-**RL**
'And then, there is also a lot of dust.' [SH, CSM 018]

In (313), *-lò* does not occur on the first predicate, because 'being bad' is a general statement about the road. But the second predicate 'being very dusty' has to occur with *-lò*, because of the logical connection between both statements: Because the road is bad (meaning that it has many potholes), the road gets dusty (as dust accumulates in the potholes).

Note that the second statement in isolation would not be marked with *-lò*. Just remarking that the road was very dusty, the most natural thing to say would be *tovar longle aduk dopik*. If one were to say it with *-lò* in isolation (outside the context of this story), i.e., *tovar longle aduk dopiklo*, it would actually better translate as 'the road was dustier now', implying a comparison with an earlier condition of the road. This implication is not present in (313). Instead of marking a change of state, maybe one could say that *-lò* here marks a conditioned state, or a conditioned quality as opposed to an intrinsic quality.

Another example of *-lò* marking a conditioned state is (314), where the cause of *ening arongpiklo* '(we) were very happy' is mentioned just before (i.e., reaching just in time to see members of the own clan perform a certain ritual).

(314)   Realis *-lò* marking a conditioned state
        <Amri asor> Amri asorsi rong-ketonglo anke
        <Amri   a-sòr>   Amrī̀   a-sòr=si   ròng-ketòng-lò   ánke
        PN   POSS-people   PN   POSS-people=FOC:RL   ceremony(kd)-RL   and.then

        netumta Amri asorbo anke chephodunloklo
        ne-tūm=tā   Amrī̀   a-sòr-bò   ánke   che-phó-dùn-lòk-lò
        1EXCL-PL=ADD   PN   POSS-people-also   and.then   RR-reach-JOIN-right.then-RL

        ening arongpiklo
        e-nīng   aróng-pìk-**lò**
        1PL.INCL-mind   be.happy-very-**RL**
        'It was the Amri people doing the *Rongketong*, and then we are also from Amri, and so we happened to reach just in time for it, and (so) we were very happy.' [SH, CSM 030]

9.6.1.5 Correcting a wrong assumption

Another context where *-lò* is used is in correcting a wrong assumption. Let us first consider (315), in which the storyteller mentions that the orphan had a shovel and a basket with him, as he went out to search for edible roots.[94]

(315) Context for (317)
chingjor epak {chingjor epak...} hak isi do
chingjòr   e-pàk   chingjòr   e-pàk   hák
shovel   one-CLF.flat   shovel   one-CLF.flat finely.woven.bamboo.basket

isī   dō
one   exist
'One shovel ... {One shovel..} (And) one basket he had.' [HK, TR 016]

The storyteller also mentions that the orphan had a small tobacco container with him, which will be of importance for the story at a later point (316).

(316) Context for (317)
atema ajerjer do mati ho
a-temá   ajerjēr   dō   matí   hò
POSS-tobacco.container(<Asm) small   exist CG   EMPH:INTERACT
'He had a small tobacco container, OK?' [HK, TR 018]

In both (315) and (316), *dō* 'exist' occurs without *-lò*. Along the lines of the previously discussed analysis of *-lò* on stative verbs, we would indeed not expect to find *-lò* here, because we are not dealing with a change of state or a conditioned state. So (315) and (316) are not problematic. However, the excerpt (317) contains essentially the same statements as (315) and (316), but here all instances of *dō* 'exist' occur with *-lò*.

(317) Realis *-lò* used in the context of correcting/clarifying wrong assumptions
{nopakke ponpema?}
{nopàk=ke   pòn-Cē=ma
dao=TOP   take.away-NEG=Q
'{He wasn't carrying a dao?}' [HK, TR 022]

nopakta dolo dak {lahe} mm
nopàk-tā   dō-**lò**   dāk   lahé   mm
dao-ADD   exist-**RL** here that.way? AFF
'He did have a dao also there. {Is it like that?} Mm.' [HK, TR 023]

---

94 Note that curly brackets in examples from the HK/TR traditional story are used for utterances (usually questions, affirmative interjections, or repeated parts of previous sentences) by a Karbi native speaker who was listening to the storyteller for a more natural storytelling situation.

nopak dolo chingjor dolo {mm} hak dolo {mm}
nopàk	dō-**lò**	chingjòr	dō-**lò**	mm	hák
dao	exist-**RL**	shovel	exist-**RL**	AFF	finely.woven.b.basket

dō-**lò**	{mm}
exist-**RL**	AFF

'He had a dao, he had a shovel, he had a finely woven bamboo basket.' [HK, TR 024]

anke hala duma kemong athongkupta dolo {mm}
ánke	hála	dumá	ke-mòng	a-thongkūp-tā
and.then	that	tobacco	NMLZ-smoke	POSS-tobacco.container-ADD

dō-**lò**	mm
exist-**RL**	AFF

'And then, he also had that tobacco container so he could smoke later.' [HK, TR 025]

What caused the storyteller to repeat those statements he just made was that the listener asked specifically whether the orphan did not also have a knife with him (as it is normal to carry a knife along when you leave the village and are on your own). So the storyteller had to correct himself, or rather, clarify: Yes, the orphan had a knife, and a shovel, and a basket – and then he also had a tobacco container. It is this pragmatically marked context of clarifying or correcting wrong assumptions that is the trigger for the use of *-lò* in this case, as native speakers have expressed that *-lò* sometimes functions to emphasize statements.[95]

Similarly, consider (318), where the realis marked existential copula *dō-lò* is used in the context of denying an allegation of lying. Also note the use of *ti* 'emphatic' here.

(318) Realis *-lò* used in objection
[..] nephan nangpakolikma {oi} nangkapachobeima {oi}
ne-phān	nang=pakolík=ma	ōi	nang=ke-pa-chobēi=ma	ōi
1EXCL-NSUBJ	1/2:NSUBJ=lie=Q	yes	1/2:NSUBJ=NMLZ-CAUS-lie=Q	yes

'[...] Are you lying to me? Are you telling me a lie?' [HK, TR 087]

"dolo ti!" pubomlo tangho, lake, <SiT laughing> "dolo!" {mm}
dō-**lò**	tì	pù-bōm-lò	tànghò	là=ke	dō-**lò**	mm
exist-RL	EMPH	say-CONT-RL	REP	this=TOP	exist-RL	AFF

'"Definitely, it's there!", this one (i.e., the orphan) kept saying, "It's there!"' [HK, TR 088]

---

[95] In this story, of course only the possession of a knife (and not the other items) is a clarifying or correcting statement – however, it seems reasonable that in this context the storyteller just clarifies overall what all things the orphan is carrying along.

9.6.1.6 Summary

Karbi -*lò* combines elements of perfective aspect as well as elements of a more abstract pragmatic category of contextuality. On the one hand, it resembles perfective aspect in occurring on event sequences in narratives, and on negated action verbs to yield a future sense (§9.6.1.2), as well as in occurring on adjectival and stative verbs to indicate a change of state (§9.6.1.3). On the other hand, there are a number of contexts, in which -*lò* occurs, which are not covered by the notion of perfectivity. Specifically, -*lò* occurs in situations of indicating a logical relationship (§9.6.1.4), or when correcting or clarifying wrong assumptions (§9.6.1.5).

9.6.1.7 Realis -*lò* on nominal predicates and focus =*lo*

While not as frequent as on verbal predicates, -*lò* 'realis' also occurs on nominal predicates. The function of adding -*lò* to nominal predicates appears to only ever be one of emphasis or (active) assertion: On nominal predicates, -*lò* only resembles verbal -*lò* where it indicates a situation of 'correcting or clarifying a wrong assumption' (§9.6.1.5). The other functions of -*lò* on stative verbs detailed in the preceding sections, i.e., change of state (§9.6.1.3), and indicating a logical relationship (§9.6.1.4), are not attested for 'nominal' -*lò*.

An example of -*lò* on a nominal predicate is (319). This folk story is about why two subclans, the Dili and the Rongchecho, split up, which goes back to two brothers of the same names that have a falling out. In this section of the text, this falling out is declared by one of them with the words 'you are Dili, I am Rongchecho', marking the 'you are Dili' assertion with -*lò*.

(319) Realis -*lò* on nominal predicate
"*nangke Dililo, <nangke> neke Rongchetcho!" lason chepulo tangho*
nàng=ke   Dilí-**lò**   <nàng=ke>   nè=ke   Rongchetchó   lasón
you=TOP   PN-**RL**   you=TOP   1EXCL=TOP   PN   that.way
che-pū-lò   tànghò
RR-say-RL   REP
'"[...] [Y]ou are Dili, <you..>, I am Rongchecho", like this they spoke to each other.' [KTa, TCS 089]

The fact that verbal -*lò* and nominal -*lò* overlap to some degree but not entirely in their functional range could be taken to consider them two different morphemes. However, it is preferable not to do that. This fact about -*lò* is analogous to the behavioral properties of irrealis -*pò* and -*jí*, which also occur on nominal predicates in examples like (320), as do other verbal affixes more generally, which is shown in §4.1.2.

(320) Irrealis *-pò* on numeral plus classifier *e-nūt* functioning as a nominal stem
anke komat aphansi kipitekangpo,
[ánke   [komāt a-phān=si]   ke-pī-tekáng-**pò**]
and.then who   POSS-NSUBJ=FOC:RL   NMLZ-give-leave.behind-**IRR1**

inutvetpo
e-nūt-vét-**pò**
one-CLF:HUM:SG-only-**IRR1**
'But who will (we) give (her) to, (she) will be alone.' [SH, CSM 063]

In light of the broader word class agnosticism of Karbi (i.e., elements from any of the larger word classes can function as predicates (§4.3)), it makes better sense to propose only one morpheme *-lò* 'realis', which occurs in both verbal and nominal predicates. (I do recognize there to be another *lo* morpheme, which does not occur on predicates, which is *=lo* 'focus', discussed below.)

A number of language consultants have suggested that there also exists a form *heló~henló*, which may be related to *-lò*. An example of this form is offered in (321). However, *heló~henló* occurs in a restricted number of contexts, almost all of which contain the demonstrative *là*. This form *heló~henló* appears to be a more formal or otherwise special variant of the simple realis. It is glossed here as 'realis:emphatic' ('RL:EMPH'). A compatible account of *heló~henló* is offered by Grüßner (1978: 132), who parses *heló* into *he* and *-lò*, with *he* analyzed as a pragmatic sentence-final type particle (see §16.3.9 on *=he*).

(321) Emphatic realis
bai pei nangingjinso'un'e nangtum aphan,
bái   pēi   nang=ingjínsō-ùn-Cē   nang-tūm   a-phān
how.bad! mother 1/2:NSUBJ=have.pity-be.able-NEG you-PL   POSS-NSUBJ

*o **lahelo** lason chungkreng kedo marjeng*
ó   la-**heló**   lasón   chungkrèng ke-dō   marjèng
EXCLAM   this-**RL:EMPH** that.way be.thin   NMLZ-exist be.thin

kedo lok'hu kedo lokphlep kedo
ke-dō   lòkhù   ke-dō   lòkphlèp ke-dō
NMLZ-exist be.pale NMLZ-exist be.pale   NMLZ-exist
'How bad! I can't tell you how much pity I feel for you, oh that's why you're so thin and so pale!' [CST, RO 040]

Finally, in addition to *-lò* on predicates, there also are a few occurrences of a *lo* marker that occurs on other elements in the clause. While not being frequent, the distribution resembles the one of realis focus =*si*, which is why this *lo* is treated as a focus marker =*lo*. Specifically, =*lo* 'focus' occurs on interrogative pronouns (322), on an NP, here the O argument (with the verb formally nominalized) (323), and on the discourse connector *amāt* 'and then' (324). This is parallel to =*si* 'focus:realis', which also occurs on interrogative pronouns and specifically on focused elements in a construction that involves a (diachronically) nominalized verb (§12.7.3.1), and on discourse connectors (§14.2.3).

(322) Focus =*lo* on interrogative pronoun
ne kopilo kevipo laho <m>
nè   kopí=lo   ke-vì-pò   là-ho
1EXCL what=FOC NMLZ-do-IRR1 this-EMPH:INTERACT
'What should I do?' [CST, HM 013]

(323) Focus =*lo* on NP (O argument)
nangphanlo nangkeponpo {mm}
nàng-phān=lo   nang=ke-pòn-pò   mm
you-NSUBJ=FOC 1/2:NSUBJ=NMLZ-take.away-IRR1 AFF
'It is you who we have to take.' [HK, TR 063]

(324) Focus =*lo* on discourse connector *amāt* 'and then'
amatlo la kroikrelo
amāt=lo   là   krōi-Cē-lò
and.then=FOC this agree-NEG-RL
'And then, she disagreed.' [SeT, MTN 009]

Also note (325), where a sentence involving focus realis =*si* produced by one speaker (not the main storyteller here, as indicated by the curly brackets) is repeated as a way of confirming it by the main storyteller. Crucially, however, in repeating it, the storyteller uses =*lo* instead of =*si*, which demonstrates that the two clitics have equivalent focus-marking functions here.

(325) Focus =*lo* used to substitute focus realis =*si*
{akejoisi longdunlokpo, eli}
a-ke-jòi=**si**   lóng-dùn-lòk-pò   è-lì}
POSS-NMLZ-be.for.free/in.vain=**FOC:RL** get-JOIN-definitely-IRR1 1PL:INCL-HON

akejoilo ili longdunpo
a-ke-jòi=**lo**   ì-li   lóng-dùn-pò
POSS-NMLZ-be.for.free/in.vain=**FOC** 1PL:INCL-HON get-JOIN-IRR1
'{We will get it without any effort!} We will get it without any effort!' [HK, TR 137]

9.6.2 Irrealis marking: -pò and -jí

There are two irrealis markers, *-pò* 'irrealis1' and *-jí* 'irrealis2', which both cover cross-linguistically typical irrealis categories associated with futurity. While *-pò* is used in the context of a more immediate, definite future/irrealis situation, *-jí* is used in more general, intentional, or indefinite future/irrealis contexts.

For example, if one says 'I will come over tomorrow', they will be more likely to use *-jí* as compared to a statement such as 'I will come over tomorrow at 2pm', in which case the use of *-pò* is more likely. That said, the suffix *-vèk* 'definitely' can be used in conjunction with *-pò* as well as with *-jí*, and it has proven difficult for my language consultants to imagine contexts in which only one of the two suffixes is truly acceptable and the other not acceptable.

An illustrative example from the corpus is (326), where a question using the more indefinite or general *-jí* 'irrealis2' receives a reply with the more definite *-pò*.

(326) Irrealis2 *-jí* in question and irrealis1 *-pò* in reply
"ahokma, methan-sibongpo?, nang neponthekjima?"
a-hōk=ma   methān-sibóngpō,   ne=pòn-thèk-**jí**=mà
POSS-truth=Q dog-SPECIES   1EXCL:NSUBJ=take.away-know.how-**IRR2**=Q

"o ne nangponthekpo ti, phu!
ó   nè   nang=pòn-thèk-**pò**   ti   phū
EXCM 1EXCL 1/2:NSUBJ=take.away-know.how-**IRR1** EMPH   grandfather:VOC

nangdunle nangdunnoi ho pulo tangho
nang=dùn=lè   nang=dùn-nōi   hò   pù-lò   tànghò
CIS=join=FOC:IRR CIS=join-INFRML.COND.IMP EMPH say-RL REP
'"Is it true, dog, you know how to take me?" "I certainly know how to take you there, grandfather. Just make sure to follow me!", he said.' [KK, BMS 034-5]

A similar example with *-jí* 'irrealis2' in the question, however the bare stem in the reply is (327).

(327) Question with *-jí* 'irrealis2' (reply with bare stem)
"chokjima?" pu nephan arjulo amatsi neta
chók-**jí**=ma   pu   ne-phān   arjū-lò amātsi   nè=tā
be.fine-**IRR2**=Q QUOT   1EXCL-NSUBJ ask-RL   and.then 1EXCL=ADD

pulo "chok; pisi chokchedetpo? Mesenloke [...]"
pù-lò   **chók**   pīsi   chók-Cē-dèt-pò   mē-sén-lò=ke
say-RL **be.fine** why   be.fine-NEG-PFV-IRR1 be.good-INTENS-RL=TOP
'"Is it fine?", they asked me, and I replied, "It's fine, why would it not be fine? It's okay [...]"' [SH, CSM 049]

The following discussion offers examples of the various future irrealis functions of *-pò* and *-jí*. In §9.6.2.2, examples of past habitual marking, which apparently only occurs with *-pò*, are offered.

9.6.2.1 Functions common to *-pò* and *-jí*

Future irrealis contexts in which both *-pò* and *-jí* are used include simple future (§9.6.2.1.1); habitual marking in procedural texts (§9.6.2.1.2); hypotheticals and counterfactuals (§9.6.2.1.3); epistemic contexts of expressing uncertainty (§9.6.2.1.4); deontic contexts of expressing necessity and obligation (§9.6.2.1.5); desideratives (§9.6.2.1.6); and purpose clauses (§9.6.2.1.7).

9.6.2.1.1 Future marking

Examples (328) and (329) are from the same text and refer to the same situation, talking about the future as indicated by the time adverb *penàp* 'tomorrow'. Perhaps somewhat unexpectedly, the first instance in (328) is marked by *-pò* 'irrealis1', which generally is the more definite, immediate future irrealis marker, and the following instances in (329) are marked by *-jí* 'irrealis2', the generally more indefinite marker, including, in the last of three repetitions, *-jí* in conjunction with *-vèk* 'definitely'. Perhaps the use of *-jí* here emphasizes the intention of the speaker.

(328) Future marking function of *-pò*
penap Rongker alongsi vangpo {mm} [...]
penàp   Ròngkèr   alòng=si   vàng-**pò**   mm
tomorrow   festival(kd) LOC=FOC:RL   come-**IRR1**   AFF
'Tomorrow we will come to the place of the *Rongker* [...].' [HK, TR 107]

(329) Future marking function of *-jí*
anke.... halake hangdunbomlo {mm} "penap vangji,
ankè   hála=ke   háng-dùn-bōm-lò   mm   penàp   vàng-**jí**
and.then   that=TOP   call-JOIN-CONT-RL   AFF   tomorrow   come-**IRR2**

penapthuke vangji, vangvekji" pu tangho [...]
penàp-thū=ke   vàng-**jí**   vàng-vék-**jí**   pu   tànghò
tomorrow-again=TOP   come-**IRR2**   come-definitely-**IRR2**   QUOT   REP
'And then, he keeps shouting, "Tomorrow I will come, when it's a new day again tomorrow, I will come, definitely I will come!" he said [...].' [HK, TR 115]

9.6.2.1.2 Habitual marking in procedural texts

In the excerpt (330), three consecutive sentences from a procedural text are offered, all of which have the final verb marked with *-pò*, as is typical.

(330) Habitual marking function of -pò in procedural text
ansi pholo ingdaklote hekpo
ánsi   pholó   ingdàk-lò-tē   hèk-**pò**
after.that cotton disperse-RL-COND remove.cover-**IRR1**
'Then, when the cotton gets dispersed, we open up (the seeds).' [KST, PSu 004]

lasí takiripen jengpo
lasì   takirí=pen   jèng-**pò**
therefore spindle(<Asm)=with spin-**IRR1**
'Then we spin/make (the thread) with a spindle.' [KST, PSu 005]

takiripen jengdette ansi thakpo
takirí=pen   jèng-dét-tē   ánsi   thàk-**pò**
spindle(<Asm)=with spin-PFV-COND after.that weave-**IRR1**
'After having spun the thread, we then weave it.' [KST, PSu 006]

Irrealis2 *-jí* occurs less frequently in procedural texts, but several instances are found, such as the ones offered in excerpt (331).

(331) Habitual marking function of *-jí* in procedural text
lasi pindeng sumpot aphan pusetame
[lasì   [pindéng   sumpót   a-phān   pùsetāmē]
therefore dress.and.ornaments EE:pindéng POSS-NSUBJ likewise

emenasi chethakji, laso apholo epensi chethakji
[e-mená=si   chV-thāk-**jí**]   lasō a-pholó   è-pen-si
1INCL-self=FOC:RL RR-weave-**IRR2** this POSS-cotton plant-NF:with-NF:RL
che-thāk-**jí**
RR-weave-**IRR2**
'And so, we weave any and all of our dresses by ourselves, after planting the cotton we weave it.' [KST, PSu 011]

ansi idunji non ahut abangta lapusonló
ánsi   ī-dūn-**jí**   [nón ahūt   abàng=tā làpusón-lò]
after.that wear-JOIN-**IRR2** now during NPDL=ADD like.this-RL
'And then, we (all of us) wear (these clothes), now also the same way.' [KST, PSu 012]

9.6.2.1.3 Hypothetical and counterfactuals

The two irrealis markers are used in both (present) hypothetical situations, as well as in counterfactual situations (in which a hypothetical alternative to a past event is expressed). First, let us examine examples of *-pò*. In (332), the speaker says 'it is okay', which is a realis assertion, but then adds 'why would it not be okay?', i.e., imagining an irrealis alternative to the realis situation, which is indicated by the use of -pò.

(332) Hypothetical reading of -pò
"chokjima?" pu nephan arjulo amatsi neta pulo "chok;
chók-jí=ma   pu   ne-phān   arjū-lò   amātsi   nè=tā
be.fine-IRR2=Q QUOT 1EXCL-NSUBJ ask-RL and.then 1EXCL=ADD
pù-lò   chók
say-RL be.fine

***pisi chokchedetpo**? Mesenloke, ennoi" pu*
pīsi   chók-Cē-dèt-**pò**   mē-sén-lò=ke   ēn-nōi
why be.fine-NEG-PFV-**IRR1** be.good-INTENS-RL=TOP take-INFRML.COND.IMP
pu
QUOT
'"Is it fine?", they asked me, and I replied, "It's fine, why would it not be fine? It's okay [...]"' [SH, CSM 049]

In (333), which is from the same personal narrative as (332), a text about a trip to a festival, which was recorded the day after the trip, the speaker imagines a hypothetical alternative to a realis situation from the trip the day before. This is thus a counterfactual situation that is marked by -pò, as the hypothetical alternative is about a past event.

(333) Counterfactual reading of -pò
anke komat aphansi kepitekangpo,
ánke   komāt   aphān=si   ke-pī-tekáng-pò,
and.then who NSUBJ=FOC:RL NMLZ-give-leave.behind-IRR1

inutvetpo
e-nūt-vét-pò
one-CLF:HUM:SG-only-IRR1
'And then, who would we have given her to, she would have been alone.' [SH, CSM 063]

Similar to the above examples of -pò in (present) hypotheticals and (past) counterfactuals, (334) and (335) offer analogous examples of -jí.

(334) Hypothetical reading of -jí
e nebangle kelengledetalangma"
e   ne-bàng=le   ke-lèng-Cē-dèt-**jí**-làng=ma
DSM 1EXCL-body=FOC:IRR NMLZ-be.fat.HUM-NEG-PFV-**IRR2**-still=Q
'"Why would I not be fat?"' [SeT, MTN 026]

(335) Counterfactual reading of *-jí*
mh elike kerenget atumke
mh [è-lì=ke   [ke-rèng-èt   a-tūm=ke]]
DSM 1PL:INCL-HON=TOP NMLZ-be.alive-all:S/O   POSS-PL=TOP

thangbaksi keleduntam thekji ason
[thàngbāk=si   ke-lè-dūn-tām   thèk-**jí**   asón]
as.if=FOC:RL   NMLZ-reach-JOIN-impossible know.how-**IRR2** like

nangpinkhattap nangpinkhatphru
nang=pinkhát-táp   nang=pinkhát-phrú
1/2:NSUBJ=advise-mindlessly   1/2:NSUBJ=advise-EE:tháp
'Since we are alive, (how can) you give so many pieces of advice as if we could reach (the place where my wife has gone after she died, when in fact we cannot).' [KK, BMS 031]

9.6.2.1.4 Epistemic reading

Expressing uncertainty, probabilities and venturing guesses is another common situation where future irrealis markers are used in Karbi. In (336), *-jí* is used in conjunction with *mene mena* 'maybe' to indicate that this is an assumption.

(336) *-jí* expressing uncertainty, probability
te "damnoi!" ante "dah! nangphihai along,
tè   dàm-nōi   ánte   dah! nang-phì-hái   alòng
OK.then go-INFRML.COND.IMP OK.then   go!   2POSS-grandmother-HON LOC

e, lothe lotha doji, mene mena" pu
e   lothē   lothā   dō-**jí**   menē   menā   pu
DSM banana EE:lothē exist-**IRR2** maybe EE:menē QUOT
'Then (she said), "Go!", and then, "Go to your grandmother, she will have bananas and other fruit maybe."' [KK, CC 024]

There are a few instances in the corpus where irrealis2 *-jí* is used in questions (see also §9.6.2). Example (337) constitutes another such instance, as a native Karbi speaker (who is listening to a folk story that is being told) is jokingly making a guess as to a detail not mentioned by the storyteller in his telling of the narrative.

(337) *-jí* expressing uncertainty, probability
{armeta jarherjima} mm jarherlo <SiT laughing>
armē=tā   jàr-hèr-**jí**=ma}   mm   jàr-hèr-lò
tail=ADD   be.standing.up-high.up-**IRR2**=Q AFF be.standing.up-high.up-RL
'{And (the tiger's) tail might have been lifted up (as he was running off)?} Yes, its tail was lifted up.' (<SiT laughing>) [HK, TR 117]

Preliminary elicitation suggests that *-pò* is also used to express uncertainty or for making guesses, although there are no instances in the corpus.

9.6.2.1.5 Expressing necessity/obligation

The deontic verb *náng* 'must, need' almost always occurs with *-jí* 'irrealis2', as in (338), and there are a few instances in the corpus where it occurs with *-pò* 'irrealis2', such as (339). Realis *-lò* cannot be directly attached to *náng*, i.e., **náng-lò* is unacceptable, but in conjunction with the intensifier *-kòk*, which also occurs in (338), it yields an acceptable verb form, i.e., *náng-kòk-lò* (although there are only three occurrences of this form in the corpus).

(338)   *-jí* on *náng* 'must'
{*lang nangkokjike*}
{làng   náng-kòk-**jí**=ke}
see   must-INTENS-**IRR2**=TOP
'{We must see (if there is a tiger there)!}' [HK, TR 086]

(339)   *-pò* on *náng* 'must'
[...] *pinipenke ne nangpen neke chekak nangpo* [...]
[pinì=pen=ke   nè   nàng=pen nè=ke   che-kák   náng-pò]
today=from=TOP 1EXCL you=from 1EXCL=TOP RR-part must-IRR1
'[...] "From today I will need to part from you." [...]' [SeT, MTN 039]

9.6.2.1.6 Expressing desiderative

Building on the conditional *-te* (§9.7.3), a desiderative construction can be formed by using one of the irrealis suffixes. This is shown in (340) and (341).

(340)   Desiderative function of *-jí*
[...] *jo... to chirijite, chirinon*
jó   tò   che-rī-**jí**-tē   che-rī-nōn
see OK   RR-search-**IRR2**-COND RR-search-SUGG.IMP1
'[...] "See! Okay, if you feel like finding yourself a wife, then find yourself one!"' [CST, RO 009]

(341)   Desiderative function of *-jí*
ako ingti tharmit ba birik jokjite, jokpo
akó   ingtí tharmìt bá   bírík   jòk-**jí**-tē, jòk-pò
then   salt   turmeric or(<Asm) chili   add-**IRR2**-if add-IRR1
'Then if you want to add salt, turmeric, or chili, you should add those!' [PI, BPR 005]

While these are the only two examples in the corpus, elicitation suggests that *-pò* 'irrealis1' can be used in this construction preceding *-te* 'conditional' as well.

9.6.2.1.7 Subordinate purpose clause marking

Purpose clauses as in (342) are typically marked with *-jí*, although using *-pò* is sometimes possible in elicitation.

(342) Subordinate purpose clause marking with *-jí* 'irrealis2'
 ethevet setame thanji pusi dak kevangló
 [e-thē-vét setāmē thán-**jí** pusi] dāk ke-vàng-lò
 one-CLF:word-only nevertheless tell-**IRR2** QUOT.COMP here NMLZ-come-RL
 'I have come here to tell just one thing.' [KK, CC 003]

This construction also occurs as a main clause insubordination construction marking the desiderative or intentionality (§15.4.2, §16.3.1.2).

9.6.2.2 Past habitual marking via *-pò*

One function of *-pò* seemingly not shared by *-jí* is the marking of past habitual ('used to') events, as in (343).

(343) Past habitual function of *-pò*
 netumta nangtum nangpipo longle thak
 [ne-tūm=tā nang-tūm nang=pī-**pò** longlē athàk
 1EXCL-PL=ADD 2-PL 1/2:NSUBJ=give-IRR1 earth on.top

 nangbokchom titisi neta
 nang=bók-chòm titī-si] nè=tā
 1/2:NSUBJ=serve.small.items-a.little habitually-NF:RL 1EXCL=ADD

 nangkechodundun
 nang=ke-chō-dūn~dūn
 CIS=NMLZ-eat-JOIN~HAB
 'You all would also give us (our food that way), you would always serve us (food) on the ground, I also used to eat like that.' [KK, BMS 060]

9.6.2.3 Summary

Irrealis1 *-pò* is more commonly used in procedural texts and is used in past habitual contexts where *-jí* 'irrealis2' appears unacceptable. Otherwise, the more frequently used irrealis marker is *-jí*: in hypotheticals and counterfactuals; expressing uncertainty and guessing; expressing necessity and obligation; occurring in the conditional desiderative construction; and marking purpose clauses.

9.7 Subordinating verbal suffixes

There are three non-final suffixes in Karbi: -*si* and -*ra* (§9.7.1), and -*pen* (§9.7.2), as well as a conditional suffix -*te* (§9.7.3), and an indirect question marker -*nē* (§9.7.4).

9.7.1 Non-final marker: Realis -*si* and irrealis -*ra* (clause-chaining)

There is a realis non-final marker -*si* and an irrealis non-final marker -*ra*, which are used in forming clause chains, see (344) and (345). Clause chaining is discussed in §15.2.1.1.

(344) Chained clauses marked with -*si* 'non-final:realis'
e anke apaita <m> pharla dam,
[e   [ánke   a-pāi=tā   <m>   pharlá   dàm]
DSM   and.then   POSS-mother=ADD   HESIT   outside.part.Karbi.house   go

theng akhangra okóksi, hem damsi,
[thēng   a-khangrá   ó-kòk-si]   [hēm
firewood   POSS-basket.for.firewood   leave-in.a.fixed.place-NF:RL   house
dàm-si]
go-NF:RL

hongkup ingnilúnsi, mok chepachusi,
[hongkūp   ingnì-lùn-si]   [mōk   che-pa-chū-si]
entrance.area.Karbi.house   sit-big:AO-NF:RL breast   RR-CAUS-suck-NF:RL

"dojoinoi, po!"
[dō-jòi-nōi   pō]
stay-quietly-INFRML.COND.IMP   father
'And then, the mother went and unloaded the firewood in the *pharla*, then went inside the house, sat down in the *hongkup*, gave the child the milk, (and said) "Be quiet, daddy!"' [KK, CC 015]

(345) Clause chain with irrealis non-final -*ra* marked clauses
[...] mo nanghem chedam ahomoike lapu chevangthurá
[mò   nang-hēm   chV-dām   a-homói=ke]   [lapú
future   your-house   RR-go   POSS-time(<Asm)=TOP   this.side
che-vāng-thū-**ra**]
RR-come-again-**NF:IRR**

langso atovarthot vangra lapen ladak
[langsō   a-továr-thót   vàng-**ra**]   [la=pen   ladāk
this   POSS-road-exactly   come-**NF:IRR** this=with   here

nanghumrira nanghem chepaletu
nang=humrí-**ra**]   [nang-hēm   che-pa-lè-tū]
CIS=visit.friends/relatives-**NF:IRR** 2:POSS-house   RR-CAUS-reach-UNCOND.IMP
'[...] [A]nd later when you go home, again come like this, come on the exact same road, and then go to the familiar place (i.e. where the dog is staying), and then go and make sure to reach your house.' [KK, BMS 089]

The use of realis *-si* or irrealis *-ra* is determined by the final verb, as shown in §15.3. Generally, in a particular context, only the realis form or the irrealis form is acceptable. However, some of my language consultants found a peculiar construction acceptable (and produced it spontaneously), whereby in a series of more than one non-final clause, the non-final markers are used in alternation. An example is (346), where a declarative, non-negated (and therefore regularly realis) final verb is preceded by two non-final clauses: the first one marked by realis *-si*, as we would expect, but the second one marked by irrealis *-ra*. Peculiar as it may seem, this is robust and fully acceptable for some of my language consultants.

(346)   Realis/irrealis alternation
        pen pasi'idunvotsi phutup humra aphi
        pèn   pasi'í-dùn-vòt-**si**   phutūp   hūm-**ra**   a-phī
        and.then   whistle-JOIN-INTENS-**NF:RL**   hat   pick.up-**NF:IRR** POSS-backside

        anat chevangthulo
        a-nát   che-vāng-thū-lò
        POSS-direction   RR-come-again-RL
        'And then, he whistled, picked up the hat and brought it back.' [SiT, PS 036]

The *-si* form for non-final markers is also found in Tibeto-Burman languages of the Himalayas, such as Tamangic languages and also East Bodish (Kurtoep) (see Georg (1996) and Hyslop (2013)).

9.7.2 Non-final *-pen*

In addition to (ir)realis-sensitive *-si* and *-ra*, there is a third non-final marker *-pen*, which also takes part in the Karbi clause-chaining system. As such it also marks semantically underspecified subordinate clauses. Further information on *-pen* in the context of clause chaining constructions in Karbi is found in §15.2.1.1.

Non-final *-pen* has presumably grammaticalized from a source construction of =*pen* 'with, from' (§10.8.1) occurring with nominalized verbs. Synchronically, *-pen* (still) frequently occurs on nominalized verbs as in (347), although there are also many instances of *-pen* on verbs not marked by *ke-* 'nominalizer', as in (348).

(347) Non-final *-pen* on nominalized verb
[...] hadak kelepen ahem asorta netum aphan
[hádāk **ke-lè-pèn**]   [a-hēm   a-sòr=tā   ne-tūm   aphān
there   NMLZ-reach-NF:with   POSS-house   POSS-people=ADD   1EXCL-PL   NSUBJ

nangkeru nangkethaita <ke>
nang=ke-rú   nang=ke-thái=tā   <ke>
1/2:NSUBJ=NMLZ-serve   1/2:NSUBJ=NMLZ-serve=ADD   <ke>

kechepameso kali [...]
ke-che-pe-mē-sō   kalī]
NMLZ-RR-CAUS-be.good-INTENS   NEG.EQU.COP
'[...] [A]nd when we arrived there, the people of the house served us really really well [...].' [SH, CSM 039]

(348) Non-final *-pen* on non-nominalized verb
lasi longku arlo chepondetpen latum ok
[lasì   longkū   arlō   che-pōn-dèt-**pen**]   [là-tūm   [ōk
therefore   cave   inside   RR-take.away-PFV-**NF:with**   this-PL   meat

han akeme keme vanpilo jatlo
hán   a-ke-mē   ke-mē]   vàn-pī-lò
prepared.vegetables   POSS-NMLZ-be.good   NMLZ-be.good   bring-BEN-RL
ját-lò
type(<Ind)-RL
'And then, (they) carried them inside the cave and they brought to them all the good meat and curry for them and everything [...].' [CST, HM 035]

9.7.3 Conditional *-te*

Conditional *-te* marks conditional clauses, as in (349). The final verb is typically marked irrealis, as with *-pò* 'IRR1' here.

(349) Conditional clause marked by *-te*
[...] neta dak dokokte, kosonpo?[...]
nè=tā   dāk   dō-kòk-**te**   kosón-pò
1EXCL=ADD   here   stay-firmly-**COND**   how-IRR1
'[...] [I]f I stay here, how will it be? [...]' [SH, CSM 062]

For information on further constructions involving conditional *-te*, see §15.2.3.1.

9.7.4 Marker of complement clauses functioning as indirect questions: -nē 'indefinite'

Indirect questions are marked by -nē, as seen in (350) (§15.2.2.2).

(350) Indirect question marked by -nē 'indefinite' followed by *chiní* 'know'
ajatnon Kohima ko'an akethe ko'an
[ajátnōn   Kóhìmà   [[[ko-án   a-ke-thè]   [ko-án
anyway   PLACE   WH-that.much   POSS-NMLZ-be.big   WH-that.much

akibilone chinine, neli [...]
a-ke-bī-lò-**nē**]]   chiní-Cē]   nè-lì]
POSS-NMLZ-be.small-RL-**INDEF** know-NEG   1EXCL-HON
'Anyway, I didn't know how big or small Kohima is [...].' [SiT, HF 019]

9.8 Aspect II: *-làng* 'still'

The aspectual suffix *-làng*, glossed as 'still,' occurs in the same temporal sense English 'still' has in instances such as (351). The context in this folk story is that before the speaker(s) can stay with their biological father, they still need to ask their adopted (tiger) parents.

(351) Aspect II: *-làng* 'still' in temporal sense
[...] ne nepei nepo aphan charjudamlang
nè   ne-pēi   ne-pō   aphān   che-arjū-dām-làng
1EXCL   1EXCL:POSS-mother   1EXCL:POSS-father NSUBJ   RR-ask-go-still
'[...] [W]e didn't agree, we still need to ask our mother and father.' [CST, HM 116]

However, *-làng* also occurs in semantically related senses (related to additivity) that are incompatible with English 'still', such as the scalar additive sense in (352), where the closest translation into English would probably be 'even'.

(352) Aspect II: *-làng* 'still' in scalar additive sense
amat hala hi'ipi abangke ekam anta
amāt   [hálasō hī'ipī   abàng=ke]   [e-kām   án=tā]
and.then that   witch   NPDL=TOP   one-step   that.much=ADD

kamkelang ha herang janglut
kàm-Cē-làng   há   herāng   jáng-lùt
step-NEG-still   over.there   trap.hole   fall-enter
'And then, the witch couldn't even take one single step, she fell down into the hole.' [CST, HM 105]

Finally, -làng is used for events that are expected to take little time or when there is a sense of the event being one step amongst several consecutive ones. For example, if there is a plan to get going to the market, but the speaker wants to go and wash her hands before leaving, she could say *rí chersām-dām-làng* 'hand wash-GO-still', with a colloquial translation along the lines of 'I'm just gonna go wash my hands real quick (and then we can go)'.[96]

9.9 Non-declarative speech act suffixes

Table 99 offers an overview of non-declarative speech act suffixes along with references to sections in which the various constructions involving these suffixes are discussed.

Table 99: Non-declarative speech act suffixes.

Speech act	Form	Function	Discussed in
Imperative/ Prohibitive	-nōi	informal conditioned imperative	§15.1.2.2, §15.1.2.6, §15.1.2.8
	-nōn	conditioned imperative	§15.1.2.3, §15.1.2.6, §15.1.2.8
	-thā	conative imperative	§15.1.2.4, §15.1.2.6, §15.1.2.8
	-tū	unconditioned imperative	§15.1.2.5, §15.1.2.6, §15.1.2.8
	-rī	prohibitive	§15.1.2.7, §15.1.2.8
Hortative	-nāng	hortative	§15.1.3.1, §15.1.3.2
	-lonāng	emphatic hortative	§15.1.3.3
	-sināng	conative hortative	

---

96 In German, *noch* 'still' is used in the same way: 'Ich gehe mir nur gerade noch schnell die Hände waschen (und dann können wir los).'

10 The noun phrase

The topic of this chapter is the structure of the noun phrase in Karbi. In §10.1, the elements of the Karbi noun phrase are introduced and an overview of the noun phrase structure is offered. Evidence for the noun phrase template is provided in §10.2.

The topic of §10.3 is the diachronic significance of the possessive construction consisting of a modifying nominal preceding an *a-* 'possessive' marked head noun. This construction has been the source construction for the grammaticalization of a number of grammatical markers. The *a-* marking of head nouns is further discussed in §10.4. This *a-* possessive marking of head nouns with preceding modifiers is also particularly significant as it occurs in more complex noun phrases with several modifiers. Here, the *a-* prefix contributes evidence to an analysis of either a flat or hierarchical/embedded structure of the preceding modifiers.

The following three sections discuss modifiers that always precede their head noun (§10.5), the plural *-tūm*, which always follows the head noun (§10.6), and property concept modifiers, relative clauses, and enumeration constructions, which may occur before or after the head noun (§10.7). Finally, §10.8 discusses the clitics that may occur at the end of a noun phrase.

10.1 Elements of the Karbi noun phrase

10.1.1 Overview: Karbi noun phrase structure

The structure of Karbi noun phrases is shown in Figure 14. Evidence for this template is offered in §10.2 below.

(DEM)	(NUM)	(RC) (PCTmodifier)	([NP]POSR)	HEAD NOUN	(PCT modifier) (RC) (NUM)	(PL)

Figure 14: Karbi noun phrase structure.

Figure 14 sorts six different types of modifiers into position classes inside the Karbi noun phrase: (1) demonstratives (DEM), (2) enumerators[97] (NUM), (3) relative clauses (RC), (4) PCT modifiers, (5) noun phrases functioning as possessors (([NP]POSR), and (6) a plural marker (PL). Of these, two only occur before the head noun: demonstratives (DEM) (§10.5.1) and possessor or modifier NPs ([NP]POSR) (§10.5.2).[98] On the right edge

---

97 The term 'enumerator' is used as a cover term for various enumeration constructions (§10.7.2).
98 Two additional types of marginal preposed modifiers are illustrated in §10.5.3.

of the noun phrase, there is one other modifier: the plural marker *-tūm* (PL) (§10.6). Finally, modifiers that may occur on either side of the head noun include relative clauses (RC) and modifiers derived from property concept terms (PCT) (§10.7.1), as well as enumeration constructions (NUM) (§10.7.2). Note that the order of these three modifier types is not only variable with respect to being pre- vs. postposed to the head noun. In cases of a preposed enumerator and a preposed relative clause or PCT modifier, the more common ordering in the corpus is for the enumerator to occur first, but the reverse order is attested as well. Finally, in postposed position vis-à-vis the head noun, the occurrence of more than one modifier of the three types NUM, RC, and PCT is not attested in the corpus. There also is no attested instance of preposed RC and PCT modifiers co-occurring.

10.1.2 Occurrence of other elements in head noun slot

While the head noun slot is typically occupied by a common noun, there are three types of coordination constructions which can go inside the head noun slot as well: a simple juxtaposition construction, and constructions involving coordinators *=pen* 'with' or *lapèn* 'and'. In addition, quotative *pu* may immediately follow the head noun.

10.1.2.1 Conjunctive coordination constructions

10.1.2.1.1 Juxtaposition
In the juxtaposition construction, two nouns are placed side by side without an overt coordinator, such as *nepiso neso* in (353) and *ahor ahan* in (354). This cannot be treated as an instance of root compounding, since any required morphology is repeated on both nouns, i.e., the first person exclusive possessive pronoun *ne-* in (353) and the general possessive/modified prefix *a-* in (354).

(353) NP coordination by juxtaposition: *nepiso neso* 'my wife and my children'
e nang nepiso neso aphan
e   nàng   [[[ne-pisò]   [ne-osō̄]]$_{HN}$ aphān]
DSM   you   1EXCL:POSS-wife   1EXCL:POSS-child   NSUBJ

la'an bondi kipi bondok kipi [...]
[[là-án   bondí]   ke-pī]   [bondòk   ke-pī]
this-that.much   captivity(<Ind)   NMLZ-give   EE:bondí NMLZ-give
'You (witch) kept my wife and my children in such bad captivity [...].' [CST, HM 094]

(354) NP coordination by juxtaposition: [DEM] – [RC] – [N N]$_{HN}$
[...] la nepei aphan keponpi ahor ahan
[là$_{DEM}$ [ne-pēi   aphān   ke-pòn-pī]$_{RC}$ [a-hōr
this   1EXCL:poss-mother NSUBJ   NMLZ-take.away-BEN   POSS-liquor
a-hán]$_{HN}$]
POSS-curry

pachomatdakji pule kopi potsi
pa-chomāt-dàk-jí   pu=le   kopí   pōt=si
CAUS-taste-sudden-IRR2   QUOT=FOC:IRR   what   reason=FOC:RL

kachekipphakma" pulo
ke-che-kīp-phàk=ma   pu-lò
NMLZ-RR-pour.out-almost.completely=Q   QUOT-RL
'"[...] **[T]his rice beer and curry that I was carrying for my mom** to let her taste it, why is almost all of it coming out by itself?", (she was thinking).' [SeT, MTN 049]

10.1.2.1.2 With coordinator =*pen* or *lapèn*

Examples of coordinating constructions with coordinators =*pen* 'with' and *lapèn* 'and' occurring in the head noun slot are (355) and (356).

(355) Coordination construction with =*pen* 'with' in head noun slot
"ponnoi jo, la ephipen
pòn-nōi   jó   [là   e-phì=pen
take.away-INFRML.COND.IMP see   this   1PL.INCL-grandmother=with

ephu aphan!" pu
e-phù   a-phān]   pu
1PL.INCL-grandfather   POSS-NSUBJ   QUOT
'"Take them, look, our grandmother and grandfather!"' [KK, BMS 106]

(356) Coordination construction with *lapèn* 'and' in head noun slot
[...] la Bey Ke'et Bey Ronghang lapen Bey Ki'ik
[là   [[Bēy   ke-èt]   [Bēy   Ronghāng]   lapèn   [Bēy
this   CLAN   NMLZ-be.yellow   CLAN   CLAN   and   CLAN
ke-ìk]]$_{HN}$
NMLZ-be.black

atum angjirta do pu
a-tūm]   a-ingjìr=tā   dō   pu
POSS-PL   POSS-sister=ADD   exist   QUOT
'[...] That Bey the Fair, Bey Ronghang, and Bey the Black, they also had a sister, it is said.' [WR, BCS 007]

Note that the same conjunctive coordination construction with =*pen* 'with' may also occur in the possessor or modifier NP slot, as in (357), as well as function to coordinate separate noun phrases, as in (358).

(357) Coordination construction with =*pen* 'with' in head noun slot
"*neke nepeipén nepo ahem chedampo*"
nè=ke   [[ne-pēi=**pen**   ne-pō]_POSR   a-hēm]_HN
1EXCL=TOP 1EXCL:POSS-mother=**with** 1EXCL:POSS-father POSS-house
che-dām-pò
RR-go-IRR1
"'I will go to my mother and father's house.'" [SeT, MTN 038]

(358) NP coordination with *lapèn* 'and'
Europe lapen kaprek kaprek adet,
[[Europe]   **lapèn**   [ke-prék   ke-prék   a-dét]
Europe(<Eng) **and**   NMLZ-be.different NMLZ-be.different POSS-country(<Ind)

America heihaipen, phorena atum dopik hadak
[America   héihái=pen]]   phorená   a-tūm   dō-pīk
America(<Eng) different.kinds.of=from foreigner(<Eng) POSS-PL exist-very
hádāk
there
'From Europe and from many different countries, (such as) from America etc., there were many foreigners there.' [SiT, HF 037]

10.1.2.2 Quotative *pu*

Quotative *pu* is used following quoted material. It may be used after sentences or words that were uttered by somebody and are then repeated (see §16.3.1 and §16.3.1.1), or in the case of names for people or things, as in (359) and (360). Note that in both these examples, *pu* simply occurs after the head noun. However, while in (359), the head noun and name *Kache Kropi* also functions as an NP by itself, in (360), *pu* occurs after the head noun *thē* 'fruit', which, in turn, is followed by the noun phrase delimiter *abàng* (§13.5). In (360), *pu* therefore specifically occurs following the head noun, not following the NP as a whole.

(359) Quotative *pu* after a personal name
nemen abangké Kache Kropi pu
[ne-mén   abàng=ke] [Kaché Krōpī **pu**]
1EXCL:POSS-name   NPDL=TOP   NAME   CLAN   **QUOT**
'My name is Kache Kropi.' [KK, CC 007]

(360) Quotative *pu* after the name of a fruit, with noun phrase delimiter following
lasi la suho athe pu abangke pe ri
lasì [là sūhō [a-thē]_HN **pu** abàng=ke] [[pé rī
therefore this thorny.plant.sp POSS-fruit QUOT NPDL=TOP cloth EE:pé

kechok aphan'iklo
ke-chòk] a-phān-īk-lò]
NMLZ-wash.clothes POSS-NSUBJ-FRML-RL
'Then, the so-called '*suho* fruit' is (used) for washing clothes.' [SiH, CW 007]

The position of *pu* following the head noun is also illustrated in (361), where both the plural and the noun phrase delimiter still follow. (Note that in the context of the story, it is more plausible to consider *Bey Ke'et* a name and simply a head noun, rather than a head noun with a following PCT modifier.)

(361) Quotative *pu* after a personal name, with further NP elements following
an Bey Ke'et pu atum abangke asomar
án [[[[Bēy ke-èt] pu] a-tūm] abàng=ke] a-oso-màr
and.then CLAN NMLZ-be.yellow QUOT POSS-PL NPDL=TOP POSS-child-PL

abang etpik tangho
abàng èt-pìk tànghò
NPDL be.yellow-very REP
'And then, with respect to the family of the so-called Bey the Fair, his children were very fair.' [WR, BCS 010]

10.1.3 The noun phrase delimiter *abàng*

The noun phrase delimiter *abàng* marks the right edge of the noun phrase. For a discussion of structural properties and functions of *abàng*, see §13.5.

10.2 Evidence for Karbi noun phrase structure

Table 100 provides an overview of noun phrase structures found in the corpus and refers to relevant examples below. The evidence from these particular noun phrase structures leads us to the position class diagram that was given at the beginning of this chapter in Figure 14. Table 100 is divided into sections I–IV for the discussion below.

Table 100: NP structure.

	(DEM)	(PCT) (RC) (NUM)	([NP] POSR)	HEAD NOUN	(PCT) (RC) (NUM)	(PL)	Example #
I	+	+NUM		+			(362)
	+	+RC		+			(363)
	+		+	+			(364)
	+			+	+NUM		(365)
II		+NUM	+PCT	+			(366)
		+NUM	+RC	+			(367)
		+RC	+NUM	+			(368)
		+NUM		+	+PCT		(369)
III		+NUM	+	+			(370)
		+RC	+	+			(371)
IV			+	+		+	(372)
			+	+	+PCT	+	(373)

Abbreviations are as follows: DEM=demonstrative; NUM=numeral or classifier-numeral-word; RC=relative clause; PCT=property concept term modifier; POSR=possessor; PL=plural.

The first four rows of Table 100 (labeled 'I') show noun phrase structures that include a demonstrative. In (362), a sequence of a demonstrative and a classifier-numeral word modify the head noun. In (363), we find a sequence of a demonstrative and a relative clause. In (364), the demonstrative is followed by a possessor, and both act as modifiers of the head noun. Whenever there is a demonstrative and one other modifier occurring before the head noun, the demonstrative goes in the first position and is followed by the modifier.

(362) NP structure: DEM – NUM – HN
hula ejon ateketa vangpo [...]
hú-la   e-jōn   a-tekè=tā   vàng-pò
over.there-this one-CLF:animal   POSS-tiger=ADD   come-IRR1
'That one tiger will come [...].' [HK, TR 169]

(363) NP structure: DEM – RC – HN
[...] Lily, la nelitum aphan nangkejapon aosopi,
[Lilý   [là   [ne-li-tūm   aphān   nang=ke-já-pòn]ʀᴄ
NAME   this   1EXCL-HON-PL   NSUBJ   1/2:NSUBJ=NMLZ-lead-take.away
[a-osopì]]ʜɴ
POSS-lady

> *elong adim dosi computer akam klemlo [...]*
> e-lòng   a-dím   dō-si]   computer   a-kám
> one-CLF:place POSS-place exist-NF:RL computer(<Eng) POSS-work
> klém-lò]
> do-RL
> '[...] Lily, the lady who took us there, she stayed in one place and did her computer work [...].' [SiT, HF 034]

(364) NP structure: DEM – [NP]$_{POSR}$ – HN[99]
> *amat la apiso abangke la jangthu abong*
> amāt   là   a-pisò   abàng=ke   **là** **jàngthù** **a-bòng**
> and.then this POSS-wife NPDL=TOP   **this** **oil**   **POSS-bottle**
>
> *cheenlo amat khalun anung vekponlok*
> che-én-lò   amāt   khalùn   anùng vēk-pōn-lòk
> RR-take-RL and.then kd.big.basket back   hang-take.away-not.main.action
> 'And then, the wife took herself the bottle of oil and hung it on the back of the *khalun* to carry it.' [SeT, MTN 044]

While a classifier-numeral word may immediately follow a demonstrative, as in (362), it may also follow the head noun, as in (365).

(365) NP structure: DEM – HN – NUM
> **hála arlèng ebeng'an** *amatsi akhalun ingpuvakló [...]*
> **hála** **arlèng** **e-bēng**-án   amātsi   a-khalùn
> **that** **slope**   **one-CLF:half**-this.much and.then POSS-kd.big.basket
> ingpú-vàk-lò
> open-RES:open-RL
> 'She (had climbed) **half of the slope** and then she opened her *khalun* basket [...].' [SeT, MTN 050]

The next section of rows of Table 100 (labeled 'II') show that PCT modifiers, relative clauses and enumerators may all occur before the head noun but their relative order may not be fixed. In (366), a classifier-numeral word precedes a PCT modifier. Likewise, the classifier-numeral word also precedes a (minimal) relative clause in (367).

---

[99] For a discussion of preposed modifier embedding, and differential analyses of these kinds of examples as [DEM – [NP]$_{POSR}$ – HN] or [[DEM – NP]$_{POSR}$ – HN], see §10.4. In following binary branching analyses, a third possibility is [DEM [[NP]$_{POSR}$ HN]$_{NP}$]. This analysis is not further discussed here, as there is currently no evidence for a tighter unit between the possessor NP and the head noun.

(366) NP structure: NUM – PCT – HN
laso ahut amat inut akaprek amonit
lasō a-hūt amāt **[e-nūt a-ke-prék**
this POSS-during and.then **one-CLF:HUM:SG POSS-NMLZ-be.different**
a-monít]
POSS-man

abangke saikel nangardonsi vanglo... [...]
abàng=ke] saikél nang=ardòn-si vàng-lò...
NPDL=TOP bicycle(<Eng) CIS=ride-NF:RL come-RL
'In this moment, another person riding on a bicycle came [...].' [SiT, PS 015]

(367) NP structure: NUM – RC – HN
[...] inut chotiki chonghoi amonit
[e-nūt [cho-tikī cho-inghói] a-monít]
one-CLF:HUM:SG AUTO.BEN/MAL-cultivate AUTO.BEN/MAL-DO POSS-man

amethang abiri arlopen eson <athe...> thesere] kelik
[[[a-metháng] a-birī] arlō=pen] e-sòn <a-thē...>
POSS-self POSS-garden inside=from one-CLF:thing POSS-fruit
theseré ke-lík
fruits IPFV-pluck
'[...] [O]ne farmer from (inside) his (own) garden is picking a kind of fruit.' [SiT, PS 002]

Since enumeration is semantically less specific than modification by a relative clause or a PCT modifier, it would be expected to find enumerators generally preceding other modifiers as is the case in these two examples (366) and (367). At the same time, there is also at least one instance in the corpus where a numeral follows a modifier (368). No doubt this more unusual order is due to the fact that the relative clause that the speaker starts with is so lengthy and complex. It seems likely that the speaker had not fully planned this noun phrase given the complexity of the relative clause. While the corpus is not large enough to test whether this ordering of RC–NUM–HN is indeed as rare as we would expect, it remains a fact about Karbi that this ordering (even if possibly being *ad hoc*) is acceptable enough that it does not require the speaker to correct himself and re-start uttering the noun phrase beginning with the numeral.

(368) NP structure: RC – NUM – HN
[...] kopipima ladak kelongdun ahormu hortar'an
[[[kopí~pí=ma làdāk ke-lóng-dùn] a-hormú hortár=án]
what~DIST.PL=Q here NMLZ-get-JOIN POSS-thing EE:hormú=all

kirim kibi isi ahem do laso
ke-rīm **ke-bí]**ʀᴄ [isī]ɴᴜᴍ **a-hēm]**ʜɴ dō lasō
ɴᴍʟᴢ-put.in.one.place ɴᴍʟᴢ-keep one **ᴘᴏss-house** exist this

langdamlonglo
làng-dām-lōng-lò
see-ɢᴏ-ɢᴇᴛ-ʀʟ
'[...] [T]here is one house where they put everything they got from the time of when the British were fighting against Japan, this we got to go and see.' [SiT, HF 056]

Example (369) shows that enumerator and PCT modifier can be distributed across both sides of the head noun. In this example, we find the classifier-numeral word before the head noun, and the PCT modifier after the head noun.

(369) NP structure: NUM – HN – PCT
"ba ko jirpo {mm} pinike ne
[ba ko jīrpō] mm [pinì=ke nè
sᴜʀᴘʀɪsᴇ(<Asm) buddy:ᴠᴏᴄ friend ᴀꜰꜰ today=ᴛᴏᴘ 1ᴇxᴄʟ

eson akhobor mesen arjulong" {mm}
[e-sòn a-khobór mē-sén] arjū-lōng] {mm}
one-ᴄʟꜰ:thing ᴘᴏss-news(<Ind) be.good-ɪɴᴛᴇɴs hear-ɢᴇᴛ ᴀꜰꜰ
'"Hey, my friend...today I got to hear (one piece of) good news."' [HK, TR 132]

Section III of Table 100 shows that a possessor always stays closest to the head noun, that is, it always immediately precedes the head noun. Any type of enumerator, as the classifier-numeral word in (370), or a relative clause, as in (371), occur before the possessor, further away from the head noun.

(370) NP structure: NUM – [NP]ᴘᴏsʀ – HN
aphrang ahut... inut arong agaonbura
a-phráng ahūt **e-nūt a-ròng**
ᴘᴏss-front during **one-ᴄʟꜰ:ʜᴜᴍ:sɢ ᴘᴏss-village**
a-gáonburá
ᴘᴏss-village.headman(<Asm)

ba arong asarthelo
bá a-ròng a-sarthè-lò
I.mean(<Asm) ᴘᴏss-village ᴘᴏss-village.headman-ʀʟ
'A long time ago, there was one village *gaonbura*, I mean, one village headman.' [CST, RO 003]

(371) NP structure: RC – [N]₍ₚₒₛᵣ₎ – HN
anke ajabok along kethapthot
ánke	[[a-jabók]		alòng	ke-thàp-thòt]
and.then	POSS-pocket(<Asm)		LOC	NMLZ-put.inside-into.opening

akriket abet ensi juiponbomlo
[a-kriket]	a-bet]]	ēn-si	jùi-pòn-bōm-lò
POSS-cricket(<Eng)	POSS-bat(<Eng)	take-NF:RL	play-take.away-CONT-RL

'And then, the cricket bat that he had put into his pocket he takes again and keeps playing while going away.' [SiT, PS 042]

The last two examples (372) and (373) illustrate the occurrence of the plural marker *-tūm* in the final slot of the noun phrase (cf. section IV of Table 100). In (372), we find a preceding possessor, while in (373), the head noun is first followed by a PCT modifier and then comes the plural marker.

(372) NP structure: [N]₍ₚₒₛᵣ₎ – HN – PL
[...] halabangso ahut elitum Karbi akhei atum
[hála-bàng-sō	ahūt	e-li-tūm	**Karbì**	**a-khéi**
that-CLF:HUM:PL-small	during	1PL.INCL-HON-PL	PN	POSS-community

a-tūm
POSS-PL

pindeng sumpot aphan kosonsonsi keklemma
pindéng	sumpót	a-phān	kosón~són=si
dress.and.ornaments	EE:pindéng	POSS-NSUBJ	how~DIST.PL=FOC:RL

ke-klém=ma
NMLZ-do=Q

'[...] [D]uring the old days, what are the (different) ways in which we, the Karbi tribe, would make/produce dresses and ornaments? (That's what I will talk about).' [KST, PSu 002]

(373) NP structure: HN – PCT – PL
[lapusonsi lasi nonpútame pini pirthe kangtang ahut
lapusón=si	lasì	nón-pù=tamē	pinì	pirthé	ke-ingtāng
like.this=FOC:RL	therefore	now-QUOT=any	today	world	NMLZ-be.strong

ahūt
during

setame ove kimi atum chethanlong] Bokolapo
setāmē	**ovè**	**ke-mī**	**a-tūm**	che-thán-lōng
nevertheless	generation	NMLZ-be.new	POSS-PL	RR-tell-GET

Bokolā-pō
NAME-male

abiha kedam pu
a-bihá   ke-dàm   pu
POSS-trade NMLZ-go   say

'That way, even today also, as the world is mature, the new generations get to tell each other (a saying), "Bokolapo is going to the market" (meaning instead of going to your destination, you're going the other way).' [HI, BPh 020]

10.3 Diachronic significance of the possessive construction

The possessive construction, schematically [N$_{POSR}$] [**a**-N$_{POSD}$], has given rise to the grammaticalization of a number of syntactic categories and grammatical functions.

Syntactic categories, or word classes, that have developed in the possessive constructions include relator nouns (§5.4), as well as, via further grammaticalization of relator nouns, a number of subordinators and adverbs (§5.4.7).

The grammatical markers that have grammaticalized in the possessive construction include a variety of nominal categories: the plural noun -*tūm* (§10.6), the emphatic reflexive with -*māt* (§6.1.2), as well as the noun phrase delimiter *abàng* (§13.5). Relator nouns have also further grammaticalized to role markers -*phān* (§14.1.2) and -*lòng* (§14.1.3). Moreover, the restrictive focus marker -*nàt* (§14.2.6.3) must have grammaticalized in the same way.

Functionally, it makes sense to treat some of the categories that have emerged, such as the plural marker -*tūm* or the emphatic reflexive -*māt*, as postposed modifiers, i.e., modifiers that follow their head noun. Structurally, however, they themselves are the head noun, the same way that in English NPs like 'the crowd of the students' or 'the students' crowd', 'the crowd' is the head noun and 'the students' acts as a modifier.

This is analogous to relator nouns, where in an NP such as 'the top of the table' or 'the table's top' (then grammaticalizing to 'on (top of) the table'), the head of the NP is 'the top' and not 'the table'.

A good illustration of the significance of the possessive construction in providing fertile ground for grammaticalization is offered in (374), where in a subordinate clause of seven words, the *a-* 'possessive' prefix occurs five times.

(374) Diachronic significance of the possessive construction
[...] Naka akhei atum aphan adunghétpen
[[[Naká   **a**-khéi   **a**-tūm]   **a**-phān]   [[**a**-dūng-hèt=pen
TRIBE   POSS-community POSS-PL   POSS-NSUBJ POSS-near-firmly=from

kethekdamlong apot ning ingsam'o, neli
ke-thèk-dām-lōng] **a**-pōt]]   nīng   ingsām-ò   nè-lì
NMLZ-see-GO-GET   POSS-because   mind   be.cold-much   1EXCL-HON
'[...] [B]ecause I could see the Naga tribes from very near, I was very happy.' [SiT, HF 058]

Within the NP *Naka akhei atum*, the first occurrence of *a-* on *khéi* marks the synchronic possessive construction (i.e., 'the tribes of the Nagas'); the second occurrence of *a-* is part of the plural construction with *-tūm*. The third *a-* occurs on the non-subject marker *-phān*, which marks the role of the NP *Naka akhei atum*.

The next word is the adverbial *adunghetpen* 'from very near', which carries *a-* because it has grammaticalized from relator noun *-dūng* 'near'. Finally, the conjunction that marks this as a subordinate clause, *apōt* 'because', must also have a history of a relator noun, to explain why *a-* occurs here.

10.4 Possessive *a-* marking of head nouns

Head nouns with postposed modifiers are not marked in any special way. Head nouns with preposed modifiers, however, are generally marked by *a-*. Those modifiers that may occur before or after the head noun illustrate this rule: if they are preposed, the head noun is marked by *a-*, if they are postposed, the head noun is not marked by *a-*.

In complex noun phrases with more than one modifier, the presence or absence of *a-* on nominal elements may be considered when trying to analyze the underlying (hierarchical or flat) syntactic structure.

First, consider the *a-* 'possessive' prefix in the first NP in (375), *la apiso abangke* 'the wife', which occurs on *pīsō* 'wife' due to the presence of the demonstrative *là* as a preposed modifier.

(375) NP structure: DEM – [N]_POSR – HN
amat la apiso abangke la jangthu abong
amāt   [là   a-pisò   abàng=ke]   **[là   jàngthù   a-bòng]**
and.then this POSS-wife NPDL=TOP   **this oil   POSS-bottle**

cheenlo [...]
che-én-lò
RR-take-RL
'And then, the wife took herself the bottle of oil [...].' [SeT, MTN 044]

In the second NP in (375), *la jangthu abong*, there are two modifiers, the demonstrative *là* and the nominal possessor/modifier, *jàngthù* 'oil'. The question is whether the structure of this NP has to be analyzed as either flat, such that both the demonstrative and the possessor modify the head noun in a linear way: [DEM – [N]_POSR – HN], or as hierarchical or embedded, such that the demonstrative modifies the possessor rather than the possessed head noun: [[DEM – N]_POSR – HN].

The answer would seem to be that it has to be analyzed as a flat structure, because if the demonstrative were modifying the possessor rather than the head noun, the possessor would have to have the *a-* prefix attached to signal that it is being modified.

Opposite from this case, it appears that the alternative, hierarchical or embedded structure of a demonstrative-possessor-head noun sequence is the only correct analysis in (376). Here, the demonstrative *laso* has to be analyzed as modifying the possessor *Karbipi* 'Karbi woman' rather than the head noun *osomar* 'children', because *Karbipi* is marked as being modified by a preposed element, i.e., *laso* 'this', via *a-*.

(376) NP structure: [DEM] [*a*-N]_{POSR} [*a*-HN]
 [...] *laso aKarbipi asomar oso cherop...* [...]
 [[**lasō a-Karbì-pī]   a-oso-màr**]   [osō   cherōp]
 this   POSS-PN-fem   POSS-child-PL   child   twin
 '[...] [T]his Karbi woman's children were twins... [...]' [CST, HM 009]

However, this evidence of *a-* on the possessor in (376) is not conclusive because *a-* may also occur on a noun in the absence of a preposed modifier (see also §7.3.1 on this issue, and specifically the discussion of (180)).

To see an example of this, consider (377). Here we have a sequence of a classifier-numeral word, *inut* 'one (CLF:HUM:SG)'; a possessor or modifier, *rong* 'village'; and the head noun, *gaonbura* 'village headman (<Asm)'.

(377) NP structure: NUM – [N]_{POSR} – HN
 aphrang ahut... inut arong agaonbura
 a-phráng   ahūt   **[e-nūt   a-ròng**
 POSS-front   during   one-CLF:HUM:SG   POSS-village
 a-gáonburá]
 POSS-village.headman(<Asm)

 ba arong asarthelo
 bá   a-ròng   a-sarthè-lò
 I.mean(<Asm)   POSS-village   POSS-village.headman-RL
 'A long time ago, there was one village *gaonbura*, I mean, one village headman.' [CST, RO 003]

In this example, we know that the classifier-numeral word *inut* modifies the head noun *gaonbura* rather than the possessor *arong* 'village', because it contains the human singular classifier *nūt*. It therefore cannot be '(the) headman of one village', but has to be 'one headman of (a) village'. Nevertheless, even though the classifier-numeral word modifies the head noun rather than the possessor *ròng* 'village', the form still occurs with the *a-* prefix, i.e., *arong*.

There are two implications of this discussion. First, an NP of the form [[MODIF] [N]_{POSR} [*a*-HN]] has to be analyzed as the flat structure [DEM – [N]_{POSR} – HN], because if the possessor or modifier noun does not carry *a-*, then it is definitely not being modified. Second, however, if the NP has the form [[MODIF] [*a*-N]~POSR~ [*a*-HN]], with the *a*- on the possessor, then the underlying structure is ambiguous. It could represent the hierarchical structure [[DEM – N]~POSR~ – HN], or it could still just represent the flat structure [DEM – [N]~POSR~ – HN].

There is more evidence that *a*- sometimes occurs on a noun without a preposed modifier present. Specifically, *a*- typically occurs on preposed (but less so on postposed) PCT modifiers, presumably because they need to be 'more' nominalized (and/or more referential) when they occur before the head noun, essentially functioning as a nominal possessor or modifier.[100] An example of a preposed PCT modifier with *a*- is (378).

(378) NP structure: NUM – PCT – HN; preposed PCT modifier with *a*- 'possessive'
laso ahut amat inut akaprek amonit
lasō a-hūt   amāt   **[e-nūt   a-ke-prék**
this POSS-during and.then one-CLF:HUM:SG POSS-NMLZ-be.different
a-monít
POSS-man

abangke saikel nangardonsi vanglo... [...]
a-bàng=ke]   saikél   nang=ardòn-si   vàng-lò...
NPDL=TOP   bicycle(<Eng) CIS=ride-NF:RL come-RL
'In this moment, another person riding on a bicycle came [...].' [SiT, PS 015]

Note, however, that there are exceptions to the rule that preposed modifiers require possessive *a*- marking of the head noun. For example, in the noun phrase *hala Bey Ki'ik atumke* in (379), the head noun *Bey Ki'ik* occurs without *a*- although *hála* is a preposed modifier that would typically require the head noun to occur with *a*-.

(379) Preposed demonstrative *hála* 'that' without *a*- on head noun
hala Bey Ki'ik atumke lo han
[hála   Bēy   ke-ìk   a-tūm=ke]   [lō   hán
that   CLAN   NMLZ-be.black   POSS-PL=TOP   banana.leaf   curry

thik'etlomati [...]
thík-ét-lò=mati
be.okay(<Asm)-PRF-RL=CG
'And then, Bey the Black and his family had already arranged everything, you know [...].' [WR, BCS 018]

---

100 For further discussion of *a*- marked preposed PCT modifiers, see the discussion of examples (181) and (182) in §7.3.1, as well more examples of preposed PCT modifiers in §10.7.1.2.

While the absence of *a-* in (379) could be due to *Bey Ki'ik* being a name, there are other cases. In (380), the same preposed demonstrative *hála* is used without adding *a-* to the head noun. In this case, we may still assume that the reason is the initial *ar-* of *arlèng* 'slope', and that we are dealing with morphophonological fusion (§3.9.2.1).

(380) Preposed demonstrative *hála* 'that' without *a-* on *ar*-initial head noun
hala arleng ebeng'an amatsi akhalun ingpuvakló [...]
hála   arlèng   e-bēng-án   amātsi   a-khalùn
that   slope   one-CLF:half-this.much and.then   POSS-kd.big.basket
ingpú-vàk-lò
open-RES:open-RL
'She (had climbed) half of the slope and then she opened her *khalun* basket [...].' [SeT, MTN 050]

Nevertheless, there are other examples, in which a preposed modifier is used without marking the head noun with *a-*, where no obvious explanation comes to mind, as in (381).

(381)   Preposed demonstrative *lasō* 'this' without *a-* on head noun
        [...] *amat laso sarpita ajo mek janglo* [...]
        [amāt   **[lasō sarpī=tā]**   a-jó   mēk   jáng-lò]
        and.then   **this   old.woman=ADD**   POSS-night eye   fall-RL
        '[...] [A]nd then also that old woman slept at night [...].' [KK, BMS 118]

My language consultants agree that the speaker in (381) did not use an *a-* prefix on *sarpī* 'old woman' but that there is no meaning difference between using *a-* or not using *a-*. Perhaps we are dealing with ongoing grammaticalization of this construction. Further research is required to find the variables that correlate with the inconsistent use of the *a-* prefix (see also the (arguably analogous) inconsistency in the occurrence of nominalizer *ke-* in nominalization constructions, §12.8, as well as §1.3.3.3).

10.5 Preposed modifiers

Frequently occurring preposed modifiers include demonstratives (§10.5.1) and nominal modifiers in the possessive construction (§10.5.2). Occasionally, interrogative pronouns and adverbs as well as derived indefinite; (general) adverbials; or non-nominalized clausal modifiers function as preposed modifiers as well (§10.5.3).

10.5.1 Demonstratives

Demonstratives (§6.1.3) precede their head noun, which, in turn, is usually marked by *a-* 'possessive', as seen in (382) (see §1.3.3.3 and §10.4 for exceptions).

(382)　Possessive *a-* on head noun with preceding demonstrative modifier
　　　　*anke halaso arni.... **laso ajangrengsoke**.... apok*
　　　　ankè　　hálasō　arnì　[lasō　**a-**jangrēngsō=ke...].　a-pōk
　　　　and.then　that　　day　this　**POSS**-orphan=TOP　POSS-stomach

　　　　ingchirdukke mati di {mm}
　　　　ingchìr-dùk=ke　　　　matì　dī　　mm
　　　　be.hungry-INTENS=TOP　CG　　Q.TAG　AFF
　　　　'On that day, this orphan was suffering from hunger, wouldn't he have been?'
　　　　[HK, TR 010]

10.5.2 Possessives

The possessive construction allows an unmarked noun ('possessor') to modify another noun, then marked by *a-* 'possessive' ('possessed'), schematically [N$_{POSR}$] [*a*-N$_{POSD}$]. An example is *rechó a-hēm* 'the king's house', where *rechó* 'king' is the possessor, and *hēm* 'house' is the possessed and marked by *a-*.

However, more complex noun phrases can also function as possessors. This includes coordination constructions such as (383); noun phrases consisting of a noun followed by a PCT modifier in (384) and (385); as well as a possessive construction in (386), thus leading to recursion.

(383)　Coordination construction with *=pen* 'with' as possessor
　　　　"*neke nepeipén nepo ahem chedampo*"
　　　　nè=ke　　**[[ne-pēi=pen**　　　　　**ne-pō]**$_{POSR}$　　　a-hēm]$_{HN}$
　　　　1EXCL=TOP　**1EXCL:POSS-mother=with**　**1EXCL:POSS-father**　POSS-house
　　　　che-dām-pò
　　　　RR-go-IRR1
　　　　"'I will go to my mother and father's house."' [SeT, MTN 038]

(384)　[N – PCT]$_{NP}$ as possessor
　　　　adet kaprek amonit kevang, haladak
　　　　[[[**a-dét**　　　　**ke-prék]**$_{POSR}$　　　a-monít]　ke-vàng　　háladāk
　　　　POSS-country　**NMLZ-be.different**　POSS-man　NMLZ-come　there

nangkelangdun do'o domestic touristta do'o
nang=ke-làng-dūn]   dō-ò]   domestic tourist=tā   dō-ò
CIS=NMLZ-see-along exist-much   domestic tourist=ADD exist-much
'There were many people who came from different countries to come and see, and there were also many domestic tourists.' [SiT, HF 038]

(385) [N – PCT]$_{NP}$ as possessor
ingnar nothongpo ano lutchok arkevaret
[[**ingnàr   nothōng-pō**]$_{POSR}$ a-nò]   lūt-chòk   arkè-varèt
elephant deaf-MODIF   POSS-ear   enter-disappearing   scratch-INTENS
'(The bird) got into the ears of a deaf elephant, and scratched around.' [RBT, ChM 024]

(386) [N$_{POSR}$ – N$_{POSD}$]$_{NP}$ as possessor
[...] amatsi netum abangke ha Chomangkan ahem
amātsi   ne-tūm   abàng=ke   [[**há**   **Chomangkán**   **a-hēm**]$_{POSR}$
and.then   1EXCL-PL   NPDL=TOP   **over.there**   **PN**   **POSS-house**

asor atumpen ako netum
a-sòr   a-tūm=pen]   akó   ne-tūm
POSS-people   POSS-PL=from   on.the.other.hand(<Asm)   1EXCL-PL

chebidaithulo ajatlo amatke vanglo
che-bidái-thù-lò   ajàt-lò   amāt=ke   vàng-lò
RR-say.goodbye(<Asm)-again-RL   GENEX-RL   and.then=TOP   come-RL
'[...] [A]nd then we said goodbye to the people from the Chomangkan house and then came back again.' [SH, CSM 066]

As illustrated in (387), the reflexive pronoun -*metháng* 'self' can function as a possessor to indicate co-reference with the subject of the clause (see also §6.1.2 on reflexives).

(387) Co-reference between subject and possessor of clause participant
[...] inut chotiki chonghoi amonit
[[e-nūt   cho-tikī   cho-inghói]   a-monít]$_i$
one-CLF:HUM:SG   AUTO.BEN/MAL-cultivate   AUTO.BEN/MAL-do   POSS-man

amethang *abiri arlopen eson <athe...> thesere] kelik*
[[[a-**metháng**]$_i$ a-birī]   arlō=pen]   e-sòn   <a-thē...>
POSS-self   POSS-garden   inside=from   one-CLF:thing   POSS-fruit
theseré   ke-lík
fruit   IPFV-pluck
'[...] [O]ne farmer from (inside) his (own) garden is picking a kind of fruit.' [SiT, PS 002]

10.5.3 Other preposed modifiers

10.5.3.1 Interrogative pronouns and derived indefinites

Both interrogative pronouns and indefinites derived from interrogative pronouns with *-nē* may function as nominal modifiers.

In (388) from a folk story, a squirrel is mad at a frog for destroying the ladder to its nest. Being sarcastic, it yells at the frog asking who it was who is so smart and strong and jumped and destroyed its ladder. Structurally, there are four coordinated noun phrases, all consisting of the interrogative pronoun *māt* 'who' modifying deverbal nominals marked by *a-* 'possessive'. A closer translation into English would be 'which knowledgeable person' and 'which strong person', but where English only has one general interrogative nominal modifier 'which', any interrogative pronoun or adverb regularly and systematically functions as a modifier in Karbi.

(388) *māt* 'who' functioning as nominal modifier
amat karlesibongpota... aning thilo... "mat akethek,
amāt   karlēsibóngpō=tā...   a-nīng   thī-lò   **[māt**
and.then   squirrel.sp=ADD   POSS-mind   be.short-RL   **who**
a-ke-thèk]
POSS-NMLZ-know.how

mat akere, mat akangtang, mat
[māt   a-ke-rè]   **[māt   a-ke-ingtāng]**   **[māt**
who   POSS-NMLZ-be.smart   **who   POSS-NMLZ-be.strong**   **who**

akangsaksi nedondon chonraima?"
a-ke-ingsàk=si]   ne-dondōn
POSS-NMLZ-EE:ingtāng=FOC:RL   1EXCL:POSS-ladder
chón-rài=ma
jump-RES:solid.obj.breaking=Q

pu, lata
pu   là=tā
QUOT   this=ADD

'And then, the squirrel... got mad, "Who is the wise one, who is the smart one, who is the strong and mighty one, who jumped on my ladder so it broke?", it (the squirrel) (said).' [RBT, ChM 019]

Similarly, in (389), which was spontaneously uttered in the context of seeing a truck crowded with people going to a market, the interrogative adverb *kodāk* 'where' modifies *bojár* 'market'.

(389) *kodāk* 'where' functioning as nominal modifier
pinì   [*kodāk* a-bojár=lo]
today **where** POSS-market(<Ind)=FOC
'Today is which market (lit., a where-market)? / Where is market day today?' (OH 121009.001)

Likewise, indefinites derived from interrogatives with -*nē* 'indefinite' function as nominal modifiers. In (390), *pine* 'some, any' is derived from *pī* 'what' and functions as a modifier of *kám* 'work'.

(390) *pí-nē* 'what-indefinite' functioning as nominal modifier
pine akam doma jirpo ho {mm}
[**pí-nē**   a-kám]   dō=ma   jīrpō   hò   mm
what-INDEF POSS-work exist=Q friend   definitely AFF
'Is there any work, friend?' [HK, TR 130]

In (391), *komāt-nē* 'who-indefinite' acts as a modifier meaning 'some, any' in the context of talking about people rather than things.

(391) *komāt-nē* 'who-indefinite' functioning as nominal modifier
komatne akurja aso vanlo, komatne
[[**komāt-nē** a-kurjà]   a-osō]   vàn-lò   [[**komāt-nē**
who-INDEF   POSS-muslim POSS-child   bring-RL   who-INDEF

abonggali aso ponlo, aphai dopiklo
a-bonggalí]   a-osō]   pòn-lò   aphái   dō-pìk-lò
POSS-Bengoli POSS-child   carry-RL   number   exist-very-RL
'He brought some young muslims, he carried some young Bengolis, he already had many of them.' [HK, TR 041]

Finally, in (392), *konát-nē* 'where-indefinite' modifies *sempu* 'shampoo' in the sense 'any shampoo; shampoo taken/bought from anywhere'.

(392) *konát-nē* 'where-indefinite' functioning as nominal modifier
[...] sabun tangho, kopine tangho, la konane asempu
[sabún   tànghò kopí-nē   tànghò   [là   **konát-nē**
soap(<Asm)   REP   what-INDEF   REP   this **where-INDEF**
a-sempú]
POSS-shampoo(<Eng?)

non'alom ke'enthapvaret, lahai abangta chokchelo
nón-alōm ke-ēn-tháp-varèt] [lahái abàng=tā chók-Cē-lò]
now-while NMLZ-take-mindlessly-INTENS these NPDL=ADD be.fine-NEG-RL
'[...] [S]oap, and whatever, shampoo from wherever, are now constantly used, and it is not okay (to use) all these things (without knowing much about them).' [SiH, CW 003]

10.5.3.2 Adverbials

Adverbials, such as *hádāk* 'there' in (393), or the more complex construction in (394), may also function as preposed nominal modifiers.

(393) Adverbial *hádāk* 'there' functioning as a preposed modifier
lapenke eson acheng do hadak achengke
[lapèn=ke e-sòn a-chēng dō] [[[hádāk]_{MODIF} a-chēng=ke]
and=TOP one-CLF:thing POSS-drum exist **there** POSS-drum=TOP

kibihek kali lake thepik thengpi
ke-bī-hèk kalī] [là=ke thè-pìk] [thengpī
NMLZ-be.small-small NEG.EQU.COP this=TOP be.big-very tree/wood

arong amatsi vandet
a-rōng amātsi vàn-dèt]
POSS-plant self bring-PFV
'And then, there was one kind of drum there, the drums there are not small, that one was very big, they had brought a tree itself.' [SiT, HF 051]

(394) Complex adverbial construction functioning as a preposed modifier
anke lapu thoi asorpen hapu Rongkhang anatthu
ánke [[lapú thói a-sòr=pen hápú Rongkháng
and.then **this.side plains POSS-people=from that.side AREA**
a-nátthū]_{MODIF}
POSS-direction

aChomangkanke neta ketheklongchenglo aronta
a-Chomangkan=ke] nè=tā ke-theklōng-chéng-lò a-rōn=tā
POSS-PN=TOP 1EXCL=also NMLZ-see-for.first.time-RL POSS-custom=also

chinidun'o'e setame ning arongpiklo
chinī-dùn-ò-Cē setāmē nīng aróng-pìk-lò
know-JOIN-much-NEG nevertheless mind be.happy-very-RL
'And then, the Chomangkan of people from this side, from the plains, and from that side, the Ronghang side, I also see for the first time.' [SH, CSM 044]

10.5.3.3 Clausal modifiers

In (395), a formally non-nominalized subordinate purpose clause (§15.2.3.2, §9.6.2.1.7) modifies the head noun *a-lám* 'POSS-matter'.

(395) Preposed, formally non-nominalized clausal modifier
lasi netum abangke ako nangchirui Diphu chirui...

lasì	ne-tūm	abàng=ke	akó	nang=chirùi	Diphú	chirùi
therefore	1EXCL-PL	NPDL=TOP	DC(<Asm)	CIS=return	PN	return

la hem chevangthuphitji pu alam do

[là	hēm	che-vàng-thū-phìt-jí		pu]	a-lám]	dō
this	house	RR-come-again-right.away-IRR2		QUOT	POSS-matter	exist

apotsi ako netum hadakpen vanglo

apōt=si	akó	ne-tūm	hádāk=pen	vàng-lò
because=FOC:RL	DC(<Asm)	1EXCL-PL	there=from	come-RL

'So we got on our way back to Diphu again..., because it was a matter of returning back home right away (i.e. not spending the night), so again we left from there.' [SH, CSM 061]

10.6 Postposed modifier: Plural marking noun *-tūm*

Plural marking of proper nouns occurs in the possessive construction, in which, structurally, the possessor is the pluralized noun, and the possessed is the plural noun *-tūm*, as in (396). (With personal pronouns, the possessor is indicated with personal possessive prefixes (§6.1.1).)

(396) Plural marking noun *-tūm*
arlosomar atumsi akele langpik

[árlosō-mār	**a-tūm**=si]	akelé	làng-pìk
woman-PL	**POSS-PL**=FOC:RL	more	see-very

'The women do a lot more of looking after things.' [KaR, SWK 040]

This plural construction with *-tūm* often has an associated plural reading. In (397), *Bey Ki'ik atum* refers to the family of *Bey Ki'ik*. In (398), *ne'ik atum* does not refer to a plurality of older brothers, but to the older brother and his wife.

(397) Associative plural function of *-tūm*
hala Bey Ki'ik atumke lo han

[hála	Bēy	ke-ìk	**a-tūm**=ke]	[lō	hán
that	CLAN	NMLZ-be.black	POSS-PL=TOP	banana.leaf	curry

> *thik'etlomati [...]*
> thík-ét-lò=mati
> be.okay(<Asm)-PRF-RL=CG
> 'And then, Bey the Black and his family had already arranged[101] everything, you know [...].' [WR, BCS 018]

(398) Associative plural function of *-tūm*
[...] ne'ik atum aphan an thonji pu
[ne-ìk   a-tūm   a-phān]   àn   thòn-jí   pu
1EXCL:POSS-older.brother POSS-PL POSS-NSUBJ rice drop-IRR2 QUOT
'"[...] I want to take rice to my brother (and sister-in-law)."' [RBT, ChM 012]

Finally, while *-tūm* cannot be used to indicate the plurality of inanimate objects, there are some contexts in which it can be used with animals. Plural *-tūm* can always be used for animals that are personified in folk stories, as in (399).

(399) Plural *-tūm* used with personified dogs in folk story
*la chonghokalosopen la misorongpo **atum** kopi*
[[[là   chonghōkalósō=pen là   misòrongpō] **a-tūm]**   kopí
 this   sp.frog=with   this   sp.ant   **POSS-PL** what

chomathalone, [...]
cho-mathà-lò-nē]
AUTO.BEN/MAL-think-RL-INDEF
'The frog and the ant thinking up whatever (bad things) [...].' [RBT, ChM 072]

10.7 Modifiers that occur preposed or postposed

10.7.1 Deverbal modifiers: PCT-based modifiers and relative clauses

It was previously assumed[102] that the noun modification constructions of property concept term (PCT) roots and prototypical verb roots show a clear syntactic difference. While both are marked morphologically the same, i.e., nominalized via *ke-*,[103] the order of head noun and modifier appeared to mark a clear difference: PCT-based modifiers

---

101 The Assamese borrowing *thík* can both refer to the state of 'things being in order, being OK', or dynamically to 'putting things in order', as is the case here.
102 See Grüßner (1978) and Konnerth (2011) (which was based on data in Grüßner (1978)).
103 See Chapter 12 on deverbal property concept term modifiers and relative clauses in the context of nominalization functions in Karbi. Also note, however, the inconsistency with which *ke-* actually occurs, as discussed in §12.8 and more generally in §1.3.3.3.

are post-head, whereas prototypical verb-based relative clauses are pre-head. Elicited PCT-based modifiers and prototypical verb-based relative clauses have shown the same pattern.

It turns out, however, that this supposedly clear distinction does not hold up against a larger body of natural data. There are instances in the corpus of pre-head PCT-based modifiers and there also is one potential instance of a post-head relative clause.

Below I will first show examples of the more typical pattern: post-head PCT-based modifiers and pre-head prototypical verb-based relative clauses (§10.7.1.1), and then discuss examples of pre-head PCT modifiers and the potential instance of a post-head relative clause (§10.7.1.2).

10.7.1.1 Post-head PCT-based modifiers and pre-head relative clauses

In (400), the PCT modifier *kemē* 'good' follows its head noun *kasú* 'plate' and *harlūng* 'bowl', respectively.

(400) PCT root following the head noun it modifies
[...] kasu keme harlung kemepen [...]
[[kasú]$_{HN}$ [ke-mē]$_{PCT}$ [harlūng]$_{HN}$ [ke-mē]$_{PCT}$=pen]
plate   NMLZ-be.good bowl   NMLZ-be.good=with
'[...] from brass (lit. good) plates and bowls [...]' [KK, BMS 056]

In (401), the relative clause *nelitum aphan nangkejapon* '(who) took us there' whose verb *nangkejapon* carries the *ke-* nominalizing prefix, precedes its head noun *a'osopi* 'lady', which is marked as being modified via *a-* 'possessive'.

(401) Relative clause verb preceding the head noun it modifies
Lilý, la nelitum aphan nangkejapon aosopi
Lilý   [là   [ne-li-tūm   aphān   nang=ke-já-pòn]$_{RC}$
NAME this 1EXCL-HON-PL NSUBJ   1/2:NSUBJ=NMLZ-lead-take.away
[a-osopì]$_{HN}$]
POSS-lady
'[...] Lily, the lady who took us there [...]' [SiT, HF 034]

Thus in these examples, both PCT and prototypical verb roots need to carry *ke-* 'nominalizer', but PCT-based modifiers follow their head noun, whereas prototypical verb-based modifiers precede them. In addition, however, a preceding relative clause requires its head noun to occur with *a-* 'possessive', whereas a following PCT-based modifier has an unmarked head noun. This follows the general pattern that head nouns with preceding modifiers are marked possessive (or modified) by *a-*, but head nouns with following modifiers remain unmarked (§10.4).

10.7.1.2 Pre-head PCT-based modifiers (and post-head relative clauses)

Contrary to what we have seen in the previous section, there also are a number of instances in the corpus in which a PCT modifier precedes rather than follows its head noun. Examples (402), (403), and (404) show pre-head PCT modifiers that themselves are marked with the *a-* 'possessive' in addition to the *ke-* 'nominalizer'.

(402) Pre-head PCT-based modifiers *èr* 'be red' and *ìk* 'be black', marked with *a-ke-* 'POSS-NMLZ-'
akeer pusetame akiik pusetame
a-ke-èr pùsetāmē **a-ke-ìk** pùsetāmē
POSS-NMLZ-be.red likewise **POSS-NMLZ-be.black** likewise

akalar pipó
a-kalár pī-pò
POSS-color(<Eng) give-IRR1
'Red or black color we will add.' [KST, PSu 009]

(403) Pre-head PCT-based modifier *mī* 'be new', marked with *a-ke-* 'POSS-NMLZ-'
lasonthotsi Lindata ketheklongpen aning kerong,
[lasón-thót=si Líndá=tā ke-theklōng-pèn] [a-nīng
that.way-exactly=FOC:RL PN=also NMLZ-see-NF POSS-mind
ke-aróng]]
NMLZ-be.happy

akimi ahormulo, amonit atum aphanta theklonglo
[a-ke-mī **a-hormú-lò]** a-monít a-tūm aphān=tā
POSS-NMLZ-be.new POSS-thing-RL POSS-man POSS-PL NSUBJ=ADD
theklōng-lòk-lò
see-happen.to-RL
'Seeing exactly this, Linda was happy, it was a new thing, she also got to see the people.' [SH, CSM 035]

(404) Pre-head PCT-based modifier *mē* 'be good', marked with *a-ke-* 'POSS-NMLZ-'
la'an akemesen atovar kedamtheksi
[la-án **a-ke-mēsén** **a-továr** ke-dàm-thēk-si]
this-that.much **POSS-NMLZ-be.good POSS-road** NMLZ-go-know.how-NF:RL

hako amonit atumke nonpu'anta ilitum
[[hakó a-monít a-tūm=ke] nón-pu-án=tā e-li-tūm
that.time POSS-man POSS-PL=TOP now-QUOT-all=ADD 1PL.INCL-HON-PL

a'ansose nangpa'okorjangdunlonglang
a-án-sosē nang=pa-okorjāng-dūn-lōng-làng
POSS-that.much-more CIS=VBLZ-girl-JOIN-GET-still

nangparisomardunlonglang
nang=pa-risō-mār-dūn-lōng-làng]
CIS=VBLZ-young.man-PL-JOIN-GET-still
'They know how to go on a good road up to a high degree (i.e., know how to do things properly, how to keep everything clean, etc.), and, because they know how to keep everything clean and nice, those people back then up until today, get to stay even more like girls and boys (i.e., young) than we do.' [SiH, CW 017]

In (405) and (406), we can see that pre-head PCT-based modifiers do not, however, obligatorily take *a-* 'possessive'.

(405) Pre-head PCT-based modifier *dúk* 'be poor'
*halata **kidukthektik** amonitlo*
hála=tā   [ke-dúk-thektík   a-monít-lò]
that=ADD   NMLZ-be.poor-as.much.v.as.it.can.be   POSS-man-RL
'That one also is an unimaginably poor man.' [HK, TR 128]

(406) Pre-head PCT-based modifier *prék* 'be different'
*Europe lapen **kaprek kaprek** adet,*
Europe   lapèn [ke-prék   ke-prék   a-dét]
Europe(<Eng) and   NMLZ-be.different NMLZ-be.different POSS-country(<Ind)

America heihaipen phorena atum dopik hadak
America   héihái=pen   phorená   a-tūm   dō-pīk
America(<Eng) different.kinds.of=from foreigner(<Eng) POSS-PL   exist-very
hádāk
there
'From Europe and from many different countries, (such as) from America etc., there were many foreigners there.' [SiT, HF 037]

The conditions for the presence or absence of *a-* on pre-head PCT modifiers has to remain a topic for further research.[104] However, some implications from the difference in ordering between pre- and post-head PCT modifiers do emerge from the preceding examples: In the marked order of pre-head PCT modifiers, there is a greater focus

---

[104] Post-head PCT modifiers may also be marked by *a-* 'possessive', see §12.2. In general, my assessment is that the presence or absence of *a-* has a morphosyntactic basis (§7.3.1) but there are so many exceptions without any obvious correlation with morphosyntactic/morphophonemic context, speaker, genre, hypoarticulated speech, or anything else that a large-scale sociolinguistic study would be needed to give us clues to a better understanding.

on the property rather than the noun that is ascribed the property.[105] In (402) above, because two colors are contrasted, clearly the specific colors are what is important here. In (403), *akimi ahormulo*, the head noun is *hormú* 'thing', which is semantically unspecific and therefore the PCT *mī* 'be new' is the crucial information. In (404), the *la'an* 'this much' in *la'an akemesen* 'this good (a way/manner)' may be considered evidence that the PCT is focused. In (405), the fact that the suffix *-thektîk* 'as (much) V as it can be' is added to the PCT root suggests that this is the semantic head. Finally, (406) has a reduplicated PCT *prék* 'be different' (and not a reduplicated 'head noun' *dét* 'country (<Ind)'), which makes it the more prominent element.

The hypothesis that pre-head order of PCT modifiers is indeed used to focus on the PCT semantics is supported by (407) and (408), which are subsequent lines in a folk story, in which a present Karbi native speaking listener interrupts the storyteller from time to time to ask for clarifications (indicated in the examples by curly brackets).

(407) Post-head *mesen* 'be good'
"*ba ko jirpo {mm} pinike ne*
[ba   ko   jīrpō]   mm   [pinì=ke   nè
SURPRISE(<Asm) buddy:VOC   friend   AFF   today=TOP   1EXCL

***eson akhobor mesen** arjulong" {mm}*
[e-sòn   a-khobór   mē-sén]   arjū-lōng]   {mm}
one-CLF:thing   POSS-news(<Ind)   be.good-INTENS   hear-GET   AFF
'"Hey, my friend...today I got to hear (one piece of) good news."' [HK, TR 132]

(408) Pre-head *mesen* 'be good'
*{"**mesen abirta**" pulohe} mm*
{[**mē-sén   a-birtá**]   pù-lò=he}   mm
be.good-INTENS   POSS-news   say-RL=AFTERTHOUGHT   AFF
'{He said "good news"?!} Mm.' [HK, TR 133]

In (407), the storyteller reports the protagonist of the story saying 'I got to hear good news', where 'good news' occurs in the standard order of the PCT-based modifier *mesen* following its head noun *khobór* 'news(<Ind)'. In (408), the Karbi speaker listening to the storyteller wants to make sure he is following the story correctly and asks to clarify: 'he said "good news"?!', which likely corresponds to what in English would be stressing the word 'good' to put it under focus.

---

105 Grüßner (1978: 123/4) also reports on two different 'adjective' constructions, with differences in greater semantic weight on either the head noun or the 'adjective' (PCT modifier). However, in Grüßner's account, this difference is what is marked by the presence or absence of *a-* on the 'adjective'. Grüßner does not report on ordering differences between pre- and postposed PCT modifiers.

Leaving behind PCT-based modifiers, there also are several examples in the corpus which look like post-head relative clauses, such as (409) and (410). It is important to note, however, that there are a number of internally-headed relative clauses in the corpus (§12.3.2), and so it is not exactly clear whether we are dealing with a post-head or an internally-headed relative clause in these instances.

(409) Post-head relative clause or internally-headed relative clause
nangso kithike enutnat [...]
[[nang-osō]$_{HN}$ [ke-thì=ke]$_{RC}$] e-nūt-nàt
2:POSS-child NMLZ-die=TOP one-CLF:HUM:SG-only
'Only one of your children has died (lit. as for your children that have died, it is just a single one) [...].' [RBT, ChM 043]

(410) Post-head relative clause or internally-headed relative clause
ansi phelo-bisir pu Karbi atum kabonai
ánsi [[phelō-bisīr pu] [Karbì a-tūm]
then alkaline-funnel.for.filtering.ashes QUOT PN POSS-PL
ke-bonái]
NMLZ-make(<Asm)

do
dō
exist
'And then, there is the so-called *phelo bisir* (funnel-like instrument for filtering the ashes) that the Karbi people make.' [SiH, KH 004]

Differences in head noun and modifier order are functionally exploited in some Tibeto-Burman languages. In Tenyidie (Angami Naga), for example, a language spoken just east of Karbi Anglong into Nagaland, (derived) adjectives only occur post-head, whereas relative clauses may be pre- or post-head. The functional difference is an "inherent or internal" interpretation if post-head (like adjectives), or an "circumstantial or external" interpretation if pre-head (Herring 1991: 58).

10.7.2 Enumeration constructions

There are four basic enumeration constructions (not counting constructional difference in pre- vs. post-head order) based on two criteria. The first criterion is whether the construction uses bound or independent numerals (see §6.4.2). The second criterion is whether the construction actually contains both a classifying element and a head noun, which I call 'complex', or whether it only has one of the two, which I call 'simple'. These four constructions based on the two criteria are shown in Table 101. The name for each construction is meant to characterize the construction with respect to classifier use.

Table 101: Enumeration constructions.

Construction	Bound vs. independent numeral	Complex vs. simple
Typical classifier	bound	complex
Self-referential classifier[a]	bound	simple
Not fully grammaticalized classifier	independent	complex
Non-classifier	independent	simple

[a] I have adopted the terms 'self-referential classifier' and 'classifier-numeral word' from DeLancey et al. (in preparation).

Table 102 shows the schematic structure of each construction and offers one example each. In the examples, we can see that the first two constructions share the bound numerals: -*ní* for 'two', as opposed to the second two constructions, which have the independent form *hiní*. The first and third 'complex' constructions both have three elements (head noun, classifier, numeral), whereas the second and fourth 'simple' constructions only have two elements (head noun/classifier, numeral).

Table 102: Examples of enumeration constructions.

Construction	Schematic structure	Example	Gloss	Translation
Typical classifier	[head noun] + [CLF-bound.NUM]	*methān jōn-ní*	dog CLF-two	'two dogs'
Self-referential classifier	[CLF.noun-bound. NUM]	*jó-ní*	night-two	'two nights'
Not fully grammaticalized classifier	[head noun] + [CLF-indep.NUM]	*monít bàng-hiní*	person CLF-two	'two people'
Non-classifier	[head noun] [indep. NUM]	*hák hiní*	b.basket two	'two finely woven bamboo baskets'

10.7.2.1 Four basic enumeration constructions

10.7.2.1.1 Typical classifier construction
The 'typical classifier' construction ([head noun] + [CLF-bound.NUM]) represents the standard classifier construction, both for Karbi as well as cross-linguistically in the Southeast Asian context. It is the most frequently used enumeration construction,

although this might be in the process of changing in the younger generation (in favor of direction enumeration, see §10.7.2.1.4). This construction is the most grammaticalized and integrated construction among the four. An example is (411), where the head noun *theseré* 'fruit' is followed by the classifier-numeral word *púm-ní*. For an overview of sortal and mensural classifiers that occur in this construction, see §5.1.1.1 and §5.1.2.1.

(411) Typical classifier construction
*laphan aning ingsamsi, **thesere pumni** tekanglo*
[là-phān   a-nīng   ingsām-si]   **[[theseré púm-ní]**   tekáng-lò]
this-NSUBJ POSS-mind be.cold-NF:RL fruits   CLF:round-two leave.for-RL
'[…] [H]e was grateful to him and gave him **two pieces of fruit**.' [SiT, PS 039]

10.7.2.1.2 Self-referential classifier construction
The 'self-referential classifier' construction ([CLF.noun-bound.NUM]) consists of one of a small subset of nouns (§5.1.3), onto which bound numerals may directly attach in order to be enumerated. They thus function both as nouns (when not counted) and as classifiers (when counted and occurring with a bound numeral attached). An example is *jó* 'day' in (412).

(412) Self-referential classifier construction
anke cholo junlo <..> ejo joni dolo
[ánke   chō-lò jùn-lò]   **[e-jó   jó-ní**   dō-lò]
and.then eat-RL drink-RL **one-night night-two** stay-RL
'And then they ate and drank… they stayed a few nights (lit., one (night), two nights).' [KTa, TCS 039]

10.7.2.1.3 Not fully grammaticalized classifier construction
In the 'not fully grammaticalized' classifier construction ([head noun] + [CLF-indep. NUM]), there is both a head noun and a classifier-numeral word. However, unlike the typical classifier construction, the classifier in this construction occurs with independent (rather than bound) numerals, which is why this is called 'not fully grammaticalized'. An example is *korte banghini* in (413). (For a list of sortal and mensural classifiers that occur in this construction, see §5.1.1.2 and §5.1.2.2.)

(413) Not fully grammaticalized classifier construction
ke latum banghini abángke korte banghini
ke   [la-tūm   bàng-hiní   abàng=ke] **[[kortè bàng-hiní]**
and.then this-PL CLF:HUM:PL-two NPDL=TOP **brother CLF:HUM:PL-two**

> *abangke aseme dokoklohe*
> abàng=ke]   a-semé   dō-kòk-lò=he
> NPDL=TOP   POSS-oath   exist-firmly-RL=EMPH
> 'And then, (between) the two of them, (between) the two brothers, the oath remains, you know.' [WR, BCS 023]

10.7.2.1.4 Non-classifier (direct enumeration) construction

On the other end of the spectrum, the least grammaticalized or integrated construction is the 'non-classifier' or 'direct enumeration' construction ([head noun] [indep. NUM]). It looks just like a simple Western Indo-European-type enumeration construction, perhaps except for the difference in ordering possibilities, as numerals may precede or follow their head noun (§10.7.2.2). (For a list of nouns that so far are attested to occur in this enumeration construction, see §5.2).

There is nothing classifier-like in this construction, and there is no evidence that this construction contains anything other than a numeral and a head noun that is modified by the numeral. Consider (414), which shows that the numerals need not be directly following or preceding their head noun.

(414) Numerals *isī, hiní* modifying *achítchit arong* in 'non-classifier construction'
> *[...] laso adak isi hini achitchit arong*
> lasō   a-dāk   [isī   hiní   [achítchit   [a-ròng]]]
> this   POSS-road.inbetween   one   two   tiny   POSS-village
>
> *kephopon do*
> ke-phō-pōn   dō
> NMLZ-reach-in.passing   exist
> '[...] [O]n the road in between / up to there, there were one or two tiny villages that we had passed.' [SiT, HF 017]

Another example from elicitation in (415) shows that in this construction, the indepedendent numeral may be removed from its head noun. In this example, the head noun is topicalized and left-dislocated, with the numeral in the main clause functioning anaphorically.

(415) Numeral functioning anaphorically in 'non-classifier construction'
> *[hák=ke   isī   dō]   [bóntā   hoton=si   avē]*
> b.basket=TOP   one   exist **but**   b.basket=FOC:RL   not.exist
> 'As for *hak* bamboo baskets, there is one, but there is no *hoton* bamboo basket.' [Elicitation SiT 130905]

10.7.2.2 Pre- vs. post-head order

The enumerator (i.e., numeral or classifier-numeral word) is placed following the head noun when the emphasis is on counting, i.e., typically in those cases, where the referent is already known (rather than newly introduced). Conversely, pre-head placement occurs in situations when a new participant is being introduced.

In (416), the classifier-numeral word *ejon* occurs after the head noun *methan-sibongpo* because the context is one of counting: 'one dog, his grandmother and his grandfather, all three'. At this point in the folk story, the dog is already known as one of the protagonists and not newly introduced.

(416) Postposed enumerator: counting (/adding up) people
"dah!" pu'ansi, methan-sibongpo ejon,
dáh   pu-ánsi   [methān-sibóngpō   **e-jōn**]
go!   QUOT-after.that   dog-SPECIES   **one-CLF:animal**

aphipen aphu, mh bangkethom
[a-phì=pen   a-phù]   mh   **bàng-kethòm**
POSS-grandmother=with   POSS-grandfather DSM   **CLF:HUM:PL-three**

vangchomchomchomchomchom
vàng-chóm~chóm~chóm~chóm~chòm
come-a.little~ITER~ITER~ITER~ITER
'"Let's go!", and then one dog, his grandmother and his grandfather, all three, went step by step by step.' [KK, BMS 099]

In (417), *bangkethom* occurs postposed to the head noun *korte* 'brother(s)', because here again, the emphasis is on the exact number, while the general referent 'Bey brothers' is already mentioned before.

(417) Postposed enumerator: specifying number after story character is introduced
hako ahut hedi Bey atum korte bangkethom do tangho
hakó   ahūt   hedī   [Bēy   a-tūm]   [kortè   **bàng-kethòm**]
that.time   during   EMPH   TITLE   POSS-PL   brother **CLF:HUM:PL-three**
dō   tànghò
exist   REP
'In the old days, you know, right?, there were three Bey brothers, they say.' [WR, BCS 001]

Finally, the pre-head placement of the enumerator *inut* in (418) is explained by the fact that a character is being newly introduced here. In fact, the use of a preposed 'one' enumerator is best understood as an indefinite article construction (§10.7.2.6.1).

(418) Preposed enumerator: newly introducing story character
laso ahut amat inut akaprek amonit
lasō   a-ahūt   amāt   **[e-nūt**   a-ke-prék
this   POSS-during   and.then   one-CLF:HUM:SG   POSS-NMLZ-be.different
a-monít
POSS-man

abangke saikel nangardonsi vanglo... laso
a-bàng=ke]   saikél   nang=ardòn-si   vàng-lo...   lasō
NPDL=TOP   bicycle(<Eng)   CIS=ride-NF:RL   come-RL   this

amonitta aphu along aphutup do
a-monít=tā   a-phú   alòng   a-phutūp   dō
POSS-man=also   POSS-head   LOC   POSS-hat   exist
'In this moment, another person riding on a bicycle came, this person also had a hat on his head.' [SiT, PS 015]

10.7.2.3 Anaphoric use of classifiers

As is typical in languages of Southeast Asia, classifiers can be used anaphorically. As such, they provide more semantic information about the referent than general third person anaphors. Two examples occur in the excerpt in (419). Note that while in the first line, *ejon* has the same distribution as a noun phrase, in the second line, *ejon* is modified by the demonstrative *halá*, thus having the distributional properties of a head noun rather than a noun phrase.

(419) Anaphoric use of classifiers
anke ejon nangtetphlut <a> nangthemuchot
ánke   **[e-jōn]**   nang=tèt-phlùt   <a>   nang=thè-mūchòt
and.then   **one-CLF:animal**   CIS=exit-suddenly.big.A/O   <a>   CIS=be.big-COMPAR
'And then, one (tiger) came out (of the jungle or some area in the Rongker ground) and he was bigger (than expected and than the previous one).' [HK, TR 172]

hala ejon nangtetphlut nangthemuchot {mm}
[hála   **e-jōn]**   nang=tèt-phlùt   nang=thè-mūchot   mm
that   **one-CLF:animal**   CIS=exit-suddenly.big.A/O   CIS=be.big-COMPAR   AFF
'That one came out and it was bigger.' [HK, TR 173]

10.7.2.4 Juxtaposition of two numerals or classifier-numeral words to indicate indefiniteness or vagueness

Juxtaposition of two numerals or classifier-numeral words is used to indicate an indefinite (or vague) amount or number. In (420), *inut banghini* is vague about the exact number of people while literally translating as 'one (or) two (people)'.

(420) Two juxtaposed classifier-numeral words: *inut banghini* 'one or two (people)'
[...] Boithalangso along neli inut banghini amonit
Boithalangsō a-lòng nè-lì **[[e-nūt bàng-hiní]** a-monít
TOWN POSS-LOC 1EXCL-HON one-CLF:HUM:SG CLF-two POSS-man

atumpen chetongji si aphrangsi nelitum
a-tūm=pen] che-tòng-jí sì a-phráng-sí
POSS-PL=WITH RR-meet-IRR2 therefore POSS-first-SPLT
ne-li-tūm
1EXCL:POSS-HON=PL

inut <'e> abangphipen chetongiklo
e-nūt a-bàngphì=pen che-tòng-īk-lò]
one-CLF:HUM:SG POSS-lady=with RR-meet-FRML-RL
'[...] [I]n Boithalangso I will meet with a few people... So first we are meeting with this lady.' [KaR, SWK 003]

In (421) and (422), the pairing of numerals or classifier-numeral words meaning 'two' and 'three' as well as 'five' and 'six' similarly represent idiomatic constructions that translate as 'a few' and 'many'.

(421) Two juxtaposed classifier-numeral words: *humni humthom* 'a few (houses)'
*laso ahem langmepik; **humni humthom** lason do*
làso a-hēm làng-mē-pīk **[hùm-ní hùm-thōm]**
this POSS-house see-be.good-very CLF:house-two CLF:house-three
lasón dō
that.way exist
'Those houses look very nice, there are a few (lit. two, three) of that kind.' [SiT, HF 049]

(422) Two juxtaposed classifier-numeral words: *bangpho bangthrok* 'many (people)'
o nelimena amatta lapu'an bangpho
o [ne-li-menà amāt=tā lapù-án **[bàng-phō**
AFF 1EXCL:POSS-HON-self self=also like.this-up.to CLF:HUM:PL-five

bangthrok osomar don rap a'osomar hem isi
bàng-thrōk osō-mār] dōn ráp a-oso-mār hēm isī
CLF:HUM:PL-six child-PL relative EE:dón POSS-child-PL house Whole

pacho'et pajun'et [...]
pa-chō-ét pa-jùn-ét]
CAUS-eat-PRF CAUS-drink-PRF
'I myself am the same, I've fed and taken care of many children and relatives' children, the whole family [...]' [KaR, SWK 067]

Juxtaposition of numerals is also used to give an estimate. In double-digit numbers, the first digit is not repeated (423).

(423) Juxtaposition in double-digit number
kiding phut krepho throk do [...]
[ke-dīng   phút   **kré-phō-thrōk**   dō]
NMLZ-be.long foot.measure(<Eng) **ten.and-five-six** exist
'It was fifteen, sixteen feet long [...].' [SiT, HF 052]

10.7.2.5 'Another' additive construction

In order to express the meaning of 'another', *nón* 'now' along with a classifier-numeral word is used as in (424), and/or the verb is marked additive by suffixes such as -*làng* 'still' and/or -*thū* 'again, yet', as in (425).

(424) 'Another' additive construction with *nón* 'now'
non ejon nangalang, neta {mm}
[**nón   e-jōn**]   náng-jí-lāng   nè=tā   mm
now   one-CLF:animal   need-IRR2-still 1EXCL=ADD   AFF
'One more I need.' [HK, TR 067]

(425) 'Another' additive construction with additive suffixes -*làng* 'still' and -*thū* 'again, yet'
isi alam dothulang
[**isī   a-lám**]   dō-**thū-làng**
one   POSS-matter exist-**again-still**
'There is still one other thing.' [SiH, KH 022]

10.7.2.6 Constructions based on 'one' enumeration

10.7.2.6.1 Preposed 'one' enumeration as an indefinite article construction

As discussed in §10.7.2.2, the placement of an enumerator before its head noun occurs in situations when a new participant is introduced. Particularly the use of a preposed 'one' enumerator can thus be understood as an indefinite article construction, as in (426).

(426) Indefiniteness marking via preposed enumeration with 'one'
erong athengpi do {mm}
[**e-rōng**   a-thengpī]   dō   mm
one-CLF:plant POSS-tree/wood   exist   AFF

athengpi khaipik ingtuipik {ingtuipik mm}
a-thengpī   khái-pìk   ingtùi-pìk   ingtùi-pìk   mm
POSS-tree/wood   grow-a.lot   be.high-a.lot be.high-a.lot AFF
'There is a (lit., one) tree; the tree is full-grown and is very high.' [HK, TR 147–8]

10.7.2.6.2 Indefinite pronoun construction
In (427), the classifier-numeral word *inut* functions as an indefinite pronoun that heads the relative clause *nangphan nangkelang* '(who) looks after you'.

(427) *e-nūt* 'one-CLF:HUM:SG' as head noun 'somebody' of relative clause
  [...] nangphan nangkelang inut do nangji [...]
  [nang-phān   nang=ke-làng   [e-nūt]]   dō   náng-jí
  you-NSUBJ   1/2:NSUBJ=NMLZ-see   one-CLF:HUM:SG   exist   need-IRR2
  '[...] [T]here needs to be **somebody to look after you** [...].' [SH, CSM 066]

10.7.2.6.3 Postposed 'one' enumeration expressing 'whole'
Postposed 'one' enumeration can also be used to indicate universal quantification as in *hem isi* 'the whole family' in (428). This meaning is understood from context.

(428) 'One' expressing 'whole'
  o nelimena amatta lapu'an bangpho
  o   [ne-li-mená   amāt=tā]   [[lapù-án   bàng-phō
  AFF(<Asm)   1EXCL-HON-self   self=ADD   like.this-up.to   CLF:HUM:PL-five

  bangthrok osomar don rap a'osomar hem isi
  bàng-thrōk   osō-mār]   [dōn   ráp   a-osō-mār]]   **[hēm   isī]**
  CLF:HUM:PL-six   child-PL   relative EE:dón   POSS-child-PL **house   one**

  pacho'et pajun'et [...]
  pa-chō-ét   pa-jùn-ét
  CAUS-eat-PRF   CAUS-drink-PRF
  'I myself am the same, I've fed and taken care of many children and relatives' children, **the whole family** [...]' [KaR, SWK 067]

10.7.2.6.4 Postposed 'one' enumeration expressing 'same'
Lastly, postposed 'one' enumeration can be also be understood to indicate 'the same'. In (429), *rong isi* means 'the same village'. As with 'one' meaning 'whole' in the previous section, the meaning of 'the same' emerges from context.

(429) Postposed 'one' enumeration expressing 'same'
mamat bamonpi aphan pen hala rong isi <a>
mamāt   [[bamón-pī   aphān] pén   hála **ròng**   isī
and.then wise.person(<Ind)-female NSUBJ and that **village** **one**

mh a'oso lata thondamrappetlo [...]
mh   a-osō]   [là=tā   thòn-dām-ràp-pèt-lò]
DSM   POSS-child this=ADD   drop-go-together-all-RL
'And then, the *bamonpi* and that child from the same village (that had died), her as well (as the *bamonpi*), they went to cremate them together [...].' [KK, BMS 121]

10.8 Noun phrase clitics

There are two slots for noun phrase clitics as shown in Figure 15. The first slot contains the comitative/instrumental/ablative clitic =*pen* (§10.8.1) and the nominal quantifier clitic =*án* (§10.8.2), whereas the second slot contains information and discourse structure clitics. Note that Figure 15 only lists the NP (as described in the previous sections of this chapter), role markers, and the clitics; another element not listed here is the noun phrase delimiter (§13.5), which, however, may occur before or after the role markers and is therefore not easily represented in a linear fashion.

NP	Role markers / (Relator nouns)	**First clitic slot** =*pen* 'with; from' =*án* 'this much; all'	**Second clitic slot** =*ke* 'TOPIC' =*tā* 'ADDITIVE' =*si* 'FOCUS:REALIS' =*le* 'FOCUS:IRREALIS' =*lo* 'FOCUS' =*he* 'AFTERTHOUGHT'

Figure 15: Noun phrase clitic slots.

Evidence for the two slots, with =*pen* and =*án* going in first position and the information and discourse structure clitics going in second position, is provided by (430) and (431).

(430) Ablative =*pen* followed by topic =*ke*
"[...] *pinipenke nangpenke ne kachekak pu*"
pinì=pen=ke   nàng=**pen=ke**   nè   ke-che-kák   pu
today=from=TOP   you=**from=TOP**   1EXCL   NMLZ-RR-part   QUOT
'"[...] [F]rom today, I am separated from you.", (she said).' [SeT, MTN 035]

(431) Quantifying clitic =án followed by additive =tā
 alang kepon athesere do'anta klolaplo
 [[[alàng ke-pòn] a-theseré] dō=**án=tā**] kló-làp-lò
 3 NMLZ-take.away POSS-fruits exist=**all=ADD** fall-completely-RL
 'All of the fruit that he was taking away fell out.' [SiT, PS 030]

10.8.1 Comitative, instrumental, ablative =pen

The clitic =*pen* has comitative and instrumental, as well as ablative functions. In (432) and (433), comitative participants are marked by =*pen*. In (433), this comitative participant is additionally indicated on the verb by -*ī* 'with' (§9.2.5.2.2). The comitative function of =*pen* also underlies its occurrence in coordination constructions (§10.1.2.1.2).

(432) Comitative NP marked by =*pen*
 apot la nangpopen chorappetlongle... [...]
 [apōt là nang-pō=**pen**] chō-ràp-pèt-lōng-Cē]
 because this 2:POSS-father=**with** eat-together-all-GET-NEG
 'Because of that, you don't get to / must not eat together with your father [...].'
 [CST, RO 019]

(433) Comitative NP marked by =*pen*; verb marked with -*ī* 'with'
 [...] pinsomar atum abangke hala osomarpen jui'irongpo [...]
 [pinsō-mār a-tūm abàng=ke] [hála osō-mār=**pen**]
 married.man-PL POSS-PL NPDL=TOP that child-PL=**with**
 jùi-**ī**-ròng-pò
 play-**with**-instead-IRR1
 '[...] [T]he men would always play with the children instead [...].' [KaR, SWK 071]

In (434), =*pen* marks an instrumental participant; here again, the instrumental participant is additionally indicated on the verb by -*ī* 'with'.

(434) Instrumental NP marked by =*pen*; verb marked with -*ī* 'with'
 nè motorsaikel=**pen**=si hethí ke-dàm-ī
 1EXCL motorcycle=**with**=FOC:RL market(<Asm) NMLZ-go-with
 'I went to the market on a motorcycle.' [Elicitation SiT 090223]

In (435), =*pen* marks a spatial ablative adverbial, 'from here', while in (436), =*pen* marks a participant whose role is apparently required by the verb, *chekak* 'part (from somebody)'. In the same example (436), the first adverbial also occurs with =*pen*, here indicating a temporal ablative: 'from today on'.

(435) (Spatial) ablative function of =*pen*
namdétsi ladakpen netum damlo
nàm-dèt-si làdāk=**pen** ne-tūm dàm-lò
buy-PFV-NF:RL here=**from** 1EXCL-PL go-RL
'After buying (these things), from here we went.' [SH, CSM 015]

(436) Ablative NP marked by =*pen*
"[...] pinipenke nangpenke ne kachekak" pu
pinì=pen=ke nàng=**pen**=ke nè ke-che-kák pu
today=from=TOP you=**from**=TOP 1EXCL NMLZ-RR-part QUOT
'"[...] [F]rom today, I am separated from you.", (she said).' [SeT, MTN 035]

Another occurrence of the temporal ablative function of =*pen* is in (437), where the meaning is 'since this morning'.

(437) Temporal adverbial marked by =*pen*
mathalo amatsi adappen chokang arsovaret
mathà-lò amātsi a-dàp=**pen** chòkàng arsō-varèt
think-RL and.then POSS-morning=**from** axe sharpen-INTENS

arsovaret arsovaretlo apiso abang arjulo
arsō-varèt arsō-varèt-lò a-pisò abàng arjū-lò
sharpen-INTENS sharpen-INTENS-RL POSS-wife NPDL ask-RL
'He was thinking, and then since early in the morning, he was sharpening his axe for a long time, and his wife asked...' [SeT, MTN 014]

The case illustrated with (438) (of which there are other similar examples in the corpus), however, is not as clearly connected semantically to the other ablative examples. The temporal adverbial *adap* 'morning' here refers to a point in time ('in the morning'), rather than a time period ('since the morning' or 'from the morning on'). The occurrence of =*pen* here could be explained, however, in that the point in time was in the past, hence there is still an implied time period, which would be from the moment in the past when the event happened until the present.

(438) Temporal adverbial marked by =*pen*
[...] misorongpoke a'ik atum atipi atum
misòrongpō=ke a-ìk a-tūm a-tepī
ant.sp=TOP POSS-older.brother POSS-PL POSS-elder.brother's.wife
a-tūm
POSS-PL

adappen rit damjuilo
a-dàp=**pen**   rīt   dàm-jùi-lò
POSS-morning=**from** field   go-away-RL
'[...] [T]he ant's older brother and his wife had gone to the *jhum* field in the morning.' [RBT, ChM 009]

Finally, there is one instance, in (439), where *=pen* marks a right-dislocated, clause-external agentive participant, or perhaps a participant with the semantic role of a source, which is how the marking with (ablative) *=pen* could be explained. (Note that ergative markers often develop from instrumentals and ablatives, especially also in other Tibeto-Burman languages.)

(439) Right-dislocated, clause-external agent (<ablative?) marked by *=pen*
lasō aphike asitin akhei aphanta
lasō   aphī=ke   a-isī-tín   a-khéi   a-phān=tā
this   after=TOP   POSS-one-each   POSS-community   POSS-NSUBJ=ADD

isisi ahem kikimpi do hadak governmentpen
isī~sī   a-hēm   ke-kìm-pī   dō   hádāk   **government=pen**
one~DIST.PL   POSS-house   NMLZ-build-BEN   exist   there   **government=from**
'After that, there was one house for every tribe, built by the government.' [SiT, HF 045]

10.8.2 Nominal quantifier constructions based on *=án* 'this much; all'

The nominal quantifier *=án* 'this much; all' occurs in several different constructions. It may cliticize directly to an NP, as in (440).

(440) Quantifying clitic *=án* 'this much; all' directly following NP
methan atum'anke abangke ha kasu keme harlung
[[methān a-tūm=**án**=ke]   abàng=ke]   há   [kasú   ke-mē   harlūng
dog   POSS-PL=**all**=TOP NPDL=TOP   over.there   plate   NMLZ-be.good   bowl

kemepen langta junlong anta cholong,
ke-mē=pen]   [lāng=tā   jùn-lōng   àn=tā   chō-lōng,]
NMLZ-be.good=with   water=ADD:COORD   drink-GET   rice=ADD:COORD   eat-GET

pirtheta bangke mh
[pirthé=tā   bàng=ke]   mh
world=ADD   NPDL=TOP   DSM
'All the dogs, there, they ate from brass (lit., good) plates and bowls, they got to drink water and they got to eat rice, everything.' [KK, BMS 056]

However, it may also occur in a more complex construction, in which it attaches to the – bare or nominalized – existential copula *dō*, see (441) and (442). (This construction with *dō* has likely functioned as the source construction for grammaticalization of *=án* as a noun phrase clitic that immediately follows the NP, as in the above example.)

(441) Quantifying clitic *=án* 'this much; all' in modifier construction with *dō* 'exist'
alang kepon athesere do'anta klolaplo
[[[alàng   ke-pòn]   a-theseré]   dō=**án**=tā]   kló-làp-lò
3   NMLZ-take.away   POSS-fruits   exist=**all**=EXH   fall-completely-RL
'All of the fruit that he was taking away fell out.' [SiT, PS 030]

(442) Quantifying clitic *=án* 'this much; all' in modifier construction with nominalized *dō* 'exist'
[...] khalun marjong along pe kedoan ri kedo'an
[khalùn   Marjòng   alòng]   [pé   **ke**-dō-**án**]   [rī
kd.big.basket kd.big.basket LOC   cloth **NMLZ**-exist-**all**   EE:pé
ke-dō-**án**]
NMLZ-exist-**all**

pe kumbor pe rinchitho penke pini
[pé   kúmbór   pé   rinchithó]   pèn=ke   pinī
cloth blanket(<Ind) cloth   kd.cloth   and=TOP   tradt.fem.waist.cloth

vankok chesik'etlo kithurpo kedampo pu [...]
vankòk   che-sík-ét-lò   ke-thùr-pò   ke-dàm-pò   pu
tradt.fem.belt RR-prepare-PRF-RL   NMLZ-get.up-IRR1   NMLZ-go-IRR1   QUOT
'[...] [I]n the big basket, she prepared all her different clothes, and blankets and cloths, and she also prepared all of her *pini* and *vankok*, and she was just about to get up and go [...].' [SeT, MTN 037]

In (443), *=án* attaches to the demonstrative *là* 'this', parallel to the interrogative amount or degree adverb *ko'an* 'how much' (§6.1.4).

(443) Quantifying clitic *=án* 'this much; all' attaching to demonstrative *là* 'this'
e nang nepiso neso aphan
e   nàng   [ne-pisò   ne-osō   aphān]
DSM   2   1EXCL-wife   1EXCL:POSS-child   NSUBJ

la'an bondi kipi bondok kipi [...]
[[là=**án**   bondí]   ke-pī]   [bondòk   ke-pī]]
this=**that.much**   captivity(<Ind) NMLZ-give   EE:bondí   NMLZ-give
'You (witch) kept my wife and my children in such bad captivity [...].' [CST, HM 094]

In several instances in the corpus, rather than just =*án*, an extended form =*ánsèt* occurs, as in (444). It is currently still unclear how the function of this extended form differs from that of the simple form.

(444) Quantifying clitic =*ánsèt* 'this much; all'
nangtum la'anset apot to
nang-tūm **là=ánsèt**   apōt   tò
you-PL   this=that.much because   OK
'Because of all this you (have been suffering), I see.'[CST, RO 041]

10.8.3 Additive, topic, and focus clitics

This section provides a first overview of the functions of additive =*tā*. Information/discourse structure functions of =*tā* as well as of the topic and focus clitics are discussed in §14.2.

10.8.3.1 Additive =*tā*

10.8.3.1.1 Overview of functions
Karbi =*tā* occurs in contexts that overlap with English 'also' or 'too', as well as in a number of other contexts. Nevertheless, from a cross-linguistic point of view, =*tā* covers a common functional range for an additive particle. For a more detailed discussion of =*tā*, see Konnerth (2014).

10.8.3.1.2 Simple additive 'also'
Karbi =*tā* functions like other additive particles to "express that the predication holds for at least one alternative of the expression in focus" (Krifka 1998).

In (445), *teke atumta* 'the tigers (also)' occurs with the additive particle, and the 'alternative expression' for which the predicate *Rongker pu do* 'celebrate (lit., have) the Rongker' holds as well is culturally implied, as the Rongker is a common festival among the Karbis.

(445) =*tā* with simple additive function
hako arnike... teke <pu> atumta Rongker pu do tangho
hakó   arnì=ke   [tekè <pu>   **a-tūm=tā**]   [Ròngkèr   pu]   dō
that.time day=TOP tiger QUOT   POSS-PL=ADD   festival(kd) QUOT   exist
tànghò
REP
'At that time (in the old days), **tigers also** (like humans/Karbis) celebrated the Rongker.' [HK, TR 035]

10.8.3.1.3 Bisyndetic coordination

Additive =tā also functions as a bisyndetic coordinator, as it occurs on each coordinated element (hence, bisyndetic). In (446), the three NPs *Bey Ki'ik*, *Bey Ke'et*, and *akibi abang* are coordinated by repeating the same clause three times, only replacing the coordinated NPs, marked by *–tā* (§15.5.1.3).

(446) Bisyndetic coordination
piso some enlo anke Bey Ki'ik abangta
pīsō	sōmē	ēn-lò]	ánke	[Bēy	ke-ìk	abàng=tā
wife	EE:pīsō	take-RL	and.then	CLAN	NMLZ-be.black	NPDL=**ADD**

ahem arit dolo Bey Ke'et abangta
a-hēm	a-rīt	dō-lò]	[Bēy	ke-èt	abàng=**tā**
POSS-house	POSS-field	exist-RL	CLAN	NMLZ-be.yellow	NPDL=**ADD**

ahem arit dolo Bey Ronghang abang,
a-hēm	a-rīt	dō-lò]	[Bēy	Ronghāng	abàng
POSS-house	POSS-field	exist-RL	CLAN	CLAN	NPDL

akibi abangta ahem arit dolo
a-ke-bī	abàng=**tā**	a-hēm	a-rīt	dō-lò]
POSS-NMLZ-be.small	NPDL=**ADD**	POSS-house	POSS-field	exist-RL

'They got married, and then Bey the Black had his (own) house and property, Bey the Fair likewise had his (own) house and property, and Bey Ronghang, the young one, also had his (own) house and property.' [WR, BCS 004]

The same parallelism construction (§16.1.1) can be used to coordinate clauses as in (447) (see §15.5.1.2).

(447) Clause coordination via additive-marked NPs
[...] langta junlong anta cholong [...]
[lāng=**tā**	jùn-lōng	àn=**tā**	chō-lōng
water=**ADD**	drink-GET	rice=**ADD**	eat-GET

'[...] [T]hey got to drink water and they got to eat rice [...].' [KK, BMS 056]

10.8.3.1.4 Scalar additive 'even'

In addition to the non-scalar additive function of 'also', =tā also indicates the scalar additive function of 'even', as in (448).

(448) Scalar additive 'even'
la abangke emekpen non'anta kethekdunlong [...]
là   abàng=ke   e-mēk=pen   nón=án=**tā**   ke-thèk-dūn-lōng
this   NPDL=TOP 1PL.INCL-eye=with now=up.to=**ADD** NMLZ-see-JOIN-GET
'(I) have seen this with my (lit., our) eyes, even nowadays (they still do this) [...].' [KaR, SWK 080]

Note that =*tā* also appears to be part of the etymology of the concessive conjunction *sitā~setā* (§15.2.3.3).

10.8.3.1.5 Universal quantification

Additive =*tā* also occurs in contexts in which it indicates universal quantification or exhaustiveness of a set. One such context are negative indefinite constructions, in which the indefinite pronoun is marked by =*tā*, while the verb is negated, as in (449) (see also §6.1.6).

(449) Negative indefinite construction with =*tā* 'additive'
[...] laso atangka atibuk halake ajatta van'un'elo [...]
[lasō a-tángká   a-tibùk]   [hála=ke]   a-ját=**tā**
this   POSS-money POSS-earthen.pot that=TOP   POSS-type=**ADD**
vàn-ūn-**Cē**-lò
bring-be.able-**NEG**-RL
'[...] [A]ll the earthen pots, that friend didn't manage to carry any (of it) [...].' [HK, TR 196]

A related element that appears to have =*tā* as a (diachronic) component is =*tamē* which is glossed as 'any' in (450) (here occurring in the general extender construction, §16.2.1). The second syllable may derive from the verb *mē* 'be good', so the literal meaning may originally have been 'also good'.

(450) =*tamē* 'any'
ansi elitum pakrengdunpo, anke horpentame
[ánsi e-li-tūm   pa-krèng-dūn-pò]   [ánke   hōr=pen=**tamē**
then   1PL.INCL-HON-PL CAUS-be.dry-JOIN-IRR1 and.then   liquor=with=**any**

jattame ingti patippo tokklingpo
ját=tamē   ingtí   patīp-pò   tokklìng-pò]
GENEX=any salt   mix-IRR1   pound.until.tight-IRR1
'And then, we need to dry it, and then either with liquor or something else we need to mix it with salt and pound until it's crushed to a paste.' [SiH, KH 013]

10.8.3.1.6 Intensifier verb construction

Like several other clitics, =tā also occurs in a copy verb construction (§16.2.3.2), in which a preposed verb copy is marked with the clitic, as in (451). With =tā, the copy verb construction functions as an intensifier construction in declarative clauses.

(451) Intensifier copy verb construction, main verb with -ò 'much'
      anke.... **paprapta paprap'olo [...]**
      ánke....   **pe-pràp=tā**   **pe-pràp-ò-lò**
      and.then CAUS-be.quick=ADD:INTENS CAUS-be.quick-much-RL
      'And then, (the tigers) did everything very quickly [...].' [HK, TR 160]

10.8.3.1.7 Discourse (information structure) function

The topic-switch function of additive =tā is discussed in §14.2.2.

10.8.3.2 Information and discourse structure clitics

Besides additive =tā, information and discourse structure clitics include =ke 'TOPIC' (§14.2.1), =si 'REALIS FOCUS' (§14.2.3), =le 'IRREALIS FOCUS' (§14.2.4), as well as the less common ones: =lo 'FOCUS' (§9.6.1.7), =he 'AFTERTHOUGHT' (§16.3.9), and restrictive focus markers (§14.2.6.3).

11 Monoclausal predicate constructions

This chapter discusses predicate constructions beyond the simple verbal predicate. It offers an overview of monoclausal, single-event predicate constructions. Clause-combining constructions are discussed in Chapter 15.

11.1 Overview

Most commonly, the predicate consists of at least one verb root, including both prototypical verb roots and property concept term roots (§4.2). This chapter gives an overview of complex predicate constructions that (appear to) involve more than one word. Specifically, §11.2 offers a discussion of markers at the monoclausal endpoint of the omplementation scale in Karbi, which may or may not be grouped with the heterogeneous category of predicate derivations (§9.2). In §11.3, adverbial constructions, including non-final marked constructions, are discussed. Two periphrastic constructions based on copulas are the topic of §11.4. In §11.5, a complex motion construction is mentioned, which requires further study. Finally, §11.6 outlines the various predicate constructions that involve noun-verb pairs.

The remainder of this overview section is dedicated to a brief note on non-verbal predicate constructions and on verbal and nominal predicate negation.

11.1.1 Non-verbal predicates

As discussed in §4.1.2, §4.1.3, and §4.3, items from a large range of different syntactic categories can function, just as they are, as the predicate of a clause. As shown in those above sections, this includes nominal stems, adverbs, interrogative pronouns and adverbs, and interjections, and it is not clear that any particular element could not function as a predicate in Karbi.

An example of a noun phrase functioning as the predicate is (452); for further examples, see the respective sections in Chapter 4.

(452) Noun phrase functioning as predicate
halata kidukthektik amonitlo [...]
[hála=tā]$_{NP}$ [ke-dúk-thektík   a-monít-lò]$_{PRED(<NP)}$
that=ADD   NMLZ-be.poor-as.much.v.as.it.can.be POSS-man-RL
'That one also is an unimaginably poor man.' [HK, TR 128]

11.1.2 Verbal and nominal predicate negation

There are two negation constructions in Karbi: a verbal negation construction and a nominal negation construction. The verbal negation construction uses the onset-reduplicative verbal suffix *-Cē* (§9.4), which repeats the onset of the last syllable of the verb stem (§3.8.6.3), as in (453), where the verb stem *lè-dūn* 'reach-JOIN' consists of a verb root and a predicate derivation suffix and is negated by *-dē*.

(453) Verbal negation of verbal predicate
bojar ledunde [...]
[bojár   lè-dūn-**Cē**
market(<Asm)   reach-JOIN-**NEG**
'He didn't reach the market [...]' [HI, BPh 023]

The nominal negation construction uses the negative equational copula *kalī* (§6.2.2.2), as in (454).

(454) Nominal negation of nominal predicate
thangta kali [...]
[tháng=tā   **kalī**]
anything=ADD   **NEG.EQU.COP**
'It's nothing [...].' [SeT, MTN 016]

The nominal negation construction can also be used to negate nominalized rather than just nominal predicates, as in (455).

(455) Nominal negation of nominalized predicate
[...] itum nangpeile kedo kalilo, [...]
[i-tūm   nang-pēi=le   **ke-dō**   **kalī-lò**]
1PL:INCL-PL   2:POSS-mother=FOC:IRR   **NMLZ-exist**   **NEG.EQU.COP-RL**
'[...] [W]e don't have your mother anymore [...].' [CST, RO 008]

However, the verbal negation construction can also be used with nominal predicates, as in (456), where a derived indefinite pronoun 'something' is derived from interrogative *pī* 'what', then reduplicated, and then negated with *-Cē*.

(456) Verbal negation of nominal predicate
"*te mo pinepinanedetjima,*
te   mò   **pí-nē~pinā-Cē**-dèt-jí=ma
and.then/therefore   future   what-INDEF~EE-NEG-PFV-IRR2=Q

ko jirpo?" pu {mm}
ko   jīrpō   pu   mm
buddy:VOC   friend QUOT   AFF
"'And there won't be anything (any difficulties, problems, dangers), my friend?'" [HK, TR 140]

And the nominal negation strategy also looks as if it could be used with verbal predicates, as in (457). However, this must rather be an instance where *a-lám* 'POSS-matter' was left out in the more complete expression *totdamlunchot alam kali* 'it is not a matter of just sitting around'. Examples of straightforward nominal negation of verbal predicates do not occur in the corpus.

(457) Nominal negation of verbal predicate
[...] rit mandu do hemtap do pusita hadak
rīt   mandú   dō   hēmtāp   dō   pu-sitā   hádāk
field field.hut   exist tree.house exist QUOT-although   there

totdamlunchot kali
tòt-dām-lùn-chòt   **kalī**
squat-go-big:AO-only   **NEG.EQU.COP**
'[...] [M]aybe there's a field hut or a tree house (i.e., places to rest and sit), but it's not about just sitting around there.' [KaR, SWK 075]

It remains a noteworthy fact that the difference between verbal and nominal negation is more pragmatic than syntactic. While further research is required to work out the details of the pragmatic functions of these different negation strategies, it appears that nominal negation is generally more emphatic than verbal negation.

Note also that the different negation constructions can be used together with differences in scope. In (458), the verbal negation construction has scope inside the participant nominalization: *kechokche* therefore means 'the one who is not good' or 'the guilty one'. The nominal negation with *kalī* can then be used to negate the predicate: *kechokche kali* '(be) not the guilty one'.

(458) Verbal negation inside participant nominalization, nominal negation of predicate
"pot nele kechokche kali [...]
pōt   [nè=le   ke-chók-**Cē**   **kalī]**
reason   1EXCL=FOC:IRR   NMLZ-be.fine-**NEG**   **NEG.EQU.COP**
"'Therefore, I'm not the guilty one [...].' [RBT, ChM 052]

11.2 Modal and other markers at the monoclausal end of the complementation scale

11.2.1 Overview

There are a small handful of markers, mostly expressing modal categories, whose morphosyntactic status is ambiguous. While the available evidence aligns them more closely with predicate derivation suffixes (§9.2) (in the sense of being bound to the preceding, semantically rich stem), there still remains some evidence of their morphosyntactic independence. Note also that all of these, unlike most predicate derivations, have an independent verb root counterpart that may form a predicate by itself, without having to follow another verb root.

I argue that the morphosyntactic status of these elements puts them on the monoclausal endpoint of a continuum of 'clause union', on which the bi-clausal endpoint is represented by independent complement-taking verbs.

As outlined by (Givón 2001a: 43 ff.), the notion of 'clause union' has a functional and a structural side that iconically go hand in hand: the cognitive-semantic integration of events on the functional side, and the syntactic integration of clauses on the structural side. Based on these functional and structural parameters involved in clause union, Givón models a 'complementation scale' for a number of constructions in English that cover various increments of the continuum.

In order to provide a context for the discussion of the modal markers of interest, §11.2.2 sketches out a model of what a complementation scale in Karbi needs to look like. With this in mind, §11.2.3 gives an overview of three morphosyntactic tests that are used to provide a more detailed descriptive account of these markers. Additional morphophonological evidence that can contribute to the problem is outlined in §11.2.4. In §11.2.5, then, the more common ones of these markers are discussed individually.

This section thus aims to highlight the morphosyntactic properties of these markers, of which especially *(-)náng* 'need, must', *(-)lōng* 'get', *(-)thēk* 'know how', and *(-)ùn* 'be able' are important modals in the language (other markers with similar properties are discussed in §11.2.5.5). The goal is to highlight their particular morphosyntactic properties vis-à-vis (non-modal) predicate derivations (as well vis-à-vis biclausal complementation constructions). Note, however, that it might ultimately be most practical to consider them part of the (already heterogeneous) category of predicate derivations.

11.2.2 Remarks on the complementation scale in Karbi

While the exact details of the complementation scale in Karbi are outside the scope of this grammar, four points on this clause union continuum are illustrated in the following discussion. At the biclausal endpoint, we have a fully finite complement clause marked with the quotative complementizer *pusi*, as in (459).

(459) Quotative complementizer *pusi* marking indirect speech CC
 amatsi Bokolapo abangke bojar dam'etlo pusi
 amātsi [[Bokolāpō abàng=ke bojár dàm-ét-lò] **pusi]**
 and.then NAME NPDL=TOP market(<Asm) go-PRF-RL **QUOT.COMP**

 asomar abang mathaló
 a-so-màr abàng mathà-lò
 POSS-child-PL NPDL think-RL
 'The children thought that he had already gone to the market.' [HI, BPh 010]

Next, there is a complementation construction involving an irrealis marked nominalized complement clause followed by the purpose or goal marker *aphān*, as in *ke-thap-ji aphan* in (460). This complement clause is more dependent than the previous type because the verb is nominalized.

(460) Nominalized complement clause with irrealis *-jí* and *aphān* 'PURP' (*bor'í* 'struggle')
 saikel along'an phatang abang vansi... la phatang
 [saikél alòng-án] [phatáng abàng] vàn-si... [[là phatáng]
 bicycle(<Eng) LOC-up.to kd.basket NPDL bring-NF:RL this kd.basket

 *saikel along **kethapji aphan** bor'ilo*
 [saikél alòng] **ke**-thàp-**jí**] **a-phān]** bor'í-lò
 bicycle(<Eng) LOC **NMLZ**-put.inside-**IRR2 POSS-PURP** try.w.great.effort-RL
 '[...] [T]o the bicycle he brings the basket, the basket he is trying to put on the cycle.' [SiT, PS 021]

One step closer to clause union, (461) offers an example of the complement-taking verb *pangchèng* 'start'. The complement clause verb *dàm* 'go' now directly precedes the main verb with no intervening material (such as the quotative complementizer *pusi* or the purpose marker *aphan*), but is marked dependent via nominalization with *ke-*.

(461) Nominalized complement clause of *pangchèng* 'start'
 *chepaklangdampen... latum **ke**damthu pangchengló*
 che-pe-klàng-dām-pen... là-tūm [**ke**-dàm-thū]$_{CC}$ pangchèng-lò
 RR-CAUS-appear-go-NF:with this-PL **NMLZ**-go-again start-RL
 'After going to show them, they again started walking.' [SiT, PS 041]

Finally, at the mono-clausal end of the continuum, we have the markers of interest in this section. They occur under the same intonation contour as the preceding main verb stem, for example *(-)thēk* 'know how' in (462).

(462) Monoclausal end of complementation scale: *(-)thēk* 'know how'
bonsita hala ahemphu abangke chipudunthekthe
bónsetā   hála   a-hēmphū   abàng=ke
but   that   POSS-house.owner.male.hon   NPDL=TOP
che-pū-dūn-**thēk**-Cē
RR-say-JOIN-**know.how**-NEG
'But that old man couldn't realize.' [SiT, PS 026]

Compared to predicate derivations such as *-dùn~-dūn* 'JOIN' in (463), the modal markers show some signs of morphosyntactic independence. This is discussed in the next section.

(463) Involvement *-dùn~-dūn* 'JOIN': acting on an object in motion
[...] akengdak arum kilut ahut amat...
[a-kèng-dàk   arúm   ke-lūt   ahūt   amāt
POSS-foot-road.inbetween   down   NMLZ-enter   during   and.then

anborpenpen chongho abang ingnidunpret
àn-bòr=pén~pén   chonghō   abàng
rice-wrapped.bundle=with~DISTR.PL   frog   NPDL
ingnì-**dūn**-prèt
sit-**JOIN**-acting.on.inflated.object
'[...] [A]nd as (the ant) was passing through between the frog's legs, with all its rice bundles, the frog sat down (pressing down the rice bundles).' [RBT, ChM 016]

11.2.3 Morphosyntactic tests for structural properties of modals

There are three morphosyntactic tests we can use to better describe the structural properties of the modals. While the first test shows the relative degree of morphological boundedness of these markers, the other two tests provide evidence for their morphological independence.

11.2.3.1 Under scope of nominalization along with main verb root?
First, markers such as *(-)thēk* 'know how' are under the scope of nominalization of the main verb, which is evidence for their morphological boundedness. In (464), the adverbial construction *kemesenpen kechothek* (see §11.3.4.1) is embedded into a nominalized adverbial clause headed by *a-joiné* 'POSS-reason' and therefore nominalized.

(464) (-)thèk~(-)thēk 'know how' under scope of nominalization along with main verb root
kemesenpen kechothek ajoine apotsi
[ke-mēsén-pen   **ke-chō-thēk**]   a-joiné
NMLZ-be.good-NF:with **NMLZ-eat-know.how**   POSS-reason
a-pōt=si
POSS-because=FOC:RL
'It's the reason why they know how to eat nicely.' [SiH, CW 022]

On the other hand, truly independent complement-taking verbs like *chèng* 'begin' are nominalized separately, as in (465).

(465) *chèng* 'begin' separately nominalized
garipen vangdét aphisi netum dakpen Hongkram
[garí=pen   vàng-dèt   aphī=si]   [ne-tūm   dāk=pen   Hongkrām
car(<Asm)=with come-PFV   after=FOC:RL 1EXCL-PL here=from PLACE

kedam kechenglo
ke-dàm   ke-chèng-lò]
NMLZ-go   NMLZ-begin-RL
'After the car came, we started going from here to Hongkram.' [SH, CSM 008]

11.2.3.2 Following adverbial construction [V]$_{\text{main verb}}$ [*pa*-V]$_{\text{adv}}$?

Part of the evidence that the modal markers of interest have some morphosyntactic independence is that they can modify complex adverbial constructions. As we can see in (466), *náng* 'need' can follow and modify the adverbial construction *kan pame* 'dance well'.

(466) (-)*náng* 'need' following an adverbial construction
[kán   pa-mé]   náng-jí
dance   CAUS-be.good   need-IRR2
'(S/he) needs to dance well.' [SiT 140127]

This is different from predicate derivations such as benefactive -*pī*, which has to occur on the main verb *tún* 'cook' inside the adverbial construction in (467), and is thus more closely bound to the verb root.

(467) -*pī* 'benefactive' on main verb inside adverbial construction
[...] *apot padap abangke, tunpi peme*
[apōt   padāp   abàng=ke   [[tún-**pī**   pe-mé]
because   this.morning   NPDL=TOP   cook-BEN   CAUS-be.good

dangpi pemenoi! [...]
[dàng-**pī**   pe-mé-nōi]]
put.on.stove-BEN   CAUS-be.good-INFRML.COND.IMP
'[...] "So this morning, cook and prepare them nicely for me [...]."' [SeT, MTN 029]

11.2.3.3 Modified itself by a predicate derivation?

Finally, there is evidence for some of the modals that, within the same predicate, they may be followed by a predicate derivation suffix that modifies the modal rather than the main verb root. An example is (468). Here *-bìn* 'unintentionally' modifies the 'non-control' marker *(-)lōng* 'GET' (§11.2.5.2.1), since *-bìn* cannot occur without *(-)lōng* 'GET', i.e., **ēn-bìn-lò* is not acceptable.

(468) *(-)lōng* 'GET' modified by following predicate derivation *-bìn* 'unintentionally'
amat nangso doke chinilo neta chekhang'un'e
amāt   nang-osō   dō=ke   chiní-lò   nè=tā   che-kháng-ùn-Cē
and.then 2POSS-child exist=TOP know-RL   1EXCL=ADD   RR-keep-be.able-NEG

amatsi nangso apran enlongbinlo
amātsi   nang-osō   a-prán   ēn-**lōng-bìn**-lò
and.then 2:POSS-child POSS-life   take-**GET-unintentionally**-RL
'And then, I knew your child was there, but I couldn't control myself and then I unintentionally took your daughter's life.' [RBT, ChM 031]

In comparison, *-prèt* 'acting on inflated object' in (469) follows *-dùn~-dūn* 'JOIN' but is not dependent on it and could occur directly on the main verb root *ingnì* 'sit', i.e., *ingnì-prèt* 'sit down (on an inflated object)' is perfectly acceptable. The fact that unlike predicate derivations, the modals may be further modified by a following predicate derivation within the same predicate is evidence for their relative degree of morphosyntactic independence.

(469) *-prèt* 'acting on inflated object' modifying main root *ingnì* 'sit'
[...] *akengdak arum kilut ahut amat...*
[a-kèng-dàk   arúm   ke-lūt   ahūt   amāt
POSS-foot-road.inbetween   down   NMLZ-enter   during   and.then

anborpenpen chongho abang ingnidunpret
àn-bòr=pén~pén   chonghō   abàng
rice-wrapped.bundle=with~DISTR.PL   frog   NPDL
ingnì-**dūn**-prèt
sit-**JOIN**-acting.on.inflated.object
'[...] [A]nd as (the ant) was passing through between the frog's legs, with all its rice bundles, the frog sat down (pressing down the rice bundles).' [RBT, ChM 016]

11.2.4 Morphophonological evidence

In addition to the morphosyntactic tests, morphophonological tone changes in some of these markers are an indicator of their morphological boundedness to the main root. Specifically, in *(-)thèk~(-)thēk* 'know how', *(-)ùn~(-)ūn* 'be able', as well as *(-)hài~(-)hāi* 'dare', the low tone form of these markers only occurs following high tone verb roots, while the mid tone form of these markers occurs following low and mid tone verb roots (§3.9.1.3).[106] When occurring as an independent verb root without a preceding verb root, only the low tone forms *thèk* 'know', *ùn* 'win, conquer', and *hài* 'win, overcome, be important' occur.

Similarly, the mid tone form of the modal *(-)lōng* 'GET' only occurs in conjunction with a preceding verb stem (of any tonal specification), while the high tone form of the independent verb *lóng* 'get' occurs if there is no other verb stem.

This tonal distinction between morphosyntactically independent and bound forms provides evidence that certain constructions are ambiguous: for example, in (470), *(-)lōng* 'GET' modifies an adverbial construction, and according to my language consultant, both bound, mid tone *(-)lōng* 'GET' and independent, high tone *lóng* 'get' are used here. (Interestingly, my language consultant feels that the high tone form is grammatically more correct, but that either one is acceptable.)

(470) *(-)lōng* 'GET' following an adverbial construction
 àn [[chō pa-mé] **lōng-lē]** (/*lóng-lē*)
 rice/food eat CAUS-be.good GET-NEG /get-NEG
 '(S/he) didn't get to eat well.' [SiT 140127]

11.2.5 The modals

The following discussion of the individual morphemes highlights their properties in light of the morphosyntactic tests (§11.2.3) and morphophonological evidence (§11.2.4) outlined above.

11.2.5.1 Deontic *(-)náng* 'need, must'
The deontic verb *(-)náng* 'need, must' (for argument structure properties, see §13.2.2.2) may occur under the scope of nominalization of the main verb stem as in (471), although this construction is not perfectly natural to my language consultant as

---

[106] For example, following low and mid tone verb roots such as *dàm* 'go' and *chō* 'eat', the mid tone form *(-)thēk* occurs: *dàm-thēk* and *chō-thēk*. However, after a high tone verb root such as *sáng* '(take) rest', the low tone form *(-)thèk* occurs: *sáng-thèk*.

indicated with the question mark. This is the case both with and without the addition of -jí 'irrealis2' following (-)náng.

(471) (-)náng 'need, must' under scope of nominalization along with main verb root
? [[ke-kán-náng(-jí)] abàng] dàm-lò
NMLZ-dance-need-IRR2 NPDL go-RL
'The one who needs to dance left.' [SiT 140127]

In (472) and (473), (-)náng modifies an adverbial construction rather than a simple main verb stem.

(472) (-)náng 'need' modifying an adverbial construction
[kán pa-mé] náng-jí
dance CAUS-be.good need-IRR2
'(S/he) needs to dance well.' [SiT 140127]

(473) (-)náng 'need' modifying an adverbial construction
lapente monit atum kedo kethak kachepangthir
lapènte monít a-tūm [[[ke-dō ke-thák]
and.then man POSS-PL NMLZ-stay NMLZ-EE:dō(<Asm)
ke-che-pa-ingthìr]
NMLZ-RR-CAUS-be.clean

nangji
náng-jí]
must-IRR2
'And then, people need to stay and live in a clean way.' [SiH, CW 001]

However, note also that in (474), (-)náng 'need' occurs inside the adverbial construction *keklem parsik* 'do thoroughly' (which is embedded in a relative clause that precedes its head noun *kám* 'work'). Specifically, (-)náng occurs on the nominalized main verb. This shows that the constructions that (-)náng occurs in are flexible, rather than syntactically fixed.

(474) (-)náng 'need' occurring inside an adverbial construction
[...] laso akhai pu kachepaklangdunji aphan
[[[lasō a-khái pu] ke-che-pe-klàng-dūn-jí] a-phān]
this POSS-community QUOT NMLZ-RR-CAUS-appear-along-IRR2 POSS-PURP

so'arlo atum **keklemnang parsik akam** *dopik*
[sō'arlō   a-tūm]   [[ke-klém-**náng** pe-arsīk]   a-kám]   dō-pìk
women:COLL POSS-PL NMLZ-do-**need** CAUS-be.deep POSS-work exist-very
'[...] [I]n order to show that this community (is okay), there is a lot of work that needs to be done thoroughly.' [KaR, SWK 033]

In (475), *-kók* 'absolutely required' modifies *(-)náng* rather than *mòng* 'smoke'.

(475) *(-)náng* 'need' modified by following predicate derivation *-kók* 'absolutely required'
{duma mongponbom nangkokjike} [...]
dumá   mòng-pōn-bōm   **náng-kók**-jí=ke}
tobacco smoke-in.passing-CONT **need-absolutely.required**-IRR2=TOP
'It's necessary to keep smoking [...].' [HK, TR 074]

Finally, *náng* 'need, must' functions as an independent verb root in (476).

(476) *náng* 'need' as independent verb root
{la monitsi kenangpohe, halatum aphanke,
là   monít=si   **ke-náng-pò=he**   hála-tum aphān=ke
this man=FOC:RL **NMLZ-need-IRR1=AFTERTHOUGHT** that-PL NSUBJ=TOP

halatum aphanke bi vosi ketheklo}
hála-tūm aphān=ke bī   võ=si   ke-thèk-lò}
that-PL NSUBJ=TOP goat chicken=FOC:RL NMLZ-see-RL
'{ [...] [T]hey will need human beings, right? They consider them goats and chickens (i.e. what is sacrificed).}' [HK, TR 042]

11.2.5.2 Non-control *(-)lōng* 'GET'

11.2.5.2.1 Function

The 'non-control' marker *(-)lōng* 'GET' occurs in the near-lexicalized instances of *thèk-lōng* 'know(?)-GET' > 'see' and *arjū-lōng* 'listen-GET' > 'hear', where it resembles similar markers in other Asian languages (see discussions by Enfield (2003) and Jenny (2012), as well as, within Northeast India, Post (2007: 491) for a discussion of the 'attainment' marker in Galo).

In addition to these near-lexicalized occurrences, *(-)lōng* 'GET' occurs in situations where the subject has a lack of control over an action or event. In contexts of desirable actions or events, a translation with English 'get to V' works. However, *(-)lōng* 'GET' is also used in contexts of non-desirable actions or events, as long as there is a lack of control on part of the subject.

In (477) and (478), *(-)lōng* 'GET' occurs in contexts of desirable actions: first, where the action could be carried out, and second, where it could not, which is frequently the case such that *(-)lōng* 'GET' often occurs in combination with negative *-Cē*.

(477) Non-control *(-)lōng* 'GET' in context of desirable action
methan atum'anke abangke ha kasu keme harlung
[[methān a-tūm-án=ke] abàng=ke] há [kasú ke-mē harlūng
dog POSS-PL-all=TOP NPDL=TOP over.there plate NMLZ-be.good bowl

kemepen langta junlong anta cholong,
ke-mē=pen] [lāng=tā **jùn-lōng** àn=tā **chō-lōng,**]
NMLZ-be.good=with water=ADD:COORD drink-GET rice=ADD:COORD eat-GET

pirtheta bangke mh
[pirthé=tā bàng=ke] mh
world=ADD NPDL=TOP DSM
'All the dogs, there, they ate from brass (lit. good) plates and bowls, they **got to** drink water and they **got to** eat rice, everything.' [KK, BMS 056]

(478) Negated non-control *(-)lōng* 'GET' in context of desirable action
<pot> tangke hala apei abang tunlongle danglonglelo,
<pōt> tángke [[hála a-pēi abàng **tún-lōng-Cē dàng-lōng-Cē-lò**]
thing and.then that POSS-mother NPDL COOK-GET-NEG put.on.stove-GET-NEG-RL

aso kachiru ajoine, si "Bai! Han
[a-osō ke-chirú a-joiné] [lasì bái hán prepared.vegetables
POSS-child NMLZ-cry POSS-reason(<Ind) therefore how.bad!

anta tunlonglelo an arni kethetangdetle!"
àn=tā **tún-lōng-Cē-lò**] [án arnì ke-thè-tāng-dèt=lē]
rice=ADD COOK-GET-NEG-RL that.much sun NMLZ-be.big-PFV2-PFV=EXCLAM
'That mother couldn't prepare the food because the child was crying, so (she exclaimed), "How bad! Neither the curry nor the rice I could cook, the sun has become so big already!"' [KK, CC 026]

In (479), *-lōng* 'GET' is used in the context of an undesirable action, specifically as a rock unintentionally (also highlighted by the use of *-bìn* 'unintentionally') kills the daughter of the king in this folk story.

(479) Non-control *(-)lōng* 'GET' in context of undesirable action
amat nangso doke chinilo neta chekhang'un'e
amāt   nang-osō   dō=ke   chiní-lò   nè=tā   che-kháng-ùn-Cē
and.then   2POSS-child exist=TOP know-RL   1EXCL=ADD RR-keep-be.able-NEG

amatsi nangso apran enlongbinlo
amātsi   nang-osō   a-prán   ēn-**lōng**-bìn-lò
and.then   2:POSS-child POSS-life take-**GET-unintentionally**-RL
'And then, I knew your child was there, but I couldn't control myself and then I unintentionally took your daughter's life.' [RBT, ChM 031]

11.2.5.2.2 Structure and distribution

In (480), *(-)lōng* 'GET' is under the scope of nominalization of *ke-kán* 'NMLZ-dance', rather than being individually nominalized.

(480) *(-)lōng* 'GET' under scope of nominalization along with main verb root
[[ke-kán-lōng]   abàng]   dàm-lò
NMLZ-dance-GET   NPDL   go-RL
'The one who got to dance left.' [SiT 140127]

When following an adverbial construction, either mid tone *(-)lōng* 'GET' or high tone, independent *lóng* 'get' can be used, as illustrated in (481) (see §11.2.4).

(481) *(-)lōng* 'GET' following an adverbial construction
àn   [[chō   pa-mé]   **lōng-lē**]   (/**lóng-lē**)
rice/food   eat   CAUS-be.good GET-NEG   /get-NEG
'(S/he) didn't get to eat well.' [SiT 140127]

In (482), *(-)lōng* 'GET' is modified by the following predicate derivation *-bìn* 'unintentionally' (see also §11.2.4).

(482) *(-)lōng* 'GET' modified by following predicate derivation *-bìn* 'unintentionally'
amat nangso doke chinilo neta chekhang'un'e
amāt   nang-osō   dō=ke   chiní-lò   nè=tā   che-kháng-ùn-Cē
and.then   2POSS-child exist=TOP know-RL   1EXCL=ADD RR-keep-be.able-NEG

amatsi nangso apran enlongbinlo
amātsi   nang-osō   a-prán   ēn-**lōng-bìn**-lò
and.then   2:POSS-child POSS-life take-**GET-unintentionally**-RL
'And then, I knew your child was there, but I couldn't control myself and then I unintentionally took your daughter's life.' [RBT, ChM 031]

Finally, (483) illustrates *lóng* 'get' functioning as an independent verb root.

(483) *lóng* 'get' as independent verb root
tangka atibuk longdunvekpo ili
tángká ɑ tibùk **lóng** dùn vék pò ì-lì
money POSS-earthen.pot **get**-JOIN-definitely-IRR1 1PL:INCL-HON
'Together we will surely get the earthen pots with money.' [HK, TR 136]

11.2.5.3 Skillful ability *(-)thèk~(-)thēk* 'know how'

The 'skillful ability' marker *(-)thèk~(-)thēk* 'know how' also does not get separately nominalized but is under the scope of negation of the preceding main verb root in (484) and (485).

(484) *(-)thèk~(-)thēk* 'know how' under scope of nominalization along with main verb root
[[ke-kán-thēk] abàng] dàm-lò
NMLZ-dance-know.how NPDL go-RL
'The one who knows how to dance left.' [SiT 140127]

(485) *(-)thèk~(-)thēk* 'know how' under scope of nominalization along with main verb root
kemesenpen kechothek ajoine apotsi
[ke-mēsén-pen **ke-chō-thēk**] a-joiné
NMLZ-be.good-NF:with **NMLZ-eat-know.how** POSS-reason
a-pōt=si
POSS-because=FOC:RL
'It's the reason why they know how to eat nicely.' [SiH, CW 022]

Example (485) also illustrates that *(-)thèk~(-)thēk* may modify an adverbial construction, which is shown in (486) as well.

(486) *(-)thèk~(-)thēk* 'know how' following an adverbial construction
lasō a-okarjāng lún [[lún pa-mé] thèk-thē]
this POSS-girl song sing CAUS-be.good know-NEG
'This girl doesn't know how to sing (well).' [SiT elicitation 090301]

In (487), *(-)thèk~(-)thēk* (and not the main verb *ningjé* 'speak') is modified by the following (reduplicated) predicate derivation *-hòi* 'little bit'.

(487) *(-)thèk~(-)thēk* 'know how' modified by following predicate derivation *-hòi* 'little.bit'
arlēng a-lám   ningjé-thèk-hòi~hōi
people POSS-language speak-know.how-little.bit~INTENS
'know how to speak Karbi a tiny little bit' [SiT 140129]

Finally, (488) presents an instance of *thèk* functioning as an independent verb root with the meaning 'be skilled', 'be knowledgeable', or 'be an expert'.

(488) *thèk* 'be skilled, knowledgeable' as an independent verb root
lasi la Hingchong musoso atomoke
[lasì   là   Hingchòng   musosō   a-tomó=ke
therefore this CONSTELLATION siblings:DL POSS-story=TOP

lapu'ik'helo Rongphar asangho kethekthe
lapù-īk-heló]   [Rongphàr a-sanghó   **ke-thèk-Cē**]
like.this-FRML-RL:EMPH   CLAN   POSS-mister:VOC **NMLZ-be.skilled-NEG**

anke nangpekengpon'iknoi
[ánke   nang=pa-kèng-pōn-īk-nōi]
and.then 1/2:NSUBJ=CAUS-be.straight-take.away-FRML-INFRML.COND.IMP
'Thus, they settled down and lived together until the end of their lives, and then that was the story of Hingchong musoso, Mister Rongphar, I'm **not an expert**, and then make it clear (i.e. correct it).' [CST, HM 120]

11.2.5.4 Physical ability *(-)ùn~(-)ūn* 'be able'

The morpheme *(-)ùn~(-)ūn* 'be able' is about physical or emotional ability rather than skillful ability. An example from an on-line narration of the pear story is (489), where the boy on the bike has an accident as he is riding over a large stone.

(489) Physical ability *(-)ùn~(-)ūn* 'be able'
amat laso damchet amat chekhang'un'elo isi
[amāt   lasō dàm-chèt] [amāt   **che-kháng-ùn-Cē-lò**]   [isī
and.then this go-a.bit   and.then **RR-keep-be.able-NEG-RL** one

arlong along tongdér
arlōng alòng tōng-dèr]
stone LOC   collide-IDEOPHONE
'And then he went just a bit further and then he **couldn't hold himself anymore**, he hit a (lit. one) stone.' [SiT, PS 029]

In (490), *(-)ùn~(-)ūn* 'be able' is shown to be under the scope of nominalization of *ke-kán* 'NMLZ-dance'.

(490) (-)ùn~(-)ūn 'be able' under scope of nominalization along with main verb root
[[ke-kán-**ùn**] abàng] dàm-lò
NMLZ-dance-be.able NPDL go-RL
'The one who can dance left.' [SiT 140127]

In (491), (-)ùn~(-)ūn 'be able' modifies the adverbial construction *kan pame* 'dance well'.

(491) (-)ùn~(-)ūn 'be able' following an adverbial construction
[kán pa-mé] **ùn-ē**
dance CAUS-be.good **be.able-NEG**
'(S/he) can't dance well.' [SiT 140127]

Finally, (492) offers an instance of *ùn* functioning as an independent verbal root with the sense of 'be (physically) strong and healthy', here negated to form an elaborate expression pair with *sò* 'hurt, be sick'

(492) *ùn* 'be able' as independent verbal root
[...] nesomar... e keso kali ki'une
ne-oso-màr e [ke-sò kalī] **[ke-ùn-Cē**
1EXCL:POSS-child-PL DSM NMLZ-hurt NEG.EQU.COP **NMLZ-be.able-NEG**

kali phuso kali kengso kali
kalī] [phú-sò kalī] [kèng-sò kalī]
NEG.EQU.COP head-hurt NEG.EQU.COP foot-hurt NEG.EQU.COP
'[...] [M]y children didn't get sick and they didn't (even) have minor sicknesses.' [CST, RO 024]

11.2.5.5 Other markers
While not as frequent as the markers discussed above, (-)hài~(-)hāi 'dare' also shares the properties of not being individually nominalized (493) and still also occurring after an adverbial construction (494).

(493) (-)hài~(-)hāi 'dare' under scope of nominalization along with main verb root
[[ke-kán-**hài**] abàng] dàm-lò
NMLZ-dance-dare NPDL go-RL
'The one who dares to dance left.' [SiT 140127]

(494) (-)hài~(-)hāi 'dare' following an adverbial construction
àn [[chō pa-mé] **hài-hē**]
rice/food eat CAUS-be.good **dare-NEG**
'(S/he) didn't dare to eat well.' [SiT 140127]

11.2 Modal and other markers at the monoclausal end of the complementation scale — 337

The verb *tengnè* 'forget', on the other hand, while also occurring under the scope of nominalization of *ke-kán* 'NMLZ-dance' in (495), cannot modify *an cho pame* 'eat well' in (496) – which may, however, be a semantic rather than morphosyntactic problem here; further research is required.

(495) *(-)tengnè* 'forget' under scope of nominalization along with main verb root
 *[[ke-kán-**tengnè**] abàng] dàm-lò*
 NMLZ-dance-dare NPDL go-RL
 'The one who forgot to dance left.' [SiT 140127]

(496) *(-)tengnè* 'forget' following *an cho pame* 'eat well' unacceptable
 àn   [[chō   pa-mé]   **tengnè-dèt]*
 rice/food   eat   CAUS-be.good **forget-PFV**
 '(S/he) forgot to eat well.' [SiT 140127]

Another interesting morpheme is *(-)bor'í(-bor'á)* 'with great effort', where *(-)bor'á* is an elaborate expression-type extension (§16.2.2.2). This morpheme also occurs in the same stem juxtaposition construction as the other markers discussed above, as seen in (497). At the same type, a morphosyntactically independent form *bor'í(-bor'á)* can take a fairly independent complement clause marked with *ke-* ... *-jí aphān* with the meaning of 'try to V' (see §11.2.2, example (460)).

(497) *(-)bor'í(-bor'á)* 'with great effort'
 [...] ajirpo abangke <keso> thengpi angsongpen nangkeklosi
 a-jirpò   abàng=ke thengpī   angsóng=pen nang=ke-kló-si
 POSS-friend NPDL=TOP tree/wood high.up=from CIS=NMLZ-fall-NF:RL

 {mm} thinilo {mm} bonseta nangdunbor'ibor'alo
 mm   thìnì-lò   mm bónsetā nang=dùn-**bor'í-bor'á**-lò
 AFF be.almost.dead-RL AFF but   CIS=join-**w.great.effort-EE:bor'í**-RL
 '[T]hat friend had fallen down from up high in the tree and hurt himself badly (lit. almost died), but by trying very hard came home.' [HK, TR 196]

Finally, a verb with modal semantics as well but with a higher degree of morphosyntactic independence is *ingtúng* 'desire', which may be individually nominalized as shown in (498).

(498) *ingtúng* 'wish' individually nominalized
 tumi nelitum Kohima kedam alamsi jerso
 [tumì   ne-li-tūm   Kóhìmà ke-dàm   a-lám=si]   jérsō
 yesterday 1EXCL-HON-PL   TOWN   NMLZ-go POSS-matter=FOC:RL a.little

> than kangtung
> thán **ke-ingtúng**
> tell **NMLZ-desire**
> 'I want to tell just a little bit about when we went to Kohima yesterday.' [SiT, HF 001]

11.3 Adverbial constructions

11.3.1 Overview

There are two proper adverbial constructions (AdvCs) in Karbi, as well as two non-final adverbial constructions (NF-AdvCs) that may function and be structured similarly to the proper adverbial constructions, and are therefore discussed here, too. All four constructions consist of a main verb and a derived adverbial element. In the two proper AdvCs, the adverbial element consists of a property concept term (PCT; see §4.2) verbal stem; it always follows the main verb, as seen in Table 103.

Table 103: Proper adverbial constructions (AdvCs).

	Schematic representation		Involved affixes
Causative AdvC	[[V]$_{main\ verb}$	[pa-V]$_{adverbial}$]	pa- 'CAUS'
Nominalization AdvC	[[ke-V]$_{main\ verb}$	[V]$_{adverbial}$]	ke- 'NMLZ'

In the 'Causative AdvC', the main verb is unmarked, while the adverbial element consists of a causative *pa-* marked PCT stem. In the 'Nominalization AdvC', the main verb is nominalized with *ke-*, while the adverbial element consists of a bare stem PCT. There is no apparent functional difference between these two proper AdvCs. Both occur in elicitation when the task is to translate from English into Karbi.

In addition to these two proper AdvCs, there are also two non-final adverbial constructions (NF-AdvCs), which resemble proper AdvCs functionally and structurally. As seen in Table 104, in NF-AdvCs the adverbial element is a non-final marked verb that has to precede the main verb.

Table 104: Non-final adverbial constructions (NF-AdvCs).

	Schematic representation		Involved affixes
Non-final *-pen* AdvC	[[ke-V-*pen*]$_{adverbial}$	[V]$_{main\ verb}$]	ke- 'NMLZ' -pen 'NF:with'
Non-final *-si* AdvC	[[ke-V-*si*]$_{adverbial}$	[V]$_{main\ verb}$]	ke- 'NMLZ' -si 'NF:RL'

While the NF-ADVC with -*pen* appears to be used with both PCT and prototypical (non-PCT) roots in the adverbial element, the NF-ADVC with -*si* 'non-final:realis' is so far only attested to occur with prototypical verb roots as the adverbial element.

NF-ADVCs thus resemble the proper ADVCs, but they of course also resemble clause chaining constructions (§15.2.1.1).

11.3.2 Causative adverbial construction [V]ₘₐᵢₙ ᵥₑᵣᵦ [*pa*-V]ₐdverbial

In the 'Causative ADVC', the main verb is unmarked, while the following adverbial element consists of a causative *pa*- marked PCT root and may take any inflectional suffixes. This is shown in (499), where the main verb *chō* 'eat' is followed by the causativized PCT root *mē* 'be good', which further has the realis suffix -*lò* attached.

(499) Causative adverbial construction
an han cho pamelo [...]
àn hán chō pa-mé-lò
rice prepared.vegetables eat CAUS-be.good-RL
'We ate well [...].' [SH, CSM 055]

It appears as though the same construction with a possibly cognate *pe*- 'causative' prefix occurs in Tenyidie (Angami) (Hutton 1921: 310) as well as in Japhug rGyalrong (Jacques 2019).

In (500), the causative adverbial construction occurs inside an elaborate expression (EE) construction, in which the verb 'cook' is expressed by the two stems *tún* 'cook' and *dàng* 'put on stove'. The two stems both suffixing -*pī* 'benefactive' occur in a parallel fashion each followed by the adverbial element *pe-mé* 'CAUS-be.good', while only the second EE element takes the inflectional imperative suffix -*nōi* (see §16.2.2.2 for syntactic properties of EE's).

(500) Causative adverbial construction in elaborate expression construction
[...] apot padap abangke, tunpi peme
[apōt padāp abàng=ke [[tún-pī pe-mé]
because this.morning NPDL=TOP cook-BEN CAUS-be.good

dangpi pemenoi! [...]
[dàng-pī pe-mé-nōi]]
put.on.stove-BEN CAUS-be.good-INFRML.COND.IMP
'[...] "So this morning, cook and prepare them nicely for me! [...]"' [SeT, MTN 029]

Finally, there are a small number of instances in the corpus in which it looks like a causativized PCT root occurs in a causative adverbial construction with an ellipsed, contextually retrievable main verb, as in (501). Here it is plausible to interpret the causativized *dér* 'be late' as the adverbial element of the ellipsed main verb *vàng* 'come' mentioned in the previous clause.

(501) Causativized PCT root without main verb?
penap vangalang... netum abang paderchotpo {mm}
[penàp vàng-jí-lāng] [[ne-tūm abàng] **pa-dér-chòt-pò**] mm
tomorrow come-IRR2-still 1EXCL-PL NPDL **CAUS-be.late-a.bit-IRR1** AFF
'Tomorrow we are coming, but we will be a bit late.' [HK, TR 106]

11.3.3 Nominalization adverbial construction [*ke*-V]ₘₐᵢₙ ᵥₑᵣᵦ [V]ₐdᵥₑᵣᵦᵢₐₗ

The nominalization adverbial construction is illustrated in (502). This construction consists of a *ke-* nominalized main verb, here *klem* 'do', followed by a PCT stem, *mesen* 'be good, be nice'.

(502) Nominalization adverbial construction
Nagalen government laso kachari atum keklem mesen
[[Nàgálén government] [lasō ke-charí a-tūm]] **[ke-klém mē-sén]**
PLACE government this NMLZ-rule POSS-PL **NMLZ-do be.good-INTENS**
'The government of Nagaland, the ruling people do a good job.' [SiT, HF 024]

Another example is (503), where the nominalization adverbial construction occurs inside a nominalized adverbial clause headed by *a-joiné* 'POSS-reason' (as well as an elaborate expression construction *ēn chō* 'live' < 'take' and 'eat'). The fact that the PCT stem *ingthìr* is nominalized as well (as opposed to being under the scope of nominalization of the *ke-* on the preceding main verb) represents evidence that we are dealing with two separate grammatical verbs.

(503) Nominalization adverbial construction inside nominalized (adverbial) clause
ke'en kangthir ajoine kecho kangthir ajoine [...]
[ke-ēn ke-ingthìr a-joiné] **[ke-chō ke-ingthír** a-joiné]
NMLZ-take NMLZ-be.clean POSS-reason **NMLZ-eat NMLZ-be.clean** POSS-reason
'because they live in a way of keeping everything clean [...]' [SiH, CW 018]

This nominalization adverbial construction may be the source construction for the grammaticalization of predicate derivations. The only formal marking of this construction is simply the nominalizer *ke-* on the preceding main verb, and the adverbial element is in the same position as predicate derivations: following the lexical verb. Since *ke-* also functions as an imperfective marker (§12.7.3.2), it is easy to imagine how an adverbial construction may be reinterpreted as imperfective marking of a complex verb stem that includes the root and a predicate derivation.

11.3.4 Non-final preposed adverbial constructions

Non-final *-pen* and *-si* may occur on a nominalized verb in order to function as an adverbial element preceding the main verb.

11.3.4.1 Non-final *-pen* construction [*ke-*V*-pen*]_{adverbial} [V]_{main verb}

In this non-final adverbial construction, the adverbial element takes *-pen* 'non-final:with'. In (504), the adverbial element is furthermore nominalized with *ke-* (while the main verb *chō-thēk* 'know how to eat' is also nominalized due to being in a nominalized adverbial clause construction headed by *a-joiné* 'POSS-reason').

(504) Non-final *-pen* construction
kemesenpen kechothek ajoine apotsi
[ke-mēsén-pen   ke-chō-thēk]   a-joiné
NMLZ-be.good-NF:with   NMLZ-eat-know.how   POSS-reason
a-pōt=si
POSS-because=FOC:RL
'(It's) the reason why they know how to eat nicely.' [SiH, CW 022]

Grüßner (1978: 60–1;89) also documents this adverbial construction, although in his data, the adverbial element is not nominalized. Note that Grüßner further reports that the adverbial element in this construction can be causativized, as in the causative adverbial construction (§11.3.2). As an example, consider (505), where data from Grüßner are repeated: In (a), this construction with the preposed adverbial element marked with *pe-* 'causative' and *-pen* 'non-final:with' is illustrated. In (b), a semantically equivalent version, the causative adverbial construction is employed (§11.3.2).

(505) Preposed adverbial construction with *pe-* 'causative' and *-pen* 'non-final:with'
(a) pe-klár   pe-mé-pen   thán-lò
    CAUS-be.clear   CAUS-be.good-NF:with   tell-RL
    '(S/he) told clearly and well.'

(b) thán   pe-klár   pe-mé-lò
    tell   CAUS-be.clear   CAUS-be.good-RL
    'id.' [Grüßner (1978:89)]

Finally, consider (506), in which nominalized, non-final -*pen* marked verbs do not constitute a single clause with the final verb *damlo* because of the lack of a single intonation contour as well as the intervening adverb *lason* 'this way'. Also, note that the non-final verbs here are all prototypical verbs rather than PCTs. This example also demonstrates the gradient nature of constructional categories.

(506) Clause chaining construction with non-final verbs marked with *ke*- 'NMLZ' and -*pen* 'non-final:with'
[...] *amatsi netum* **chepenangpen kangnekpen**
amātsi   ne-tūm   che-penáng-**pen**   **ke**-ingnēk-**pen**
and.then 1EXCL-PL RR-make.fun-**NF:with** **NMLZ**-laugh-**NF:with**

kachingnipen, *lasonsi damlo*
ke-che-ingnì-**pen,**   làsón=sì   dàm-lò
NMLZ-RR-EE:ingnēk-**NF:with**   that.way=FOC:RL   go-RL
'[...] [A]nd then teasing each other and laughing, that's how we go (there).'
[SH, CSM 021]

11.3.4.2 Non-PCT root construction [*ke*-V-*si*]_{adverbial} [V]_{main verb}

Lastly, prototypical verbs (i.e., non-PCT roots) can be marked non-final with -*si* 'non-final:realis' and (typically) nominalized with *ke*- in order to express a simultaneous, and sometimes specifically manner indicating, event. In (507), *ingvāi* 'choose' occurs with nominalizer *ke*- and non-final -*si* indicating the manner in which the main event *chō* 'eat' occurred.

(507) Non-PCT root non-final adverbial construction
amat "mai pei! kaita nangtum lasonloma?" "o
amāt   mái   pēi   kái=tā   nang-tūm lasón-lò=ma   ó
and.then how.bad! mother always=ADD   you-PL   that.way-RL=Q vocative

po! lasonlo netum khali
pō   lasón-lò   ne-tūm   khalí
father   that.way-RL   1EXCL-PL   always(<Asm)

kechongvailoksi kecho"
ke-cho-ingvāi-lók-si   **ke-chō**
NMLZ-AUTO.BEN/MAL-choose-only-NF:RL   **NMLZ-eat**
'And then, "How mean, mother, was it always for you like this?" "O father, like this we (can) always eat only what we (carefully) pick and choose.'" [CST, RO 037]

In (508), *dáng* 'put on stove' (here: 'cook tea') is nominalized and marked non-final with *-si*, indicating simultaneity with the main verb *tòt* 'squat'.

(508) Non-PCT root non-final simultaneity construction
[...] hongpharlasi sa
hòng-pharlá=si   sá
outside-outside.Karbi.house=FOC:RL   tea(<Ind)

kachodangsi totborlo apenan
ke-cho-dáng-si   **tòt-bòr-lò**
NMLZ-AUTO.BEN/MAL-put.on.stove-NF:RL   squat-appearing.small:S-RL
a-penàn
POSS-husband

abangke
abàng=ke
NPDL=TOP
'[...] [O]utside the Karbi house, preparing himself tea, (he) sat there, the husband.'
[SeT, MTN 040]

Finally, (509) suggests that the non-final marked adverbial element does not need to be nominalized, as *ardòn* 'ride' clearly indicates the manner in which the directional motion verb *vàng* occurred, but there is no *ke-* prefix on *ardòn*. Further research is required for a more detailed account of non-final marked clauses functioning as adverbial elements.

(509) Non-nominalized prototypical verb in non-final adverbial construction
laso ahut amat inut akaprek amonit
lasō   a-ahūt   amāt   e-nūt   a-ke-prék
this   POSS-during and.then   one-CLF:HUM:SG   POSS-NMLZ-be.different
a-monít
POSS-man

abangke saikel nangardonsi vanglo... laso
a-bàng=ke   saikél   **nang=ardòn-si   vàng-lò...**   lasō
NPDL=TOP   bicycle(<Eng)   **CIS=ride-NF:RL   come-RL**   this

amonitta aphu along aphutup do
a-monít=tā   a-phú   alòng   a-phutūp   dō
POSS-man=also   POSS-head   LOC   POSS-hat   exist
'In this moment, another person riding on a bicycle came, this person also had a hat on his head.' [SiT, PS 015]

11.4 Periphrastic constructions based on copulas

The simple existential and possessive constructions are discussed in §13.2.2.3. In addition to the two simple constructions, there is a progressive and an indirect argument quantification construction that are worth mentioning.

11.4.1 Progressive construction with non-final suffix -si plus copula dō

A -si non-final marked main verb may be followed by the existential copula dō to form a construction with a progressive reading. An example is (510), which is from an on-line narration of the Pear Story. Since the speaker is telling the story as he is seeing it unfold in the video clip, there are many occurrences of progressive and imperfective constructions in this text.

(510) Progressive construction with non-final suffix -si plus copula dō
adunghet osomar banghini bangkethom do... halatumke
adūng-hét osō-mār bàng-hiní bàng-kethòm dō... hála-tūm=ke
near-INTENS child-PL CLF:HUM:PL-two CLF:HUM:PL-three exist that-PL=TOP

juirekraksi do
jùi-rek~rāk-si   dō
play-silently~DIST.PL-NF:RL exist
'Nearby, there were a few children, they were there playing silently.' [SiT, PS 031]

The beginning of the same text also serves as a good example to show the use of imperfective ke- (§12.7.3.2) in the same context as the V-si dō construction (511).[107]

(511) Progressive construction with non-final suffix -si plus copula dō
vo kiku...
vō   ke-kú
chicken IPFV-crow
'A rooster is crowing...' [SiT, PS 001]

vota kujengsi do... inut
vō=tā   **kú-jèng-si**   dō   [e-nūt
chicken=ADD crow-for.long.time(sound)-NF:RL exist one-CLF:HUM:SG

---

[107] In addition to the aspectual component, there may also be a pragmatic component of a presentational or sentence focus that is part of the function of this construction. More research on a larger number of examples is needed.

chotiki chonghoi amonit amethang
cho-tikī   cho-inghói   a-monít]   [a-metháng
AUTO.BEN/MAL-cultivate   AUTO.BEN/MAL-do   POSS-man   POSS-self

abiri arlopen eson <athe...> thesere kelik
a-birī   arlō=pen]   [e-sòn   <a-thē...>   theserḗ]   ke-lík
POSS-garden   inside=from   one-CLF:thing   POSS-fruit   fruits   IPFV-pluck
'There's a chicken crowing... One cultivator (/farmer) from (inside) his own garden is picking one kind of fruit.' [SiT, PS 002]

Note that the Tamangic language Thakali has an identical construction, structurally and seemingly also functionally, which, to make the match perfect, has the same form *-si* for the non-final marker (Georg 1996: 120).[108]

11.4.2 Copula argument quantification construction

There are nominal constructions to express argument quantification, such as the quantifying noun phrase clitic *=án* 'this much; all' (§10.8.2), or using universally quantifying pronouns such as *kadókavē* 'all, everybody' (§6.1.6) as a modifier. But the more frequent way to express argument quantification is via (indirect) verbal constructions. These verbal constructions are based on argument quantification predicate derivations (PDs; §9.2.5.1). While these suffixes can attach to the main verb, there also is a nominalization-based construction: specifically, this involves an event or a participant nominalization of the main verb on the one hand, and, on the other hand, the existential copula with quantifying PDs attached to it.[109]

An example is (512), which actually was produced by my language consultant when asked for a translation of the English sentence 'many people came', which suggests that this construction is pragmatically neutral.[110]

(512) Copula argument quantification construction
monít   ke-vàng   dō-ò
person   NMLZ-come   exist-much:s/o
'Many people came.' [SiT 090302]

---

[108] A non-final form *-si* occurs in a number of Himalayan Tibeto-Burman languages (§9.7.1).
[109] In the case of an event nominalization, this then is an instance of the nominalization plus copula construction, see §12.7.1.
[110] While it is the simpler analysis to consider *monit kevang* an event nominalization, it is technically also possible to consider it an internally headed relative clause, with *monit* as the head noun.

A corpus example is (513), where the -ò quantification suffix on the copula has scope over the subject of the nominalized clause, *so'arlo atum* 'the women'.[111]

(513) Corpus example of copula argument quantification construction
[...] angtan akam kachongdatdunji
[[a-ingtán   a-kám]   ke-cho-ingdát-dùn-jí
POSS-outside POSS-work   NMLZ-AUTO.BEN/MAL-make.a.living-JOIN-IRR2

aphanta so'arlo atum kabor'i do'olo
a-phān=tā]   [sō'arlō   a-tūm]   ke-bor'í   dō-**ò**-lo
POSS-PURP=also women:COLL POSS-PL NMLZ-try   exist-**much:S/O**-RL
'[...] **[M]any** women also try to get outside work.' [KaR, SWK 064]

Similarly, in (514), the parsing of *nangkelelesi* suggests an interpretation of this word as a participant nominalization and therefore the *=si* as the focus marker. Another possibility is to interpret this as a non-final construction such that there is no focus marker *=si* but the realis non-final marker *-si*.

(514) Copula argument quantification construction
ha nangkelelesi ke'onglang {mm}
há   nang=ke-lè-Cē=si   ke-óng-làng   mm
over.there CIS=NMLZ-reach-NEG=FOC:RL   NMLZ-exist.much-still AFF
'Over there still many of them haven't arrived.' [HK, TR 183]

11.5 Complex motion construction

There is a complex motion construction in Karbi (or perhaps more than one construction) but this topic requires further research. An example is *vekponbom dambomlo* in (515). The fact that *-bōm* 'continuative' occurs twice suggests that this is a sequence of two independent verbs, but the fact that inflectional *-lò* 'realis' only occurs once at the end suggests that we are dealing with a juxtaposition of two stems.[112]

---

[111] Despite being structurally different from English due to the use of argument quantification predicate derivations, there may be a similar pragmatic function of this kind of construction in both Karbi and English, such that the nominalization construction with the existential copula serves a presentational function (i.e., the difference between 'many women try to get a job' and 'there are many women trying to get a job').

[112] Note that this kind of stem juxtaposition also occurs in the parallelism type of elaborate expression construction (§16.2.2.2).

(515) Complex translocative motion construction with verbs in juxtaposition
saikel vekponbom dambomlo, atheta
[saikél **vèk-pōn-bōm dàm-bōm-lò**] [a-thē=tā
bicycle(<Eng) **steer-on.the.way-CONT go-CONT-RL** POSS-fruit=ADD

kloponpresi tovar soding kloponbomlo
kló-pòn-prè-si továr sodíng kló-pòn-bōm-lò
fall-take.away-scattered-NF:RL road all.along fall-take.away-CONT-RL
'He is steering the bicycle away and going away, and the fruits are falling down here and there and all along the road they keep falling down.' [SiT, PS 025]

While (515) illustrates a direct juxtaposition of verb stems, (516) illustrates a case where a noun intervenes. What is furthermore different in this example, is that while *-pòn~-pōn* 'on the way' is involved here as well, it is the element that is repeated across both verb stems. Note that there is still only one final inflectional element *-làng* 'still' at the end of the second part *junpon* of this construction.

(516) Complex translocative motion construction with noun intervening
si ladakpen damlo Dimapur vurpon sa
sì ladāk=pen dàm-lò Dimápúr **vùr-pōn** sá
therefore here=from go-RL PLACE **drop.in-in.passing** tea(<Ind)

junponlang
jùn-pōn-làng
drink-in.passing-still
'And then, from here we went, we stopped by in Dimapur and just had tea.' [SiT, HF 009]

11.6 'Noun plus verb' predicate constructions

11.6.1 Non-possessed noun incorporation

Noun incorporation constructions are predicates that require the presence of a particular noun that remains unmarked for role and not available for any kind of modification. In the construction type discussed here, the noun also remains without possessive prefixes. This is different from the construction type discussed in the next section §11.6.2, which involves obligatorily possessed nouns.

The noun in the incorporation construction typically has a particular semantic role in the event denoted by the construction, but it is not always the same semantic role across different noun-verb pairs. Table 105 offers four sample noun incorporation expressions.

Table 105: Noun incorporation.

Noun incorporation expression		Incorporated noun		Semantic role of noun
arnì tè	'dry in sun'	arnì	'sun'	Force, Instrument
lāng chinglu	'take bath'	lāng	'water'	Instrument
àn ingchìr	'be hungry'[a]	àn	'rice; food'	?Patient
pirthé haché	'be born'[b]	pirthé	'world'	?Goal

[a]In addition to *àn ingchìr* for 'be hungry', one can also say *-pōk ingchìr* with *-pōk* 'stomach' as the incorporated noun, see §11.6.2.
[b]For the expression *pirthé haché* as well, there is a possessed noun incorporation construction that can be used instead (§11.6.2). Note that using *pirthé* 'world' in an expression meaning 'be born' also exists in German *auf die Welt kommen* 'lit.: come onto the world > be born'.

Evidence that a noun inside an incorporation construction cannot be modified is offered in (517). Just changing the noun *lāng* 'water' in *lang kachinglu* 'take bath' to *lang keso* 'hot water' in (a) is not acceptable. In order to say 'take a bath with hot water', a full instrumental noun phrase needs to be added in (b): *lang kesopen(si)* 'with hot water'. Interestingly, in that case, the bare noun *lāng* from the noun incorporation construction becomes optional.

(517) Modifying the noun inside a noun incorporation construction
    (a) **Klìrbon [lāng ke-sò]   ka-chinglú*
         NAME   water NMLZ-be.hot NMLZ-take.bath
         Attempted: 'Klìrbon is taking a bath with hot water.'

    (b) *Klìrbon [lāng ke-sò=pen=si]   (lāng) ka-chinglú*
         NAME   water NMLZ-be.hot=with=FOC:RL water NMLZ-take.bath
         'Klìrbon is taking a bath with hot water.' [BIK 110205]

The optionality of *lāng* 'water' in (b) shows that this is still a somewhat loose noun incorporation construction, which is also evidenced by the fact that it is not possible to fully integrate the noun into the verb stem: it is not acceptable to say **ka-lang-chinglu* '*NMLZ-water-take.bath' or **ka-che-lang-inglu* '*NMLZ-RR-water-take.bath'.

Further evidence that these noun incorporation constructions are not entirely grammaticalized and semantically bleached comes from (518). This is from a folk story, and there are two abandoned babies that are crying because they are hungry. The storyteller first says *an kangchir* for 'be hungry', and then seemingly decides that there is still too much semantics associated with *àn* 'rice, food' that he adds the non-final marker *-si* and specifies: *mok kangchir* 'be hungry (for breast milk)'.

(518) Noun incorporation construction: *àn kangchìr* 'be hungry'
[...] banghini hangjolo... an kangchirsi mok
[bàng-hinî háng-jò-lò]   àn   ke-ingchìr-si
CLF:HUM:PL-two call-many.continuously:S-RL rice NMLZ-be.hungry-NF:RL
mōk
breast

kangchir
ke-ingchìr
NMLZ-be.hungry
'[...] [T]he two of them (i.e., babies), were crying loudly, they were (food-)hungry, they were hungry for milk.' [CST, HM 027]

11.6.2 Psycho-collocations and possessed noun incorporation

Southeast and East Asian languages commonly have a construction termed 'psycho-collocation' by Matisoff (1986:4): "a polymorphemic expression referring as a whole to a mental process, quality, or state, one of whose constituents is a psychonoun, i.e. a noun with explicit psychological reference (translatable by English words like HEART, MIND, SPIRIT, SOUL, TEMPER, NATURE, DISPOSITION, MOOD)".[113]

Karbi also has such psycho-collocations, with *-nīng* 'mind, heart' as the 'psychonoun',[114] and various PCT and non-PCT verb roots as the other constituent. A few sample psycho-collocations are offered in Table 106. The right-hand column in the table offers glosses for those verbs that also occur outside the psycho-collocation. Note that several verb roots only occur in the psycho-collocation construction with *-nīng* and not otherwise: *aróng* 'be happy', *ói* 'be sad', and *hāng* 'want'.

As can be seen in Table 106, psycho-collocations include emotions and inner states, as well as bodily functions such as *-nīng vàng* 'throw up'.

While Karbi native speakers agree that in careful speech *-nīng* is obligatorily possessed, there are a number of counter-examples in the corpus. In elicitation, *(nè)*

---

[113] In a way, this type of construction can be seen as the converse to possessor-raising constructions: instead of generalizing to an affected possessor, the psycho-collocation (and other possessed noun incorporation with incorporated body part terms, as discussed further below in this section) specifies the 'possessed' locus of the impact of an event, which in psycho-collocations is *-nīng* 'heart, mind', but may be other body part terms.
[114] Karbi *-nīng* goes back to Proto-Tibeto-Burman *niŋ* 'heart' (Matisoff 2003). Apparent cognates in Meitei are *-niŋ* 'wish to V' and a homophonous root with the meaning 'head/mind' (Chelliah 1997: 215;333;512).

Table 106: Sample psycho-collocations.

Form		Meaning	Meaning without -nīng
-nīng	aróng	'be happy'	n/a
	ói	'be sad'	n/a
	thī	'be mad'	<'be short'
	ingsām	'be glad, be grateful'	<'be cold'
	mē	'be calm, well-tempered'	<'be good'
	siksāk	'be troubled'	<'be difficult'
	thè	'hope'	<'be big'
	hāng	'want'	n/a
	vàng	'throw up'	<'come'

ne-nīng aróng '(1EXCL) 1EXCL:POSS-mind be.happy' is typically used to translate 'I'm happy' into Karbi. In spontaneous language use, however, examples such as (519), where just *nīng* without a possessive prefix are used, are not uncommon.

(519) Psycho-collocation with no overt possessive prefix on *-nīng*
anke lapu thoi asorpen hapu Rongkhang anatthu
ánke   lapú   thói   a-sòr=pen   hápú   Rongkháng
and.then   this.side plains   POSS-people=from   that.side AREA
a-nátthū
POSS-direction

aChomangkanke neta ketheklongchenglo aronta
a-Chomangkan=ke   **nè**=tā   ke-theklōng-chéng-lò   a-rōn=tā
POSS-PN=TOP   **1EXCL**=also NMLZ-see-for.first.time-RL POSS-custom=also

chinidun'o'e setame ning arongpiklo
chiní-dùn-ò-Cē   setāmē   **nīng** **aróng-pìk-lò**
know-JOIN-much-NEG   nevertheless   **mind** **be.happy-very-RL**
'And then, the Chomangkan of people from this side, from the plains, and from that side, the Ronghang side, I also see for the first time. While I don't know their customs much, I'm very happy.' [SH, CSM 044]

While psycho-collocations generally express inner states or emotions, or at least generally only intransitive predicates, the expression *-nīng ingsām* 'be happy' is used transitively as 'be grateful to (somebody)' in (520). Also, in (521), the reciprocal prefix *che-* is used with *-nīng ói* 'be sad' to express 'be upset with one another'.

(520) Psycho-collocation used transitively
[...] *laphan aning ingsamsi thesere pumni tekanglo*
[là-phān **a-nīng ingsām-si**] [theseré púm-ní tekáng-lò]
this-NSUBJ POSS-mind be.cold-NF:RL fruits CLF:round-two leave.for-RL
'[...] [H]e (the bicycle boy) was grateful to him (the boy who had picked up his hat for him) and gave him two pieces of fruit.' [SiT, PS 039]

(521) Psycho-collocation used with reciprocal *che-*
[...] *anke ha aphike la Bey Ke'etpen*
ánke há aphī=ke [là Bēy ke-èt=pen]
and.then over.there after=TOP this CLAN NMLZ-be.yellow/fair=with

Bey Ki'ik abangke aning che'oitanglo
Bēy ke-ìk abàng=ke] **a-nīng che-ói-táng-lò**
CLAN NMLZ-be.black NPDL=TOP POSS-mind RR-be.sad-finish-RL
'[...] [A]nd then quite some time later, Bey the Fair and Bey the Black got upset with each other.' [WR, BCS 017]

In addition to psycho-collocations, there are a few other noun incorporation expressions which also occur with an 'obligatorily possessed' noun (although with these also, spontaneous speech allows for their use as free forms). Three such expressions are attested so far, which are listed in Table 107. Note that in all three expressions, the incorporated noun refers to a body part that is saliently involved in the event.[115]

Table 107: Possessed noun incorporation expressions (non-psycho-collocations).

Noun incorporation expression		Incorporated noun	
-mēk prāng	'wake up'	*-mēk*	'eye'
-maháng thèk	'be born'	*-maháng*	'face'
-pōk ingchìr	'be hungry'	*-pōk*	'stomach'

Two of the possessed noun incorporation expressions are illustrated in (522) and (523).

(522) Noun incorporation construction: *-mēk prāng* 'wake up'
dunjuiló anké adap amek nangpranglo
dùn-jùi-lò ánke a-dàp **a-mēk nang=prāng-lò**
join-away-RL and.then POSS-morning **POSS-eye CIS=wake.up-RL**
'She had joined him and gone away with him, and then, in the morning, they woke up.' [KK, BMS 119]

---

[115] Beyond a notion of 'salient involvement', it is not possible to characterize the role of the referent with respect to a particular semantic role (which is generally possible with nouns in non-possessed noun incorporation expressions (§11.6.1)).

(523) Noun incorporation construction: *maháng thèk* 'be born'
hem arlo osomar amahang theklo [...]
[hēm   arlō]   [osō-mār]   **[a-maháng   thèk-lò]**
house inside child-PL   **POSS-face   see-RL**
'Inside the house, the children were born [...].' [CST, HM 009]

An analogous construction is a 'measuring' construction, which includes overt reference to the dimension along which the measuring takes place. In (524), the description of a person as being short includes the noun *-jōn* 'height'.

(524) Incorporated noun as reference dimension in measuring expressions
amat amonitta ajon thihek
amāt   a-monít=tā   **a-jōn**   **thī-hèk**
and.then   POSS-man=also POSS-height   be.short-small
'And then, the person is short.' [SiT, PS 022]

Finally, an interesting example illustrating the same basic possessed noun incorporation construction is (525). Here the property of *léng* 'be fat/healthy' is highlighted as a physical property by including the possessed noun *-bàng* 'body'.

(525) Reference noun construction
anke dak chevangpó, "pi apotsi nang nangbang
ánke   [dāk   che-vāng-pò]   [pí   a-pōt=si]   **nàng**
and.then   here   RR-come-IRR1   what   POSS-reason=FOC:RL   **you**
nang-bàng
2:POSS-body

lengvaretmati, sarbura" pu
léng-varèt=mati,   sàrburá   pu
be.fat.HUM-INTENS=CG   old.man   QUOT
'And then he would return (and she said), "Why are you so fat/healthy, man? (That's very strange!)"' [SeT, MTN 025]

11.6.3 Light verb construction

In light verb constructions, the semantics of a predicate is provided by a noun, while the verb only contributes structural verbhood. In (526) and (527), the verbs *pī* 'give' and *klém* 'make, do' act as light verbs with the nouns *rón* 'fight' and *kám* 'do, make'.

(526) Light verb construction *rón ka-chi-pí* 'fight NMLZ-RR-give'
misorongpopen chongho ron kachipi atomo [...]
[misòrongpō=pen chonghō **rón ke-che-pí** a-tomó]
sp.ant=with frog **fight NMLZ-RR-give** POSS-story
'[...] the story of when the ant fought with the frog [...]' [RBT, ChM 007]

(527) Light verb construction *kám klém* 'do work'
Hydro-Electric-Project alongsi kam klem'ikbom
Hydro-Electric-Project a-lòng=si **kám klém-īk-bōm**
NAME POSS-LOC=FOC:RL **work do-FRML-CONT**
'I work for the Hydro-Electric Project.' [KaR, SWK 010]

In (528), the light verb *táng*, which does not occur by itself, is used with the noun *semé* 'vow'.

(528) Light verb construction: *semé táng* 'take a vow'
anke latumta hedi seme tangdetlo
ánke la-tūm=tā hedī **semé táng**-dèt-lò
and.then this-PL=ADD Q.TAG **vow(<Khs) LV**-PFV-RL
'And then, they also, you know, took a vow.' [WR, BCS 032]

11.6.4 Cognate object construction

In cognate object constructions the verb and the object noun are derived from the same etymological root. Examples in Karbi are *lún lún* 'sing a song' (529) and *dondón dón* 'place a ladder' (530).

(529) Cognate object construction: *lún lún* 'sing a song'
*lasō a-okarjāng **lún** [[lún pa-mé] thèk-thē]*
this POSS-girl song sing CAUS-be.good know-NEG
'This girl doesn't know how to sing (well).' [SiT elicitation 090301]

(530) Cognate object construction: *dondón dón* 'place a ladder'
dondon chedonsi... anke amonit abang
[**dondón che-dón-si...**] [ánke [a-monít abàng]
ladder RR-place.ladder/bridge-NF:RL and.then POSS-man NPDL

<a> pe akelokpen keroi isi ajamborong
[[pé a-ke-lòk=pen ke-ròi isī a-jamboróng
cloth POSS-NMLZ-be.white=with NMLZ-sew one POSS-bag

> *arlosi lahai kethap lapen arum kevan*
> arlō=si]   [lahái]   ke-thàp]]   lapèn   [arúm   ke-vàn]]
> inside=FOC:RL these   NMLZ-put.inside   and   down   NMLZ-bring
> 'He's placed himself a ladder... and then, the man, into one bag sown from white cloth he puts these (fruits), and then brings them down.' [SiT, PS 003]

The use of the cognate object construction is only optional in the sense that the verb can also occur without the cognate object. An example for *lún* 'sing' being used without *lún* 'song' is (531). For *dón* 'place.ladder' being used without *dondón* 'ladder' (and instead with the Assamese borrowing *dolóng* 'bridge'), see (532). This shows that using cognate objects is in fact more of a rhetorical choice than a grammaticalized construction.

(531) Use of *lún* 'sing' without cognate object *lún* 'song'
> *kaningje kosonma ape ari kosonma jutang-jubat*
> ke-ningjé   kosón=ma   a-pé   a-rī   kosón=mà   jutáng-jubát
> NMLZ-speak how=Q   POSS-cloth POSS-EE:pé how=Q   custom-EE:jutáng
>
> *kosonma kilun kosonma kekan kosonma*
> kosón=mà   **ke-lún**   kosón=mà   ke-kán   kosón=mà
> how=Q   NMLZ-sing   how=Q   NMLZ-dance   how=Q
>
> *ahokpetpenke theklonglelang nelita*
> a-hōk-pèt-pen=ke   thèklōng-Cē-làng   nè-lì=tā
> POSS-truth-all-ADVBZ=TOP   see-NEG-still   1EXCL-HON=ADD.also
> 'How do they talk, how their attires look, how their customs are, how they sing and how they dance, how all these things really are, I myself hadn't seen yet either.' [SiT, HF 006]

(532) Use of *dón* 'place.ladder' without *dondón* 'ladder'
> *laso ser honjeng rup honjeng adolong*
> lasō   sér   honjèng   rúp   honjèng   a-dolóng
> this   gold(<Khs)   thread   silver   thread   POSS-bridge(<Asm)
>
> *donji*
> **dón-jí**
> place.ladder/bridge-IRR2
> 'We will fix a bridge (made) of this gold thread and this silver thread.' [CST, HM 095]

11.6.5 Hybrid construction

We also find a hybrid between a non-possessed incorporation construction and a cognate object construction in the case of *sái tikì* (533). While not actually being from the same etymological root and therefore not qualifying as a cognate object construction, the noun *sái* and the verb *tikì* have the same reference. The noun *sái* is furthermore non-possessed and cannot be modified. (Note that the demonstrative *là* preceding *sái* modifies the whole nominalized adverbial clause here, not *sái* specifically.)

(533) Hybrid construction *sái tikì* 'cultivate'
 te la'an abangke la sai katiki
 te là=án abàng=ke là **sái ke-tikì**
 and.then/therefore this=up.to NPDL=TOP this **labor NMLZ-cultivate**

 alonglo chotiki chonong alonglo [...]
 alòng-lò cho-tikì cho-nōng alòng-lò
 LOC-RL AUTO.BEN/MAL-cultivate AUTO.BEN/MAL-loosen.soil LOC-RL
 'And then, this much, it's for cultivating and loosening the soil [...].'
 [KaR, SWK 095]

11.7 Other complex predicate constructions discussed elsewhere

In addition to the complex predicate constructions discussed in this chapter, there are several other constructions which serve rhetorical purposes and are therefore discussed in Chapter 16: the general extender construction (§16.2.1); complex predicates based on elaborate expressions (§16.2.2); and copy verb constructions (§16.2.3).

12 Nominalization

Nominalization is at the core of clausal grammar in Karbi as in other Tibeto-Burman languages (see Matisoff (1972); Noonan (1997); Bickel (1999); Genetti et al. (2008); DeLancey (2011); other contributions in Yap, Grunow-Hårsta, and Wrona (2011); among others). In addition to being the underlying construction of subordinate clause types, nominalization is also the diachronic source construction for main clause types, including focus and imperfective constructions. This chapter lays out the various synchronic and diachronic functions of nominalization in Karbi.

In Karbi, there is only one nominalizer, which is *ke-* (with allomorphs *ki-~ka-*; see §3.9.2.1). This nominalizing velar prefix has many apparent cognates across several branches of Tibeto-Burman both inside and outside Northeast India, which suggests that it is reconstructible to Proto-Tibeto-Burman (Konnerth 2016).

This chapter begins with a discussion of *ke-* deriving nouns from verbs (§12.1). Nominal modifiers derived from PCT roots are briefly discussed in §12.2, although the main discussion of this construction is found in §10.7.1. The next three sections are dedicated to the three major nominalized subordinate clause types: relative clauses in §12.3; complement clauses in §12.4; and adverbial clauses in §12.5. A summary of irrealis *-jī* marked subordinate clauses from all three types is offered in §12.6. In §12.7, nominalized main clause types are discussed, which includes both synchronic and diachronic nominalization constructions. Finally, §12.8 addresses the issue of the inconsistent occurrence of *ke-* on structurally nominalized verbs or clauses.

12.1 Derivational nominalization

In its most basic function, *ke-* derives nouns from verbs. In (534), *kú* 'crow' undergoes event nominalization via *ke-*, and then functions as a noun and furthermore as a noun phrase, as it takes on the role of the S argument in the clause *akiku jume'ong* 'his crowing is very nice to hear'. In addition to *ke-*, the *a-* 'possessive' prefix is attached. This prefix occurs in a wide range of grammatical contexts (§7.3.1; §10.3; §10.4). Here, it marks the third person possessive, referring to the rooster as the 'possessor'.

(534) *ke-* deriving an event nominalization (with *a-* 'possessive')
"[...] hala alo abangta thatnangnelang, <piku>
[hála a-lò abàng=tā thàt-náng-Cē-làng]   <pe-ku>
that POSS-male.animal NPDL=ADD slaughter-need-NEG-still CAUS-crow

akiku jume'ong" pusi pukok pu
[a-ke-kú   arjū-mē-óng]   pusi   pù-kòk   pu
POSS-NMLZ-crow hear-be.good-be.much QUOT.COMP say-firmly QUOT
'"[...] [L]et's not kill that rooster, (let it cr...), his crowing is very nice to hear", (she) said firmly.' [SeT, MTN 010]

In (535), *ke-* functions as a participant nominalizer on the PCT root *bī* 'be small'. Here again, *a-* occurs in addition to *ke-*, but with a different function from that in (534). Here, *a-* apparently contributes to the noun-hood or referentiality of *akibisi* 'the youngest one' (see §7.3.1).

(535) *ke-* deriving a participant nominalization (with *a-* 'possessive')
*latumke **akibisi** atumlo, latumta*
[la-tūm=ke   **a-ke-**bī-sí   a-tūm-lò]   [la-tūm=tā
this-PL=TOP POSS-NMLZ-be.small-SPLT POSS-PL-RL   this-PL=ADD

piso some enlo potsi ahem arit dolo
pīsō   sōmē   ēn-lò]   [pōt=si   a-hēm   a-rīt   dō-lò]
wife   EE:pīsō take-RL reason=FOC:RL   POSS-house POSS-field exist-RL
'They were (the children/descendants of) the youngest, they also had gotten married and so they had their house and property.' [WR, BCS 027]

Example (536) shows that *ke-* may also occur without *a-* 'possessive' as the sole element deriving the noun *kakirla* 'change' from the verb *kirlá* 'turn over'.

(536) *ke-* deriving a participant nominalization (without *a-* 'possessive')
bonta non adin abang asapso kakirla
bóntā [nón a-dín   abàng] asàp-sō   **ke-kirlá**
but   now POSS-day(<Asm)   NPDL   little.bit-DIM NMLZ-turn.over

dochetlo [...]
dō-chèt-lò
exist-a.bit-RL
'But nowadays, there's some change [...].' [KaR, SWK 064]

Finally, (537) and (538) are instances of nominalized verbs occurring with the demonstrative *lasō* 'this', which serves as an additional indicator of the noun-hood of the event nominalizations. In (537), *kabor'i* 'struggle' is derived from *bor'i* 'try hard, make an effort' and in (538), the event nominalization is *laso kekoi abangke* 'this rubbing', also featuring the noun phrase delimiter *abàng* (§13.5).[116]

---

116 Interestingly, *a-* 'possessive' does not occur on *kabor'i* or *kekoi*, even though nouns modified by preceding elements such as demonstratives generally take *a-* (see §10.4 and §10.5.1). See §1.3.3.3 for more information.

(537) ke- deriving an event nominalization, marked with demonstrative *lasō* 'this'
lapen laso kabor'i ajokpen non inut
lapèn   [[lasō **ke-borʼí**]   ajōk=pen]   nón
and.then this **NMLZ-make.great.effort** because=with now
e-nūt
one-CLF:HUM:SG

banghini atum… o nelimena amatta
bàng-hiní   a-tūm]   a-thē   o   ne-lì-mená   amāt=tā
CLF:HUM:PL-two POSS-PL POSS-reason AFF 1EXCL:POSS-HON-self self=ADD
'And then, because of this effort (they make), another few people (are able to go out to make money)…, I myself (am) the same.' [KaR, SWK 065]

(538) Complement clause functioning as a topical argument
ansi ilitum lapu pe along koipó, laso kekoi
[ánsi   i-li-tūm   lapù   [pé   alòng] kòi-pò]   **[[lasō**
after.that 1PL:incl-HON-PL like.this cloth   LOC   rub-IRR1 **this**
ke-kòi
NMLZ-rub

abangke mane angpip dopiklo, siri-sabun
abàng=ke] CC (>TOP) mane   angpìp   dō-pìk-lò]   [sirí-sabún
NPDL=TOP   I.mean(<Asm) foam   exist-very-RL Shree.soap(<Asm)

anijom asonlo
a-nijóm   asón-lò]
POSS-procedure(<Asm) like-RL
'And then, like this we rub the cloth, this rubbing, I mean, it creates a lot of foam, like using *Shree* soap.' [SiH, CW 006]

12.2 Property concept term (PCT)-based noun modification

Property concept term (PCT) verbal roots need to be nominalized in order to function as nominal modifiers. An example is (539), where *mē* 'be good' is nominalized to modify *kasú* 'plate' and *harlūng* 'bowl'. While post-head noun order is more common, pre-head noun order also occurs, as detailed in §10.7.1.

(539) PCT root following the head noun it modifies
methan atum'anke abangke ha kasu keme
[[methān a-tūm-án=ke]   abàng=ke]   há   [[kasu]HN
dog   POSS-PL-all=TOP NPDL=TOP over.there(<Pnr) plate
[ke-mē]PCT
NMLZ-be.good

12.2 Property concept term (PCT)-based noun modification

*harlung keme*pen langta junlong anta
[harlūng]$_{HN}$ [ke-mē]$_{PCT}$=pen] [[lāng=tā jùn-lōng]
bowl NMLZ-be.good=with water=ADD:COORD drink-GET
[àn=tā
rice=ADD:COORD

cholong, pirtheta bangke, mh
chō-lōng]] [pirthé=tā bàng=ke] mh
eat-GET world=ADD NPDL=TOP DSM
'All the dogs, there, they ate from brass (lit. good) plates and bowls, they got to drink water and they **got to** eat rice, everything.' [KK, BMS 056]

Most PCT modifiers in the corpus are not complex and do not have any affixes in addition to nominalizer *ke-*. However, it is possible to add predicate derivation suffixes (§9.2), as in the preposed PCT modifier *kidukthektik* 'unimaginably poor' in (540).

(540) Pre-head PCT-based modifier *dúk* 'be poor'
*halata **kidukthektik** amonitlo*
hála=tā **[ke-dúk-thektík** a-monít-lò]
that=ADD NMLZ-be.poor-as.much.V.as.it.can.be POSS-man-RL
'That one also is an unimaginably poor man.' [HK, TR 128]

As pointed out in §10.7.1.2, PCT modifiers preposed to their head noun are sometimes marked by *a-* 'possessive'. In the corpus, this occurrence of *a-* is only found on preposed PCT modifiers but not on postposed ones. However, elicitation examples such as (541), as well as data reported by Grüßner (1978: 123–4) demonstrate that PCT modifiers following their head noun may also be marked by *a-* 'possessive'. Further research is needed to determine what functional difference there may be in adding or not adding *a-* on PCT modifiers.

(541) PCT modifiers following their head noun, marked with *a-* 'possessive'
    (a) *mír* ***a-ke-làng-mē***
        flower **POSS-NMLZ-**look-be.good
        'a pretty flower'

    (b) *mír* ***a-ke-làng-mē-mē***
        flower **POSS-NMLZ-**look-be.good-NEG
        'an ugly flower' [SiT 090301]

Note that like the clausal nominalization constructions, PCT modifiers inconsistently occur with *ke-* in the corpus (§12.8).

12.3 Relativization

Relativization in Karbi as in most other Tibeto-Burman languages is based on nominalization. In Karbi, relative clauses are indeed clausal modifiers rather than forming derived noun phrases. Evidence for this analysis is that relative clause participants are normally expressed in the relative clause (rather than being possessors of the nominalized verb).

There are two relative clause constructions, which are both marked with the *ke-* prefix: standard (externally-headed) relativization (§12.3.1) and internally-headed relative clauses (§12.3.2). In the standard, externally-headed relative clause, the participant that is relativized on is gapped. In the internally-headed relative clause, all participants may be overtly expressed or left out via zero anaphora, just as in main clauses (§13.4.3). In internally-headed relative clauses, the indicators of dependency are the nominalizer as well as the position in the sentence, i.e. preceding an *a-* marked head noun.

Co-relative constructions are best analyzed as diachronic nominalization constructions similar to focus constructions, and are discussed in §12.7.3.1.4.

12.3.1 Standard (externally-headed, pre-head) relativization

In the standard relativization construction, which is the more frequent one in the corpus, the head noun occurs external to the relative clause, with the relative clause preceding. The only instances in which a relative clause looks like it is following its head noun (§10.7.1.2) are instances that may instead be interpreted as being internally-headed (discussed in the next section §12.3.2).

12.3.1.1 Relativization on different clause participants

In Karbi, syntactic roles such as S, A, O, R, and T are not grammatically prominent concepts in clausal organization (§13.1.2). Nevertheless, as in Chapter 13, the discussion below also uses these syntactic role labels for descriptive purposes. As we can see, any syntactic or semantic type of clause participant (argument or oblique) can be relativized on. Specifically, the data below show relativization on S, A, and O arguments, on locative and instrumental participants, as well as possessors.

S argument relativization is illustrated in (542), as the head noun *a-monít* 'POSS-man' would be an S argument in the relative clause *kachingkoidup* 'who had fallen down'.

(542) S relativization
 [...] lapenke <la> kachingkoidup
 [lapèn=ke   <là>   **[ke-chingkoí-dùp**
 and.then=TOP this   **NMLZ-fall.down.HUM-falling.sound.from.high.solid.obj**

amonit <a> aphan <la> <thesere aphatang heihai thesere along>
[a-monít] a-phān] <theseré a-phatáng héihái
POSS-man POSS-NSUBJ fruits POSS-kd.basket different.kinds.of
theseré alòng>
fruits LOC

aphatang along thesere thapdunlo rapdunlo laphan
a-phatáng alòng theseré thàp-dūn-lò ráp-dùn-lò là-phān
POSS-kd.basket LOC fruits put.inside-JOIN-RL help-JOIN-RL this-NSUBJ
'[...] [A]nd then for the person who had fallen down, they put with him the fruit in the basket, they helped him.' [SiT, PS 032]

Relativization of A arguments that occur in conjunction with O arguments (specifically, the O-high argument *nelitum* 'we' and the O-low argument *theseré* 'fruit', see §13.2.1.2) is illustrated in (543) and (544), respectively.

(543) A relativization (with O-high)
[...] Lily, la nelitum aphan nangkejapon aosopi,
Lilý [là [ne-li-tūm aphān nang=ke-já-pòn]$_{RC}$
NAME this 1EXCL-HON-PL NSUBJ 1/2:NSUBJ=NMLZ-lead-take.away
[a-osopì]]$_{HN}$
POSS-lady

elong adim dosi computer akam klemlo
e-lòng a-dím dō-si computer a-kám klém-lò]
one-CLF:place POSS-place exist-NF:RL computer(<Eng) POSS-work do-RL
'[...] Lily, the lady who took us there, she stayed in one place and did her computer work [...].' [SiT, HF 034]

(544) A relativization (with O-low)
[...] nangchithurkrikrisi laso <la> thesere kelik amonit
nang=chithùr-krì~krì-si] [lasō <là> theseré ke-lík]$_{RC}$
CIS=drag-follow.closely~ITER-NF:RL **this** this fruits NMLZ-pluck
a-monít]$_{HN}$
POSS-man

adungan nanglelo
adūng=án] nang=lè-lò
near=up.to CIS=reach-RL
'[...] [D]ragging along a female goat, he got near this fruit picking man.' [SiT, PS 010]

Two examples of O relativization are offered in (545) and (546) (specifically, O-low relativization on *theseré* 'fruit' and *jamboróng* 'bag').

(545) O-low relativization
alang kepon athesere do'anta klolaplo
[[alàng ke-pòn]~RC~   **a-theseré**~HN~   dō-án=tā   kló-làp-lò
3   NMLZ-take.away   POSS-fruits   exist-all=EXH   fall-completely-RL
'All of the fruit that he was taking away fell out.' [SiT, PS 030]

(546) O-low relativization
dondon chedonsi... anke amonit abang
[dondón che-dón-si...]   [ánke   [a-monít   abàng]
ladder   RR-place.ladder/bridge-NF:RL   and.then   POSS-man   NPDL

<a> pe akelokpen keroi isi ajamborong
[[pé   a-ke-lòk=pen   ke-ròi]~RC~   isī   **a-jamboróng**~HN~
cloth   POSS-NMLZ-be.white=with   NMLZ-sew   one   POSS-bag

arlosi lahai kethap lapen arum kevan
arlō=si]   [lahái]   ke-thàp]]   lapèn   [arúm   ke-vàn]]
inside=FOC:RL   these   NMLZ-put.inside   and   down   NMLZ-bring
'He's placed himself a ladder... and then, the man, into one bag sown from white cloth he puts these (fruit), and then brings them down.' [SiT, PS 003]

There are only a few ditransitive constructions in the corpus and none involving relativization. Therefore the above shown S, A, and O relativization constructions represent all attested instances of the relativization of particular syntactic roles. However, it is also possible to relativize on other types of (oblique) clause participants. For example, (547) and (548) show that it is possible to relativize on locative NPs.

In (547), *[[hala] [ka-ngni] a-dim]]* is 'that place where (one) sits'.

(547) Locative relativization
lapenke hala kangni adim along
lapèn=ke   [[hála]   **[ke-ingnì]**~RC~   **a-dím]]**~HN~   alòng
and.then=TOP   that   **NMLZ-sit**   **POSS-place**   LOC

ingnithekthesi <a> si ingchin apum along
ingnì-thēk-Cē-si   sì   ingchìn   a-púm   alòng
sit-see-NEG-NF:RL   therefore   iron   POSS-CLF:round   LOC

ingnisi... saikel kevekponlo
ingnì-si...   saikél   ke-vèk-pōn-lò
sit-NF:RL   bicycle(<Eng)   NMLZ-steer-take.away-RL
'And then, he doesn't know how to sit down on that sitting place (seat), and then on the iron bar he sits and steers the bicycle away.' [SiT, PS 024]

In (548), the O-low relative clause *[[kopipima ladak ke-longdun] a-hormu hortar'an]* 'the things that (people) have collected here' is embedded into the locative relative clause *[[ki-rim ki-bi] isi a-hem]* 'one house where one keeps (the things that people have collected here)'.

(548) Locative relativization
[...] kopipima ladak kelongdun ahormu hortar'an
[[[**kopí~pí=ma** **làdāk** **ke-lóng-dùn]** **a-hormú** **hortár-án]**
what~DIST.PL=Q here NMLZ-get-JOIN POSS-thing EE:hormú-all

kìrim kibi isi ahem do [...]
ke-rīm **ke-bi]**_{RC} isī **a-hēm]**_{HN} dō
NMLZ-put.in.one.place NMLZ-keep one POSS-house exist
'[...] [T]here is one house where they put everything they got (from the time of when the British were fighting against Japan, i.e., the War Museum) [...].' [SiT, HF 056]

In (549) and (550), relativization on instrumental clause participants is illustrated. In (549), this instrumental relativization is indicated on the relative clause verb with *-ī* 'with' (§9.2.5.2.2).

(549) Instrumental relativization
*[[lasō a-monít bī ke-thu-ī]*_{RC} *a-nopak]*_{HN} *lahé-ló*
this **POSS-man** **goat** **NMLZ-slaughter-with** **POSS-knife** this-RL
'This is the knife that the man killed the goat with.' [Elicitation SiT 090223]

However, marking the verb with *-ī* is not obligatory, as illustrated in (550), where *-ī* does not occur.

(550) Instrument relativization
lasi la thap ketok alengpumta
lasì [[là] [**thàp** **ke-tòk]**_{RC} **a-lengpūm=tā]**_{HN}
therefore this **cake.for.rice.beer** NMLZ-pound POSS-pestle=ADD

otdunno [...]
ót-dùn-nō]
touch-JOIN-be.bad
'The pestle with which the rice beer cake is ground is bad to touch (i.e., shouldn't be touched) [...].' [WR, BCS 037]

Finally, (551) offers an example of possessor relativization: *[[arlong achetpen sarnung ki-dip] a-hem]* 'the houses, whose roofs (they) cover with slabs of stone'.

(551) Possessor relativization
[...] *lapenke arlong achetpen sarnung kidip ahemta*
lapèn=ke [arlōng a-chèt=pen   sarnūng ke-dìp]_RC
and=TOP   stone   POSS-small.piece=with roof   NMLZ-cover
a-hĕm=tă]_HN
POSS-house=ADD

nelitum thekdamlong
ne-li-tūm   thèk-dām-lōng
1EXCL-HON-PL   see-GO-GET
'[...] [A]nd then, we also went to see the houses, whose roofs (they) cover with slabs of stone.' [SiT, HF 048]

12.3.1.2 Irrealis-marked relative clauses

While the relative clause verb typically remains unmarked for aspectual or modal categories, it is possible to add *-jí* 'irrealis2' for a future or irrealis reference (see also the general discussion of irrealis-marked nominalized subordinate clauses in §12.6). For example, in (552), the speaker refers to the matter she is going to talk about as *ne kethanji alamthe*.

(552) Future relative clause
ne kethanji alamtheke jo dak rong'aje along
[[nè   ke-thân-**jí**]   a-lamthē=ke]   [jó   dāk   ròng'ajé alòng
1EXCL NMLZ-tell-**IRR2** POSS-matter=TOP see here festival LOC

nangkachetongdunsi
nang=ke-chetòng-dūn-si]
CIS=NMLZ-meet-JOIN-NF:RL
'The matter that I will talk about... after meeting here at the festival...' [KK, CC 002]

Only a few sentences later in (553), however, she refers to that same matter she is about to narrate as *ne kethan atomo*, without using *-jí*. This shows that the simple relative clause verb (not marked with *-jí*) has a wide range of default interpretations, including irrealis contexts, and that using *-jí* is an optional way of specifically highlighting a future or irrealis reference.

(553) Non-purpose relative clause
ta ne kethan atomo abangke
tā   [[nè   **ke-thán**] a-tomó   abàng=ke]
but 1EXCL **NMLZ-tell** POSS-story NPDL=TOP

pachekengdamthekthedet tahai meneta
[pe-che-kèng-dàm-thèk-Cē-dèt   tahài   menē=tā]
CAUS-RR-be.straight-go-know.how-NEG-PFV   DUBIT   maybe=ADD

nangthanpo
nang=thán-pò
1/2:NSUBJ=tell-IRR1
'The story I'll be telling now, maybe I can't tell it perfectly (lit. straight), but I will still tell (it).' [KK, CC 008]

12.3.1.3 Head noun occurring with personal possessive prefix

The noun *bé* 'habit' occurs in a construction in which it takes a relative clause but, surprisingly, is additionally marked by a personal possessive prefix rather than just the general *a-* possessive prefix. An example is (554).

(554)   Head noun *bé* 'habit' occurring with personal possessive prefix
         o <nang> mota nangtum kachekoi nangbe doji
         o   <nang>   mó=tā   **nang-tūm**   **ke-che-kói**   **nang-bé**
         DSM   you   future=ADD   **you-PL**   **NMLZ-RR-accuse**   **2POSS-habit**
         dō-jí
         exist-IRR2
         '"You will (continue to) have a habit of accusing each other in the future."'
         [RBT, ChM 077]

Two analyses are possible based on interpreting the existential copula as being more intransitive-like ('X exists') or more transitive-like ('X has Y'). In the intransitive analysis, the example needs to be bracketed as follows: *[[[nangtum kachekoi] nangbe]$_S$ doji]* 'lit., your habit of you accusing each other will exist'. In the transitive analysis, it would instead be: *[[nangtum]$_A$ [[kachekoi] nangbe]$_O$ doji]* 'lit., you will have your/a habit of accusing each other'.

The second analysis as a more transitive-like possessive construction may be considered preferable because it follows the basic possessive construction that requires the 'O argument' to be marked possessive (§13.2.2.3.2).

This construction has so far only been found to occur with this head noun *bé* 'habit'.

12.3.2 Internally-headed (or post-head) relativization

In addition to the standard relativization construction discussed above, there is another relativization construction that involves the relative clause verb following the head noun. Almost all examples of this construction only consist of the head noun and the relative clause verb, in which case this construction is structurally ambiguous: it could represent either an internally-headed relative clause or a relative clause that follows its head noun rather than preceding it (see also §10.7.1.2). The only example that appears to offer clarification is (555), where the relative clause A argument precedes the head noun, suggesting that head noun is truly embedded in the relative clause.

(555) Internally-headed RC?
*jumepik, phu, **nang tomo kethan;***
arjū-mē-pìk   phū   [nàng   [tomó]$_{HN}$ ke-thán]$_{RC}$
hear-be.good-very grandfather:VOC you   story   NMLZ-tell

penapta nangthantha dei {oi to} mm
penàp=tā   nang=thán-thā   déi   ōi   tò   mm
tomorrow=ADD 1/2:NSUBJ=tell-CON.IMP right? yes   OK   AFF
'(This) was very nice to hear, grandfather, **the story you've told (or: you telling a story)**; tomorrow also you'll need to tell us a story, OK?' [HK, TR 200]

However, (555) may also simply be treated as a nominalized clause functioning as the S argument of the verb *jumepik* 'be very nice to hear', which is why the analysis of this relativization construction as either internally-headed or post-head remains inconclusive.

This relativization construction is much less frequent than the standard relativization construction. While determining its pragmatic function requires a larger corpus with more instances, the occurrences discussed here suggest that this marked construction may be used in emphatic or dramatic discourse contexts.

There are a few examples of S argument relativization, such as (556) and (557). In (556), the relative clause verb *kithike* '(who) have died' occurs after the head noun *nangso* 'your children'. As we can see in the context of this intonation unit, the sentence with the relative clause is in contrast with the next sentence, as the speaker is comparing the death of the addressee's child to the death of many of her own children. In this quasi-parallelism between the two sentences, the relativized noun *nangso kithike* occurs in the same subject position as the topic =*ke* marked NP consisting of the simple possessed noun *neso* 'my children' in the following clause.

(556) Internally-headed or post-head RC: relativizing on S argument
Neso tangte avelo, nesu tangte avelo.
[ne-osō   tángtē avē-lò   ne-sū   tángtē
1EXCL:POSS-child   TOP   not.exist-RL 1EXCL:POSS-grandchild TOP
avē-lò]
not.exist-RL

Nangso kithike enutnat, nesoke
[[[nang-osō]ₕₙ ke-thì=ke]ᴿᶜ   e-nūt-nàt]   [ne-osō=ke
2:POSS-child   NMLZ-die=TOP one-CLF:HUM:SG-only   1EXCL:POSS-child=TOP

bangthrok phosi kithi.
bàng-thrōk   phō-si   ke-thì]
CLF:HUM:PL-six   five=FOC:RL NMLZ-die
'I don't have any children anymore, no grandchildren anymore. Only one child of yours has died, but of mine, so many have died.' [RBT, ChM 043]

In (557), the construction again only consists of the head noun, i.e, the S argument that is being relativized on, and the RC verb. The S argument is *nangpiso, Karbipi asomar, aso*, where there are two appositional constructions: first, *nangpiso, Karbipi asomar* 'your wife, the Karbi woman', and second, *asomar, aso* '(her) children, (her) child'.[117]

(557) Internally-headed or post-head RC: relativizing on S argument
"Nangpiso, Karbipi asomar aso <ke.. ke> kehacheke
[[nang-pisò Karbì-pī   a-oso-màr   a-osō]ₕₙ   ke-haché=ke]ᴿᶜ
2:POSS-wife PN-fem   POSS-child-PL   POSS-child   NMLZ-be.born=TOP

thengpi abeng angse! Jaho! Hini!"... pu anke hala
thengpī   a-bēng   angsé   jaho   hiní   pu   ánke   hála
tree/wood POSS-piece   only   look.there!   two   QUOT   and.then   that

richo abangta chelangdamlo, "Bai!"
richó   abàng=tā   che-lāng-dām-lò   bái
king   NPDL=ADD   RR-see-go-RL   how.bad!
'"Your wife, the Karbipi's children that were born, they are only two pieces of wood (rather than real humans), look there at the two!", and then, that king also went himself to look (and exclaimed), "My goodness!"' [CST, HM 022]

Finally, (555) above, repeated here as (558), may be analyzed as an instance of an internally-headed RC relativizing on the O argument *tomó* 'story' (keeping in mind the caveat mentioned above).

---

[117] Switching from plural *asomar* to singular *aso* may be because the fact that this is about two children is not well captured by either the plural form (which may be implying more than two) or the unmarked form (which may be implying one). Perhaps that is why further on, the speaker adds *hiní* 'two' in a grammatically odd way as it is disconnected from any NP and also without the human classifier *bàng*.

(558) Possibly internally-headed RC relativizing on O-low argument
jumepik, phu, **nang tomo kethan;**
arjū-mē-pìk   phū   **[nàng   tomó   ke-thán]**
hear-be.good-very grandfather:VOC **you   story   NMLZ-tell**

penapta nangthantha dei {oi to} mm
penàp=tā   nang=thán-thā   déi   ōi   tò   mm
tomorrow=ADD 1/2:NSUBJ=tell-CON.IMP right? yes OK AFF
'(This) was very nice to hear, grandfather, **the story you've told (or: you telling a story)**; tomorrow also you'll need to tell us a story, OK?' [HK, TR 200]

12.4 Complementation

12.4.1 Standard complementation

Complement clauses (CCs) are typically nominalized, although there also are (formally) non-nominalized CC constructions, as discussed in §15.2.2. Also see §11.2 for a discussion of modal and other markers at the monoclausal endpoint of the complementation scale.

Examples (559) through (563) illustrate complement clauses functioning as O arguments of complement-taking verbs *pangchèng* and *chèng*, both meaning 'start'; *jūt*, *tāng*, and *ingtòn*, all meaning 'finish' or 'conclude'; and *làng-dūn* 'see-JOIN' > 'watch'.

(559) Nominalized complement clause of *pangchèng* 'start'
*chepaklangdampen... latum **kedamthu** pangchengló*
[che-pe-klàng-dām-pen] là-tūm **[ke-dàm-thū]**$_{CC\,(>O)}$[118] pangchèng-lò
RR-CAUS-appear-go-NF this-PL **NMLZ-go-again** start-RL
'After going to show them, they again start walking.' [SiT, PS 041]

(560) Nominalized complement clause of *chèng* 'start'
garipen vangdét aphisi netum dakpen Hongkram
[garí=pen   vàng-dèt aphī=si]   ne-tūm **[dàk=pen Hongkrām**
car(<Asm)=with come-PFV after=FOC:RL 1EXCL-PL **here=from PLACE**

kedam kechenglo
ke-dàm] ke-chèng-lò
NMLZ-go NMLZ-begin-RL
'After the car came, we started going from here to Hongkram.' [SH, CSM 008]

---

[118] This notation indicates that this is a complement clause (CC) functioning as the O argument of the matrix verb.

(561) Nominalized complement clause of *jūt* 'finish' and *tāng* 'finish'
amatsi la apenan abangke adapprang la chokang

amātsi	[là	a-penàn	abàng=ke	a-dapprág	**[là**	**chòkàng**
and.then	this	POSS-husband	NPDL=TOP	POSS-dawn	**this**	**kd.axe**

karso kejutpen laso athengpi along

ke-arsō]	ke-jūt-pèn]	[lasō	a-thèngpī	alòng
NMLZ-sharpen	NMLZ-finish-NF:with	this	POSS-tree/wood	LOC

hongdamvaret hongdamvaret [...]

hōng-dām-varèt	hōng-dām-varèt
make.hole.in.tree-GO-INTENS	make.hole.in.tree-GO-INTENS

[...] "kehong tanglobo choklobo" pulo [...]

[ke-hōng]	tāng-lò=bo	chók-lò=bo	pù-lò
NMLZ-make.hole.in.tree	finish-RL=RQ	be.fine-RL=RQ	say-RL

'And then early in the morning, after having finished sharpening his axe, the husband kept making a hole for a long time, [...] "I'm finished making the hole, right, it's okay, right?", (he) said [...].' [SeT, MTN 017]

(562) Nominalized complement clause of *ingtòn* 'conclude'
[...] atomo kethan kangton'iklo; kardom'iklo ho

[[**a-tomó**	**ke-thán]**	ke-ingtòn-ìk-lò]	kardóm-īk-lò
POSS-story	**NMLZ-tell**	NMLZ-conclude-FRML-RL	GREETING-FRML-RL

ho]
EMPH:INTERACT

'[...] I've finished telling the story, thank you.' [SeT, MTN 052]

(563) Nominalized complement clause of *làng-dūn* 'see-JOIN' > 'watch'
ansi la sa jun'et ajat'et aphisi netum

ánsi	là	sá	jùn-ét	aját-ét	aphī=si	ne-tūm
after.that	this	tea(<Ind)	drink-PRF	GENEX-PRF	after=FOC:RL	1EXCL-PL

la cheng kethiplo... cheng kethip langdunlo

là	cheng	ke-thip-lò	**[chēng**	**ke-thīp]**cc (>0)	làng-dūn-lò
this	drum	NMLZ-beat.drum-RL	**drum**	**NMLZ-beat.drum**	see-JOIN-RL

'After we drank tea and everything they were beating drums, we... (they) were drumming... (we) watched the drum beating.' [SH, CSM 041]

The dividing line between complement clauses and derivational event nominalization is blurred in many cases, especially when the complement clause only consists of the verb. This is because both CC and event nominalization constructions are formally marked the same way, with nominalizer *ke-*, but also because of the typical absence of overt NPs referring to recoverable participants (i.e., zero anaphora, §13.4.3). Therefore, in (563) and perhaps even more so in (564), *cheng kethip langdunlo* and *kekan kilun langdunlo* could be translated both as complement clauses (i.e., 'watched them beat the drums' and 'watched them sing and dance') as well as event nominalizations (i.e., 'watched the drum beating' and 'watched the singing and dancing').

(564) Nominalized complement clause of *làng-dūn* 'see-JOIN' > 'watch'
 amat Kavonpen nelitum kekan kilun langdunlo
 amāt Kavón=pen ne-li-tūm **[ke-kán ke-lún]**
 and.then NAME=with 1EXCL-HON-PL **NMLZ-dance NMLZ-sing**
 làng-dūn-lò
 see-JOIN-RL
 'And then, with Kavon we watched the dancing and singing [...].' [SiT, HF 035]

Besides representing the O argument of a complement-taking verb, CCs also function as S arguments, illustrated in (565) and (566). In both of these examples, the complement clause S arguments are followed by nominal predicates.

(565) Complement clause functioning as S argument
 inutvet kedunke pine dinghakjak amatsi
 [[e-nūt-vét ke-dùn=ke]_{CC (>S)} [pí-nē dìnghakják]_{PRED}]
 one-CLF:HUM:SG-only NMLZ-join=TOP what-INDEF odd
 amātsi
 and.then

 la elitum ajirpo alangli Ju'espensi
 là e-li-tūm a-jirpò alàng-lì Ju'és=pen=si
 this 1PL:INCL-HON-PL POSS-friend 3-HON COUNTRY=from=FOC:RL

 kevang Kavon Kavon aphanta cheponlo
 ke-vàng Kavón Kavón aphān=tā che-pōn-lò
 NMLZ-come NAME NAME NSUBJ=ADD RR-take.away-RL
 'Going alone along with (Lily) is a strange thing, and so, this friend of ours, he who has come from the US, Kavon, Kavon we also took along with us.' [SiT, HF 008]

(566) Complement clause functioning as S argument
 neli kachoklemke Habepi ahabekong'iklo
 [nè-lì ke-cho-klém=ke]_{CC (>S)} [Habepī
 1EXCL-HON NMLZ-AUTO.BEN/MAL-do=TOP DISTRICT
 a-habekóng-īk-lò]_{PRED}
 POSS-main.headman-HON-RL
 'What I work as is Habekong of the Habepi district (of Rongkhang).' [SeT, MTN 003]

Finally, in (567), the complement clause *laso ahormu abangke kadokave akheita kacharlidun* is marked as a topic with *=ke* and functions pragmatically as a conditional (i.e., 'it would be good if everybody learned this') (see Haiman (1978) for a discussion of the functional similarity between conditionals and topics).

(567) Topic *=ke* marked nominalized clause functioning as a conditional
laso ahormu abangke kadokave akheita
[[[lasō   a-hormú   abàng=ke]$_O$ [kadókavē   a-khéi=ta]$_A$
this   POSS-thing   NPDL=TOP   all   POSS-community=ADD

kacharlidunke mesen pusi neli matha
ke-charlì-dūn=ke]$_{CC}$ [mē-sén]$_{PRED}$]   pusi   nè-lì   mathà
NMLZ-study-JOIN=TOP   be.good-INTENS   QUOT.COMP   1EXCL-HON   think
'I think for this thing, it would be good for (everybody from) every tribe (i.e. everybody in the world) to learn it.' [SiT, HF 044]

12.4.2 Irrealis-marked complement clauses

Complement clauses may also be marked irrealis by *-jí* and followed by one of two nominal elements: either *aphān*, glossed below as 'purp' but (historically) the same morpheme as the non-subject marker *-phān* (§14.1.2); or the (semantically bleached) noun phrase delimiter *abàng* (§13.5). The addition of irrealis *-jí* as well as *aphān* or *abàng* is structural evidence for a lesser degree of clausal integration exhibited by this irrealis complementation construction. Following Givón (2001a), this lesser degree of clausal integration is expected to have a functional equivalent of a lesser degree of event integration (see also §11.2.2). For a general discussion of irrealis-marked nominalized subordinate clauses, see §12.6.

12.4.2.1 Irrealis-marked complement clauses with purpose marker *aphān*
The irrealis complementation construction with *aphān* is illustrated in (568) and (569). In (568), the complement clause functions as the O argument of the complement-taking verb *bor'í* 'try (with great effort)', which occurs in this construction in several instances in the corpus.

(568) Nominalized complement clause with irrealis *-jí* and *aphān* 'PURP'
saikel along'an phatang abang vansi... la phatang
[saikél   alòng-án]   [phatáng   abàng]   vàn-si...   [[là   phatáng]
bicycle(<Eng)   LOC-up.to   kd.basket   NPDL   bring-NF:RL   this   kd.basket

saikel along **kethapji aphan** *bor'ilo*
[saikél alòng] **ke**-thàp-**jí]** **a-phān]** bor'í-lò
bicycle(<Eng) LOC NMLZ-put.inside-IRR2 POSS-PURP try.w.great.effort-RL
'[...] [T]o the bicycle he brings the basket, the basket he is trying to put on the cycle.' [SiT, PS 021]

In (569), the complement clause *[[pirthe along ka-cheklangdunji] aphan]* functions as the S argument of *sungkrung* 'be difficult'.

(569) Nominalized complement clause with irrealis *-jí* and *aphān* 'PURP' (*sùng* 'be difficult')
[...] isi akhai mane pirthe along
[isī a-khái mane [pirthé a-lòng
one POSS-community I.mean(<Asm) world POSS-LOC

kacheklangdunji aphan sungkrung [...]
ke-che-klāng-dūn-**jí** **aphān]** sùng-krùng]
NMLZ-RR-appear-JOIN-IRR2 PURP be.difficult-INTENS
'[...] [F]or a community... I mean, to show itself to the world is difficult [...].' [KaR, SWK 051]

12.4.2.2 Irrealis-marked complement clause with noun phrase delimiter *abàng*

Besides *aphān*, the noun phrase delimiter *abàng* can also mark the end of an irrealis complement clause. While *aphān* inherently has the semantics of marking a goal, purpose, or intention and also marks adverbial clauses with that semantic range (see §12.5), *abàng* represents a structural-only, semantically empty marker of the end of the noun phrase (see also the discussion in §13.5).

An example is (570), where the *abàng* irrealis CC functions as the O argument of *thèk* 'know how'.

(570) Complement clause of *thèk* 'know how' marked with *abàng* 'NPDL'
"*Kevang akoke ne nanglong nangdunjuilo;*
[ke-vàng akó=ke] [nè nang-lòng nang=dùn-jùi-lò]
NMLZ-come when=TOP 1EXCL 2-LOC CIS=join-away-RL

ne non chedamji abang thekthedetpo!"
[nè nón chV-dām-**jí**] **abàng]** thèk-Cē-dèt-pò]
1EXCL now RR-go-IRR2 NPDL know.how-NEG-PFV-IRR1
"'When we came, I followed you along far away, I wouldn't know how to find my way back now [...].'" [KK, BMS 097]

12.4.3 Functional types of complement-taking verbs

According to Givón (2001a,b), there are three functional types of complement-taking verbs: modality verbs, manipulation verbs, and perception-cognition-utterance (PCU) verbs. In the above discussion as well as the discussion in §11.2, both modality and PCU verbs are illustrated. For an example of a manipulation verb, consider (571), where *doi* 'send' takes the complement clause *lang kesok* '(to) get water', with the causee *Kungri* marked non-subject with *-phān*.

(571) Manipulation complement clause
 Kungri a-phān [lāng ke-sòk]$_{CC}$ **doi-thā**
 NAME POSS-NSUBJ water NMLZ-get.water send-IMP:CON
 'Send Kungri to get water!' [Elicitation SiT 090228]

12.5 Adverbial subordination

The following subsections discuss nominalized adverbial subordination. For further types of adverbial clauses that are not (formally) nominalized, see §15.2.3 on non-nominalized adverbial clause types, as well as §15.2.1 on clause-chaining.

12.5.1 Nominalized adverbial subordination: Subordinators from relator nouns

The most frequent type of adverbial subordination consists of a subordinator derived from a relator noun (§5.4) following a nominalized clause. An example is (572), where *aphī* marks a temporal anteriority ('after') relationship of the nominalized subordinate clause to the main clause.

(572) Nominalized anteriority adverbial clause
 ***laso hem nangkachiri aphi**, apenan abang sunjoi*
 [[lasō] [hēm] nang=**ke**-che-rī aphī] a-penàn abàng
 this house CIS=**NMLZ**-RR-search after POSS-husband NPDL
 sūn-jòi
 descend-quietly
 '[...] [A]fter she went back to search for it in the house, the husband quietly came down [...].' [SeT, MTN 042]

From a functional perspective, *aphī* in (572) needs to be considered a subordinator (see also §5.4.7.1). Structurally, however, a nominalized clause followed by a (relator noun-derived) subordinator is equivalent to a noun phrase followed by a relator noun – which is, of course, how this construction developed.

However, there are also some instances in the corpus where a relator noun-derived subordinator follows a non-nominalized clause. The subordinator *aphī* occurs in this construction in (573). Since the clause is no longer nominalized in this construction, there now is structural evidence that grammaticalization has occurred and that this is a new construction that is no longer equivalent to a nominal relator noun construction. Here, *aphī* is unambiguously a subordinator with the *a-* prefix as a frozen (because non-alternating and function-less) element that can only be explained through reconstruction of *aphī* as a relator noun.

(573) Non-nominalized anteriority adverbial clause
garípen vangdét aphisi, *netum dakpen Hongkram*
[garí=pen **vàng-dèt** aphī=si] ne-tūm dāk=pen Hongkrām
car(<Asm)=with **come-PFV** after=FOC:RL 1EXCL-PL here=from PLACE

kedam kechenglo
ke-dàm ke-chèng-lò
NMLZ-go NMLZ-begin-RL
'After the car came, we started going from here to Hongkram.' [SH, CSM 008]

12.5.2 Semantic types

In the following discussion of semantic types, all those constructions are included that are based on a relator noun-derived subordinator, even though in some instances, the adverbial clause verb is no longer nominalized with *ke-*, as discussed in the preceding section §12.5.1 (but see also the discussion in §12.8 on the overall inconsistent occurrence of *ke-* on nominalized subordinate clause verbs). As shown in Table 108, nominalized adverbial subordination covers a wide-range of interclausal semantic relations, including the categories of place, time, and causality, as well as several other ones. The terminology for the semantic types listed in Table 108 is from Kortmann (1996: 138), except for the last type, 'topic'.

Table 108 shows the relator noun-derived subordinators used to express the particular semantic types of adverbial clause, as well as lists references for the examples that illustrate each type.

Table 108: Semantic types of nominalized adverbial subordinate clauses.

Semantic Type		Subordinator		Example
Place		alòng	'LOC'	(574)
Time	Anteriority	aphī	'after'	(575)
	Posteriority	akò	'before'	(576)

Table 108 (continued)

Semantic Type		Subordinator		Example
	Simultaneity overlap	akò	'when'	(577)
		alòng		(578)
	Simultaneity duration	ahūt	'while'	(579), (583)
Causality		apōt	'because'	(580)
		ajoiné		(581)
		ajōk		(582)
Other	Purpose	aphān	'PURP'	(583)
	Comparison/Similarity	asón	'like'	(584)
	Topic	alòng	'regarding'	(585)
		abàng		

There is one subordinator, *akó* 'before', which is different from the other subordinators in that it requires the adverbial clause verb to be negated. Obligatory verbal negation in posterior adverbial clauses is typical in Tibeto-Burman; it exists in languages as diverse as Kurtoep (Hyslop 2011: 633–4), Galo (Post 2007: 828),[119] and Burmese (Konnerth 2008).[120]

In the following discussion, each semantic type of nominalized adverbial subordination is illustrated by an example from the corpus, as referenced in Table 108.

In (574), a (non-nominalized and negated) locative adverbial clause is marked by *alòng* 'locative'.[121]

(574) Locative adverbial clause
   [...] *laso aosomar Hingchong musoso atum aphan*
   lasō   a-oso-màr   Hingchòng   musōsō   a-tūm   a-phān
   this   POSS-child-PL CONSTELLATION siblings:DL   POSS-PL   POSS-NSUBJ

   ha same sadu akrong alat,
   há   samé   sadú   a-króng   a-lat
   over.there   path   EE:samé POSS-CLF.road   POSS-EE:króng

---

119 According to Post, there is no form in Galo that directly expresses posteriority. The form quoted here to occur with obligatory verbal negation is a "combination of subordinate clause predicate negation and achievement marking", which, however, according to Post, comes closest to expressing posteriority in Galo.
120 There is, of course, also a clear functional motivation for negating a 'before' clause, since the inherent nature of this event type consists of not being realized (yet) in relationship to the event expressed by the main clause.
121 The relator noun *-lòng* that this subordinator is derived from covers a wide range of semantics (§5.4.1), and also represents one of the two basic role markers (§14.1.3).

votek ingrengre voso ingrengre along
[[vōtèk   ingrèng-Cē]   [vōsō   ingrèng-Cē]
wild.bird call(small.animals)-NEG EE:vōtèk call(small.animals)-NEG
alòng]_LOC
LOC

osomar ponpidam'et thondam'et
osō-mār   pòn-pī-dām-ét   thòn-dām-ét
child-PL   take.away-BEN/MAL-go-PRF   drop-go-PRF
'[...] [T]hese Hingchong sisters, over there, she went to carry the children to a place where the roads cross, where the birds don't sing, and left them there.' [CST, HM 014]'

In (575), *aphī* 'after' marks an anteriority relationship to the following main clause event.[122]

(575) Nominalized anteriority adverbial clause
laso hem nangkachiri aphi, *apenan abang sunjoi*
[[lasō]   [hēm]   nang=**ke**-che-rī   aphī]_ANTE a-penàn   abàng
this   house   CIS=**NMLZ**-RR-search   after   POSS-husband   NPDL
sūn-jòi
descend-quietly
'[...] [A]fter she went back to search for it in the house, the husband quietly came down [...].' [SeT, MTN 042]

As mentioned above, the verb of a posteriority marking adverbial clause is obligatorily negated, as in (576).

(576) Posteriority adverbial clause with *akò* 'before, when'
bang vangve ako eli damnangji {mm}
[**bàng**   **vàng-Cē**   **akò**]_POST   è-lì   dàm-náng-jí   mm
CLF:HUM:PL **come-NEG**   **before**   1PL:INCL-HON   go-must-IRR2   AFF
'[...] [W]e need to go (there) before anybody gets (there).' [HK, TR 142]

The subordinator *akò* indicates anteriority with a negated verb as in (576), but indicates simultaneity overlap ('before') when occurring with a non-negated verb, as illustrated in (577).[123]

---

[122] The relator noun *-phī* is also used in the locative sense of 'back(side)' (§5.4.3).
[123] The same root *-kò* or *-kó* for 'time' appears to be part of the word *hakó*, with the distal demonstrative formative *há* (§6.1.3) being the other part. This word *hakó* occurs in the folk story introductory phrase *hako ahut*, translatable as the English fairy tale introductory phrase 'once upon a time'.

(577) Simultaneity overlap adverbial clause with *akò* 'when'
"*Kevang akoke ne nanglong nangdunjuilo*
[ke-vàng akò=ke]_{SIOVER} [nè nang-lòng nang=dùn-jùi-lò]
NMLZ-come when=TOP 1EXCL 2POSS-LOC CIS=join-away-RL

ne non chedamji abang thekthedetpo
[nè nón chV-dām-jí abàng thèk-Cē-dèt-pò]
1EXCL now RR-go-IRR2 NPDL know.how-NEG-PFV-IRR1

nangthondunnoi" pulo tangho
nang=thòn-dūn-nōi] pù-lò] tànghò
1/2:NSUBJ=drop-JOIN-INFRML.COND.IMP say-RL REP
'"When we came, I followed you along far away, I now won't find my way back, (so) come along and drop (the bamonpi)!", (the bamonpo) said, as they say.' [KK, BMS 097]

In addition to *akò*, the general locative form *alòng* can be used to indicate simultaneity overlap as well, in a common metaphorical extension from place to time. An example is (578).

(578) Simultaneity overlap adverbial clause with *alòng* 'locative'
ingparke bhari arleng dingpo karlu alongke,
ingpár=ke **[bharí arlèng dīng-pō ke-arlū**
besides=TOP **very.big(<Ind) slope be.long-big NMLZ-climb**
alòng=ke]_{SIOVER}
LOC=TOP

la apenan abangke barso kedo kangtung [...]
là a-penàn abàng=ke barsō ke-dō ke-ingtúng]
this POSS-husband NPDL=TOP peeing NMLZ-exist NMLZ-desire
'And then, when she was climbing up the long slope, the husband had to pee [...].' [SeT, MTN 048]

Simultaneity duration is marked by *ahūt* 'while', which also functions as a relator noun 'during' following noun phrases (§5.4.4). The use of *ahūt* is illustrated in (579).

(579) Simultaneity duration adverbial clause with *ahūt* 'during, while'
[...] halabangso kiridam ahut jangreso aphan
[hálabàngsō ke-rì-dām ahūt]_{SIDUR} jangrēsō a-phān
that NMLZ-search-go during single.parent.child POSS-NSUBJ

chetonglok [...]
che-tòng-lòk
RR-meet-happen.to
'[...] [W]hile he was looking for (more), he ran into the orphan [...].' [HK, TR 048]

Causality can be expressed by one of three subordinators: *apōt*, *ajoiné*, and *ajōk* (see also §5.4.5). While (580) illustrates the use of *apōt* by itself, in (581), both *ajoiné* and *apōt* are used in a sequence.

(580) Causality adverbial clause with *apōt* 'because'
[...] thoisi kedo apot rit pine akam
[**thói=si** **ke-dō** **apōt**]_{CAUSE} [rīt pí-nē a-kám
plains=FOC:RL **NMLZ-stay** **because** jhum.field what-INDEF POSS-work

abangke pu'an mane ebe ave [...]
abàng=ke] pù=án mane e-bé avē
NPDL=TOP like.this=up.to I.mean(<Asm) 1PL.INCL-habit not.exist
'[...] [B]ecause we have been staying in the plains, we don't have any experience in going to the *jhum* field [...].' [KaR, SWK 083]

(581) Causality adverbial clause, double-marked with both *ajoiné* and *apōt*
[...] alanglitum kecho kejun, kedo kethak kangthir
[[alang-li-tūm ke-chō ke-jùn ke-dō ke-thák
3-HON-PL NMLZ-eat NMLZ-drink NMLZ-stay NMLZ-EE:dō(<Asm)
ke-ingthìr
NMLZ-be.clean

ajoine apotsi nonpu'an pusetame alanglitumpen
a-joiné **apōt=si**]_{CAUSE} nón-pu-án pùsetamē
POSS-reason **because=FOC:RL** now-QUOT-till even.though
alang-li-tūm=pen
3-HON-PL=with

itumke lapu do thak ekdom chingnek
e-tūm=ke lapù dō thák ékdóm chV-ingnék
1PL.INCL-PL=TOP like.this stay EE:dō(<Asm) EXCM(<Asm) RR-laugh

chingni arong alon kedo'ikraplonglo
chV-ingnì aróng alón ke-dō-īk-ràp-lōng-lò]
RR-EE:ingnēk be.happy elegance NMLZ-stay-FRML-together-GET-RL
'[...] [B]ecause everything they eat or drink and everything related to their lifestyle is very clean, therefore up to today, we stay and we laugh and we get to happily stay together with them (i.e., they are still alive).' [SiH, CW 024]

An example of *ajōk* is (582). Note that the verb of the nominalized adverbial clause, *ke'ong*, is further marked with the non-final suffix *-pen*. According to my language consultants, this use of *-pen* is "not necessary", but it appears to be constructionalized for some speakers.

(582) Causality adverbial clause marked with *ajōk*
[...] *ako ahut asomar ke'ongpen ajok sarpi*
[akó   ahūt   **[a-so-màr   ke-óng-pen   ajōk]**_{CAUSE}
that.time during **POSS-child-PL NMLZ-exist.much-NF:with because**
sarpī
old.woman

sarbura atum ha ritlo vopi
sàrburá   a-tūm   há   rītlō   vō-pī
old.man   POSS-PL over.there inhabited.field   chicken-female

chopangrengdamlo
cho-pangrēng-dām-lò
AUTO.BEN/MAL-rear-GO-RL
'[...] [O]nce upon a time, because they had many children, the old woman and the old man went over there to the field, to rear hens.' [SeT, MTN 004]

Purpose adverbial clauses are marked by *aphān*, which is related to the non-subject marker *-phān* (§14.1.2). An example of *aphān* is (583), where it is embedded into a simultaneity duration adverbial clause marked by *ahūt*.

(583) Purpose adverbial clause with *aphān* 'purpose' (embedded in a simultaneity duration adverbial clause)
laso ateke pilolo kechopan aphan kevang
[[[lasō   a-tekè   pilolō]   **ke-chopān   aphān]**_{PURP}
this   POSS-tiger female.and.male.animal   **NMLZ-graze   PURP**
ke-vàng
NMLZ-come

ahut, haso aHingchong musoso osomar kechiru
ahūt]_{SIDUR} [[hásō   a-Hingchòng   musosō   osō-mār   ke-chirú
during   that   POSS-CONSTELLATION   siblings:DL child-PL NMLZ-cry

banghini hangjolo [...]
bàng-hiní   háng-jò-lò]
CLF:HUM:PL-two   call-many.continuously:S-RL
'This tiger couple had come to look for food, at that moment, the Hingcho sisters, the two of them, were crying loudly [...].' [CST, HM 027]

Adverbial clauses indicating a 'comparison' or 'similarity' relationship to the main clause are marked by *asón* 'like'. In clauses with the irrealis meaning of 'as if' as in (584), the main clause predicate is marked by *-jí* 'irrealis2'.

(584) Comparison/Similarity adverbial clause with *asón* 'like'
mh elike kereng'et atumke
mh   è-lì=ke   ke-rèng-èt   a-tūm=ke
DSM   1PL:INCL-HON=TOP   NMLZ-be.alive-all:S/O   POSS-PL=TOP

thangbaksi keleduntam thekji ason
[thàngbāk=si   ke-lè-dūn-tām   thèk-jí
as.if=FOC:RL   NMLZ-reach-JOIN-impossible   know.how-IRR2
asón]COMPAR/SIMIL
like

nangpinkhattap nangpinkhatphru
nang=pinkhát-táp   nang=pinkhát-phrú
1/2:NSUBJ=advise-mindlessly   1/2:NSUBJ=advise-EE:tháp
'Since we are alive, (how can) you give so many pieces of advice as if (i.e., pretend that) we could reach (the place where my wife has gone after she died).' [KK, BMS 031]

Finally, *alòng* may also function as a general subordinator that marks a topical subordinate clause with a meaning like 'with respect to', as in (585).

(585) Topical adverbial clause with *alòng*
neli karjulong <a>... hako ahut abang
[nè-lì   ke-arjū-lōng]   <a> [[[hakó   a-hūt   a-bàng
1EXCL-HON   NMLZ-hear-GET   AFF that.time   POSS-during   POSS-CLF:HUM:PL

<a> *rit ke'en rit kepan, chonong*
rīt   ke-ēn   rīt   ke-pān   cho-nōng
field   NMLZ-take   field   NMLZ-clear.vegetation   AUTO.BEN/MAL-loosen.soil

chosim alongle pusitame pinsomar
cho-sīm   alòng=le]TOP   pu-setamē]   pinsō-mār
AUTO.BEN/MAL-EE:nōng   LOC=FOC:IRR   QUOT-nevertheless married.man-PL

atum mute arlosomar atumsi akele klempik pu [...]
a-tūm   mutē   árlosō-mār   a-tūm=si   akelé   klém-pìk   pu
POSS-PL   compared.to   woman-PL   POSS-PL=FOC:RL   more   do-very   QUOT
'I have heard this: (I could learn this:), in the old days, while cultivating the *jhum* field, while working on loosening the soil and doing these kinds of works or whatever, compared to the men, it was the women who did much more [...].' [KaR, SWK 070]

Similarly, in (586), there is an adverbial clause marked by the noun phrase delimiter *abàng*. Here also, the function is that of a topical element: 'with respect to (the plan/

intention of) making you meet my grandmother', where the idea of a plan or intentionality lies in the irrealis marking with -jí.[124]

(586) Topical adverbial clause with abàng 'NPDL'
lasi "to tangte nephi aphan
lasì   tò   tángtē   **[ne-phì   a-phān**
therefore   OK   if   1EXCL:POSS-grandmother   POSS-NSUBJ

nangkapachetongji abangke pathe'anganang"
nang=ke-pa-chetòng-jí   abàng=ke]   pa-the'āng-sināng
1/2:NSUBJ=NMLZ-CAUS-meet-IRR2   NPDL=TOP   CAUS-be.bright-si.HORT
'And then, "Okay then, in order to make you meet my grandmother, let's wait a little while until it's bright (lit., make it/let it get bright)."' [KK, BMS 062]

12.5.3 Adverbial subordination constructions with additional marking

As discussed in the previous section, several semantic types of adverbial subordination are marked by constructions that have another morphosyntactic element in addition to clausal nominalization followed by a subordinator. Specifically, temporal posteriority with *akò* 'before' requires verbal negation (without the nominalizer *ke-*); causal subordinator *ajōk* induces non-final marking with *-pen* 'NF:with' for some native speakers; and, the adverbial clause is marked irrealis with *-jí* when evoking a comparison ('as if') with *asón*, or when indicating a plan or an intention, in an adverbial clause marked with the noun phrase delimiter *abàng*.

12.6 Irrealis-marked nominalized subordinate clauses

The verbs inside nominalized subordinate clauses typically only consist of the stem with nominalizer *ke-*. The one exception is that subordinate clauses of all three types (relative, complement, and adverbial clauses) may be marked with *-jí* 'irrealis2'. If marked irrealis, the meanings expectedly change to intentional futures, purposives, or other types of hypotheticals.

Relative clauses marked by *-jí* may indicate an intentional future event pertaining to the head noun, as in (587), where *ne kethanji alamthe* refers to 'the matter that I will talk about' or 'want to talk about'. Note that this marking is not obligatory in the case of future reference; as discussed in §12.3.1, a few moments later, another relative

---

[124] Compare this construction to complementation with the noun phrase delimiter *abàng* discussed in §12.4.2.2, as well as irrealis-marked nominalized subordinate clauses discussed more generally in §12.6.

clause is produced by the same speaker about the same topic (i.e., with the same future reference), but without *-jí*.

(587) Irrealis-marked relative clause indicating intentional future
ne kethanji alamtheke jo dak rong'aje along
[nè **ke**-thán-**jí** a-lamthē=ke] [jó dāk ròng'ajé alòng
1EXCL **NMLZ**-tell-**IRR2** POSS-matter=TOP see here festival LOC

nangkachetongdunsi
nang=ke-chetòng-dūn-si]
CIS=NMLZ-meet-JOIN-NF:RL
'The matter that I will talk about… after meeting here at the festival…'
[KK, CC 002]

Another situation where *-jí* may be used on a relative clause verb is in a noun complement purpose construction. In (588), *[[asaikel kapasangkokra parjaplun ki-bi-ji] a-son]* refers to 'a device to keep the bicycle parked and standing.

(588) Irrealis-marked relative (/nominal complement) clause indicating a purpose
<sangkok> asaikel kapasangkokra
<sáng-kòk> [[a-saikél ke-pe-sáng-kòk-rà
take.rest-firmly POSS-bicycle(<Eng) NMLZ-CAUS-take.rest-firmly-NF:IRR

parjaplun kibiji a-son avedet amat
pe-arjàp-lùn **ke**-bí-**jí**] a-sòn] avē-dèt]
CAUS-stand-big:AO **NMLZ**-keep-**IRR2** POSS-thing not.exist-exhaustive
amāt
and.then

asaikel abang pakrepkhram
a-saikél a-bàng pe-krēp-khràm
POSS-bicycle(<Eng) POSS-CLF:HUM:PL CAUS-fall.over-with.loud.noise
'He stops the bicycle and there is no device to keep it standing up, and then he let the bicycle fall over with a loud noise.' [SiT, PS 019]

Similarly, in (589), the irrealis marked clause *[aso mok ka-chepechu-ji]* '(to) breastfeed their children' represents another nominal complement purpose construction, here with the head noun *pór* 'time'.

(589) Irrealis-marked relative (/nominal complement) clause indicating a purpose
thap ketoklok jo arníta sanglongle,
[thàp ke-tòk-lók] [jó arnì=tā sáng-lōng-Cē]
cake.for.rice.beer IPFV-pound-only night day=ADD take.rest-GET-NEG

thap ketoklok ketoklok, aso mok
[thàp   ke-tòk-lók   ke-tòk-lók]   **[[[a-sō   mōk**
cake.for.rice.beer IPFV-pound-only IPFV-pound-only **POSS-child breast**

kachepechuji apor ave tangho
ke-che-pa-chū-jí]   a-pór]   avē   tànghò]
NMLZ-RR-CAUS-suck-IRR2 **POSS-time** not.exist REP
'They just kept grinding the rice for the rice beer cake, the whole time they didn't get to take rest, they were grinding (for) the rice beer cake, they didn't even have time to breast-feed their children.' [WR, BCS 030]

In nominalized complementation, *-jí* often occurs in complement clauses of *bor'í* 'try' (590), as they inherently indicate an intention.

(590) Irrealis-marked complement clause indicating an intention
angtan akam kachongdatdunji
[[a-ingtán   a-kám]   **ke-**cho-ingdát-dùn-**jí**
POSS-outside POSS-work **NMLZ-**AUTO.BEN/MAL-make.a.living-JOIN-**IRR2**

aphanta so'arlo atum kabor'i do'olo
aphān=tā]   sõ'arlō   a-tūm   ke-bor'í dō-ò-lò
PURP=ADD women:COLL POSS-PL NMLZ-try exist-much-RL
'[...] [M]any women also try to get outside work.' [KaR, SWK 064]

Finally, consider irrealis-marked nominalized adverbial clauses. As discussed in §12.5.2, *-jí* occurs on adverbial clauses in conjunction with subordinator *asón* 'like' to indicate an imagined comparison. Another semantic type of adverbial clause where we would expect to find robust irrealis marking is in purpose adverbial clauses. Surprisingly, though, there are a number of instances such as (583) in §12.5.2, where purpose adverbial clauses are not marked irrealis. While the corpus does also contain purpose adverbial clauses that are marked with *-jí* 'irrealis2', such as (591) and (592), there is no obvious explanation as to why purpose adverbial clauses do not exhibit more consistent irrealis marking.

(591) Irrealis-marked adverbial clause indicating purpose
[...] laso akhai pu kachepaklangdunji aphan
[[[lasō   a-khái   **pu]   ke-che-pe-klàng-dūn-jí]**
this   POSS-community   **QUOT NMLZ-RR-CAUS-appear-along-IRR2**
aphān]
PURP

so'arlo atum keklemnang parsik akam dopik
sō'arlō   a-tūm   ke-klém-náng   pe-arsīk   a-kám   dō-pìk
women:COLL   POSS-PL   NMLZ-do-need   CAUS-be.deep   POSS-work   exist-very
'[...] [I]n order to show that this community (is okay), there is a lot of (things to think) deeply about and work to do.' [KaR, SWK 033]

(592) Irrealis-marked adverbial clause indicating purpose
phinu chojordamji aphan hu kulat
[[phinū   cho-jōr-dām-jí]   a-phān]   hú   kulát
banana   AUTO.BEN/MAL-sell-GO-IRR2   POSS-PURP   over.there   shop(<Asm)

anat damlo
a-nát   dàm-lò
POSS-direction   go-RL
'In order to go and sell bananas there he went towards the shop.' [HI, BPh 005]

12.7 Main clause constructions

The following discussion is dedicated to constructions in which the *ke-* prefix occurs on main clause verbs. In order for the *ke-* prefix to synchronically still be the nominalizer, there has to be an element, such as a copula, that serves as the finite verb in order for the construction to overall become finite. If there is no such element, then *ke-* no longer functions as a nominalizer in that construction, and we may instead refer to that construction as a diachronic nominalization construction.

Four main clause constructions are attested that involve *ke-*. The 'nominalization plus copula' construction (§12.7.1) involves the existential copula *dō*, while adverbial constructions involve an adverbial element that renders the construction finite, as discussed in the previous chapter in §11.3.3 and §11.3.4 above (see §12.7.2 below).

Finally, there are two diachronic nominalization construction involving *ke-* that lack an element to render them finite, meaning that reanalysis of the nominalizer *ke-* has to have occurred (§12.7.3).

12.7.1 Nominalization plus existential copula construction

Instead of a simple verbal predicate, there are some instances in the corpus where speakers choose to use a nominalization construction involving the existential copula *dō*. An example is (593), where the nominalization plus copula construction is further embedded in a declarative intensifier copy verb construction of the structure '*V=ke V-suffixes*' (§16.2.3.1).

(593) Nominalization plus copula construction
Naka anglong pu bihek akopenta arjulong
Náká   a-inglóng   pu   bī-hèk   akó=pen=tā   arjū-lōng
TRIBE   POSS-hill   QUOT   be.small-small   then=from=ADD   listen-GET

Naka akhei puta arjulong lapenke... Naka
Náká   a-khéi   pu=tā   arjū-lōng   lapèn=ke   Náká
TRIBE   POSS-community   QUOT=ADD:although   ask-GET   and.then=TOP   TRIBE

akhei amonit so'arlopen pusetame sopinsopen
a-khéi   a-monít   so'àrlō=pen   pùsetāmē   sopìnsō=pen
POSS-community   POSS-man   women:COLL=with   likewise   boy:COLL=with

pusetame elong longni lason kechetong doke
pùsetāmē   e-lòng   lòng-ní   lasón   **ke-chetòng**   **dō=ke**
likewise   one-CLF:place   CLF:place-two   that.way   **NMLZ-meet**   **exist=TOP**

dohe
dō=he
exist=AFTERTHOUGHT
'Since my childhood, I got to hear about the Naga hills, the Naga people, but of both the women and men, (only some), like that, I got to meet in a place or two.' [SiT, HF 004]

In (593), instead of *kechetong doke dohe*, a simple verbal predicate could have been used in the same copy verb construction as well: *chetongke chetonghe*. Although we would expect that the nominalization construction is somehow more emphatic than using a simple verbal predicate, the pragmatic difference is if anything very subtle, as my language consultants did not perceive a clear functional difference.

Similarly, in (594), instead of the simple verbal predicate *chungkrenglo*, a nominalization construction is used: *kechungkreng dolo*. Oddly enough, the speaker does not use *ke-* on the remaining three PCT predicates (for further discussion of this, see §12.8).

(594) Nominalization plus copula construction
[...] kechungkreng dolo, marjeng dolo, lok'hu dolo, lokphlep dolo;
[ke-chungkrèng   **dō-lò**]   [marjèng   dō-lò]   [lòk'hù   dō-lò]
NMLZ-be.thin   **exist-RL**   be.thin   exist-RL   be.pale   exist-RL
[lòkphlèp   dō-lò]
be.pale   exist-RL

kithita kedothupo, kejangta
[**ke-**thì=tā   ke-**dō**-thū-pò]   [**ke-**jāng=tā
NMLZ-die=ADD   NMLZ-**exist**-again-IRR1   **NMLZ-**hang.down=ADD

kedothupo
ke-**dō**-thū-pò]
NMLZ-**exist**-again-IRR1
'[...] [T]hey became thin, they became pale, and they were about to die.' [CST, RO 022]

In the second line of (594), *thì* 'die' occurs in an elaborate expression (EE) construction with *jāng*. The verb pair further occurs in a nominalization construction: *kithita kedothupo* and *kejangta kedothupo*, instead of *thipo* and *jangpo*. Here, however, it seems that the nominalization construction serves the structural purpose of allowing the speaker to coordinate the EE verb pair with the use of =*tā* 'additive' on the preposed verb copies (§15.5.1.2).

In another type of nominalization plus copula construction, there appears to be an underlying structural ambiguity. Consider (595), where under one analysis, the nominalized clause could be interpreted as a direct S argument of the existential copula, i.e., *[[laso adak isi hini achitchit arong kephopon]ₛ do]*. Alternatively, it could be interpreted as an internally-headed relative clause, with the head noun being the S argument of the existential copula: *[[[laso adak [isi hini achitchit arong]_{HN} kephopon]_{RC}]ₛ do]*.

(595)   Nominalization plus copula construction with presentational function
penke damsi isi aporke Kohima rongsopi lelo...
[pèn=ke   dàm-si   isī   a-pór=ke   Kóhìmà   ròngsōpī   lè-lò]
and.then=TOP go-NF:RL one   POSS-time=TOP   PLACE   town   reach-RL

laso adak isi hini achitchit arong
[[lasō   a-dāk]   [isī   hiní   achítchít   a-ròng]
this   POSS-road.inbetween one   two   tiny   POSS-village

kephopon do
ke-phō-pōn   dō]
NMLZ-reach-in.passing   **exist**
'And then we went and at one o'clock, we reached Kohima Town..., on the road in between / up to there, there were several tiny villages that we had crossed.' [SiT, HF 017]

There is a structural and a functional argument to be made in evaluating these two analyses. On the one hand, the RC analysis is more marked in that internally-headed (and/or post-head) relative clauses occur with low frequency (see §12.3.2). Structurally, this analysis is therefore less preferable, all things being equal. On the other hand, however, the RC analysis makes sense functionally, as this appears to be a kind of presentational construction used to introduce the head noun. Consider the intonation unit following (595), which is offered in (596).

(596) Intonation unit following (595)
amen heihai nangthanpon... ta ning ave
a-mén   héihái   nang=thán-pòn   tā   nīng   avē
POSS-name different.kinds.of 1/2:NSUBJ=tell-in.passing but   mind   not.exist
'Their names they had told us in passing... but I can't remember (now).' [SiT, HF 018]

Since this following intonation unit comments on the 'several tiny villages', this suggests that the nominalization construction in (595) served the information-structural function of introducing the 'several tiny villages' to the interlocutor/listener.
For another example, consider the excerpt in (597), which contains both the intonation unit (IU) with the nominalization construction and the subsequent IU.

(597) Nominalization plus copula construction with presentational function
ansi phelo-bisir pu Karbi atum kabonai do
ánsi   **[phelō-bisīr**   **pu]**   [Karbì   a-tūm
then   **alkaline-funnel.for.filtering.ashes**   **QUOT**   PN   POSS-PL
ke-bonái]   **dō**
NMLZ-make(<Aśm)   **exist**
'And then, there is the so-called *phelo bisir* (funnel-like instrument for filtering the ashes) that the Karbi people make.' [SiH, KH 004]

laso aphelo-bisir alongsi laso aphelo
[lasō   a-phelō-bisīr   alòng=si]
this   POSS-alkaline-funnel.for.filtering.ashes   LOC=FOC:RL
[lasō   a-phelō
this   POSS-alkaline

ingkrunget humdun'etpo, ingkrung'et arje'etpo
ingkrùng-èt   hūm-dūn-ét-pò]   ingkrùng-ét   arjè-ét-pò
separate-PRF   pick.up-JOIN-PRF-IRR1   strain-PRF   separate-PRF-IRR1
'In this ash funnel, we sieve the ashes and pick them up, we thoroughly sieve the ashes.' [SiH, KH 005]

Here again, functional considerations suggest that the relative clause analysis is more appropriate than the event nominalization analysis, as this construction serves the function of introducing the participant 'the so-called *phelo bisir*'. This function can be deduced from the next text unit, which comments on this participant, specifically on how this *phelo bisir* is used as a tool in the process of preparing alkaline food by using ashes.

The relative clause analysis implies an underlying structure that can be schematically represented as: *[[phelo-bisir pu]$_{HN}$ Karbi atum kabonai]$_s$ do]*. Note that here, the construction is again structurally ambiguous between an internally-headed or a post-head relative clause, as discussed in §12.3.2. It could be internally-headed:

[[[[phelo-bisir pu]$_{HN}$ Karbi atum kabonai]$_{RC}$]$_s$ do], or post-head relativization:
[[[phelo-bisir pu]$_{HN}$ [Karbi atum kabonai]$_{RC}$]$_s$ do].

In addition to the instances discussed here, the function of a presentational construction might also be underlying the copula argument quantification construction discussed in §11.4.2.

12.7.2 Adverbial constructions

Several adverbial constructions (including constructions based on non-final marking) involve synchronic nominalization. This is discussed in §11.3.

12.7.3 Diachronic nominalization constructions in main clause grammar

In diachronic nominalization constructions, the *ke-* prefix occurs on the main clause but there is no other element to render the clause finite. Therefore, the *ke-* must have been reanalyzed in those instances, and cannot synchronically be considered a nominalizer despite its historical origin (hence, diachronic nominalization). There are two types of diachronic nominalization constructions: focus constructions (with several subtypes), and an imperfective-marking construction.

12.7.3.1 Focus constructions

There are three subtypes of focus constructions. First, there is the general argument focus construction, which may occur in all clause types including non-declarative speech acts (§12.7.3.1.2). Second, specifically in content questions, the interrogative pronoun or adverb is typically marked as being under focus (although another element can be under focus as well, then belonging to the first type of focus construction) (§12.7.3.1.3). Third, there is a co-relative construction that is best analyzed as a focus construction as well, with the co-related elements across the two clauses being under focus (§12.7.3.1.4).

All focus constructions have two structural properties in common. First, there is an element in the clause that occurs with one of three focus clitics: mostly with *=si* if the verb is realis, or with *=le* if it is irrealis (§15.3), but in a few cases also with *=lo* (§9.6.1.7). Second, in a substantial number of occurrences (though not in all, see the next section §12.7.3.1.1), the verb is marked with *ke-* without a copula present that would render the clause finite. Since these are not imperfective constructions (see §12.7.3.2 below) (although some may be as well, see §12.7.3.3), there has to be a different historical explanation for why the verb is diachronically nominalized in the focus construction. The typologically most plausible explanation is to assume that the Karbi focus construction originates in a cleft construction. This historical development is sketched out in §12.7.3.1.5.

12.7.3.1.1 Inconsistent occurrence of ke-

While we find inconsistent occurrence of *ke-* in synchronic nominalization constructions (§12.8), this is even more prominent in diachronic nominalization, specifically focus constructions. In the general argument focus construction (§12.7.3.1.2), only about a third of the clauses that contain an element marked by *=si* 'focus:realis' have *ke-* on the verb. In content questions, the proportion is higher, but it is still only about two thirds of clauses that contain a focus-marked interrogative pronoun that also occur with *ke-*. As for co-relative focus constructions, there only are very few instances in the corpus, but all of those are nominalized.

My hypothesis is that the occurrence of *ke-* is so inconsistent in these focus constructions because it is a fossilized element that no longer serves a grammatical function and is thus not a salient element in these constructions (see §12.7.3.1.5 for a historical account of the focus construction).

12.7.3.1.2 General argument focus construction

In the general argument focus construction, about a third of the occurrences of focus marker *=si* are coupled with diachronic nominalization of the main verb, i.e., the presence of the *ke-* prefix. This is found in elicitation, such as the contrastive focus construction in (598), which was elicited via translation of the contrastive focus structure from English into Karbi.

(598) General argument focus construction: elicited contrastive focus construction
[nè   phàk-ōk=**le**   *ki-tún*   kalī]   [vō-ōk=**si**
1EXCL   pig-meat=**FOC:IRR**   NMLZ-cook   NEG.EQU.COP   bird-meat=**FOC:RL**

ki-tún]
NMLZ-cook
'I don't/won't cook pork, I (will) cook chicken.' Or: 'It is not me cooking meat, it is (me) cooking chicken.' [Elicitation SiT 090303]

Here, the first clause is negated and the element under contrastive focus is hence marked with *=le*, while the second clause is asserted and the element under contrastive focus therefore marked with *=si*. In both clauses, the main verb is marked with *ke-*.

Corpus examples that also illustrate the co-occurrence of focus marked elements with *ke-* marked verbs follow: with realis focus marker =*si* in (599); with irrealis focus marker =*le* in (600); and with focus marker =*lo* in (601). Again, note that these examples only illustrate a subset of focus construction instances; more than half of the instances occur without *ke-* on the verb.

(599) General argument focus construction with realis focus marker =*si*
amatsi itum aphanke dak habit angbongsi
amātsi   e-tūm   a-phān=ke   dāk   habít   angbòng=**si**
because   1PL.INCL-PL   POSS-NSUBJ=TOP   here   jungle   in.middle.of=**FOC:RL**

nangkethonti
nang=**ke**-thòn-tí
1/2:NSUBJ=**NMLZ**-drop-get.rid.off
'And then, she took us here in the middle of the jungle and abandoned us.'
[CST, HM 052]'

(600) General argument focus construction with irrealis focus marker =*le*
[...] "*itum nangpeile kedo kalilo*" [...]
[i-tūm   nang-pēi=**le**   **ke**-dō   kalī-lò]
1PL:INCL-PL   2:POSS-mother=**FOC:IRR**   **NMLZ**-exist   NEG.EQU.COP-RL
'[...] "We don't have your mother anymore." [...]' [CST, RO 008]

(601) General argument focus construction with realis focus marker =*lo*
bang nekengdak arumloklo kedam
bàng   ne-kèng-dàk   arúm-lòk=**lo**   **ke**-dàm
CLF:HUM:PL   1EXCL:POSS-foot-road.inbetween   down-just=**FOC**   **NMLZ**-go
'The other people simply walked through between my legs.' [RBT, ChM 015]

12.7.3.1.3 Content question focus construction

Interrogative pronouns and adverbs often occur with a focus clitic: mostly with =*si* but sometimes also with =*lo*. Looking at those instances of content questions in the corpus that have a focus-marked interrogative pronoun or adverb, about two thirds have verbs marked with *ke-* in the clause. Examples that illustrate this are (602) and (603).[125]

---

[125] Note that content questions may have another focus-marked element in addition to a focus-marked interrogative pronoun or adverb; see the discussion of (851) in §15.3.2.

(602) Content question focus construction with realis focus marker =si
nesomar pule kosonsi thengpi abeng
ne-oso-màr   pu=le   **kosón=si**   thengpī   a-bēng
1EXCL:POSS-child-PL QUOT=FOC:IRR   **how=FOC:RL**   tree/wood   POSS-piece

nangketetroiroidetlo
nang=**ke**-tèt-ròi~rōi-dèt-lò
CIS=**NMLZ**-exit-PL.solid.obj~DIST.PL-PFV-RL
'If they are my children, how did they come out as pieces of wood?' [CST, HM 023]

(603) Content question focus construction with realis focus marker =lo
ne kopilo kevipo laho <m>
nè   kopí=**lo**   **ke**-vì-pò   là-ho
1EXCL   what=**FOC**   **NMLZ**-do-IRR1   this-EMPH:INTERACT
'What should I do?' [CST, HM 013]

12.7.3.1.4 Co-relative focus construction

The co-relative construction might have also developed as a focus construction, although the evidence is less clear, partly because this is a rare construction in the corpus.

This construction is based on corresponding interrogative pronouns or adverbs (§6.1.3) and demonstrative/deictic pronouns and adverbs (§6.1.4) across two nominalized clauses (see also §6.1.5). In this construction, the interrogative pronouns or adverbs are marked with the question particle =*ma* in order to function as indefinite or universal relative pronouns 'whoever', 'whatever', etc.

In (604), the first clause contains the derived universal relative pronoun *ko'anma* 'how(ever) much', while the second clause contains the =*lo* focus-marked demonstrative counterpart *la'anlo* 'that much'. Both clauses are nominalized, meaning that this co-relative construction has the same structural properties as the two other focus construction subtypes discussed above.

(604) Co-relative construction
ha thepai thereng longku longdang pirthe methan ko'anma
há   thepài   therēng   longkū   longdāng   pirthé   methān
over.there   cliff   EE:thepài   cave   crevice   world   dog
ko'án=ma
how.much=Q

kedam bamonpota la'anlo kidun
ke-dàm   bamón-pō=tā   **la'án=lo**   **ke**-dùn
NMLZ-go   wise.person(<Ind)-male=ADD   **that.much**=FOC   **NMLZ**-join
'There, over all kinds of difficult terrain, over caves and crevices, as much as the dog went, that much the bamonpo followed him.' [KK, BMS 041]

12.7.3.1.5 Historical development

It is typologically well attested that a focus construction can be diachronically based on nominalization, as in the following scenario. As sketched out in Figure 16, the historical development involves a cleft as a source construction. In this 'Stage 1', the focus marker is (still) an equational copula. That is, a sentence like *nè=si ke-dàm*, with *nè* being the first person exclusive pronoun and *dàm* being the verb root 'go' is historically interpreted as a cleft: '(it) [[is]cop [me]NP] [who is going]NP'. The structure is that of an equational copula clause, with the clefted NP ('me') occurring with the copula clause-initially because it is under focus, and with the other NP ('who is going') being a headless relative clause. Since relative clauses are nominalized with *ke-* in Karbi, this historical scenario would explain how the two structural pieces of the focus construction, i.e., the focus clitic and the *ke-* on the verb, go together.

Stage 1: NP(=COP) [[...] *ke*-V]_REL]_NP

→ reanalysis of copula as focus marker

Stage 2: NP(=FOC) [...] *ke*-V

Figure 16: Grammaticalization scenario for =*si* 'focus' (starting as copula).

After reanalysis of the copula as a focus marker,[126] we now have a focus construction that still has the same two elements as the original cleft construction, although *ke-* can no longer synchronically be interpreted as a nominalizer, since that would leave the construction non-finite. Therefore, *ke-* has to be analyzed as a fossil in the synchronic focus construction. Note, however, that the fact that this construction is negated with the nominal negation construction (using the negative equational copula *kalī* rather than the verbal suffix -*Cē*; §11.1.2), as seen in (605), still shows the nominal character of the construction.

(605) General argument focus construction with irrealis focus marker =*le*
 [...] "*itum nangpeile kedo kalilo*" [...]
 [i-tūm nang-pēi=**le** **ke-dō** kalī-lò]
 1PL:INCL-PL 2:POSS-mother=**FOC:IRR** **NMLZ**-exist NEG.EQU.COP-RL
 '[...] "We don't have your mother anymore." [...]' [CST, RO 008]

This account for the historical development of the focus construction in Karbi is well supported by cross-linguistic case studies. Focus markers grammaticalizing from a cleft

---

[126] The reanalysis might have been facilitated if the original copula was most commonly used in this construction. Since a simple juxtaposition construction for equational clauses might have always been an option, the copula would have only been used in pragmatically marked contexts, of which a cleft would be a prime example.

construction involving a copula are attested in many languages of the world including the Uto-Aztecan language Cora (Casad 1984); the Afro-Asiatic languages Lamang and Rendille (Heine and Reh 1984); Japanese (Harris and Campbell 1995); and Papiamentu (S. Kouwenberg and Muysken 1995; Holm 1988); see also Heine and Kuteva (2002).

In addition to the typological support for this reconstruction, there is Tibeto-Burman internal evidence as well, in particular for the =*si* realis focus clitic. The evidence comes from Central 'Kuki-Chin' languages, where there is a *sii* equational copula in Hakha Lai (Peterson 2003: 424), and a *si* equational copula in Falam Lai (King 2010), filling in comparative evidence for Karbi =*si* originating in an equational copula. Moreover, in Falam Lai, there also is a *si* focus marker that occurs with interrogative pronouns and adverbs the same way Karbi =*si* does (§12.7.3.1.3). Falam Lai has therefore both the reanalyzed focus marker *si* as well the copula source form *si*, providing direct evidence that this development has occurred in this language.

As for the other two, much less frequent focus clitics in Karbi, =*le* and =*lo*, the evidence is not as clear. However, it could very well be that =*le* can be historically linked to the second syllable in the negative equational copula *kalī*, since there is comparative evidence that the velar-initial first syllable can be linked to negative forms in Tibeto-Burman, and the lateral-initial second syllable to copular forms (§6.2.2.2). While the vowels do not match, this is still a strong hypothesis for functional reasons, because it can explain the irrealis-sensitivity of the focus marker =*le* with the negative polarity association of *kalī*.

An investigation into the historical origin of =*lo* will need to consider realis -*lò* (§9.6.1.7), but whether both forms ultimately reconstruct back to an equational copula is not clear at present.

12.7.3.2 Imperfective construction

Another construction that represents an instance of diachronic nominalization is the imperfective marking of main clauses with *ke-*, i.e., the reanalyzed nominalizer (see further below for a discussion of the historical scenario). This aspectual function of *ke-* marked main clauses was also pointed out by Grüßner (1978: 95), who more narrowly calls it progressive aspect. In order to include those instances where *ke-* occurs on PCT roots functioning as main clause verbs, however, I refer to it more broadly as an imperfective construction. Examples of *ke-* occurring on PCT-based verbs are offered in (606) and (607).

(606) Diachronic nominalization: imperfective marking on PCT roots
 [...] nangong adakvam ahemsi kene asopi
 [nang-ōng adakvám a-hēm=si] kenē
 2:POSS-maternal.uncle second.child POSS-house=FOC:RL HESIT
 [a-oso-pì
 POSS-child-female

arje kemerintihe po nang hadak Bey
arjè   **ke**-mē-rintí=he]   [pō   nàng
appearance   **IPFV**-be.good-equally:PL:S/A=AFTERTHOUGHT   father you
hádāk   Bēy
there   CLAN

Ki'ik ahemsi nang piso hangdamrong
ke-ìk   a-hēm=si   nàng pīsō hàng-dām-ròng]
NMLZ-be.black   POSS-house=FOC:RL   2   wife call-GO-instead
'[…] [A]t your second-born maternal uncle's house, his daughters are all equally beautiful, you know, father, you went there to the house of Bey the Black to ask for a wife instead.' [WR, BCS 013]

(607) Diachronic nominalization: imperfective marking on PCT roots
"*nangpran nang'en'etji*" *pulo… osomar ante kephere*
nang-prán nang=ēn-èt-jí   pù-lò   osō-mār ánte   **ke**-pheré
2:POSS-life 1/2:NSUBJ=take-PFT-IRR2   say-RL child-PL OK.then **IPFV**-fear
'"Your lives I will take", (she) said, so the children were scared.' [CST, RO 020]

In (608) and (609), *ke-* occurs on active verbs *tòk* 'pound, grind' and *tūk* 'dig' in constructions that further highlight their imperfectivity: in (608) with the suffix *lók* 'only' that translates as 'keep V-ing (without doing anything else)', and in (609) in a construction that repeats the same verb a number of times to indicate the durative nature of the event.

(608) Diachronic nominalization: imperfective marking on non-PCT verbs
*thap **ketoklok** jo arníta sanglongle,*
[thàp   **ke-tòk-lók]**   [jó   arnì=tā   sáng-lōng-Cē]
cake.for.rice.beer   **IPFV-pound-only**   night day=ADD   take.rest-GET-NEG

*thap **ketoklok ketoklok**, aso mok*
[thàp   **ke-tòk-lók**   **ke-tòk-lók]**   [[[a-sō   mōk
cake.for.rice.beer **IPFV-pound-only**   **IPFV-pound-only**   POSS-child breast

kachepechuji apor ave tangho
ke-che-pa-chū-jí]   a-pór]   avē   tànghò]
NMLZ-RR-CAUS-suck-IRR2   POSS-time   not.exist   REP
'They just kept pounding the rice for the rice beer cake, the whole time they didn't get to take rest, they were pounding the rice beer cake, they didn't even have time to breast-feed their children.' [WR, BCS 030]

(609) Diachronic nominalization: imperfective marking on non-PCT verbs
laso ajangrengsoke phurui kituk kituk kituk kituk...
lasō	a-jangrēngsō=ke	phurùi	ke-tūk	ke-tūk	ke-tūk	ke-tūk
this	POSS-orphan=TOP	yam	NMLZ-dig	NMLZ-dig	NMLZ-dig	NMLZ-dig

chelangledetlohe {mm} chelangledetlo
che-làng-Cē-dèt-lò=he	mm	che-làng-Cē-dèt-lò
RR-see-NEG-PFV-RL=DM	AFF	RR-see-NEG-PFV-RL

'This orphan, as he was digging and digging and digging... he didn't look around.' [HK, TR 051]

Imperfective *ke-* occurs frequently in one particular text in the corpus, which is an on-line narration of the pear story, where the speaker is commenting on the video clip as he is watching it. Examples are (610) and (611).

(610) Imperfective *ke-* in the pear story narration
vo kiku
vō	**ke**-kú
chicken	**IPFV**-crow

'A chicken (rooster) is crowing.' [SiT, PS 001]

(611) Imperfective *ke-* in the pear story narration
dondon chedonsi... anke amonit abang
[dondón	che-dón-si...]	[ánke	[a-monít	abàng]
ladder	RR-place.ladder/bridge-NF:RL	and.then	POSS-man	NPDL

<a> pe akelokpen keroi isi ajamborong
[[pé	a-ke-lòk=pen	ke-ròi	isī	a-jamboróng
cloth	POSS-NMLZ-be.white=with	NMLZ-sew	one	POSS-bag

arlosi lahai kethap lapen arum kevan
arlō=si]	[lahái]	**ke**-thàp]]	lapèn	[arúm	**ke**-vàn]]
inside=FOC:RL	these	**IPFV**-put.inside	and	down	**IPFV**-bring

'He's placed himself a ladder... and then, the man, into one bag sown from white cloth he puts these (fruit), and then brings them down.' [SiT, PS 003]

A typologically well-supported way to model the historical development of the imperfective construction from a nominalization construction is to assume a locational construction as the source construction. As sketched out in Figure 17, the locational construction at Stage 1 would include an S argument, a locational NP that structurally consists of a nominalized clause, and the locational copula, which is the same as the existential copula in Karbi, *dō*. This hypothesized source construction for the Karbi imperfective is structurally analogous to the source construction of the English progressive (i.e., 'S be on/at V-ing'), except that in English, a preposition 'on' or 'at' was required, where in Karbi nothing but the locational copula *dō* is required.

Stage 1: ([NP]s) [[...] *ke*-V]LOC [*dō*]be.at

⟶ loss of locational copula *dō* 'be at'

Stage 2: ([NP]S/A) [...] *ke*-V

Figure 17: Possible grammaticalization pathway for the imperfective construction.

In the absence of closely related languages, it is not clear what kind of comparative evidence could help put this reconstruction on a stronger footing. It appears that there is no possible evidence that could substantially contribute to strengthen or weaken this hypothesis, but the fact that this is a cross-linguistically well-attested development suggests that this is a plausible reconstruction.

12.7.3.3 Ambiguity between focus and imperfective interpretation

In some instances, such as (612), there is an ambiguity as to what triggers the *ke*-prefix on the main clause verb, as this is an imperfective context but there is also a focused element *lují=si* 'mirror=FOC:RL' in the clause.

(612) Ambiguity between focus and imperfective interpretation
anke laso athongkup along lujisi
ánke   [lasō   a-thongkūp   a-lòng]   lují=**si**
and.then this   POSS-tobacco.container   POSS-LOC   mirror=FOC:RL

kapabon
ke-pa-bōn
NMLZ-CAUS-be.attached
'And then, on this tobacco container, there was a mirror attached.' [HK, TR 026]

Similarly, in (613), which is from the on-line narrated pear story (see (610) and (611) in the preceding section §12.7.3.2), the *ke*- can be interpreted as being the fossilized nominalizer from the focus construction evoked by *=si* 'focus:realis', but it can also be interpreted as marking imperfective aspect, as the speaker is commenting on the event as it is occurring in the video clip.

(613) Ambiguity between focus and imperfective interpretation
lake phatang alongsi kethap
là=ke   phatáng   alòng=**si**   **ke**-thàp
this=TOP   B.BASKET   LOC=**FOC:RL**   **NMLZ**-put.inside
'He is putting them in a *phatang* bamboo basket.' [SiT, PS 004]

Note that in examples like these, *ke-* is glossed as 'nominalizer' because it is the more neutral label and better reflects the ambiguity between the two possible interpretations.

12.8 Inconsistent occurrence of *ke-* 'nominalizer' in nominalization constructions

This section aims to draw attention to the inconsistency with which *ke-*'nominalizer' occurs in synchronically nominalized constructions, across all types of synchronically nominalized constructions (though less so in nominalized complementation constructions, as discussed further below).

In (614) and (615), *ke-* is absent from PCT modifiers, both preposed and postposed. Note that (614) is an elicited sentence (produced when asked for a translation of the English sentence), which strongly suggests that the absence of *ke-* cannot be accounted for as being due to fast colloquial or hypo-articulated speech.

(614) Lack of *ke-* 'NMLZ' on preposed PCT modifier
 là=ke **[[làng-mē-sén]** a-mír] kalī
 this=TOP **look-GOOD-INTENS** POSS-flower NEG.EQU.COP
 'This is not a pretty flower.' [Elicitation SiT 090220]

(615) Lack of *ke-* 'NMLZ' on postposed PCT modifier
 ba ko jirpo {mm} pinike ne
 ba ko jīrpō mm pinì=ke nè
 SURPRISE(<Asm) buddy:VOC friend AFF today=TOP 1EXCL

 eson akhobor mesen arjulong {mm}
 [[e-sòn] a-khobór **[mē-sén]]** arjū-lōng {mm}
 one-CLF:thing POSS-news(<Ind) **be.good-INTENS** hear-GET AFF
 'Hey my friend...today I got to hear good news.' [HK, TR 132]

In (616), *ke-* is absent on a relative clause verb, and similarly, in (617), a construction that can be interpreted as a relative clause verb or a participant nominalization also occurs without *ke-*.

(616) Lack of *ke-* 'NMLZ' on relative clause verb
 [...] *"he matsi", hala apiso abang pulo,*
 he komāt=si hála a-pisò abàng pù-lò
 hey! who=FOC:RL that POSS-wife NPDL say-RL

"he therak thekthe apinso"
he   [[**therāk   thèk-Cē**]   a-pinsò]
hey!   **be.ashamed know.how-NEG**   POSS-married.man
'[...] "Hey, who is that!", the wife said, "hey, (you are) a man who doesn't feel any shame".' [SeT, MTN 034]

(617)   Lack of *ke-* 'NMLZ' on relative clause verb / participant nominalization
[...] e kasu harlung pirthe... rim abang ave,
e   kasú   harlūng pirthé [[[[**rīm**]   a-bàng]   avē]
DSM   plate bowl   world   **keep.in.order**   POSS-CLF:HUM:PL   not.exist

bi abang ave... hem hormu hortar
[[[**bí**   a-bàng]   avē]]   hēm   [hormú   hortár]
keep   POSS-CLF:HUM:PL   not.exist house   thing   EE:hormú

rikcho rikhaplo pu
rík-chò   rík-hàp-lò   pu
be.scattered-everything.neg.1/2 be.scattered-everything.neg.2/2-RL   QUOT
'[...] [T]he plates and bowl and everything (are scattered) because nobody kept them in place, everything is scattered.' [KK, BMS 093]

In (618), (619), and (620), adverbial clause verbs occur without *ke-*. Note that in (620), there are three parallel nominalized, non-final marked verbs, but only the last two are marked with *ke-*.

(618)   Lack of *ke-* 'NMLZ' on adverbial clause verb
phinu chojordamji aphan hu kulat
[[phinū   **cho-jōr-dām-jí**]   a-phān]   hú   kulát
banana   **AUTO.BEN/MAL-sell-GO-IRR2**   POSS-PURP   over.there   shop(<Asm)

anat damlo
a-nát   dàm-lò
POSS-direction   go-RL
'In order to go and sell bananas there he went towards the shop.' [HI, BPh 005]

(619)   Lack of *ke-* 'NMLZ' on PCT root functioning as an adverbial clause verb
lasi laso adakke tovarta mesen apot
lasì   [[[lasō   a-dàk=ke]   továr=tā   **mē-sén**]
therefore   this   POSS-road.inbetween=TOP   road=ADD   **be.good-INTENS**
apōt]
because

12.8 Inconsistent occurrence of ke- 'nominalizer' in nominalization constructions

leta ledappranglo Bokolia'an
lè=tā lè-dàppràng-lò Bokoliá-án
reach=ADD reach-early-RL PN-till
'So on this stretch, the road was good, and so we reached Bokolia early.' [SH, CSM 012]

(620) Lack of *ke-* 'NMLZ' on adverbial clause verb
*[...] amatsi netum **chepenangpen kangnekpen***
amātsi ne-tūm che-penáng-pèn **ke**-ingnēk-pèn
and.then 1EXCL-PL RR-make.fun-NF:with NMLZ-laugh-NF:with

***kachingnipen**, lasonsi damlo*
ke-che-ingnì-pèn, làsón=sì dàm-lò
NMLZ-RR-EE:ingnēk-NF:with that.way=FOC:RL go-RL
'We get to join and watch the Chomangkan, and so we are happy and everything, and then teasing each other and laughing each other, that's how we went (there).' [SH, CSM 021]

Finally, complement clauses have a different status, because there are a number of different complementation constructions that can be situated on a scale of clause union (§11.2.2). Therefore, the presence or absence of *ke-* may (or should) be interpreted as an actual functional difference between two constructions, which is different from the absence of *ke-* on relative and adverbial clause verb, which have to be interpreted as being nominalized independent of whether *ke-* is actually used on the verb or not.[127] That said, there is one nominalized complementation construction that structurally resembles relative and adverbial clauses due to the noun phrase delimiter *abàng* functioning as a complementizer (which is an element structurally equivalent to the head noun of relative clauses and the subordinator of adverbial clauses). As (621) shows, however, *ke-* may also be absent in this case of a nominalized complementation construction.

(621) Complement clause of *thèk* 'know how' marked with *abàng* 'NPDL'
"kevang akoke ne nanglong nangdunjuilo;
[ke-vàng akó=ke] [nè nang-lòng nang=dùn-jùi-lò]
NMLZ-come when=TOP 1EXCL 2-LOC CIS=join-away-RL

---

[127] Note, however, that it is also possible to interpret the absence of *ke-* on adverbial clause verbs as an indicator of advanced grammaticalization (and thus as a functional element), as discussed in §12.5.1.

> *ne non chedamji abang thekthedetpo! [...]"*
> [nè   nón   chV-dām-jí]   abàng]   thèk-Cē-dèt-pò]
> **1EXCL   now   RR-go-IRR2   NPDL**   **know.how-NEG-PFV-IRR1**
> '"When we came, I followed you along far away, I now won't find my way back [...]."' [KK, BMS 097]

It is not clear at this point what may be behind the inconsistent occurrence of *ke-* on synchronically nominalized verbs. The two most plausible reasons do not actually fully explain it: first, it does not seem to be a (purely) phonological issue, such that *ke-* does not occur if the verb stem already has a certain number of syllables, because there are instances such as (620), where the trisyllabic *chepenangpen* occurs without *ke-*, but instances such as (542), where an equally trisyllabic *chingkoidup* occurs with *ke-*. Second, it is not (only) an issue of colloquial versus careful speech, since the lack of *ke-* also occurs in elicitation as in (614) above. This issue has to be left to future study but see §1.3.3.3 for more discussion based on seemingly analogous cases of non-obligatoriness in other grammatical domains.

13 Clause participants: Overview, participants, noun phrase delimiter

This and the next chapter together deal with clause participants, both arguments and obliques, which are argued not to be two discrete types of participants but to rather represent different points on a continuum in Karbi. The discussion treats the expression of clause participants and the ways they are marked, depending on their functions and roles. Starting with brief sections on terminological and conceptual issues in §13.1, §13.2 offers an overview of what is to be said about the expression of clause participants from the perspective of the predicate. Here I discuss argument roles in typical declarative clauses as well as constructions that deviate from the typical patterns. While these two chapters focus on the discussion of clause participant structure in declarative clauses, §13.2 also surveys what can be said about grammatical relation constructions in domains other than declarative clauses.

In §13.3, an overview is provided of the ways participants are expressed and marked. Still within this chapter, §13.4 discusses argument expression (as lexical noun phrases, pronouns, or zero anaphora), whereas §13.5 offers an overview of how the Karbi noun phrase delimiter marker *abàng* interacts with participant marking. Role marking and core information/discourse structure marking are discussed in Chapter 14.

13.1 Preliminaries

13.1.1 Terminology

This section gives an overview of how terminology is used in this chapter. While the noun phrase is the smallest unit that is relevant in this chapter, in §13.4 I distinguish between pronouns and lexical noun phrases, where 'lexical noun phrase' is intended to refer to a noun phrase with a lexical head noun, i.e., in opposition to a pronoun.

In order to be able to independently refer to the structural and the functional elements of relevance in this chapter, I use the following terminology. Functionally, we can distinguish between arguments, which are required by the predicate, and obliques (also called adjuncts), which are not required by the predicate but instead offer additional information. Structurally, we can distinguish between noun phrases, which are unmarked for local role marking, and 'relator noun phrases', which are marked by a relator noun. There is also one postposition =*pen*, and noun phrases marked with this postposition I will refer to as 'postpositional phrases'.

In §13.1.2 and throughout the chapter, I argue that there is no strict divide between arguments and obliques. Nevertheless I find the syntactic primitives or macroroles (depending on the viewpoint) of S, A, O, R, and T useful labels for the description of 'argument' structure. The syntactic roles of S, A, O, R, and T define the number of arguments in a given construction, i.e., one, two, or three arguments, with (attempted) minimal reference to semantics, originally going back to Comrie (1978) and Dixon (1979).[128] Within this framework, S is the single argument of an intransitive predicate; A is the more agent-like argument of a transitive clause, and O (or P) is the other argument of a transitive clause; and in ditransitive clauses, R is the recipient-like argument and T is the theme-like argument.

13.1.2 The argument-oblique continuum and the syntax, semantics, and pragmatics in role marking

The distinction between participants that are required by the predicate and those that are not, that is, the distinction between arguments and obliques, is not straightforward in Karbi.[129] First, there is a practical challenge in examining argument structure in Karbi (shared by, in fact, many and presumably the majority of languages across the world), which is that Karbi pervasively uses zero anaphora. The consequence is that large amounts of texts have to be considered in order to get a sense for what typical patterns are, and what patterns may be exceptional or irregular. Nevertheless, what we find after consideration of large amounts of text is that Karbi does not have clear, syntactic case marking, such that each syntactic role of S, A, O, R, and T is always marked the same way. The only one of these syntactic roles that is consistently represented is the S argument, which is always unmarked for role. However, that does not necessarily mean that there is an S argument category in Karbi. Instead, within the system as a whole, it makes sense to also interpret the consistently unmarked status of S arguments pragmatically, i.e., as being due to the fact that S arguments by definition are the only argument in a clause. The pragmatic principle is: 'Don't mark an argument if it's obvious what its role is with respect to the predicate!'

Even more broadly, it is not true that a direct relationship exists between a particular type of marking or not-marking and core versus non-core or oblique status. Unlike in English, where at least in transitive clauses the generalization holds fairly

---

[128] Note that Comrie actually used the label 'P' instead of 'O'.
[129] In fact, it is not clear how a theory that posits a strong division between core arguments and obliques would hold up to cross-linguistic examination. Croft (2001: 272 ff.) in his 'Radical Construction Grammar' examines the distinction in English, and finds arguments in favor of a sharp distinction insufficient. He concludes that "under scrutiny, arguments and adjuncts as global syntactic roles evaporate."

well that core arguments are unmarked while obliques occur as prepositional phrases, no such generalization works in Karbi. As shown in §14.1.1, an unmarked NP may take on any 'syntactic' or semantic role. Nevertheless, there is a sense that unmarked NPs, NPs marked by -*phān* 'non-subject', and NPs marked by -*lòng* are more typically have core status in the sense of a non-semantically-specific status. It seems, however, that in Karbi, the non-semantic end of the continuum is more strongly influenced by pragmatic factors such as contextual role assignment, rather than syntactic factors such as valence.

Semantics plays a role in local marking as O-high[130] arguments (see §13.2.1.2), which are marked by *aphān*, tend to have human referents while O-low arguments, which remain unmarked, do not have human referents. Similarly, goal arguments with human referents are always marked by *alòng*, while those with non-human referents are more typically unmarked (§13.2.2.1). The generalization in these cases appears to be that arguments with human referents are always marked, whereas arguments with non-human referents are typically unmarked, but may be marked if pragmatically important or salient. These issues are further discussed in Chapter 14.

13.2 The predicate: Defining argument roles

This section discusses the generalizations we can make about how predicates define their argument roles. Section §13.2.1 discusses the common mono-, bi-, and trivalent constructions in typical declarative clauses. Section §13.2.2 deals with other common constructions that deviate from the patterns discussed in §13.2.1, including the 'need' construction, existential and possession constructions, and motion constructions. Section §13.2.3 provides an overview of predicates with derivationally changed argument structures. In §13.2.4, the only type of 'agreement' in Karbi is discussed, which is the proclitic *nang=* as a marker of non-subject speech act participants. Finally, §13.2.5 discusses (largely, the absence of) constructions in other grammatical domains that reflect argument structural properties.

13.2.1 Argument roles in typical declarative clauses

Following standard practice in approaching argument structure, I will start out by assuming that there are typically one, two, or three core arguments in a clause, and that the predicate defines how many argument roles exist in a given construction,

---

[130] Karbi exhibits differential O marking. O-high arguments are those marked by -*phān* 'non-subject', while O-low arguments are those not marked by -*phān*; see §13.2.1.2 and §14.1.5.

i.e., how many required roles there are. This is also referred to as the valence of the predicate. There may be one (S only), two (A and O), or three (A, R, and T) required argument roles, and the predicate is, respectively, monovalent or intransitive, bivalent or transitive, or trivalent or ditransitive. In each of these three cases, there are one or two default patterns of marking each role. In the monovalent construction, S is always unmarked (§13.2.1.1). In bivalent constructions, A is always unmarked, while O may be unmarked (O-low) or marked by *-phān* 'non-subject' (O-high) (§13.2.1.2). In trivalent constructions, A is also always unmarked, while R may be marked with *-phān* 'non-subject' and T unmarked (R-centered construction), or T may be marked with *-phān* 'non-subject' or unmarked, and R marked with *-lòng* 'locative' or unmarked (T-centered constructions) (§13.2.1.3). Nevertheless, certain predicates may require that one of these roles be marked in a way that deviates from the default pattern (§13.2.2).

13.2.1.1 Monovalent predicate: Unmarked S argument

Monovalent predicates require one core argument only, which never receives any kind of role marking, but may occur with *abàng* 'noun phrase delimiter' (§13.5) and/or one of the information and discourse structure clitics (§14.2). In (622), the predicate *bihek'hak'lang* based on the PCT *bī* 'be small' requires exactly one argument, which is filled by *nesomar* 'my children'.

(622)   Unmarked S argument
        e nesomarta bihek'hak'lang
                 [NP]_S

        e   **[ne-oso-màr=tā]**_S   bī-hek~hāk-làng
        DSM   **1EXCL-child-PL=ADD**   be.small-small~DISTR.PL-still
        'My children are still so small!' [CST, RO 006]

In (623) and (624), we find examples of monovalent clauses that feature an oblique participant in addition to the S argument. In (623), the oblique is a topic, and specifically the possessor of the S argument (see §13.2.2.4), and in (624), the oblique is a topic as well, but specifically a participant to whom the proposition applies.

(623)   Monovalent clause with additional oblique
        *[...] **halata** asomar thelo dinglo*
          [NP]_{OBL}   [NP]_S

        [hála=tā]   [a-oso-màr]   thè-lò   dīng-lò
        that=ADD   POSS-child-PL be.big-RL be.long-RL
        '[...] [A]nd so as for him also, his children grew up.' [WR, BCS 006]

(624) Monovalent clause with oblique
neliphanke ø me'ongchotlo

[NP]₀ʙʟ	[ø]s
[ne-li-phān=ke]	[ø] mē-óng-chòt-lò
1EXCL-HON-NSUBJ=TOP	ø be.good-be.much-very-RL

'This is very good (i.e. a very good opportunity) for me.' [SiT, HF 003]

13.2.1.2 Bivalent predicates: Marking of A and O arguments

In bivalent predicates, which require two arguments, the A argument is always unmarked, just like the S argument, but there is a split in O argument marking. Some O arguments remain unmarked, while other O arguments are marked by -*phān* 'non-subject' (§14.1.5), with various semantic and pragmatic factors probabilistically pushing O arguments towards one or the other. Following Bickel (2010), I call one end of the emerging continuum, where O is unmarked, O-low, and the other end, where O is marked by -*phān*, O-high.

In (625) and (626), we find examples of these two constructions in bivalent clauses. Example (625) features an O-low argument, which remains unmarked. Example (626) features an O-high argument, marked by -*phān*. In both examples, the respective A arguments are unmarked.

(625) Typical bivalent predicate with O-low: Both A and O unmarked
ba ko jirpo {mm} pinike ne

	[NP]ᵥₒc				[NP]ᴀ
ba	[ko	jīrpō]	mm	pinì=ke	nè
SURPRISE(<Asm)	buddy:VOC	friend	AFF	today=TOP	1EXCL

eson akhobor mesen arjulong {mm}

[NP]ₒ-ₗₒw			
[e-sòn	a-khobór	mē-sén]	arjū-lōng {mm}
one-CLF:thing	POSS-news(<Ind)	be.good-INTENS	hear-GET AFF

'Hey my friend...today I got to hear good news.' [HK, TR 132]

(626) Typical bivalent predicate with O-high: A unmarked and O marked with *aphān* 'primary object'
hala bamonpopen bamonpita

[NP]ᴀ	
[hála bamón-pō=pen	bamón-pī=tā]
that wise.person(<Ind)-male=with	wise.person(<Ind)-female=ADD

la methan aphanta inghonpik

[NP *aphān*]_{o-high}

[là   methān   **aphān**=tā]   inghōn-pìk
this   dog   NSUBJ=ADD love-very
'That Bamonpo and Bamonpi, both of them, also loved the dog a lot.'
[KK, BMS 005]

Other possibilities in marking transitive A and O arguments are as follows. The 'A' argument may be marked by -*lòng* 'locative' in the possession construction (§13.2.2.3), or by -*phān* 'non-subject' in the 'need' construction (§13.2.2.2). The O argument may be marked by -*lòng* 'locative' in the motion construction, particularly if the goal is a human referent (§13.2.2.1).

13.2.1.3 Trivalent predicates: Marking of A, R, and T arguments

Trivalent predicates have three required arguments: the most agent-like A argument, the recipient-, location- or goal-like R argument, and the T argument, which is the one that is most clearly conceptualized as being transferred or moved. While the A argument is always unmarked, there are three basic trivalent constructions, which differ in whether -*phān* 'non-subject' marking occurs on R, on T, or on neither of them, as shown in Table 109. Note that no ordering between T and R is implied here, as the order is not based on syntactic factors but instead appears based on pragmatic factors (see also §14.2.6.1).

Table 109: Object marking in trivalent constructions.

	T argument		R argument	
R-marked	T	Ø	R	-*phān*
T-marked	T	-*phān*	R	(-*lòng*/RNs)
Unmarked	T	Ø	R	(-*lòng*/RNs)

13.2.1.3.1 R-marked trivalent construction

In the R-marked construction, exemplified by (627) and (628), the human R argument is marked by -*phān* 'non-subject', while both A and (inanimate) T remain unmarked. Verbs that occur in this construction include *pī* 'give', *paklàng* 'show' (< *pa-klàng* 'CAUS-appear'), and *thòn* 'drop; take T to R'. This last verb *thòn* also frequently occurs in the T-marked trivalent construction (§13.2.1.3.2).

(627) Trivalent predicate with *aphān*-marked R argument
an laso a'oso abang thesere pumni

[NP]₍A₎			[NP]₍T₎	
án	[lasō	a-osō	abàng]	[theseré púm-ní]
and.then	this	POSS-child	NPDL	fruits CLF:round-two

hala ajirpo banghini aphan chepaklangdamlo

[NP *aphān*]₍R₎		
[hála a-jirpò	bàng-hiní	aphān] che-pa-klàng-dām-lò
that POSS-friend	CLF:HUM:PL-two	NSUBJ RR-CAUS-appear-GO-RL

'And then, this child went to show the two pieces of fruit to those two friends.'
[SiT, PS 040]

(628) Trivalent predicate with *aphān*-marked R argument
e misorongpoke <...> a'ik aphan... an kethondam

[NP]₍A₎	[NP *aphān*]₍R₎		[NP]₍T₎	
e	misòrongpō=ke	a-ìk aphān	àn	ke-thòn-dām
DSM	ant.sp=TOP	POSS-older.brother NSUBJ	rice	NMLZ-drop-GO

'The ant was on the way to drop off rice for his older brother.' [RBT, ChM 010]

There is one example in the corpus where both T and R have human referents, and the R-marked construction is used here (629).

(629) Human T and R referents in R-marked construction, corpus example
asomarke asoke aphi aphan

[∅]₍A₎	[NP]₍T₎	[NP]₍T₎	[NP *aphān*]₍R₎	
∅	a-so-màr=ke	a-osō=ke	[a-phì	aphān]
∅	POSS-child-PL=TOP	POSS-child=TOP	POSS-grandmother	NSUBJ

tekangbuplo
tekáng-bùp-lò
leave.for-RES:gone-RL
'She left her child with the grandmother.' [KK, CC 011]

In elicited (translated) examples, additional cases where both R and T have human referents are more commonly expressed via the R-marked construction (three out of four) than the T-marked construction. These examples include events of handling a baby (630); marriage (631); and showing or presentation (632).

(630) Human T and R referents in R-marked construction

[PRO]₍A₎	[NP *aphān*]₍R₎		[NP]₍T₎	

alang-li-tūm a-pēi aphān=si kong'er ke-pī
3-HON-PL POSS-mother NSUBJ=FOC:RL baby NMLZ-give
'They gave the baby to the mother.' [Elicitation SiT 190508]

(631) Human T and R referents in R-marked construction

penān ke-pa-cho-pí apharman
husband NMLZ-CAUS-AUTO.BEN/MAL-give for

[PRO-*phān*]₍R₎	[NP]₍T₎

alangli-phān a-sopì
3:HON-NSUBJ POSS-daughter

che-pí-dèt-lò
RR-give-PFV-RL
'He gave his daughter to him (for marriage).' [Elicitation SiT 190508]

(632) Human T and R referents in R-marked construction

[PRO]₍A₎	[NP *aphān*]₍R₎		[NP]₍T₎	

alàng-lì a-pēi aphān a-sō pa-klàng-lò
3-HON POSS-mother NSUBJ POSS-child CAUS-appear-RL
'He showed the boy to his mother.' [Elicitation SiT 190508]

In sum, the R-marked trivalent construction appears to be the preferred construction whenever there is a human R referent. The T participant may or may not have a human referent.

13.2.1.3.2 T-marked trivalent constructions

In the T-marked trivalent construction, the T argument is by definition marked by -*phān*. The R argument is typically marked by either the general locative relator noun -*lòng* (see §14.1.3 and §5.4.1) or a relator noun with more specific semantics, but may remain unmarked.

In these constructions, the R argument may only have a human referent if the T argument has a human referent as well (but even then, the R-marked construction appears to be the preferred choice, see the previous section). Otherwise, the R argument is a non-human location and the T argument is human or non-human. This construction is not used in the combination of a non-human T argument and a human R argument, because this constellation occurs in the R-centered trivalent construction (§13.2.1.3.1). A recurring verb in these constructions is *thòn*, which is glossed as 'drop' and translates as 'take T to R' or 'leave T with/at R', where both T and R may or may not have human referents (although it may be a requirement that at least one of the two have a human referent). Note that this verb also occurs in the R-centered trivalent construction. Another verb that occurs in this construction is *thàp* 'put inside', where R is the location or item in which T is put.

Examples (633) and (634) are from the same story, talking about the same event of a witch abandoning children in the forest. Therefore, in both clauses, the T argument has a human referent, while the R argument is a non-human location. The T argument is marked by *-phān* in both instances. The R argument is marked by the general locative marker *-lòng* in (633), but it is marked by the more semantically specific relator noun *-ngbòng* 'in the middle of' in (634).

(633) Trivalent predicate with *-phān* marked +human T argument and *-lòng* marked locative non-human R argument
[...] itum aphanke ha nampi namdur alongsi

[NP *aphān*]ᴛ			[NP *alòng*]ʀ		
e-tūm	aphān=ke	há	nāmpī	nāmdūr	alòng=si
1PL.INCL-PL	NSUBJ=TOP	over.there	big.forest	EE:nampī	LOC=FOC:RL

ekethondamlo
e=ke-thòn-dām-lò
1INCL:NSUBJ=NMLZ-drop-GO-RL
'[...] (The witch) abandoned us over there in the deep forest.' [CST, HM 076]

(634) Trivalent predicate with *-phān*-marked +human T argument and *-ngbòng*-marked locative non-human R argument
amatsi itum aphanke dak habit angbongsi

	[NP *aphān*]ᴛ		[NP *angbòng*]ʀ	
amātsi	e-tūm	aphān=ke	dāk habít	angbòng=si
because	1INCL-PL	NSUBJ=TOP	here jungle	in.middle.of=FOC:RL

nangkethonti
nang=ke-thòn-tí
1/2:NSUBJ=NMLZ-drop-get.rid.off
'And then, she abandoned us here in the middle of the jungle.' [CST, HM 052]

Example (635) is from the same story as the previous two examples, but is from earlier in the story where the T argument is a third person instead of the first person. Interestingly, the storyteller first uses the non-subject marker *-phān* on the T argument, then mentions the locative R argument, which is rather complex and lengthy, and then again mentions the T argument, this time without *-phān*. The reason for this change in marking could be that the storyteller corrected himself and wanted to leave the T argument unmarked, perhaps because he decided to use -*pī* to indicate the mother of the children as the maleficiary and hence primary non-subject argument in a quasi-applicative construction (see §13.2.3.2). However, a possibly better, pragmatically-based explanation is that the storyteller simply wants to remind the listeners of the identity of the T referent, and leaves it unmarked for predicate role, following the pragmatic principle of 'if the role of an argument is obvious, leave it unmarked' (see §13.1.2, Chapter 14).

(635) Trivalent predicate with unmarked(?) T argument and -*lòng*-marked locative non-human R argument

pu amat la Karbipi langhe kedam aphi
[pu   amāt   là   Karbì-pī   lànghē   ke-dàm   aphī
QUOT and.then this PN-FEM washing.place NMLZ-go after

laso aosomar, Hingchong musoso atum aphan

[NP *aphān*]$_T$

[lasō   a-oso-màr   Hingchòng   musōsō   a-tūm   aphān]
this POSS-child-PL CONSTELLATION siblings:DL POSS-PL NSUBJ

ha same sadu akrong alat votek

[NP *alòng*]$_R$

há   samé   sadú   a-króng   a-lat   vōtèk
over.there path EE:samé POSS-CLF:road POSS-EE:króng wild.bird

ingrengre voso ingrengre along

ingrèng-Cē   vōsō   ingrèng-Cē   alòng
call(small.animals)-NEG EE:vōtèk call(small.animals)-NEG LOC

osomar ponpidam'et thondam'et

[NP]$_T$

osō-mār pòn-pī-dām-ét   thòn-dām-ét
child-PL take.away-BEN/MAL-GO-PRF drop-GO-PRF

'And then, after the Karbi woman has gone to the water place, these Hingchong sisters, over there, she went to carry the children to a place where the roads cross, where the birds don't sing, (she) took the children and left them there.' [CST, HM 014]

In (636), the verb is again *thòn* 'drop; take T to R', and the T argument again has a human referent while the R argument again has a non-human referent. This example demonstrates, however, that the R argument may remain unmarked, as *skúl* does here.

(636) Trivalent predicate with *aphān*-marked human T argument and unmarked non-human R argument
[...] *apai abangsi mane kechengpenke*

[NP]₀			
a-pāi	abàng=si	mane	ke-chèng=pen=ke
POSS-mother	NPDL=FOC:RL	I.mean(<Asm)	NMLZ-begin=from=TOP

osomar aphan skul thondunnangji

[NP *aphān*]ₜ		[NP]ᵣ	
[osō-mār	a-phān]	skúl	thòn-dūn-náng-jí
child-PL	POSS-NSUBJ	school(<Eng)	drop-JOIN-need-IRR2

'[...] The mothers, from the beginning on (when the children start going to school), they have to take the children to school.' [KaR, SWK 048]

Finally, an elicited (translated) example shows that this construction may also be used when both T and R have human referents (637). Note, however, that this entirely independently elicited example has the same basic meaning as the corpus example in (629) above, which instead occurs in the R-marked construction. This illustrates clearly the pragmatic basis of the differences between these trivalent constructions.

(637) Human T and R referents in T-marked construction

[NP]₀		[NP *alòng*]ₜ		[NP *aphān*]ᵣ		
alàng-lì	a-phì		alòng=si	osō	aphān	tekáng-bùp
3-HON	POSS-grandmother		LOC=FOC:RL	child	NSUBJ	leave.for-RES:gone

'She left the child with the grand mother.'

In sum, the T-marked construction in all cases has a human T referent, whereas the R participant may or may not have a human referent.

13.2.1.3.3 Unmarked trivalent construction

Verbs such as *thàp* 'put inside' require a T and an R object but both are typically inanimate, as in (638) and (639). In both examples, T remains unmarked. R is marked by the general locative *-lòng* in (638), and by the more semantically specific *arlō* 'inside' in (639).

(638) Trivalent predicate with unmarked non-human T argument and *alòng*-marked non-human R argument
lapenke... phatang along thesere thaplelo... [...]

	[NP *alòng*]ᵣ		[NP]ₜ	
lapèn=ke	[phatáng	alòng]	theseré	thàp-lè-lò
and.then=TOP	BASKET	LOC	fruits	put.inside-again-RL

'And then, he again put fruits in the *phatang* basket [...].' [SiT, PS 044]

(639) Trivalent predicate with unmarked non-human T argument and *arlō*-marked non-human R argument
[...] *anke amonit abang<a> pe akelokpen keroi isi*

[NP]_A			[NP *arlō*]_R		
[ánke	[a-monít	abàng]	[[pé a-ke-lòk=pen	ke-ròi	isī
and.then	POSS-man	NPDL	cloth POSS-NMLZ-be.white=with	NMLZ-sew	one

ajamborong arlosi lahai kethap lapen arum kevan

		[NP]_T		
a-jamboróng	arlō̄=si]	[laháI] ke-thàp]]	lapèn	[arúm
POSS-bag	inside=FOC:RL	these NMLZ-put.inside	and	down
ke-vàn]]				
NMLZ-bring				

'[...] [A]nd then, the man, into a bag sown from white cloth he puts these (fruit), and then brings them down.' [SiT, PS 003]

The unmarked construction appears to be the preferred choice when both T and R have non-human referents (but see (635) above).

13.2.1.3.4 Summary: Trivalent constructions

The previous sections have shown three trivalent constructions: R-marked, T-marked, and unmarked. One possible analysis is to consider the T-marked and the unmarked constructions as two subtypes of the same basic construction. Example (635) above, where a T-marked construction 'changes' to an unmarked construction in spontaneous speech may be considered to provide some support for such an analysis.

If we combine the T-marked and the unmarked types into a single basic construction, we can then analyze this single basic construction as a 'transitive' motion construction where 'R' is actually the goal argument, and 'T' is actually 'O'. Doing that would at first seem like an improvement in making the facts about Karbi look more systematic: the differential marking of T (with or without -*phān*; i.e., the T-marked and the unmarked subtypes) is really just the differential marking of O (with or without -*phān*); and motion constructions, which exist for 'intransitives' (which then have an S plus a goal argument), also exist for 'transitives' (which then have an A plus an O plus a goal argument).

At present, this analysis remains a hypothesis, and further research will need to investigate whether the T-marked/unmarked construction and the basic transitive construction have further commonalities.

Finally note that there may be at least three factors that play a role in the choice of the trivalent construction. First, certain verbs may always occur in a single construction. For example, *paklàng* 'show' only occurs in the R-marked construction in the evidence shown above. Second, the referential properties of R and T may call for (or at least rule out) certain constructions. For example, the combination of a human R referent and a non-human T referent may only occur in the R-marked construction.[131] Note that these first two factors are not independent from each other since a verb such as *paklàng* requires a human (or personified) R referent. Third, pragmatic factors play an important role. As we have seen above (compare (629) and (637)), the same event, once in an example of spontaneous speech and once in an (independently) elicited example based on translation, is expressed in either the R-marked or the T-marked construction.

13.2.1.4 Alignment in typical declarative clauses

Cross-linguistically, there are two types of alignment. First, alignment is about whether S aligns with A or with O, or neither in mono- and bivalent constructions. Second, it is about whether O aligns with R or with T, or neither in bi- and trivalent constructions.

By comparing the typical monovalent and bivalent declarative clause constructions, we can see that S and A are both unmarked, while there is a split in O marking such that O-low is unmarked and O-high is marked by *-phān*. Therefore, the O-high construction has O marked different from S and A, suggesting nominative alignment for S and A. However, in the O-low construction, O is equally unmarked, just like S and A, suggesting a neutral alignment system.

For the other type of alignment across bi- and trivalent constructions, the situation is even more complex, because there is not only O-high and O-low, but there are also several trivalent constructions. In the R-marked construction, R is marked the same as O-high via *-phān* 'non-subject', and T is unmarked like O-low. In the T-marked construction, T is marked the same as O-high via *-phān* 'non-subject', while R is either unmarked like O-low or marked locative via *-lòng* or a semantically more specific relator noun. In the unmarked construction, neither R nor T are marked by *-phān* and are thus equally treated like O-low participants. As suggested in the previous section, it may be possible to analyze the T-marked/unmarked constructions as a 'transitive motion' construction, but this requires more research.

These issues that arise in the attempt to identify alignment in Karbi serve as evidence that participant marking in Karbi does not have a firm syntactic basis.[132]

---

[131] Furthermore, the same verb *thòn* 'take T to R' participates in the R-centered construction if T has a non-human referent and R has a human referent, and it participates in a T-centered construction if T has a human referent and R has a non-human referent.

[132] Note that constituent order does not help with clarifying questions about alignment in Karbi. Karbi is predominantly verb-final, and the position of a constituent relative to the verb is therefore generally not helpful. At the same time, clause participants may occur following the verb, but this is argued to be determined by pragmatic rather than syntactic factors in §14.2.6.1.

13.2.2 Declarative clause constructions with non-typical role marking of arguments

The following subsections discuss declarative clause constructions that deviate from the typical role-marking shown above, most of them in favor of more semantically-based role marking.

13.2.2.1 Motion constructions with unmarked and -*lòng* marked goals

Motion verbs such as *dùn* 'follow; join', *dàm* 'go', *lè* 'reach', or *vùr* 'drop in; stop by', often occur with overtly expressed goal participants.

However, it depends on the particular verb, how overt goal participants are marked, or whether we may even consider them goal arguments (i.e., conceptually required participants). And overt goal participant marking also depends on the referent, particularly whether it is human or non-human. Finally, pragmatic factors also appear to play a role.

First, let's consider *dùn* 'follow; join'. Example (640) has a non-human referent goal, which remains unmarked, while (641) has a human referent goal, which in both clauses of this example is marked by the general locative -*lòng*.

(640) *dùn* 'join' with unmarked non-human goal
*ansi **ha hithi** dunlo [...]*
ánsi   **[há   hithi]**_{GOAL/?O}   dùn-lò
after.that **over.there market(<Asm)**   join-RL
'And then, there they **went to the market** [...].' [KK, BMS 081]

(641) *dùn* 'join' with -*lòng*-marked human goal
***apiso along** chidunkri*
[[a-pisò   alòng]_{GOAL/O} chV-dūn-krì]
POSS-wife LOC   RR-join-follow.closely

*laso **abamonpi along** dunkrilo*
[[lasō a-bamón-pī   alòng]_{GOAL/O} dùn-krì-lò]
this   POSS-wise.person(<Ind)-female LOC   join-follow.closely-RL
'He **followed his wife** closely, he **followed this *bamonpi*** closely.' [KK, BMS 082]

The same pattern of leaving a non-human referent goal unmarked but marking a human referent with -*lòng* is found with *dàm* 'go' in (642) and (643).

(642) *dàm* 'go' with unmarked non-human goal
*amatsi "Bokolapo abangke **bojar** dam'etlo"[...]*
amātsi   Bokolāpō abàng=ke   **[bojár]**_{GOAL/?O} dàm-ét-lò
and.then NAME   NPDL=TOP   **market(<Asm)**   go-PRF-RL
'[The children thought that] Bokolapo had already **gone to the market**.' [HI, BPh 010]

13.2 The predicate: Defining argument roles — 415

(643) *dàm* 'go' with *alòng*-marked human goal
*[...] **nangphihai along** damnói dei*
[nang-phì-hái   alòng]_GOAL/?O   dàm-nōi   déi
2POSS-grandmother-HON LOC   go-INFRML.COND.IMP OK?
'[...] **[G]o to your grandmother**, ok?' [KK, CC 016]

Example (644) shows that with *vùr* 'drop in, stop by', the location where one 'stops by' has a non-human referent here and is also left unmarked.

(644) *vùr* 'drop in, stop by' with unmarked non-human goal
sì ladakpen damlo Dimapur vurpon sa
sì   ladāk=pen dàm-lò [Dimápúr]_GOAL/?O vùr-pōn   sá
therefore here=from go-RL   PLACE   drop.in-in.passing tea(<Ind)

junponlang
jùn-pōn-làng
drink-in.passing-still
'And then, from here we went, we stopped by Dimapur and just had tea.'
[SiT, HF 009]

Examples (645) and (646) once again show that with *lè* 'reach', we get the same pattern of marking a human referent goal with *-lòng* while leaving a non-human referent goal unmarked.

(645) *lè* 'reach' with *-lòng*-marked +human goal
*lapenke **la thesere kelikbom amonit along** nanglelo*
lapèn=ke [[là [theseré ke-lík-bòm]   a-monít] alòng]_GOAL/?O
and=TOP   this fruit   NMLZ-pluck-CONT   POSS-man LOC
nang=lè-lò
CIS-reach-RL
'And then, he came to the fruit picking man.' [SiT, PS 016]

(646) *lè* 'reach' with unmarked non-human goal
*penke damsi isi aporke **Kohima rongsopi** lelo... [...]*
pèn=ke   dàm-si   isī a-pór=ke   [Kóhìmà ròngsōpī]_GOAL/?O
and.then=TOP go-NF:RL one POSS-time=TOP   PLACE   town
lè-lò
reach-RL
'And then (we) went and at one o'clock, we reached Kohima Town [...].'
[SiT, HF 017]

However, (647) shows that a non-human referent goal may also be marked with *-lòng* 'locative', not just +human referent goals, here also with *lè* 'reach'.

(647) *lè* 'reach' with *-lòng*-marked non-human goal
 [...] festival aground along lele ako abángke...
 [festival a-ground along]~GOAL/?O~ lè-Cē akó abàng=ke]
 festival POSS-ground LOC reach-NEG before NPDL=TOP
 '[...] [B]efore we reached the festival grounds...' [SiT, HF 026]

The same is true for the goal of *vàng* 'come', where non-human referent goals may also be marked with *-lòng* as in (648), or unmarked as in (649).

(648) *vàng* 'come' with *-lòng*-marked non-human goal
 *penap **Rongker alongsi** vangpo {mm} [...]*
 penàp [Ròngkèr alòng=si]~GOAL/?O~ vàng-pò mm
 tomorrow **festival(kd) LOC=FOC:RL** come-IRR1 AFF
 'Tomorrow we will come to (the place of) the *rongker* [...].' [HK, TR 107]

(649) *vàng* 'come' with unmarked non-human goal
 *an ansi **ahem arit** chevánglo, [...]*
 [án ánsi [a-hēm a-rīt]~GOAL/?O~ che-vāng-lò]
 that.much after.that **POSS-house POSS-field** RR-come-RL
 'And then they came home to their house and property [...].' [KK, BMS 113]

It is perhaps surprising that *vàng* 'come' allows the same options for marking goals as more inherently goal-oriented motion verbs, considering that *vàng* is inherently more source-oriented and more frequently occurs with overtly expressed source participants in the text corpus, which, however, are then marked with ablative =*pen*.

While the required argument status of goals for motion verbs has been argued for other Tibeto-Burman languages such as Galo (Post 2007: 417), in Karbi any motion verb may take unmarked goal participants, and even non-motion verb may take unmarked locative participants. This is further shown in §14.1.1.

13.2.2.2 'Need' construction
The verb *náng* 'need' requires two arguments: the participant who needs something, which I will refer to as the A argument, and the participant that is needed, which I will refer to as the O argument. As shown in the elicited sentence in (650), the A argument may be marked by *-phān* 'non-subject', but this is in fact optional in the sense that some speakers will mark the A argument of *náng* 'need' with *-phān*, and others

will not.[133] It is an open question at this point, whether this is a dialectal difference. According to my consultants, it is 'more correct' to use *-phān* here.

(650) 'Need' construction

[PRO (*-phān*)]_A	[NP]_O

ne-li(-phān)   kolóm   náng-jí
1EXCL-HON-NSUBJ   pen   need-IRR2
'I need a pen.' [Elicitation]

13.2.2.3 Existential copula constructions: Simple locative and possessive constructions

There are several constructions indicating location and possession that involve the existential copula *dō*, with the suppletive negative form *avē* (§6.2.2.1.1). Besides the simple locative construction, there are two different possession constructions that differ in how A and O are marked, with unclear effects on the semantic or pragmatic interpretation.

13.2.2.3.1 Simple locative construction

The simple locative construction expresses 'X is.at Y', where 'Y' represents the location. The 'subject' X is always unmarked for role, while the location Y may be unmarked as well or marked by either the general locative *-lòng* or by a more semantically specific relator noun. This is demonstrated with (651), where the location is marked by *-lòng*, and by (652), where the location is unmarked.

(651) Simple locative (with relator noun)
"[...] *richoke ha pharla alongsi pohui moidai along doji* [...]"
richó=ke   [há   pharlá alòng=si]_{LOC}   [[pohùi mòidāi]
king=TOP   over.there   porch LOC=FOC:RL   pillow backrest
alòng]_{LOC}   dō-jì
LOC   exist-IRR2
"'[...] [T]he king will be over there in his *pharla*, on his comfortable bed (lit., on his pillows and back cushions) [...].'" [CST, HM 044]

---

133 There is no example of *náng* 'need' with overt A and O arguments in the corpus of recorded texts. The following example demonstrates, however, an unmarked O argument of *náng* despite having a human referent:

[...] {e la **monitsi** kenangpohe [...]}
e   là   **monít=si**   ke-náng-pò=he
INTERJ this **man=FOC:RL** NMLZ-need-IRR1=AFTERTHOUGHT
'[...] {Human beings (they) need [...].}' [HK, TR 042]

(652) Simple locative (without relator noun)
*anke <tovar> **tovar** longle adukta dopiklo*
ánke   <továr>   **[továr]**_{LOC}   [lònglē a-dūk=tā]   dō-pìk-lò
and.then road   **road**   earth   POSS-dust=ADD   exist-very-RL
'And then, there is also a lot of dust on the road.' [SH, CSM 018]

Since the verb used in the simple locative construction is the existential copula, it perhaps comes as no surprise that the existential construction may be structurally identical, if a locative participant is added. Examples (653) and (654) show that existential clauses with added locatives are parallel to simple locatives in that the locative may also be either unmarked or marked by a locative relator noun.

(653) Existential with locative (without relator noun)
*hako arni tangho {mm} **enut arecho***
hákó   arnì tànghò {mm} [[e-nūt   a-rechó]
that.time day   REP   AFF   **one-CLF:HUM:SG**   POSS-king

***arong** {mm} jangreso.... do tangho {mm}*
a-ròng]_{LOC}   {mm}   jàngrēsō....   dō   tànghò   {mm}
POSS-village   AFF   single.parent.child   exist   REP   AFF
'In the old days (once upon a time), in a king's village, there was an orphan.' [HK, TR 002]

(654) Existential with locative (with relator noun)
*[...] **aphong arong along** <theng> vo ikpo*
[a-phòng   **a-rōng**   **alòng]**_{LOC}   <theng>   vō   ík-pō
POSS-wild.jackfruit   **POSS-plant**   **LOC**   <tree..> bird   be.black-MODIF

vo thepo do
vō   thè-pō   dō]
bird   be.big-MODIF   exist
'[...] [B]y the wild jackfruit tree, there is <a tr(ee)..> a huge black bird.' [SeT, MTN 018]

13.2.2.3.2 Predicational possession construction with unmarked A/possessor and possessive-marked O/possessed

In one of the two predicational possession constructions, the possessor (or arguably, A argument) is unmarked, while the possessed (or arguably, O argument) is also unmarked with respect to role marking, but carries the appropriate possessive prefix. Examples (655) through (657) illustrate this construction.

In the main corpus, this construction is used when the possessed element is a bound noun that requires a possessive prefix (§5.5). Preliminary elicitation suggests that the same construction can be used even if the possessed element is not a bound noun; see also the discussion in the next section.

(655) Possession construction with unmarked A, 2nd person possessive-marked O
"*nangdun nangne*" *puta, kroikredetlo,*
[nang-dùn　　náng-Cē　　pu=tā]　　　　　　　　[krōi-Cē-dèt-lò]
CIS-join　　need-NEG　QUOT=ADD:although　agree-NEG-PFV-RL

"***nangke nangdin*** *dolang*"
[nàng=ke]$_{A/POSR}$　[nang-dín]$_{O/POSD}$　dō-làng]
2=TOP　　　　　　2POSS-day(<Asm)　exist-still
'Although (she) said, "(You) shouldn't follow me!", he didn't agree (saying), "You still have your life to live (lit. days)."' [KK, BMS 084]

(656) Possession construction with unmarked A and 1st person exclusive possessive-marked O
*[...] amat **neta neri** ave **nekeng** ave [...]*
amāt　　　[nè=tā]$_{A/POSR}$　[ne-rí]$_{O/POSD}$　　avē　　　[ne-kèng]$_{O/POSD}$
and.then　1EXCL=ADD　　1EXCL:POSS-hand　not.exist　1EXCL:POSS-foot
avē
not.exist
'[...] [A]nd then also, I don't have hands or feet [...].' [RBT, ChM 030]

(657) Possession construction with unmarked A and 3rd person possessive-marked O
*[...] jongsi **phakok abang athu** do pulote...*
jóngsi　[phàk-ōk　abàng]$_{A/POSR}$　[a-thú]$_{O/POSD}$　dō　　pulote
if　　　pig-meat　NPDL　　　　　POSS-fat　　　　exist　if
'[...] [I]f there is fat on the pork...' [PI, BPR 002]

Note that marking of O as possessed by A is a semantic, not syntactic requirement, hence examples like (658) are possible, where the A referent 'we (inclusive)' includes the O referent 'you'.

(658) Possession construction with first inclusive A and second-person-possessive O
[...] "itum nangpeile kedo kalilo" [...]
[[i-tūm]$_{A/POSR}$　[nang-pēi=le]$_{O/POSD}$　　ke-dō　　　　kalī-lò
1INCL=PL　　　　2:POSS-mother=FOC:IRR　NMLZ-exist　NEG.EQU.COP-RL
'[...] "We don't have your mother anymore." [...]' [CST, RO 008]

This possession construction is best considered a specific type of the topical possessor construction (§13.2.2.4).

13.2.2.3.3 Predicational possession construction with locative-marked A and unmarked O argument

Possession can also be expressed in a construction that marks the possessor A as a locative and leaves the O unmarked with respect to both role marking as well as possessive marking. This is the construction that speakers typically use when translating a simple possessive clause from English if the possessed element is not a bound noun root (see previous section). The elicited sentence in (659) can be used in contexts of both having money in general (being a rich person) as well as having money on oneself in the present moment.

(659) Possession construction with locative marked A and unmarked O
 [ne-lòng]$_{POSR}$ [tángká]$_{POSD}$ dō
 1EXCL-LOC money exist
 'I have money.' SiT 190515

There are no clear examples of this construction in the corpus because the possessor is always left out. This fact is actually suggestive of a functional difference between the two possession constructions discussed in this and the previous section: the unmarked O and the possessive-marked O constructions. If the unmarked O construction typically occurs without an overt possessor A argument then it is clear that the A argument is not highlighted in this construction. On the other hand, in the possessive-marked O construction, the possessor is more commonly overtly expressed as well as again marked on the possessed noun via a possessive prefix. Therefore this construction highlights the possessor. A text example of the unmarked O construction with no possessor overtly expressed is (660). In this example, the possessor is a continuing topic and the focus is on the various possessions of his. This illustrates that in the unmarked O construction the emphasis is more on the possessed items, which can be contrasted with the possessive-marked O construction in the previous section where the emphasis is on the possessor.

(660) Unmarked O possession construction
 nopak dolo chingjor dolo {mm} hak dolo {mm}
 nopàk dō-**lò** chingjòr dō-**lò** hák dō-**lò**
 dao exist-**RL** shovel exist-**RL** finely.woven.b.basket exist-**RL**
 '(He) had a dao, he had a shovel, he had a finely woven bamboo basket.' [HK, TR 024]

13.2.2.4 Topical possessor construction

The topical possessor construction presents the possessor of a (logical) argument of the clause as the actual argument that receives role marking, while at the same time treating it as a (left-dislocated) topic (§14.2.5). In (661), the logical O argument *a-prán (a-múi)* 'her life' of the verb *ēn* 'take' does not receive non-subject marking via *-phān*, but the 'possessor' of 'her life', *nepiso* 'my wife' is marked with *-phān* instead while being left-dislocated.

(661) Topical possessor construction
*kosonloma ne laso... <e> **nepiso aphan** ne*
[kosón=lo=ma nè lasō] <e> **[[ne-pisò a-phān]$_{POSR}$** nè
how=FOC=Q 1EXCL this <e> **1EXCL-wife POSS-NSUBJ** 1EXCL

apran endet amui endetta bang
a-prán ēn-dèt a-múi ēn-dèt-tā] bàng
POSS-life take-PFV POSS-EE:prán(<Ind) take-PFV-if CLF:HUM:PL

sankur sankamaita echethanpo
sán-kúr sán-kamái=tā e=che-thán-pò
five(<Pnr)-clan five(<Pnr)-EE:kúr=ADD 1PL.INCL=RR-tell-IRR1
'How I (should do) this...? If I take my wife's life, everybody will criticize us.'
[CST, RO 045]

This kind of external possessor marking construction is common in Tibeto-Burman as well as cross-linguistically (see Bickel (2001) and references therein as well as van Driem (1991)).

In (662), the verb *luksón* is intransitive and *aso* 'its children' is the S argument, while the possessor is left-dislocated. There is no role marking on the possessor since S arguments are not role-marked.

(662) Left-dislocated topical possessor, not role-marked
*[...] **lata** aso kaluksonlo*
[là=tā]$_{POSR}$ [a-sō]$_S$ ke-luksón-lò
this=ADD POSS-child NMLZ-be.lost(<Asm)-RL
'[...] [A]nd so as for it (the bird), its offspring were lost.' [RBT, ChM 022]

While the previous two examples suggest that this construction may indicate that the possessor is strongly affected by the event, this is not actually always the case. In the last line in (663), *halata* refers to 'Bey the Fair', and the following proposition is about his children: *asomar thelo dinglo* 'his children grew up'. That is, the possessor construction can also be used to keep the possessor a topic, not only if the possessor is conceptualized as being affected.

(663) Left-dislocated possessor, not affected
asomar thelo dinglo anke Bey Ke'et
a-oso-màr   thè-lò   dīng-lò   ánke   [[Bēy   ke-èt
POSS-child-PL be.big-RL be.long-RL and.then   CLAN   NMLZ-be.yellow

abangta lason thakthaklo piso some enlo potsi
abàng=tā]   lasón   thakthāk-lò]   [pīsō   sōmē   ēn-lò]   apōt=si
NPDL=ADD   that.way   same-RL   wife   EE:pīsō take-RL   reason=FOC:RL

halata asomar thelo dinglo
[[hála=tā]~POSR~   [a-oso-màr]~s~   thè-lò   dīng-lò]
that=ADD   POSS-child-PL   be.big-RL be.long-RL
'His children were growing up and then Bey the Fair also did the same and he got married and as for him also, his children grew up.' [WR, BCS 006]

The possession construction with unmarked A and possessive-marked O (§13.2.2.3.2) is best considered a subtype of this topical possessor construction.

13.2.2.5 Comparative constructions

Finally, there are several different comparative constructions that employ different types of role marking. In one type, the comparative construction structurally resembles a transitive construction in Karbi. In (664) and (665), the standard of comparison is marked by *-phān* 'non-subject', while the participant that is being compared remains unmarked. The verb may or may not be marked by *-mū~-mūchòt* 'comparative' in this construction. Note that in (664), the standard of comparison is additionally marked by *-te*, which could be the conditional *-te* (§9.7.3).

(664) Comparative *-mū~-mūchòt* with overtly mentioned standard of comparison
[methān   a-phān-te]   ingnàr   thè-mū
dog   POSS-NSUBJ-COND?   elephant   be.big-COMPAR
'Elephants are bigger than dogs.' [SiT 090221]

(665) Comparative construction without *-mū~-mūchòt*
opeija nephanta halasi nangsarlang
opeija   ne-phān=tā   hála=si   nang=sàr-làng
my.goodness! 1EXCL-NSUBJ=ADD   that=FOC:RL   1/2:NSUBJ=be.old-still
'Oh my goodness! This one is even older than me! (*both laughing*)' [HK, TR 098]

This *-te* in *aphante* in (664) may further be the same element as the second syllable in *mutē* 'compared to' in (666), which marks the standard of comparison here. The first syllable could be related to *-mū* 'comparative'.

(666) Comparative construction with *mutē* 'compared.to', *akelé* 'more', *-pìk* 'very'
[...] pinsomar atum mute arlosomar atumsi
pinsō-mār   a-tūm   mutē   árlosō-mār a-tūm=si
married.man-PL POSS-PL compared.to woman-PL POSS-PL=FOC:RL

akele klempik pu [...]
akelé   klém-pìk pu
more   do-very   QUOT
'[...] [C]ompared to the men, it was the women who did much more (work), (I heard) [...].' [KaR, SWK 070]

13.2.3 Predicates with derivationally changed argument structure

Causative *pe-~pa-* and benefactive/malefactive (affective) *-pī* have an effect on argument structure as demonstrated by the examples and discussion below. These changes in argument structure that the two affixes cause make them different from instrumental/comitative *-ī*, which leaves the instrumental/comitative participant marked with *=pen* (§9.2.5.2.2).

13.2.3.1 Causative *pe-~pa-*
If the causative *pe-~pa-* occurs on monovalent verbs such as *thì* 'die' in (667), the original S argument becomes the new causee, which in Karbi appears to be treated like an O argument. In (667), the causee *osōmār* is marked non-subject via *-phān*.

(667) Former S becomes *aphān*-marked O
osomar aphan pathietnangta, kopu manalangma

[NP *aphān*]_{CAUSEE / O (<S)}

[[osō-mār   aphān]   pa-thì-èt-nangtā]   kopù
child-PL   NSUBJ   CAUS-die-all:S/O-if.alternatively how
mán-jí-lāng=ma
become-IRR2-still=Q
'Also if I kill the children, how will it be? (i.e., it won't be good either).' [CST, RO 047]

As causative *pe-~pa-* occurs on bivalent verbs, the effect on argument structure varies. In (668), the causee and former A argument is marked non-subject via *-phān*, while the former O argument remains unmarked.

(668) Former A becomes *aphān*-marked ?R
si methan-sibongpo aphansi hem pahonlo [...]

[NP *aphān*]_{CAUSEE / ?R (<A)}		[NP]_{?T(<O)}	
[sì	[methān-sibóngpō aphān=si]	hēm	pa-hón-lò]
therefore	dog-SPECIES NSUBJ=FOC:RL	house	CAUS-look.after-RL

'Therefore, they made the dog look after the house [...].' [KK, BMS 011]

However, in (669), the causee and former A argument is not marked by *-phān*, but is unmarked.

(669) Former A becomes unmarked ?R
[...] "nangpai an patunnang" pu

[NP]_{CAUSEE / ?R (<A)}	[NP]_{?T(<O)}		
nang-pāi	àn	pa-tún-nāng	pu]
2-mother	rice	CAUS-cook-HORT	QUOT

'[...] "Let (or let's let) your mother cook rice.", (she said).' [KK, CC 018]

The text example (670) and elicitation based on this example provided in (671) show that further argument marking options exist, perhaps specifically with the verb *chetòng* 'meet' and a human referent O argument. Example (670) shows that the former O argument may also be marked by *-phān*, and it is unclear how the former A argument would be marked in that case. Alternatively, as shown in (671), the former O argument may be marked by *=pen* 'with' (§14.1.4.1.1), while the former A argument may receive marking via *-phān*. It is impossible, however, to mark both arguments with *-phān*.

(670) Former O becomes *aphān*-marked ?T
ne nephi aphan nangpachetongvekji [...]

[NP]_{CAUSER / A}	[NP *aphān*]_{?T(<O)}	
nè	ne-phì	aphān nang=pV-chetòng-vék-jí
1EXCL	1EXCL-grandmother	NSUBJ 1/2:NSUBJ=CAUS-meet-definitely-IRR2

'I will definitely make you meet my grandmother [...].' [KK, BMS 029]

(671) Former O becomes *=pen*-marked ?T, A becomes *aphān*-marked ?R
ne nephipen nangphan

[NP]_{CAUSER / A}	[NP=*pen*]_{?T(<O)}	[NP -*phān*]_{?R(<A)}
nè	ne-phì=pen	nang-phān
1EXCL	1EXCL-grandmother=with	2-NSUBJ

nangpachetongvekji
nang=pV-chetòng-vék-jí
1/2:NSUBJ=CAUS-meet-definitely-IRR2
'I will definitely make you meet my grandmother.' [Elicitation based on KK, BMS 029]

13.2.3.2 Benefactive/malefactive (affective) -*pī*

Adding the suffix -*pī* to the verb indicates that there is an argument that is affected by the particular event described by the predicate; the affected argument may be a beneficiary or a maleficiary (§9.2.5.2.1). If overtly expressed, the beneficiary or maleficiary is non-subject-marked with -*phān*, as shown in (672).

(672) Beneficiary marked with *aphān* 'non-subject'
[...] *hadaksi **kadokave la Diphu asor aphan** kecho*
[hádāk=si   [kadókavē   là   Diphú [a-sòr   aphān]]_BEN ke-chō
there=FOC:RL all   this PN   POSS-people   NSUBJ   NMLZ-eat

*kejun nangsik**pi**lo hadaksi netum an*
ke-jùn   nang=sík-**pī**-lò]   [hádāk=si   ne-tūm   àn
NMLZ-drink   1/2:NSUBJ=prepare-**BEN/MAL**-RL   there=FOC:RL   1EXCL-PL   rice

cholo han cholo
chō-lò   hán   chō-lò]
eat-RL   prepared.vegetables   eat-RL
'[...] [T]here, they prepared meals **for all of us Diphu people**, there we had our meal.' [SH, CSM 054]

However, (673) shows that the affected argument may also remain unexpressed via zero anaphora (§13.4.3). We know that this is a case of zero anaphora because the verb is marked by -*pī*. Context makes it clear that here the maleficiary (rather than a beneficiary) is the mother of the children, *la Karbipi*, mentioned at the beginning of this text unit.

(673) Maleficiary as zero anaphora
*pu amat **la Karbipi** langhe kedam aphi*
[pu   amāt   là   Karbì-**pī**   lànghē   ke-dàm   aphī]
QUOT   and.then this PN-FEM   washing.place   NMLZ-go   after

laso aosomar Hingchong musoso atum aphan
[[lasō   a-oso-màr   Hingchòng   musōsō   a-tūm   aphān]
this   POSS-child-PL   CONSTELLATION   siblings:DL   POSS-PL   NSUBJ

ha same sadu akrong alat votek
[há   samé sadú   a-króng   a-lat   vōtèk
over.there path EE:samé POSS-CLF:road POSS-EE:króng wild.bird

ingrengre voso ingrengre along
ingrèng-Cē   vōsō   ingrèng-Cē   alòng]
call(small.animals)-NEG EE:vōtèk call(small.animals)-NEG LOC

*osomar pon**pi**dam'et thondam'et*
[osō-mār]   pòn-**pī**-dām-ét   thòn-dām-ét]
child-PL   take.away-**BEN/MAL**-GO-PRF drop-go-PRF
'And then, after the Karbi woman has gone to the water place, these Hingchong sisters, over there, she went to carry the children to a place where the roads cross, where the birds don't sing, (she) took the children and left them there.' [CST, HM 014]

Finally, (674) suggests that an affected argument, here the beneficiary *arnám* 'god(s)', may be included and marked by *-phān* without the verb being marked by *-pī*.

(674) Beneficiary marked with *-phān* 'non-subject' without benefactive marking on verb
*tangka atibuksi **ronji la arnam aphan**,*
[[tángká a-tíbùk=si]   **ròn-jí**]   [[là   arnàm aphān]
money POSS-earthen.pot=FOC:RL **distribute-IRR2** this god   NSUBJ

latum a'arnam aphan {avan along} avan
[là-tūm a-arnàm aphān]]$_{\text{BEN}}$ {[a-ván   alòng]} [a-ván
this-PL POSS-god NSUBJ   POSS-share LOC   POSS-share

*along tangka atibuk **nunrenpo** lasi*
alòng] [tángká a-tíbùk]   **nún-rèn-pò**   lasì
LOC   money POSS-earthen.pot place.container-in.a.row-IRR1 therefore
'(The tigers) distribute/offer the money pots **for the god, for their gods**, {on their plates (of offerings)}, and they will put the money pots in one long row' [HK, TR 111]

This raises the question of whether we can actually ascribe an argument-structure-changing force to *-pī*. The example in (674) shows that the argument structure can be changed in the same way in the absence of *-pī*. Of course, there should be more examples than just this one.[134] But if this turns out to be a more productive pattern, then it

---

[134] Note, however, that this example was judged grammatically unproblematic by two independent native speakers, in the course of working through the analysis of this folk story.

13.2.4 Non-subject speech act participant indexing on the verb

The only participants cross-referenced on the verb are speech act participants (SAPs) in non-subject roles. The details about this phenomenon are discussed in §8.3.1.

What should be added here is that there are instances of *nang=* that follow in line with evidence presented by Bickel (2001) on different agreement relations in Tibeto-Burman. An example is (675), where the beneficiary NP '(for) all of the Diphu people' is cross-referenced on the verb by *nang=*, which through context is disambiguated to be first person plural 'we'. This is similar to Bickel's (2001: 586) 'partitional' agreement, "where the NP denotes a subset of the referents denoted by the agreement marker", though in an inverted sense, because here the 'agreement' *nang=* represents the subset of the referent denoted by the NP.

(675) (Inverted) 'partitional agreement' (Bickel 2001)
*[...] hadaksi **kadokave la Diphu asor aphan** kecho kejun*

hádāk=si	[kadókavē	là	Diphú	a-sòr	aphān]	ke-chō
there=FOC:RL	all	this	PN	POSS-people	NSUBJ	NMLZ-eat

ke-jùn
NMLZ-drink

***nang**sikpilo hadaksi netum an cholo*

nang=sík-pī-lò	hádāk=si	ne-tūm	àn	chō-lò
1/2:NSUBJ=prepare-BEN/MAL-RL	there=FOC:RL	1EXCL-PL	rice	eat-RL

han cholo
hán   chō-lò
prepared.vegetables   eat-RL
'[...] [T]here, they prepared meals **for all of us Diphu people**, there we had our meal.' [SH, CSM 054]

In (676), *nang=* cross-references the affected possessor of the O argument, which is a typical construction that *nang=* occurs in (§8.3.1.3). Interestingly, however, this example shows that the 'affected SAP possessor marking' of *nang=* 'frees up' the NP to highlight a different property of the possessor, which in this example is number information in the form of *bàng-hiní* 'two people'.

(676) nang= cross-referencing possessor
[...] ne banghini aphanta nangpran **nang**en'etji
nè   [bàng-hiní   aphān=ta]$_{POSR}$ [nang-prán]$_o$
1EXCL CLF:HUM:PL-two   NSUBJ=ADD   2:POSS-life
nang=ēn-èt-jí
1/2:NSUBJ=take-all:S/O-IRR2
'[...] I will take the lives of the both of you.' [CST, RO 019]

Note that the verbal proclitic nang= does not 'agree with' a particular syntactic role. The only generalization that holds (so far) is that it does not occur with subjects. It therefore does not represent a grammatical relations construction.

13.2.5 Other grammatical relations constructions

Apart from the dubious status of grammatical relations marking in declarative clauses, one grammatical domain in which grammatical relations appear to matter is in the set of predicate derivations which modify an argument. Some predicate derivations seem to modify or classify arguments that take on a particular syntactic role (§9.2.5.3). For example, -èt 'all:S/O' can be used with intransitive verb stems such as hingnō 'be bad' in (677), where it modifies the S argument.

(677) -èt 'all:S/O' with scope over S argument of hingnō 'be bad'
"nehem hingnoet nerit hingnoetsi..."
ne-hēm   hingnō-**èt**   ne-rīt   hingnō-**èt**-si
1EXCL:POSS-house   bad-**all:S/O**   1EXCL:POSS-field   bad-**all:S/O**-NF:RL
"'My house and everything is all destroyed and so...'" [RBT, ChM 071]

It also occurs with transitive verb stems such as pivir 'destroy' in (678), in which case the scope is over the O argument, i.e., the item destroyed.

(678) -èt 'all:S/O' with scope over O argument of pivir 'destroy'
"nangrong nangrim nangpiviretji sala"
nang-rōng   nang-rīm   nang-pi-vír-**èt**-jí   sala
2POSS-plant 2POSS-EE:rōng   1/2:NSUBJ-CAUS-be.lost-**all:S/O**-IRR2   damn.you!
"'I will destroy your stem and everything (i.e., your species), damn you!'"
[RBT, ChM 061]

This S/O or absolutive argument modification appears to be consistent in typical transitive construction (as discussed in §13.2.1.2). However, an example of the motion verb construction (§13.2.2.1) with lè 'reach' and its S (or A?) argument in (679) serves as a reminder that the unsolved status of grammatical relations in basic declarative clauses makes it difficult to talk about grammatical relations in other grammatical domains.

(679) *-èt* 'all:s/o' with scope over ?S argument of *lè* 'reach'
ladak nangkeleke abarika.... asarthe laheiheike
ladāk   nang=ke-lè=ke   a-bariká   a-sàrthè
here   CIS=NMLZ-reach=TOP   POSS-OFFICER   POSS-village.headman
lahei~hei=ke
these~DIST.PL=TOP

nangle'etlo {oi}
nang=lè-**èt**-lò   {ōi}
CIS=reach-**all:s/o**-RL yes
'As for those that have already arrived here, the *barika* and the *sarthe* and all the other important tigers have already arrived.' [HK, TR 186]

Nevertheless, certain predicate derivations do seem to reflect alignment of arguments across both intransitive and transitive constructions (in particular, alignment of S with O). In contrast, constructions in other grammatical domains often cited to reflect grammatical relations, such as agreement (§13.2.4), clause-chaining and clause coordination or pivots (§15.2.1 and §15.5), or relativization (§12.3) generally do not reflect alignment.

13.3 Overview: Clause participant marking

For each clause participant, choices need to be made as to whether or how it should be expressed, depending on a host of pragmatic, syntactic, and semantic factors. Figure 18 offers a representation of the options speakers have in argument expression. The arrows between slots 2 and 3, i.e., between the optional use of the noun phrase delimiter *abàng* and the role markers, indicate that either order occurs, i.e., 2 before 3 but also 3 before 2.

The remainder of this chapter as well as the next chapter together discuss the argument expression options as laid out in Figure 18. We start out with a participant in slot 1. The speaker has to decide to leave the argument unexpressed, i.e., as a zero anaphora, or to use a pronoun or a lexical noun phrase; this is discussed in §13.4. Then, Karbi has an element that may or may not be added, the 'noun phrase delimiter' *abàng*, discussed in §13.5. The options in role marking and in information/discourse structure marking are the topic of Chapter 14.

13.4 Lexical noun phrase versus pronoun versus zero anaphora

The choice of using either a lexical noun phrase, a pronoun, or zero anaphora depends on how the speaker models the information and activation status of the argument in

1	2 ↔	3	4
[Participant]	NPDL	Role	Inform./Discourse structure
[LEXICAL NP]	abàng	-ø	-ø
[PRONOUN]		-phān 'NSUBJ'	=ke 'TOP'
		-lòng 'LOC'	=tā 'ADD'
		[Other RNs/	=si 'FOC:RL'
		=pen]	=le 'FOC:IRR'
[ZERO ANAPHORA --]			

Figure 18: Schematic overview of argument expression in Karbi.

the addressee's mind, often relying quite strongly on the context to aid in the identification of the referent. While this is a highly complex process, where many sociolinguistic in addition to pragmatic variables determine the outcome, in what follows, I give text examples to illustrate some basic cases of this three-way distinction in argument expression.

13.4.1 Lexical noun phrase

A clause participant is expressed via a lexical noun phrase if the speaker assumes the addressee cannot uniquely identify its referent. This is the case when a referent is not activated – either because it is newly introduced or reintroduced – or if it is contrasted with another referent.

The term 'lexical noun phrase' is underspecified as to how much information is provided. A lexical noun phrase may consist of just a noun, or it may include a combination of modifiers (see Chapter 10). I use the term 'lexical noun phrase' in contrast with just 'noun phrase' in order to exclude pronouns. In (680), two new referents are introduced, one is the oblique participant 'in a king's village', the other is the S argument 'orphan'.

(680) Two newly introduced participants: locative *inut arecho arong* and S argument *jangreso*
hako arni tangho {mm} inut arecho
hákó   arnì tànghò {mm} [[e-nūt   a-rechó]
that.time day   REP   AFF one-CLF:HUM:SG POSS-king

*arong {mm} **jangreso**.... do tangho {mm}*
a-ròng]$_{OBL}$ {mm} **[jàngrēsō]**$_s$ ....   dō   tànghò {mm}
POSS-village AFF   **single.parent.child** exist   REP   AFF
'In the old days (once upon a time), in a king's village, there was an orphan (lit. the child of a single parent).' [HK, TR 002]

Sometimes a speaker uses zero anaphora or a pronoun in a clause, and then, apparently as an afterthought, judges the referent not uniquely identifiable and uses a lexical noun phrase to ensure correct identification of the argument, as with *jirpopo* in (681).

(681) Postposed full NP
anke damlo adapprang halatum damlo tangho, jirpopo {mm}
ánke   dàm-lò a-dappráng   hála-tūm dàm-lò tànghò **jīrpō~pō**
and.then go-RL POSS-dawn   that-PL   go-RL   REP   **friend~DUAL**
'And then, they went, early in the morning they went, the two friends.'
[HK, TR 146]

13.4.2 Pronoun

Pronouns are in a sense intermediate between a lexical noun phrase, which occurs when a participant is first introduced, and zero anaphora, which represents the absence of an overt reference to the argument. Example (682) starts out with a lexical noun phrase: 'among the Bey, there were three brothers'. In the following text unit, this participant is first referred to by the pronoun *latum* 'they', and then left out via zero anaphora in the next clause.

(682) Full NP *Bey atum / korte bangkethom* changing to pronoun *latum* (and to zero anaphora)
Bey atum korte bangkethom *do aklengsi abangke*
[**Bēy   a-tūm   kortè   bàng-kethòm**   dō] [a-klèng-sí
CLAN POSS-PL brother CLF:HUM:PL-three   exist POSS-old.one-SPLT
abàng=ke
NPDL=TOP

Bey Ki'ik adakvam abangke Bey Ke'et
Bēy   ke-ìk]   [adakvám   abàng=ke Bēy   ke-èt
CLAN NMLZ-be.black second.child NPDL=TOP CLAN NMLZ-be.yellow

akibi abangke Bey Ronghang
[a-ke-bī   abàng=ke Bēy   Ronghāng]
POSS-NMLZ-be.small   NPDL=TOP CLAN SUBCLAN
'(Among) the Bey, there were three brothers, the oldest one was Bey the Black, the second one was Bey the Fair, and the small one was Bey Ronghang.'
[WR, BCS 002]

anke **latum** thelo dinglo, ø piso some enlo tangho						
ánke	**la-tūm**	thè-lò	dīng-lò	ø	pīsō	sōmē
and.then	**this-PL**	be.big-RL	be.long-RL	**zero.anaphora**	wife	EE:pīsō
ēn-lò	tànghò					
take-RL	REP					

'And then, they grew up and they got married, so they say.' [WR, BCS 003]

13.4.3 Zero anaphora

Zero anaphora, i.e., the phenomenon of leaving highly topical continuing arguments unexpressed, is very frequent in Karbi discourse. Because highly topical continuing arguments are typically subjects rather than objects, zero anaphora more commonly refers back to subjects. The excerpt in (683) contains two text units. In the first, *misòrongpō* 'ant' is expressed as a full NP. It was already mentioned before, but in contrast with another protagonist, i.e., *chonghōkalósō* 'frog', so in this first intonation unit, the full NP is repeated, but is marked as a topic via =*ke*. In the second intonation unit, the continuing topic *misòrongpō* 'ant' is not overtly expressed, which is indicated by a 'ø' symbol for zero anaphora in the position where we would otherwise expect a topic NP, i.e., clause-initially. Note that the at that point discontinued topic *chonghōkalósō* 'frog' is mentioned again at the end of the second text unit, expressed via a lexical NP and marked with =*ke* 'topic'.

(683) Full NP *misorongpo* 'ant' changing to zero anaphora
*e **misorongpoke** <...> a'ik aphan... an*

e	**misòrongpō=ke**	a-ìk	aphān	àn
DSM	**ant.sp=TOP**	POSS-older.brother	NSUBJ	rice

kethondam
ke-thòn-dām
NMLZ-drop-GO
'The ant was on the way to drop off rice for his older brother.' [RBT, ChM 010]

amat ø horbong anbor...

amāt	ø	hōr-bōng	àn-bòr
and.then	**ZERO.ANAPHORA**	liquor-gourd	rice-wrapped.bundle

*inghorpontanlo **chonghokalosoke** tovar dakkrang*

inghór-pòn-tàn-lò	**chonghōkalósō=ke**	továr
carrying.load-take.away-S/O:big-RL	**frog.sp=TOP**	road

dàk-kràng
spread.out-INTENS
'And then, the ant was carrying the large liquor gourd and rice bundle, and the frog had spread out on the road (blocking the way).' [RBT, ChM 011]

Another example is (684). Here, *harlōng* 'stone, rock' is a lexical NP in the first two clauses of the intonation unit (where its role changes from an O argument to an S argument). Then, the topic switches to the daughter of the king and the third and fourth clause of this intonation unit are only about her. Then, in the last clause, the rock again becomes the A argument but remains unexpressed via zero anaphora, although the topic had in the meantime switched to the daughter of the king. Context unambiguously identifies the A argument as the rock, making zero anaphora possible here.

(684) Full NP *harlōng* 'stone, rock' changing to zero anaphora
harlong turpurlo aharlong ingplonglo richo
[harlōng túr-pùr-lò]   [a-harlōng   ingplòng-lò]   [richó
stone   kick-move.over-RL POSS-stone   run.away.animal-RL king

asopi abang ha langhe lang kachinglu...
a-oso-pì   abàng há   lānghē   lāng ke-chinglú]
POSS-child-female NPDL   over.there washing.place water IPFV-take.bath

amat lang kachinglu ketangpen kevang amat
[amāt   lāng ke-chinglú   ke-tāng-pen   ke-vàng   amāt
and.then water NMLZ-take.bath NMLZ-finish-NF   NMLZ-come and.then

ø richo asopi aphan baplam
ø   richó a-oso-pì   a-phān
ZERO.ANAPHORA king POSS-child-female POSS-NSUBJ
báp-làm]
press.down-RES:paste.like
'(The elephant) kicked the stone, the stone rolled away, the daughter of the king was taking a bath there at the washing place, and then after having finished taking her bath, (she) was coming (home), and then (the stone) rolled over the king's daughter pressing on her.' [RBT, ChM 026]

13.5 Noun phrase delimiter *abàng*

The 'noun phrase delimiter' (NPDL) *abàng* occurs very frequently in the corpus of recorded texts. There are close to 300 instances, depending on whether some occurrences are counted as *a-bàng* 'POSS-CLF(:HUM:PL)' instead (§13.5.2), i.e., the source form of the grammaticalized *abàng*. The noun phrase delimiter marks noun phrases and relator noun phrases in any clausal role and with any information status, although it most frequently occurs on noun phrases unmarked for clausal role and either unmarked for information/discourse structure status or marked with topic =*ke*. It thus appears to correlate with subject and topic to a large degree. Its function is difficult to narrow down but has to do with marking contrast between clausal or discourse participants, and perhaps also to emphasize the referential status of a noun phrase. This section will discuss various aspects in the ways that the noun phrase delimiter is used in order to help understand its function(s) better but a definitive account cannot be provided here. The position of the noun phrase delimiter is at the end of an NP, either preceding or following any role markers, and always before any information/discourse structure clitics.

Examples of *abàng* are given in (685), where both an extraclausal possessor NP and the clausal S argument are marked by *abàng*.

(685) Noun phrase delimiter *abàng* on extraclausal possessor NP and on possessed S argument
*an Bey Ke'et pu atum **abangke***
án	[Bēy	ke-èt		pu	a-tūm	**abàng=ke**]
and.then	CLAN	NMLZ-be.yellow		QUOT	POSS-PL	**NPDL=TOP**

*asomar **abang** etpik tangho*
[a-oso-màr	**abàng**]	èt-pìk	tànghò
POSS-child-PL	**NPDL**	be.yellow-very	REP

'And then, with respect to the so-called Bey the Fair and his family, his children were very fair.' [WR, BCS 010]

In the story that (685) is taken from, *abàng* is used particularly frequently (§13.5.5). The story is about three brothers from the Bey Clan in mythological times, and gives an account of why each brother started a subclan and how the relationships between the subclans came about. One reason for the frequent use of *abàng* may be that there are three protagonists, which are constantly contrasted. A further example that highlights this is (686).

(686) Noun phrase delimiter with contrastive function
*[...] anke Bey Ki'ik **abangta** ahem arit dolo*
ánke	[[Bēy	ke-ìk	**abàng=tā**]	a-hēm	a-rīt
and.then	CLAN	NMLZ-be.black	**NPDL=ADD**	POSS-house	POSS-field

dō-lò]					
exist-RL					

*Bey Ke'et **abangta** ahem arit dolo*
[[Bēy	ke-èt	**abàng=tā**]	a-hēm	a-rīt	dō-lò]
CLAN	NMLZ-be.yellow	**NPDL=ADD**	POSS-house	POSS-field	exist-RL

*Bey Ronghang **abang**, akibi **abangta**,*
[[[Bēy	Rònghāng	**abàng**]	[a-ke-bī		**abàng=tā**]]
CLAN	CLAN	**NPDL**	POSS-NMLZ-be.small		**NPDL=ADD**

ahem arit dolo
a-hēm   a-rīt   dō-lò]
POSS-house POSS-field   exist-RL

'[...] Bey the Black had his (own) house and property, Bey the Fair likewise had his (own) house and property, and Bey Ronghang, the young one, also had his (own) house and property.' [WR, BCS 004]

13.5.1 Distribution of noun phrase delimiter *abàng*

The noun phrase delimiter *abàng* occurs in a wide variety of semantic and pragmatic contexts, as further discussed in §13.5.3 and §13.5.4. In the corpus of recorded texts, it occurs with NPs that have singular referents as well as with NPs that have plural referents. It occurs with lexical NPs but also with pronouns, such as *alàng* 'he', *netūm* 'we (exclusive)', and *ilitūm* 'we (inclusive; formal)'. It also occurs with uniquely referential proper names, e.g., *Bokolapo abangke*.

The 'noun phrase delimiter' most typically occurs on noun phrases, but there are some instances where *abàng* occurs on adverbs (or on (nominalized) subordinate clauses, see §13.5.2). Its occurrence on adverbs generally leads to a (nominal-like) interpretation of adverbs as referring to bounded entities, which can then be contrasted with other bounded entities. For example, (687) is about a character in the story, who takes his grandmother's advice and changes his mind about which of his two uncles' daughters he wants to marry. As a consequence, (687) states that at the house of the uncle that had been his original choice for marriage, referred to as *hadak abangke* 'there', all the food that had already been prepared for the wedding got rotten, because the wedding never took place. The expression of interest, *hadak abangke* 'there', clearly contrasts the original house/family with the newly chosen house/family to marry into. It appears that adding *abàng* results in the vague adverb *hádāk* 'there' receiving a more specific interpretation of referring to the original house/family (i.e., what could be translated as 'at the there one (i.e., house)').

(687) Noun phrase delimiter on *hádāk* 'there'
*[...] an **hadak abangke** lo han thuruilo, hala*
[án   [**hádāk   abàng=ke**]   lō   hán   thū-rùi-lò]   [hála
and.then **there**   **NPDL=TOP** banana.leaf   curry   rot-many-RL   that

aphi alam karju an Bey Ke'et
a-phì   a-lám   ke-arjū   án]   [Bēy   ke-èt
POSS-grandmother   POSS-word   NMLZ-hear   because   CLAN   NMLZ-be.yellow

ahem hedi hadak asopi la Bey Ke'et
a-hēm   hedī]   [hádāk a-oso-pì]   [là   Bēy   ke-èt
POSS-house   NP.EMPH   there POSS-child-female   this   CLAN   NMLZ-be.yellow

asopi aphansi hedi piso hangdamrong
a-oso-pì   aphān=si   hedī]   [pīsō   hàng-dām-ròng]
POSS-child-female   NSUBJ=FOC:RL   NP.EMPH   wife   call-GO-instead

hadaksi pangri pangdonrong tangho
[hádāk=si   pangrí   pangdòn-ròng   tànghò]
there=FOC:RL   reconcile   even.out-instead   REP
'[…] [A]nd then there all the food got rotten, and then he followed his grandmother's advice and to Bey the Fair's house, you know, there (that man's) daughter, to the daughter of Bey the Fair, you know, he went to ask for her as a wife instead, there he went to get married instead.' [WR, BCS 016]

A similar use of *abàng* with an adverb is shown in (688). Here, *nón* 'now' is used with *abàng* again to restrict the unbounded adverb 'now' to a bounded reading of 'this time'.

(688) Noun phrase delimiter on *nón* 'now'
laso kematha amatsi "o do nangnelo, non abangke"
lasō   ke-mathà   amātsi   o   dō   nāng-Cē-lò   **[nón   abàng=ke]**
this   NMLZ-think   and.then INTERJ stay   need-NEG-RL   **now   NPDL=TOP**
'We were thinking this, and (thought), "Oh, no need to stay, this time."' [SH, CSM 065]

The noun phrase delimiter may also occur with an entire adverbial clause, as in (689). A parallel example without the NPDL in (690) shows that *abàng* in (689) does not function as a syntactic head when it occurs on adverbial subordinate clauses.

(689) *Abang* 'heading' a semantically unspecified adverbial subordinate clause
lasi "to tangte nephi aphan
lasì   [tò   tángtē   ne-phì   a-phān
therefore OK   if   1EXCL:POSS-grandmother   POSS-NSUBJ

nangkapachetongji abangke pathe'anganang"
nang=ke-pa-chetòng-jí   **abàng=ke]**   pa-the'āng-sināng
1/2:NSUBJ=NMLZ-CAUS-meet-IRR2   **NPDL=TOP**   CAUS-be.bright-si.HORT
'And then, "Okay then, in order to make you meet my grandmother, let's wait a little while until it's bright (lit., make it/let it get bright)."' [KK, BMS 062]

(690) Semantically unspecified adverbial subordinate clause not 'headed' by *abang*
[...] nephi nangkidunjike si ne
ne-phì   nang=ke-dùn-jí=ke]   [sì   nè
1EXCL:POSS-grandmother CIS=NMLZ-join-IRR2=TOP therefore 1EXCL

nangponpo pulo
nang=pòn-pò]   pù-lò
1/2:NSUBJ=take.away-IRR1 say-RL
'"[...] (There) my grandmother will come and so I will take you there", (the dog) said.' [KK, BMS 064]

Finally, (691) offers an example of *abàng* with demonstratives apparently for an added sense of referentiality (see also §6.1.3).

(691) Noun phrase delimiter on demonstratives
lasi laso ahonjeng komatma keteroiun
lasì   lasō   a-honjèng   komāt=ma ke-teròi-ùn
therefore this   POSS-thread who=Q   NMLZ-walk.cautiously-be.able

labangke *ahoklo*
là-abàng=ke   a-hōk-lò
this-NPDL=TOP   POSS-truth-RL
'Therefore, whoever can walk (over) this thread, that one is true (i.e., not a liar).' [CST, HM 096]

13.5.2 Diachronic source construction: Human classifier as syntactic head noun

The noun phrase delimiter likely originates in a construction where the human classifier *-bàng* (itself originating in the lexical noun *-bàng* 'body') functions as the head noun of a relative clause, as in (692).

(692) *Abang* heading a relative clause
[...] la saikel kevek abang puthot chevekponthulo [...]
[là   saikél   ke-vèk   **a-bàng]**   puthōt
this   bicycle(<Eng) NMLZ-steer **POSS-CLF:HUM:PL** again
che-vēk-pōn-thū-lò
RR-steer-away-again-RL
'[...] [T]he one riding a bicycle again got on his way [...].' [SiT, PS 033]

Occurrences of *abang* following a nominalized verb are glossed as the human classifier if they indeed have a human referent. In examples such as (693), involving action nominalizations and therefore no human referent, *abàng* is glossed as the noun phrase delimiter.

(693) *Abang* marking an action nominalization
*[...] laso kekoi **abangke** mane angpip dopiklo,*
[[lasō ke-kòi **abàng=ke**] mane angpìp dō-pìk-lò]
this NMLZ-rub **NPDL=TOP** I.mean(<Asm) foam exist-very-RL

siri-sabun anijom asonlo
[sirí-sabún a-nijóm asón-lò]
Shree.soap(<Asm) POSS-procedure(<Asm) like-RL
'[...] [T]his scrubbing, I mean, it creates a lot of foam, like using *Shree* soap.'
[SiH, CW 005-6]

13.5.3 Coocurrence of *abàng* with role markers

Most commonly, *abàng* occurs with NPs unmarked for role (see §14.1 on role marking). It rarely occurs with 'non-subject' *-phān* marked NPs or 'locative' *-lòng* marked NPs. There are only four instances of *abàng* occurring with the non-subject marker in the corpus of recorded texts, one of which is given in (694). The typical order of *abàng* preceding the roler marker is reversed in one of these four instances, where instead of *abàng aphān* as in (694), the order is *aphān abàng*, with no clear semantic or pragmatic difference.

(694) Noun phrase delimiter *abàng* occurring with 'non-subject' *-phān* marked NP
*anke la apenan **abang aphanke** aning*
[ánke là a-penān **abàng aphān=ke**] a-nīng
and.then this POSS-husband **NPDL NSUBJ=TOP** POSS-mind

kaparongji pupo, ok paka paka, han
ke-pa-aróng-jí pu-pò] [ōk paká paká hán
NMLZ-CAUS-be.happy-IRR2 QUOT-IRR1 meat very.good very.good curry

paka paka lopen thuidun pame pamepo
paká paká lō=pen thùi-dūn pa-mé
very.good very.good banana.leaf=with wrap-JOIN CAUS-be.good
pa-mé-pò]
CAUS-be.good-IRR1
'And then, in order to satisfy her husband, she wrapped very good meat and very good curry very nicely for him to take along (to the field).' [CST, RO 014]

Likewise, there are only four instances of *abàng* occurring with 'locative' *-lòng*, one of which is with a nominalized adverbial clause in (695). In contrast with the non-subject marker, all four instances have the same order of the role marker or subordinator *-lòng* preceding *abàng*. Note that all four instances come from the same speaker in the text KaR SWK.

(695) Noun phrase delimiter *abàng* occurring with 'locative' *-lòng* marked NP
si un'an abangke elitum
[sì   ùn=án   abàng=ke   e-li-tūm
therefore be.able=up.to   NPDL=TOP   1PL.INCL-HON-PL

*kachethan **along abangke**... akaprek alam abang*
ke-che-thán   **alòng**   **abàng=ke]**   [[a-ke-prék   a-lám
NMLZ-RR-tell   **LOC**   **NPDL=TOP**   POSS-NMLZ-be.different   POSS-language
abàng]
NPDL

humponpera pareponpera
hūm-pōn-Cē-rà   parē-pōn-Cē-rà
pick.up-on.the.way-NEG-NF:IRR   use.tool-on.the.way-NEG-NF:IRR

ningjeponpera Karbi alampen un'an abangke
ningjé-pòn-Cē-rà]   [Karbì   a-lám=pen   ùn=án
speak-on.the.way-NEG-NF:IRR   TRIBE   POSS-language=with   be.able=up.to
abàng=ke]
NPDL=TOP

Karbi alampen kachethanponji aphan...
[Karbì   a-lám=pen   ke-che-thán-pòn-jí   aphān]
TRIBE   POSS-language=with   NMLZ-RR-tell-take.away-IRR2   PURP

si bor'ilonang hedi?
[sì   bor'í-lonāng   hedī]]
therefore   try-HORT:EMPH   okay?
'So as much as we can, regarding our talking to each other, without picking up another language, without speaking another language, in Karbi as much as we can, let's try to speak in (pure) Karbi to each other, okay?' [KaR, SWK 016]

Example (695) also exemplifies the use of *abàng* on (nominalized or non-nominalized) subordinate clauses without a head noun or subordinator, in *un'an abangke* 'as much as we can'. This is best analyzed as an instance of a topic-marked subordinate clause (§12.5.1).

13.5.4 Co-occurrence of *abàng* with core information/discourse structure clitics

The noun phrase delimiter mostly occurs with NPs marked with =*ke* 'topic' and NPs unmarked for core information/discourse structure (cf. §14.2 on these markers).

Table 110 shows that in more than half of the occurrences of the noun phrase delimiter in the main corpus of this grammar (with a total of 12,485 words), it occurs with =*ke* 'topic' (55%). This evidence from usage shows that the pragmatic function of the noun phrase delimiter is highly compatible with the function of =*ke* 'topic'. Conversely, just over a quarter of the occurrences of =*ke* 'topic' include the noun phrase delimiter. This shows that also from the perspective of the topic marker, co-occurrence with the noun phrase delimiter is quite typical although the topic marker has a larger functional range that covers more diverse contexts.

Table 110: Co-occurrence of *abàng* with core information/discourse structure clitics.

	Perspective of NPDL		Perspective of clitic	
	# co-occurrences with NPDL	% co-occurrence (relative to NPDL total)	# occurrences of clitic total	% co-occurrence (relative to clitic total)
=*ke* 'TOP'	161	55%	591	27%
=*tā* 'ADD'	22	7.5%	367	6%
=*si* 'FOC:RL'	7	2.4%	208	3.4%
=*le* 'FOC:IRR'	1	0.3%	89	1.1%
Unmarked	103	35%		
TOTAL	294	100%		

Less commonly, the noun phrase delimiter remains unmarked for core information/discourse structure, which is the case in another third of its occurrences. Much less common are co-occurrences with any of the other three core information/discourse structure clitics, which altogether make up 10% of the occurrences of the noun phrase delimiter.

Examples of the uncommon co-occurrence of the noun phrase delimiter with the three clitics other than =*ke* 'topic' are given below: with additive =*tā* in (696), with focus =*si* in (697), and with irrealis focus =*le* in (698).

(696) Noun phrase delimiter *abàng* with =*tā* 'additive'
  [...] *laso arni abangke hala osomar atum mandu kecho*
  [[lasō arnì abàng=ke] [hála osō-mār a-tūm mandú ke-chō]
  this day NPDL=TOP that child-PL POSS-PL field.hut NMLZ-eat

apo abangta nangsuntuklo [...]
[[a-pō   **abàng=tā**]   nang=sūn-tùk-lò]]
POSS-father **NPDL=ADD**   CIS=descend-sd.of.stepping-RL
'[...] [T]hat day, (in order for) those children to eat (in) the *mandu*, the father in turn came down (from the tree house) [...].' [CST, RO 030]

(697) Noun phrase delimiter *abàng* with *=si* 'focus'
latum <la> hi'ipi abangsi laso kethondamtilo
là-tūm   <là> hī'ipī **abàng=si**   lasō   ke-thòn-dām-tí-lò
this-PL   this witch   **NPDL=FOC:RL**   this   NMLZ-drop-GO-get.rid.off-RL
'(Nobody else than) the witch abandoned them.' [CST, HM 083]

(698) Noun phrase delimiter *abàng* with *=le* 'focus:irrealis'
hala alo abangle chothatnang [...]
[hála a-lò   **abàng=le**]   cho-thāt-nāng
that   POSS-male.animal   **NPDL=FOC:IRR**   AUTO.BEN/MAL-slaughter-HORT
'"Let's kill that rooster!" [...]' [SeT, MTN 010]

13.5.5 Differences between speakers, texts, genres

Since the function(s) of the noun phrase delimiter have remained elusive, this section briefly explores usage of this marker in the corpus. Table 111 shows how often the noun phrase delimiter occurs in the different texts of the main corpus. The texts are listed according to the frequency of occurrence of the noun phrase delimiter starting on the top with the text where it occurs the most frequently. In this text BPh, there are 15 occurrences of this marker, while the text consists of a total of 226 words. Therefore, the noun phrase delimiter represents 6.6% of the words of this text. The average occurrence of the noun phrase delimiter is at 2.6%, the short text BPR is therefore approximately representing the average frequency; this is indicated by the horizontal bold lines in the table. The vertical bold line marks off the information about the texts from the information about the frequency of the noun phrase delimiter. The standard deviation is 1.7%.

Table 111: Occurrence of *abàng* across texts.

	Speakers	Recording	Genre[a]	# words	# NPDL	% of occurrence
1	HI	BPh	FS	226	15	6.6%
2	WR	BCS	FS	630	36	5.7%
3	KK	CC	N	338	14	4.1%

Table 111 (continued)

	Speakers	Recording	Genre[a]	# words	# NPDL	% of occurrence
4	SiT	PS	OEN	502	20	4.0%
5	SeT	MTN	FS	710	28	4.0%
6	KaR, BT	SWK	I/C	1,128	42	3.7%
7	KsT	PSu	PT	131	4	3.1%
8	CST	HM	FS	1,140	33	2.9%
9	PI	BPR	PT	118	3	2.5%
10	KK	BMS	FS	1,317	26	2.0%
11	SiH	CW	PT	371	6	1.6%
12	CST	RO	FS	649	10	1.5%
13	KTa	TCS	FS	1,006	15	1.5%
14	HK, SiT	TR	FS	1,516	22	1.5%
15	SiT	HF	PN	852	8	0.9%
16	SH	CSM	PN	827	6	0.7%
17	SiH	KH	PT	291	2	0.7%
18	RBT	ChM	FS	733	4	0.5%

[a] FS: folk story; I/C: interview/conversation; N: narrative; OEN: online elicited narrative; PN: personal narrative; PT: procedural text.

We see in Table 111 that there is substantial variation in the frequency of the noun phrase delimiter across the different texts, ranging from 6.6% to 0.5%. There is no correlation between the length of the text and the frequency of the noun phrase delimiter. The average frequency of occurrence is found in the shortest text.

There are three speakers that have each contributed two texts for the main corpus. While speaker SiH (numbers 11 and 17 in Table 111) uses fairly similar NPDL frequencies at 1.6% and 0.7% (the difference being within the standard deviation), speakers KK (numbers 3 and 10) and SiT (numbers 4 and 15) vary more across texts. For speaker KK, the NPDL frequency varies between 4.1% and 2.0%, and for speaker SiT the range is even more striking between 4.0% and 0.9%.

While this brief quantitative exploration evidently requires a follow-up at a larger scale, I want to hypothesize based on these data that genre matters for the frequency of the noun phrase delimiter. In particular, we see a tendency that more spontaneously produced texts involve a higher NPDL frequency. I believe this is part of the explanation for the large difference in the two texts of speaker SiT. The frequency of 0.9% is associated with a spontaneous yet self-paced, self-'directed' narration. On the other hand, the frequency of 4.0% occurs where SiT provides a commentary on the video clip of the pear story as he is watching it. Clearly in this latter case, the speaker would have trouble fully planning even just individual sentences. The NPDL may thus be a useful 'bulk provider', a hesitation device of a substantive sesquisyllable that clearly demarcates noun phrase and provides some small amount of time for the speaker to (re-)plan the remainder of the utterance. Still, even if this tendency were to prove more stable when more data are considered, it is clear that it would still only partly motivate the frequency of occurrence of the noun phrase delimiter. It is clearly not just a hesitation device but also lends prominence to noun phrases, in particular to those that are 'topical', as well as may serve to highlight the referentiality of noun phrases that may not have a regular nominal head noun.

14 Role marking and core information/discourse structure marking

This chapter represents part two of the discussion of clausal participants. In §14.10, syntactic and semantic role marking is discussed. Here, the three major types of marking participants (i.e., unmarked and marked by -*phān* 'non-subject' or -*lòng* 'locative') are discussed in a section each to demonstrate the range of contexts in which they occur. Other issues in role marking are also discussed in this section. Finally, §14.2 offers an overview of the four main information and discourse structure clitics as well as several other information and discourse structure constructions.

14.1 Role marking

I use the term 'role marking' to refer to a type of marking or non-marking that relates a participant to the verb. This term intentionally remains inexplicit whether these are syntactic or semantic roles, as well as between core and oblique participants. Figure 19 shows the four basic possibilities in role marking on a continuum of the parameter of 'syntacticity' and/or, in fact, 'pragmaticity' (least semantic information and most likely to be 'core argument') and 'semanticity' (most semantic information and most likely to be 'oblique'). These four possibilities are: (1) leave the NP unmarked; (2) the 'non-subject' marker -*phān*; (3) the 'locative' marker -*lòng*; and (4) one of a set of (semantically specific) relator nouns (§5.4) or the comitative/instrumental/ablative =*pen*.

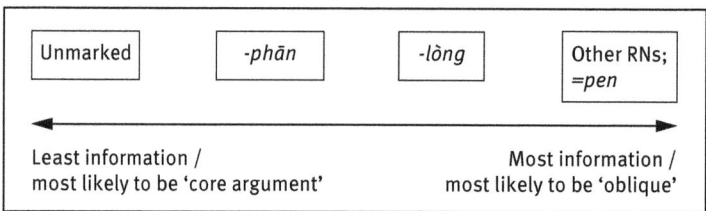

Figure 19: Role marking possibilities.

Figure 19 represents these four possibilities on a continuum based on evidence that an unmarked NP can fill any semantic role (§14.1.1); while an NP marked with -*phān* 'non-subject' is somewhat more restricted in its role interpretation (§14.1.2); an NP marked with -*lòng* 'locative' is even more restricted in its role interpretation (§14.1.3); and finally, an NP marked with one of the other relator nouns or with =*pen* very specifically fills particular roles (§14.1.4). Note, however, that there is variation as to how semantically specific a member of the category on the semantic end of the continuum is. For example, =*pen* is in fact not as semantically specific because it covers comitative, instrumental, and ablative roles.

While the left end of the continuum in Figure 19 could be considered the syntactic pole, I believe there is a very strong sense that it is more of a pragmatic pole. That is, at this pole, pragmatic factors enable the language comprehender to determine the particular role an NP has. In particular, instead of offering concrete semantic information, the use of an unmarked NP means that the speaker relies on the addressee to be able to unambiguously figure out the role of the NP. The two middle points on the continuum, -*phān* and -*lòng* may be analyzed as having some syntactic basis, because -*phān* generally never marks S/A (except for, arguably, in the semantic marking of arguments of *náng* 'need', §14.1.2.4), and -*lòng* generally never marks S/A (except for, again arguably, in the semantic marking of possessors, §14.1.3.4), and never O or T, pending the analysis of motion/goal constructions (§13.2.2.1, §14.1.3.2, §14.1.3.3).

14.1.1 Unmarked noun phrases

Unmarked noun phrases in a clause may fill any 'syntactic' or 'semantic' role, i.e., they may fill in for 'core' arguments as well as any type of additional 'oblique' participant. It therefore makes sense to think of them as truly unmarked, rather than 'zero-marked', i.e., leaving them without a marker is not to be understood in opposition or in a paradigm with the actual markers, but as not specified for a syntactic or semantic role. Instead, then, unmarked is best understood as a pragmatic default, which represents the assumption on part of the speaker that the addressee is able to identify the syntactic or semantic role the unmarked noun phrase takes in the clause (see also §13.1.2). 'Unmarked' then instructs the listener to interpret the noun phrase as the most obvious or expected syntactic or semantic role. In addition, 'unmarked' NPs predominate where the semantic role is non-salient or most typical. For example, a locative NP that could receive the general locative marker -*lòng* is more likely to remain unmarked than a locative NP whose locational properties are unexpected or salient, such as -*ngsóng* 'high up' (§14.1.1.7). Examples that demonstrate the occurrence of unmarked noun phrases in all types of syntactic and semantic roles follow.

14.1.1.1 S argument

Examples (699) and (700) show that NPs unmarked for role can function as S arguments both of predicates consisting of PCT roots and those consisting of active verbs.

(699) Unmarked S argument (PCT root)
jangrengso abangta repik tangho {mm}
jangrēngsō abàng=tā rè-pìk tànghò mm
orphan NPDL=ADD be.smart-very REP AFF
'(But) the orphan is very smart.' [HK, TR 064]

(700) Unmarked S argument
*lasi ha **nangpai** vanglo jaho damnoi mok*

lasì	há	**nang-pāi**	vàng-lò	jáho
therefore	over.there	**2-mother**	come-RL	look.there!

dàm-nōi	mōk			
go-INFRML.COND.IMP	breast			

chudamnoi dah pulo

chū-dām-nōi	dáh	pù-lò
suck-GO-INFRML.COND.IMP	go!	say-RL

'And then, "From there your mom has come, look there! Go! Go and drink milk, go!" said (the grandmother).' [KK, CC 014]

14.1.1.2 A argument

A arguments are always unmarked, here in a transitive clause with an O-low argument *phurùi* 'yam' in (701).

(701) Unmarked A argument
laso ajangrengsoke phurui kituk kituk kituk kituk...

lasō	a-jangrēngsō=ke	phurùi	ke-tūk	ke-tūk	ke-tūk	ke-tūk
this	POSS-ORPHAN=TOP	yam	NMLZ-dig	NMLZ-dig	NMLZ-dig	NMLZ-dig

chelangledetlohe {mm}
che-làng-Cē-dèt-lò=he
RR-see-NEG-PFV-RL=AFTERTHOUGHT

'This orphan, as he was digging yam and digging and digging... he didn't look around.' [HK, TR 051]

14.1.1.3 O-low argument

Example (702) and (703) show that O arguments both with non-human and human referents may remain unmarked. Unmarked O arguments are defined as O-low arguments (§13.2.1.2), so by definition, only O-low arguments are unmarked, while O-high arguments are marked by *-phān* 'non-subject'.[135]

(702) Unmarked O-low argument with non-human referent
*nepo **kecho ahormu** vanpo*

ne-pō	[ke-chō	a-hormú]	vàn-pò
1EXCL-father	NMLZ-EAT	POSS-THING	bring-IRR1

'Our father will have brought something to eat.' [HI, BPh 016]

---

[135] Note that in (703), the reason why the O argument *nechor* is unmarked is not because the verb is marked reflexive by *che-*; O arguments of reflexive-marked verbs can still be O-high (see §8.4.3).

14.1 Role marking

(703) Unmarked O-low argument with human referent
"ne nahokpen setame... e ne nechor

nè	nahōk=pen	setāmē	e	nè	**ne-chór**
1EXCL	anywhere=from	nevertheless	DSM	1EXCL	**1EXCL:POSS-SPOUSE**

chirithupo" pu [...]

che-rī-thū-pò	pu
RR-search-again-IRR1	QUOT

'"No matter from where but I will find another wife!" (he thought by himself) [...].' [CST, RO 009]

14.1.1.4 T argument
T arguments in R-marked and unmarked ditransitive constructions (§13.2.1.3) remain unmarked, as in (704).

(704) Unmarked T argument in R-marked trivalent construction
lapenke aphutup pidetlo laphan

	[NP]₁		[NP *aphān*]ᵣ
lapèn=ke	**a-phutūp**	pī-dèt-lò	là-phān
and.then=TOP	**POSS-HAT**	give-PFT-RL	this-NSUBJ

'And then, he gave him his hat.' [SiT, PS 038]

14.1.1.5 R argument (T-marked trivalent construction)
In the T-marked trivalent constructions, the R argument may be unmarked, as in (705), where the verb *thòn* means 'take T to R'.

(705) Unmarked R argument in T-centered trivalent construction
[...] apai abangsi mane kechengpenke

	[NP]ₐ		
a-pāi	abàng=si	mane	ke-chèng=pen=ke
POSS-mother	NPDL=FOC:RL	I.mean(<Asm)	NMLZ-begin=from=TOP

osomar aphan skul thondunnangji

[NP *aphān*]₁		[NP]ᵣ	
[osō-mār	a-phān]	**skúl**	thòn-dūn-náng-jí
child-PL	POSS-NSUBJ	**school(<Eng)**	drop-JOIN-need-IRR2

'[...] [T]he mothers, I mean, from the beginning on (when the children start going to school), they have to take the children to school.' [KaR, SWK 048]

14.1.1.6 Goal/locative argument/participant of motion verbs

Both the verb *dàm* 'go' and the verb *ingnì* 'sit' in (706) take goal participants. While we may consider 'go' to be a motion goal verb and 'sit' a motion manner verb, both take equally unmarked goal/locative participants: *pharlá* 'outside part of Karbi house' and *hēm* 'house' in the case of *dàm* 'go', and *hongkūp* 'entrance area of Karbi house' in the case of *ingnì* 'sit'.

(706) Unmarked goal argument of motion verbs
*e anke apaita <m> **pharla** dam,*
e   [ánke   a-pāi=tā   <m>   **pharlá**   dàm]
DSM and.then POSS-mother=ADD HESIT **outside.part.Karbi.house** go

*theng akhangra okóksi, **hem** damsi,*
[thēng   a-khangrá   ó-kòk-si]
firewood POSS-basket.for.firewood leave-in.a.fixed.place-NF:RL
[hēm   dàm-si]
house go-NF:RL

***hongkup** ingnilúnsi, mok chepachusi,*
[hongkūp   ingnì-lùn-si]   [mōk   che-pa-chū-si]
entrance.area.Karbi.house sit-big:AO-NF:RL breast RR-CAUS-suck-NF:RL

"Dojoinoi, po!"
[dō-jòi-nōi   pō]
stay-quietly-INFRML.COND.IMP father
'And then, the mother went and unloaded the firewood in the *pharla*, then went inside the house, sat down in the *hongkup*, breastfed the child (and said), "Be quiet, father!"' [KK, CC 015]

14.1.1.7 Other types of participants

As shown in §14.1.1.6, both goals of motion goal verbs, which should therefore be considered arguments, i.e., required roles, and locatives of motion manner verbs are often unmarked. Another example of a different motion manner verb, *chón* 'jump', with an unmarked goal participant is offered in (707).

(707) Unmarked goal participant with manner motion verb *chón* 'jump'
amat chonghota chonthap chonphrulo
amāt   chonghō=tā   chón-tháp   chón-phrú-lò
and.then frog=ADD   jump-mindlessly jump-EE:tháp-RL

kesolo... karlesibongpo adon chonrai
ke-sò-lò   **[karlēsibóng-pō   a-dón]**   chón-rài
NMLZ-hurt-RL **squirrel.sp-male POSS-BRIDGE** jump-solid.obj.breaking
'And then, the frog was jumping everywhere because he was hurt, and he jumped on the ladder of the squirrel and it broke.' [RBT, ChM 018]

Locatives may also be unmarked with predicates that we do not conceptualize as involving a locative core argument. This is the case in (708), where the locative *mandú* '(in) the field hut' is an oblique participant of *chō* 'eat'. In the same sentence, however, the previous conditional clause has a different oblique locative, *hemtap angsong* 'up in the tree house', here marked with the relator noun *-ngsóng* 'high.up'.

(708)   Unmarked (non-salient) locative NP with *chō* 'eat', but marked salient locative NP (*angsóng* 'high up')
[...] nangpole **hemtap angsong** *chote, nangtumke mandule*
[[nang-pō=le   **[hēmtāp   a-ngsóng]**   chō-tē]   nang-tūm=ke
2-father=FOC:IRR **tree.house POSS-HIGH.UP** eat-if   2-PL=TOP
[mandú=le]
field.hut=FOC:IRR

cho
chō]
eat
'[...] "[I]f your father takes his meal in the *hemtap*, you eat in the *mandu*."' [CST, RO 017]

The fact that in the same sentence, the locative NP *mandú* '(in) the field hut' is unmarked, but the other locative NP *hemtap angsong* 'high up in the treehouse', provides further evidence that 'unmarked' really does mean 'unmarked' in the sense that a role does not need to be marked if it is unambiguously and expectedly defined by context (as judged, of course, by the speaker). Here, the unusual and salient location 'up in the tree house' is marked by the specifically semantic relator noun *-ngsóng*, while the ordinary and default location on the ground '(in) the field hut' remains unmarked.

Finally, (709) and (710) demonstrate that NPs in unusual and typically oblique roles such as 'instrument' and 'path' may be unmarked if the speaker judges the context to satisfactorily disambiguate their roles.

(709)   Unmarked instrumental NP
[...] laphanke ha <e> sirkut ingdeng krehini arlo
là-phān=ke   há   \<e\>   sirkút   ingdēng   kré-hiní   arlō
this-NSUBJ=TOP over.there HESIT room   level   ten.and-two inside

> *bengdamcheklo <ta> <e>* **sabi** *maricheklo*
> bèng-dām-chèk-lò <e>   [sabí]$_{INSTR}$ marí-chèk-lò
> lock-GO-firmly-RL HESIT **key(<Asm)** lock(<Asm)-firmly-RL
> '[...] [H]e locked (her) away firmly far inside the house in a room 12 levels inside, he locked it firmly with a key.' [CST, HM 024]

(710) Unmarked path participant
> *[...]* ***langso atovarthot*** *vangra lapen ladak*
> [[langsō a-továr-thót]$_{PATH}$ vàng-ra]   [la=pen   ladāk
> this   POSS-ROAD-EXACTLY   come-NF:IRR   this=from   here
>
> *nanghumrira nanghem chepaletu*
> nang=humrí-ra]   [nang-hēm   chV-pa-lè-tū]
> CIS=visit.friends/relatives-NF:IRR   2:POSS-house   RR-CAUS-reach-IMP
> '[...] [C]ome on the exact same road, and then go to the familiar place (i.e. where the dog is staying) and then go and make yourself reach your home.' [KK, BMS 089]

14.1.2 Functions of 'non-subject' -*phān*

The 'non-subject' marker -*phān* may occur with any roles except for S and A arguments, which is why it is glossed as 'non-subject'. The only instance where -*phān* marks an argument that might be argued to have A-like properties is the 'subject' of *náng* 'need' (§14.1.2.4). In its more syntactic functions, -*phān* marks O arguments (§14.1.2.1); R arguments in the R-marked trivalent construction (§14.1.2.2); and T arguments in the T-marked trivalent construction (§14.1.2.3); finally, -*phān* marks other types of participants (§14.1.2.6).

14.1.2.1 O-high argument

O arguments are differentially marked by -*phān* (§14.1.5); if marked by -*phān*, they are referred to as O-high (§13.2.1.2). Almost all -*phān* marked O arguments in the corpus of recorded texts have human referents as in (711).

(711) -*phān* marking O argument with human(/personified) referent
> <h> **halaphansi** *apei apo chitinloklo*
> **hála-phān=si**   a-pēi   a-pō   che-tīn-lòk-lò
> **that-NSUBJ=FOC:RL**   POSS-mother   POSS-father   RR-mistake-happen.to-RL
> 'They mistakenly considered them (i.e., the tigers) mother and father.' [CST, HM 109]

However, there are three instances of O-arguments with non-human referents, all with the same referent in the same recording: a procedural text which is mostly about how traditional clothes are made. One of these instances is (712). The O-high argument in three different sentences is *pindeng sumpot* a collective elaborate expression that refers to 'dress and ornaments', which is the topic of the larger discourse or text, and perhaps because of that is treated as an O-high argument.

(712) *-phān marking inanimate O argument*
asumpot halabangso ahut elitum Karbi
a-sumpót]   [hála-bàng-sō   ahūt   e-li-tūm   Karbì
POSS-EE:pindéng that-NPDL-DEM during 1PL.INCL-HON-PL   PN

akhei atum **pindeng sumpot aphan**
a-khéi   a-tūm   **[pindéng   sumpót   aphān]**
POSS-community POSS-PL **dress.and.ornaments EE:PINDÉNG   NSUBJ**

kosonsonsi keklemma
kosón~són=si   ke-klém=ma
how~DIST.PL=FOC:RL   NMLZ-do=Q
'[...] [D]uring the old days, what are the (different) ways in which we, the Karbi tribe, would make/produce dresses and ornaments? (That's what I will talk about).' [KST, PSu 002]

Finally, in another instance of O-high arguments, the apparently typically intransitive predicate *nīng ingsām* 'be glad' takes an O-high argument and is then interpreted as 'be grateful to somebody' in (713).

(713) *-phān marked participant of predicate nīng ingsām 'be glad; be grateful'*
lapenke la phutup <kapa...> kipidunthu apot
lapèn=ke   [là   phutūp ke-pī-dūn-thū   apōt]
and.then=TOP   this   hat   NMLZ-give-JOIN-again   because

laphan aning ingsamsi, thesere pumni tekanglo
[là-phān   a-nīng   ingsām-si]   [theseré   púm-ní   tekáng-lò]
this-NSUBJ POSS-mind   be.cold-NF:RL fruits   CLF:round-two   leave.for-RL
'And then, because he returned the hat, (the bicycle boy) was grateful to him and gave him two pieces of fruit.' [SiT, PS 039]

14.1.2.2 R argument (R-marked trivalent construction)

R arguments may be marked by *-phān*, as in (714). Note that in this example, the speaker first uses the plural form *asomarke* (i.e., with *-mār* 'plural') for the T argument, and then corrects herself and uses the singular form *asoke*. This construction is defined as the R-marked trivalent construction (§13.2.1.3.1).

(714) *-phān* marked R argument
asomarke asoke aphi aphan

[ø]_A	[NP]_T	[NP]_T	[NP *aphān*]_R
ø	a-só-màr=ke	a-osō=ke	[a-phì aphān]
ø	POSS-child-PL=TOP	POSS-child=TOP	POSS-grandmother NSUBJ

tekangbuplo
tekáng-bùp-lò
leave.for-RES:gone-RL
'She left her child with the grandmother.' [KK, CC 011]

14.1.2.3 T argument (T-marked trivalent construction)

In the T-marked trivalent constructions (§13.2.1.3.2), T is marked with *-phān*, as in (715).

(715) *-phān*-marked human T argument and *alòng*-marked locative R/goal argument
[...] itum aphanke ha nampi namdur alongsi

[NP *aphān*]_T			[NP *alòng*]_R		
e-tūm	aphān=ke	há	nāmpī	nāmdūr	alòng=si
1PL.INCL-PL	NSUBJ=TOP	over.there	big.forest	EE:nampī	LOC=FOC:RL

ekethondamlo
e=ke-thòn-dām-lò
1INCL:NSUBJ =NMLZ-drop-GO-RL
'[...] (The witch) abandoned us over there in the deep forest.' [CST, HM 076]

14.1.2.4 Semantic marking with *náng* 'need'

As discussed in §13.2.2.2, the verb *náng* 'need' takes an A-like argument that is optionally marked by *-phān*.

14.1.2.5 Marking the standard of comparison

Example (716) shows that *-phān* often marks the standard of comparison in comparative constructions (cf. §13.2.2.5).

(716) *-phān* marked standard of comparison
*opeija **nephanta** halasi **nang**sarlang* (both laughing)
opeija **ne-phān**=tā hála=si nang=sàr-làng
my.goodness! 1EXCL-NSUBJ=ADD that=FOC:RL 1/2:NSUBJ=be.old-still
'Oh my goodness! This one is even older than me! (*both laughing*)' [HK, TR 098]

14.1.2.6 Other types of participants

The 'non-subject' marker -*phān* also marks different types of participants in the corpus of recorded texts. In (717), (718), and (719), it occurs in a clause with a PCT verb, an equational clause, and in an existential construction, respectively, marking a topical participant to whom the stated proposition applies.

(717) -*phān* marking an oblique participant of *mē* 'be good'
neliphanke *me'ongchotlo*
ne-li-phān=ke mē-óng-chòt-lò
1EXCL-HON-NSUBJ=TOP be.good-be.much-very-RL
'This is very good (i.e. a very good opportunity) for me.' [SiT, HF 003]

(718) -*phān* marking an oblique participant in an equational clause
isi great inspiration **neliphan,** *laso hormu neli atumi*
isī great inspiration **ne-li-phān** lasō hormú nè-lì
one great inspiration 1EXCL-HON-NSUBJ this thing 1EXCL-HON
tumì
yesterday

thekdamlonglokpenke ning ingsam'olo
thèk-dām-lōng-lòk-pèn=ke nīng ingsām-ò-lò
see-GO-GET-happen.to-NF=TOP mind be.cold-much-RL
'It was one great inspiration for me, that I got to see this thing yesterday I was very glad.' [SiT, HF 032]

(719) -*phān* marking an oblique participant of *avē* 'not exist'
mh nephanke aker apar nangkethanke
mh **ne-phān=ke** a-kēr apár nang=ke-thán=ke
DSM 1EXCL-NSUBJ=TOP POSS-bad.omen besides 1/2:NSUBJ=NMLZ-tell=TOP

avelo <bu>
avē-lò
not.exist-RL
'To me, this is nothing but a bad omen.' [KK, BMS 021]

In (720), -*phān* marks a beneficiary despite the absence of the benefactive suffix -*pī* in the verb stem (see also §13.2.3.2).

(720) Beneficiary marked with -*phān* 'non-subject' without benefactive -*pī* on verb
tangka atibuksi ronji **la arnam aphan,**
[[tángká a-tíbùk=si] **ròn-jí]** [[là arnàm aphān]
money POSS-earthen.pot=FOC:RL **distribute-IRR2** this god NSUBJ

latum a'arnam aphan {avan along} avan
[là-tūm   a-arnàm   aphān]]_BEN {[a-ván   alòng]} [a-ván
this-PL   POSS-GOD   NSUBJ   POSS-share   LOC   POSS-share

*along tangka atibuk **nunrenpo** lasi*
alòng] [tángká   a-tíbùk]   **nún-rèn-pò**   lasì
LOC   money   POSS-earthen.pot **place.container-in.a.row-IRR1**   therefore
'(The tigers) distribute/offer the money pots **for the god, for their gods**, {on their plates (of offerings)}, and they will put the money pots in one long row' [HK, TR 111]

The discussion of the above examples in this subsection imply that *-phān* occurs on participants with different clausal functions. Another way of looking at this, which would certainly be a fruitful, complementary approach to describe the way the language works, is from the perspective of construction grammar. Specifically, it would be useful to try and identify various argument structure constructions and to see how verbs can occur in one or more such constructions. As a result, (717), (718), and (719) may be considered instances of a two-argument construction; and a verb such as *mē* 'be good' may occur in such a construction without additional marking the same way it may occur in the more common construction which includes only a single argument.[136] Such an approach takes argument structure constructions as the basic units, rather than particular role-(un)marked participants. See also §14.1.6.

Finally, it should be noted that *aphān* has grammaticalized to function as a subordinator marking nominalized adverbial clauses as in (721).

(721)   *aphān* as subordinator with adverbial clause
        laso ateke pilolo kechopan aphan kevang
        [[[lasō a-tekè   pilolō]   **ke-chopān**   **aphān**]_PURP
        this   POSS-tiger female.and.male.animal   **NMLZ-GRAZE**   **PURP**
        ke-vàng
        NMLZ-COME

        ahut, haso aHingchong musoso osomar kechiru
        ahūt]_SIDUR   [[hásō   a-Hingchòng   musosō   osō-mār   ke-chirú
        during   that   POSS-CONSTELLATION   siblings:DL child-PL   NMLZ-cry

        banghini hangjolo [...]
        bàng-hiní   háng-jò-lò]
        CLF:HUM:PL-two   call-many.continuously:S-RL
        'This tiger couple had come to look for food, at that moment, the Hingcho sisters, the two of them, were crying loudly [...].' [CST, HM 027]

---

136 I am grateful to Pattie Epps for this suggestion.

Evidence for considering the subordinator *aphān* not (yet) a separate morpheme from the non-subject role marker is offered by (722).[137] Here we can see that two *(a)-phān* phrases are coordinated: one an NP, the other a purpose subordinate clause, which indicates that they are treated as having the same syntactic status. See §12.5.2 for the paradigmatic context of the subordinator *aphān*.

(722) Coordination of two *-phān* marked constituents: NP and purpose clause
tun dangpikang'etsi
[tún dàng-pī-káng-ét-si]
cook put.on.stove-BEN/MAL-leaving-PRF-NF:RL

chinghorponkingsi rit kedo atum
[che-inghór-pòn-kìng-si]   [[[rīt ke-dō
RR-carry.load-on.the.way-small.weight:O-NF:RL field NMLZ-STAY
a-tūm]
POSS-PL

aphanta ba hadak keklemdamji aphan
a-phān=tā]   bá   [[hádāk ke-klém-dàm-jí]   aphān]
POSS-NSUBJ=ADD or(<Asm) there   NMLZ-DO-GO-IRR2 PURP

chinghorponkingsi rit dampo [...]
che-inghór-pòn-kìng-si]   rīt dàm-pò
RR-carry.load-on.the.way-small.weight:O-NF:RL field go-IRR1
'They cook for others at home, carrying the load (of food) on her own (to) the ones staying in the field or carrying it to go there and work, thus they would go to the field [...].' [KaR, SWK 075]

14.1.3 Functions of 'locative' *-lòng*

14.1.3.1 Locative/goal R argument (T-marked/unmarked trivalent constructions)
'Locative' *-lòng* marks R arguments in T-marked and unmarked trivalent constructions (§13.2.1.3.2, §13.2.1.3.3). The *-lòng* marked argument may have a non-human or a human referent, as in (723) and (724), respectively.

---

[137] This example then also provides evidence for the gradient nature of categories as caused by grammaticalization (DeLancey 1997), here specifically for *-phān* being 'in between' an NP marking relator noun (with a syntacticized function) and a subordinator.

(723) *-lòng*-marked locative non-human R argument
lapenke... phatang along thesere thaplelo... [...]

[NP *alòng*]ᴿ	[NP]ᴛ
lapèn=ke... **[phatáng alòng]**	theseré thàp-lè-lò...
and.then=TOP **BASKET LOC**	fruit put.inside-again-RL

'And then, he again put fruit in the *phatang* basket [...].' [SiT, PS 044]

(724) *-lòng*-marked locative human R argument
lasi anke tharunvirsi, aoso ha padok

			([NP]ᴛ)	
lasì	ánke	tharún-vìr-si	a-osō	há
therefore	and.then	rock-gently-NF:RL	POSS-child	then.much.later

pa-dòk
CAUS-be.sweet

padoksi, aphi along thondamkoklo

	[NP *alòng*]ᴿ	
pa-dòk-si	**a-phì**	**alòng**
CAUS-be.sweet-NF:RL	**POSS-GRANDMOTHER**	**LOC**

thòn-dām-kòk-lò
drop-GO-in.a.fixed.place-RL

'And then, gently she was rocking the child and then consoling it, and she left (the child) with the grandmother.' [KK, CC 032]

14.1.3.2 Locative O-like argument

'Locative' *-lòng* marks O-like arguments of verbs *tōng* 'collide' in (725), *kòi* 'rub, scrub' in (726), and *dùn* 'follow, join' in (727).

(725) *-lòng* marked locative O-like argument of *tōng* 'collide'
amat laso damchet amat chekhang'un'elo isi arlong along

amāt	lasō	dàm-chèt	amāt	che-kháng-ùn-Cē-lò	[isī
and.then	this	go-a.bit	and.then	RR-keep-be.able-NEG-RL	**one**
arlōng	**alòng]**				
stone	**LOC**				

tongdér
tōng-dèr
collide-IDEOPHONE

'And then he went just a bit further and then he couldn't hold himself anymore, he hit one stone.' [SiT, PS 029]

(726) *-lòng* marked locative O-like argument of *kòi* 'rub, scrub'
[...] laso athe phlakdakpó ansi ilitum lapu
[lasō a-thē phlàk-dàk-pò [ánsi i-li-tūm lapù
this POSS-fruit split-RES:split-IRR1 after.that 1PL:INCL-HON-PL like.this

pe along koipó, laso kekoi abangke mane angpip
[pé along] kòi-pò] [[lasō ke-kòi abàng=ke] mane angpìp
cloth LOC rub-IRR1 this NMLZ-rub NPDL=TOP I.mean(<Asm) foam

dopiklo, siri-sabun anijom asonlo
dō-pìk-lò] [sirí-sabún a-nijóm asón-lò]
exist-very-RL Shree.soap(<Asm) POSS-procedure(<Asm) like-RL
'We split this (*vo'arkokpo*) fruit, and then, like this we scrub the cloth, this scrubbing, I mean... it creates a lot of foam, like using *Shree* soap.' [SiH, CW 005-6]

(727) *-lòng* marked locative O-like argument of *dùn* 'follow, join'
***apiso along** chidunkri*
[[a-pisò alòng]$_{\text{GOAL/O}}$ chV-dūn-krì]
POSS-WIFE LOC RR-join-follow.closely

*laso **abamonpi along** dunkrilo*
[[lasō a-bamón-pī alòng]$_{\text{GOAL/O}}$ dùn-krì-lò]
this POSS-WISE.PERSON(<IND)-FEMALE LOC join-follow.closely-RL
'He followed his wife closely, he followed this *bamonpi* closely.' [KK, BMS 082]

14.1.3.3 Motion verb locative/goal

While (727) in the previous section has already demonstrated that goal/O-like arguments may be marked by 'locative' *-lòng*, further examples of goals or locatives are offered below. The goal of the verb *dàm* 'go' has a human referent that is marked by *-lòng* in (728), and, similarly, the locative of the verb *dō* 'stay' has a human referent that is marked by *-lòng* in (729).

(728) *-lòng* marked goal of *dàm* 'go'
ne han an tunpó ajatpó, chirurinoi!
[nè hán àn tún-pò aját-pò] [chirú-rī-nōi]
1EXCL curry rice cook-IRR1 GENEX-IRR1 cry-PROH-INFRML.COND.IMP

***nangphihai along** damnói dei]*
[[nang-phì-hái alòng] dàm-nōi déi]
2POSS-GRANDMOTHER-HON LOC go-INFRML.COND.IMP OK?
'I will cook food and everything, don't cry, go to your grandmother, ok?' [KK, CC 016]

(729) -*lòng* marked locative of *dō* 'stay'
aphihai alongle donoi
[a-phì-hái   alòng=le]   dō-nōi
POSS-GRANDMOTHER-HON   LOC-FOC:IRR stay INFRML.COND.IMP

chirurinói pu tangho
chirú-rī-nōi   pu   tànghò
cry-PROH-INFRML.COND.IMP QUOT REP
'"Stay with your grandmother, don't cry!" (she) said.' [KK, CC 017]

14.1.3.4 Semantic marking with possessor construction

There is one type of possessor construction, in which the 'A' argument is marked locative by *-lòng*, see §13.2.2.3.3.

14.1.4 Semantically marked participants

This section discusses relator noun phrases (and the one postpositional phrase of Karbi, with *=pen* 'with, from') other than those with *-phān* 'non-subject' (§14.1.2) and *-lòng* 'locative (§14.1.3). These participants marked with elements other than *-phān* and *-lòng* may also occur both as core roles (§14.1.4.1 below) and as 'obliques' (§14.1.4.2 below), in the (not easily operationalizable) sense of required or not required by the predicate. This is evidence that they are not, in fact, categorically different from *-phān* and *-lòng*, which is why the various role markers are represented as being on a continuum in §13.1.2. Nevertheless, there is a gradient difference between *-phān*, *-lòng* and the more semantically specific relator nouns (and *=pen*), in two interrelated senses. First, *-phān* and *-lòng* are semantically bleached, which makes them applicable in a greater variety of contexts. Second, this leads to a higher frequency with which *-phān* and, to a lesser extent, *-lòng* are used, compared to the lower frequency that each of the more semantically specific relator nouns are used. This in turn leads me to the hypothesis that to the extent that we can differentiate between core arguments and obliques, *-phān* and *-lòng* more often mark core arguments, and the more semantically specific relator nouns more often mark obliques.

14.1.4.1 Semantically specific marking of functionally core roles

There are two constructions in which core arguments are marked by elements other than *-phān* and *-lòng*. One is with *=pen* 'comitative, instrumental, ablative', the other is with various specific locative relator nouns.

14.1.4.1.1 Comitative, instrumental, ablative =pen

The predicates in both (730) and (731) require a comitative argument: in (730) through the predicate derivation -ràp 'together (with)', and in (731) through the comitative/instrumental predicate derivation -ī. In both clauses, however, the comitative argument is marked by =pen.

(730) Semantically required comitative NP marked by =pen
 apot "la nangpopen chorappetlongle... [...]"
 [apōt là **nang-pō=pen** chō-**ràp**-pèt-lōng-Cē]
 because this **2POSS-FATHER=WITH** eat-**together**-all-GET-NEG
 'Because of that, you don't get to / must not eat together with your father [...].'
 [CST, RO 019]

(731) Semantically required comitative NP marked by =pen
 [...] pinsomar atum abangke hala osomarpen jui'irongpo [...]
 [pinsō-mār a-tūm abàng=ke] **[hála osō-mār=pen]**
 married.man-PL POSS-PL NPDL=TOP **that child-PL=with**
 jùi-**ī**-ròng-pò
 play-**with**-instead-IRR1
 '[...] [T]he men would always play with the children instead [...].' [KaR, SWK 071]

The same, seemingly obligatory, marking with =pen occurs on the instrumental NP in (732), where, again the verb stem contains the predicate derivation -ī, which means that the instrument role is indicated in the verb stem.

(732) Projected instrumental NP marked by =pen
 nè **motorsaikel=pen=si** hethí ke-dàm-**ī**
 1EXCL **motorcycle=with=FOC:RL** market(<Asm) NMLZ-go-**with**
 'I went to the market on a motorcycle.' [Elicitation SiT 090223]

Finally, the verb stem *chekak* 'part/separate (from)' in (733) also semantically requires an ablative or comitative role, which is fulfilled by the second person pronoun marked by =pen.

(733) Projected ablative/comitative NP marked by =pen
 "[...] pinipenke nangpenke ne kachekak" pu
 pinì=pen=ke **nàng=pen=ke** nè ke-che-kák pu
 today=from=TOP **you=from=TOP** 1EXCL NMLZ-RR-PART QUOT
 '"[...] [F]rom today, I am separated from you." (she said).' [SeT, MTN 035]

It thus appears that while comitative, instrumental, and ablative roles may be unmarked (§14.1.1.7), if they are marked, they are always and only marked by =*pen*. Even with the 'applicative-like' (though not actually applicative) -*ī* suffix, comitatives and instrumentals are never marked by -*phān* 'non-subject'. This suggests that there is a sense in which comitative, instrumental, and ablative roles are never afforded a syntactically high status (while they can arguably be afforded a pragmatically high status if left unmarked).

14.1.4.1.2 Goal arguments marked with semantically specific relator nouns

While R arguments may be unmarked (§14.1.1.5), or marked by -*phān* (§14.1.2.2), or marked by -*lòng* (§14.1.3.1), they can in fact also be marked by more semantically specific relator nouns, such as *arlō* 'inside' in (734) or -*ngbòng* 'in the middle of' in (735).

(734) Trivalent predicate with unmarked non-human T argument and *arlō*-marked non-human R argument

[...] anke amonit abang<a> pe akelokpen keroi isi

[NP]ₐ			[NP *arlō*]ᵣ	
[ánke	[a-monít	abàng]	**[[pé**	**a-ke-lòk=pen**
and.then	POSS-man	NPDL	**cloth**	**POSS-NMLZ-BE.WHITE=WITH**
ke-ròi	**isī**			
NMLZ-SEW	**one**			

ajamborong arlosi lahai kethap lapen arum kevan

		[NP]ₜ			
a-jamboróng	arlō=si]	[lahái]	ke-thàp]]	lapèn [arúm	ke-vàn]]
POSS-bag	inside=FOC:RL	these	NMLZ-put.inside	and down	NMLZ-bring

'[...] [A]nd then, the man, into a bag sown from white cloth he puts these (fruit), and then brings them down.' [SiT, PS 003]

(735) Trivalent predicate with -*phān* marked T argument and -*ngbòng* marked locative non-human R argument

amatsi itum aphanke dak habit angbongsi

	[NP *aphān*]ₜ		[NP *angbòng*]ᵣ	
amātsi	e-tūm	aphān=ke	dāk habít	angbòng=si
because	1INCL-PL	NSUBJ=TOP	here jungle	in.middle.of=FOC:RL

nangkethonti
nang=ke-thòn-tí
1/2:NSUBJ=NMLZ-drop-get.rid.off

'And then, she abandoned us here in the middle of the jungle.' [CST, HM 052]

14.1.4.2 Semantically specific relator noun marking of obliques

Semantically specific relator nouns presumably most often mark obliques, i.e., roles not required by the predicate. Examples of the semantically specific roles marked by the various relator nouns are offered in §5.4; a sample instance of -*ngsóng* 'high up' marking a semantically specific location is provided in (736). In this example, the non-specific or non-salient locative role of *mandú* '(in) the field hut' remains unmarked (see also §14.1.1.7).

(736) 'Salient' locative NP marked by -*ngsóng* 'high up'
       [...] nangpole **hemtap angsong** chote, nangtumke
       [[nang-pō=le   **[hēmtāp   a-ngsóng]**   chō-tē]   nang-tūm=ke
       2:POSS-father=FOC:IRR   **tree.house   POSS-HIGH.UP**   eat-if   2-PL=TOP

       mandule cho
       [mandú=le]   chō]
       field.hut=FOC:IRR   eat
       '[...] "[I]f your father takes his meal in the *hemtap*, you eat in the *mandu*."'
       [CST, RO 017]

14.1.5 Differential marking

O arguments as well as goal arguments are differentially marked. For O arguments, this means that certain O arguments are marked by -*phān* 'non-subject' while others remain unmarked (§13.2.1.2). For goal arguments, this means that some are marked by -*lòng* 'locative' while others remain unmarked.

Both semantic and pragmatic factors underlie this differential marking, and they do so in a probabilistic way. For example, an important semantic factor is +/-human. A human referent is very likely to be marked by -*phān* or -*lòng*, while a non-human referent is very likely to remain unmarked. Nevertheless, not all O and goal arguments with human referents are marked and not all arguments with non-human referent are unmarked. Comprehensive corpus study of the interplay of semantic and pragmatic factors involved in differential argument marking in Karbi needs to be carried out in future research.

Nevertheless, just to offer a glimpse of the pragmatic aspects of differential marking, consider (737) and (738). These examples show that in the same context, within the same story and just four text units apart, in the same proposition 'we still need to ask our mother and father', the O argument 'our mother and father' may be unmarked or marked by -*phān* 'non-subject'. This may have something to do with *nepei nepo* 'our mother and father' just having been mentioned in the preposed subordinate clause in (737). But in any event, it clearly shows that differential O marking may be triggered solely by pragmatic factors, because these two examples are semantically identical.

(737) [NP] *charjudamlang*
'mh' "nepei nepo hadak do apot nepei
['mh'   ne-pēi   ne-pō   hádāk dō   apōt]
NEG.INTERJ 1EXCL-mother 1EXCL-father there stay because
[[ne-pēi
1EXCL:POSS-MOTHER

nepo charjudamlang" pu amatsi halaso ateke along
ne-pō]   che-arjū-dām-làng   pu]   [amātsi   [hálasō
1EXCL:POSS-FATHER   RR-hear-go-still   QUOT   because   that
a-tekè   alòng]
POSS-tiger   LOC

ako chedamlo
akó   che-dām-lò]
again(<Asm) RR-go-RL
'No! "Because our mother and father are there, let's still go and ask our mother and father, and then they went to the tigers.' [CST, HM 112]

(738) [[NP] aphān] *charjudamlang*
pu netum kroikredet ne nepei
pu   ne-tūm   krōi-Cē-dèt   nè   [[ne-pēi
QUOT 1EXCL:POSS-PL   agree-NEG-PFV   1EXCL   1EXCL:POSS-mother

nepo aphan charjudamlang
ne-pō]   **aphān]**   che-arjū-dām-làng
1EXCL:POSS-father   **NSUBJ**   RR-ask-go-still
'[...] [W]e didn't agree, we still need to ask our mother and father.' [CST, HM 116]

14.1.6 Marking variation

Below I show two examples where the same verb stem can, to some extent, participate in different argument structure constructions, as shown below with two different verb stems: *che(-)tòng* '(RR-)meet' and *arjū-dām* 'ask-go'.

14.1.6.1 *che-tòng* 'RR-meet'

The verb *chetòng* 'meet' can be diachronically analyzed into the reflexive/reciprocal prefix *che-* and the root *tòng*, although *tòng* does not occur by itself, so *chetòng* is a lexicalized unit. As the following examples show, the argument structure that occurs with *chetòng* is not fixed, but there is variation. In (739), *chetòng* is used intransitively with a plural S argument, here *rát* 'the public', in the sense of 'meet' or 'gather'.

(739) Intransitive plural
rat chetongte ako, {mm} ladak nangkeleke abarika....
[rát   che-tòng-Cē   akò]   {mm}   [ladāk nang=ke-lè=ke
public RR-meet-NEG before AFF   here   CIS=NMLZ-reach=TOP
a-bariká
POSS-OFFICER

asarthe laheiheike nangle'etlo {oi}
a-sàrthè]   [lahéi~héi=ke   nang=lè-èt-lò]   {ōi}
POSS-village.headman these~DIST.PL=TOP CIS=reach-all:S/O-RL yes
'Before the tigers gathered, as for those that had already arrived here, the *barika* and the *sarthe* and all the other important tigers have already arrived.' [HK, TR 185-6]

Examples (740) and (741) show that alternatively, and more often in the corpus of recorded texts, *chetòng* is used transitively. In (740), the O argument is marked by *=pen* 'comitative', and in (741), the O argument is marked by *-phān* 'non-subject'.

(740) O argument of *chetòng* 'meet' marked with *=pen* 'comitative'
e <ne> <nang> nephipen mo
e   <nè>   <nàng>   **ne-phì=pen**   mò
DSM 1EXCL 2   **1EXCL:POSS-GRANDMOTHER=WITH** future

chetongvekpo <ne>
chetòng-vék-pò   <nè>
meet-definitely-IRR1 1EXCL
'I will definitely meet my grandmother later.' [KK, BMS 028]

(741) O argument of *chetòng* 'meet' marked with *-phān* 'non-subject'
[...] halabangso kiridam ahut jangreso aphan
[hálabàngsō ke-rì-dām   ahūt]   **[jangrēsō**   **a-phān]**
that   NMLZ-search-go during **single.parent.child POSS-NSUBJ**

chetonglok [...]
che-tòng-lòk
RR-meet-happen.to
'[...] [W]hile he was looking for (more), he ran into the orphan [...].' [HK, TR 048]

14.1.6.2 *arjū-dām* 'ask-GO'
Another instance of marking variation occurs with *arjū-dām* 'ask-go', and in this case it appears to be due to this being a complex stem that involves serialization of *arjū* 'ask' and *dàm* 'go' (also see §9.2.4 on the grammaticalized predicate derivation *-dàm~-dām* 'GO'). Examples (742) and (743) show that the 'non-subject' argument can

be marked either by *-phān* 'non-subject' or *-lòng* 'locative', which suggests that the argument structure reflects either *arjū* 'ask', leading to marking by *-phān*, or *dàm* 'go', leading to marking by *-lòng*.

(742) [[NP] aphān] *arjudamlo*
"Matlo ante kechokcheke?", o ha <ingnar
[māt=lo   ánte   ke-chók-Cē=ke]   [ó   há   <ingnàr
who=FOC OK.then   NMLZ-be.fine-NEG=TOP   EXCM over.there elephant

nothongpole> ingnar nothongpo aphan arjudamlo
nothōng-pō=le>   **[ingnàr   nothōng-pō   aphān]** arjū-dām-lò]
deaf- MODIF =FOC:IRR **elephant deaf-MODIF   NSUBJ** ask-go-RL
'"Who then is the guilty one?", o there <the deaf elephant> he went to ask the deaf elephant.' [RBT, ChM 032]

(743) [[NP] alòng] *arjudamlo*
ha karlesibongpo along arjudamlo
[há   karlēsibóng-pō   alòng] arjū-dām-lò
over.there squirrel.sp-male   LOC   ask-go-RL
'Over there he went and asked the squirrel [...].' [RBT, ChM 066]

14.2 Core information/discourse structure marking

The four sections below discuss each of the four core information/discourse structure clitics: topic *=ke* in §14.2.1; additive *=tā*, which acts as a topic-switch marker, in §14.2.2; furthermore, (realis) focus *=si* in §14.2.3; and irrealis focus *=le* in §14.2.4. They are called 'core information/discourse structure clitics' because they occur more frequently – and are hence at the core of Karbi grammar – than other markers with related functions, such as *=lo* 'FOCUS' (cf. §9.6.1.7), the markers and constructions of restrictive focus (§14.2.6.3), or other information and discourse marking constructions (§14.2.6). They are referred to as 'information/discourse structure' clitics as a way of acknowledging that their functional ranges extend beyond strictly information structural functions at the sentence level, which is cross-linguistically common among markers and constructions of this type (Matić and Wedgwood 2013; Ozerov 2015).

The four core information/discourse structure clitics occur in the corpus with significantly different frequencies. Table 112 shows that the two more topic-like markers *=ke* and *=tā* occur much more frequently than the two more focus-like markers *=si* and *=le*. In addition, *=ke* 'topic' occurs almost as often as all the three other markers together. A partial explanation for the higher frequency of *=ke* is that this marker can occur on more than a single participant in a clause in contrast to the other clitics.

Table 112: Frequencies of occurrence of core information/discourse structure clitics.

	# occurrences in corpus	% occurrences in corpus
=ke 'TOP'	591	4.7
=tā 'ADD'	367	2.9
=si 'FOC:RL'	208	1.7
=le 'FOC:IRR'	89	0.7

14.2.1 Topic =ke

In calling =ke a topic marker, I follow the traditional notion of 'topic' as 'what the sentence is about'. Since this does not serve as an operationalizable definition, this section instead offers examples to provide an overview of typical occurrences of topic =ke, which coincide with typical topic functions in the linguistic literature. Note that in all instances, =ke indicates an element at the beginning of the clause, only following any discourse connectors (or another element marked by =ke). NPs marked by =ke may be participants that are not required by the verb semantics, or they may be core arguments that are required by the semantics of the verb. NPs marked (or unmarked) for any syntactico-semantic role (§14.1) may be marked with =ke. Topic =ke also occurs on adverbs, as well as on entire clauses.

The topic marker =ke optionally marks the S argument of equational clauses, as it does in (744).

(744) Topic =ke on S argument in equational clause
 kortete apoke richo
 [kortetè   a-pò=ke]   [richó]
 2.siblings.of.same.gender   POSS-FATHER=TOP   king
 'The father of the sisters was a king.' [CST, HM 004]

Topic =ke marks framing elements at the beginning of clauses, which indicate the setting of the event expressed in the clause. In (745), a temporal NP is marked with =ke, while in (746), a temporal adverb occurs in the same construction.

(745) Topic =ke on framing NP
 [...] laso arni abangke hala osomar atum mandu kecho [...]
 [[lasō arnì abàng=ke] [hála osō-mār a-tūm   mandú   ke-chō]
 this   day   NPDL=TOP   that child-PL POSS-PL   field.hut IPFV-eat
 '[...] [T]hat day, those children were eating in the *mandu* [...].' [CST, RO 030]

(746) Topic =ke on framing adverb
'mh' o pei atum pinike itum an chorappetsinang

'mh'	[ó	pēi	a-tūm]	**[[pinì=ke]**	e-tūm	àn
NEG	vocative	mother	POSS-PL	**today=TOP**	1INCL-PL	rice

chō-ràp-pèt-sināng]
eat-together-all-CON.HORT
'No, o mothers, today let's eat together (and see what's going to happen)!'
[CST, RO 027]

Examples (747) and (748) show that there may be more than one topic-marked element, in which case both topics occur at the beginning of the clause. In (747), the second person pronoun *nàng*, which is an oblique or non-core person participant of the nominal predicate '(these) are new people', represents the first topic; the locative adverb *dāk* 'here' represents the second topic.

(747) Double topic (person participant and locative adverb)
[...] *"nangke dakke arleng kimi apot la siksakji" pu* [...]

[[[nàng=ke]₁	[dāk=ke]₂	arlēng	ke-mī	apōt]	là
you=TOP	**here=TOP**	person	NMLZ-be.new	because	this

siksāk-jí]   pu
be.difficult-IRR2   QUOT
'[...] [F]or you, here, these are new people, so it will be difficult [...]' [SH, CSM 066]

In (748), the temporal postpositional phrase *laso arnipenke* 'from this day on' represents the first topic. The O argument of the verb stem *pavē* 'cause to not exist', *hala hi'ipi* 'that witch', represents the second topic, which is reactivated here after having been an important character in the story before.

(748) Double topic (temporal NP and person participant)
lasi laso arnipenke hala hi'ipi aphanke pavedetlo,

lasì	[lasō arnì=pen=ke]₁	[hála hī'ipī aphān=ke]₂
therefore	**this day=from=TOP**	that witch NSUBJ=TOP

pe-avē-dèt-lò
CAUS-not.exist-PFV-RL

la Karbipipensi alangtum choboche chosonse, aosomarpen

là	Karbì-pī=pen=si	alàng-tūm	chobochè	chosonsé
this	PN-female=with=FOC:RL	3-PL	settle.down	EE:chobochè

a-osō-mār=pen
POSS-child-PL=with
'From that very day on, he killed the witch (lit. made her not exist), with the Karbi woman they settled down, with the children.' [CST, HM 119]

In (749) and (750), =*ke* occurs on each of two contrasting topics in two different clauses. In (749), the two clauses are constructed parallel to one another, which makes it very straightforward to see how =*ke* marks contrastive topics.

(749) Topic =*ke* in contrastive topic construction
       inutke hi'ipi, inutke arlengpi, Karbipi
       [e-nūt=ke   hī'ipī] **[e-nūt=ke**   [arlēng-pī   Karbì-pī]]
       one-CLF:HUM:SG=TOP witch   **one-CLF:HUM:SG=TOP** person-FEM   PN-FEM
       '**One** is a witch, **one/the other** is a woman, a Karbi woman.' [CST, HM 006]

In another example of the contrastive topic construction in (750), the clauses are not structured exactly parallel to one another, but the contrast is still very clear: '*you* have already reached', and '*we* don't know how to get there'.

(750) Topic =*ke* in contrastive topic construction
       e nanghem nangritlo, nangke nangcheleroklo
       [e   nang-hēm   nang-rīt-lò]   **[nàng=ke** nang=chV-lē-ròk-lò]
       DSM   2POSS-house   2POSS-field-RL **you=TOP**   CIS=RR-reach-completed-RL

       netumke damthekthelo, nangphipen
       [ne-tūm=ke   dàm-thèk-Cē-lò   nang-phì=pen
       1EXCL-PL=TOP go-know.how-NEG-RL   2POSS-grandmother=with

       nangphuké
       nang-phù=ke]
       2POSS-grandfather=TOP
       'It's your house and property, **you**'ve already reached, (but) **we** won't know how to go, your grandmother and your grandfather.' [KK, BMS 096]

The next example is part of a story, in which a dog takes his owner to *Chom Arong* 'Chom's Village', the place in Karbi mythology where the dead people reside. In (751), the dog and its owner have reached a huge body of water on their journey. In this sentence, the dog is speaking, and =*ke* occurs on the first person pronoun subject. It appears that the function of =*ke* here is to indicate the despair of the dog over the difficulty of the task; =*ke* may thus serve to evoke a set of candidates more likely to succeed in the challenge. This is similar to the contrastive topic function discussed before.

(751) Topic =*ke* evoking a set of more likely candidates?
       kopusi neke nangkepaparponpoma
       kopù=si   **nè=ke**   nang=ke-pa-pár-pòn-pò=ma
       how=FOC:RL   **1EXCL=TOP** 1/2:NSUBJ=NMLZ-CAUS-cross(<Asm)-take.away-IRR1=Q
       'How will I (of all people) take you across the water?' [KK, BMS 045]

Finally, while the above examples suggest that =ke is only used with given and referential, or definite, participants, (752) shows that the derived indefinite pronoun *komatne* 'somebody' may also occur with =ke.

(752) Topic-marked indefinite pronoun
komatneke... la ser kapali'et asonsi
[komāt-nē=ke... là sér ke-pa-lì-èt asón=si]
who-INDEF=TOP this gold NMLZ-CAUS-flow-RES:yellow like=FOC:RL

acharpen ketheklong langmepik [...]
[[a-chár=pen ke-theklōng] [làng-mē-pīk]]
POSS-far.away=from NMLZ-see see-be.good-very
'As if somebody had colored it with gold to make it look yellow and shiny, from far away it's very pretty [...].' [SiT, HF 021]

Finally, a construction that 'topic' =ke as well as 'additive' =tā occur in is the (affected) possessor construction (see §14.2.5 and §13.2.2.4).

14.2.2 Additive =tā

Additive =tā fulfills a number of non-pragmatic functions (§10.8.3.1). As an information/discourse structure clitic, it occurs in two particular types of constructions, with the overarching function of marking what may be referred to as 'topic-switch'.

In one construction type, it occurs in the context of converse verb pairs, such as 'ask'–'answer', 'give'–'take', or 'throw'–'catch'. If a speaker describes an event using converse verb pairs and therefore describes an event from two perspectives, =tā typically occurs on the subject of the second part of the converse verb pair description. This is shown in (753) and (754), where the converse verb pairs are 'ask'–'answer' and 'take (interview)'–'give (interview)'.

(753) =tā signaling the perspective-switch from asking to answering (converses)
"chokjima?" pu, nephan arjulo,
[[chók-jí=mà] pù ne-phān arjū-lò]
be.fine-IRR2=Q QUOT 1EXCL-NSUBJ ask-RL

amatsi neta pulo, "chok [...]"
[amātsi nè=**tā** pù-lò chók]
and.then 1EXCL=**ADD** say-RL be.fine
'"Is it fine?", they asked me, and I replied, "It's fine [...]."' [SH, CSM 049]

(754) =tā signaling the perspective-switch from taking to giving (converses)
*latum interview enlo, alang**ta** interview chepidunlo*
[la-tūm   interview ēn-lò]   [alàng=**tā** interview che-pí-dùn-lò]
DEM.PROX-PL interview take-RL   3=**ADD**   interview RR-give-JOIN-RL
'They took interviews (from her), and she also gave them interviews.'
[SH, CSM 050]

In the other construction type, =tā marks a reactivated topic that contrasts with the current topic. This function of =tā is argued here to indicate discourse continuity, i.e., as telling the listener to understand the utterance as being strongly connected to the previous discourse despite the fact that the topic has changed (cf. also Kaplan's (1984: 514) explanation of obligatory English 'too' as "to emphasize the similarity between contrasting constituents"). This strong connection is typically afforded by a causal, resultative, or reactive relationship to the previous event, as demonstrated with the following examples.

In the folk story *Chonghokaloso lapen Misorongpo* 'The Frog and the Ant' (see Appendix B), there are numerous instances of topic-switch =tā due to the structure of the story, which is built on the idea of a chain reaction of events: after a fight between an ant and a frog, the ant bites the frog, the frog is mad and jumps around and destroys a squirrel's ladder, the squirrel gets mad and gnaws a fruit off a tree, which then falls on the back of a pig, and so on. In the end, a rock kills the king's daughter, and as the king tries to find out who he can hold responsible, he traces the chain reaction back to the frog and the ant and punishes them. This story that is built on this chain reaction of events offers a number of natural topic-switch situations that are marked by =tā. For example, in (755), the first clause states that the frog, ellipsed via zero anaphora (§13.4.3), is in rage and jumps on the squirrels ladder, which then breaks. As a consequence, the squirrel, marked by =tā, gets angry. It is this topic switch to the squirrel as it reacts to the frog's action that is marked by =tā.

(755) Topic-switch: =tā marking new topic reacting to action by previous topic
karlesibongpo adon chonrai
[karlēsibōngpō a-dón]   chōn-rài
squirrel.sp   POSS-bridge   jump-RES:solid.obj.breaking

amat karlesibongpota aning thilo
amāt   karlēsibōngpō=**tā** [a-nīng   thī-lò]
and.then   squirrel.sp=**ADD**   POSS-mind   be.short-RL
'(The frog) jumped on the ladder of the squirrel so it broke, and then the squirrel **in turn** got angry.' [RBT, ChM 018-9]

In (756), Bamonpo's wife passes away, as expressed euphemistically in the first clause with the expression *Chom chevoi* 'return to Chom (i.e., the mythological village of the dead)'. As a consequence, Bamonpo, marked by =tā, is desperate and full of worries.

(756) Topic-switch: =tā indicating a consequence
so Chom chevoijuilo, ansi "mai! kopusi
[sō]   [Chóm che-vói-jùi-lò]   [ánsi   mái   kopù=si
DEM.PROX PLACE RR-return-away-RL after.that how.bad! how=FOC:RL

kedothek apotloma?", mh, bamonpota ningrilo
ke-dō-thèk   apōtlo=ma]   [bamón-pō=**tā**   ningrī-lò]
NMLZ-stay-know.how should= Q   wise.person(<Ind)-male=**ADD**   worry-RL
'She returned to Chom, **and so Bamonpo** worried, "How bad! How should I be able to live on?"' [KK, BMS 015]

The next example is from a story about an orphan who encounters a tiger. Here, over the last few text units, the tiger has just threatened the orphan and said that he will take away the orphan. In (757), the storyteller switches back to the orphan protagonist. This kind of topic-switch after the end of direct speech (i.e., topic-switch to the addressee of the direct speech) is very commonly marked by =tā on the new topic.

(757) Topic-switch in larger context (057–063: tiger threatening orphan)
*jangrengso abang**ta** repik tangho*
[jangrengsō abàng=**tā**]   rè-pìk   tànghò
orphan   NPDL=**ADD** be.sharp-very REP
'(But) the orphan is very smart.' [HK, TR 064]

As a last example, consider (758), where the topic-switch does not involve a subject-switch as has been the case in the previous examples. This is from a story where a king's children are abandoned in a jungle without the king ever knowing they existed. Here, at the end of the story, the children return and the king recognizes that they are in fact his children. In (758), the first clause is the direct speech of the king proclaiming to the children that he considers them to be indeed his children. In the second clause, the topic switches from the king to the children, as the action of the king taking his children home consequentially follows from the recognition that they are his children.

(758) Topic-switch: =tā on -*phān* marked argument
"o nangtum nesolo" pusi... laso aHingchong
[[o   nang-tūm   ne-osō-lò]   pusi]   [[lasō   a-Hingchòng
AFF 2-PL   1EXCL:POSS-child-RL QUOT.COMP this   POSS-PN

musoso aphanta hem chehangponlo
musōsō]   aphān=**tā**]   hēm   che-háng-pòn-lò
siblings:DL   NSUBJ=ADD   house   RR-call-take.away-RL
'"O, you are my children!" he said, **and so** he called **these two Hingchong siblings** home.' [CST, HM 106]

Finally, a construction that 'additive' =*tā* as well as 'topic' =*ke* occur in is the (affected) possessor construction (see §14.2.5 and §13.2.2.4).

Recent research has shown that additive particles with similar pragmatic functions to Karbi =*tā* exist in a wide range of languages all across the world. Within the Afroasiatic language family, Tosco's (2010: 330 ff.) account of the Gawwada additive particle as a "topic-switching device" very strongly resembles Karbi =*tā*. Similarly and also within Afroasiatic, the Amharic -*mm* enclitic discussed by Demeke and Meyer (2008) has very clear parallels with Karbi =*tā*. Likewise, within Niger-Congo, the Avatime additive particle covers a similar pragmatic function (Putten 2011). Outside Africa, Öpengin (2013) reports the same type of pragmatic functions for the Central Kurdish additive particle, and Diana Forker (June 2013, p.c.) for several Nakh-Daghestanian languages in the Caucasus.[138]

14.2.3 Realis focus =*si*

Realis focus =*si* occurs in affirmative, declarative main clauses and appears to be in complementary distribution with =*le* 'irrealis focus', which occurs in a number of irrealis-type constructions (see §14.2.4 on =*le*, and see §15.3 on the notion of realis vs. irrealis in focus clitics). I call =*si* and =*le* focus markers because they both mark contrastive/corrective focus, schematically 'not X=*le*, but Y=*si*' (§14.2.5). However, =*si* also occurs in a range of other, more or less focus-like, constructions.

In (759) we see an example of corrective/contrastive focus from natural text, which can be schematically represented as 'not X=ADD, not Y=ADD, but Z=*si*'.

(759) Contrastive/corrective focus with =*si* in text (with nominalizer *ke*-)
la-tūm   [[phelāng=pen=tā kalī]   [tín=pen=tā   kalī]]
this-PL   thatch=with=ADD   NEG.EQU.COP   tin(<Eng)=with=ADD   NEG.EQU.COP

---

[138] It thus may be the case that is cross-linguistically common that additive particles are used as topic-switch devices, and that Western Indo-European languages are cross-linguistically odd in this respect.

[arlōng   a-chèt=pen=**si**]   ki-dìp [...]
stone   POSS-piece=with=**FOC:RL**   NMLZ-cover
'Neither with thatch nor with tin, but with slabs of stone they cover (their roofs) [...]' [SiT, HF 050]

In (760) we see an example of restrictive focus: the orphan 'all by himself' performed the action. For a discussion of additional and more specific restrictive focus constructions, which optionally involve =si, see §14.2.6.3.

(760)   Restrictive focus with =si 'focus'
        [lasō   a-tángká-án=ke]   jangrēngsō=**si**   ke-vàn-thū-lò
        this   POSS-money-all=TOP   orphan=**FOC:RL**   NMLZ-bring-again-RL
        'All this money the orphan brought back by himself.' [HK, TR 197]

In (761), which is from the same story about the orphan, =si occurs on *lují* 'mirror' in a clause that describes a mirror being attached to a tobacco container. This mirror ends up being instrumental in the orphan's successful lie to a tiger, which helps him reverse his role from being a victim to scaring the tiger off. The =si marking could thus be signaling the importance of this referent, as a way to indicate that this referent should be paid attention to.

(761)   Focus =si to indicate an important referent?
        anke laso athongkup along lujisi kapabon [...]
        ánke   lasō   a-thongkūp   alòng lují=**si**
        and.then   this   POSS-tobacco.container   LOC   mirror=**FOC:RL**
        ke-pa-bōn
        NMLZ-CAUS-be.attached
        'And then, on this tobacco container, there was a mirror attached [...].' [HK, TR 026]

Focus =si frequently occurs on content question words, such as *kopù* 'how' in (762), which represents another argument to call it a focus marker; content question words are naturally under focus as they represent new or sought-for information.[139]

(762)   Focus =si on content question word
        kopusi neke nangkepaparponpoma
        kopù=**si**   nè=ke   nang=ke-pa-pár-pòn-pò=ma
        how=**FOC:RL**   1EXCL=TOP   1/2:NSUBJ=NMLZ-CAUS-cross(<Asm)-take.away-IRR1=Q
        'How will I take you across the water?' [KK, BMS 045]

---

[139] For the use of realis focus =si as opposed to irrealis focus =le on content question words, see §15.3.2.

There are a range of elements which often have =*si* attached, while the force of the focus is weak and the forms appear to be semi-lexicalized. One such type of element is discourse connectors ('and then') such as *amāt* or *amātsi*, and apparently also in the forms *lasì* and *ánsi* (§16.1.3). Another type of elements are adverbs meaning 'like this', such as *lasón* in (763).

(763)   Focus =*si* on *lasón* 'this way' (weak focus)
       lasi Bokolapo atomo lasonsí monit atum non

lasì	Bokolāpō	a-tomó	lasón=**si**	monít	a-tūm	nón
therefore	NAME	POSS-story	that.way=**FOC:RL**	man	POSS-PL	now

       chethanbom
       che-thán-bòm
       RR-tell-CONT
       'And so that's how people continue to tell each other the story of Bokolapo nowadays.' [HI, BPh 021]

Focus =*si* also fairly frequently occurs on subordinators such as *aphī* 'after', *apōt* 'because', or *aphān* 'in order to', without a clear change in semantics or pragmatics. Marking a subordinator with =*si* does not yield a restrictive sense along the lines of 'only after' or 'only because'. In (764), *aphī* 'after' occurs with =*si* in a simple personal narration of a sequence of activities: 'after we drank tea, we watched the drumming'. There is no sense of any special status of this sequence of events.

(764)   Subordinator *aphī* 'after' with =*si* 'focus'

ánsi	là	sá	jùn-ét	a-ját-ét	aphī=**si**
after.that	this	tea(<Ind)	drink-already	POSS-type-already	after=**FOC:RL**

ne-tūm	chēng	ki-thīp	làng-dūn-lò
1EXCL-PL	drum	NMLZ-beat.drum	see-JOIN-RL

       'After we drank tea and everything, we watched the drumming.' [SH, CSM 041]

Finally, there are also a number of instances in which =*si* occurs on locative NPs, as in (765). Future study will need to address whether these can be somehow subsumed under the general focus marking function, or whether they need to be accounted for otherwise.

(765)   =*si* 'focus' with locative function

nè	ke-dō	a-jakát	abàng=ke	hápú	kenē
[1EXCL	NMLZ-exist	POSS-place(<Asm)	NPDL=TOP]	that.side	HESIT

Sochēng-Dhenta	a-nátthū	Duarsalona=**si**	ke-dō
[TOWN	POSS-direction]	AREA=**FOC:RL**	NMLZ-exist

       'The place where I live is that side, it's towards Socheng Dhenta, in Duarsalona.' [KK, CC 004]

Focus =*si* may have its origin in a copula, as apparent copula *si(i)* cognates exist in 'Kuki-Chin'. This then would also explain the common occurrence of *ke-* 'nominalizer' on predicates in clauses that have an NP marked with =*si*. The diachronic nominalization scenario that accounts for copulas grammaticalizing to focus markers is discussed in §12.7.3.1. Another (or perhaps in the end the same) possibility for the etymology and apparent cognates of =*si* is to link it to demonstrative *si* in Meitei (Chelliah 1997: 81).

Note that there are a few instance of a =*lo* focus marker in the corpus, which must be linked historically to the realis predicate suffix -*lò*. As discussed in §9.6.1.7, judging from the few occurrences of =*lo* in the corpus, there is no functional difference to realis focus =*si*. As further research is required, however, =*lo* will not be further discussed here.

14.2.4 Irrealis focus =*le*

Irrealis focus =*le* occurs in complementary distribution with realis focus =*si*. The irrealis contexts in which =*le* occurs include non-declarative speech acts (§15.1), subordinate clauses, deontic predicates that involve *náng* 'need', and negated predicates. For a discussion of irrealis clause types, see §15.3.

In (766), =*le* occurs in the first clause with a negated predicate and in the second clause with an imperative. The focus marking here suggests that there is a set of alternatives to the focus marked element, and that a previous false preconception is being corrected. In the first clause, the first person pronoun is focus-marked. While it is clear that there is somebody who is guilty in this context, the speaker asserts – and corrects the wrong belief – that it is not him. In the second clause of this example, the focus marking again highlights the existence of a set of alternatives. This time, one alternative is the speaker himself and that alternative is contrasted and corrected with the focus-marked participant, the Vo'arbipi bird.

(766) =*le* marking contrastive/corrective focus
"Apot nele kechokche kali, richo. Hala
[apōt   **nè=le**   ke-chók-Cē   **kalī**   richó] [[hála
because **1EXCL=FOC:IRR**   NMLZ-be.fine-NEG   **NEG.EQU.COP** king   that

vo'arbipi aphanle arjudamnoi!"
võarbí-pī   **a-phān=le**]   arjū-dām-**nōi**]
bird.sp-female **POSS-NSUBJ=FOC:IRR** ask-go-**INFRML.COND.IMP**
'"Therefore, I'm not the guilty one, king, go ask that Voarbipi!"' [RBT, ChM 037]

The next example shows that it is, however, not always contrastive/corrective focus which is marked by =*le*. In this story, the mother of two little children dies. In (767), the father desperately addresses his children.[140] One thing he says is *itum nangpei=le kedo kalilo* 'we don't have your mother anymore', where *=le* occurs on *nangpei* 'your mother'. It is clear that 'your mother' does not contrast with any concrete alternative here, in the sense that there was any belief that somebody else could have died. It does make sense, however, to think of the function of *=le* here as emphasizing how compared to the death of any person, the loss of the mother is the most difficult loss to cope with.

(767) *=le* not marking contrastive/corrective focus
si asomar aphan charjulo "o pei atum
[sì   a-oso-màr   a-phān   che-arjū-lò]   [ó   pēi   a-tūm
therefore POSS-child-PL POSS-NSUBJ RR-ask-RL   vocative mother   POSS-PL

te kopujilangma? itum nangpeile kedo
tē   ko-pù-jí-lāng=ma]   [e-tūm   **nang-pēi=le**   ke-dō
if   WH-like.this-IRR2-still=Q 1INCL-PL   **2:POSS-MOTHER=FOC:IRR** NMLZ-exist

kalilo, nangpeita arnam mandamlo arni
kalī-lò]   [nang-pēi=tā   arnàm   mán-dàm-lò
NEG.EQU.COP-RL 2:POSS-mother=ADD god   become/happen-go-RL
arnì
EE:arnàm

mandamlo apot
mán-dàm-lò   apōt]
become/happen-go-RL because
'Therefore, he asked his children, "O mothers, so then, what else could we do?", We don't have your mother anymore, because your mother has gone to become god (i.e., has died).' [CST, RO 008]

See the next section, §14.2.5, for more information on how *=le* relates to, and interacts with, the other core information/discourse structure clitics.

A possibility for the etymology of *=le* is to relate it to the negative equational copula *kalī* (§6.2.2.2). As *kalī* is likely to diachronically consist of two morphemes, where the first, velar onset syllable is the negative morpheme and the second, lateral-onset syllable is the copula, this second morpheme in *kalī* could very well be historically the same morpheme as *=le*. Copulas often grammaticalize to focus markers in cleft constructions, which, in fact, likely happened with *=si* as well (§12.7.3.1). The fact that it is specifically (the copula portion of) the negative equational copula that may be

---

140 Note that it is common in Karbi to address one's children as *pēi~pāi* 'mother' and *pō* 'father'.

the grammaticalization source of =*le* would have further explanatory force given that =*le* marks focus in irrealis contexts only.

14.2.5 Relationships between core information/discourse structure clitics

As mentioned above, both =*ke* and =*tā* occur in the (affected) possessor construction (see §13.2.2.4), as in (768) and (769).

(768) Possession construction with unmarked A, 2nd person possessive-marked O
"nangdun nangne" puta, kroikredetlo,
[nang=dùn   náng-Cē   pu=tā]   [krōi-Cē-dèt-lò]
CIS=join   need-NEG   QUOT=ADD:although   agree-NEG-PFV-RL

"nangke nangdin dolang"
[nàng=ke]$_{A/POSR}$ [nang-dín]$_{O/POSD}$ dō-làng]
2=TOP   2POSS-DAY(<ASM)   exist-still
'Although (she) said, "(You) shouldn't follow me!", he didn't agree (saying), "You still have your life to live (lit. days)."' [KK, BMS 084]

(769) Possession construction with unmarked A and 1st person exclusive possessive-marked O
*[...] amat **neta neri** ave **nekeng** ave [...]*
amāt   [nè=tā]$_{A/POSR}$ [ne-rí]$_{O/POSD}$ avē   [ne-kèng]$_{O/POSD}$
and.then   1EXCL=ADD   1EXCL:POSS-HAND   not.exist   1EXCL:POSS-FOOT
avē
not.exist
'[...] [A]nd then also, I don't have hands or feet [...].' [RBT, ChM 030]

In a different construction, =*ke* and =*tā* can co-occur in the same clause as they mark different constituents. This is perhaps not surprising considering that =*ke* can occur on two different elements in the same clause as shown above in §14.2.1 (note, however, that topic-switch =*tā* does not occur twice in the same clause). Example (770) shows that within the same clause, the -*phān* 'non-subject' marked R argument may occur with =*tā* and the unmarked A argument with =*ke*. The context of this folk story that allows this coocurrence of =*tā* and =*ke* is as follows. Bokolapo, a folk story fool character, asks his children why they are calling him their father, as Bokolapo thinks that he is in a different village. Example (770) directly follows Bokolapo's direct speech talking to his children, and =*tā* thus occurs after direct speech, which is typical (see §14.2.2). After this sentence, which explains how Bokolapo mistakenly talks to his children not knowing that they are his children, the topic does indeed switch to the children. In this sentence, however, Bokolapo still is the topic, and is marked as such by =*ke*.

(770) Additive topic-switch =tā and =ke marking two arguments in the same clause
asomar aphantá Bokolapo abangké lasonsi lam
[a-so-màr   aphān=**tā**]   [Bokolā-pō abàng=**ke**] lasón=si   lám
POSS-child-PL NSUBJ=**ADD**   NAME-male   NPDL=**TOP**   that.way=FOC:RL   word

thakdunronglo
thàk-dūn-ròng-lò
answer-JOIN-instead-RL
'(To) his (own) children, Bokolapo mistakenly answered like this.' [HI, BPh 013]

Next the relationship between the two focus clitics needs to be considered. Example (771), which is elicited, shows their complementary distribution in corrective focus statements, which schematically are: 'not X=*le*, but Y=*si*'.

(771) Contrastive/corrective with irrealis focus =*le* and realis focus =*si*
[nè   phàk-ōk=**le**   ki-tún   kalī]   [vō-ōk=**si**
1EXCL   pig-meat=**FOC:IRR** NMLZ-cook   NEG.EQU.COP bird-meat=**FOC:RL**

***ki**-tún*]
NMLZ-cook
'I don't/won't cook pork, I (will) cook chicken.' [Elicitation SiT 090303]

Nonetheless, =*si* and =*le* can co-occur (on different constituents) in the same clause. The construction in which this is possible is content questions. Here, the content question word is often marked by =*si*, while another element in the same clause can be marked as focus as well, then receiving irrealis focus marking via =*le* (see also §15.3.2). An example is (772).

(772) Realis focus =*si* on content question word; irrealis focus =*le* on other element
[...] nonke methan-sibongpopen banghinivetle kopusi pirthe
nón=ke   methān-sibóngpō=pen   bàng-hiní-vèt=**le**
now=TOP   dog-SPECIES =with   CLF:HUM:PL-two-only=**FOC:IRR**
kopù=**si**   pirthé
how=**FOC:RL**   world

mindar dodunthekpoma pulo
mindár   dō-dūn-thèk-pò=ma   pu-lò
world(<Pnr) stay-JOIN-know.how-IRR1=Q   QUOT-RL
'[...] "Now, how will I manage to stay in the world just the two of us with the dog?" (he thought).' [KK, BMS 016]

Finally, let us examine data that document how topic and focus marking can interact. As shown in (773), both contrastive topic and contrastive focus can be marked within the same sentence. The example consists of two parallel clauses, which have the same verb *chō* 'eat', while both the A arguments and the locatives are contrasted. The contrasting A arguments are *nangpo* 'your father' and *nangtum* 'you (both)'. The contrasting locatives are *hemtap angsong* 'up in the tree house' and *mandu* '(in) the field hut'. While the two participants are marked as we would expect in the second clause, i.e., the A as topic and the locative as focus, the first clause has the A marked as focus and the locative unmarked. This may be because the speaker had not planned the whole sentence as he was producing the first clause. The second clause does give us evidence, however, of how topic and focus marking can interact in an expected pattern. Note that irrealis focus *=le* occurs in both clauses for different reasons: in the first clause because it is a (subordinate) conditional clause, in the second clause because it is an unmarked imperative.

(773) Contrastive topic and contrastive focus: *=le* 'irrealis focus' and *=ke* 'topic'
 [...] *nangpole hemtap angsong chote nangtumke mandule cho*
 [[nang-pō=**le**   hēmtāp   angsóng   chō-tē]   nang-tūm=**ke**
 2-father=**FOC:IRR** tree.house high.up   eat-if   2-PL=**TOP**
 mandú=**le**   chō]
 field.hut=**FOC:IRR** eat
 '"[...] [I]f your father takes his meal in the *hemtap*, you eat in the *mandu*!"'
 [CST, RO 017]

Lastly, (774) shows that *=tā*, *=ke* and *=le* can occur within the same clause. Here, we have two topics marked by *=tā* and *=ke* as also seen above in (770), and in addition a focused adverb marked by *=le*.

(774) Interaction of additive *=tā*, topic *=ke* and irrealis focus *=le*
 amat "anborta pinike nangtum hadakle an
 [amāt   àn-bòr=**tā**   pinì=**ke**   nang-tūm
 and.then rice-wrapped.bundle=**ADD** today=**TOP** you-PL
 hádāk=**le**   àn
 there=**FOC:IRR** rice

 chodunnoi! kaita dah nangtumta
 chō-dūn-nōi]   [kái=tā   dáh   nang-tūm=tā
 eat-JOIN-INFRML.COND.IMP   always=ADD   go!   you-PL=ADD

 chodunnoi! [...]"
 chō-dūn-nōi]
 eat-JOIN-INFRML.COND.IMP
 'And then, "The rice bundles, today, eat them there!" (She would) always (say), "Go! You too eat together (there) [...]!"' [CST, RO 017]

While all of the data presented above demonstrate that we can group topic markers =*ke* and =*tā* on the one hand, as well as focus markers =*si* and =*le* on the other hand, there is a single construction that suggests a different grouping, which is the intensifier copy verb construction. Here, the the irrealis construction uses =*le* (§16.2.3.3), while the realis construction uses =*tā* rather than =*si* (§16.2.3.2).

14.2.6 Other information/discourse status constructions

14.2.6.1 Constituent order

This section offers some evidence for the pragmatic basis of constituent order variation. Karbi is verb-final like most Tibeto-Burman languages. However, it is relatively easy to find clauses with arguments placed after the verb if they represent old or given information. The following examples demonstrate this for mono-, bi-, and trivalent clauses. In (775), the S argument occurs after the verb as it represents old information, which is evidenced by the preceding question with verb focus rather than argument focus.

(775) SV in question followed by VS in answer
"*pine akam doma jirpo ho?*" {*mm*}

[NP]$_S$	V

[pí-nē   a-kám]   dō=ma jīrpō   hò   mm
what-INDEF POSS-work   exist=Q friend EMPH:INTERACT   AFF
'Is there any work, friend?' [HK, TR 130]

"*ave **akamke**, seta vangthahe*".... *damlo* {*mm*}

V	[NP]$_S$

avē   a-kám=ke   setā vàng-thā=he....   dàm-lò mm
not.exist **POSS-WORK=TOP**   but   come-CON.IMP=EMPH   go-RL   AFF
'"There is no work, but come here (anyway)", and he went.' [HK, TR 131]

In (776) and (777), the A argument and the O argument, respectively, occur after the verb as they represent old information. In (776), this is evidenced by the use of the distal demonstrative *hála*, which is frequently used for discourse-old information. In (777), the evidence lies in how the speaker corrects herself after first saying 'men and women' to saying 'mothers and fathers', thereby clearly making the O argument 'children' given information, because the terms 'mothers and fathers' versus 'women and men' imply that this is about children.

(776) OVA
damchot aphi... phutup kitirok theklongloklo

	[NP]ₒ	V
[dàm-chót a-phì]	[phutūp ke-tī-ròk]	thèklōng-lòk-lò
go-a.bit POSS-after	hat NMLZ-leave.behind-COMPL	see-just-RL

hala bol ke'otdong a'oso abang

[NP]ₐ
[hála [ból ke-ót-dòng] a-osō abàng]]
that ball(<Eng) NMLZ-touch-attached POSS-child NPDL

'And then, after going just a bit, (he) saw the hat that had (fallen down and) been left behind, that boy that was holding the ball.' [SiT, PS 035]1[141]

(777) AVO
lasi pinso arlo ba apai apota

		[NP]ₐ			
lasì	[pinsō	arlò]	bá	[a-pāi	a-pō=tā]
therefore	married.man	woman	or(<Asm)	POSS-mother	POSS-father=ADD

pachehoman osomar aphan, laso

V	[NP]ₒ	
pe-che-homán	[osō-mār a-phān]]	lasō
CAUS-RR-be.equal(<Asm)	child-PL POSS-NSUBJ	this

adaito che'en pute,] [bangbang
a-daitó che-én pu-tē bàng~bāng
POSS-responsibility(<Asm) RR-take QUOT-COND CLF:HUM:PL-DIST.PL

akhai ason] mane undunjima pusi
a-khái asón mane ùn-dūn-jí=ma pusi
POSS-community like I.mean(<Asm) be.able-JOIN-IRR2=Q QUOT.COMP

---

[141] The literal translation imitates the constituent order of Karbi. The comma before the A NP in the translation is only intended to facilitate reading and is not supposed to imply that the speaker is pausing. The recording is very clear that the A NP is part of the same intonation unit as the preceding O NP and predicate and therefore a clause-internal (rather than extra-clausal) participant.

nelita kamatha
nè-lì=tā   ke-mathà
1EXCL-HON=ADD   NMLZ-think

'So the men and women, or the mothers and fathers, if they make themselves equal for the children, if they take this their own responsibility, then like other peoples' tribes we will be successful (on a par with other peoples' tribes), (that is what) I think.' [KaR, SWK 052]

In (778), the R argument in this trivalent clause is given information, because the T argument *aphutup* is marked possessive and the R argument is the possessor, so the T argument makes the R argument old or given information.

(778) TVR
lapenke aphutup pidetlo laphan

[NP]₍T₎	V	[NP]₍R₎
lapèn=ke	a-phutūp pī-dèt-lò	là-phān
and.then=TOP	POSS-hat give-PFV-RL	this-NSUBJ

'And then, he gave him his hat.' [SiT, PS 038]

Finally, although zero anaphora (§13.4.3) is very common and clauses with all arguments overtly expressed are rare in the corpus of recorded texts, the default is for A arguments to go in sentence-initial position, presumably because A arguments tend to be topics. Whether there is a default for positioning of R and T arguments in trivalent constructions is unclear (see §13.2.1.3). Due to the seeming default of sentence-initial A arguments and the verb-final structure of Karbi, however, we can say that there is a default for bivalent clauses with overtly expressed NPs to be AOV. However, there certainly are examples where that is not the case, as already shown above with A and O occurring after the verb. Another example of a bivalent clause that is not AOV is (779), where the order instead is OAV. The first two lines offer the context for the OAV clause: The king has two children, which, however, he never knew, because they were taken by a witch right after they were born. After many years, the king finally meets his children and finds out the truth. The example below starts with an exclamation by the king: 'They are indeed my children!'

(779) OAV
apot laso aricho abang mathalo, "ai!
apōt   [lasō a-rechó   abàng] mathà-lò ái
because this POSS-king NPDL   think-RL how.strange!

nesomarlo laho!" pu
ne-oso-màr-lò   làho   pu
1EXCL:POSS-child-PL-RL   EXCLAM   QUOT

'Therefore, the king thought, "How strange! They are indeed my children!"' [CST, HM 084] *aosomar aphan halaso aricho abang hangpon'et*

[NP]₀	[NP]ₐ	[NP]ᵥ
[a-osō-mār aphān]	[hálasō a-rechó abàng]	háng-pòn-ét
POSS-child-PL NSUBJ	that POSS-king NPDL	call-take.away-PRF

'The king called his children to take them with him.' [CST, HM 085]

The next text unit describes the subsequent action by the king, which is to take his children home. At this point, the king has been the topic, and the fact that the children are his children (marked possessive by *a-*) is new information. This could explain why we find OAV order here.

14.2.6.2 New participant marking

As discussed in more detail in §10.7.2.6.1, new participants are typically marked by an indefiniteness construction that is built on pre-head enumeration with 'one'.

14.2.6.3 Restrictive focus markers

There are at least six restrictive focus markers, which differ in morphological status, syntactic distribution, and semantic and pragmatic functions. Table 113 gives an overview of the forms and distributions; the abbreviation 'CLF/NUM/QUANT' stands for 'classifiers/numerals/quantifiers'. Note that all markers are glossed as 'only' in examples.

Table 113: Distribution of restrictive focus markers.

Occurs on/with >	CLF/NUM/QUANT	Noun	Verb
angsé	–	+	+
anàt ~	–	+	+
-nàt	+	–	–
-vèt	+	–	–
-lòk	–	+	+
-dèt	–	+	–
-chòt	?	–	+

'+' means that the marker occurs with the particular element, '–' means it does not, and '?' means that there is currently no evidence to tell for sure.

With respect to morphological status, there is a lot of variation. We find one full word, *angsé*; one element that occurs as a full word *anát* when it syntactically modifies a noun or predicate but occurs as a suffix on classifiers, numerals, and quantifiers; and finally, there are four markers that only occur as suffixes. Full words occur as post-head modifiers.

Table 114: Functions of restrictive focus markers.

Function >	Exclusively	Exclusively and constantly	Does not meet numeric/measurable expectation	Does not meet semantic/pragmatic expectation ('merely')
Associated with >	entity	event	entity	entity / event
Marked on >	noun	noun / verb	CLF/NUM/QUANT	noun / verb
angsé	–	?	–	+
(a-)nàt	+	+	+	+
-vèt	–	–	+	–
-lók	–	+	–	?
-dèt	+	–	–	?
-chòt	–	+	+	+

As for their syntactic distribution, the markers differ in whether they attach to classifiers/numerals/quantifiers, nouns, predicates, or a combination of these, as shown in Table 113. Note that *anàt~-nàt* is the only marker whose form differs depending on which type of head it modifies. Finally, note that *angsé* is the only element for which a likely historical origin still exists in the language: the verb *angsé* 'be naked'. While *anàt* looks like a relator noun, there is no homophonous lexical item in modern Karbi that could represent its grammaticalization source element. The *-dèt* suffix is homophonous with exhaustive perfective *-dèt* (§9.5.1), and the exhaustive semantic component does make a relationship between the two suffixes likely, as does the fact that restrictive focus *-dèt* does not occur on verbs.

Table 114 shows which restrictive focus markers indicate which particular function, of which four have so far been identified.

The function described by the adverb 'exclusively' indicates that the referent of the noun marked as such is asserted to be the exclusive and only referent for which the proposition is correct. An elicited example with *-dèt* is (780). Here, if it ended up being the case that somebody besides or along with Kasang was bringing food, the sentence would not be truthful.

(780) *-dèt* marking 'exclusively' function
 Kasang-**dèt**=si àn ke-thòn-dām
 NAME-**only**=FOC:RL rice NMLZ-drop-GO
 'Only/exclusively Kasang (nobody else and nobody accompanying her) is bringing food.' [Elicitation SiT 111104]

An elicited minimal pair of (780) is (781). It illustrates the function of *-lók* to indicate the function described in Table 114 as 'exclusively and constantly'. Specifically this means that if there was anybody besides Kasang who kept bringing food or also if

Kasang only brings or brought food once, the sentence would not be truthful. Note that in both (780) and (781), the restrictive focus marked NP is additionally marked by the general focus particle =*si* (§14.2.3).

(781) *-lók* marking 'exclusively and constantly' function
*Kasang-**lók**=si   àn   ke-thòn-dām*
NAME-**only**=FOC:RL   rice   NMLZ-drop-GO
'Only/exclusively Kasang (nobody else and nobody accompanying her) keeps bringing food.' [Elicitation SiT 111104]

An example of this 'exclusively and constantly' marking function of *-lók* from the corpus of recorded texts is (782). Here the context makes it very clear that the action is going on 'constantly'.

(782) *-lók* marking 'exclusively and constantly' function
thap ketoklok jo arníta sanglongle,
[thàp   ke-tòk-lók]   [jó   arnì=tā   sáng-lōng-Cē]
cake.for.rice.beer IPFV-pound-only night day=ADD   take.rest-GET-NEG

thap ketoklok ketoklok, aso mok
[thàp   ke-tòk-lók   ke-tòk-lók]   [[[a-sō   mōk
cake.for.rice.beer IPFV-pound-only IPFV-pound-only   POSS-child breast

kachepechuji apor ave tangho
ke-che-pa-chū-jí]   a-pór]   avē   tànghò]
NMLZ-RR-CAUS-suck-IRR2   POSS-time   not.exist   REP
'They just kept pounding the rice for the rice beer cake, the whole time they didn't get to take rest, they were pounding the rice beer cake, they didn't even have time to breast-feed their children.' [WR, BCS 030]

In (783) we find a text example that shows *-vèt* occurring on classifier-numeral words. The restrictive focus here indicates that there is an expectation in this context that there should be a higher number than the one that the 'only' marker has scope over.

(783) *-vèt* for numeric/measuring only: No more than X
[…] api jonni alo
[a-pī   jōn-ní]   [a-lò
POSS-female/mother CLF:animal-two   POSS-male.animal

jonnivetlo jonphlivetlo
jōn-ní-**vèt**-lò]   [jōn-phlī-**vèt**-lò]
CLF:animal-two-**only**-RL   CLF:animal-four-**only**-RL
'[…] (It) was two hens and two roosters only, (it) was only four (that were left).' [SeT, MTN 028]

Lastly, the function 'not meeting the full expectation' with respect to a referent or event presupposes a contextually defined semantic and pragmatic scale of referent and events that fulfill a particular expectation more or less. In the folk story example in (784), a witch has previously taken the Karbi woman's children and abandoned them in the jungle, while putting two pieces of firewood in the cradle, which were meant to imitate the shape of the children. In (784), the witch says to the father, i.e., the king, that the Karbi woman had given birth to 'only' or 'merely' two pieces of firewood. Pieces of firewood clearly do not fulfill the expectation of actual human babies and would be ranked lower in an intuitive scale on what a woman should give birth to.

(784) *angsé* 'merely': does not meet full expectation (semantic/pragmatic scale)
nangpiso Karbipi asomar aso <ke.. ke> kehacheke
[[nang-pisò Karbì-pī a-oso-màr a-osō ke-haché=ke
2:POSS-wife PN-fem POSS-child-PL POSS-child NMLZ-be.born=TOP

thengpi abeng angse jaho hiní... pu
[thengpī a-bēng angsé] jaho hiní pu
tree/wood POSS-piece only look.there! two QUOT

anke hala richo abangta chelangdamlo bai
ánke hála richó abàng=tā che-lāng-dām-lò bái
and.then that king NPDL=ADD RR-see-go-RL how.bad!
'"Your wife's, the Karbipi's children that were born, they are only two pieces of wood (rather than real humans), look there at the two!", and then, that king also went himself to look (and exclaimed), "My goodness!"' [CST, HM 022]

15 Clause types and clause combining

This chapter offers an overview of different main and subordinate clause types. It does not go over nominalized and historically nominalized clause types, as they are discussed in Chapter 12. Likewise, it does not discuss declarative main clause types; intransitive, transitive, and ditransitive clauses – or mono-, bi-, and trivalent verbs – are the topic of §13.2.

The structure of this chapter is as follows. It begins with non-declarative main clause types in §15.1: interrogatives, imperatives, and hortatives. In §15.2, subordinate clause types and constructions are discussed, again, excluding any discussion of nominalization. In §15.3, an overview of irrealis clause types is provided, which emerge as a function of irrealis-sensitive non-final and focus markers. The next section §15.4 deals with (non-nominalized) insubordination constructions, i.e., formally subordinate clauses functioning as main clauses. In §15.5, the grammatically less prominent domain of clause coordination (as compared to clause chaining and other subordination) is discussed. Finally, §15.6 offers a few remarks on the lack of a grammaticalized syntactic pivot in Karbi to determine participant role continuity across clauses.

15.1 Non-declarative main clause types

Non-declarative main clause types represent the core of 'irrealis' constructions (see §15.3.2). This includes interrogatives (§15.1.1), imperatives (§15.1.2), and hortatives (§15.1.3). Another non-declarative main clause type discussed in Chapter 16 is exclamatives (§16.3.8).

15.1.1 Interrogatives

This overview of interrogatives begins with content questions in §15.1.1.2. After a terminological note on 'polar' and 'disjunctive' interrogatives in §15.1.1.3, the following four subsections discuss four (sets of) constructions that lie on a continuum with respect to the degree of the speaker's expectation that the reply will confirm the truth of the proposition. On this continuum, polar interrogatives (§15.1.1.4) are neutral and open, while tag questions (§15.1.1.7) indicate a strong expectation towards the truth of the proposition. Inbetween we find disjunctive interrogatives (§15.1.1.5), which are closer to polar interrogatives, and interrogative assumptions (§15.1.1.6), which are closer to tag questions. The last subsection is dedicated to the feedback request construction (§15.1.1.8).

15.1.1.1 Question particle =ma

The question particle =ma occurs mostly in polar interrogatives (§15.1.1.4.1) and disjunctive interrogatives (§15.1.1.5), as well as, in a pragmatically marked way, in content questions (§15.1.1.2.2).

A polar interrogative particle of the form *ma* is found in a large number of Tibeto-Burman languages. As pointed out by Thurgood (1983), there is a clear historical link between the interrogative *ma* and the common **ma* Tibeto-Burman or Trans-Himalayan preverbal negative, such that the interrogative must have developed from the negative. The reconstruction takes the common 'A-not-A' disjunctive question construction[142] as a starting point. In this construction, a polar question like 'do/did you eat?' is expressed as 'eat not-eat'. In order for the negative to be reanalyzed as a polar interrogative particle, all that has to happen is for the second repetition of the verb to be dropped.

15.1.1.2 Content questions with interrogative pronouns and adverbs

Content questions contain an interrogative pronoun or adverb, i.e., 'what', 'who', 'where', and so on (see §6.1.4). In the corpus, roughly two thirds of content questions are nominalized via the *ke-* prefix. This fact is best understood if we consider the content question construction to be a grammaticalized cleft construction, where the content question word is the element under focus. This is not only plausible in terms of content question words cross-linguistically being a very typical element under focus, but also with respect to Karbi internal evidence of =si 'focus:realis' frequently occurring on content question words. For further discussion, see §12.7.3.1.

In Karbi, there is no dedicated content question particle. The question particle =ma, however, which marks polar interrogatives may occur at the end of content questions.

15.1.1.2.1 Verb occurring without =ma

When eliciting content questions via translation from English, the verb is not marked by the question particle =ma, and also in texts, it appears that not using =ma is pragmatically more neutral.

Examples (785) and (786) are content questions in which the verb occurs without the question particle =ma. In both examples, the verb is nominalized (§12.7.3.1). In (785), the content question word *pīsi* 'why' apparently diachronically contains =si 'focus:realis' (see also §15.3.2) and, presumably as a result, cannot occur with either =si 'focus:realis' or =lo 'focus', which is otherwise common for interrogative pronouns and adverbs. In (786), *nát* 'where' is marked by =lo 'focus'.

---

142 See §15.1.1.5.1 for the equivalent, though structurally somewhat different, construction in Karbi.

(785) Content question without =ma
[...] "bai! pisi nang kardikphlilo?" pu [...]
bái **pīsi** nàng ke-ardīk-phlì-lò pu
how.bad! **why** you NMLZ-peep-for.awhile-RL QUOT
'[...] "How bad! Why are you looking?" [...]' [SeT, MTN 034]

(786) Content question without =ma
{latum natlo kedo ante?}
{là-tūm **nát=lo** ke-dō ánte}
this-PL **where=FOC** NMLZ-exist OK.then
'{Where are they staying then?}' [HK, TR 162]

While most questions have the content question word in clause-initial position, this is not necessarily the case, as shown in (786). Note that (786) is not an echo question that asks the addressee to reconfirm something already said, but the question asks for previously not addressed information. It is said by somebody listening to a storyteller tell this folk story (as indicated by the curly brackets), and the question is getting at the location of two protagonists of the story. It could therefore be the case, however, that the speaker in (786) knew the answer to his question, as he might have known the plot of the folk story.

15.1.1.2.2 Verb occurring with =ma

If the question particle =ma occurs at the end of a content question, then the question becomes rhetorical and is either not intended to elicit an answer, or at least signals that there is no 'correct answer' to the question that would satisfy the person asking. An elicited minimal pair is (787). Whereas (a) without =ma is pragmatically neutral and simply asks for new information, (b) may be asked in a situation where everybody had been worried about the absence of the addressee and the utterance has a strong pragmatic component of complaining about the addressee's absence.

(787) Content question minimal pair with and without =ma 'question particle'
(a) tumì **konát=si** ke-dàm-lò?
yesterday **where=FOC:RL** NMLZ-go-RL
'Where did you go yesterday?'

(b) tumì **konát=si** ke-dàm=ma?
yesterday **where=FOC:RL** NMLZ-go-Q
'Where did you possibly go yesterday?' [Elicitation KT 111208]

Examples from the corpus provide more evidence. In (788), from a folk story, the king asks a rock why it had killed his daughter. Since it was an accident, which the king is aware of, there is of course no satisfactory answer to the question but obviously the king is upset and therefore =*ma* is used here.

(788) Content question with =*ma*
[...] "***Kopisi** nang nesopi aphan kipithi**ma**?*" [...]
[**kopīsi** nàng [ne-oso-pì a-phān] ke-pV-thì=**ma**]
why 2 1EXCL:POSS-child-female POSS-NSUBJ NMLZ-CAUS-die=Q
'[...] "For what possible reason did you kill my daughter?" [...]' [RBT, ChM 028]

Similarly, in the folk story from which (789) is taken, the question 'why didn't you get up?' is not intended to elicit an answer, because it is followed up by a command that the addressed group of tigers should hurry up.

(789) Content question with =*ma*
"***Pīsi** kithurvangvedet**ma**?*" {mm} "*Paprapnang ho!*" {mm}
pīsi ke-thùr-vàng-Cē-dèt=**ma** mm pe-pràp-nàng
why NMLZ-get.up-PL-NEG-PFV=Q AFF CAUS-be.quick-HORT:CON
hò mm
EMPH:INTERACT AFF
'"Why didn't you get up? Let's try to be quick!"' [HK, TR 154-5]

15.1.1.3 Polar interrogatives and disjunctive interrogatives

In the terminology used here, polar interrogatives aim to elicit agreement or rejection (§15.1.1.4), while disjunctive interrogatives present the addressee with two alternatives, of which one is expected to be confirmed and the other rejected (§15.1.1.5). While different constructions are used for polar and disjunctive interrogatives, there is also some constructional overlap. First, both types may make use of the question particle =*ma*, although =*ma* may also occur in content questions. Second, the answers to polar and disjunctive interrogatives most commonly follow the same pattern, which is to repeat (the positive or negative version of) the predicate whose proposition the addressee confirms.

15.1.1.4 Polar interrogatives

15.1.1.4.1 Polar interrogatives with =*ma*

Polar interrogatives may simply be marked by adding =*ma* 'question particle' on the predicate. Examples of this type of polar interrogative along with corresponding answers, which consist of a parallel declarative clause without =*ma*, are offered in (790), where the predicate is the adverb *lasón* 'this way', and in (791), where the predicate is based on the verb *chók* 'be fine, be okay'.

(790) Polar interrogative with =ma and with answer
amat "mai pei! kaita nangtum lasonloma?"
amāt   mái   pēi   kái=tā   nang-tūm   **lasón-lò=ma**
and.then how.bad! mother   always=ADD   you-PL   that.way-RL=Q

"O po! lasonlo netum khali
ó   pō   **lasón-lò**   ne-tūm   khalí
vocative father that.way-RL 1EXCL-PL always(<Asm)

kechongvailoksi kecho"
ke-cho-ingvāi-lók-si   ke-chō
NMLZ-AUTO.BEN/MAL-choose-only-NF:RL NMLZ-eat
'And then, "How mean, mother, was it always for you like this?" "O father, like this we (can) always eat only what we (carefully) pick and choose."' [CST, RO 037]

(791) Polar interrogative with =ma and with answer
"chokjima?" pu, nephan arjulo,
[[**chók-jí=mà**]   pù   ne-phān   arjū-lò]
be.fine-IRR2=Q   QUOT   1EXCL-NSUBJ ask-RL

amatsi neta pulo, "chok [...]"
[amātsi   nè=tā   pù-lò   **chók**]
and.then   1EXCL=ADD   say-RL   **be.fine**
'"Is it fine?", they asked me, and I replied, "It's fine [...]"' [SH, CSM 049]

Example (792) shows that this type of interrogative with =ma also allows the verb to be negated.

(792) Polar interrogative with =ma and with answer[143]
{nopakke ponpema?}
nopàk=ke   **pòn-Cē=ma**
dao=TOP   take.away-NEG=Q
'{He wasn't carrying a dao?}' [HK, TR 022]

nopakta dolo dak {lahe} mm
nopàk=tā   **dō-lò**   dāk   lahé   mm
dao=ADD   exist-RL   here   that.way? AFF
'He did have a dao also there. {Is it like that?} Mm.' [HK, TR 023]

---

[143] The curly brackets mark off utterances by an active listener who occasionally interrupts the storyteller in this story.

15.1.1.4.2 Polar interrogatives with prosody only

Another polar interrogative construction is formed by using a rising intonation. An example is offered in excerpt (793), which starts out with a storyteller talking about the protagonist of the story and saying that he he had no parents or siblings. As a reaction, another Karbi native speaker listening to the storyteller asks *enutvetlo?* '(so) he was alone?', to which the answer by the storyteller is agreement through repeating the predicate *enutvetlo*.

(793) Prosodic polar question
apei avelo apo avelo...
a-pēi   avē-lò   a-pō   avē-lò
POSS-mother   not.exist-RL   POSS-father   not.exist-RL

a'ik avelo ate avelo
a-ìk   avē-lò   a-tè   avē-lò
POSS-older.brother   not.exist-RL   POSS-elder.sister   not.exist-RL
'He didn't have a mother anymore, he didn't have a father anymore.... He didn't have any brothers or sisters anymore.' [HK, TR 004]

{*enuvelo?*}
e-nūt-vét-lò
one-CLF:HUM:SG-only-RL
'{He was alone?}' [HK, TR 005]

enuvelo {to}
e-nūt-vét-lò   tò
one-CLF:HUM:SG-only-RL   OK
'He was alone. {OK.}' [HK, TR 006][144]

Figure 20 offers the spectrogram and waveform of the question *enutvetlo?* and the answer *enutvetlo*, with the blue line representing F_0 and the yellow line representing intensity (figure made with Praat (Boersma and Weenink 2013)).[145]

While the first *enutvetlo*, which represents the question, shows the expected rise in F_0, it is perhaps surprising that the answer appears to mirror the interrogative F_0, as more clearly seen in Figure 21, which only displays F_0 over time (also produced with Praat). As we can see in Figure 21, F_0 goes up to just over 200 Hz in the question and to just below 200 Hz in the answer, and these are both male speakers. However, in

---

[144] The audio file for HK, TR 005-6 is available available at https://scholarsbank.uoregon.edu/xmlui/handle/1794/13657.
[145] Note that in both speakers' productions, both alveolar stops are elided as is common in hypoarticulated speech (§3.7.1). Segmentically, they therefore both produce *"enuvelo."*

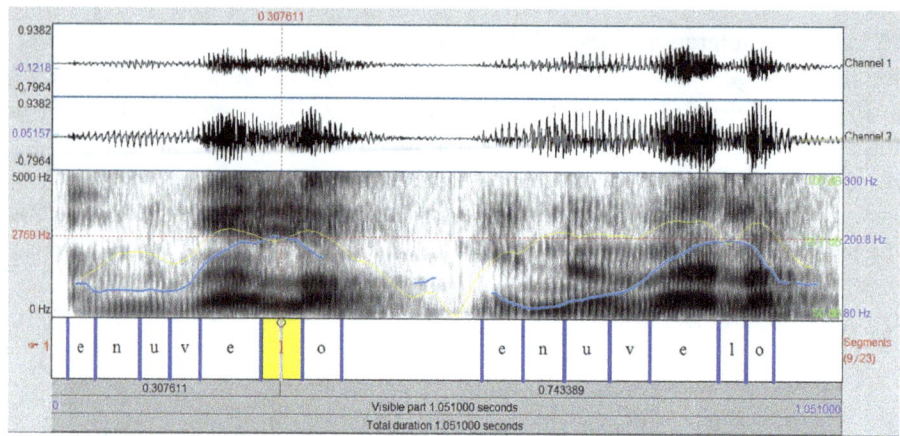

Figure 20: Waveform and spectrogram of interrogative and subsequent declarative *enutvetlo* 'he was alone' (HK, TR 005-6).

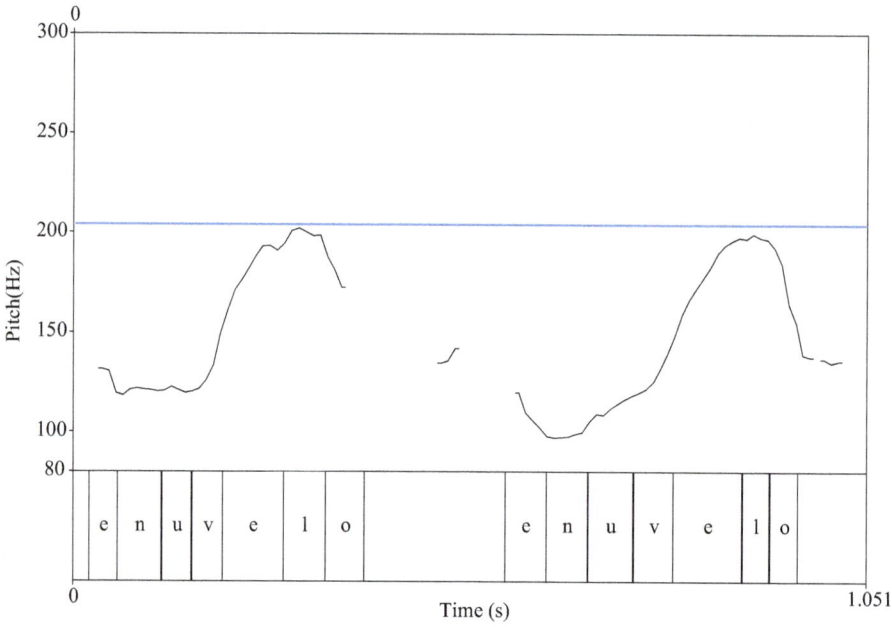

Figure 21: F_0 contour of interrogative and subsequent declarative *enutvetlo* 'he was alone' (HK, TR 005-6).

the answer the pitch clearly goes down to under 150 Hz on the last syllable, the realis marker *-lò*, unlike in the question. What seems to be underlying the high pitch on *-vét* 'only' in the answer is stress or emphasis that the orphan indeed was alone.

15.1.1.5 Disjunctive interrogatives

There are four different disjunctive interrogative constructions in Karbi, as shown in Table 115.

Table 115: Disjunctive interrogative types.

Type	Schematically
1	A=*ma* A-NEG
2	A=*ma* B
3	A=*ma* B=*ma*
4	A=*ma ma* B=*ma*

15.1.1.5.1 Type 1: A=*ma* A-NEG

The type [A=*ma* A-NEG] is a typical disjunctive question construction in languages of Southeast Asia. Burling (2004: 338) refers to the exact same construction in Garo as the 'balanced question' construction, whereas Li and Thompson (1981: 532) use the term 'A-not-A' for a similar construction in Mandarin Chinese.[146]

An example of the construction is shown in (794). It appears that only verbal predicates participate in this construction in Karbi.

(794) Disjunctive interrogative: A=*ma* A-NEG
 sáng-jí=ma   sáng-sē
 take.rest-IRR2=Q take.rest-NEG
 'Should we take rest or not?' [Notebook OH 121010.004]

15.1.1.5.2 Type 2: A=*ma* B

Examples of the second type, 'A=*ma* B', are provided in the question-answer pair in (795) as well as in (796), which both have nominal predicates.

(795) Disjunctive interrogative: A=*ma* B
 {jangresoma jangrengsolo?}
 jangrēsō=ma   jangrēngsō-lò
 single.parent.child= Q orphan-RL
 '{Was it a child with one parent left or no parents at all?}' [HK, TR 011]

---

[146] However, while in Mandarin Chinese, the construction involves simply an affirmative predicate followed by its negated counterpart, both Karbi and Garo require the first affirmative predicate to be additionally marked by the question particle =*ma*, i.e., 'A=*ma* A-NEG'.

       jangrengsolo
       jangrēngsō-lò
       orphan-RL
       'It was an orphan with no parents left.' [HK, TR 012]

(796) Disjunctive interrogative: A=*ma* B
       [*hálasō*   *a-hūt*   *abàng=ke*]   *Nagaòn=ma*   *Karbi_Anglong-lò?* [...]
       that   POSS-during   NPDL=TOP   DISTRICT=Q   DISTRICT-RL
       'At that time, was it Nagaon or Karbi Anglong? [...]' [KCT, SWK 014: SiT]

However, verbal predicates may also occur in this construction, for example *chō-mē=ma chō-nō?* 'eat-GOOD=Q eat-BAD > is it edible or not?'. It is not clear whether verbs can only occur in this construction if they denote opposites (in which case they mirror the 'A=*ma* A-NEG' construction shown above).

15.1.1.5.3 Type 3: A=*ma* B=*ma*
The third disjunctive interrogative construction consists of a simple juxtaposition of two polar questions, both marked with =*ma* clause-finally. An example is (797).

(797) Disjunctive interrogative: A=*ma* B=*ma*
       [...] *lasō*   *a-ron*   *a-tang=pen*   *ke-dō-dē=ke*   [*rong=si*
       this   POSS-custom   POSS-EE:ron   NMLZ-stay-NEG=TOP   village=FOC:RL

       óng=ma],   **[town** *a-lòng=si*   *óng=ma,*   *rongsopī a-lòng*]?
       be.much=Q   town   POSS-LOC=FOC:RL   be.much=Q   town   POSS-LOC
       'The people that don't behave well (lit. stay with the customs), is it mostly the village people or the town people, from the *rongsopi*?' [JB, SWK 174: SiT]

15.1.1.5.4 Type 4: A=*ma ma* B=*ma*
Finally, Type 4 is characterized by using an apparently further grammaticalized version of =*ma* 'question particle', which has turned into a disjunctive clause coordinator 'or' in questions only. In this construction then, both disjunctive interrogative clauses are marked by =*ma* clause-finally, and they are additionally linked via coordinator *ma*. An example of this construction is (798), reported by Grüßner (1978).

(798) Disjunctive interrogative: A=*ma ma* B=*ma*
       [*a-hotón*   *a-béléng*   *mamát-làng=ma*],
       POSS-basket   POSS-strainer   ?self-still=Q

```
       ma     [a-ki-mī            cho-lóng-lò=ma?]
       or:Q   POSS-NMLZ-be.new    AUTO.BEN/MAL-get-RL=Q
```
'Do you still have the same baskets and strainers, or did you get new ones?'
(Grüßner 1978: 129; glosses LK)

Another, incomplete instance of the same construction occurs in (799). In this example, the speaker begins with a content question. He then presumably decides that he has more knowledge and asks for the same information more directly, rephrasing it as a disjunctive question. He stops, however, after the coordinating *ma*, leaving the alternative of the disjunctive question unexpressed.

(799)   Disjunctive interrogative: A, or?
```
        [...] kolosō   a-deng=pen=si                ke-vàng-īk-lò?
        which         POSS-district=from=FOC:RL    NMLZ-come-FRML-RL

        Kamrup        a-deng=pen=ma,               ma...?
        DISTRICT      POSS-district=from=Q         Q
```
'Which district are you from? From the Kamrup district, or...?' [JB, SWK 021: SiT]

15.1.1.6 Interrogative assumption =bo

The 'interrogative assumption' clitic *=bo* marks statements whose proposition the speaker assumes is true while still eliciting a reply that is expected to confirm the truth of the proposition.

An example of a *=bo* marked interrogative assumption is (800), in which the curly brackets indicate a native Karbi speaker different from the main storyteller of this text. In this example, there are two *=bo* marked interrogative assumptions, both with a third person subject. In both cases, they are confirmed: the first question via the affirmative interjection *a*, and the second question via affirmatively repeating the predicate.

(800)   Interrogative assumption =bo
```
        {anke inghonghelobo?} a {kekatchon
        {ánke       inghòng-Cē-lò=bo}              a     {ke-kàt-chón
        and.then    wait-NEG-RL=ITROG.ASSUM        AFF   NMLZ-run.HUM-very.quickly

        pulobo?} kekatchonlo
        pù-lò=bo}                    ke-kàt-chón-lò
        like.this-RL=ITROG.ASSUM     NMLZ-run.HUM-very.quickly-RL
```
'{And so, he is not waiting, huh?} Mm. {Is he running away?} He is running away.' [HK, TR 116]

In (801), the subject of the *=bo* marked clause is second person. Here also, a full reply follows the interrogative assumption.

(801) Interrogative assumption =bo
ke methan-sibongpoke "hem **chirimkangetlobo,**
kè   methān-sibóngpō=ke]   [hēm
and.then dog-SPECIES=TOP   house
che-rím-káng-ét-lò=**bo**
RR-keep.in.order-leaving-PRF-RL=ITROG.ASSUM

phu?" pu "hem chirim'et chibi'etlo"
phū]   pu   [hēm   che-rím-ét   che-bí-ét-lò]
grandfather:VOC QUOT   house RR-keep.in.order-PRF   RR-keep-PRF-RL
'And then, the dog (said), "I assume you already put everything in its place?"
(he said). "Yes, I've put everything in order."' [KK, BMS 039]

15.1.1.7 Tag question *dī*

Tag questions marked by *dī* are used to seek confirmation for the truth of a proposition that the speaker strongly believes in. In (802), a tag question marked by *dī* is confirmed in a reply with the same adverbial predicate.

(802) Tag question with *dī* 'question.tag' with reply
"ba! Lasonloklo, di?", "o! Lasonloklo, po!"
[bá   lasón-lók-lò   **dī]**   [ó   lasón-lók-lò   pō]
how.bad!   that.way-only-RL   **Q.TAG** AFF   that.way-only-RL   father
'"How mean, like that it's always (lit. only) been, right?", "Yes, it's been just like that, father!"' [CST, RO 039]

15.1.1.8 Feedback request with *déi*

Whereas *dī* 'question tag' occurs after realis clauses and elicits confirmation of the truth of a proposition, *déi* 'OK?' occurs after irrealis clauses and represents a request to the addressee to confirm their 'having taken notice'. Irrealis contexts in which *déi* is used for feedback request include imperatives (§15.3.2), as in (803), and deontic clauses with *náng* 'need' (§15.3.4), as in (804).

(803) Feedback request with *déi* following imperative clause
*[...] ladakle dotha **dei**? jattha dak lang*
ladāk=le   dō-thā   **déi**   ját-thā   dāk   lāng
here=FOC:IRR   stay-CON.IMP **OK?**   GENEX-CON.IMP   here   water

chinglunoi juinoi pu amat [...]
chinglú-nōi   jùi-nōi   pu   amāt
take.bath-INFRML.COND.IMP   play-INFRML.COND.IMP   QUOT   and.then
'[...] [S]tay here, okay? Here do everything, and take your bath and play" he said, and then [...]' [CST, RO 049]

(804) Feedback request with *déi* following deontic clause
 *lasi osomar aphan pulo adapprang thurdap nangji **dei?***
 lasì   osō-mār aphān pù-lò   a-dappráng thùr-dàp   náng-jí
 therefore child-PL NSUBJ say-RL POSS-dawn get.up-early need-IRR2
 déi
 OK?
 'So I said to the children, "We need to get up early in the morning, okay?"'
 [SH, CSM 002]

Feedback request *déi* 'OK?' is also commonly used in a formulaic expression following *dàm-pò* 'go-IRR1' > 'I'm leaving' (i.e., *dampo, dei?*), which is used as a 'good-bye' expression after being done visiting.

15.1.2 Imperatives and prohibitives

The following subsections discuss the various imperative and prohibitive constructions, including the bare stem imperative (§15.1.2.1); the informal suggestive imperative with *-nōi* (§15.1.2.2); the (non-informal) suggestive imperative with *-nōn* (§15.1.2.3); the conative imperative *-thā* (§15.1.2.4); and the most command-like imperative with *-tū* (§15.1.2.5). Section §15.1.2.6 discusses the differences between *-nōn*, *-thā*, and *-tū*. Prohibitive *-rī* is discussed in §15.1.2.7, and the prohibitive construction that combines an imperative with the prohibitive suffix is shown in §15.1.2.8.

15.1.2.1 Bare stem imperative

The structurally simplest imperative construction is to use the bare stem, as in (805). As a prohibitive counterpart to the bare stem imperative construction, a simple negated verb may be used, e.g., *ót-ē* 'touch-NEG' > 'don't touch (it)!'[147]

(805) Bare stem imperative
 "*ako nangpole mandu cho tangte...*
 akó   nang-pō-le   mandú   chō tángtē
 on.the.other.hand(<Asm) 2:POSS-father-FOC:IRR field.hut eat if

 *nangtumke ha hemtap angsongle **cho**!*"
 nang-tūm=ke há   hēmtāp   angsóng=le   **chō**
 you-PL=TOP   over.there tree.house high.up=FOC:IRR   **eat**
 '"On the other hand, when your father eats in the *mandu*, you eat up there in the *hemtap*!"' [CST, RO 018]

---

147 I have heard this used by somebody who was talking to a four-year old child.

15.1.2.2 Informal conditioned imperative -*nōi*

Imperative -*nōi* is the more informal version of the conditioned imperative -*nōn* (§15.1.2.3). The description as 'conditioned' refers to the typically underlying implication of a consequence or circumstance that underlies the imperative. In written Karbi, -*nōn* is generally used instead of -*nōi*. However, Grüßner's (1978: 96) characterization of -*nōi* as an "impolite and harsh command" appears overstated; consider the folk story example (806), where -*nōi* is used in addressing the king.[148]

(806) Informal conditioned imperative -*nōi*
"*Apot nele kechokche kali, richo. Hala*
[apōt   nè=le   ke-chók-Cē   kalī   richó]   [[hála
because 1EXCL=FOC:IRR NMLZ-be.fine-NEG NEG.EQU.COP   king   that

vo'arbipi aphanle arjudamnoi!"
võarbí-pī   a-phān=le]   arjū-dām-**nōi**]
bird.sp-female POSS-NSUBJ=FOC:IRR ask-go-**INFRML.COND.IMP**
"'Therefore, I'm not the guilty one, king, go ask that Voarbipi!'" [RBT, ChM 037]

In this part of the story, the king is looking for somebody he can hold responsible for the death of his daughter. The elephant, who is speaking here, explains why he is not responsible, and suggests the king ask the *vo'arbipi* bird instead as somebody who would be able to provide further information. It is this implication of an expected consequence that will follow from the suggested action that is encoded in -*nōi* (and -*nōn*).

Another example is (807), where the function of -*nōi* is to highlight a negative consequence if the suggested action is not performed. In the given part of this folk story, a stepmother is speaking to her stepchildren, who she has been mistreating. Here, she wants to prevent them from eating together with their father, so their father will not notice what bad food she has them eat.

(807) Informal conditioned imperative -*nōi*
amat "anborta pinike nangtum hadakle an
amāt   [àn-bòr=tā   pinì=ke   nang-tūm   hádāk=le
and.then   rice-wrapped.bundle=ADD   today=TOP   you-PL   there=FOC:IRR
àn
rice

---

148 It is admittedly still surprising that an informal form is used in talking to the king. Note, however, that the first person pronoun *nè* in the previous clause also occurs without the honorific suffix -*lī* (§6.1.1), which suggests that this interaction with the king is indeed occurring on a rather informal level.

chodunnoi! kaita dah nangtumta
chō-dūn-**nōi]** [kái=tā dáh nang-tūm=tā
eat-JOIN-**INF.COND.IMP** always=ADD go! you-PL=ADD

chodunnoi nangpole hemtap angsong chote
chō-dūn-**nōi]** [[nang-pō=le hēmtāp angsóng chō-tē]
eat-JOIN-**INF.COND.IMP** 2:POSS-father=FOC:IRR tree.house high.up eat-if

nangtumke mandule cho
nang-tūm=ke mandú=le chō]
you-PL=TOP field.hut=FOC:IRR eat
'And then, "The rice bundles, today, eat them there!" (She would) always (say), "Go! You too eat together (there)! If your father takes his meal in the *hemtap*, you eat in the *mandu*!"' [CST, RO 017]

Note also in (807) that the bare stem imperative (§15.1.2.1) occurs in the last clause of this text unit, thus appearing functionally equivalent to *-nōi* here.

15.1.2.3 Conditioned imperative *-nōn*

The suffix *-nōn* indicates an imperative that suggests (rather than commands) an action under particular circumstances. It is the more formal counterpart to *-nōi* (§15.1.2.2). In (808), children whose mother has died are saying to their father that if he wants to look for a new wife, he should go ahead.

(808) Conditioned imperative *-nōn*
 [...] to chirijite, chirinon!
 tò che-rī-jí-te che-rī-**nōn**
 OK RR-search-IRR2-COND RR-search-**COND.IMP**
 '[...] "Okay, if you feel like finding yourself a wife, then find yourself one!"'
 [CST, RO 009]

15.1.2.4 Conative imperative *-thā*

Conative imperative *-thā* is used when the speaker suggests the addressee try and do something and see what happens. Compared to *-nōi* and *-nōn* (§15.1.2.2, §15.1.2.3), *-thā* is less direct or immediate, although they may be used in the same context suggesting that their functions are not very different. This can be seen in (809). In this folk story, a father desperately sees no other way to deal with a difficult situation than to abandon his children. In (809), he has taken them to a place in the jungle and tells them to try and stay there, using *-thā*; and that they should take baths and play there, using *-nōi*.

(809) Conative imperative *-thā*
bahari alongtar along ponlo amatsi... "o pei! ladakle
baharí   a-longtàr   alòng   pòn-lò   amātsi   ó   pēi
very.big(<Ind)   POSS-rock   LOC   take.away-RL and.then VOC mother
ladāk=le
here=FOC:IRR

dotha dei jattha dak lang chinglunoi
dō-**thā**   déi   ját-thā   dāk   lāng   chinglú-nōi
stay-**CON.IMP** OK?   GENEX-CON.IMP   here   water take.bath-INF.COND.IMP

juinoi" [...]
jùi-nōi
play-INF.COND.IMP

'He took them to the place of a very big rock, and then, (he said) "Mothers, try to stay here, okay? Here do everything, and take your bath and play!" [...]'
[CST, RO 049]

15.1.2.5 Unconditioned imperative *-tū*

Imperative *-tū* is quite different from *-nōi*, *-nōn*, and *-thā*. Unlike those three imperative constructions, *-tū* has more force; i.e., while the latter three suffixes are more like suggestions that take circumstances and the context into consideration, *-tū* is more command-like and applies in general. The only occurrence of imperative *-tū* in the corpus of recorded texts is (810), which deviates from the above description that was obtained through elicitation.[149] Still, *-tū* in (810) might indicate a general instruction for how to reach home, which may be why this imperative construction is used here, rather than one of the other ones.

(810) Imperative *-tū*
[...] mo nanghem chedam ahomoike lapu chevangthurá
[mò   nang-hēm   chV-dām   a-homói=ke]   [lapú
future   your-house   RR-go   POSS-time(<Asm)=TOP this.side
che-vāng-thū-ra]
RR-come-again-NF:IRR

langso atovarthot vangra lapen ladak
[langsō   a-továr-thót   vàng-ra]   [la=pen   ladāk
this   POSS-road-exactly   come-NF:IRR   this=with   here

---

149 Elicited examples of when *-tū* rather than one of the other imperative constructions would be used centered on moral imperatives, such as '(You must) love your parents!' or '(You must) love the poor!' Using, for example, the conative imperative *-thā* (§15.1.2.4) instead in this context, the meaning would be 'Love them and see what happens / what the consequences are.'

nanghumrira nanghem chepaletu
nang=humrí-ra]   [nang-hēm   che-pa-lè-**tū**]
CIS=visit.friends/relatives-NF:IRR   2:POSS-house RR-CAUS-reach-**UNCOND.IMP**
'[...] [A]nd later when you go home, again come like this, come on the exact same road, and then go to the familiar place (i.e. where the dog is staying), and then go and make sure to reach your house.' [KK, BMS 089]

15.1.2.6 Imperatives -nōn, -thā, and -tū and Grüßner's (1978) account of politeness differences

Elicitation sessions conducted for this research suggest that Grüßner's (1978: 96–7) classification of imperative suffixes on a politeness continuum is a secondary (and therefore less consistent) pragmatic dimension to these constructions. The primary functional differences appear to be as follows. First, if the speaker suggests for the addressee to do something given particular circumstances and resulting consequences, then the conditioned imperative suffixes -nōi and -nōn are used. Second, if the implication is that the addressee should try to do something and see what will happen, then the conative imperative suffix -thā can be used instead. Third, if the addressee should do something unconditionally, the imperative suffix -tū is the most appropriate.

15.1.2.7 Prohibitive -rī

There is only one prohibitive in Karbi, which is -rī, as shown in (811). The prohibitive may, however, co-occur with one of the imperative suffixes (§15.1.2.8).

(811) Prohibitive -rī
ai nepran neenri, nemui
ái   [ne-prán   ne=ēn-**rī**]   [ne-múi
how.bad! 1EXCL:POSS-life 1EXCL:NSUBJ=take-**PROH** 1EXCL:POSS-EE:prán(<Ind)]

neenri, richo
ne=ēn-rī]   richó
1EXCL:NSUBJ=take-PROH   king
'"Please, don't take my life, king!"' [RBT, ChM 068]

15.1.2.8 Prohibitive construction via combination of prohibitive and imperative suffix

One set of prohibitive constructions combine -rī 'prohibitive' with one of the imperative suffixes. Example (812) below illustrates the combination of -rī with -nōi 'informal conditioned imperative', and (813) the combination of -rī with -thā 'conative imperative.'

(812) Prohibitive construction with -rī 'prohibitive' and -nōi 'informal conditioned imperative'

richo kipu "tangte damrinoi! nangtumke
richó   ke-pù   tángtē   dàm-**rī-nōi**   nàng-tūm=ke
king   NMLZ-say then   go-**PROH-INF.COND.IMP** 2POSS-PL=TOP

nesomarlo!"
ne-oso-màr-lò
1EXCL:POSS-child-PL-RL
'The king said, "Don't go then! You are my children!"' [CST, HM 115]

(813) Prohibitive construction with -rī 'prohibitive' and -thā 'conative imperative'
vung-**rī-thā**!
pull-**PROH-CON.IMP**
'Don't pull (yet)!' [Notebook AT 121009.005]

The form *vungritha* in (813) is used in a context of a friend trying to open a car door from outside, which is still locked from inside. Thus the speaker asks the addressee to suspend the action just for a moment, not in general. It therefore appears that combining prohibitive -rī with imperative suffixes serves to convey the pragmatic distinctions inherent in the different imperative markers, which are otherwise undifferentiated in the single prohibitive -rī.

The same type of construction that combines a prohibitive with an imperative suffix is also found in Rongmei Naga, a Western Naga language (cf. Post and Burling 2017) spoken in the Tamenglong district of Manipur and Barak Valley of Assam (Deb and Singha 2014). The prohibitive suffix in Rongmei is also -ri, which suggests that language contact may be the reason why the same type of construction is found in both languages.

15.1.3 Hortatives

There is one general hortative suffix, -nāng, in Karbi, as well as extended forms -lonāng and -sināng (§15.1.3.3); the jussive construction that serves as a third person command ('s/he should V') is formed via affixation of causative pa- and hortative -nāng (§15.1.3.2).

15.1.3.1 General hortative -nāng

The general hortative marker that indicates that the speaker suggests they themselves together with the addressee, i.e., first and second person, perform an action (also cross-linguistically referred to as 'cohortative') is the suffix -*nāng*.[150] Several instances of -*nāng* 'hortative' occur in (814).

(814) Hortative -*nāng*
ne kedam aling nangdunnoi setame, chonang junnang!
[nè   ke-dàm   alíng   nang=dùn-nōi   setāmē]   [chō-**nāng**
1EXCL   NMLZ-go INDEF   CIS=join-INF.COND.IMP nevertheless eat-**HORT**
jùn-**nāng**]
drink-**HORT**

hormu horton chirim chibikangvetra, dunnang,
[hormú   hortón   chV-rím   chV-bí-káng-vèt-rà]
thing   EE:hormú RR-put.in.one.place   RR-keep-give.leave-nicely-NF:IRR
[dùn-**nāng**
join-**HORT**

ha nephi along!
há   ne-phì   a-lòng]
over.there   1EXCL:POSS-grandmother   POSS-LOC
'Join me, wherever I go, but let's eat and drink and let's keep everything nicely (here, i.e. put everything in order before we leave), let's go there, to my grandmother's place.' [KK, BMS 033]

The negative hortative is formed with the verbal negative suffix -*Cē* (§9.4). An example is (815).

(815) Negated hortative -*nāng*
" [...] *ningveke elitumta e vopi ejon*
[[ningvē=ke   e-li-tūm=tā   e   vō-pī   e-jōn
evening=TOP   1PL.INCL-HON- PL=ADD   DSM   chicken-female   one-CLF:animal

chothatnang" pulo amat hala apiso abang pulo
cho-thāt-nāng]   pù-lò]   [amāt   hála a-pisò   abàng pù-lò
AUTO.BEN/MAL-slaughter-HORT   say-RL   and.then   that POSS-wife   NPDL   say-RL

"***thatnangne*** *ti sarbura*"
[**thàt-nāng-Cē**   ti   sàrburá]]
slaughter-HORT-NEG   EMPH   old.man
'"[...] [L]et's kill ourselves a hen tonight", he said, (but) the wife said, "Let's not, old man (and I won't change my mind)!"' [SeT, MTN 007]

---

[150] Grüßner (1978: 97) lists this suffix with a low tone. According to my language consultants, there is a low tone form of this suffix, which, however, is used to convey a conative sense, see below.

Interestingly, the hortative can be turned into a question by adding the question particle =ma (§15.1.1). For example, dàm-nāng=ma? 'go-HORT=Q' means 'should we go?'

A change in tone can be used for a change in pragmatic function. While the regular mid tone form -nāng carries the connotation of a more immediate 'let's (do) right now!', a low tone form -nàng is used for a more general and/or conative interpretation, i.e., 'let's (in general) (do) (or try to do)', as in (816).[151]

(816) Low tone -nàng with conative interpretation
paprapnang ho! {mm}
pe-pràp-nàng   ho   mm
CAUS-be.quick-HORT:CON EMPH:INTERACT   AFF
'Let's try to be quick!' [HK, TR 155]

There may be a historical link between -nāng 'hortative' and deontic náng 'need, must', as was also suggested by Grüßner (1978: 97). Note, however, that there is also a -ning hortative in other Tibeto-Burman languages such as Hakha Lai (Kuki-Chin; Peterson 2003: 415), which may be cognate with the Karbi hortative, in which case we have to assume a much larger time depth.

15.1.3.2 Jussive construction with causative pa- and hortative -nāng

The jussive construction, which is generally directed towards a third person argument with the meaning 'let him/her/them V', is formed with causative pa- and hortative -nāng (see also Grüßner (1978: 98)). In (817), the meaning is 'let your mother cook (rice)!'

(817) Jussive construction with causative pa- and hortative -nāng
"nangpai an patunnang" pu
nang-pāi   àn   **pa-tún-nāng**   pu]
2:POSS-mother rice   **CAUS-cook-HORT**   QUOT
'[...] "Let (or let's let) your mother cook rice!" (she said).' [KK, CC 018]

As (818) and (819) show, verbs marked with pa- 'causative' plus -nāng 'hortative' may also be directed towards speech act participants, as the verbs here are marked with the SAP non-subject marker nang= (§8.3.1). The examples also show that this construction is negated via negation of the verb stem, followed by -nāng 'hortative.'

---

151 See also §15.1.3.3 on the extended hortative form -sināng, which also carries a conative connotation.

(818) Hortative -nāng directed towards first person plural
thap toklongle mó pirthe kangtang sita la
thàp   tòk-lōng-Cē   mò   pirthé ke-ingtāng   setā   là
cake.for.rice.beer pound-GET-NEG future world NMLZ-be.strong but   this

netum Bey Ronghang atumke thap
ne-tūm   Bēy   Ronghāng   a-tūm=ke   thàp
1EXCL-PL   CLAN   CLAN   POSS-PL=TOP   cake.for.rice.beer

nangpatoklonglenang pu
nang=pa-tòk-lōng-**Cē-nāng**   pu
1/2:NSUBJ=CAUS-pound-GET-**NEG-HORT**   QUOT
'"We don't get to pound the rice for the rice beer, even in the future when the world is mature (lit. strong), we, the Bey Ronghang shouldn't (be requested to) have to pound the rice for rice beer cake", (he) said' [WR, BCS 034]

(819) Hortative -nāng on negated verb stem, directed towards first person plural
mó pirthe kangtangta nang Bey Ke'etpen
mò   pirthé ke-ingtāng=tā   nàng   Bēy   ke-èt=pen
future world   NMLZ-be.strong=even you   CLAN   NMLZ-be.yellow=with

Bey Ki'ikke nangpachiunenang pu tangho
Bēy   ke-ìk=ke   **nang**=pa-che-ūn-**Cē-nāng**   pu
CLAN   NMLZ-be.black=TOP   1/2:NSUBJ=CAUS-RR-be.able-**NEG-HORT**   QUOT
tànghò
REP
'Up into the future when the world is mature (lit. strong), you (my offspring), Bey the Fair and Bey the Black, let's make us not be able (to tolerate) each other!' [WR, BCS 022]

15.1.3.3 Extended forms: Emphatic hortative *-lonāng* and conative hortative *-sināng*

In addition to simply *-nāng*, two other, apparently bi-morphemic forms occur: *-lonāng* and *-sināng*.[152] The simplest diachronic analysis, which is to consider the *lo* the realis suffix *-lò* and the *si* the realis non-final suffix *-si*, is very plausible given the semantics of these hortative variants, which have emphatic and conative connotations, respectively. Structurally, it is less clear how the realis and non-final suffixes might have ended up fused with hortative *-nāng*.

---

[152] Grüßner (1978: 97) additionally reports a form *-ponàng*, which is, however, not known to my consultants. It also needs to be noted that Grüßner spells what is here called the 'conative hortative' as *-senàng*, and suggests that its function is that of an immediate hortative rather than a conative hortative.

The *-lonāng* form is glossed as 'emphatic hortative', as it typically occurs in a context where the speaker expects or confronts disagreement. This emphatic connotation in the context of a disagreement makes realis *-lò* a plausible diachronic component in *-lonāng* as *-lò* 'realis' has that use independently as well (§9.6.1.5). In (820), the addressee of the direct speech is depressed and worried, and so the emphatic hortative *-lonāng* (here shortened to *-anāng*, see §3.7.3) serves to emphatically suggest to do something that the speaker knows the addressee does not want to do.

(820) Emphatic hortative *-lonāng*
[...] *"choklembom chobomanang! nephi*
cho-klém-bòm   chō-bōm-**lonāng**   ne-phì
AUTO.BEN/MAL-do-CONT   eat-CONT-**HORT:EMPH**   1EXCL:POSS-grandmother

aphanke rira jonghe setame, theklonglelo"
a-phān=ke   rí-rà   jonghé   setāmē   theklōng-Cē-lò
POSS-NSUBJ=TOP   search-NF:IRR   as.much.as   nevertheless   see-NEG-RL
'[...] "Let's keep working and eating (i.e., let's live as usual), even if we keep searching for my grandmother, we won't see her."' [KK, BMS 017]

The *-sināng* form is glossed as 'conative hortative', as it means 'let's try and V and see what is going to happen'.[153] This conative connotation of *-sināng* is also shared by the conative imperative *-thā* (§15.1.2.4). Examples from the same folk story that show the different pragmatics underlying the use of *-sināng* and *-lonāng* are (821) and (822). In (821), the negative interjection *'mh'* at the beginning of the direct speech does not (yet) indicate disagreement of the speaker (a father) with the addressee (his children), but the speaker's decision that he and his children need to have their meals together so he can find out why his children are so sickly. In (821), the speaker uses the conative *-sināng*, 'let's try and eat together (and find out what the problem is)!'

(821) Conative hortative *-sināng*
'mh' o pei atum pinike itum an
'mh'   ó   pēi   a-tūm   pinì=ke   i-tūm   àn
NEG.INTERJ   vocative   mother   POSS-PL   today=TOP   1INCL-PL   rice

chorappetsinang
chō-ràp-pèt-**sināng**
eat-together-all-**HORT:CON**
'No, o mothers, today let's eat together (and see what's going to happen)!' [CST, RO 027]

---

[153] A conative hortative is also expressed via tone change. If the low tone instead of the mid tone is used on the basic hortative *-nāng*, then it also carries a conative connotation, see §15.1.3.1 above.

The children (as the addressees) disagree with this suggestion in (821), and, as a consequence, in (822), the father, now emphatically using -lonāng, makes an executive decision saying that they should have their meal together.

(822) Emphatic hortative -lonāng
to pei, pinike an chorappetanang
tò   pēi   pinì=ke   àn   chō-ràp-pèt-**lonāng**
OK   mother today=TOP rice eat-together-all-**HORT:EMPH**
"'Okay, mother, today, let's eat together!'" [CST, RO 033]

15.2 Non-nominalized subordinate clause types

Subordinate clauses are often nominalized in Karbi, as discussed in Chapter 12, and specifically §§12.3, 12.4, 12.5. However, there also exist a variety of non-nominalized types of subordinate clauses. This includes three larger functional types: non-final clauses that occur in a clause-chaining construction (§15.2.1); complement clauses (§15.2.2); and adverbial clauses (§15.2.3).

15.2.1 Non-final clauses in clause chains

15.2.1.1 Morphologically marked clauses: -si 'non-final:realis', -ra 'non-final:irrealis', -pen 'non-final:with'

There are three suffixes in Karbi that indicate the non-final status of a verb: -si 'non-final:realis' (§9.7.1), -ra 'non-final:irrealis' (§9.7.1), and -pen 'non-final:with' (§9.7.2). While -si and -ra are realis/irrealis-sensitive counterparts of one another (depending on the realis/irrealis specification of the final verb, §15.3), -pen historically originates in the postposition =pen 'with; from' (§10.8.1). Non-final -pen is younger than -si and still shows traces of nominal affiliation in that it very often (but not obligatorily) attaches to nominalized verbs. The most frequent non-final marker is -si with 104 occurrences in the corpus. Non-final -pen only has 73 occurrences. Irrealis non-final -ra only occurs 21 times.

The realis non-final marker -si occurs in typical clause chains that denote subsequent events. In (823), four non-final -si marked clauses occur in temporal sequence. Note, however, that is very rare to find such long clause chains. It is most common to only find one non-final clause marked by -si, followed by a final clause. Nevertheless, while both -si and -ra may, if rarely, occur in chains of several clauses, -pen never occurs on more than one non-final clause to denote a temporal sequence.

(823) Chained clauses marked with *-si* 'non-final:realis'
e anke apaita <m> pharla dam,
e   [ánke   a-pāi=tā   <m>   phailá   dàm]
DSM   and.then   POSS-mother=ADD   HESIT outside.part.Karbi.house go

*theng akhangra **okóksi**, hem **damsi**,*
[thēng   a-khangrá   ó-kòk-si]   [hēm
firewood   POSS-basket.for.firewood leave-in.a.fixed.place-NF:RL house
dàm-si]
go-NF:RL

*hongkup **ingnilúnsi**, mok **chepachusi**,*
[hongkūp   ingnì-lùn-si]   [mōk   che-pa-chū-si]
entrance.area.Karbi.house   sit-big:AO-NF:RL breast RR-CAUS-suck-NF:RL

"Dojoinoi, po!"
[dō-jòi-nōi   pō]
stay-quietly-INFRML.COND.IMP   father
'And then, the mother went and unloaded the firewood in the *pharla*, then went inside the house, sat down in the *hongkup*, breastfed the child (and said), "Be quiet, father!"' [KK, CC 015]

In addition, non-final clauses may bear other types of semantic relationship to the final clause, besides temporal sequence. In (824), *-si* occurs on a manner motion verb *vèk* 'steer' (here: 'ride a bike'), while the final verb *vàng* 'come' indicates the deictic direction towards the reference point.

(824) Non-final clause marked with *-si*: Manner adverbial clause
kidun a'oso...] halata saikel nangveksi
ke-dùn   a-osō   hála=tā   saikél   nang=vèk-si
NMLZ-join   POSS-child that=also   bicycle(<Eng) CIS=steer-NF:RL

vangbomlo... menmen latum chetonglok amat
vàng-bōm-lò...   ménmèn   la-tūm   che-tòng-lòk   amāt
come-CONT-RL   suddenly   this-PL   RR-meet-just   and.then
'He keeps going, and then, as he's going, from that side (i.e., the opposite side), one girl, one school girl, she's also riding a bike and coming, suddenly they meet.' [SiT, PS 027]

In (825), *-si* marks a subordinate clause that has a causal relationship to the final clause.

(825) Non-final clause marked with -si: Causal adverbial clause
[...] laphan aning ingsamsi thesere pumni tekanglo
[là-phān   a-nīng   ingsām-si]   [theseré púm-ní   tekáng-lò]
this-NSUBJ   POSS-mind   be.cold-NF:RL fruits   CLF:round-two   leave.for-RL
'[...] [H]e (the bicycle boy) was grateful to him (the boy who had picked up his hat for him) and gave him two pieces of fruit.' [SiT, PS 039]

The high degree of clausal integration exhibited by clause chaining with -*si* is shown in (826) and (827). Here the O argument of the final verb is placed at the beginning of the sentence, thus appearing to be structurally under the scope of the non-final clause.

(826) O argument of final clause inside non-final clause
Rasinja aphanta damsi ne ingthurdamlo
[[**Rasínjá   aphān=tā**   dàm-si]   nè   **ingthùr-dām-lò**]
 PN   NSUBJ=ALSO   go-NF:RL   1EXCL   **wake.up-GO-RL**
'I also went and woke up Rasinja.' [SH, CSM 006]

(827) O argument of final clause inside non-final clause
laso osomar banghini aphan juja'e
[**lasō   osō-mār   bàng-hiní   a-phān]   juja'ē**
 this   child-PL   CLF:HUM:PL-TWO   POSS-NSUBJ   cradle

homtekangsi thaptekanglo
hóm-tekáng-**si**   thàp-tekáng-**lò**]
fix.by.tying-leaving-**NF:RL** **put.inside-leaving-RL**
'So (the mother) fixed the cradle, and went to wash clothes, and then, she fixed the cradle for the two children, and put them inside.' [CST, HM 010]

All three non-final markers may also occur on negated verbs. An example is with -*si* in (828), where the semantic relationship between the non-final and the final clause is one of causality.

(828) Non-final marked negated verb
anke apai abangke an tundamlo ajatlo, anke
[ánke   [a-pāi   abàng=ke]   àn   tún-dàm-lò   aját-lò]   ánke
and.then   POSS-mother   NPDL=TOP   rice   cook-GO-RL   GENEX-RL   and.then

> hala aso abangke kroithekthesi chiruthuvaret
> [hála a-osō abàng=ke] krōi-thēk-**Cē-si** chirú-thù-varèt]
> that POSS-child NPDL=TOP agree-know.how-**NEG-NF:RL** cry-again-INTENS
> 'And then, the mother went and cooked food and everything, and then, that child couldn't agree and kept crying a lot.' [KK, CC 019]

In the excerpt in (829), -si marks the 'head' part of the tail-head linkage construction (§16.1.2). Both -si and -pen commonly occur in the tail-head linkage construction in this way.

(829) Non-final -si marked clause in tail-head linkage construction
lasi netum ha nete netepo
lasì   ne-tūm   há   ne-tè
therefore 1EXCL-PL over.there 1EXCL:POSS-elder.sister
ne-tepō
1EXCL:POSS-brother.in.law

> aphanta **ingthumponlo**
> a-phān=tā **ingthùm-pōn-lò**
> POSS-NSUBJ=ADD **go.and.bring-take.away-RL**
> 'So we went there to pick up my elder sister and brother-in-law as well.' [SH, CSM 010]

> **ingthumponsi** netum dakpen baji throksi
> **ingthùm-pōn-si**   ne-tūm   dāk=pen   bají
> **go.and.bring-take.away-NF:RL** 1EXCL-PL here=from o'clock(<Asm)
> thrōksí
> seven

> ra achitim aporlo netum dakpen barlo
> rà   a-chitìm   a-pór=lo   ne-tūm   dāk=pen   bár-lò
> and POSS-half POSS-time=FOC 1EXCL-PL here=from start-RL
> 'We went to pick them up and from here... it was at seven thirty, from here we started.' [SH, CSM 011]

15.2.1.2 Prosodically marked clauses

Unsurprisingly, the non-final status of a clause is often also marked by prosody, specifically with extra high pitch. If the non-final status is not additionally marked morphologically (i.e., by a non-final suffix), the extra high tone typically occurs on the last syllable, e.g. on -lò 'realis' in (830).

(830) Prosodic extra high pitch on -*lò* 'realis' as marker of non-final status
*amat la apiso abangke akhalun **chinghortangló***
amāt [là a-pisò abàng=ke] a-khalùn
and.then this POSS-wife NPDL=TOP POSS-kd.big.basket
che-inghór-tāng-lò
RR-carry.load-finish-RL

ha kedamlo
há ke-dàm-lò
over.there NMLZ-go-RL
'And then, the wife put the basket rope around her head and was just leaving (to go over) there (to her parents' place).' [SeT, MTN 041][154]

The prosodic extra high tone to indicate 'non-final' is sometimes also used in addition to 'non-final' suffixes, in which case it is typically the syllable preceding the 'non-final' suffix that receives the extra high tone, specifically -*kòk* 'in a fixed place' and -*lùn* 'big:AO' in (831), and -*lòk* 'right then' in (832).

(831) Prosodic extra high pitch preceding -*si* 'non-final:realis'
e anke apaita <m> pharla dam,
e [ánke a-pāi=tā <m> pharlá dàm]
DSM and.then POSS-mother=ADD HESIT outside.part.Karbi.house go

*theng akhangra **okóksi**, hem damsi,*
[thēng a-khangrá ó-kòk-si] [hēm dàm-si]
firewood POSS-basket.for.firewood leave-in.a.fixed.place-NF:RL house go-NF:RL

*hongkup **ingnilúnsi**, mok chepachusi,*
[hongkūp ingnì-lùn-si] [mōk che-pa-chū-si]
entrance.area.Karbi.house sit-big:AO-NF:RL breast RR-CAUS-suck-NF:RL

"Dojoinoi, po!"
[dō-jòi-nōi pō]
stay-quietly-INFRML.COND.IMP father
'And then, the mother went and unloaded the firewood in the *pharla*, then went inside the house, sat down in the *hongkup*, breastfed the child (and said), "Be quiet, father!"' [KK, CC 015]

---

[154] The audio file for SeT, MTN 041 is available at https://scholarsbank.uoregon.edu/xmlui/handle/1794/13657.

(832) Prosodic extra high pitch preceding -*pen* 'non-final:with'
la **chetheklókpen** {mm} aharchi chethekloklo mati {mm} [...]
là   che-thēk-lòk-pen   mm   a-harchī   che-thēk-lòk-lò
this   RR-see-right.then-NF:with   AFF   POSS-image   RR-see-right.then-RL
mati {mm}
DM   AFF
'As he was looking, he of course saw the image [...].' [HK, TR 101][155]

15.2.2 Complement clauses

Complement clauses (CCs) may be nominalizations (§12.4). In addition, there are four complement clause constructions that are not (formally) nominalized: verb juxtaposition (§15.2.2.1), CCs marked with -*nē* 'indefinite' in the case of indirect questions (§15.2.2.2), CCs marked with =*ke* 'topic' (§15.2.2.3), and CCs followed by quotative *pu* or quotative complementizer *pusi* (§15.2.2.4).

15.2.2.1 Verb juxtaposition

In (833) and (834), the verb *thèk* 'know how' occurs in the CC juxtaposition construction. In most instances of this construction, it looks like a serialization construction, in which the root of the CC verb and the root of the CC-taking verb appear directly serialized with no other elements intervening. However, (834) shows that a more complex predicate in an adverb construction (§11.3.2) may also be followed by complement-taking *thèk* 'know how'.

(833) Complement-taking verb *thèk* 'know.how' in juxtaposition construction
"*ahokma, methan-sibongpo?, nang nepon thekjima?*" [...]
a-hōk=ma   methān-sibóngpō,   ne=pòn
POSS-truth=Q   dog-SPECIES   1EXCL:NSUBJ=take.away
thèk-jí=ma
know.how-IRR2=Q
'"Is it true, dog, you know how to take me?" [...]' [KK, BMS 034]

(834) Complement-taking verb *thèk* 'know.how' in juxtaposition construction
lasō a-okarjāng lún   [[lún pa-mé]   **thèk-thē]**
this POSS-girl   song sing   CAUS-be.good   know-NEG
'This girl doesn't know how to sing (well).' [SiT elicitation 090301]

---

[155] The audio file for HK, TR 101 is available at https://scholarsbank.uoregon.edu/xmlui/handle/1794/13657.

In (835), the verb *tengnè~tennè* 'forget (to do something)' is linked to its complement clause 'carry along a bottle of oil' by simple juxtaposition of complement clause verb and complement-taking verb.

(835) Complement-taking verb *tengnè~tennè* 'forget' in juxtaposition construction
[...] anke amat eson abang, jangthu abong,
ánke	amāt	[e-sòn	abàng]	jàngthù	a-bòng
and.then	and.then	one-CLF:thing	NPDL	oil	POSS-gourd

***chepon tennedet** pu amat laso hem nangkachiri*
che-pōn	tengnè-dèt	pu	amāt	lasō	hēm
RR-TAKE.AWAY	**forget-PFV**	QUOT	and.then	this	house

nang=ke-che-rī
CIS=NMLZ-RR-search

aphi, apenan abang sunjoi [...]
aphī	a-penàn	abàng	sūn-jòi
after	POSS-husband	NPDL	descend-quietly

'[...] [A]nd then, one thing, a bottle of oil, she forgot to carry along, and so after she went back to search for it in the house, then the husband quietly came down [...].' [SeT, MTN 042]

15.2.2.2 Indirect questions

Complement clauses functioning as indirect questions are marked by *-nē* 'indefinite (INDEF)' (see also §6.1.4.1). In (836), the complement-taking verb *chiní* 'know' takes the CC 'how big or small it is', which is an indirect disjunctive question that occurs with *-nē* 'indefinite' after its second part.

(836) Indirect question marked by *-nē* 'indefinite' followed by *chiní* 'know'
ajatnon Kohima ko'an akethe ko'an
[ajátnōn	Kóhìmà	[[[ko-án	a-ke-thè]	[ko-án
anyway	PLACE	WH-that.much	POSS-NMLZ-be.big	WH-that.much

*akibilo**ne** chinine, neli [...]*
a-ke-bī-lò-**nē**]]		chiní-Cē]	nè-lì]
POSS-NMLZ-be.small-RL-**INDEF**	know-NEG	1EXCL-HON

'Anyway, I didn't know how big or small Kohima is [...].' [SiT, HF 019]

In (837), three separate indirect questions are all marked with *-nē* 'indefinite' and then anaphorically picked up on in the following topic NP *laso alam* '(about) this matter'.

(837) Indirect questions marked by -nē 'indefinite'
[...] "[...] kolosonlone aning rongne rongrene
[[kolosón-lò-**nē**]   [a-nīng   aròng-nē   aróng-Cē-**nē**]
how-RL-**INDEF**   POSS-mind be.happy-INDEF be.happy-NEG-**INDEF**

kolosontong alang kemunthilone laso alam
[kolosón-tōng   alàng ke-múnthí-lò-**nē**]]   [lasō a-lám
how-INDIR.ITROG 3   NMLZ-think.deeply-RL-**INDEF** this POSS-matter

netum intervyu enji, alomso enji"
ne-tūm   intervyu   ēn-jí   alōm-sō   ēn-jí]
1EXCL-PL interview(<Eng) take-IRR2 while-small take-IRR2
'[...] "[...] how is it (for her), is she happy or not, how is she thinking about it, about this matter, we want to take interviews, for awhile (we want to) take (interviews)"' [SH, CSM 048]

Note that in the third indirect question CC *kolosontong alang kemunthilone* 'how is she thinking about it', the interrogative pronoun *kolosón* 'how' has the suffix *-tōng* 'indirect interrogative pronoun' attached to it, see §6.1.4.2.

15.2.2.3 Topic =*ke* marked complement clauses
Topic =*ke* may also mark CCs, as in (838). However, this construction is rare in the corpus.

(838) Complement clause of *chiní* 'know' marked with topic =*ke*
amat nangso doke chinilo [...]
amāt   [[nang-osō   dō=**ke**]   chiní-lò]
and.then   2POSS-child exist=**TOP** know-RL
'And then, I knew your child was there [...].' [RBT, ChM 031]

15.2.2.4 Quotative *pu* and *pusi* complementizers
Both the simple quotative *pu* and the more complex form *pusi*, which is a fusion of *pù-si* 'say-NF:RL',[156] function as complementizers. In (839), both *pu* and *pusi* occur within the same intonation unit, both times marking the end of direct speech. First, we have *pu* occurring after the CC *nepo kajoklu* 'our father is a fool', which represents direct speech as evidenced by the use of the first person exclusive possessive prefix *ne-* rather than the general and third person possessive prefix *a-*. Similarly, further

---

156 Analogous quotative complementizers derived from a non-final marked verb 'say' are found in various subbranches of Tibeto-Burman, for example, in the Tamangic language Chantyal (Noonan 2006: 4), the Tani language Galo (Post 2007: 848), and the 'Kuki-Chin' language Daai Chin (So-Hartmann 2009: 321).

along, we have *pusi* occurring after the direct speech CC *nepo [...] bojar kidunpensi kevanglo* 'our father [...] has come back after going to the market'.

(839) Examples of *pu* and *pusi* functioning as complementizers of direct speech
*setame asomar abangke **nepo kajoklu pu***
[setāmē   [a-so-màr   abàng=ke]   [[ne-pō
nevertheless POSS-child-PL NPDL=TOP 1EXCL:POSS-father
ke-joklū]   **pu]**
NMLZ-be.foolish **QUOT**

*chininedetsí **nepo** <bojar kidunpen>*
chiní-Cē-dèt-si]   [[ne-pō   <bojár   ke-dùn-pen>
know-NEG-PFV-NF:RL 1EXCL:POSS-father market(<Asm) NMLZ-join-NF:with

bojarsi kidun apot bojar kidunpensi
bojár=si   ke-dùn   apōt   bojár
market(<Asm)=FOC:RL NMLZ-join because market(<Asm)
ke-dùn-pen-si
NMLZ-join-NF:with-NF:RL

***kevanglo pusi** asomar abang mathalo*
ke-vàng-lò]   **pusi]**   [a-so-màr   abàng]   mathà-lò
NMLZ-come-RL **QUOT.COMP** POSS-child-PL NPDL think-RL
'But the children didn't know at all "Our father is a fool." They thought, "Our father has come back after going to the market."' [HI, BPh 014]

In the same story, talking about the same event, the same construction using *pusi* is also used to indicate the end of indirect, rather than direct, speech, where instead of *nepo* 'our father', the same referent is referred to by his character name Bokolapo, see (840).

(840) Quotative complementizer *pusi* marking indirect speech CC
amatsi Bokolapo abangke bojar dam'etlo pusi
amātsi   [[Bokolāpō abàng=ke bojár   dàm-ét-lò] **pusi]**
and.then NAME   NPDL=TOP market(<Asm) go-PRF-RL **QUOT.COMP**

asomar abang mathaló
a-so-màr   abàng mathà-lò
POSS-child-PL NPDL think-RL
'The children thought that Bokolapo had already gone to the market.' [HI, BPh 010]

15.2.3 Adverbial clauses

15.2.3.1 Conditional -te

Conditional clauses are marked by -te 'conditional (COND)', as in (841), where the final verb of the main clause is marked irrealis, here by -pò.

(841) Conditional clause
[...] neta dak dokokte, kosonpo?[...]
nè=tā   dāk   dō-kòk-**te**   kosón-pò
1EXCL=ADD here stay-firmly-**COND** how-IRR1
'[...] [I]f I stay here, how will it be? [...]' [SH, CSM 062]

Conditional -te is also used in procedural texts where it appears to indicate temporal precedence. In this case, it may either co-occur with -dèt 'perfective', as in (842), or -lò 'realis', as in (843). But although the English translations of these two examples require 'realis' phrasing (i.e., 'after' or 'when', rather than 'if'), note that in Karbi procedural texts, the main verbs are marked irrealis, typically using -pò (cf. §9.6.2.1.2). That is to say, even in these two examples, the conditional clauses remain 'irrealis' (even if the translation suggests otherwise).

(842) Perfective -dèt and conditional -te marking temporal precedence
takiripen jengdétte ansi thakpo
[takirí=pen   jèng-dèt-**te**]   ánsi   thàk-pò
spindle(<Asm)=with   spin-PFV-**COND** after.that weave-IRR1
'After having spun the thread, we then weave it.' [KST, PSu 006]

(843) Realis -lò and conditional -te marking temporal precedence
ansi pholo ingdaklote hekpo
ánsi   [pholó ingdàk-lò-tē]   hèk-pò
after.that cotton disperse-RL-COND   remove.cover-IRR1
'Then, after the cotton gets dispersed, we open up (the seeds).' [KST, PSu 004]

A counterfactual conditional can be expressed by using the construction [V asón-te], as in (844). The same construction can be used for a simple, non-counterfactual conditional in order to be more polite, as in (845).

(844) Counterfactual conditional with asón-te
Lindale do asonte ansose ning arongji
Líndá=le   dō   asón-te   án-sosē   nīng aróng-jí
NAME=FOC:IRR exist like-COND that.much-more   mind be.happy-IRR2

apotlo... pu anchotlo
apōtlò   pù   án-chòt-lò
COUNTERFACT like.this that.much-only-RL
'If Linda would have been there, I would have been even happier, that's all.'
[SiT, HF 061]

(845) Polite conditional with *asón-te*
si aphrangsi nanglimen chethan asonte <'e>
sì   aphráng-sí   nang-li-mén   che-thán   asón-tē
therefore   first-SPLT   2POSS-HON-name   RR-tell   like-COND

me'iksenji
mē-īk-sén-jí
be.good-FRML-INTENS-IRR2
'So first, if you could tell us your name, that would be wonderful.'
[KaR, SWK 004]

15.2.3.2 Purpose clauses with quotative complementizers
Purpose clauses may be nominalizations (§12.5), but they may also be finite clauses followed simply by quotative *pu* or by the quotative complementizer *pusi*, as in (846).[157]

(846) Purpose clause with quotative complementizer
ethevet setame thanji pusi dak kevangló
[e-thē-vét   setāmē   thán-jí   **pusi]**   dāk   ke-vàng-lò
one-CLF:word-only nevertheless   tell-IRR2 **QUOT.COMP** here   NMLZ-come-RL
'I have come here to tell just one thing.' [KK, CC 003]

15.2.3.3 Concessive *sitā~setā*
Concessive *sitā~setā* is sometimes used at the end of a finite clause to mark it as a concessive subordinate clause, as in (847). Otherwise, *sitā~setā* or variants such as *setāmē* or *bónsitā~bóntā* may be used as adversative coordinating conjunctions (§15.5.3).

(847) Concessive *setā ~ sitā* marking a subordinate clause
[...] ok hanta thiktheilo seta, hala
[[ōk   hán=tā   thík-théi-lò   **setā]**   [hála
meat   curry=ADD   be.okay(<Asm)-all:EXH:S/O-RL **even.though**   that

---

[157] The use of a quotative-derived complementizer in a purpose construction is found in other Tibeto-Burman languages as well, e.g., Chantyal (Noonan 2006).

> *aphi sarpi alam karju apot, anke Bey*
> a-phì   sarpī   a-lám   ke-arjū   apōt]
> POSS-grandmother   old.woman   POSS-word   NMLZ-hear   because
> [ánke   Bēy
> and.then   CLAN
>
> *Ke'et ahem chepangri chepangdonronglo [...]*
> ke-èt   a-hēm   che-pangrí   che-pangdòn-ròng-lò
> NMLZ-be.yellow   POSS-house   RR-reconcile   RR-even.out-instead-RL
> '[...] [A]lthough they (i.e., Bey the Black's family) had prepared all the food, because (he) had followed his grandmother's advice, he had instead married into Bey the Fair's family [...].' [WR, BCS 018]

Note that *sitā~setā* likely originates in a sequence of *-si* 'non-final:realis' and *=tā* 'additive' because the combination of the non-final marker plus the additive particle yields concessive conjunctions in other TB languages as well. An example is *lüphi* 'even though' (< *lü* 'non-final' + *phi* 'additive') in the Southern 'Kuki-Chin' language Daai Chin (So-Hartmann 2009: 343).

15.3 Irrealis clause types: Irrealis-sensitivity in non-final and focus markers

15.3.1 Overview

In both non-final verb suffixes (*-si* 'non-final:realis' and *-ra* 'non-final:irrealis', see §9.7.1 and §15.2.1.1) and focus clitics (*=si* 'focus:realis', §14.2.3, and *=le* 'focus:irrealis', §14.2.4), a binary distinction exists between a realis version of the marker and an irrealis version of the marker. In both cases, this means that the realis version occurs if the final verb is realis, and the irrealis version occurs if the final verb is irrealis. They are thus sensitive to the (ir)realis context they occur in, similar to negative polarity items (Israel 2011).

In both grammatical domains of non-final and focus marking, irrealis is the marked context with respect to frequency: *-si* 'non-final:realis' occurs 104 times in the corpus, while *-ra* 'non-final:irrealis' occurs 21 times in the corpus; similarly, *=si* 'focus:realis' has 208 occurrences, while *=le* 'focus:irrealis' has 89 occurrences. The following subsections show what counts as 'irrealis' for the binary distinction in non-final and focus markers – which is in fact slightly different for the two domains.[158]

---

[158] 'Irrealis' is a commonly applied descriptive label, but has also been argued not to constitute a (single) grammatical category (Bybee, Perkins, and Pagliuca 1994; Mithun 1995; Chafe 1995; Bybee 1998) – a claim these Karbi data certainly lend support to if we compare the irrealis categories of *-ra*

Table 116 gives an overview of the irrealis contexts in which -*ra* and =*le* occur, as evidenced by corpus examples, in the order discussed in the subsections to follow. Note that -*ra* appears to occur in a more limited range of irrealis contexts, which, however, may also be due to its overall lower frequency compared to =*le* (89 vs. 21 occurrences).[159] Nevertheless, an interesting grammatical context is that of negation, where =*le* is undoubtedly correct and frequently used, while -*ra* is only accepted by some native speakers to be the correct form and other native speakers prefer using realis non-final -*si*.

Table 116: Irrealis contexts for -*ra* 'NF:IRR' and =*le* 'FOC:IRR'.

Grammatical context		-*ra* 'NF:IRR'	=*le* 'FOC:IRR'
Non-declarative speech acts	Questions	X	X
	Imperatives	X	X
	Hortatives	X	X
Negation		(X)	X
Deontic clauses (with *náng* 'need')		–	X
Conditional subordinate clauses		–	X

15.3.2 Non-declarative speech acts

Both the irrealis non-final marker and the irrealis focus marker occur in all three types of non-declarative speech acts: questions, imperatives, and hortatives. Respective examples of -*ra* are offered in (848), (849), and (850).

(848) Irrealis non-final -*ra* in question
  [...] *ladak kachedandunra <kithipen> kithidunma?*
  ladāk ke-che-dán-dùn-**ra**   <ke-thì-pèn>   ke-thì-dūn=ma
  here NMLZ-RR-fight-JOIN-**NF:IRR** NMLZ-die-NF:with NMLZ-die-JOIN=Q
  '[...] [D]id they fight here, and did they die?' [SiT, HF 028]

---

and =*le* as well as -*pò* 'irrealis1' and -*jí* 'irrealis2' (§9.6.2). The best explanation for the functional overlap and differences between the irrealis ranges of the four markers no doubt lies in their differential diachronic developments, as a general principle also argued by Cristofaro (2012) and Mauri and Sansò (2012).

159 Preliminary attempts to elicit -*ra* in deontic and conditional subordinate clauses suggest that -*ra* can be used in those contexts as well.

(849) Irrealis non-final -ra; imperative-marked final verb
[...] mo nanghem chedam ahomoike lapu chevangthurá
[mò   nang-hēm   chV-dām   a-homói=kc]   [lapú
future   your-house   RR-go   POSS-time(<Asm)=TOP this.side
che-vāng-thū-**ra**]
RR-come-again-**NF:IRR**

langso atovarthot vangra lapen ladak
[langsō   a-továr-thót   vàng-**ra**]   [la=pen   ladāk
this   POSS-road-exactly   come-**NF:IRR** this=with   here

nanghumrira nanghem chepaletu
nang=humrí-**ra**]   [nang-hēm   che-pa-lè-tū]
CIS=visit.friends/relatives-**NF:IRR** 2:POSS-house RR-CAUS-reach-UNCOND.IMP
'[...] [A]nd later when you go home, again come like this, come on the exact same road, and then go to the familiar place (i.e. where the dog is staying), and then go and make sure to reach your house.' [KK, BMS 089]

(850) Irrealis non-final -ra; hortative-marked final verb
hormu horton chirim chibikangvetra, dunnang,
hormú   hortón   chV-rím   chV-bí-káng-vèt-rà]
thing   EE:hormú RR-put.in.one.place RR-keep-give.leave-nicely-NF:IRR
[dùn-nāng
join-HORT

ha nephi along!
há   ne-phì   a-lòng]
over.there 1EXCL:POSS-grandmother   POSS-LOC
'Join me, wherever I go, but let's eat and drink and let's keep everything nicely (here, i.e. put everything in order before we leave), let's go there, to my grandmother's place.' [KK, BMS 033]

Examples of =le in all three types of non-declarative speech acts are given in (851), (852), and (853). Note that (851) is interesting, because in questions, both focus markers may occur: realis focus =si only ever occurs on interrogative pronouns, like *kopù* 'how' here, whereas irrealis focus =le may occur on an additional focused element, here *banghinivet* 'the two (of us)'.

(851) Irrealis focus =le in question
[...] nonke methan-sibongpopen banghinivetle kopusi pirthe
nón=ke   methān-sibóngpō=pen   bàng-hiní-vèt=le
now=TOP   dog-SPECIES=with   CLF:HUM:PL-two-only=FOC:IRR
kopù=si   pirthé
how=FOC:RL   world

mindar dodunthekpoma pulo
mindár   dō-dūn-thèk-pò=ma   pù-lò
world(<Pnr)   stay-JOIN-know.how-IRR1=Q   say-RL
'[…] "Now, how will I manage to stay in the world just the two of us with the dog?" (he thought).' [KK, BMS 016]

(852)   Irrealis focus =*le*; imperative-marked final verb
       aphihai alongle donoi […]
       a-phì-hái   a-lòng=**le**   dō-nōi
       POSS-grandmother-HON   POSS-LOC=**FOC:IRR**   stay-INF.COND.IMP
       '"Stay with your grandmother […]!"' [KK, CC 017]

(853)   Irrealis focus =*le*; hortative-marked final verb
       […] temole chethanikronglonang mh
       temó=**le**   che-thán-īk-ròng-lonāng   mh
       story=**FOC:IRR**   RR-tell-FRML-instead-HORT:EMPH   DSM
       '[…] [L]et's tell a story instead!' [CST, HM 002]

In (854), both markers co-occur: =*le* occurs on the subject NP in a non-final clause marked by -*ra*, where the final verb is a hortative form marked by -*nāng* 'hortative'.

(854)   Irrealis focus =*le* and irrealis non-final -*ra*; hortative-marked final verb
       "dah! etumle arveng chepachap chepachapra,
       dáh   e-tūm=**le**   arvēng   che-pa-cháp
       go!   1PL.INCL-PL=**FOC:IRR**   feather   RR-CAUS-pile.up
       che-pa-cháp-**ra**
       RR-CAUS-pile.up-**NF:IRR**

       rungponra, ha purthimi along thondamnang!"
       rùng-pōn-**ra**   [há   purthimí   alòng]   thòn-dām-nāng
       lift-take.away-**NF:IRR**   over.there   earth(<Asm)   LOC   drop-GO-HORT
       '"Let's go, let's put our wings together, and lift him up and put him there on the ground!"' [KTa, TCS 066]

15.3.3 Negation

In negative contexts, irrealis focus =*le* has to be used, as on *inglóng* 'hill' in (855). (Note that in this contrastive focus situation here, the subsequent positive clause has the alternative *thói* 'plains' marked with realis focus =*si*.)

(855) Irrealis focus =le; negated final verb
nelitumke bihekpenta inglongle
[ne-li-tūm=ke   bī-hèk=pen=tā   inglóng=**le**
1EXCL:POSS-HON-PL=TOP   be.small-INTENS=from=ADD   hill=**FOC:IRR**

kedoke kali non ason thoisi kedo apot [...]
ke-dō=ke   kalī]   [nón   asón   thói=si
NMLZ-stay=TOP NEG.EQU.COP   now   like   plains=FOC:RL
ke-dō   apōt]
NMLZ-stay   because
'Since my childhood we have not been living in the hills; because we have been living in the plains [...].' [KaR, SWK 083]

For non-final suffixes, negative contexts are ambiguous. Some native speakers are happy to use either *-ra*, as in elicited (856), or *-si*, while others only accept *-si* and ban *-ra* entirely from negative contexts.

(856) Irrealis non-final *-ra*; negated final verb
alàng   ōk   a-hán   tún-**ra**   chō-ò-ē
3   meat   POSS-curry   cook-**NF:IRR** eat-much-NEG
'He cooked food but didn't eat much.' [SiT 090302]

15.3.4 Deontic clauses (expressing necessity/obligation; with *náng* 'need, must')

In deontic clauses involving *náng* 'need', elements in focus are marked by irrealis focus *=le*, as in (857). Note that this is the only context in which the use of one of the irrealis-sensitive markers (i.e., *-ra* or *=le*) overlaps with the use of *-pò* 'irrealis1' and *-jí* 'irrealis2', see §9.6.2.1.5.

(857) Irrealis focus *=le*; deontic final verb
[...] nephi aphanle kamatha nangalang [...]
[ne-phì   a-phān=**le**   ke-mathà
1EXCL:POSS-grandmother   POSS-NSUBJ=**FOC:IRR**   NMLZ-think
náng-jí-lāng
need-IRR2-still
'[...] "You still need to think of my grandmother!" [...]' [KK, BMS 022]

Preliminary elicitation suggests irrealis non-final *-ra* can be used as well if the final verb is a complex predicate involving *náng* 'need, must'.

15.3.5 Conditional subordinate clauses

Inside a conditional subordinate clause, a focused element is also marked by irrealis =*le* rather than realis =*si*, as seen in (858). Note that the second occurrence of =*le* in this example is due to the bare stem imperative form of the final verb.

(858) Irrealis focus =*le* in conditional subordinate clause
"[...] nangpole hemtap angsong chote, nangtumke
[[nang-pō=**le**   hēmtāp   angsóng chō-te]   nang-tūm=ke
2:POSS-father=**FOC:IRR** tree.house high.up eat-COND you-PL=TOP

mandule cho!"
mandú=le   chō]
field.hut=FOC:IRR eat
'"[...] [I]f your father takes his meal in the *hemtap*, you eat in the *mandu!*'"
[CST, RO 017]

In this context as well, preliminary elicitation suggests irrealis non-final -*ra* can be used if a non-final claused is linked to a following conditional subordinate clauses (schematically, '[V_x-*ra*]$_{\text{Clause.1}}$ [V_y-COND]$_{\text{Clause.2}}$, then ... ').

15.4 Non-nominalized insubordination (formally non-finite declarative main clause types)

While (historically) nominalized main clauses are discussed in §12.7, this section deals with insubordinated constructions that are not based on nominalization. Following Evans (2007: 367), insubordination is defined here as "the conventionalized main clause use of what, on prima facie grounds, appear to be formally subordinate clauses".

15.4.1 Main clauses marked with =*ke* 'topic': Background information construction

Main clauses marked with =*ke* 'topic' provide a background against which a statement just mentioned (or about to be mentioned) is meant to be understood (see §16.3.10). Since clauses marked with =*ke* may function as subordinate clauses (§15.2.2.3), main clauses marked with =*ke* are best treated as instances of insubordination.

A =*ke* marked clause may follow or precede a main clause that it is contextually linked to, as in (859) and (860).

(859) 'Topic' =ke marked clause following its contextually related clause
ingsām-hòi... arvè ke-jáng=**ke**
be.cold-a.bit rain NMLZ-fall=**TOP**
'It's a bit cold... it's raining (that's why).' [Notebook OH 121011: 001]

(860) 'Topic' =ke marked clause preceding its contextually related clause
apok ingchirdukke...
a-pōk ingchìr-dùk=**ke**
POSS-stomach be.hungry-INTENS=**TOP**

anke inglong arloksi phurui chosot
ánke [inglóng arlòk=si] [phurùi chosòt]
and.then hill foot.of.hill=FOC:RL yam kd.vegetable

choridamlo tangho [...]
cho-rī-dām-lò tànghò
AUTO.BEN/MAL-search-go-RL REP
'He was suffering from hunger, and so, he went here and there (lit. up and down the hills) to look for wild vegetables [...].' [HK, TR 014-5]

If the context is provided by a question, a =*ke* marked main clause may also be used in the answer, as in (861).

(861) 'Topic' =ke marked clause in answer to question
<ha> *Misorongpo arju, "Chonghoisi nang chongho*
misòrongpō arjū chonghói=si nàng chonghō
sp.ant ask reason=FOC:RL you frog

ami korrakmati?" "Tovar nangdangthipke"
a-mí kòr-ràk=mati] **továr nang=dāng-thìp=ke**
POSS-buttocks bite-RES:little.wound=CG **road CIS=BLOCK-FIRMLY=TOP**
'He asked the ant, "Why did you bite the frog in the butt?", "He had come and was blocking the road... and so..."' [RBT, ChM 076]

15.4.2 Main clauses marked with *pu* 'quotative': Desiderative construction

Quotative *pu* used as a sentence-final particle marks a desiderative or intention construction (see also §16.3.1.2). This main clause construction must have developed from the complementizer function of quotative *pu* occurring with complement clauses (§15.2.2.4) and subordinate purpose clauses (§15.2.3.2). Ellipsis of a following main clause would have then lead to the development of the insubordinated construction. Examples of the desiderative construction are given in (862), (863), and (864).

15.4 Non-nominalized insubordination (formally non-finite declarative main clause types) — 525

Note that in all examples, the verb preceding *pu* 'quotative' is marked irrealis with *-jí* 'irrealis2' as in the subordinate purpose clause construction (§9.6.2.1.7), and that in (864), the quotative *pu* is additionally marked with realis *-lò* (see §16.3 for further cases of particles that take inflectional suffixes).

(862) Main clause marked with *pu* 'quotative': desiderative construction
adapprang netum thurlo Hongkram Chomangkan dunji pu
a-dappráng   ne-tūm   thùr-lò   Hongkrām   Chomangkán
POSS-dawn   1EXCL:POSS-PL   get.up-RL   PN   PN
dùn-jí   **pu**
join-IRR2   **QUOT**
'We got up early in the morning, we wanted to join the Chomangkan in Hongkram.' [SH, CSM 001]

(863) Main clause marked with *pu* 'quotative': desiderative construction
ai tovar nangpektha ti ko jirpo,
ái   továr   nang-pèk-thā   tì   ko   jīrpō,
how.bad!   road   1/2:NSUBJ-give.way-IMP:CON EMPH   buddy:VOC   friend

ne'ik atum aphan an thonji pu
ne-ìk   a-tūm   a-phān   àn   thòn-jí   **pu**
1EXCL:POSS-older.brother   POSS-PL   POSS-NSUBJ   rice   drop-IRR2   **QUOT**
'"How bad! Please do give way to me. I want to take rice to my brother (and sister-in-law)."' [RBT, ChM 012]

(864) Desiderative construction with *pu* 'quotative' additionally marked realis *-lò*
lasi <ling> juja'e homtekangsi halaso ape ari
[lasì   juja'ē   hóm-tekáng-si]   hálasō   a-pé   a-rī
therefore   cradle   fix.by.tying-leaving-NF:RL   that   POSS-cloth   POSS-EE:pé

kechechokdamji **pulo** *amatsi laso osomar banghini*
[ke-che-chōk-dām-jí   **pu-lò**   [amātsi   [lasō   osō-mār
NMLZ-RR-wash.clothes-go-IRR2   **QUOT-RL**   and.then this   child-PL
bàng-hiní
CLF:HUM:PL-two

aphan juja'e homtekangsi thaptekanglo
a-phān]   juja'ē   hóm-tekáng-si   thàp-tekáng-lò]
POSS-NSUBJ   cradle   fix.by.tying-leaving-NF:RL   put.inside-leaving-RL
'So (the mother) fixed the cradle and (she) wanted to go wash those clothes, and then, she fixed the cradle for the two children, and put them inside.' [CST, HM 010]

15.4.3 Stand-alone indirect questions

Indirect question complement clauses such as '[I do not know [whether he leaves or stays]ₒₒ]' are discussed in §15.2.2.2. They are typically based on a disjunctive or polar question 'X or not X', or 'X or Y'. The two clauses X and Y are then marked by *-nē* 'indefinite'.

In the following two examples, indirect question complement clauses are used without a main clause, making them instances of insubordination. In (865), the function is to ask a polar question (for Karbi polar and disjunctive question structure, see §15.1.1.4 and §15.1.1.5) in an indirect way, as can be done in English with 'I wonder if you heard of this' instead of the direct 'Have you heard of this?'[160]

(865) Using stand-alone indirect question instead of direct polar question
si nanglitumta lason arjulongne
sì   nang-li-tūm=tā   lasón   arjū-lōng-**nē**
therefore   2POSS-HON-PL=ADD   that.way   hear-GET-**INDEF**

arjulonglene angko lason thakthak atomo
arjū-lōng-Cē-**nē**   akó   lasón   thakthāk
hear-GET-NEG-**INDEF** on.the.other.hand(<Asm) that.way   same
a-tomó
POSS-story

pine ason nanglitum karjulong doma lason
pí-nē   asón   nang-li-tūm   ke-arjū-lōng   dō=ma   lasón
what-INDEF like   2POSS-HON-PL   NMLZ-hear-GET exist=Q   that.way
'And so, whether you have heard this or not (I wonder), is there any such story like this that you've heard, like that?' [KaR, SWK 072]

Another example is (866), where the ellipsed main clause has to be understood as 'we don't know' rather than 'I wonder'.

(866) Stand-alone indirect question with conventionalized ellipsis of main clause
netumke arlengpi asolone kaline
ne-tūm=ke   arlēng-pī   a-sō-lò-**nē**   kalī-**nē**
1EXCL:POSS-PL=TOP   person-female   POSS-child-RL-INDEF   NEG.EQU.COP-**INDEF**
'Whether we are the children of the Karbi woman or not (we don't know).' [CST, HM 087]

---

[160] Less direct questions are a common politeness (because face-saving) strategy; insubordinated constructions cross-linguistically often serve this kind of function (Evans 2007).

15.5 Clause coordination

Clause coordination, i.e., coordinating two main clauses into one unit, is not common in Karbi, as in clause-chaining languages in general. However, there are a few strategies available, which are discussed below. Note that it is a cross-linguistic problem to define coordination as involving two truly 'equal' clauses with none showing any signs of dependency on the other (Haspelmath 2004). In Karbi, it is still up to future research to investigate this further, including, for example, the question of whether or not the constructions discussed below allow for the subject to change across coordinated clauses.

15.5.1 Conjunctive coordination

15.5.1.1 Conjunctive coordinator *lapèn* 'and'

One rarely used conjunctive coordination construction consists of using *lapèn* (< *là* 'this' and =*pen* 'with, from') between the first and the second clause. An example is in the text unit (867), which actually begins with the more typical clause-chaining construction, i.e., the verb *chedon* 'place (him)self a ladder' marked non-final with *-si*. The next two clauses, however, are both main clauses with verbs marked progressive with *ke-*, linked by *lapèn* 'and'.

(867) Conjunctive coordination with *lapèn* 'and'
      dondon chedonsi... anke amonit abang
      [dondón che-dón-si...]   [ánke   [a-monít abàng]
      ladder   RR-place.ladder/bridge-NF:RL and.then POSS-man NPDL

      <a> pe akelokpen keroi isi ajamborong
      [[pé a-ke-lòk=pen   ke-ròi   isī   a-jamboróng
      cloth POSS-NMLZ-be.white=with NMLZ-sew one POSS-bag

      arlosi lahai kethap lapen arum kevan
      arlō=si]   [lahái] ke-thàp]]   **lapèn** [arúm ke-vàn]]
      inside=FOC:RL these PROG-put.inside **and** down PROG-bring
      'He's placed himself a ladder... and then, the man is putting these (pieces of fruit) into one bag sown from white cloth and is bringing them down.' [SiT, PS 003]

15.5.1.2 Additive particle clause/VP coordination constructions

Two other conjunctive coordination constructions, which perhaps rather than actually linking clauses may only be linking verb phrases,[161] involve the additive particle =*tā*

---

[161] This is a matter for future research. That said, it is cross-linguistically often difficult to distinguish between clause and VP coordination, and therefore sometimes useful to group them as 'verbal conjunction' (Haspelmath 2004, 2005).

(§10.8.3.1). In one construction, =tā occurs on NPs, as in (868). In this example, we have two different verbs that are linked, jùn 'drink' and chō 'eat'. Note, however, that the otherwise identical construction can also be used to coordinate NPs only, with the verb remaining the same, as discussed below (§15.5.1.3).

(868) Clause coordination via additive-marked NPs
  […] langta junlong anta cholong […]
  [lāng=**tā**   jùn-lōng   àn=**tā**   chō-lōng
  water=**ADD** drink-GET   rice=**ADD** eat-GET
  '[…] [T]hey got to drink water and they got to eat rice […].' [KK, BMS 056]

In the other construction, the additive particle may be used in a copy verb construction, in which a copy of the verb root occurs with =tā, followed by the verb root with optional addition of morphology (see also §16.2.3 for other copy verb constructions that have discourse functions). In (869), the two events 'cook much' and 'eat much' are coordinated via this construction.

(869) Clause coordination via additive-marked verb copy
  ōk   a-hán   [tún=**tā**   tún-ò]   [chō=**tā**   chō-ò]
  meat POSS-curry cook=**ADD**   cook-much   eat=**ADD**   eat-much
  '(S/he) often cooks and often eats.' [SiT 100515]

Note that conjunctive coordination via a copy verb construction with the additive particle also exists in Hakha Lai (Central 'Kuki-Chin') (Peterson and VanBik 2004: 348).

15.5.1.3 Clausal NP coordination

Clausal NP coordination puts every participant in a separate clause by repeating the verb each time, and connects the participants across clauses with additive =tā. The result is a parallelism structure (§16.1.1). A folk story example is (870), in which three clauses are structured in parallel, which are about the three protagonists of this story.

(870) Parallelism based on coordination indicated by additive =tā (folk story)
  […] **anke Bey Ki'ik abangta** *ahem arit dolo*
  ánke   [[Bēy   ke-ìk   abàng=tā]   a-hēm   a-rīt
  and.then   CLAN   NMLZ-BE.BLACK   NPDL=ADD   POSS-house   POSS-field
  dō-lò]
  exist-RL

  Bey Ke'et abangta *ahem arit dolo*
  [[Bēy   ke-èt   abàng=tā]   a-hēm   a-rīt   dō-lò]
  CLAN   NMLZ-BE.YELLOW   NPDL=ADD   POSS-house   POSS-field   exist-RL

Bey Ronghang abang, akibi abangta,
[[[Bēy   Ronghāng abàng]   [a-ke-bī   abàng=tā]]
 CLAN   CLAN   NPDL   POSS-NMLZ-BE.SMALL   NPDL=ADD

ahem arit dolo
a-hēm   a-rīt   dō-lò]
POSS-house   POSS-field   exist-RL
'[...] Bey the Black had his (own) house and property, Bey the Fair likewise had his (own) house and property, and Bey Ronghang, the young one, also had his (own) house and property.' [WR, BCS 004]

Examples from personal narratives are (871) and (872). Example (871) connects S arguments while repeating the verb. Example (872) is a more complex case involving negation, which requires translation into English as 'neither ... nor ... '.

(871) Parallelism based on coordination (personal narrative)
       Samprita dunji Rasinjata dunji Lindata
       [**Sàmprì=tā**   dùn-jí]   [**Rasínjá=tā** dùn-jí]   [**Líndá=tā**
       PN=ADD   join-IRR2   **PN=ADD**   join-IRR2 **PN=ADD**

       dunji pulo
       dùn-jí]   pu-lò
       join-IRR2   QUOT-RL
       'Sampri, Rasinja, and Linda (all) wanted to join.' [SH, CSM 004]

(872) Parallelism based on coordination (personal narrative)
       *latum **phelangpenta kali** tinpenta*
       [là-tūm   [[phelāng=pen=tā   kalī]   [tín=pen=tā
       this-PL   thatch=with=ADD   NEG.EQU.COP   tin(<Eng)=with=ADD

       kali, *arlong achetpensi kidip [...]*
       kalī]]   [arlōng   a-chèt=pen=si]   ke-dìp]
       NEG.EQU.COP   stone   POSS-piece=with=FOC:RL   NMLZ-cover
       'Neither with thatch nor with tin, but with slabs of stone they cover (their roofs) [...].' [SiT, HF 050]

15.5.2 Disjunctive coordination

In a disjunctive indirect question, both clauses are sufficiently marked by *-nē* 'indefinite', as shown in §15.2.2.2. However, apparently if the first clause ends up very long, disjunctive *màtè* 'or' may be inserted for more obvious marking, as evidenced in (873).

(873) Disjunctive coordinator *màtè* linking two subordinate clauses
lapen latum haladak... la botor bokan areng kelok
lapèn   là-tūm   háladāk   [la   botór   bokán   a-rèng
and.then   this-PL   there   this   climate(<Asm)   EE:botór   POSS-skin
ke-lòk
NMLZ-be.white

alampenke climate pulo laso kemesen
a-lám=pen=ke   climate   pù-lò   lasō   ke-mē-sén
POSS-language=with=TOP   climate(<Eng)   say-RL   this   NMLZ-be.good-INTENS

apotlone mate la Naka atum aphan ketheklongpen
a-pōt-lò-nē]   **màtè**   [là   Naká   a-tūm   aphān   ke-theklōng-pèn]
POSS-reason-RL-INDEF   **or**   this   TRIBE   POSS-PL   NSUBJ   NMLZ-see-NF:with

akele aning kangsampik apotlone
[akelé   a-nīng   ke-ingsām-pīk]   a-pōt-lò-nē
more.than.expected   POSS-mind   NMLZ-be.cold-very   POSS-reason-RL-INDEF
'And then, they there... whether the reason was that the *botor bokan*, 'climate' in English (lit. the white skin language), was good or whether the reason was seeing the Nagas and because of that everybody being exceedingly happy (I don't know).' [SiT, HF 036]

15.5.3 Adversative coordination

Adversative coordination may be expressed by using the coordination conjunction *bóntā* 'but', as in (874)

(874) Adversative coordination with *bóntā* 'but'
atomo abangke neli pu'an than pajirmi
a-tomó   abàng=ke   nè-lì   pù=án   thán   pa-jirmī
POSS-story   NPDL=TOP   1EXCL-HON   like.this=up.to   tell   CAUS-elaborate

thekthe bonta non akai'anta emekpen
thēk-Cē   **bóntā**   nón   a-kái=án=tā   e-mēk=pen
know.how-NEG   **but**   now   POSS-time(<Asm)=up.to=even   1INCL-eye=with

kethekdunlong ba kachinivek asonlo
ke-thèk-dūn-lōng   bá   ke-chiní-vék   asón-lò
NMLZ-see-JOIN-GET   or(<Asm)   NMLZ-know-definitely   like-RL
'Such a story I can't tell any details about, but even up to today with eyes I could see or anyway definitely know, that's how it is.' [KaR, SWK 073]

15.6 Lack of a syntactic pivot

There does not appear to be a grammaticalized syntactic pivot in Karbi, although further research is necessary to confirm this claim. The lack of a syntactic pivot is understood to mean that the mapping of participant roles across clauses is not determined by syntactic principles, and if clausal roles of participants change, this is not indicated by any kind of overt marking. Instead, it is left to pragmatics to solve ambiguities in cross-clausal continuity.

An example that illustrates the role of pragmatics in cross-clausal continuity of participant roles is offered in (875). There are three clauses here, and the interesting change in participant roles occurs between the first two clauses. The first clause '(X) returned the hat to (Y)' has both the A argument X and the R argument Y unexpressed via zero anaphora. In the following clause '(Y) was grateful to X', the former R argument Y becomes the new A argument, while the former A argument X becomes perhaps an R argument, or in any event the recipient of Y's gratefulness. This change in participant roles is not overtly marked.

(875) Unmarked change in participant roles across clauses
lapenke ø la phutup <kapa..> kipidunthu apot

$[\varnothing]_{A:X}$ $[\varnothing]_{R:Y}$

lapèn=ke	[ø	là	phutūp	ø	ke-pī-dūn-thū	apōt]
and.then=TOP		this	hat		NMLZ-give-JOIN-again	because

laphan aning ingsamsi, thesere pumni tekanglo

$[\varnothing]_{A:Y}$ $[NP]_{R:X}$

[ø là-phān a-nīng ingsām-si] [theseré púm-ní
  this-NSUBJ POSS-mind be.cold-NF:RL fruits CLF:round-two
tekáng-lò]
leave.for-RL

'And then, because he returned the hat, (the bicycle boy) was grateful to him and gave him two pieces of fruit.' [SiT, PS 039]

16 Discourse constructions

This chapter discusses Karbi discourse constructions as encountered in the corpus of recorded texts. Since the major text genre represented in the corpus is narratives, this chapter offers more detailed description of the constructions that occur in this particular genre.

The chapter begins with an overview of constructions that pervade the texts in the corpus and serve to structure the discourse (§16.1). This is followed by a discussion of rhetorical constructions, which serve emphatic or intensifying purposes (§16.2). An overview of particles is offered in §16.3, and a list of interjections is provided in §16.5. Finally, §16.6 offers text samples that show how hesitation and correction words are used.

16.1 Discourse structuring constructions

This section discusses discourse structuring constructions including clause parallelism in §16.1.1, tail-head linkage in §16.1.2, discourse connectors that have a function similar to English 'and then' in §16.1.3, and, finally, a description of the two discourse structuring markers *e* and *'mh* in §16.1.4.

16.1.1 Clause parallelism

Solnit (1995: 127) defines parallelism as "the binary repetition of linguistic features for rhythmic, esthetic or other expressive effect". There are two constructions that systematically result in this kind of parallelism in Karbi.[162] One is the elaborate expression (EE) construction (§16.2.2); the other is biclausal NP coordination (see §10.8.3.1.3 and §15.5.1.2). EE use is far more prevalent in folk stories and formulaic language like ceremonial chants; in spontaneous, colloquial language, EE's occur less often. Frequency of NP coordination at the clausal level appears not to be influenced by text genre. Below I discuss first EE parallelism and then biclausal NP coordination parallelism.

EE constructions may be built on nouns or verbs. In example (876) from a folk story, the EE *võtèk võsõ* 'birds' is the basis for the parallelism in the relative clause *votek ingrengre voso ingrengre along*. A similar example from a personal narrative is (877), where the parallelism is based on the verbal EE *sík dáng* 'prepare', which occurs in an adverb construction (§11.3.2).

---

[162] Acoustically, parallel structures are often accompanied by prosodic marking, which is what I understand much of Solnit's notion of "rhythmic effect" in his definition to refer to.

(876) Parallelism based on elaborate expression construction (folk story)
[...] hi'ipi abangke etum aphan ha **votek ingrengre**
[hī'ipī abàng=ke] [e-tūm aphan] há **[[vōtèk**
witch NPDL=TOP 1PL.INCL-PL NSUBJ over.there wild.bird
ingrèng-Cē]
call(small.animals)-NEG

***voso ingrengre along** ekethondamti*
[vōsō ingrèng-Cē] alòng] e=ke-thòn-dām-tí
EE:vōtèk call(small.animals)-NEG LOC 1PL.INCL=NMLZ-drop-GO-get.rid.off
'[...] [T]hat witch took and abandoned us over there where the birds don't chirp.' [CST, HM 062]

(877) Parallelism based on elaborate expression construction (personal narrative)
[...] pu amat alangtum te lang keso kecho
pu amāt alàng-tūm te [lāng ke-sō] [ke-chō
QUOT and.then 3-PL and.then/therefore water NMLZ-be.hot NMLZ-eat

kejun haihui'anta nangsikpi pame
ke-jùn] háihúi-án=tā **nang=sík-pī pa-mé**
NMLZ-drink GENEX-all=ADD 1/2:NSUBJ=prepare-BEN CAUS-be.good

nangdangpi pame
nang=dáng-pī pa-mé
1/2:NSUBJ=put.on.stove-BEN CAUS-be.good
'[...] [A]nd so they had nicely prepared and gotten ready (some) tea (lit. hot water) and food and drink and such things.' [SH, CSM 040]

The other construction that results in parallelism is clausal NP coordination. This construction expresses that a particular proposition is true for two or more participants. Instead of coordinating the NPs representing the participants inside a single clause, this construction puts each participant in a separate clause but keeps the verb constant. An example is (878), where the coordinated *neri nekeng* 'my hands and feet' occur in two different clauses, both ending in the negative existential copula *avē*.

(878) Clausal NP coordination
[...] amat neta neri ave nekeng ave [...]
amāt nè=tā [[ne-rí avē] [ne-kèng
and.then 1EXCL=ADD **1EXCL:POSS-hand** not.exist **1EXCL:POSS-foot**
avē]]
not.exist
'[...] [A]nd then also, I don't have hands or feet [...].' [RBT, ChM 030]

Another example of parallelism, which is only loosely built on clausal NP coordination, is (879). What contributes to the impression of parallelism here (as in other instances of clausal NP coordination, see §15.5.1.2), is (diachronically, here) the occurrence of additive =*tā* on both coordinated elements.

(879) Further occurrence of parallelism
arvi suinangta dannokso ar'e suinangta dannokso
[arvī **sùi-nangtā** dannoksō] [ar'ē **sùi-nangtā** dannoksō]
left turn-if.alternatively danger right turn-if.alternatively danger
'If I turn left, it will be dangerous, if I turn right, it will also be dangerous.'
[RBT, ChM 013]

16.1.2 Tail-head linkage

Tail-head linkage consists of the sentence-initial repeating of information from the previous sentence. This phenomenon of narrative structure was first described by Longacre (1968), and has since been reported in other Tibeto-Burman languages such as Galo (Tani) (Post 2007) and Dolakha Newar (Genetti 2011), as well as a range of languages from all across the world (see overview in Guillaume (2011) and De Vries (2005)). Despite the fact that tail-head linkage is an extremely common phenomenon cross-linguistically, the actual form it takes varies. In Karbi, the typical pattern is that the last clause is repeated verbatim, including arguments and predicate (although typically not including the reportative particle). An example is (880), in which the final clause *piso some enlo* '(they) got married' is repeated at the beginning of the next intonation unit, where it is followed by *ánke* 'and then' (§16.1.3), leading into the new information.

(880) Tail-head linkage: identical repetition
*anke latum thelo dinglo **piso some enlo** tangho*
ánke la-tūm thē-lò dīng-lò **pīsō sōmē ēn-lò** tànghò
and.then this-PL be.big-RL be.long-RL **wife EE:pīsō take-RL** REP
'And then, they grew up and got married, so they say.' [WR, BCS 003]

***piso some enlo** anke Bey Ki'ik abangta*
pīsō sōmē ēn-lò] ánke [Bēy ke-ìk abàng=tā
wife EE:pīsō take-RL and.then CLAN NMLZ-be.black NPDL=ADD

ahem arit dolo Bey Ke'et abangta
a-hēm a-rīt dō-lò] [Bēy ke-èt abàng=tā
POSS-house POSS-field exist-RL CLAN NMLZ-be.yellow NPDL=ADD

ahem arit dolo Bey Ronghang abang
a-hēm　　　a-rīt　　　dō-lò]　[Bēy　　Ronghāng　abàng
POSS-house　POSS-field　exist-RL　CLAN　　CLAN　　　　NPDL

akibi abangta ahem arit dolo
a-ke-bī　　　　　　　abàng=tā　　a-hēm　　　a-rīt　　　dō-lò]
POSS-NMLZ-be.small　NPDL=ADD　　POSS-house　POSS-field　exist-RL
'They got married, and then Bey the Black had his (own) house and property, Bey the Fair likewise had his (own) house and property, and Bey Ronghang, the young one, also had his (own) house and property.' [WR, BCS 004]

The excerpt in (881) starts with a sentence that is much longer and more complex. For the tail-head linkage construction, the storyteller only repeats a simplified version of the predicate, i.e., shortening *ponpidam'et thondam'et* at the "tail" to simply *thondamtilo* at the "head", without including any NPs.

(881) Tail-head linkage: slightly modified repetition
pu amat la Karbipi langhe kedam aphi, laso
[pu　　　amāt　　　là　　　Karbì-pī　　lànghē　　　　ke-dàm　　aphī]　[lasō
QUOT　and.then　this　PN-fem　washing.place　NMLZ-go　after　this

aosomar Hingchong musoso atum aphan
a-oso-màr　　　　Hingchòng　　　　musōsō　　　　a-tūm　　a-phān]
POSS-child-PL　　CONSTELLATION　siblings:DL　POSS-PL　POSS-NSUBJ

ha same sadu akrong alat votek
há　　　　　　samé　sadú　　a-króng　　　　a-lat　　　　　　vōtèk
over.there　path　EE:samé　POSS-CLF.road　POSS-EE:króng　wild.bird

ingrengre voso ingrengre along osomar
ingrèng-Cē　　　　　　　　　vōsō　　　　ingrèng-Cē　　　　　　　　　　alòng　osō-mār
call(small.animals)-NEG　EE:vōtèk　call(small.animals)-NEG　LOC　　child-PL

ponpidam'et thondam'et
pòn-pī-dām-ét　　　　　　　**thòn-dām-ét**
take.away-BEN/MAL-go-PRF　drop-go-PRF
'And then, after the Karbi woman has gone to the water place, these Hingchong sisters, over there, she went to carry the children to a place where the roads cross, where the birds don't sing, (she) took the children and left them there.' [CST, HM 014]

***thondamtilo** anke halaso aKarbipi ahem*
[thòn-dām-tí-lò　　　　　　ánke]　　[[hálasō　a-Karbì-pī]　　　a-hēm
drop-go-get.rid.off-RL　and.then　that　　POSS-PN-fem　POSS-house

nangchevanglo ja'e along nangchelanglo asomar ave
nang=che-vāng-lò ja'ē alòng nang=che-lāng-lò [a-oso-màr avē]
CIS=RR-come-RL cradle LOC 1/2:NSUBJ=RR-see-RL POSS-child-PL not.exist
'(The witch) abandoned (the children there), and then that Karbi woman came home, she looked in the cradle, her children were not there.' [CST, HM 015]

16.1.3 Discourse connectors

Discourse connectors are elements that typically occur between the end of one paragraph and the beginning of a new paragraph in narratives, such as English 'and then'. An overview of so far attested forms in Karbi is offered in Table 117. They are sorted by being based on either *án* 'this much; all' (§10.8.2) or the demonstrative *là* (§6.1.3). Apparent combining elements are listed in the right-hand column. Glosses are not given; they all carry out equivalent functions translatable into English as 'and then'.

Table 117: Discourse connectors.

Based on ...	Form	Possibly combined with ...
án 'this much'	*ánke*	=*ke* 'topic'
	ánsi	=*si* 'focus:realis'
	ánte	-*te* 'conditional'
	ánpen(ke)	=*pen* 'with', =*ke* 'topic'
lá 'this'	*lasì*	=*si* 'focus:realis'
	(la)pèn(ke)	=*pen* 'with', =*ke* 'topic'
	(la)pèn(te)	=*pen* 'with', -*te* 'conditional'

The placement of discourse connectors in narratives either at the end of a paragraph, the beginning of a new paragraph, or in a neutral position in-between two paragraphs merits further study. It appears that all types of placement occur, but it is currently not clear what functions may be associated with the differences. Another interesting aspect of discourse connector placement also in need of further investigation is that they occur in second position following the subject in several clauses in the corpus. Examples (882) and (883) exemplify this construction.

(882) Discourse connector *ánke* occurring after subject
"*to tangte" pu*
tò tángtē pu
OK if QUOT
'"Okay then", (said the *bamonpo*).' [KK, BMS 091]

*methan-sibongpota **anke** inghongdinglo*
methān-sibóngpō=tā **ánke** inghòng-dìng-lò
dog-SPECIES=ADD **and.then** wait-steadily-RL
'And then the dog waited and waited.' [KK, BMS 092]

(883) Discourse connector *ánte* occurring after subject
"*nangpran nang'en'etji" pulo... osomar **ante** kephere*
[nang-prán nang=ēn-èt-jí   pù-lò] [osō-mār **ánte** ke-pheré]
2:POSS-life 1/2:NSUBJ=take-all:S/O-IRR2 say-RL child-PL **thus** NMLZ-fear
'"I will take your lives", she said, so the children were scared.' [CST, RO 020]

The fact that both instances of post-subject occurrence of discourse connectors are immediately following direct speech may be a coincidence. There is, however, a correlation in topic-switch often occurring after the end of direct speech, which is one of the typical instances where topic-switch is marked by additive *=tā* (§14.2.2), as is the case in (882) with the subject *methān-sibóngpō=tā*. I suspect that discourse connectors are further markers of topic-switch where they occur following a (subject) argument.

16.1.4 Discourse structuring markers *e* and *'mh*

There are two markers that are particularly involved in structuring discourse. I have glossed them both as 'discourse structuring marker' or 'DSM', but I describe their distributions and functions in more detail below. They both have unusual phonological shapes that ally them with interjections: one is *e* with a long vowel that typically hosts a salient intonation contour; the other is *'mh*, which is similar to (but shorter and with a lower voice than) the English backchanneling 'mm' – essentially a glottal stop initial, voiced /m/.

The *e* marker frequently occurs in narratives by different speakers at the beginning of direct speech, as in (884) and (885).

(884) Discourse structuring marker *e* at beginning of direct speech
"***e** pedo'osinang" pusi kipu*
e   pe-dō-ò-sināng   pusi   ke-pù
DSM CAUS-exist-much-CON.HORT   QUOT.COMP   NMLZ-say
'"Let them remain in abundance for now", (she) said.' [SeT, MTN 008]

(885) Discourse structuring marker *e* at beginning of direct speech
"***e** epo do epoke doke do do setame*
e   [e-pō   dō]   [e-pō=ke   dō=ke   dō]   [[dō setamē]
DSM 1INCL-father exist 1INCL-father=TOP exist=TOP exist exist nevertheless

> *apiso banghini"*
> [a-pisò   bàng-hiní]]
> POSS-wife CLF:HUM:PL-two
> '"We have a father, though we have a father, he has two wives."' [CST, HM 046]

Example (886) shows that *e* also occurs inside direct speech, not only at the beginning. At the same time, parallel to the previous examples, this instance of *e* likewise occurs after a pause. The position of *e* following a pause appears to be typical but more research is needed.

(886) Discourse structuring marker *e* inside direct speech
> *"bai! an adín ningke an ajo ningke*
> bái   [[án   a-dín   nīngke] [án   a-jó   nīngke]
> how.bad! that.much POSS-day(<Asm) even   that.much POSS-night even
>
> *nesomar... e keso kali ki'une*
> ne-oso-màr   e   ke-sò   kalī   ke-ùn-Cē
> 1EXCL:POSS-child-PL   **DSM** NMLZ-hurt NEG.EQU.COP NMLZ-be.able-NEG
>
> *kali phuso kali kengso kali*
> kalī   phú-sò   kalī   kèng-sò   kalī
> NEG.EQU.COP head-hurt NEG.EQU.COP foot-hurt NEG.EQU.COP
> 'How bad! Not even in this long time did my children get sick
> and they didn't have minor sicknesses.' [CST, RO 024]

Example (887) further shows that while *e* most frequently occurs in direct speech, this is not exclusively the case. In this example, however, *e* also occurs at the beginning of an intonation unit, and specifically at the beginning of a narration (which follows an introduction by the speaker).

(887) Discourse structuring marker *e* at beginning of intonation unit (/narration), no direct speech
> *e ha apai abang theng endamjuiló*
> e   há   [a-pāi   abàng] thēng   ēn-dām-jùi-lò
> **DSM** over.there POSS-mother NPDL   firewood take-GO-away-RL
> 'Over there/far away, a mother went away to get firewood.' [KK, CC 010]

Examples (888) and (889) illustrate the use of the discourse structuring marker *'mh*. In both cases, *'mh* occurs either right after or right before an important event in the storyline is told. After uttering *'mh*, the storytellers pause for effect. In (888), *'mh* is uttered after mentioning that the Karbi woman gave birth to the two children that end up being the protagonists of the story.

(888) Discourse structuring marker *'mh* after narrating an important event
hala apenan abang mei thei kedam aphi la
hála   a-penān   abàng [méi   théi]   ke-dàm   aphī]   [[là
that   POSS-husband NPDL   assembly   EE:méi   NMLZ-go   after   this

Karbipi abangke osomar hachelo ha hem
Karbì-pī   abàng=ke   osō-mār   haché-lò   [há   hēm
PN-female/mother   NPDL=TOP   child-PL   be.born-RL   over.there house

arlo 'mh
arlō]]   **'mh**
inside   DSM
'After her husband had gone for meetings, the Karbi woman gave birth to children there inside the house.' [CST, HM 008]

In (889), the storyteller utters *'mh* and pauses after mentioning one of the protagonists as topic via *=ke*, then goes on to say that she passed away. In the course of the story, her husband will follow her and temporarily succeeds in bringing her back to the living.

(889) Discourse structuring marker *'mh* in middle of sentence, before narrating an important event
amat aphu kesopen amat bamonpi
amāt   a-phú   ke-sò-pèn   amāt   bamón-pī
and.then   POSS-head   NMLZ-hurt-NF   and.then   wise.person(<Ind)-female

abangke 'mh Chom chevoijuilo
abàng=ke   **'mh**   Chóm   che-vói-jùi-lò
NPDL=TOP   DSM   PLACE   RR-return-away-RL
'And then she had a fever and so the *bamonpi* returned to Chom (i.e., died).' [KK, BMS 014]

16.2 Rhetorical constructions

Rhetorical constructions add stronger force to an utterance or to a particular phrase. General extender constructions are discussed in §16.2.1, elaborate expression constructions in §16.2.2, copy verb constructions in §16.2.3, two constructions that involve the negative equational copula *kalī* in §16.2.4, and, finally, prosodic emphasis in §16.2.5.

16.2.1 General extender constructions

General extenders are expressions like English 'and so on', 'etcetera', 'and stuff', 'and everything', 'or anything', 'or whatever', as discussed by Overstreet (1999). Overstreet shows that the intuitive idea that general extenders in English function to indicate that there is a larger set involved is typically correct. For example, in 'apples and oranges and stuff', the general extender 'and stuff' is indeed usually interpreted to set up a category (e.g., 'fruit') and thus include further members of this category. However, this does not actually explain why general extenders are used. Overstreet shows that general extenders are often used because they are built on intersubjective knowledge of what else may belong to a category invoked by general extenders, which represents a politeness or in-group marking strategy. Furthermore, general extenders are also often used in particular emphatic constructions, where they may not even imply that there are further category members. For example, one such construction takes the form *X and everything, but Y* (as in, 'she is nice and everything, but I still don't like her'). Here, the purpose of the general extender 'and everything' is to assert X to build up to the contrast with Y (Overstreet 1999: 91).

In Overstreet's study, English general extenders most frequently occur in the construction "[1 item + general extender]," for example, 'apples and stuff', although a three-part construction [2 items + general extender] as in 'apples and oranges and stuff,' and longer expressions also occur (1999: 25–7). In Karbi, the construction is always binary: one noun phrase or verb plus general extender, i.e., '[NP/V] [GENEX]'. The general extender is typically *aját*, but may also be *háihúi* (and dialectal variants of the same word) for NPs.

The typical general extender *aját* has grammaticalized from *ját* 'type, thing' – which also occurs as an indefinite pronoun, see §6.1.6 – and the possessive/modified *a-* prefix.[163]

In (890), the predicate occurs in the *aját* general extender construction. While the main verb *(lāng) chinglú* only takes perfect *-ét*, the general extender *aját* repeats the perfect suffix and also adds realis *-lò*. The general extender here invokes a category of grooming activities.

(890) Predicate general extender: [V-PRF] [*aját*-PRF-RL]
 lasi nemethangta thurdappranglo lang
 lasì ne-metháng=tā thùr-dàppràng-lò lāng
 therefore 1EXCL-self=ADD:PRL get.up-very.early-RL water

 chinglu'et ajat'etlo osomar aphanta ingthurlo
 chinglú-ét aját-ét-lò osō-mār aphān=tā ingthùr-lò
 take.bath-PRF **GENEX-PRF-RL** child-PL NSUBJ=ADD:PRL wake.up-RL
 'So I got up early in the morning and took a bath and everything and also woke up the children.' [SH, CSM 003]

---

163 Galo (Tibeto-Burman; Tani) also has a general extender construction based on an indefinite marker that occurs in the negative indefinite construction, although in Galo it is the same marker as the interrogative pronoun of content 'what', *jòo* (Post 2007: 344 ff.).

In (891), the verb and general extender are marked the same, with -*pò* 'IRR1'. Here, it is not clear whether the general extender invokes a category of activities that involve cooking. There could be a category of household chores, but there is no mention in this text of anything other than cooking. The general extender may then rather serve as an intensifier construction, which contrasts the obligation of the mother to cook with the infant's crying that prevents her from doing so.

(891) Predicate general extender: [V-IRR1] [*aját*-IRR1]
*ne han an **tunpó ajatpó**, chirurinoi!* [...]
[nè   hán   àn   **[tún-pò   aját-pò]]**   [chirú-rī-nōi]
1EXCL   curry   rice   cook-IRR1   **GENEX**-IRR1   cry-PROH-IMP: SUGG2
'I will cook food and everything, don't cry! [...]' [KK, CC 016]

Further along in the same text, the speaker picks up again on the same issue, stating that the mother couldn't cook because the baby was crying. In (892), the speaker uses an elaborate expression construction (§16.2.2) instead of the general extender. Since the same content is communicated in (891) and (892), this suggests that the functions of general extender and elaborate expression constructions overlap in Karbi.

(892) Elaborate expression: [V1-GET-NEG] [V2-GET-NEG-RL]
<*pot*> *tangke hala apei abang **tunlongle***
tángke   [[hála   a-pēi   abàng   **tún-lōng-Cē**
and.then   that   POSS-mother   NPDL   **cook-GET-NEG**

***danglonglelo**, aso kachiru ajoine* [...]
dàng-lōng-Cē-lò]   [a-osō   ke-chirú   a-joiné]
put.on.stove-GET-NEG-RL   POSS-child   NMLZ-cry   POSS-reason(<Ind)
'That mother couldn't cook at all, because the child was crying [...].' [KK, CC 026]

In (893), the verb is marked imperfective with the *ke-* prefix and *aját* is unmarked. The general extender construction here invokes a category of mad or disturbed elephant behavior, which is clear from the context, which tells us that a bird had just scratched the elephant's ears. This example shows then that categories invoked by general extenders are always context-dependent, which is also what Overstreet has found for English and has called the 'intersubjective' property of general extender constructions.

(893) Predicate general extender: [IPFV-V] [*aját*]
*angnarta **kangrong ajat** <ku> turthap turphrulo...*
a-ingnàr=tā   **ke-ingròng   aját**   túr-tháp   túr-phrú-lò
POSS-elephant=ADD   **IPFV-roar   GENEX**   kick-mindlessly   kick-EE:tháp-RL

harlong turpur
harlōng túr-pùr
stone kick-move.over
'This elephant was roaring and everything and kicked around mindlessly, and kicked over a rock.' [RBT, ChM 025]

The general extender *aját* also occurs with NPs, as in (894). In this instance, it is not clear whether the general extender implies a category of other items that caused people getting sick with a cold besides all the dust on the roads (a common cause for getting sick). The general extender construction may rather serve an intensifying function here.

(894) NP general extender: [NP=*pen*] [*aját*=*pen*]
anke osomar atumta anuttinta arep
ánke osō-mār a-tūm=tā a-nūt-tín=tā a-rēp
and.then child-PL POSS-PL=ADD POSS-CLF:HUM:PL-each=ADD POSS-waist

amoi kesolo singjam **longle adukpen**
a-mòi ke-sò-lò singjám **[lònglē a-dūk=pen**
POSS-back NMLZ-hurt-RL have.a.cold **earth POSS-dust=from**

ajatpen *lapu amanke netum hapupen vanglo*
aját=pen] lapù mánke ne-tūm hápú=pen vàng-lò
GENEX=from like.this and.then 1EXCL-PL that.side=from come-RL
'And then, (as for) the children, each of them, their waists and backs were hurting, and they had cold (symptoms), from the dust and everything, and like this we then came from that side.' [SH, CSM 070]

Finally, (895) and (896) show that *háihúi* (and its dialectal variants) also functions as an NP general extender. In (895), this invokes a category of snacks for the road, which here likely just replaces a tedious enumeration at an irrelevant level of specificity. In (896), however, saying *America heihaipen* may be parallel to Overstreet's (1999: 83) observation that general extenders may function to indicate "a maximum extreme", i.e., the least likely item or fact from a category. In this interpretation of (896), America is presented as the least likely country to have visitors from, among the category of countries that visiting foreigners may be from. The general extender would then have a scalar additive function translatable with 'even'.

(895) General extender construction with *háihúi*; function: invoking set of snacks
anke **thesere haihuita** *namponlo <kecho> tovar*
ánke **theseré háihúi=tā** nàm-pōn-lò <ke-cho>
and.then **fruit different.kinds.of=also** buy-take.away-RL NMLZ-eat
továr
road

    *kecho aphan **lang haihui** namponlo*
    ke-chō   a-phān   **lāng   háihúi**   nàm-pōn-lò
    NMLZ-eat   POSS-PURP   **water different.kinds.of** buy-take.away-RL
    'And then, we also bought some fruit etc. to carry along, to eat on the road, and we bought some water etc. to carry along.' [SH, CSM 014]

(896) General extender construction with *héihái*; function: scalar additive?
    Europe lapen kaprek kaprek adet
    Europe   lapèn ke-prék   ke-prék
    Europe(<Eng) and NMLZ-be.different NMLZ-be.different
    a-dét
    POSS-country(<Ind)

    ***America heihaipen** phorena atum*
    America   **héihái=pen**   phorená   a-tūm
    America(<Eng) **different.kinds.of=from** foreigner(<Eng) POSS-PL

    dopik hadak
    dō-pīk   hádāk
    exist-very there
    'From Europe and from many different countries, (even) from America etc., there were many foreigners there.' [SiT, HF 037]

General extender constructions are frequent in the corpus of recorded texts, particularly in personal narratives. They are thus an important device in structuring discourse and balancing the level of specificity and relevance of information, and reflect on the relationship between speaker and addressee.

16.2.2 Elaborate expression constructions

Elaborate expressions (EE's) are a common phenomenon in Southeast Asian languages (Matisoff 1973; Goddard 2005; Peterson 2010). They represent a binary construction, in which two elements are used instead of a single one. In Karbi, it is the first element of the two which is the head of the construction and which also occurs otherwise independently.

The patterns of formal relationships between the two elements are discussed in §16.2.2.1, and §16.2.2.2 shows how EE's are embedded into the sentence. The functions of EE's are discussed in §16.2.2.3.

16.2.2.1 Forms of elaborate expressions

In Karbi, EE's always have their head first, followed by the EE complement, as in *ingnēk ingnì* 'laugh', where *ingnēk* is the head and *ingnì* is the EE complement. The head also exists as an independent item, outside the EE construction (with so far only one exception), i.e., *ingnēk* 'laugh' is a full lexical verb by itself. Some EE complements also exist as independent items, although the majority of complements from EE's in the corpus, are items that only occur as EE complements and do not actually have a meaning by themselves. I gloss EE complements that are independent items with their existing gloss, e.g., in the EE *sáp thèng*, I gloss *sáp* as 'beat with something flexible' and *thèng* as 'beat with something solid'. Other EE complements I just gloss as 'EE:X', where X is the EE head. In some cases, the EE complement is homophonous with an independent item that has no semantic relationship with the EE head, for example in the EE *ingnēk ingnì* 'laugh', *ingnì* is homophonous with the verb 'to sit'. Since there is no apparent semantic relationship between laughing and sitting, I have glossed the EE complement *ingnì* as 'EE:ingnēk'.

Both monosyllabic and disyllabic roots participate in EE's. In EE's based on monosyllabic roots, either a prefix or suffix often occurs on both the head lexeme and the EE complement, which results in the characteristic four-syllable structure, although two-syllable structures, as in (897) occur (as well as structures with more than four syllables in total, e.g., six syllables); EE's are always symmetrical in terms of syllable structure such that the head lexeme and the EE complement always have the same amount of syllables.

(897) Elaborate expression with two syllables only
*lasi la suho athe pu abangke **pe ri***
[lasì   là   sūhō   a-thē   pu   abàng=ke] **[[pé   rī**
therefore this sp.thorny.plant POSS-fruit QUOT   NPDL=TOP   **cloth EE:pé**

kechok aphan'iklo
ke-chòk]   a-phān-īk-lò]
NMLZ-wash.clothes   POSS-PURP-FRML-RL
'Therefore, the *suho* fruit is for washing clothes.' [SiH, CW 007]

Table 118 represents a subset of the 55 EE complements so far attested (that are not also independent items), which show the range of formal relationships between head lexeme and EE complement. It begins with monosyllabic and then lists disyllabic (and two trisyllabic) nouns and verbs, and then offers some sample items from other word (sub-)classes that also have EE complements. I represent different syllables (between head and complement) by different letters ('A' through 'E') and identical syllables by using the same letter; quasi-reduplication (e.g., using the same syllable but switching a vowel) is indicated by adding an apostrophe (e.g., A'). The right-most column 'Meaning of EE (if changed)' notes if a particular EE has a consistent semantic effect (for EE functions, see §16.2.2.3).

In the corpus, the most frequent pattern for monosyllables is A-B, and the most frequent pattern for disyllables is AB-AC, followed by AB-AB'. The other patterns are very rare, and identical syllables in AB-BC and AB-CB may, in fact, be coincidence.

16.2 Rhetorical constructions

Table 118: Formal patterns in elaborate expressions.

Type	EE head	Gloss	EE complement	Meaning of EE (if changed)
Monosyllables (N/V)				
A-B	rīt	'field'	jāi	
	úm	'cage'	kràng	
	dō	'to stay'	thák (<Asm)	
A-A'	àn	'cooked rice'	ùn	
[A-A'	méi	'assembly'	théí]	
Disyllables (N/V)				
AB-AC	arnàm	'god'	arnì	
	chojūn	'celebration(kd)'	chokú	'celebrations' (COLL)
	hormú	'thing'	hortár / (hortón)	
	jutáng	'custom'	jubát	'customs, culture' (COLL)
	ingnēk	'to laugh'	ingnì	
AB-AB'	bor'í	'to try; struggle'	bor'á	
	lōthē	'banana'	lōthā	
AB-CD	ingjìr	'sister'	arlô	
	Chománg	'Khasi'	Kechè	
AB-BC	pīsō	'wife'	sōmē	
AB-CB	rītlō	'inhabited field'	jàilò	
Trisyllable (N)				
ABC-A**DE**	theseré	'fruit'	thekumbōng	
ABC-D**BC**	alohí	'guest'	dolohí	
Other word (sub-)classes				
Rel N (**AB-AC**)	atèng	'according.to'	amàng	
PCT verb (**AB-AC**)	ingtāng	'to be strong'	ingsàk	
Adverb (AB-A'B)	parái	'this.side'	harái	'this riverbank and that riverbank' (COLL)
Verb suffix (A-B)	-sō	'intensifier' (§16.2.4.2)	-vír	
	-tháp	'mindlessly'	-phrú	'here and there'
[(A-A')	-nèk	N/A	-nòk	'doing bad unnecessarily']

Table 118 shows that in both monosyllables and disyllables, there are instances of quasi-reduplicated EE complements with vowel switch (§3.8.6.2), such as *àn ùn* 'rice' or *lōthē lōthā* 'banana'. This vowel switch quasi-reduplication is a frequent pattern; other quasi-reduplication types are not frequent and more likely coincidental, such as *méi théi* 'assembly', which I have put in square brackets due to this reason.

In the subset of forms given in Table 118, there is only one instance where the EE complement represents a borrowing, i.e., *dō thák* 'stay', but there are other forms that follow the same pattern (of using a borrowing as EE complement). It would be expected that an in-depth study of EE complements will identify more borrowings, as this was also reported to be a common source for EE complements in Lahu by Matisoff (1973: 83).[164]

A third source of EE complements may be the Karbi song language although the origins of many words in the song language themselves are unclear and form an interesting historical mystery (§1.1.3.3).

One item, *hormú* 'thing', occurs with two different EE complements in the corpus, *hortár* and *hortón*, although *hortár* is more typically used, according to my consultants. Curiously, the same speaker in the same text uses first *hortón* and then *hortár*. Generally, EE heads only occur with one specific EE complement.

There are a few instances, where using an EE instead of just the head by itself has a consistent semantic effect, which is recorded in the right-most column in Table 118. Specifically, there is a tendency for noun EE's to convey a collective interpretation.

The verb suffix pair *-nèk -nòk* resembles EE's due to the phonological relationship between the two elements, but in this case the 'head' is not used independently, which is evidence that this is not actually an EE. The suffix pair *-nèk -nòk* is therefore different from the suffix pair *-tháp -phrú*. The suffix pair *-nèk -nòk* and another suffix pair where both elements have to co-occur are treated as discontinuous predicate derivations in §9.2.1.1.2.

EE's may be formed with any word (sub-)class, as shown in Table 118. Text examples (898) and (899) show elaborate expressions based on a relator noun and on a verb suffix, respectively.

(898) Relator noun elaborate expression
choboche choingtung **hako ateng hako**
[choboché   cho-ingtúng   [hákó   atèng]   [hákó
settle.down AUTO.BEN/MAL-desire that.time according.to that.time

---

[164] Note also the EE *motór garí* 'car', where both *motór* and *garí* are ultimately borrowed from English. The second part *garí* must have been borrowed through Assamese because of the initial /g/, and this may be true for *motór* too although there is no phonological evidence of the same type. As Pattie Epps (p.c.) points out, this EE may in fact originate in the archaic English compound 'motorcar', which would have then been reanalyzed as an EE.

amangle kali setame [...]
amàng=le]　　　　kalī　　　　setāmē]
EE:atèng=FOC:IRR　NEG.EQU.COP　nevertheless
'Although it is not like before when they settled down [...].' [KK, BMS 115]

(899)　Verb suffix elaborate expression
*amat chonghota **chonthap chonphrulo***
amāt　　　chonghō=tā　chón-**tháp**　　　chón-**phrú-lò**
and.then　frog=ADD　　jump-**mindlessly**　jump-**EE:tháp-RL**

kesolo... karlesibongpo adon chonrai
ke-sò-lò　　　karlēsibóngpō　a-dón　　　chón-rài
NMLZ-hurt-RL　sp.squirrel　　POSS-bridge　jump-RES:solid.object.breaking
'And then, the frog was jumping everywhere, (because) he was hurt, and he jumped on the ladder of the squirrel and it broke.' [RBT, ChM 018]

16.2.2.2 Embedding into parallelism or compound construction

In texts, elaborate expressions occur embedded in either a parallelism construction or a compound construction. Examples (900) and (901) represent a minimal set on the EE *méi théi* 'assembly'. The two examples are from the same story, communicating the same proposition, first as a main clause, then in a repetition as background information. In (900), the EE occurs in a clause-level parallelism construction, *[mei kedam], [thei kedam]*. In (901), the EE occurs in an NP-level compound construction, *[[mei thei] kedam]*.

(900)　Nominal elaborate expression in parallelism construction
richolo amat apoke mei kedam thei kedam [...]
[richó-lò]　amāt　　a-pò=ke　　　　**[[méi**　　ke-dàm]　**[théi**　　ke-dàm]]
king-RL　　and.then　POSS-father=TOP　**assembly**　NMLZ-go　**EE:méi**　NMLZ-go
'He is a king, so their father (often) goes to meetings [...].' [CST, HM 005]

(901)　Nominal elaborate expression in compound construction
hala apenan abang mei thei kedam aphi la
hála　a-penān　　　　abàng　**[[méi**　　　**théi]**　　ke-dàm　aphī]]　[là
that　POSS-husband　　NPDL　　**assembly**　**EE:méi**　NMLZ-go　after　　this

Karbipi abangke osomar hachelo ha hem arlo mh
Karbì-pī　　　　　　　abàng=ke　　osō-mār　　haché-lò　　[há　　　　hēm
PN-female/mother　　NPDL=TOP　　child-PL　　be.born-RL　over.there　house
arlō]]　mh
inside　DSM
'After her husband had gone for meetings, the Karbi woman gave birth to children there inside the house.' [CST, HM 008]

The same options are available in forming elaborate expressions off verbs. Consider the following three examples based on the elaborate expression *tún dáng* 'cook'. While in (902), the elaborate expression occurs in a parallelism construction such that the imperative suffix *-nōi* is repeated on both roots, the roots form a compound stem in (903). Note that (904) is somewhat of an intermediate type, as the derivational complex occurs on both roots, but the inflectional imperative suffix *-nói* only occurs on the second root.

(902) Verbal elaborate expression in parallelism construction
ne nephi aphan nangpachetongvekji
nè   ne-phì   a-phān
1EXCL 1EXCL:POSS-grandmother   POSS-NSUBJ
nang=pV-chetòng-vék-jí
1/2:NSUBJ=CAUS-meet-definitely-IRR2

e tunnoi dangnoi chonang junnang
e   **tún**-nōi   **dáng**-nōi   chō-nāng   jùn-nāng
DSM cook-INF.COND.IMP put.on.stove-INF.COND.IMP eat-HORT   drink-HORT
'I will definitely make you meet my grandmother; (now) cook and prepare, let's eat and drink (so we can start our journey).' [KK, BMS 029]

(903) Verbal elaborate expression in compound construction
so'arlo atum adapprang ha the'ang'e
sō'arlō   a-tūm   a-dàpprāng   há   the'āng-Cē
women:COLL POSS-PL   POSS-very.early   over.there be.bright-NEG

akopen hem kedo atum aphanta
akò=pen   [hēm   ke-dō   a-tūm   a-phān=tā]
before=from   house   NMLZ-stay   POSS-PL   POSS-NSUBJ=also

tun-dangpikang'et nangjilang
tún-dàng-pī-káng-ét   náng-jí-lāng
cook-put.on.stove-BEN/MAL-leaving-PRF   need-IRR2-still
'Early in the morning, over there, the women have to cook and do all the household works from before dawn also for those who stay at home (besides food for themselves).' [KaR, SWK 074]

(904) Nominal elaborate expression in intermediate parallelism/compound construction
[...] *apot padap abangke, tunpi peme*
[apōt   padāp   abàng=ke   [**tún**-pī   pe-mé]
because   this.morning   NPDL=TOP   cook-BEN   CAUS-be.good

dangpi pemenoi! [...]
[**dàng**-pī   pe-mé-**nōi**]]
put.on.stove-BEN CAUS-be.good-**INF.COND.IMP**
'[...] [T]his morning, cook and prepare them nicely for me! [...]' [SeT, MTN 029]

16.2.2.3 Functions of elaborate expressions

According to Matisoff's (1973: 82) definition, EE's do not have a semantic function but represent "[the use of] four syllables where two would have conveyed the same information". This is largely true for Karbi as well, although there are some noun EE's which apparently do have a consistent semantic effect of conveying a collective interpretation (see Table 118 above in §16.2.2.1).

Instead of creating a change in semantics, EE's are typically considered a stylistic device used by sophisticated speakers. However, Peterson (2010) demonstrates that EE's also frequently function as intensifiers in Khumi (Kuki-Chin), across the border in Bangladesh. In Karbi, EE's also have intensifying functions similar to what Peterson has pointed out for Khumi. For example, the use of EE's in a situation of "heightened emotional intensity" is shown in (905), where the speaking participant of the story threatens to kill the addressee participant.

(905) Elaborate expressions: *nangpran_nangmui; nangsapji_nangthengji*

"[...] pinike **nangpran** damji **nangmui** damji,
pinì=ke   **nang-prán** dàm-jí **nang-múi**   dàm-jí]
today=TOP 2:POSS-life   go-IRR2 2:POSS-EE:prán(<IND) go-IRR2

<nangsapdamji> **nangsapji**
<nang=sáp-dàm-jí>   nang=sáp-jí
1/2:NSUBJ=beat.w/sth.flexible-go-IRR2 1/2:NSUBJ=beat.w/sth.flexible-IRR2

nangthengji!"
nang=thèng-jí
1/2:NSUBJ=beat.w/sth.solid-IRR2
'[...] [T]oday your life will definitely go, I will beat the hell out of you!" [RBT, ChM 033]

A similar level of intensity can also be argued to underlie (906), where two babies abandoned in the jungle by a witch are saved by a tiger couple. In (906), the female tiger says to the male tiger that they should not leave the two crying babies in the jungle, but that they should take them with them and take care of them. The reason why they should do that, according to the tigress, is because the babies are *monit monor* 'human beings'. The use of the EE evokes a number of (perhaps, noble) connotations, which is why the tigress can use it as a reason for why they should go through the trouble of taking care of them.

(906) Elaborate expression: *monít__monór*
"[...] *lake **monít monór** aso apot itum*
là=ke   [[**monít   monór**]   a-osō]   apōt   e-tum
this=TOP **man**   **EE:monít** POSS-child because 1INCL-PL

orapondetnang"
orá-pòn-dèt-nāng
take.care-take.away-PFV-HORT
'[...] "[B]ecause they are human beings, let's carry them away and take care of them!"' [CST, HM 033]

A matter for future research is the relationship between EE's and general extenders in Karbi. There is a functional overlap between the two in that both may add an intensifying force to the utterance (§16.2.1). Mauri (2017) discusses both EE's (or *echo word formation*) and general extenders as two cross-linguistic types of strategies used in the expression of *ad hoc* categories. In Karbi, a predicate can simultaneously occur in the elaborate expression construction and in the general extender construction, such as *nangcharkok nangcharpheklo ajatlo* in (907).

(907) Elaborate expression and general extender used in combination
[...] bang hako ahem hako arit e
[bàng   hakó   a-hēm   hakó   a-rīt   e
CLF:HUM:PL that.time POSS-house that.time POSS-field DSM

nangcharkok nangcharpheklo ajatlo, *ahem arit*
nang=chV-arkòk nang=chV-arphèk-lò aját-lò]   [a-hēm   a-rīt
CIS=RR-clean   CIS=RR-EE:arkòk-RL GENEX-RL   POSS-house POSS-field

<*chevangsi*> *nangchotun nangchodanglo*
<che-vāng-si>   nang=cho-tún   nang=cho-dāng-lò]
RR-come-NF:RL CIS=AUTO.BEN/MAL-cook CIS=AUTO.BEN/MAL-put.on.stove-RL
'[...] [A]nd then they cleaned their old house and property and everything, and they came home and cooked there for themselves.' [KK, BMS 113]

16.2.3 Copy verb constructions

There are a range of copy verb constructions, which consist of a preposed copy of the verb root that is marked with one of the core information/discourse structure clitics (see §14.2) or the question clitic (see §15.1.1.2.2), followed by the actual main verb, which may carry derivational and inflectional morphology. Their functions have to do with adding force to the predicate, which we can consider iconic given the phonological force created through repetition of the verb. For a comparative perspective on copy verb constructions across Tibeto-Burman languages, see Ozerov and Daudey (2017).

Note that the resulting predicates resemble parallelism constructions (§16.1.1) although in the case of copy verb constructions, the number of syllables may differ between the two parallel verb units.[165]

In addition to the four copy verb constructions presented in what follows, there is another copy verb construction that has the function of coordinating clauses, as discussed in §15.5.1.2.

16.2.3.1 Assertive (with =ke 'topic')

The assertive copy verb construction consists of the root of the main verb marked with =ke 'topic', followed by the full main verb with additional suffixes if applicable, schematically 'V=ke V-suffixes'. The function of this construction is to strongly assert a proposition. As a result, the construction is often employed to set up a contrast, as in *X is indeed the case, but Y*, which is evidenced by the fact that this construction is frequently followed by a concessive conjunction.[166] An example is (908), where the assertive copy verb construction occurs in the clause *epoke doke do* 'we do have a father', which sets up a contrast to 'he has two wives' as marked by the concessive *do setame* – a contrast presumably in the sense that although there is one father, the maternal side is unusual, because there are two women.

(908) Assertive =ke copy verb construction followed by contrast (*do setame*)
*e epo do, epoke **doke do**, do setame,*
e   [e-pō   dō]   [e-pō=ke   **dō=ke   dō]**   [[dō
DSM   1INCL-father   exist   1INCL-father=TOP   **exist=TOP   exist**   exist
setamē]
nevertheless

apiso banghini
[a-pisò   bàng-hinî]]
POSS-wife   CLF:HUM:PL-two
'We have a father, though we do have a father, he has two wives.' [CST, HM 046]

Similarly, in (909), there is a contrast built up by *kechetong doke dohe* '(I) have indeed met (some of them)', which follows in the next intonation, offered in (910), which starts with *setā* 'but'.

---

165 For example, *haita haipik* in (914) below resembles other parallelism constructions closely but *leta ledappranglo* in (915) does not to the same extent. Still the similarity with parallelism constructions indicates that the underlying repetition is a recurrent rhetorical device in the language. I am grateful to Pattie Epps for raising this point.
166 While English does not have a dedicated marker for this kind of strong assertion in anticipation of a contrast, German has *zwar*, which always has to be followed by *aber* 'but'. The particle *zwar* has the telling etymology *es ist wahr* 'it is true'.

(909) Assertive =*ke* copy verb construction followed by contrast in next text unit (*seta*)

Naka anglong pu bihek akopenta arjulong
Náká	a-inglóng	pu	bī-hèk	akó=pen=tā	arjū-lōng
TRIBE	POSS-hill	QUOT	be.small-small	then=from=ADD	hear-GET

Naka akhei puta arjulong lapenke... Naka
Náká	a-khéi	pu=tā	arjū-lōng	lapèn=ke	Náká
TRIBE	POSS-community	QUOT=ADD	ask-GET	and.then=TOP	TRIBE

akhei amonit so'arlopen pusetame sopinsopen
a-khéi	a-monít	so'àrlō=pen	pùsetāmē	sopìnsō=pen
POSS-community	POSS-man	women:COLL=with	likewise	boy:COLL=with

*pusetame elong longni lason **kechetong doke***
pùsetāmē	e-lòng	lòng-ní	lasón	**ke-chetòng**	**dō=ke**
likewise	one-CLF:place	CLF:place-two	that.way	**NMLZ-meet**	**exist=TOP**

***do**he*
dō=he
exist=AFTERTHOUGHT
'Since my childhood, I got to hear about the Naga hills, the Naga people, from both the women and men, in one or two places, like that, I actually have met (some of them).' [SiT, HF 004]

(910) Text unit after (909)

seta adunghetpen alanglitum arong alanglitum
setā	adūng-hét=pen	alang-li-tūm	a-ròng	alang-li-tūm
but	near-very.near=from	3-HON-PL	POSS-village	3-HON-PL

ahem alanglitum kedo kethak kosonma
a-hēm	alang-li-tūm	ke-dō	ke-thák	kosón=mà
POSS-house	3-HON-PL	NMLZ-stay	NMLZ-EE:dō(<Asm)	how=Q

'But from very near, their villages, their houses, how do they stay and live?' [SiT, HF 005]

This assertive copy verb construction does not necessarily occur in a larger contrast construction. In (911), there is no contrast involved. The speaker states that she saw a particular ceremony performed in a different region that has somewhat different customs. She says she saw it for the first time and that she liked it. Then she says *prekke prekchot* 'it really is slightly different', referring to the ceremonial customs in that region. Apparently, the assertive copy verb construction is used here because the speaker just stated that she saw it for the first time and so it was perhaps a surprise to find out that the ceremony is indeed performed in a slightly different way in West Karbi Anglong.

(911) Assertive =ke copy verb construction without contrast
anke lapu thoi asorpen hapu Rongkhang anatthu
ánke   [lapú   thói   a-sòr=pen   hápú   Rongkháng
and.then this.side plains   POSS-people=from that.side AREA
a-nátthū
POSS-direction

aChomangkanke neta ketheklongchenglo aronta
a-Chomangkan=ke] nè=tā   ke-theklōng-chéng-lò   a-rōn=tā
POSS-PN=TOP   1EXCL=also NMLZ-see-for.first.time-RL POSS-custom=also

chinidun'o'e setame ning arongpiklo
chiní-dùn-ò-Cē   setāmē   nīng   aróng-pìk-lò
know-JOIN-much-NEG   nevertheless mind   be.happy-very-RL

prekke prekchot *lapu anatthupen*
prék=ke   **prék-chòt**   lapú   a-nátthū=pen
be.different=TOP **be.different-slightly** this.side   POSS-direction=from
'And then, the Chomangkan of people from this side, from the plains, and from that side, the Rongkhang side, I also saw it for the first time, and I don't know their customs, but still I was happy (to see it); it really is slightly different from this side.' [SH, CSM 044-5]

16.2.3.2 Intensifier declarative (with =tā 'additive')

The intensifier declarative copy verb construction consists of the root of the main verb marked with =tā 'additive', followed by the full main verb with additional suffixes if applicable, schematically 'V= tā V-suffixes'. The function of this construction is intensification, which is evidenced by the fact that the main verb typically carries quantifying and intensifying suffixes, such as *-óng* '(too) much', *-ò* 'much, very', or *-pìk* 'very'.

In (912), the context is that one of the tigers tells the other tigers that they need to be quick in performing a ceremony and explains why that is of tremendous importance. Example (912) occurs after the direct speech and states that the tigers did indeed do everything very quickly.

(912) Intensifier copy verb construction, main verb with *-ò* 'much'
*anke... **paprapta paprap'olo***
ánke   **pe-pràp=tā**   **pe-pràp-ò-lò**
and.then   **CAUS-be.quick=ADD** **CAUS-be.quick-much-RL**
'And then, (the tigers) did everything very quickly[...].' [HK, TR 160]

In (913), a grandmother talks to her infant grandchild and says that the child has cried too much, using the intensifier construction.

(913) Intensifier copy verb construction, main verb with -óng '(too) much'
chiruta chiru'ongchotlo nang piba chevanra
chirú=tā   chirú-óng-chòt-lò   nàng   pibā   che-vān-ra
cry=ADD   cry-too.much-a.bit-RL   2   baby.carrying.cloth   RR-bring-NF:IRR

hong vannoi ho
hòng   vàn-nōi   ho
outside   bring-INFRML.COND.IMP   definitely
'(You) have cried too much, bring your *piba* and bring it outside!' [KK, CC 022]

In (914), an evil stepmother mistreats her stepchildren, and so the storyteller says this sentence, using the intensifier construction to emphasize how evil the stepmother was.

(914) Intensifier copy verb construction, main verb with -*pìk* 'very'
haita haipik
hài=tā   hài-pìk
have.bad.character=ADD   have.bad.character-very
'(She) really had a very bad character [...].' [CST, RO 016]

In (915), the speaker talks about travel by car to a place relatively far away. The first portion is the way up to Bokolia, as mentioned in this sentence. She says that because the road is good, they reached Bokolia really early, employing the intensifier construction.

(915) Intensifier copy verb construction, main verb with -*dàppràng* 'early'
lasi laso adakke tovarta mesen
lasì   lasō   a-dàk=ke   továr=tā   mē-sén
therefore this   POSS-road.inbetween=TOP   road=ADD   be.good-INTENS

apot **leta ledappranglo** *Bokolia'an*
apōt   **lè=tā**   **lè-dàppràng-lò**   Bokoliá-án
because   **reach=ADD**   **reach-early-RL**   PN-till
'So for this stretch, the road was good, and so we reached Bokolia very early.' [SH, CSM 012]

16.2.3.3 Intensifier non-declarative (with =*le* 'focus:irrealis')
The available data on the =*le* 'focus:irrealis' construction suggest that it also has an intensifier function, like the copy verb construction with =*tā* (§16.2.3.2), but that it occurs specifically with non-declarative speech acts.

In (916), the construction is used to intensify an imperative 'follow me!', which has further emphatic marking through use of the interactive emphatic particle *ho* (§16.3.6).

(916) Intensifier copy verb construction with =*le*, imperative main verb
"*o ne nangponthekpo ti, phu!*
ó nè nang=pòn-thèk-pò ti phū
EXCLAM 1EXCL 1/2:NSUBJ=take.away-know.how-IRR1 EMPH grandfather:VOC

nangdunle nangdunnoi
nang=dùn=le nang=dùn-nōi
1/2:NSUBJ=join=FOC:IRR 1/2:NSUBJ=join-INFRML.COND.IMP

ho" pulo tangho
hò pù-lò tànghò
EMPH:INTERACT say-RL REP
'"I certainly know how to take you there, grandfather. Just make sure to join me", (he) said.' [KK, BMS 035]

16.2.3.4 Perseverance construction (with =*ma* 'question particle')

In addition to the above mentioned copy verb constructions that involve core information/discourse structure clitics, there also is a parallel construction that instead uses the question clitic =*ma* (§15.1.1.2.2). While this construction does not occur in the corpus of recorded texts, I have collected one example through elicitation, and Grüßner (1978: 129–30) offers further examples. It appears that this construction has a durative function, indicating that the agent persevered in a particular activity. The elicited example (917) in particular suggests that this construction indicates perseverance.

(917) Perseverance copy verb construction with =*ma* 'question particle'
[arvī che-lāng-lē] [ar'ē che-lāng-lē,] [ke-tòk=ma ke-tòk]
left RR-see-NEG right RR-see-NEG NMLZ-write=Q NMLZ-write
'Without looking left or right, (s/he) keeps writing.' [Elicitation SiT 090228]

In Grüßner's examples (918) and (919), no context is offered, but his translations suggest that the construction indicates durativity.

(918) Copy verb construction with =*ma* 'question particle'
pé=ma pé-lò
look.for.lice=Q look.for.lice-RL
'She was looking for lice for awhile.' (Grüßner 1978: 130)

(919) Copy verb construction with =ma 'question particle'
che-mīn=ma   che-mīn-lò
RR-complain=Q RR-complain-RL
'They were complaining for awhile.' (Grüßner 1978: 130)

Lastly, Grüßner's example (920) shows that the second verb may be marked by additive =tā, i.e., 'V=ma V=tā'. The additive marking results in a concessive meaning that combines with the durative function: 'despite persevering in V-ing, (something else happened)'.

(920) Copy verb construction with =ma 'question particle'
[rì=ma   rì=tā,]   ōk   lóng-lē-dèt-lò
search=Q   search=ADD   meat   get-NEG-PFV-RL
'However much he was searching (for it), he didn't get the meat.' (Grüßner 1978: 129)

16.2.4 Constructions with negative equational copula *kalī*

There are two constructions that employ the negative equational copula *kalī*; the disagreement construction, which does not require a nominalized verb; and the intensifier construction, which does require nominalization of the main verb.

16.2.4.1 Disagreement construction based on quasi-reduplication and negative equational copula

The disagreement construction uses the same quasi-reduplication pattern with vowel change found elsewhere in the grammar (§3.8.6.2), followed by the negative equational copula *kalī*.

Example (921) is from a story, and this particular text unit is uttered by a dog addressing a tree. Previously, the dog had told the tree that the tree should help the dog owner cross a large body of water. The tree does not want to do that, whereupon the dog says (921), telling the tree that whether or not he wants to do it, he has to, using the disagreement construction, which includes the vowel change in *ponpe ponpa*, followed by *kali*. Note that the main verb here is not nominalized, but only carries the negative suffix.

(921) Reduplicative copy verb construction based on *pòn-pē* 'take.away-NEG'
"ponpe ponpa kalilo, ponnoi
[[pòn-Cē   pònpā   kalī-lò]   [pòn-nōi]]
take.away-NEG   DISAGR   NEG.EQU.COP-RL   take.away-INFRML.COND.IMP

```
hadak pirthe mindar ponnoi, nangta"
[[hádāk   pirthé   mindár      pòn-nōi]                          nàng=tā]
there     world    world(<Pnr)  take.away-INFRML.COND.IMP        you=ADD
```
"'It's not about whether you want to or don't want to take them, just take them, there to the world take them, you (have to).'" [KK, BMS 109]

Example (922) is from a different story, where an orphan encounters a tiger. Scared to death, the orphan asks what his fault is, because according to Karbi traditional belief, only those who violate cultural norms are eaten by tigers. The tiger replies by using the disagreement construction, dismissing the orphan's question about the fault.

(922) Reduplicative copy verb construction based on *ke-dō* 'NMLZ-exist'
```
kedo keda kaliloke; {e} pap kedo keda,
ke-dō         kedā      kalī-lò=ke            e    páp    ke-dō
NMLZ-exist    DISAGR    NEG.EQU.COP-RL=TOP    AFF  fault  NMLZ-exist
kedā
DISAGR

nangphanke nangkeponpo {nangponpo}
nang-phān=ke    nang=ke-pòn-pò                      {nang=pòn-pò}
2-NSUBJ=TOP     1/2:NSUBJ=NMLZ-take.away-IRR1       1/2:NSUBJ=take.away-IRR1
```
'There is no matter of existence (of a sin); there is no matter of a sin or no sin, but I'll carry you away!' [HK, TR 058-9]

16.2.4.2 Nominalization-based intensifier construction *ke-V-sō kalī*

This construction involves a nominalized verb with an attached *-sō* suffix, followed by the negative equational copula. The final syllable of the root (i.e., the syllable before the *-sō* suffix) is typically lengthened to further add prosodic emphasis. The function is to mark a positive, highly emphatic statement. An example is (923), where the transitive *inghōn* 'love' occurs in the construction.

(923) Nominalization-based intensifier construction with *inghōn* 'love'
```
methan-sibongpo ante <pini> bamonpo atum aphan
methān-sibóngpō    ántè       <pinì>  bamón-pō              a-tūm     aphān
dog-SPECIES        OK.then    today   wise.person(<Ind)-male POSS-PL  NSUBJ

kanghonso kali
ke-inghōn-sō              kalī
NMLZ-love-INTENS          NEG.EQU.COP
```
'The dog loved the *bamonpo* and *bamonpi* so much!' [KK, BMS 004]

In (924), the construction occurs with the PCT root *thè*. It is further combined with an elaborate expression construction (§16.2.2) based on the *-sō* suffix element of this construction.

(924) Nominalization-based intensifier construction with *thè* 'be big' (involving elaborate expression construction)
[...]langta ketheso kethevir kali, langso

lāng=tā	**ke-thè-sō**	**ke-thè-vír**	**kalī**
water=ADD	NMLZ-be.big-INTENS	NMLZ-be.big-EE:SŌ	NEG.EQU.COP

[langsō
this

atalo bhari
a-taló   bharí]
POSS-sea very.big(<Ind)
'[...] [T]he water was so infinitely big, this was a huge sea.' [KK, BMS 044]

16.2.5 Prosodic emphasis

An important matter for future study is the investigation of prosodic constructions that serve as rhetorical devices. As just mentioned in §16.2.4.2 above, there is a large amount of vowel lengthening used to convey prosodic emphasis in the nominalization-based intensifier construction, although this type of prosodic emphasis also occurs in other constructions. One such example is a full verb reduplication construction that occurs in KK, CC 012. Figure 22 shows the large amount of lengthening occurring on the last syllable of the first repetition of the predicate, i.e., *baithekthe: baithekthe* '(she) just did not know how to possibly calm down (the child)' (*bài* 'to console, calm'; *thèk* 'know how'; *-thē* 'negation').

16.3 Particles

This section discusses the various particles attested so far. A comprehensive examination of the distributional properties of each of the particles is beyond the scope of this grammar. However, it should be noted that the majority of the particles only occur in sentence-final position, but some other ones may occur after NPs (as noted where information is available). Furthermore, a subset of these particles may actually occur in constructions with suffixes from the mood/non-final paradigm (§9.1), specifically with *-lò* 'realis' or *-pò* 'irrealis1', or with *-si* 'non-final:realis'. This includes the desiderative construction based on *pu* in §16.3.1.2, dubitative *tahái* in §16.3.3, and 'always' *titī* in §16.3.4.

16.3 Particles — 559

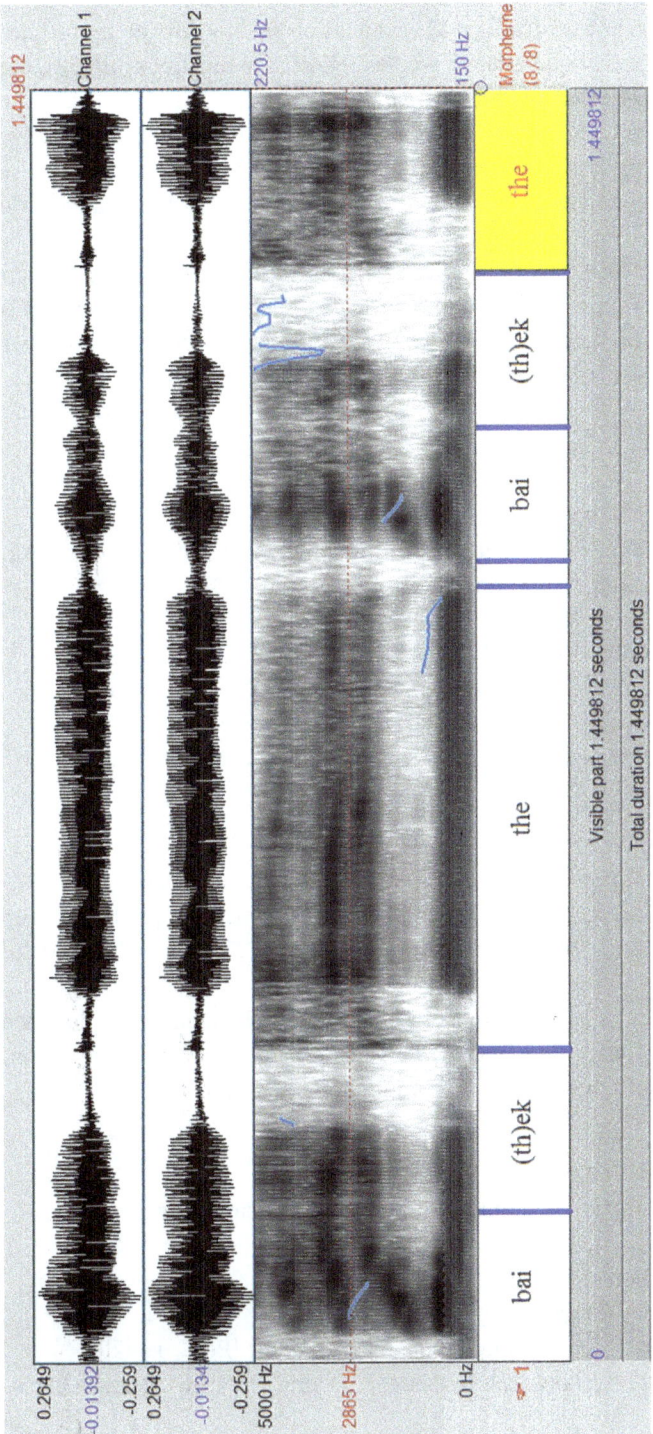

Figure 22: Prosodic emphasis in full predicate reduplication of *baithekthe* (KK, CC 012). The audio file for KK, CC 012 is available at https://scholarsbank.uoregon.edu/xmlui/handle/1794/13657.

The majority of particles, however, do not appear to allow for any affixation: the quotative particle *pu* in its purely quotative as well as reportative functions (§16.3.1), the reportative particle *tànghò* (§16.3.2), dubitative *bón* (§16.3.3), emphatic *ti* (§16.3.5), the 'interactive emphatic' *ho* (§16.3.6), the vocative particle *ó* (§16.3.7), the exclamative construction based on the irrealis focus marker =*le* (§16.3.8), the afterthought =*he* (§16.3.9), the common ground marker =*mati* (§16.3.11), and, finally, the narrative style marker *hedī* (§16.3.12).

In the discussion of these particles, I offer my current understanding of their functions. However, my understanding of the intricate details of particle functions is limited. Future research on Karbi particles as well as further typological study of these types of discourse markers in languages across the world are required.

16.3.1 Quotative *pu*

Quotative *pu*, grammaticalized from *pù* 'say', follows after, and indicates the end of, direct speech, as in the reported exchange in the text unit in (925).

(925) Quotative *pu* marking the end of direct speech
"*chininedetlo, po. Te mo nechenekvaretjima,*
[[[chiní-Cē-dèt-lò pō]   [tē mò   ne=chenék-varèt-jí=ma
know-NEG-PFV-RL father if future 1EXCL:NSUBJ=torture-INTENS-IRR2=Q

po?" pu, "nangchenekne, pei atum" pu
pō] **pu]** [[nang=chenék-Cē   pēi   a-tūm]   **pu]**
father **QUOT** 1/2:NSUBJ=torture-NEG mother POSS-PL **QUOT**
'"I don't know, father, if in the future (you take a new wife), will she keep torturing us, father?", "She won't torture you, mothers", he said.' [CST, RO 010]

Quotative *pu* also functions as a semantically neutral complementizer (as does the related element *pusi* 'quotative complementizer (QUOT.COMP)') (§15.2.2.4). In addition, quotative *pu* functions as a purpose clause conjunction (§15.2.3.2).

16.3.1.1 Reportative function of *pu*
Quotative *pu* may also function as a reportative marker. An example is (926).

(926) Reportative function of quotative *pu*
[...] *la Bey Ke'et Bey Ronghang lapen Bey Ki'ik*
[là   [[Bēy ke-èt]   [Bēy Ronghāng] lapèn [Bēy ke-ìk]]
this CLAN NMLZ-be.yellow CLAN CLAN   and   CLAN NMLZ-be.black

> *atum angjirta do pu*
> a-tūm]   a-ingjìr=tā   dō   **pu**
> POSS-PL   POSS-sister=ADD   exist   QUOT
> '[...] That Bey the Fair, Bey Ronghang, and Bey the Black, they also had a sister, it is said.' [WR, BCS 007]

As a reportative particle, *pu* is functionally equivalent to *tànghò* (§16.3.2) and in fact, they sometimes co-occur as *pu tànghò*, as in (927).

(927) Combined use of both reportative particles *pu* and *tànghò*
> *nangong akleng ahemke nangong*
> [nang-ōng   a-klèng   a-hēm=ke]   [nang-ōng
> 2:POSS-maternal.uncle POSS-old.one   POSS-house=TOP   2:POSS-maternal.uncle
>
> *ahemripo ahemke la'an abang*
> a-hēmrī-pō   a-hēm=ke]   la-án   abàng
> POSS-oldest.son-male   POSS-house=TOP   this-that.much   NPDL
>
> *ki'ikrintile **putangho***
> ke-ìk-rintí=le   **pu-tànghò**
> NMLZ-be.black-equally:PL:S/A=FOC:IRR   QUOT-REP
> 'The family of your oldest maternal uncle, the family of your uncle who is the eldest son of the family, all of them are so black (so you shouldn't take your wife from them)!' [WR, BCS 014]

16.3.1.2 Desiderative function of *pu*

The desiderative function of *pu* has presumably grammaticalized via insubordination of the purpose clause conjunction *pu* (§15.2.3.2). The verb preceding *pu* 'quotative' is marked irrealis with *-jí* 'irrealis2' (§9.6.2.1.7). An example is (928).

(928) Purpose/desiderative marking function of *pu* (main clause)
> *ai tovar nangpektha ti ko jirpo,*
> ái   továr   nang-pèk-thā   tì   ko   jīrpō,
> how.bad!   road   1/2:NSUBJ-give.way-IMP:CON   definitely   buddy:VOC   friend
>
> *ne'ik atum aphan an thonji **pu***
> ne-ìk   a-tūm   a-phān   àn   thòn-jí   **pu**
> 1EXCL:POSS-older.brother   POSS-PL   POSS-NSUBJ   rice   drop-IRR2   QUOT
> '"How bad! Please do give way to me. I want to take rice to my brother (and sister-in-law)."' [RBT, ChM 012]

Example (929) shows that *pu* in the desiderative construction may take *-lò* 'realis'.

(929) Purpose/desiderative marking function of *pu*; with realis *-lò*
lasi <ling> juja'e homtekangsi halaso ape ari
[lasì   juja'ē   hóm-tekáng-si]   hálasō   a-pé   a-rī
therefore cradle   fix.by.tying-leaving-NF:RL that   POSS-cloth   POSS-EE:pé

kechechokdamji **pulo** amatsi laso osomar banghini
[ke-che-chōk-dām-jí   **pu-lò**]   [amātsi   [lasō   osō-mār
NMLZ-RR-wash.clothes-go-IRR2   **QUOT-RL**   and.then this   child-PL
bàng-hiní
CLF:HUM:PL-two

aphan juja'e homtekangsi thaptekanglo
a-phān]   juja'ē   hóm-tekáng-si   thàp-tekáng-lò]
POSS-NSUBJ   cradle   fix.by.tying-leaving-NF:RL put.inside-leaving-RL
'So (the mother) fixed the cradle and (she) wanted to go wash those clothes, and then, she fixed the cradle for the two children, and put them inside.' [CST, HM 010]

16.3.2 Reportative *tànghò*

The reportative particle *tànghò* typically occurs at the end of a clause. It marks information as being indirectly known, because somebody has told it to the speaker. In the corpus, *tànghò* is frequently used in folk stories. As orally transmitted texts, folk stories of course fully consist of reported information. In certain parts of the narrative, the storyteller typically adds *tànghò*; further research is required to understand where and for what purpose exactly *tànghò* is used in the narrative structure of folk stories. So far, it appears that one such part of the story that is typically marked by *tànghò* is the beginning of the story. For example, in (930), this particular text starts out by introducing the three protagonists, followed by a *tànghò* at the end of the clause.

(930) Reportative *tànghò* at the end of an utterance in a folk story
hako ahut hedi Bey atum korte bangkethom do **tangho**
[hakó   ahūt   hedī]   Bēy   a-tūm   kortè   bàng-kethòm   dō
that.time during   DM   CLAN   POSS-PL   brother   CLF:HUM:PL-three   exist
tànghò
REP
'In the old days, you know, right?, there were three Bey brothers, they say.'
[WR, BCS 001]

In ordinary conversation, using *tànghò* at the end of an utterance marks reported information, which may have been acquired just moments earlier. For example, Speaker A can relay information of Speaker B reporting to have already eaten to Speaker C by saying *Chō-ét-lò tànghò*. 'eat-PRF-RL REP' > '(S/he) said (s/he) has already eaten'.

Example (931) shows that *tànghò* may also occur after an NP if the scope is intended to be particularly over that NP.

(931) Reportative *tànghò* after an NP
ansi la hepi ason ingmoipo **hepipen thijok**
[ánsi là hepī asón ingmōi-pò]   [[[hepī=pen thijōk
then this brinjal like cook.with.alkaline-IRR1 **brinjal=with deer**

a'ok tangho pine lason
a-ōk] tànghò] pí-nē lasón
POSS-meat REP what-INDEF that.way

kechongmoi
ke-cho-ingmōi]
NMLZ-AUTO.BEN/MAL-cook.with.alkaline
'And then, we cook eggplant or something similar with the alkaline, we cook eggplant and deer meat, so they say, or whatever like that with baking soda.'
[SiH, KH 008]

The disyllabic form of *tànghò* suggests that diachronically there are two morphemes involved. In fact, there is one instance in the corpus where apparently the first syllable is used independently of the second syllable. In (932), *-tàng* is used as a verbal suffix in a predicate that is marked as a question via *=ma*. Apparently, *-tàng* here has the same function of indicating that the requested information is not directly known by the addressee, but is information that the addressee only knows if at all as reported information.

(932) Reportative *tàng* in question
the'o'o**tang**ma atibukta} mm
thè-ò~ò-**tàng**=ma a-tibùk=tā} mm
be.big-much~DIST.PL-**REP**=Q POSS-earthen.pot=ADD AFF
'{Are the earthen pots all very big?}' [HK, TR 177]

It appears that *-tàng*, or *tàngma*, is more generally the interrogative counterpart of *tànghò*, because attempts to elicit the use of *-tàng* in other contexts have only yielded questions, e.g., (933).

(933) Reportative *tàng* in question
a-rèng ke-lòk a-tūm=ke àn chō-**tàng**=ma?
POSS-skin NMLZ-be.white POSS-PL=TOP rice eat-**REP**=Q
'Are white people said to eat rice?'

In addition to *tànghò*, quotative *pu* also functions as a reportative marker (§16.3.1.1).

16.3.3 Dubitatives *bón, tahái, menē*

There are three dubitative particles, *bón*, *tahái*, and *menē*. There are no instances of *bón* in the recorded text corpus, but (934) offers an elicited example.

(934) Dubitative *bón*
 jáng-jē-dèt-jí   **bón**
 fall-NEG-PFV-IRR2   **DUBIT**
 'It probably won't rain.' [SiT 090221]

According to Grüßner's (1978: 130–2) account of *bón*, this particle occurs at the end of quoted clauses (but before the quotative marker). In his view, this is the distributional difference between *bón* and *=bo*, which he suggests are functionally equivalent (for information on *=bo*, see §15.1.1.6); *=bo* only occurs as a sentence-final particle. Further research is required to offer a semantic analysis of the differences between *tahái*, *bón*, and *=bo*. Note that *bón* may be the first element in *bóntā* 'but' (with the additive *=tā* as a second element; see §15.5.3).

Another dubitative particle is *tahái*. In (935), *tahái* occurs after a negated verb ('may not be able to tell it well') and co-occurs with another dubitative marker, *menē* 'maybe'.

(935) Dubitative *tahái*, followed by *menē* 'maybe'
 ta ne kethan atomo abangke
 tā   [nè   ke-thán   a-temó   abàng=ke]
 but 1EXCL NMLZ-tell   POSS-story   NPDL=TOP

 *pachekengdamthekthedet **tahai** meneta*
 [pe-che-kèng-dàm-thèk-Cē-dèt   **tahái**   menē=tā]
 CAUS-RR-be.straight-go-know.how-NEG-PFV   **DUBIT**   maybe=ADD:although

 nangthanpo
 nang=thán-pò]
 1/2:NSUBJ=tell-IRR1
 'The story I'll be telling now, maybe I can't tell it perfectly (lit. straight), but I will still tell (it).' [KK, CC 008]

Example (936) shows that *-lò* 'realis' can be attached to *tahái*, apparently to convey a higher likelihood of the proposition. We may thus translate *tahái-lò* as 'probably' rather than 'maybe'.

(936) Dubitative *tahái* with realis *-lò*
 <a> *nangli aphrangphrang, hakoko alam sitame*
 nàng-lì   [aphráng~phràng   hakó~kò   a-lám   sitāmē]
 you-HON   first~DIST.PL   that.time~DIST.PL   POSS-matter   nevertheless

arju'iklong **tahailo**
arjū-īk-lōng **tahài-lò**
hear-FRML-GET **DUBIT-RL**
'You probably have heard the different matters about the old days.' [KaR, SWK 059]

In (937) and (938), two instances of *menē* 'maybe' are provided.

(937) Dubitative *menē* 'maybe'
te "damnoi!" ante "dah! nangphihai
tè dàm-nōi ánte dah! nang-phì-hái
OK.then go-INFRML.COND.IMP OK.then go! 2POSS-grandmother-HON

along, e, lothe lotha doji, mene mena" pu
alòng e lothē lothā dō-jí **menē** menā pu
LOC DSM banana EE:lothē exist-IRR2 maybe EE:menē QUOT
'Then (she said), "Go!", and then, "Go to your grandmother, (she) will have bananas and other fruit maybe."' [KK, CC 024]

(938) Dubitative *menē* 'maybe'
do'an atangka amethang choke cholo mene
dō-án a-tángká a-metháng chō=ke chō-lò **menē**
stay-all POSS-money POSS-self spend=TOP spend-RL **maybe**

chochelo mene chinidunde [...]
chō-Cē-lò **menē** chiní-dùn-Cē
spend-NEG-RL **maybe** know-JOIN-NEG
'All the money, whether they (the government) may have spent the money for themselves (i.e. have had issues with corruption) or not, I don't know [...].' [SiT, HF 025]

16.3.4 Always *titī*

The particle *titī* means 'always' or 'habitually'. In (939), *titī* indicates that the situation described is a typical, habitual scenario: this is how it always was.

(939) 'Always' *titī*
so'arlo atumsi keklem abang dopo
[[sō'arlō a-tūm=si] [ke-klém a-bàng] dō-pò]
women:COLL POSS-PL=FOC:RL NMLZ-do POSS-CLF:HUM:PL exist-IRR1

> *pinso atum abangke osomarpen chelemrong*
> [[pinsō   a-tūm   abàng=ke]   osō-mār=pen   che-lém-ròng
> married.man   POSS-PL   NPDL=TOP   child PL=with   RR-play.with.toys-instead
>
> *titi; lason arjulonghe*
> **titī]**   [lasón   arjū-lōng=he]
> always   that.way   hear-GET=AFTERTHOUGHT
> '[...] [T]he women would be the working ones, the men would always play with the children instead, this is actually what I've heard.' [KaR, SWK 071]

In (940), *titī* surprisingly occurs with what may be *-si* 'NF:RL', or possibly *=si* 'focus:realis'. It is currently not clear how to analyze *titisi* here, but this demonstrates that *titī* belongs to the subset of particles that may occur with morphological marking (§16.3).[167]

(940) 'Always' *titī* with *-si* 'non-final:realis'
netumta nangtum nangpipo longle thak
[ne-tūm=tā   nang-tūm   nang=pī-pò   longlē   athàk
1EXCL-PL=ADD   2-PL   1/2:NSUBJ=give-IRR1   earth   on.top

*nangbokchom **titisi** neta*
nang=bók-chòm   **titī-/=si]**   nè=tā
1/2:NSUBJ=serve.small.items-a.little   **always-NF:RL/=FOC:RL?**   1EXCL=ADD

nangkechodundun
nang=ke-chō-dūn~dūn
CIS=NMLZ-eat-JOIN~HAB
'You all would also give us (our food that way), you would always serve us (food) on the ground, I also used to eat like that.' [KK, BMS 060]

The etymology of *titī* could be a reduplication of emphatic *ti* (see §16.3.5), which would make sense given that cross-linguistically, habituality often correlates with reduplicative marking.

16.3.5 Emphatic *ti*

The emphatic particle *ti* occurs at the end of a sentence and can be translated into English via lexical emphatics such as 'really' or 'definitely', or the *do*-emphatic construction. It occurs in positive and negative declarative clauses, as well as in non-declarative clauses, such as imperatives and hortatives.

---

[167] Evidence that *titisi* is indeed the habitual marker *titī* plus a /si/ element comes from the fact that the habitual function is additionally indicated by the following, reduplicated main verb *nangkechodundun*.

In (941), the first line represents a question that expresses the lack of confidence of the person asking (i.e., the owner of the dog, or 'grandfather') that the dog might actually be able to take him (across a huge body of water). The question starts with *ahokma?* 'is it true?', and then asks *neponthekjima?* 'will you be able to take me?'. In his reply, the dog tries to reassure his owner that he will indeed be able to take him across the water, and he does that by adding *ti*. He then also uses a copy verb construction, *nangdunle nangdunnoi*, which is another type of emphatic construction (see §16.2.3.3).

(941) Emphatic *ti* with declarative, positive verb
"*ahokma, methan-sibongpo?, nang neponthekjima?*"
a-hōk=ma   methān-sibóngpō,   ne=pòn-thèk-jí=mà
POSS-truth=Q dog-SPECIES   1EXCL:NSUBJ =take.away-know.how-IRR2=Q

"*o ne **nangponthekpo ti**, phu!*
ó   nè   **nang=pòn-thèk-pò**   **ti**
EXCM 1EXCL   **1/2:NSUBJ=take.away-know.how-IRR1**   **EMPH**
phū
grandfather:VOC

nangdunle nangdunnoi ho pulo tangho
nang=dùn=le   nang=dùn-nōi   hò   pù-lò
CIS=join=FOC:IRR   CIS=join-INFRML.COND.IMP   EMPH:INTERACT   say-RL
tànghò
REP
'"Is it true, dog, you know how to take me?" "I certainly know how to take you there, grandfather. Just make sure to follow me!", he said.' [KK, BMS 034-5]

In (942) we find an example o6f emphatic *ti* co-occurring with *ho* 'EMPH:INTERACT' (see §16.3.6), of which there are several instances in the corpus.

(942) Emphatic *ti* with declarative, positive verb (with *ho* 'EMPH:INTERACT')
*o... neta lasi ho **kiribom ti ho***
o   nè=tā   lasì   hò   **ke-rì-bōm**   **tì**
AFF   1EXCL=ADD   thus   EMPH:INTERACT   **NMLZ-search-CONT**   **EMPH**

hò
EMPH:INTERACT
'Oh (I see). I also am searching for somebody just like you (lit. like this).' [HK, TR 065]

In (943) and (944), *ti* occurs with directives, specifically the conative imperative *-thā* and the hortative *-nāng*.

(943) Emphatic *ti* with imperative *-thā*
ai tovar **nangpektha ti***, ko jirpō*
ái	továr	**nang-pèk-thā**	**tì**	kʊ	jīrpō,
how.bad!	road	**1/2:NSUBJ-give.way-IMP:CON**	**EMPH**	buddy:VOC	friend

ne'ik atum aphan an thonji pu
ne-ìk	a-tūm	a-phān	àn	thòn-jí	pu
1EXCL:POSS-older.brother	POSS-PL	POSS-NSUBJ	rice	drop-IRR2	QUOT

"'How bad! Please do give way to me. I want to take rice to my brother (and sister-in-law).'" [RBT, ChM 012]

(944) Emphatic *ti* with hortative *-nāng*
[anke laso <la> kepholok abarika
[ánke	lasō	ke-phō-lòk	a-bariká
and.then	this	NMLZ-reach-happen.to	POSS-OFFICER

abangke ningjelemdetlo tangho
abàng=ke	ningjé-lemdet-lò	tànghò]
NPDL=TOP	speak-repeatedly-RL	REP

***paprapnang ti** komarli ho {mm}*
[**pe-pràp-nāng**	**tì**	ko-marlí	hò]	mm
CAUS-be.quick-HORT	**EMPH**	buddy:VOC-PL:VOC	EMPH:INTERACT	AFF

'And then, that head tiger that had encountered (the orphan) kept saying, "Let's make it quick, friends!"' [HK, TR 153]

Lastly, in (945), *ti* occurs after a negated verb, here a negative hortative.

(945) Emphatic *ti* with negative hortative
" *[...] ningveke elitumta e vopi ejon*
[[ningvē=ke	e-li-tūm=tā	e	vō-pī	e-jōn
evening=TOP	1PL.INCL-HON- PL=ADD	DSM	chicken-female	one-CLF:animal

chothatnang" pulo amat hala apiso abang
cho-thāt-nāng]	pù-lò]	[amāt	hála	a-pisò	abàng
AUTO.BEN/MAL-slaughter-HORT	say-RL	and.then	that	POSS-wife	NPDL

*pulo **"thatnangne ti** sarbura"*
pù-lò	[**thàt-nāng-Cē**	**tì**	sàrburá]]
say-RL	**slaughter-HORT-NEG**	**EMPH**	old.man

"'[...] [L]et's kill ourselves a hen tonight", he said, (but) the wife said, "Let's not, old man (and I won't change my mind)!"' [SeT, MTN 007]

16.3.6 Interactive emphatic *ho*

Compared to 'emphatic' *ti*, 'interactive emphatic' *ho* is more frequent in the recorded text corpus of 12,485 words (i.e., 30 instances of *ho* versus 8 instances of *ti*). While *ti* may be the only indicator of emphasis, *ho* more typically occurs in conjunction with other emphatic elements and constructions. Also, *ho* often occurs in non-declarative speech acts. In (946), it occurs with the *=le* copy verb construction (§16.2.3.3).

(946)   Interactive emphatic *ho* after verb in emphatic copy verb construction
"*o ne nangponthekpo ti, phu!*
ó   nè   nang-pòn-thèk-pò   tì   phū
EXCM   1EXCL   1/2:NSUBJ-take.away-know.how-IRR1   EMPH   grandfather:VOC

nangdunle nangdunnoi ho"
nang=dùn=le   nang=dùn-nōi   **hò**
1/2:NSUBJ=join=FOC:IRR   1/2:NSUBJ=join-INFRML.COND.IMP   **EMPH:INTERACT**

pulo tangho
pù-lò   tànghò
say-RL   REP
"'I certainly know how to take you there, grandfather. Just make sure to join me", (he) said.' [KK, BMS 035]

In (947) and (948) we find examples of *ho* occurring together with the feedback or back-channel requesting *déi* (§15.1.1.8).

(947)   Interactive emphatic *ho* after feedback request marker *déi*
tangte osomar atum... ne eson atomo
tángtē   osō-mār   a-tūm   nè   e-sòn   a-tomó
if   child-PL   POSS-PL   1EXCL   one-CLF:thing   POSS-story

nangthanpo dei ho {to}
nang=thán-pò   **déi**   **ho**   {to}
1/2:NSUBJ=tell-IRR1 **OK?**   **EMPH:INTERACT**   OK
'If so then, (dear) children, I will tell you one story, ok? {OK.}' [HK, TR 001]

(948)   Interactive emphatic *ho* after feedback request marker *déi*
jamborong along hako arnike luji puhe
jamboróng   a-lòng   hakó   arnì=ke   lují   pu=he
bag   POSS-LOC   that.time   day=TOP   mirror   QUOT=AFTERTHOUGHT

> *{mm} dei ho*
> mm **déi hò**
> AFF **OK? EMPH:INTERACT**
> 'In the bag, in the old days, (they used to keep) a so-called *luji*, a mirror (container), you know, right?' [HK, TR 017]

In (949), *ho* occurs along with the 'common ground' marker *mati*. This shows that *ho* may emphasize information that the speaker expects the listener to know. The use of *ho* here implies that the tobacco container will play a key role in the story, so the storyteller wants to make sure the listener pays attention to the mentioning of the tobacco container.

(949) Interactive emphatic *ho* after *mati* 'common ground'
atema ajerjer do mati ho
a-temá   ajerjēr   dō   matí   **hò**
POSS-tobacco.container(<Asm) small   exist   CG   **EMPH:INTERACT**
'So he had this small tobacco container.' [HK, TR 018]

In (950), *ho* marks information that the speaker knows will be surprising to the listener and may be taken with disbelief. In anticipation of that, *ho* emphatically asserts the information.

(950) Interactive emphatic *ho* in expecting surprise, together with *ti* 'emph'
*o... neta lasi **ho**, kiribom ti **ho***
o   [nè=tā   lasì   **hò**]   [ke-rì-bōm   tì
AFF 1EXCL=ADD thus   **EMPH:INTERACT**   NMLZ-search-CONT   EMPH
hò]
EMPH:INTERACT
'Oh (I see). I also am searching for somebody just like you (lit. like this).' [HK, TR 065]

16.3.7 Vocative *ó*

The vocative particle is used before the name or kinship term when calling for somebody. For example, somebody with the name 'Rasinza' is usually called by saying *ó Rasinza!*, while the mother is usually called by saying *ó pēi/pāi*, where *pēi~pāi* is the lexical noun for 'mother'. In situations of simply addressing, rather than calling, somebody, the vocative particle is generally not used. The vocative forms of *phù* 'grandfather' and *phì* 'grandmother' take the mid tone, see (951).

(951) Vocative *phū* 'grandfather'
jumepik phu [...]
arjū-mē-pìk   phū
listen-be.good-very   grandfather:VOC
'Very nice to hear, grandfather [...]!' [HK, TR 200]

16.3.8 Exclamative function of irrealis focus =*le*

The irrealis focus marker =*le* (see §14.2.4) may occur at the end of a sentence to convey exclamative force, as in (952) and (953).

(952) Irrealis focus =*le* with exclamative function
ai nesomarlole laho! thengbeng
ái   [ne-oso-màr-lò=le   laho]   [thēng-bēng
how.strange!   1EXCL:POSS-child-PL-RL=FOC:IRR   EXCLM   firewood-piece

kalilo, nesomarlole laho!
kalī-lò]   [ne-oso-màr-lò=**le**   laho]
NEG.EQU.COP-RL   1EXCL:POSS-child-PL-RL=**FOC:IRR** EXCLM
'How strange, they are my children! They are not pieces of wood anymore, they are my children!' [CST, HM 082]

(953) Irrealis focus =*le* with exclamative function
mh "an akai adin ne nangkapangreng
mh   [án   a-kái   a-dín   nè
DSM   that.much   POSS-time(<Asm)   POSS-day(<Asm)   1EXCL
nang=ke-pangrèng
1/2:NSUBJ=NMLZ-rear

ningke, nang keningjejepinpi amethan-sibongpole!"
nīngke]   [nàng   [ke-ningjé-Cē-pín-pī   a-methān-sibóngpō=**le**]]
even   you   NMLZ-speak-NEG-never-truly   POSS- dog-SPECIES=**FOC:IRR**
'"Even though all this time I have had you, you have been the dog who never talked before at all!"' [KK, BMS 019]

In both (952) and (953), the exclamation is a result of surprise over a novel insight. This is probably the more common cause for exclamations. However, the surprise element is not necessary for the use of sentence-final =*le*, as shown in (954). The fact that the members of the uncle's family all have a dark skin complexion is not something the speaker just found out. The exclamation here serves the purpose of adding force to the argument that the addressee should not marry that uncle's daughter.

(954) Irrealis focus =*le* with exclamative function (not expressing a surprise)
nangong akleng ahemke nangong
[nang-ōng   a-klèng   a-hēm=ke]   [nang-ōng
2:POSS-maternal.uncle POSS-old.one POSS-house=TOP 2:POSS-maternal.uncle

ahemripo ahemke la'an abang
a-hēmrī-pō   a-hēm=ke]   la-án   abàng
POSS-oldest.son-male POSS-house=TOP this-that.much NPDL

ki'ikrintile putangho
ke-ìk-rintí=**le**   pù-tànghò
NMLZ-be.black-equally:PL:S/A=**FOC:IRR**   QUOT-REP
'The family of your oldest maternal uncle, the family of your uncle who is the eldest son of the family, all of them are so black (so you shouldn't take your wife from them)!' [WR, BCS 014]

16.3.9 Afterthought =*he*

The afterthought marker =*he* usually occurs on right-dislocated NPs, as in several instances in (955). In the first instance, we have the NP *la Beyhem asarpihe*. This represents an afterthought to the previous clause *anke hala aphi sarpi dolang tangho* 'and then, there still was that old woman'. The storyteller decides that she needs to clarify who 'that old woman' is, and utters the afterthought NP *la Beyhem asarpihe* 'the old woman from the Bey family'. After this clarification, the storyteller picks up from where she digressed and repeats the last clause from the story line, *aphi sarpi dolang* 'the old woman was still here'.

(955) Several instances of =*he* 'AFTERTHOUGHT' on right-dislocated NPs
[...] anke hala aphi sarpi dolang tangho,
[ánke   [hála a-phì   sarpī   dō-làng   tànghò]
and.then that   POSS-grandmother   old.woman   exist-still REP

*la Beyhem **asarpihe**...] aphi*
[là   Bēy-hēm   a-sarpī=he...   [a-phì
this CLAN-house   POSS-old.woman=AFTERTHOUGHT   POSS-grandmother

sarpi dolang, anlo aphi abang kipu tangho,
sarpī   dō-làng]   [ánlo   a-phì   abàng   ke-pù
old.woman exist-still and.then POSS-grandmother   NPDL   NMLZ-say
tànghò]
REP

*hala asupo **aphanlohe**, asopi*
[hála   a-su-pò   aphān-lò=he]
that   POSS-grandchild-male   NSUBJ-RL= AFTERTHOUGHT
[a-oso-pì
POSS-child-female

*aso **aphanlohe** [hala a'ik*
a-osō   a-phān=lo=he]   [hála a-ìk
POSS-child   POSS-NSUBJ=FOC=AFTERTHOUGHT   that   POSS-older.brother

abangke Bey Ki'ik pu apot... anke kene
abàng=ke   Bēy   ke-ìk   pu   apōt]   [ánke   kenē
NPDL=TOP   CLAN NMLZ-be.black QUOT because and.then HESIT

aphi sarpi abang kipu tangho...
a-phì   sarpī   abàng   ke-pù   tànghò]
POSS-grandmother old.woman NPDL   NMLZ-say   REP
'And then there was still their grandmother, the old woman. The old woman of the Bey house, you know. His grandmother, the old woman was still there. This was how it was, up to here. And then the grandmother was saying, to her grandson, you know. To her daughter's son, you know. The eldest brother, because he was called Bey the Black... The grandmother, the old woman said...' [WR, BCS 012]

The second instance of *=he* in (955) is in *hala asupo aphanlohe* '(to) the grandson', which adds or clarifies the O argument of the previous clause *anlo aphi abang kipu tangho* 'the grandmother said'. The third instance follows right after the second instance, where the storyteller clarifies which grandson it is when she says *asopi aso aphanlohe* '(to) her daughter's son'.

While *=he* more frequently occurs on NPs in the corpus, there are some instances where it occurs on full clauses that are added as an afterthought to the previous utterance. An example is (956), where the speaker makes a strong statement by adding *titī* 'always' at the end. She then apparently decides that she does not want to take responsibility for this strong claim, and adds *lason arjulonghe* 'that is (anyway) what I've heard'.

(956) 'AFTERTHOUGHT' *=he* on full clause
so'arlo atumsi keklem abang dopo
[[sō'arlō   a-tūm=si]   [ke-klém a-bàng]   dō-pò]
women:COLL POSS-PL=FOC:RL NMLZ-do POSS-CLF:HUM:PL exist-IRR1

pinso atum abangke osomarpen chelemrong titi;
[[pinsō   a-tūm   abàng=ke]   osō-mār=pen   che-lém-ròng
married.man POSS-PL NPDL=TOP child-PL=with RR-play.with.toys-instead
titī]
always

lason arjulonghe
[lasón   **arjū-lōng=he**]
that.way hear-GET=AFTERTHOUGHT
'[...] [T]he women would be the working ones, the men would always play with the children instead, this is actually what I've heard.' [KaR, SWK 071]

Particle =*he* further occurs more broadly than just in afterthought contexts in the folk story WR, BCS. In this text, =*he* appears to functionally overlap with *hedī* (§16.3.12), which in turn is best analyzed as a combination of =*he* and the tag question marker *dī* (§15.1.1.7). An example of =*he* functioning as a marker of narrative style analogous to *hedī* is (957).

(957)   =*he* as a marker of narrative style
        an lasi latum korte banghini alóngpén 'Bey
        án   lasì   la-tūm kortè   bàng-hiní   a-lòng=pen
        and.then therefore this-PL brother CLF:HUM:PL-two POSS-LOC=from
        [Bēy
        CLAN

        Ki'ik' pu abang ahemsi angjirpi abang
        ke-ìk   pu   abàng a-hēm=si]   [a-ingjìr-pī   abàng]
        NMLZ-be.black QUOT NPDL   POSS-house=FOC:RL POSS-sister-female NPDL

        piso hangdamlohe
        pīsō   hàng-dām-lò=**he**
        wife   call-GO-RL=**EMPH**
        'And then, therefore, among the two brothers, their sister went to the so-called 'Bey the Black', to his house, to ask for a wife, you know.' [WR, BCS 011]

16.3.10 Background information: =*ke* 'topic' marked main clauses

Clauses marked with =*ke* 'topic' provide a background against which a statement just mentioned (or about to be mentioned) is meant to be understood. Typically, the semantic link is one of causality, with the =*ke* marked main clause commonly providing a reason. This construction is discussed as an instance of insubordination in §15.4.1.

Two examples, in which a =*ke* marked clause follows a main clause and is semantically linked to it via causality, are (958) and (959).

(958)   'Topic' =*ke* marked clause following its contextually related clause
        *ingsām-hòi... arvè ke-jáng=**ke***
        be.cold-a.bit rain NMLZ-fall=**TOP**
        'It's a bit cold... it's raining (that's why).' [Notebook OH 121011: 001]

(959) 'Topic' =*ke* marked clause following its contextually related clause
     arvè   jáng-làng, ingtìng-ò-lò=ke,   jó!
     rain   fall-still   be.dark-much-RL=TOP look!
     'It's still raining, (so) it's very dark, look!' [Notebook AT 121011: 002]

In (960), the first clause *apok ingchirdukke* represents a separate intonation unit and is thus prosodically marked as a main clause. However, since it is marked with =*ke*, it signals to the listener that this is background information providing context for an event that is more relevant to the storyline.

(960) 'Topic' =*ke* marked clause preceding its contextually related clause
     apok ingchirdukke...
     a-pōk   ingchìr-dùk=**ke**
     POSS-stomach be.hungry-INTENS=**TOP**

     anke inglong arloksi phurui chosot
     ánke   [inglóng arlòk=si]   [phurùi chosòt]
     and.then hill   foot.of.hill=FOC:RL yam   kd.vegetable

     choridamlo tangho [...]
     cho-rī-dām-lò   tànghò
     AUTO.BEN/MAL-search-GO-RL REP
     'He was suffering from hunger, and so, he went here and there to look for wild vegetables [...].' [HK, TR 014-5][168]

In the excerpt in (961) and in the following text unit in (962), =*ke* marked main clauses are used as answers to 'why'-questions. It appears that using the background information construction rather than a direct 'because'-clause is a more indirect way of answering. This makes sense in the context here, because both the frog and ant are accused by an enraged king of ultimately being responsible for the death of his daughter.

(961) 'Topic' =*ke* marked clause in answer to question
     chongho aphan arjulo, "Pi chonghoisi nangke karle
     [chonghō a-phān   arjū-lò]   [pí   chonghói=si   nàng=ke karlē
     frog   POSS-NSUBJ ask-RL   what reason=FOC:RL you=TOP squirrel

---

[168] The audio file for HK, TR 014-5 is available at https://scholarsbank.uoregon.edu/xmlui/handle/1794/13657.

adon chonraimati?" pu
a-dón chón-rài=mati] pu
POSS-bridge/ladder jump-solid.obj.breaking=as.you.know QUOT
'He asked the frog, "Why did you jump on the ladder of the squirrel?"' [RBT, ChM 074]

misorongpota nemi nangkorrakke
misòrongpō=tā ne-mí nang=kòr-ràk=ke
sp.ant=ADD 1EXCL:POSS-buttocks 1/2:NSUBJ=bite-RES:little.wound=TOP
'The ant bit me in the butt... (and so...)' [RBT, ChM 075]

(962) 'Topic' =*ke* marked clause in answer to question
<ha> Misorongpo arju, "Chonghoisi nang chongho
misòrongpō arjū chonghói=si nàng chonghō
sp.ant ask reason=FOC:RL you frog

*ami korrakmati?" **"Tovar nangdangthipke"***
a-mí kòr-ràk=mati] **továr nang=dāng-thìp=ke**
POSS-buttocks bite-RES:little.wound=CG **road CIS=block-firmly=TOP**
'He asked the ant, "Why did you bite the frog in the butt?", "He had come and was blocking the road... and so..."' [RBT, ChM 076]

Finally, in excerpt (963) from an interview, the interviewee first speaks and says that she is a Terang family member. The interviewer takes his turn and essentially repeats the information he was just given, using tag questions, which occur after main clauses marked by topic =*ke*.

(963) Tag question with *dī* 'question.tag'
neli dak Ran habe arong Terang hem asor
nè-lì dāk [Ran habē] a-ròng]] [[Teràng hēm] a-sòr]
1EXCL-HON here NAME headman POSS-village CLAN house POSS-people
'I am here at Ran Habe village, a member of the Terang family.' [KaR, SWK 006: KaR]

Terang hemsi nangli kedoloke di?, Terang
[Teràng hēm=si nàng-lì ke-dō-lò=**ke** **dī**] [Teràng
CLAN house=FOC:RL you-HON NMLZ-stay-RL=**TOP** **Q.TAG** CLAN

hem asorloke di?
hēm a-sòr-lò=**ke** **dī**]
house POSS-people-RL=**TOP** **Q.TAG**
'So you live in the Terang house, don't you, you're a member of the Terang family, aren't you?' [KaR, SWK 007: BTi]

Here, the tag questions are clearly not intended to elicit confirmation of the truth of the proposition, as they represent a repetition of already provided information,[169] which is marked by clause-final=*ke* 'topic'.

16.3.11 Common ground marker =*mati*

The sentence-final particle =*mati* appears to indicate that the information conveyed in a sentence represents common ground between the speaker and the addressee either through knowledge gained from context, or universal or cultural knowledge. In (964), the storyteller had just previously asserted that Bey the Fair and Bey the Black cannot tolerate each other. In this example, she connects this new information to old information mentioned earlier in the story about this being ultimately the grandmother's fault.

(964) =*mati* indicating old information, here connected to new information
[...] Bey Ke'etpen Bey Ki'ik kechiune
[Bèy   ke-èt=pen   Bēy   ke-ìk   ke-che-ūn-Cē
CLAN   NMLZ-be.yellow=with CLAN   NMLZ-be.black NMLZ-RR-be.able-NEG

athaike <hala piso> aphi sarpi abang
a-thái=ke]   <hála pīsō> a-phì   sarpī   abàng
POSS-place(<Asm)=TOP   that   wife   POSS-grandmother   old.woman   NPDL

chokchedétlomati
chók-Cē-dèt-lò=**mati**
be.fine-NEG-PFV-RL=CG
'[...] And the reason (lit. place) why Bey the Fair and Bey the Black can't (tolerate) each other is that <that wife...>, that grandmother made that mistake (lit. was not okay).' [WR, BCS 019]

Example (965) tells the reason why the orphan protagonist of a story is leaving the village, which is because he is hungry and so needs to go look for vegetables. The common ground marker =*mati* here indicates that the orphan being hungry is not new information: because he is an orphan, of course he will be hungry because he doesn't have a family to provide for him. The use of the question tag *dī* suggests that the storyteller is making sure that the orphan being hungry can indeed be considered common ground, and a logical reason for the orphan to leave the village.

---

169 In fact, the video of this interview shows that the interviewer is not even looking at the interviewee as he is uttering the tag questions, but instead is looking down to his notes. The use of tag questions here seems to rather be a sociopragmatic device because it is likely considered impolite to simply assert statements about the addressee.

(965) =*mati* indicating that statement is uncontroversial
*apok ingchirdukke***mati** *di {mm}*
a-pōk   ingchìr-dùk=ke=**mati**   dī   mm
POSS-stomach   be.hungry-INTENS=TOP=CG   Q.tag   AFF
'This orphan was suffering from hunger, wouldn't he have been?' [HK, TR 010]

In (966), =*mati* occurs in a question, which at first glance poses a problem for the interpretation that =*mati* marks common ground. It appears, however, that =*mati* here marks the common ground, or presupposition, that the *hanthar* fruit fell on the back of the pig, and the information sought by the question is only why it did that.

(966) =*mati* in a question
Ha hanthar aphan arjudamlo... "Kopisi nang
há   hanthàr   a-phān   arjū-dām-lò   kopīsi   nàng
over.there vegetable.sp POSS-NSUBJ   ask-go-RL   why   2

*phakbelengpi amoi klodup***mati**, *hanthar?"*
phàkbeléngpī   a-mòi   kló-dùp=**mati**
pig.sp   POSS-back   fall-falling.sound.from.high.solid.obj=CG
hanthàr
vegetable.sp
'There to the hanthar he went and asked, "Why did you possibly fall down on the back of the pig, Hanthar?"' [RBT, ChM 060]

16.3.12 Narrative style *hedī*

The particle *hedī* appears to have different functions depending on the dialect. In a number of dialects, it may be used as a synonym of the question tag marker *dī* (§15.1.1.7), as in (967) or a synonym of the feedback request marker *déi* (§15.1.1.8), as in (968).

(967) *hedī* with question tag function (like *dī*)
[...] athakke aina do {mm}
athàk=ke   ainá   dō   mm
on.top=TOP   mirror(<Ind)   exist   AFF

lují pu **hedi** *{lují do} lují do {mm}*
lují   pu   **hedī**   lují   dō}   lují   dō   mm
mirror   QUOT   **Q.TAG**   mirror   exist   mirror   exist   AFF
'[...] It had an *aina* on top; it had what we call a mirror, right? {It had a mirror?} It had a mirror.' [HK, TR 019-20]

(968) *hedī* with feedback request function (like *déi*)
[...] *si bor'ilonang,* **hedi***?*
sì   bor'í-lonāng   **hedī**
therefore try-HORT:EMPH   **okay?**
'[...] Let's try, okay?' [KaR, SWK 016]

In the West Karbi Anglong Amri dialect, *hedī* is highly frequent in folk stories, where it occurs after topical noun phrases, as in (969). In that use, it apparently also functions as a feedback requesting device, but with less force. In this dialect, it has grammaticalized as a marker of narrative style.[170]

(969) *hedī* as noun phrase emphatic marker
latumke **hedi** *la Bey Ke'et kele*
la-tūm=ke   **hedī**   là   Bēy   ke-èt   ke-lè
this-PL=TOP **NP.EMPH** this CLAN   NMLZ-be.yellow   NMLZ-reach

ahemlote Bey Ki'ik le'un'e pu
a-hēm-lò-te   Bēy   ke-ìk   lè-ūn-Cē   pu
POSS-house-RL-COND   CLAN   NMLZ-be.black   reach-be.able-NEG   QUOT

laso adohai dokoklo aseme dokoklo
lasō a-dohái   dō-kòk-lò   a-semé   dō-kòk-lò
this POSS-oath(<Ind)   exist-firmly-RL   POSS-oath   exist-firmly-RL
'And so they, you know, when there's a house that (a daughter of) Bey the Fair has reached (i.e. got married there), there (a daughter of) Bey the Black can't reach (i.e. can't get married), there's a *dohai*, there's an oath.' [WR, BCS 025]

Note that just *=he* functions quite similarly to *hedī* as a marker of narrative style in this dialect (§16.3.9).

16.4 Honorific and formality marking

There are three markers for a honorific or formal speech style. First, there is a suffix *-lī*, which occurs on pronouns and addressing words (§16.4.1). Second, there is a verbal

---

[170] When I recorded the folk story that example (969) is taken from, I was staying in Umswai in West Karbi Anglong. After the recording was finished, then 10-year old Platinum Hanse suggested I record him telling a folk story as well, which we did. Although the folk story that (969) is taken from struck me as abounding with *hedī*, in Platinum's narration, he probably used *hedī* twice as much. He clearly knew that *hedī* was a marker of narrative style in the local dialect, and so made sure to show that he knew it and that he was telling a folk story the way folk stories are supposed to sound.

suffix -*īk* (§16.4.2). And lastly, there is an honorific suffix -*héi* ~ -*hái*, which occurs on kinship terms (§16.4.3).

16.4.1 Honorific -*lì* on pronouns and addressing words

The honorific suffix -*lì* attaches to pronouns (and personal possessive prefixes) as shown in §6.1.1. Adding -*lì* to all pronouns (i.e., first, second, and third person) indicates the social relationship between speaker and addressee. There are clear rules on when -*lì* has to be used and when it should not be used, depending on the speaker's and addressee's clan affiliations. However, particularly in the towns, the younger generation does not follow the rules that strictly anymore.

Honorific -*lì* also occurs on -*mār* pluralized nouns (§7.4.4), apparently only in forms of address, such as *komarli*, which is used by male speakers to address their fellow men from different clans (from *ko*, which is used for singular address male-to-male address among non-relatives), or *jirpomarli* (from *jīr-pō* 'friend-male'), or *ongmarli* (from *ōng* 'maternal uncle'), etc.

16.4.2 Formal -*īk* on predicates

The suffix -*lì* on pronouns has to be used consistently on every pronoun if required by the social relationship between speaker and addressee. This is different from the verb suffix -*īk* 'formal' ('FRML'), which is not used on every single verb, even if the relationship between speaker and addressee requires a formal register. The pattern that underlies the use of -*īk* requires further research, but the following generalizations can be made. First, -*īk* occurs with any kind of request, including indirect requests, as in (970).

(970) Formal marker -*īk* in indirect request
si aphrangsi, nanglimen chethan asonte, <e>
sì   a-phráng-sí   nang-li-mén   che-thán   asón-tē
therefore   POSS-first-SPLT   2-HON-name   RR-tell   like-COND

me'iksenji
mē-**ik**-sén-jí
be.good-**FRML**-INTENS-IRR2
'So first, if you could tell us your name, that would be wonderful!' [KaR, SWK 004]

Besides requests, -*īk* also occurs commonly in simple assertive clauses. It appears as though -*īk* in assertive clauses is often used at the end of a paragraph or episode in, for example, procedural texts. The reason for this could be that the end of an episode serves as a good moment to use *-īk* as a reminder of the formal speech style. In (971), which is a procedural text about traditional washing and cleaning methods and the traditional status of cleanliness, the *-īk* suffix is used here at the end of a short paragraph that discusses the *suho* fruit; in what follows (971), the speaker moves on to talk about a different fruit that is used for washing the head.

(971) Formal marker *-īk* at the end of a paragraph
lasi la suho athe pu abangke pe ri
[lasì   là   sūhō   a-thē   pu   abàng=ke]   [[pé   rī
therefore this sp.thorny.plant POSS-fruit QUOT   NPDL=TOP   cloth EE:pé

kechok aphan'iklo
ke-chòk]   a-phān-**īk**-lò]
NMLZ-wash.clothes POSS-PURP-**FRML**-RL
'Therefore, the *suho* fruit is for washing clothes.' [SiH, CW 007]

In the corpus of recorded texts, *-īk* does not occur in folk stories, but it does occur in procedural texts. There is one exception, where *-īk* does, however, occur in a folk story in the corpus, which is provided in (972); this text unit represents the last one of this recording.

(972) Formal marker *-īk* in last sentence of folk story
lasi choboche chosonsesi akai jangikraplo
lasì   chobòché   chosonsé-si   a-kái
therefore settle.down EE:choboché-NF   POSS-time(<Asm)
jáng-**īk**-rāp-lò
fall-**FRML**-together-RL

lasi la Hingchong musoso atomoke
lasì   là   Hingchòng   musosō   a-tomó=ke
therefore this CONSTELLATION   siblings:DL   POSS-story=TOP

lapu'ik'helo Rongphar asangho kethekthe anke
lapù-**īk**-heló   Rongphàr   a-sanghó   ke-thèk-Cē
like.this-**FRML**-RL:EMPH   CLAN   POSS-mister:VOC   NMLZ-know.how-NEG
ánke
and.then

nangpekengpon'iknoi
nang=pa-kèng-pōn-**īk**-nōi
1/2.NSUBJ=CAUS-be.straight-take.away-**FRML**-INFRML.COND.IMP
'Thus, they settled down and lived together until the end of their lives, and then that was the story of *Hingchong musoso*, Mister Rongphar, I'm not an expert, so make it clear (i.e. correct it) please.' [CST, HM 120]

What the use of -ĩk here suggests is that the storyteller says the last sentence of the story not as part of actually telling the story, but as a statement about the story, i.e., on a meta-level.

16.4.3 Honorific -héi ~ -hái on kinship terms

The honorific suffix -héi ~ -hái only occurs on kinship terms. It is used both in terms of address and in terms of reference, especially for one's spouse's relatives (e.g., phì-hái 'grandmother-kin:HON' and phù-hái 'grandfather-kin:HON', or lok-hái 'brother.in.law-kin:HON'). According to Grüßner (1978: 73–4), -héi ~ -hái has lexicalized in some cases such that the root with the suffix and the root without the suffix refer to two different kin relations; this requires further study.

16.5 Interjections

Interjections are words that always represent an utterance by themselves. Table 119 presents a list of interjections collected so far. In addition to the interjections listed below, there are also conventionalized interjections that are used to interact with animals, such as [doʷ.doʷ.doʷ] for calling dogs to feed them, or [suʃ] to chase away chickens. Further research is required to provide a more comprehensive list.

Note that several items in Table 119 have unusual phonological shapes. The glottal fricative /h/ does not usually occur as a coda consonant (§3.1.2.3), and the off glide [ʷ] is likewise not part of the regular phonological inventory of Karbi (§3.2.2).

Table 119: Interjections.

Domain	Form	Gloss	Use
Replies to questions	kalàng	'yes'	reply to polar interrogatives, expressing (dis-)agreement[a]
	kalī	'NEG.EQU.COP'	
	'mh' [ʔmm̂ʔ]	'no'	
	ōi	'yes'	
	tò	'yes, okay, I see'	
	o	'AFF'	backchanneling
	hói		reply when called by name
Directives	dáh	'(let's.)go!'	typically a hortative, literally meaning 'let's go!'; but also used when directed to addressee only, as 'go!'

Table 119 (continued)

Domain	Form	Gloss	Use
	díh	'leave.me!'	when speaker is held by somebody
	jó	'look.here!'	directing addressee to look at something right in front
	jáho	'look.there!'	directing addressee to look at something further away
	hoʷ	'here.you.go!'	when handing something to addressee
Surprise, fear, shock, etc.	bóh	'surprise'	expressing surprise
	ái	'how.bad!'	expressing desperation, disapproval, fear
	mái	'how.bad!'	
	lahó	'EXCLAM'	'exclamation' (only used by one particular speaker, at the end of exclamatory sentences)
	ékdóm	'EXCLAM(<Asm)'	'exclamation', used by many speakers, after the constituent that is stressed or emphasized
	lahé	'really?', 'is it so?'	reaction to (sometimes only mildly) surprising information

ᵃNote that a very typical way to reply to polar interrogatives is to repeat the verb (and, as the case may be, adding negation).

Example (973) illustrates how exclamative *ékdóm*, a borrowing from Assamese, is used in a sentence. It is typical for *ékdóm* to occur in the middle of a sentence, where it has scope over the following item.

(973) *ékdóm* 'exclamation(<Asm)'
anke lapusi ekdom nangkangthuloklo
ánke   làpù=sì   **ékdóm**   nang=kangthú-lók-lò
and.then like.this=FOC   EXCM(<Asm)   CIS=bounce-only-RL
'And then, like this we were constantly bouncing up and down.' [SH, CSM 019]

Generally, interjections do not occur embedded into a clause. In (974), however, *kalī* 'no' and *kalàng* 'yes' are embedded. Here, *kali kalang kejekthek* is an idiomatic expression, 'know what to do and what not to do'.

(974) *kalī* 'no' and *kalàng* 'yes' embedded into clause
kali kalang *kejekthek ajoine, laso*
kali   **kalàng**   ke-jék-thèk   a-joiné
NEG.EQU.COP   **yes**   NMLZ-know.do's.and.don't's-know.how   POSS-reason
lasō
this

> *apotsi*
> apōt=si
> because=FOC:RL
> 'Because they know what to do and what not to do.' [SiH, CW 019]

16.6 Hesitation and correction words

This section offers description and examples of how hesitation and correction words are used in Karbi.

16.6.1 Hesitation words *kenē* and *mane* (<Assamese)

The hesitation word *kenē* (also pronounced as *ekenē*) can be used when having difficulties in retrieving or choosing a word while wanting to avoid just pausing in silence. *Kenē* may be used by itself with no further marking, in which case it simply indicates that the speaker is thinking of the next things to say. An example of this is in (975), where in actually a very long text unit that is cut down here to just the last two clauses for presentational purposes, the speaker uses the discourse connector *ánke* and apparently then is not sure how to proceed, and rests for a short moment on the hesitation word *kenē*.

(975) *kenē* 'hesitation' not adjusted grammatically
[...] *hala a'ik abangke Bey Ki'ik pu apot...*
[hála a-ìk   abàng=ke Bēy ke-ìk   pu   apōt]
that POSS-older.brother NPDL=TOP CLAN NMLZ-be.black QUOT because

*anke **kene** aphi sarpi abang kipu tangho*
[ánke **kenē** a-phì   sarpī   abàng ke-pù   tànghò]
and.then **HESIT** POSS-grandmother old.woman NPDL   NMLZ-say REP
'[...] [T]he eldest brother, because he was called Bey the Black... and then, um, the grandmother, the old woman said' [WR, BCS 012]

Examples (976) and (977) show that *kenē* may also function as a "pro-lexeme" similar to what Post (2007: 678) has described for the Galo hesitation word *məráa*. This means that *kenē* can substitute for any noun or verb. This is evidenced by the fact that in (976), *kenē* takes the the (nominal) focus clitic *=si*, and in (977), it takes the (verbal) hortative suffix *-nāng*.

(976) *kenē* 'hesitation' with realis focus =*si*
  [...] lapenke haladak... kelecheng nelitum, **kenesi**
  lapèn=ke háladāk [ke-lè-chéng   ne-li-tūm]
  and=TOP   there   NMLZ-reach-for.first.time 1EXCL-HON-PL
  [kenē=si
  HESIT=FOC:RL

  kelang...la kosonloma... festival aground
  ke-làng]   [là   kosón-lò=ma] [festival a-ground
  NMLZ-see   this how-RL=Q   festival   POSS-ground

  along lele ako abángke...
  alòng lè-Cē   akó   abàng=ke]
  LOC   reach-NEG   before NPDL=TOP
  '[...] [A]nd then, there... the place where we reached first, I mean, we saw...
  how was it, before we reached the festival grounds...' [SiT, HF 026]

(977) *kenē* 'hesitation' with -*nāng* 'hortative'
  anke pinike <the> kenenang bong tharve
  ánke   pinì=ke   <thē> **kene-nāng**   bōng   tharvē
  and.then   today=TOP fruit **HESIT-HORT** younger.sibling:VOC mango

  athele endamnang tharve menpiklo
  a-thē=lè   ēn-dām-nāng   tharvē mèn-pìk-lò
  POSS-fruit=FOC:IRR take-go-HORT mango   be.ready.to.eat-very-RL

  pusi pu tangho tharve athe endamnang
  pusi   pù   tànghò tharvē a-thē   ēn-dām-nāng
  QUOT.COMP   say REP   mango   POSS-fruit   take-GO-HORT
  'And then, "today, younger brother, let's, let's go and get mangos, the
  mangos are very ripe", (the older brother) said, "Let's go and get mangos!"'
  [KTa, TCS 041]

Karbi has borrowed the Assamese hesitation word *mane*. An example of *mane* used in Karbi is (978). Here the speaker apparently is trying to remember the word for 'hill field' while saying *mane*, then just uses a descriptive possessive construction, then says *kopunelo* 'what do you call it?', but still does not remember and leaves it at that.

(978) Hesitation marker *mane* (<Assamese)
  mane *hu inglong aritsi elitum*
  mane   hú   inglóng a-rīt=si   e-li-tūm
  I.mean(<ASM) over.there hill   POSS-field=FOC:RL 1PL.INCL-HON-PL

> *kopunelo la inglong arit panpó*
> ko-pu-nē-lò   là   inglóng a-rīt   pān-pò
> WH-QUOT-INDEF-RL this hill POSS-field clear.vegetation-IRR1
> 'I mean... up there on the fields on the hill, what do you call it? We clear the vegetation from the hill fields.' [SiH, KH 002]

16.6.2 Correction words *chē* and *bá* (<Assamese)

When a speaker accidentally uses a word or misconstructs an entire phrase, the normal way to correct oneself is to use *chē* and then say what was intended. In (979), the speaker accidentally says *thàk* 'answer', then realizes that was not the intended verb of saying, so she says *chē* and then corrects herself and uses the intended *pinkhát* 'advise' with the realis suffix *-lò*.

(979) Corrective marker *chē* after using *thàk* 'answer' instead of *pinkhát* 'advise'
ne nangchethondunpo pusi methan-sibongpo
[[nè   nang=che-thōn-dūn-pò]   pusi   methān-sibóngpō
1EXCL 1/2:NSUBJ=RR-drop-join-IRR1 QUOT.COMP dog-SPECIES

*thak **che** pinkhatlo*
thàk   **chē**   pinkhát-lò
answer **I.mean** advise-RL
'"I will drop you home", the dog answered, I mean, advised.' [KK, BMS 090]

Similarly in (980), the speaker wants to say that those people of a particular clan, who are not allowed to touch a pestle due to a type of curse but do so, will violate a cultural code and therefore be punished by the common consequence of such behavior, which is to be eaten by a tiger. Instead of just saying 'tiger', however, the speaker intends to use a conventional euphemism: 'the one who does not have a headstrap' (because tigers do not carry baskets on their back). The speaker makes a mistake and makes the *avē* 'not exist' the main verb instead of nominalizing it in order for it to go inside the relative clause to qualify the tiger as the one who does not have a headstrap. She says *chē*, and then corrects herself and nominalizes *avē* and adds the correct main verb *pondetji*.

(980) Corrective marker *chē* after making a mistake in constructing the sentence
bang thap ketok alengpum otdunlote
[bàng   thàp   ke-tòk   a-lengpūm
CLF:HUM:PL cake.for.rice.beer NMLZ-pound POSS-pestle
ót-dùn-lò-tē]
touch-along-RL-COND

ekene Karbi atum kipu asingnam avedetji
ekenē [Karbì a-tūm ke-pù a-singnām [avē-dèt-jí
HESIT PN POSS-PL NMLZ-say POSS-head.strap not.exist-PFV-IRR2

che asingnam kave pondetji pu ekene
chē] a-singnām ke-avē pòn-dèt-jí pu ekenē
I.mean POSS-head.strap NMLZ-not.exist take.away-PFV-IRR2 QUOT HESIT

teke pondetji tangho
teké pòn-dèt-jí tànghò
tiger take.away-PFV-IRR2 REP
'If somebody touches the pestle used for pounding the rice for the rice beer cake, um, then what the Karbis call the one won't have a headstrap, I mean, the one that doesn't have a head strap will take him away, um, (i.e.) the tiger will take him away, it is said.' [WR, BCS 036]

Finally, another correction word that is used is *bá*, which, like *mane*, is a borrowing from Assamese. Ironically, the speaker uses the Assamese borrowing *bá* in (981) after noticing that he used an Assamese word, *gáonburá* 'village head man' instead of the native Karbi equivalent *sarthè*.

(981) Corrective *bá* (<Assamese) after unintentional use of an Assamese borrowing
aphrang ahut... inut arong agaonbura
a-phráng ahūt e-nūt a-ròng
POSS-front during one-CLF:HUM:SG POSS-village
a-gáonburá
POSS-village.headman(<Asm)

ba arong asarthelo
bá a-ròng a-sarthè-lò
I.mean(<ASM) POSS-village POSS-village.headman-RL
'A long time ago, there was one village *gaonbura*, I mean, one village headman.' [CST, RO 003]

Appendix A

Abbreviations

(kd)	a kind of
<Asm	from Assamese
<Eng	from English
<Ind	from Indic
<Khs	from Khasi
<Pnr	from Pnar
1/2/3	first/second/third person
A	'agent-like' argument of transitive clause
ADD	additive focus (=tā)
ADV	adverbial
AFF	affirmative
ASSUM	assumption
CAUS	causative (pe-~pa-)
CC	complement clause
CG	common ground (=matî)
CIS	cislocative (nang=)
CLF	classifier
COLL	collective
COMP	complementizer
COMPAR	comparative
COMPL	completive
CON	conative
COND	conditional (-te)
CONT	continuative (-bōm)
COP	copula
DEM	demonstrative
DIM	diminutive (-sō)
DISAGR	disagreement
DISTR	distributive
DM	discourse marker
DSM	discourse section marker
DUBIT	dubitative
EE	elaborate expression
EMPH	emphatic
EQU	equational
EXCL	exclusive
EXCLAM	exclamative
EXH	exhaustive
FEM	female
FOC	focus
FRML	formal
GENEX	general extender
GO	grammaticalized 'go'
HESIT	hesitation word
HON	honorific

HORT	hortative
IMP	imperative
INCL	inclusive
INDIR	indirect
INFRML	informal
INTENS	intensifier
INTERACT	interactive
INTERJ	interjection
IRR	irrealis
IRR1	irrealis1 (*-pò*)
IRR2	irrealis2 (*-jî*)
ITER	iterative
ITROG	interrogative
JOIN	grammaticalized 'join'
LOC	locative
LV	light verb
MODIF	modifier
NEG	negative
NF	non-final
NMLZ	nominalizer
NPDL	noun phrase delimiter
NSUBJ	non-subject
NUM	numeral
O	'other' argument of transitive clause
PCT	property concept term
PFV	perfective
PRF	perfect (*-ét*)
PL	plural
POSD	possessed
POSR	possessor
POSS	possessive
PRL	parallel
PROH	prohibitive
PURP	purpose
Q	question particle
Q.TAG	question tag
QUOT	quotative (*pu*)
RC	relative clause
RDL	right dislocation
REP	reportative (*tànghò*)
RL	realis (*-lò*)
RR	reflexive/reciprocal
S	single argument of intransitive clause
SG	singular
SPLT	superlative
TOP	topic
TS	topic-switch
UNCOND	unconditional
VOC	vocative

Appendix B

Folk story: Chonghokaloso lapen Misorongpo (RBT, ChM)

This folk story is about a chain reaction of events that sets off when a frog blocks the road and sits down on an ant that in turn bites the frog; from there on, one animal suffers from being disturbed or hurt by another animal, and as a consequence accidentally disturbs or hurts another animal, and so on: the ant disturbs the frog, the frog disturbs the squirrel, the squirrel disturbs the pig, the pig disturbs the bird, the bird disturbs the elephant, the elephant kicks a rock, which then kills the daughter of the king. The king traces back the chain reaction to the frog and the ant, and punishes both of them.

The audio file for the entire text RBT, ChM is available at https://scholarsbank. uoregon.edu/xmlui/handle/1794/13657.

<nelike...> nelimenke Rongbang Teron,
<nè-lì-ke...>   ne-li-mén=ke   Ròngbàng Terón
1EXCL-HON=TOP 1EXCL:POSS-HON-name=TOP NAME   CLAN

motiyar <arpu>, kedoke Ujandongka Teron arong
motíyár   <arpū>   ke-dō=ke   Ujándongká Terón a-ròng
OFFICER   responsibility NMLZ-stay=TOP   VILLAGE   CLAN   POSS-village
'I... my name is Rongbang Teron, I have the responsibility of a *Motiyar*, (where) I live (is) Ujandongka, Teron Village.' [RBT, ChM 002]

choklemdun habe bangphli aso;
[cho-klém-dùn   habē   bàng-phlī   a-sō]
AUTO.BEN/MAL-do-JOIN headman.assistant   CLF:HUM:PL-four   POSS-child

habe bangphli atum alongsi, nem chodun
[[habē   bàng-phlī   a-tūm   alòng=si]   [ném   chō-dūn]
headman.assistant   CLF:HUM:PL-four   POSS-PL   LOC=FOC:RL custom eat-JOIN

rakom chodun ajor chodun akri chodun
[rakóm   chō-dūn]   [a-jòr   chō-dūn]   [a-krì   chō-dūn]]
EE:ném eat-JOIN   POSS-slice.of.meat   eat-JOIN   POSS-EE:jòr   eat-JOIN
'Working together, there are children of four *Habe* (in this area), (together) with the four *Habe*, we accept the responsibility of this post (lit. eat the customs), we carry out the rituals (lit. eat together the long slices of meat).' [RBT, ChM 003]

matsi ajor akri pinchongma lake chu
[māt=si   a-jòr   a-krì   pinchóng=ma] [là=ke   chú]
who=FOC:RL POSS-slice.of.meat POSS-EE:jòr   create=Q   this=TOP long.ago

Socheng Rengbonghompensi bang habe atum haren
Sochēng Rengbonghōm=pen=si bàng   habē   a-tūm   harēn
VILLAGE   NAME=from=FOC:RL   somebody   headman.assistant   POSS-PL   EE:habē

atum... e kethe atum kiding atum
a-tūm   e   ke-thè   a-tūm   ke-dīng   a-tūm
POSS-PL   DSM   NMLZ-be.big POSS-PL   NMLZ-be.long POSS-PL

solangdo arnam pharo atumsi bang ajor
solangdō   arnàm   pharó   a-tūm=si   bàng   a-jòr
four.chieftains(<Khs) god   hundred POSS-PL=FOC:RL   CLF   POSS-slice.of.meat

pinchongkang akri pinchongkang
pinchóng-káng   a-krì   pinchóng-káng
create-give.leave   POSS-EE:jòr   create-give.leave
'Who has established these customs of *Ajor Akri*? It was, long ago, from (the time of) *Socheng Rengbonghom* that the *Habe* and *Haren*, the dignitaries (lit. the big and long ones), the four chieftains, the hundred gods established the *Ajor* and established the *Akri*.' [RBT, ChM 004]

lasi ajor chodun akri chodun
lasì   a-jòr   chō-dūn   a-krì   chō-dūn
therefore   POSS-slice.of.meat   eat-JOIN   POSS-EE:jòr eat-JOIN
'That way, we carry out the rituals (lit. eat the *Ajor* and eat the *Akri*).' [RBT, ChM 005]

nelilam nelitomoke lapuhelo; tomo
[ne-li-lám   ne-li-tomó=ke   lapù-heló]   [tomó
1EXCL:POSS-HON-word   1EXCL:POSS-HON-story=TOP   like.this-RL:EMPH story

thannangji pulotangte, tomoke...
thán-náng-jí   pùlotángtē]   [tomó=ke
tell-need-IRR2   if   story=TOP
'My topic, my story is like this, if I should tell a story, the story...' [RBT, ChM 006]

puhelo, misorongpopen chongho ron kachipi atomo:
pù-heló   [misòrongpō=pen   chonghō   rón   ke-che-pí   a-tomó]
like.this-RL:EMPH   ant.sp=with   frog   fight   NMLZ-RR-give   POSS-story

arnisi
[arnì-sī]
day-one
'...(it's) like this, the story of when the ant fought with the frog, one day.' [RBT, ChM 007]

<chongh..> misorongpo atum korte banghini
<chongh..>   misòrongpō   a-tūm   kortè   bàng-hiní
<fro(g)...>   ant.sp   POSS-PL   brother   CLF-two
'There were two <fro(g)>... ant brothers.' [RBT, ChM 008]

chonghoke ejonvet misorongpoke a'ik
[chonghō=ke   e-jōn-vét]   [misòrongpō=ke   a-ìk
frog=TOP   one-CLF:animal-only   ant.sp=TOP   POSS-older.brother

atum atipi atum adappen rit damjuilo
a-tūm   a-tepī   a-tūm   a-dàp=pen   rīt   dàm-jùi-lò]
POSS-PL   POSS-elder.brother's.wife   POSS-PL   POSS-morning=from   field   go-away-RL
'The frog was alone, as for the ant, its older brother and his wife had gone to the *jhum* field in the morning.' [RBT, ChM 009]

e misorongpoke <...> a'ik aphan... an kethondam
e   misòrongpō=ke   a-ìk   a-phān   àn   ke-thòn-dām
DSM   ant.sp=TOP   POSS-older.brother   POSS-NSUBJ   rice   NMLZ-drop-GO
'The ant was on the way to take rice to its older brother.' [RBT, ChM 010]

amat horbong anbor... inghorpontanlo
amāt   hōr-bōng   àn-bòr   inghór-pòn-tàn-lò
and.then   liquor-gourd   rice-wrapped.bundle   carrying.load-take.away-S/O:big-RL

chonghokalosoke tovar dakkrang
chonghōkalósō=ke   továr   dàk-kràng
frog.sp=TOP   road   assume.spreadout.position-VSE
'And then, the ant was carrying the large liquor gourd and rice bundle, and the frog had spread out on the road (blocking the way).' [RBT, ChM 011]

ai tovar nangpektha ti ko jirpo,
ái   továr   nang=pèk-thā   ti   ko   jīrpō,
how.bad!   road   1/2:NSUBJ=give.way-IMP:CON   EMPH   buddy:VOC   friend

ne'ik atum aphan an thonji pu
ne-ìk   a-tūm   a-phān   àn   thòn-jí   pu
1EXCL:POSS-older.brother   POSS-PL   POSS-NSUBJ   rice   drop-IRR2   QUOT
'"How bad! Please do give way to me. I want to take rice to my brother (and sister-in-law)."' [RBT, ChM 012]

arvi suinangta dannokso ar'e suinangta dannokso
[arvī   sùi-nangtā   dannoksō]   [ar'ē   sùi-nangtā   dannoksō]
left   turn-if.alternatively   danger   right   turn-if.alternatively   danger
'If I turn left, it will be dangerous, if I turn right, it will also be dangerous.' [RBT, ChM 013]

la nekengdak arum lutponchoksi
[là   ne-kèng-dāk   arúm   lūt-pōn-chòk-si
this 1EXCL:POSS-foot-road.inbetween down   enter-CARRY-disappearing-NF:RL

apotlo ko mopen pu kedam
apōtlo   ko]   [mó=pen   pú   ke-dàm
should   buddy:VOC   while=from   this.side   NMLZ-go

chingkiponklung atum'anta
che-ingkī-pōn-klùng   a-tūm-án=tā]
RR-talk-CARRY-echoing.sound   POSS-PL-all=ADD
"'You should pass through between my legs, buddy, just awhile earlier, all of these people that are talking there have also gone this side.'" [RBT, ChM 014]

"bang nekengdak arumloklo kedam"
bàng   ne-kèng-dàk   arúm-lòk=lo   ke-dàm
CLF:HUM:PL   1EXCL:POSS-foot-road.inbetween down-just=FOC   NMLZ-go
"'The other people simply walked through between my legs.'" [RBT, ChM 015]

pulo akengdak arum kilut ahut amat...
pù-lo   [a-kèng-dàk   arúm   ke-lūt   ahūt   amāt]
say-RL   POSS-foot-road.inbetween down   NMLZ-enter   during   and.then

anborpenpen chongho abang ingnidunpret
àn-bòr=pén~pén   chonghō   abàng   ingnì-dūn-prèt
rice-wrapped.bundle.with~DISTR.PL frog   NPDL   sit-JOIN-acting.on.inflated.obj
'(This) the frog said, and as the ant was passing through below (the frog) between its legs, with all its rice bundles, the frog sat down (pressing down the rice bundles)' [RBT, ChM 016]

amat misorongpo abang... aning siksaklo jo an
[amāt   misòrongpō   abàng   a-nīng   siksāk-lò]   [jó]   [àn
and.then ant.sp   NPDL   POSS-mind   be.difficult-RL look!   rice

ingnipipretlo chongho ami korlut
ingnì-pī-prèt-lò]   [[chonghō   a-mí]   kòr-lùt]
sit-BEN/MAL-acting.on.inflated.obj-RL   frog   POSS-buttocks bite-enter
'And then, the ant was at a loss, look! The frog sat down on the rice bundles (to the detriment of the ant), and the ant bit the frog's butt with its teeth entering.' [RBT, ChM 017]

amat chonghota chonthap chonphrulo
amāt   chonghō=tā   chón-tháp   chón-phrú-lò
and.then   frog=ADD   jump-mindlessly   jump-EE:tháp-RL

kesolo... karlesibongpo adon chonrai
ke-sò-lò   karlēsibóng-pō   a-dón   chón-rài
NMLZ-hurt-RL   squirrel.sp-male POSS-bridge jump-solid.obj.breaking
'And then, the frog was jumping everywhere, (because) he was hurt, and he jumped on the ladder of the squirrel and it broke.' [RBT, ChM 018]

amat karlesibongpota... aning thilo: "mat
[amāt   karlēsibóng-pō=tā... a-nīng   thī-lò]   [māt
and.then   squirrel.sp-male=ADD POSS-mind   be.short-RL who

akethek mat akere mat akangtang
a-ke-thèk   māt   a-ke-rè   māt   a-ke-ingtāng
POSS-NMLZ-know.how   who   POSS-NMLZ-be.smart   who   POSS-NMLZ-be.strong

mat akangsaksi ne dondon chonraima?"
māt   a-ke-ingsàk=si   ne-dondōn   chón-rài=ma]
who   POSS-NMLZ-EE:ingtāng=FOC:RL   1EXCL-ladder jump-RES:solid.obj.breaking=Q

pu, lata
pu   là=tā
QUOT   this=ADD
'And then, the squirrel... got mad, "Who is the wise one, who is the smart one, who is the strong and mighty one, who jumped on my ladder so it broke?", it (the squirrel) (said).' [RBT, ChM 019]

aning kithi, thengpi arongtin thengphrang
[a-nīng   ke-thī]   [thengpī   a-rōng-tín   thēngphráng
POSS-mind   NMLZ-be.short   tree/wood   POSS-CLF:plant-each   EE:thengpī

arongtin rikang asitin rotthap
a-rōng-tín   rikāng   a-sī-tín   ròt-tháp
POSS-CLF:plant-each   creeper   POSS-one-each   cut-mindlessly

rotphrulo, hanthar athe rotpet
ròt-phrú-lò]   [hanthàr   a-thē   ròt-pèt]
cut-EE:tháp-RL   vegetable.sp   POSS-fruit   cut-RES:cut.off
'(The squirrel) was mad, and then, (it) gnawed each tree and creeper, and it gnawed off the *Hanthar* fruit.' [RBT, ChM 020]

phakbelengpi amoi peklodup
phàkbeléngpī   a-mòi   pe-kló-dùp
pig.sp   POSS-back   CAUS-fall-falling.sound.from.high.solid.obj
'It made it (the fruit) fall down onto the back of a pig.' [RBT, ChM 021]

mat laso aphakta kathirikpenlo, lata
māt   [lasō   a-phàk=tā   ke-thirík-pen-lò],   [là=tā
and.then this   POSS-pig=ADD   NMLZ-startle-NF:with-RL   this=ADD

timurthap timurphru, lobong timurphlut, vo'arbipi
timùr-tháp   timùr-phrú],   [lobōng   timùr-phlùt]   [võ'arbí-pī
root-mindlessly root-EE:tháp   plantain   root-miss/fail   bird.sp-female

atar saprai, an aso
a-tār   sáp-rài]   [án   a-sō
POSS-nest beat.w/sth.flexible-solid.obj.breaking that.much POSS-child

joningkoi jonthomkep kedoji, lata
jōn-ingkòi   jōn-thòm-kēp   ke-dō-jí   [là=tā
CLF:animal-twenty CLF:animal-three-ten NMLZ-exist-IRR2 this=ADD

aso kaluksonlo
a-sō   ke-luksón-lò
POSS-child NMLZ-lose(<Asm)-RL

'And then, (as a consequence) this pig startled and then it also was lifting up things with its snout here and there, and then it lifted and uprooted the plantain plant with its snout, (the plantain plant) beat (i.e., hit as it fell down) the nest of the *Vo'arbipi* and then there will be many offspring (lit. 20, 30), as for this one (the *Vo'arbipi*), its offspring were also lost.' [RBT, ChM 022]

amatsi voarbipita... aning chipithithudet
amātsi   võarbí-pī=tā...   a-nīng   che-pa-thī-thū-dét
and.then bird.sp-female=ADD POSS-mind RR-CAUS-be.short-again-PFV

lutthap lutphru, arkethap arkephru amat
lūt-tháp   lūt-phrú   arkè-tháp   arkè-phrú   amāt
enter-mindlessly enter-EE:tháp scratch-mindlessly scratch-EE:tháp and.then
'And so the *Vo'arbipi* in turn got mad, it entered here and there and scratched around here and there, and then.' [RBT, ChM 023]

ingnar nothongpo ano lutchok arkevaret
[[ingnàr   nothōng-pō] a-nò]   lūt-chòk   arkè-varèt
elephant deaf-MODIF POSS-ear enter-disappearing scratch-INTENS
'(The bird) got into the ears of a deaf elephant, and scratched around.' [RBT, ChM 024]

angnarta kangrong ajat, <ku> turthap
a-ingnàr=tā   ke-ingròng   aját   <ku>   túr-tháp
POSS-elephant=ADD NMLZ-roar GENEX <ku> kick-mindlessly

turphrulo... harlong turpur
túr-phrú-lò   harlōng túr-pùr
kick-EE:-tháp-RL stone   kick-move.over
'This elephant was roaring and everything and kicked around mindlessly, and kicked over a rock.' [RBT, ChM 025]

harlong turpurlo, aharlong ingplonglo, richo
[harlōng túr-pùr-lò],   [a-harlōng   ingplòng-lò],   [richó
stone   kick-move.over-RL   POSS-stone   run.away.animal-RL king

asopi abang ha langhe lang kachinglu...
a-oso-pì   abàng há   lānghē   lāng   ke-chinglú]
POSS-child-female   NPDL   over.there washing.place   water   NMLZ-take.bath

amat lang kachinglu ketangpen kevang amat richo
[amāt   lāng   ke-chinglú   ke-tāng-pen   ke-vàng   amāt   richó
and.then water   NMLZ-take.bath   NMLZ-finish-NF:with NMLZ-come   and.then king

asopi aphan baplam
a-oso-pì   a-phān   báp-làm]
POSS-child-female   POSS-NSUBJ   press.down-RES:paste.like
'(The elephant) kicked the stone, the stone rolled away, the daughter of the king was taking a bath there at the washing place, and then after having finished taking her bath, (she) was coming (home), and then (the stone) roled over the king's daughter pressing on her.' [RBT, ChM 026]

amat "an arni tiliphak potsi
amāt   [[án   arnì   tilí-phák   pōt=si
and.then   that.much   sun   decline-almost.completely reason=FOC:RL

neso langhe kedam vangverekma?" pulo richo,
[ne-osō   lānghē   ke-dàm]   vàng-Cē-rèk=ma]   pù-lò   richó]
1EXCL:POSS-child   washing.place   NMLZ-go   come-NEG-late=Q   say-RL   king

donsuri arat chingthumdunlo...,
[dón-surí   a-rát   che-ingthùm-dūn-lò]
CLF:household-thousand   POSS-public(<Asm)   RR-go.and.bring-JOIN-RL

harlong baplam
harlōng báp-làm
stone   press.down-RES:paste.like
'And then, "Even though it's already past mid-day (lit. the sun has almost set), why has my child having gone to the washing place still not come back?",said the king and all the subjects joined (him) to go and bring (the king's daughter)... and (she) was flattened by the stone.' [RBT, ChM 027]

amat harlong aphan arjulo, "Kopisi nang
[amāt   harlōng a-phān   arjū-lò] [kopīsi nàng
and.then stone   POSS-NSUBJ   ask-RL   why   2

nesopi aphan kipithima?", "O, ne
ne-oso-pì   a-phān   ke-pV-thì=ma]   [o   nè
1EXCL:POSS-child-female   POSS-NSUBJ   NMLZ-CAUS-die=Q   SURPRISE   1EXCL

kali."
kalī]
NEG.EQU.COP
'And then (the kind) asked the stone, "For what possible reason did you kill my daughter?", "Oh it wasn't me!"' [RBT, ChM 028]

"komatlo tangte"
komāt=lo   tángtē
who=FOC   if
'"Who then?"' [RBT, ChM 029]

"ingnar nothongposi bang nemi
[ingnàr   nothōng-pō=si   bàng   ne-mí
elephant   deaf-MODIF=FOC:RL   CLF   1EXCL:POSS-buttocks

netimurphit, amat neta neri
ne=timùr-phìt]   [amāt   nè=tā   ne-rí
1EXCL:NSUBJ=root-w/sudden.movement   and.then   1EXCL=ADD   1EXCL:POSS-hand

nekeng ave, pulo neta ave
avē   ne-kèng   avē]   [pù=lo   nè=tā
not.exist   1EXCL:POSS-foot   not.exist like.this=FOC   1EXCL=ADD

vangnangkoklo"
vàng-náng-kòk-lò]
come-must-absolutely.required-RL
'"The deaf elephant lifted up my butt, and then also, I don't have hands or feet and like this, I had to come (rolling)."' [RBT, ChM 030]

"amat nangso doke chinilo neta chekhang'un'e
amāt   nang-osō   dō=ke   chiní-lo   nè=tā   che-kháng-ùn-Cē
and.then   2POSS-child   exist=TOP   know-RL   1EXCL=ADD   RR-keep-be.able-NEG

amatsi nangso apran enlongbinlo"
amātsi   nang-osō   a-prán   ēn-lōng-bìn-lò
and.then   2:POSS-child   POSS-life   take-GET-unintentionally-RL
'And then, I knew your child was there, but I couldn't control myself and then I unintentionally took your daughter's life.' [RBT, ChM 031]

"matlo ante kechokcheke?", <*"o ha ingnar*
[māt=lo   ánte   ke-chók-Cē=ke]   [ó   há   <ingnàr
who=FOC OK.then NMLZ-be.fine-NEG=TOP INTERJ over.there elephant

nothongpole"> ingnar nothongpo aphan arjudamlo
nothōng-pō=le>   [ingnàr   nothōng-pō   a-phān]   arjū-dām-lò]
deaf- MODIF =FOC:IRR   elephant   deaf- MODIF   POSS-NSUBJ   ask-GO-RL

'"Who then is the guilty one?", o there <the deaf elephant> he went to ask the deaf elephant.' [RBT, ChM 032]

"pi chonghoisi nang harlongle <nang>
[pí   chonghói=si   nàng   harlōng=le   <nang>
what   reason=FOC:RL   you   stone=FOC:IRR   your

kiturnek kiturnok? Neso apran
ke-túr-nèk   ke-túr-nòk]   [ne-osō   a-prán
NMLZ-kick-doing.bad.unnecessarily   NMLZ-kick-EE:-nèk   1EXCL:POSS-child   POSS-life

damjuilo, pinike nangpran damji nangmui
dàm-jùi-lò]   pinì=ke   nang-prán   dàm-jí   nang-múi
go-away-RL   today=TOP   2:POSS-life   go-IRR2   2:POSS-EE:prán(<Ind)

damji, <nangsapdamji>
dàm-jí]   <nang=sáp-dàm-jí>
go-IRR2   1/2:NSUBJ=beat.w/sth.flexible-go-IRR2

nangsapji nangthengji!"
nang=sáp-jí   nang=thèng-jí
1/2:NSUBJ=beat.w/sth.flexible-IRR2   1/2:NSUBJ=beat.w/sth.solid-IRR2

'"What did you kick the rock for? The life of my daughter is gone, today your life will definitely go, I will beat the hell out of you!" [RBT, ChM 033]

pulo ingnar nothongpo chethakdunlo, "o bang
pù-lò   [ingnàr   nothōng-pō   che-thāk-dūn-lò]   [o   bàng
say-RL   elephant deaf- MODIF   RR-answer-JOIN-RL   VOC   CLF

voarbipi, akam kechomathale neno
võarbípī   a-kám   ke-chomathā=le   ne-nò
bird.sp   POSS-work   NMLZ-think.with.bad.intentions=FOC:IRR   1EXCL:POSS-ear

nanglutchok nangarkerakrakdetkema?"
nang=lūt-chòk   nang=arkè-ràk~ràk-dèt=ke=ma]
CIS=enter-disappearing   CIS=scratch-RES:little.wound~DISTR.PL-PFV=TOP=Q

'He said (this) and the deaf elephant answered, "O Voarbipi, what were you thinking, coming into my ears and scratching and wounding me?!"' [RBT, ChM 034]

amat "neta dothekthe sangthekthelo,
amāt [nè=tā dō-thèk-Cē sáng-thèk-Cē-lò]
and.then 1EXCL=ADD stay-know.how-NEG take.rest-know.how-NEG-RL

neno kangthak neno kangthong amat neta
[ne-nò ke-ingthàk ne-nò ke-ingthōng] amāt [nè=tā
1EXCL:POSS-ear NMLZ-itch 1EXCL:POSS-ear NMLZ-be.deaf and.then 1EXCL=ADD

turthap turphrulo, ahoklo, neke harlong
túr-tháp túr-phrú-lò] [a-hōk-lò] [nè=ke harlōng
kick-mindlessly kick-EE:tháp-RL POSS-truth-RL 1EXCL=TOP stone

turpurlo"
túr-pùr-lò]
kick-move.over-RL
'And then, "I also didn't know how to stay or how to rest, my ears were itching, my ears are deaf, and then I was kicking here and there, and it's true, and I kicked the rock."' [RBT, ChM 035]

ha nangso aphan rodamji marek pupe
há nang-osō a-phān rō-dām-jí marēk pu-Cē
over.there 2:POSS-child POSS-NSUBJ hit-GO-IRR2 unexpectedly QUOT-NEG
'Over there (the stone) went and unintentionally hit your child.' [RBT, ChM 036]

"Apot nele kechokche kali, richo. Hala
[apōt nè=le ke-chók-Cē kalī richó] [[hála
because 1EXCL=FOC:IRR NMLZ-be.fine-NEG NEG.EQU.COP king that

vo'arbipi aphanle arjudamnoi!"
vōarbí-pī a-phān=le] arjū-dām-nōi]
bird.sp-female POSS-NSUBJ=FOC:IRR ask-go-INFRML.COND.IMP
'"Therefore, I'm not the guilty one, king, go ask that *Voarbipi*!"' [RBT, ChM 037]

voarbipi along richo atum damlilo
[vōarbí-pī a-lòng] [richó a-tūm] dàm-lì-lò
bird.sp-female POSS-LOC king POSS-PL go-again-RL
'The people of the king in turn (lit. 'again') went to the *Voarbipi*.' [RBT, ChM 038]

"O voarbipi, nangbang doma?", pulo, "Do."
o vōarbí-pī nang-bàng dō=ma pù-lò dō
VOC bird.sp-female 2:POSS-body stay=Q say-RL stay
'"O *Voarbipi*, are you there?", (the king and his people) said, "(I) am (here)".' [RBT, ChM 039]

"Piloma richo?" "Richo kali! Pisi nang ingnar
[pílo=ma richó]   [richó kalī]   [pīsi nàng ingnàr
what=Q   king   king   NEG.EQU.COP why you   elephant

nothongpo ano lutchokmati? Nang pinike
nothōng-pō a-nò   lūt-chòk=mati]   [nàng pinì=ke
deaf- MODIF POSS-ear enter-disappearing=CG   you   today=TOP

nangpran damji nangmui damji!"
nang-prán dàm-jí nang-múi   dàm-jí]
2:POSS-life go-IRR2 2:POSS-EE:prán(<Ind) go-IRR2
'"What's the matter, king?", "(It's) not (about calling me the) king! Why the heck did you get into the elephant's ear? Today your life will go!"' [RBT, ChM 040]

"Ai richo, nepran nangenri nemui
ái   richó ne-prán   nang=ēn-rī   ne-múi
how.bad! king   1EXCL:POSS-life 1/2:NSUBJ=take-PROH 1EXCL:POSS-EE:prán(<Ind)

nangenri"
nang=ēn-rī
1/2:NSUBJ=take-PROH
'"Oh no, king, don't take my life!"' [RBT, ChM 041]

"pisi ne ingnar nothongpo ano lutledetjima?"
pīsi nè   ingnàr   nothōng-pō a-nò   lūt-Cē-dèt-jí=ma
why   1EXCL elephant deaf- MODIF POSS-ear enter-NEG-PFV-IRR2=Q
'"How could I've not entered into the deaf elephant's ears?"' [RBT, ChM 042]

Neso tangte avelo, nesu tangte avelo.
[ne-osō   tángtē avē-lò   ne-sū   tángtē avē-lò]
1EXCL:POSS-child TOP   not.exist-RL 1EXCL:POSS-grandchild TOP   not.exist-RL

Nangso kithike enutnat, nesoke
nang-osō   ke-thì=ke   e-nūt-nàt   ne-osō=ke
2:POSS-child   NMLZ-die=TOP   one-CLF.hum.one-only   1EXCL:POSS-child=TOP

bangthrok phosi kithi.
bàng-thrōk phō=si   ke-thì
CLF-six   five=FOC:RL   NMLZ-die
'I don't have any children anymore, no grandchildren anymore. Only one child of yours has died (lit. as for your children that have died, it is just a single one), but of mine, so many (lit. six, five) have died.' [RBT, ChM 043]

"laso alobongle netar
[lasō   a-lobòng=le   ne-tār
this   POSS-plantain=FOC:IRR   1EXCL:POSS-nest

sapraike, jo!, lobong aphanle
sáp-rài=ke]   jó   [lobōng   a-phān=le
beat.w/sth.flexible-solid.obj.breaking=TOP look! plantain POSS-NSUBJ=FOC:IRR

arjudamnoi, richo, nangmasi!"
arjū-dām-nōi,   richó]   nàng-masi
ask-go-INF.COND.IMP king   you-the.only.one
'"(It's because) this plantain destroyed my nest, look! Go and ask the plantain, King! You're the only one (who can settle this issue)!"' [RBT, ChM 044]

mat richo atum <che> damthulelo, lobong along,
māt   richó   a-tūm   dàm-thū-lè-lò,   lobōng   a-lòng,
and.then king   POSS-PL   go-again-again-RL plantain   POSS-LOC
'And so, the king and his people went again, to the plantain.' [RBT, ChM 045]

"O lobong, chonghoisi nang... voarbipi atar
o   lobōng,   chonghói=si   nàng...   võarbí-pī   a-tār
VOC plantain   reason=FOC:RL   2   bird.sp-female   POSS-nest

kesapraimati? Nangpran damji,
ke-sáp-rài=mati   nang-prán   dàm-jí
NMLZ-beat.w/sth.flexible-solid.obj.breaking=CG   2:POSS-life go-IRR2

nangmui damji, nangjat nangkhong
nang-múi   dàm-jí   nang-ját   nang-khóng
2:POSS-EE:prán(<Ind) go-IRR2   2:POSS-type   2:POSS-tribe

nangpavir'etji. Sala!", Therdamlo.
nang=pa-vír-èt-jí   sala   thér-dàm-lò
1/2:NSUBJ=CAUS-lose-all-IRR2   damn.you!   threaten-GO-RL
'"O plantain, why the heck did you destroy the nest of the *Vo'arbipi*, your life will go, I will destroy your tribe and your species, damn you!", (he) went and threatened (the plantain).' [RBT, ChM 046]

lobong chethakdunlo
lobōng   che-thāk-dūn-lò
plantain   RR-answer-JOIN-RL
'The plantain answered.' [RBT, ChM 047]

"Ai! Ne kali, richo"
ái   nè   kalī   richó
how.bad! 1EXCL NEG.EQU.COP   king
'"Oh, it wasn't me, king!"' [RBT, ChM 048]

"phakbelengpisi nemi nangtimurphlut"
phàkbeléngpī=si   ne-mí   nang=timùr-phlùt
pig.sp=FOC:RL   1EXCL:POSS-buttocks   1/2:NSUBJ=root-quickly:bad
'"The pig had just like that uprooted my butt with its snout."' [RBT, ChM 049]

"amatsi neta dothekthedetlo, neta
amātsi   [nè=tā   dō-thèk-Cē-dèt-lò]   [nè=tā
and.then 1EXCL=ADD stay-know.how-NEG-PFV-RL   1EXCL=ADD

ingnilun anat"
ingnì-lùn   a-nàt]
sit-big:AO:not.suddenly   POSS-only
'"And then, I also couldn't stay still, I also just sat down big as I am."' [RBT, ChM 050]

"amat ahoklo, voarbipi atar do marek
amāt   a-hōk-lò   vōarbí-pī   a-tār   dō
and.then POSS-truth-RL bird.sp-female POSS-nest exist
marēk
unintentionally/unexpectedly

chinine amat neke kreprailo"
chinī-Cē   amāt   [nè=ke   krēp-rài-lò]
know-NEG   and.then   1EXCL=TOP   fall.over-solid.obj.breaking-RL
'"And then it's the truth, I had no idea it was the *Vo'arbipi's* nest, and then I fell over (and the nest) was destroyed."' [RBT, ChM 051]

"pot nele kechokche kali. Phakbelengpi
pōt   [nè=le   ke-chók-Cē   kalī]   [phàkbeléngpī
reason   1EXCL=FOC:IRR   NMLZ-be.fine-NEG NEG.EQU.COP   pig.sp

aphanle... arjudamnoi, nangmasi!", pulelo
a-phān=le   arjū-dām-nōi]   nàng-masi   pù-lè-lò
POSS-NSUBJ=FOC:IRR   ask-go-INF.COND.IMP   2-the.only.one   say-again-RL
'"Therefore, I'm not the guilty one. Go and ask the pig, you're the only one (who can ask and find out)!" he also said.' [RBT, ChM 052]

so aricho thakthak charjudamthulelo..., "O phakbelengpi"
sō   a-richó   thàkthāk   che-arjū-dām-thū-lì-lò...,   ó   phàkbeléngpī
this   POSS-king   same   RR-ask-go-again-again-RL   VOC   pig.sp
'So this king, all the same, again went to ask in this matter of his own, "O Phakbelengpi!"' [RBT, ChM 053]

"Pinike, nangjat nangkhong nangpivir'etji, sala!
pinì=ke   nang-ját   nang-khóng   nang=pi-vír-èt-jí   sala
today=TOP   2:POSS-type   2:POSS-tribe   1/2:NSUBJ=CAUS-lose-PFT-IRR2   damn.you!

Nangpithitheiji!"
nang=pi-thì-théi-jí
1/2:NSUBJ=CAUS-die-all:S/O-IRR2
'"Today, I will destroy your tribe and kind, damn you! I will kill all of you!"' [RBT, ChM 054]

"Nangtum kopisi lobong katimurthap katimurphru? <ar>
[nang-tūm kopīsi lobōng ke-timùr-tháp   ke-timùr-phrú]
2:POSS-PL why   plantain NMLZ-root-mindlessly NMLZ-root-EE:tháp

Vo'arbipi atar kesaprai athema!"
[võarbí-pī   a-tār   ke-sáp-rài   athēma]
bird.sp-female POSS-nest NMLZ-beat.w/sth.flexible-solid.obj.breaking because
'"Why do you (pigs) go around lifiting up plantains here and there? That's why you destroyed the nest of the *Vo'arbipi*."' [RBT, ChM 055]

"Ai! Ne kali, richo"
ái   nè   kalī   richó
how.bad! 1EXCL NEG.EQU.COP king
'"Oh, it wasn't me, king!"' [RBT, ChM 056]

"bang hantharsi nemoi nangklodup,
[bàng hanthàr=si   ne-mòi   nang=kló-dùp]
CLF   vegetable.sp=FOC:RL 1EXCL:POSS-back   CIS=fall-falling.from.high:solid.obj

neta keso kasiksaksi"
[nè=tā   ke-sò   ke-siksāk-si]
1EXCL=ADD NMLZ-hurt   NMLZ-be.difficult-NF:RL
'A *hanthar* fruit fell on my back, so I was hurt and disturbed.' [RBT, ChM 057]

"ahoklo neta timurthap timurphru amat
a-hōk-lò   nè=tā   timùr-tháp   timùr-phrú   amāt
POSS-truth-RL   1EXCL=ADD root-mindlessly   root-EE:tháp   and.then

ahok, lobong timurpur"
a-hōk   lobōng   timùr-pùr
POSS-truth   plantain root-move.over
'"It's the truth, I was lifting up things with my snout, and then (it's) the truth, I uprooted the plantain."' [RBT, ChM 058]

<...> *"hanthar aphan arjudamnoi!"*
hanthàr   a-phān   arjū-dām-nōi
vegetable.sp POSS-NSUBJ   ask-go-INF.COND.IMP
'"Go and ask the *Hanthar*!"' [RBT, ChM 059]

ha hanthar aphan arjudamlo... "Kopisi nang
há   hanthàr   a-phān   arjū-dām-lò   kopīsi   nàng
over.there vegetable.sp POSS-NSUBJ ask-go-RL   why   2

phakbelengpi amoi klodupmati, hanthar?"
phàkbeléngpī   a-mòi   kló-dùp=mati   hanthàr
pig.sp   POSS-back   fall-falling.sound.from.high.solid.obj=CG   vegetable.sp
'There to the hanthar he went and asked, "Why did you possibly fall down on the back of the pig, *Hanthar*?"' [RBT, ChM 060]

"nangrong nangrim nangpiviretji, sala!"
nang-rōng   nang-rīm   nang=pi-vír-èt-jí   sala
2:POSS-plant   2:POSS-EE:rōng   1/2:NSUBJ=CAUS-lose-all:S/O-IRR2 damn.you!
'"I will destroy your stem and everything (i.e., your species), damn you!"' [RBT, ChM 061]

"Ai richo, nejat nepivirri, nekhong
ái   richó   ne-ját   ne=pi-vír-rī,   ne-khóng
how.bad!   king   1EXCL:POSS-type 1EXCL:NSUBJ=CAUS-lose-PROH 1EXCL:POSS-tribe

nepivirri!"
ne=pi-vír-rī
1EXCL:NSUBJ=CAUS-lose-PROH
'"O king, don't kill the ones of my kind, don't kill my tribe!"' [RBT, ChM 062]

"nele kechokche kali. Ne neri
[nè=le   ke-chók-Cē   kalī]   nè   ne-rí
1EXCL=FOC:IRR   NMLZ-be.fine-NEG   NEG.EQU.COP   1EXCL   1EXCL:POSS-hand

ehongvetsi chiripling anat"
e-hòng-vét=si   che-ríp-lìng   a-nàt]
one-CLF:long.cylindrical-only=FOC:RL RR-hold.firmly-sth.small.hanging   POSS-only
'"I'm not the guilty one, I was just holding myself with one hand only."' [RBT, ChM 063]

"karlesibongpo abang neri nangrotpet amat
[karlēsibóng-pō   abàng   ne-rí   nang=ròt-pèt]
squirrel.sp-male   NPDL   1EXCL:POSS-hand   1/2:NSUBJ=cut-sd.of.resulting.event
amāt
and.then

neta ahoklo phakbelengpi amoi
[nè=tā   a-hōk-lò   phàkbeléngpī   a-mòi
1EXCL=ADD   POSS-truth-RL   pig.sp   POSS-back

chonduplo"
chón-dùp-lò]
jump-falling.from.high:solid.obj-RL
"'The squirrel gnawed off my hands and then, as for me also it's true, I jumped on the pig's back.'" [RBT, ChM 064]

apot nangle arjudamnoi, ha karlesibongpo aphan
apōt   nàng=le   arjū-dām-nōi,   há   karlēsibóng-pō
because you=FOC:IRR   ask-go-INF.COND.IMP   over.there   squirrel.sp-male
a-phān
POSS-NSUBJ
"'Therefore, you (only you), go and ask, there, the squirrel.'" [RBT, ChM 065]

ha karlesibongpo along arjudamlo... "Te
há   karlēsibóng-pō   alòng   arjū-dām-lò   tè
over.there   squirrel.sp-male   LOC   ask-go-RL   and.then

karlesibongpo, pisi nang hanthar athe
karlēsibóng-pō   pīsi   nàng   hanthàr   a-thē
squirrel.sp-male   why   you   vegetable.sp   POSS-fruit

kerotpetle... phakbelengpi amoi
ke-ròt-pèt=le   phàkbeléngpī   a-mòi
NMLZ-cut-sd.of.resulting.event=FOC:IRR   pig.sp   POSS-back

peklodup athema?"
pe-kló-dùp   athēma
CAUS-fall-falling.sound.from.high.solid.obj   because
'Over there he went and asked the squirrel, "So then, squirrel, why were you gnawing (where) the *Hanthar* (was hanging)? Because it fell down on the back of the pig."'
[RBT, ChM 066]

"apot pinike nangreng sopikji"
apōt   pinì=ke   nang-rèng   sò-pìk-jí
reason   today=TOP   2:POSS-skin   hurt-very-IRR2
"'Therefore, today, your skin will hurt badly.'" [RBT, ChM 067]

"ai nepran neenri, nemui
ái   ne-prán   ne=ēn-rī   ne-múi
how.bad!   1EXCL:POSS-life   1EXCL:NSUBJ=take-PROH   1EXCL:POSS-EE:prán(<Ind)

neenri, richo!"
ne=ēn-rī   richó
1EXCL:NSUBJ=take-PROH   king
"'Please, don't take my life, king!'" [RBT, ChM 068]

"nele kechokche kali"
nè=le   ke-chók-Cē   kalī
1EXCL=FOC:IRR   NMLZ-be.fine-NEG NEG.EQU.COP
"'I'm not the guilty one!'" [RBT, ChM 069]

"neta nehem ave nerit ave"
nè=tā   ne-hēm   avē   ne-rīt   avē
1EXCL=ADD   1EXCL:POSS-house   not.exist 1EXCL:POSS-field   not.exist
"'I don't have any property (lit. a house or a field).'" [RBT, ChM 070]

"nehem hingnoet nerit hingnoetsi..."
ne-hēm   hingnō-èt   ne-rīt   hingnō-èt-si...
1EXCL:POSS-house   bad-all:S/O   1EXCL:POSS-field   bad-all:S/O-NF:RL
"'My property (lit. house and field) is all destroyed and so...'" [RBT, ChM 071]

"la chonghokalosopen la misorongpo atum kopi
[[là   chonghōkalósō=pen   là   misòrongpō   a-tūm]   kopí
this   frog.sp=with   this   ant.sp   POSS-PL   what

chomathalone, nedon
cho-mathà-lò-nē]   [ne-dón
AUTO.BEN/MAL-think-RL-INDEF   1EXCL:POSS-ladder

chonraikemati; pot neta
chón-rài=ke=mati]   [pōt   nè=tā
jump-RES:solid.obj.breaking=TOP=CG   therefore 1EXCL=ADD

nedon kachithu"
ne-dón   ke-che-thú]
1EXCL:POSS-bridge/ladder   NMLZ-RR-cut
"'The frog and the ant thinking up whatever (bad things), (they) just jumped on my ladder and destroyed it; because of that I was just collecting the materials to (re-)build my ladder.'" [RBT, ChM 072]

amat <chongho... aphan misorongpo arjulo pichonghoisi o>
amāt   [chonghō   a-phān]   misòrongpō   arjū-lò   pí-chonghói=si
and.then   frog   POSS-NSUBJ   ant.sp   ask-RL   what-reason=FOC:RL
'And then <the ant asked the frog, why...>.' [RBT, ChM 073]

chongho aphan arjulo, "Pi chonghoisi nangke karle
[chonghō   a-phān   arjū-lò]   [pí   chonghói=si   nàng=ke   karlē
frog   POSS-NSUBJ   ask-RL   what   reason=FOC:RL   you=TOP   squirrel

adon chonraimati?" pu
a-dón   chón-rài=mati]   pu
POSS-bridge/ladder jump-RES:solid.obj.breaking=as.you.know   QUOT
'He asked the frog, "Why did you jump on the ladder of the squirrel?"' [RBT, ChM 074]

"misorongpota nemi nangkorrakke"
misòrongpō=tā   ne-mí   nang=kòr-ràk=ke
ant.sp=ADD   1EXCL:POSS-buttocks   1/2:NSUBJ=bite-RES:little.wound=TOP
'The ant bit me in the butt... (and so...).' [RBT, ChM 075]

<ha> Misorongpo arju, "Chonghoisi nang chongho
misòrongpō arjū   chonghói=si   nàng   chonghō
sp.ant   ask   reason=FOC:RL   you   frog

ami korrakmati?"
a-mí   kòr-ràk=mati]
POSS-buttocks bite-RES:little.wound=CG
'He asked the ant, "Why did you bite the frog in the butt?", "He had come and was blocking the road... and so..."' [RBT, ChM 076]

o <nang> mota nangtum kachekoi
o   <nang> mó=tā   nang-tūm   ke-che-kói
DSM   you   future=ADD   you-PL   NMLZ-RR-accuse

nangbe doji
nang-bé   dō-jí
2:POSS-habit exist-IRR2
'"You will (continue to) have a habit of accusing each other in the future."' [RBT, ChM 077]

misorongpo aphan chujengpen avam kokdong
misòrongpō a-phān   chūjēng=pen   a-vám   kòk-dòng
ant.sp   POSS-NSUBJ single.hair=with   POSS-waist   tie-attached

pechengran
pe-chēng-ràn
CAUS-be.narrow.inbetween-delicate/about.to.break
'(The king) took the ant on its hair and tied it up on its waist.' [RBT, ChM 078]

chongho aphan jamir abupen
chonghō a-phān   jamír   a-bú=pen
frog   POSS-NSUBJ grain.sp   POSS-bundle=with

sapphratphratdet amat abang
sáp-phrát~phrát-dèt   amāt   a-bàng
beat.w/sth.flexible-sd.beating~DISTR.PL-PFV   and.then   POSS-CLF:HUM.PL

pevangphrok
pe-vàng-phròk
CAUS-come-bulging.out
'And with a bundle of *jamir* they kept beating the frog so its skin got swollen.' [RBT, ChM 079]

ansi ingtonlo
ánsi   ingtòn-lò
after.that   conclude-RL
'And then it's finished.' [RBT, ChM 080]

Appendix C

Stimuli-based narrative: Pear Story (SiT, PS)

This text is an online narration of the Pear Story (Chafe 1980). The speaker was asked to describe what was happening as he was watching the video clip.

The audio file for the entire text SiT, PS is available under the DOI name 10.7264/N3P55KRP at https://scholarsbank.uoregon.edu/xmlui/handle/1794/13657

vo kiku
vō   ke-kú
chicken IPFV-crow
'A rooster is crowing.' [SiT, PS 001]

vota kujengsi do... inut
[vō=tā   kú-jèng-si   dō]   [e-nūt
chicken=also crow-for.long.time(sound)-NF:RL exist one-CLF:HUM:SG

chotiki chonghoi amonit amethang abiri
cho-tikī   cho-inghói   a-monít] [a-metháng   a-birī
AUTO.BEN/MAL-cultivate AUTO.BEN/MAL-do POSS-man   POSS-self   POSS-garden

arlopen eson <athe...> thesere kelik
arlō=pen]   e-sòn   <a-thē...> theseré ke-lík
inside=from one-CLF:thing POSS-fruit   fruits   IPFV-pluck
'There's a rooster crowing (in the background)... One farmer inside his own garden is picking a type of fruit.' [SiT, PS 002]

dondon chedonsi... anke amonit abang
[dondón   che-dón-si...]   [ánke   [a-monít   abàng]
ladder   RR-place.ladder/bridge-NF:RL   and.then   POSS-man   NPDL

<a> pe akelokpen keroi isi ajamborong
[[pé   a-ke-lòk=pen   ke-ròi   isī   a-jamboróng
cloth POSS-NMLZ-be.white=with   NMLZ-sew one   POSS-bag

arlosi lahai kethap lapen arum kevan
arlō=si]   [laháí] ke-thàp]]   lapèn   [arúm   ke-vàn]]
inside=FOC:RL these   NMLZ-put.inside and   down   NMLZ-bring
'He's placed himself a ladder (and)... and then, the man, into a bag sown from white cloth he puts these (fruit), and then brings them down.' [SiT, PS 003]

lake phatang alongsi kethap
là=ke   [phatáng   a-lòng=si]   ke-thàp
this=TOP B.BASKET   POSS-LOC=FOC NMLZ-put.inside
'He is putting them in a *phatang* bamboo basket.' [SiT, PS 004]

ajahak atheke longle athak klobom lapusonta do
[[ajahák a-thē=ke]   [longlē a-thàk]   kló-bòm]   [làpusón=tā   dō]
some   POSS-fruit=TOP   earth   POSS-on.top fall-CONT like.this=ADD exist
'Some (pieces of) fruit keep falling on the ground, that's also happening.' [SiT, PS 005]

so amonit achethok along peta do <aphutup
[[sō   a-monít]   a-chethōk   a-lòng   pé=tā   dō]   <a-phutūp
this   POSS-man   POSS-neck   POSS-LOC   cloth=ADD exist   POSS-hat

alongke> aphu alongke phutupsi kachekup choi
a-lòng=ke>   [a-phú   a-lòng=ke   phutūp=si   ke-che-kúp]   [chói
POSS-LOC=TOP   POSS-head   POSS-LOC=TOP   hat=FOC:RL NMLZ-RR-cover   shirt

ki'iksi kachingchoi
ke-ìk=si   ke-chingchói]
NMLZ-be.black=FOC:RL NMLZ-wear
'This man also has a cloth on his neck, on his head he's wearing a hat, he's wearing a black shirt.' [SiT, PS 006]

dondon do arongta the'o, laso athesere <e>
[dondón   dō]   [a-rōng=tā   thē-ò]   [lasō   a-theseré
ladder   exist   POSS-plant=ADD   be.big-much   this   POSS-fruits

arong... bita nangkangreng ase
a-rōng]   [bī=tā   nang=ke-ingrèng   a-sè
POSS-plant   goat=even   CIS=NMLZ-call(small.animals)   POSS-disease

kethepar
ke-thè-pār]
NMLZ-be.big-very
'There's a ladder, the tree is very big; this fruit tree..., the voice of a goat is also very loud.' [SiT, PS 007]

laso kethap aphrang aphrang <la> longle keklo alongpen
lasō   ke-thàp   aphráng~aphráng   <là>   longlē   ke-kló   alòng=pen
this   NMLZ-put.inside   before~INTENS   this   earth   NMLZ-fall LOC=from

humsi laso aketer athesere <la> longle
hūm-si   lasō   a-ke-tèr   a-theseré   <là>   longlē
pick.up-NF:RL this   POSS-NMLZ-be.dirty   POSS-fruits   this   earth

kero'anke halaso apepensi venlo
ke-rō=án=ke   hálasō   a-pé=pen=si   vēn-lò
NMLZ-hit-all-TOP that   POSS-cloth=with=FOC:RL wipe-RL
'Just before putting them into (the basket), he picks them up from having fallen onto the ground, and these dirty pieces of fruit, all the ones that had hit the ground, with this cloth, he wiped them clean.' [SiT, PS 008]

anke lasonsi thapbomlo
ánke   lasón=si   thàp-bōm-lò
and.then that.way=FOC:RL put.inside-CONT-RL
'And then, like this he kept putting them inside (the baskets).' [SiT, PS 009]

ha achar tovar kengkeng inut phutup
[[há   achár   továr   kengkèng]   [e-nūt   phutūp
over.there far.away road   all.the.way   one-CLF:HUM:SG   hat

kachikupdong amonit... bi api
ke-che-kúp-dòng   a-monít]... [bī   a-pī]
NMLZ-RR-cover-attached POSS-man   goat   POSS-female

nangchithurkrikrisi laso <la> thesere
nang=chithùr-krì-krì-si]   [lasō   <là> theseré
CIS=drag-follow.closely-follow.closely-NF:RL this   this   fruits

kelik amonit adung'an nanglelo
ke-lík   a-monít   adūng-án]   nang=lè-lò
NMLZ-pluck POSS-man   near-up.to   CIS=reach-RL
'Over there, far away, all the way down the road, one man wearing a hat, dragging along a female goat, close up to this man who was picking fruit he reached.' [SiT, PS 010]

laso amonitta... <a> lapu bi ponlo <la> abi abangke
lasō a-monít=tā...   lapù   bī   pòn-lo   <là>   a-bī   abàng=ke
this   POSS-man=ADD   like.this   goat   take.away-RL   this   POSS-goat   NPDL=TOP

kedun mo
ke-dùn   mō
NMLZ-join hesitate
'This person also... like this (he's) taking away the goat, this goat is hesitating to go along.' [SiT, PS 011]

ne <kechokang...> kachopanji aning
[nē   <ke-chō-káng...>   ke-chopān-jí   a-nīng
something   NMLZ-eat-just   NMLZ-look.for.food-IRR2   POSS-mind

kehang ason bonsita halaso amonit chingtontesi
ke-hàng   asón]   bónsetā hálasō a-monít   chingtòn-Cē-si
NMLZ-want   like   but   that   POSS-man   stop.for.awhile-NEG-NF:RL

chithurponbomlo
chithùr-pōn-bōm-lò
drag-take.away-CONT-RL
'It's as if the goat wants to graze, but that man without stopping keeps dragging (the goat) away.' [SiT, PS 012]

abi ponbomlo ha helovinglo
a-bī   pòn-bōm-lò   há   helō-víng-lò
POSS-goat take.away-CONT-RL   over.there   be.far-very-RL
'He keeps taking the goat away, over there, it's far away.' [SiT, PS 013]

anke laso amonit abangke, la chotiki
ánke   [lasō a-monít   abàng=ke]   [là   cho-tikī
and.then   this   POSS-man   NPDL=TOP   this   AUTO.BEN/MAL-cultivate

chonghoipen kecho amonit abangke... puthot
cho-inghói-pen   ke-chō   a-monít   abàng=ke]   puthōt
AUTO.BEN/MAL-do-NF:with   NMLZ-eat   POSS-man   NPDL=TOP   next/again

angsong arlusi... thengpi arong arlusi athe likbomlo
angsóng   arlū-si...   thengpī   a-rōng   arlū-si   a-thē   lík-bòm-lò
high.up   climb-NF:RL tree/wood POSS-plant   climb-NF:RL POSS-fruit   pluck-CONT-RL
'And then, this man, the man who lives off of (lit., eats from) cultivating, again climbed up high, climbed up the tree and kept picking the fruit.' [SiT, PS 014]

laso ahut amat inut akaprek amonit
[lasō   a-hūt   amāt]   [e-nūt   a-ke-prék   a-monít
this   POSS-during   and.then   one-CLF:HUM:SG   POSS-NMLZ-be.different   POSS-man

abangke saikel nangardonsi vanglo... laso amonitta
a-bàng=ke]   saikél   nang=ardòn-si   vàng-lo   lasō   a-monít=tā
NPDL=TOP   bicycle(<Eng)   CIS=ride-NF:RL   come-RL   this   POSS-man=ADD

aphu along aphutup do
a-phú   a-lòng   a-phutūp   dō
POSS-head   POSS-LOC   POSS-hat   exist
'In this moment, another person came, riding a bicycle, this person also had a hat on his head.' [SiT, PS 015]

lapenke la thesere kelikbom amonit along nanglelo
lapèn=ke	là	theseré	ke-lík-bòm	a-monít	a-lòng	nang=lè-lò
and–TOP	this	fruits	NMLZ-pluck-CONT	POSS-man	POSS-LOC	CIS=reach-RL

'And then, he reached (the place) where the fruit picking man was.' [SiT, PS 016]

thengpi arum nanglelo amonit abangke angsongsi do
thengpī	a-rúm	nang=lè-lo	a-monít	abàng=ke	angsóng=si	dō
tree/wood	POSS-down	CIS=reach-RL	POSS-man	NPDL=TOP	high.up=FOC:RL	exist

'He reached underneath the tree, that man (who's picking the fruit) is up high (in the tree).' [SiT, PS 017]

lapenke arum la dondon adunghet amat... <a>
lapèn=ke	arúm	là	dondón	adūng-hét	amāt...
and.then=TOP	down	this	ladder	near-INTENS	self

phatang hini plengchongchong... <a> thesere kiliktang
phatáng	hiní	plèng-chóng~chòng...	theseré	ke-lík-táng
kd.basket	two	be.full-slightly.high~INTENS	fruits	NMLZ-pluck-PFV

theklonglo lapenke saikel pasangkoklo
thèklōng-lò	lapèn=ke	saikél	pa-sáng-kòk-lò
see-RL	and.then=TOP	bicycle(<Eng)	CAUS-take.rest.firmly-RL

'And then, down below (the tree), in the place itself very close by the ladder, two baskets were full, he sees the fruit that had already been picked, and then he stopped the bicycle.' [SiT, PS 018]

<sangkok> asaikel kapasangkokra
<sáng-kòk>	a-saikél	ke-pe-sáng-kòk-ra
take.rest-firmly	POSS-bicycle(<Eng)	NMLZ-CAUS-take.rest.firmly-NF:IRR

parjaplun kibiji a-son avedet amat
pe-arjàp-lùn	ke-bí-jí	a-sòn	avē-dèt	amāt
CAUS-stand-big:AO	NMLZ-keep-IRR2	POSS-thing	not.exist-PFV	and.then

asaikel abang pakrepkhram
a-saikél	abàng	pe-krēp-khràm
POSS-bicycle(<Eng)	NPDL	CAUS-fall.over-with.loud.noise

'He stops the bicycle and there is no device to keep it standing up, and then he made the bicycle fall over with a noise.' [SiT, PS 019]

lapenke amonit kopisi keklemma, hala
lapèn=ke	a-monít	kopī=si	ke-klém=ma	hála
and.then=TOP	POSS-man	what=FOC:RL	NMLZ-do=Q	that

ahemphu abang la langrei amat
a-hēmphū abàng là làng-rèi amāt
POSS-house.owner.male.HON NPDL this see-sideways and.then
'And then, what is the man doing, that old man, he glances to the side briefly, and then...' [SiT, PS 020]

<aphatang along'an saikel...> <a> saikel along'an
<a-phatáng alòng-án saikél...> saikél a-lòng=án
POSS-kd.basket LOC-up.to bicycle(<Eng) bicycle(<Eng) POSS-LOC=up.to

phatang abang vansi... la phatang saikel along
[phatáng abàng] vàn-si... là phatáng saikél a-lòng
kd.basket NPDL bring-NF:RL this kd.basket bicycle(<Eng) POSS-LOC

kethapji aphan bor'ilo
ke-thàp-jí aphān bor'í-lò
NMLZ-put.inside-IRR2 PURP try.w.great.effort-RL
'<The bicycle to the baskets> To the bicycle he takes the basket, the basket he is somehow trying to put on the bicycle.' [SiT, PS 021]

amat amonitta ajon thihek
amāt a-monít=tā a-jōn thī-hèk
and.then POSS-man=ADD POSS-height be.short-INTENS
'And then, the person is short.' [SiT, PS 022]

lapenke saikel along aphrang anatsi
lapèn=ke saikél a-lòng a-phráng a-nát=si
and.then=TOP bicycle(<Eng) POSS-LOC POSS-first POSS-direction=FOC:RL

kethap
ke-thàp
NMLZ-put.inside
'And then he puts it on the bicycle in the front.' [SiT, PS 023]

lapenke hala kangni adim along ingnithekthesi
lapèn=ke [hála ke-ingnì a-dím a-lòng] ingnì-thēk-Cē-si
and.then=TOP that NMLZ-sit POSS-place POSS-LOC sit-see-NEG-NF:RL

<a> si ingchin apum along ingnisi... saikel
sì ingchìn a-púm a-lòng ingnì-si... saikél
therefore iron POSS-CLF:round POSS-LOC sit-NF:RL bicycle(<Eng)

kevekponlo
ke-vèk-pōn-lò
NMLZ-steer-away-RL
'And then, he doesn't know how to sit down on that sitting place (saddle), and then on the iron bar he sits and steers the bicycle away.' [SiT, PS 024]

saikel vekponbom dambomlo atheta
[saikél   vèk-pòn-bōm   dàm-bōm-lò]   a-thē=tā
bicycle(<Eng)   steer-away-CONT go-CONT-RL   POSS-fruit=ADD

kloponpresi tovar soding kloponbomlo
kló-pòn-prè-si   továr sodíng   kló-pòn-bōm-lò
fall-on.the.way-scattered-NF:RL   road   all.along   fall-on.the.way-CONT-RL
'He is steering the bicycle away and going away, and the fruit is falling out here and there and all along the road it keeps falling out.' [SiT, PS 025]

bonsita hala ahemphu abangke chipudunthekthe
bónsetā hála a-hēmphū   abàng=ke   che-pū-dūn-thēk-Cē
but   that POSS-house.owner.male.HON NPDL=TOP   RR-say-JOIN-know.how-NEG
'But that old man couldn't realize.' [SiT, PS 026]

<la> dambomlo... anke kedambom ahut ha
<là>   dàm-bōm-lò... ánke   ke-dàm-bōm   ahūt   há
this   go-CONT-RL   and.then   NMLZ-go-CONT during   over.there

<punu> anatthupen inut arloso oso, skul
a-nátthū=pen   e-nūt   árlosō osō   skúl
POSS-direction=from   one-CLF:HUM:SG   woman   child school(<Eng)

kidun a'oso... halata saikel nangveksi
ke-dùn   a-osō   hála=tā   saikél   nang=vèk-si
NMLZ-join   POSS-child   that=also   bicycle(<Eng)   CIS=steer-NF:RL

vangbomlo... menmen latum chetonglok amat
vàng-bōm-lò...   ménmèn   la-tūm   che-tòng-lòk   amāt
come-CONT-RL   suddenly   this-PL   RR-meet-just   and.then
'He keeps going, and then, as he's going, from that side (i.e., the opposite side), one girl, one school girl, she's also riding a bike and coming, suddenly they meet, and then...' [SiT, PS 027]

<la> <saikel...> <a> <la> arlososo abangpen
<là>   <saikél...>   <là>   árlosō~sō   abàng=pen
this   bicycle(<Eng)   this   woman~DUAL   NPDL=with

chetongder amat aphutup klophit
che-tōng-dèr   amāt   a-phutūp   kló-phìt
RR-collide-IDEOPHONE   and.then   POSS-hat   fall-right.away
'The bicycle..., with the girl he collided and then his hat fell down.' [SiT, PS 028]

amat laso damchet amat chekhang'un'elo isi arlong
amāt   lasō   dàm-chèt   amāt   che-kháng-ùn-Cē-lò   isī   arlōng
and.then   this   go-a.bit   and.then   RR-keep-be.able-NEG-RL   one   stone

along tongdér
a-lòng   tōng-dèr
POSS-LOC   collide-IDEOPHONE
'And then he went just a bit further and then he couldn't hold himself anymore, he hit a stone.' [SiT, PS 029]

alang kepon athesere do'anta klolaplo
[[alàng   ke-pòn]   a-theseré   dō=án=tā]   kló-làp-lò
3   NMLZ-take.away   POSS-fruits   exist=all=ADD   fall-completely-RL
'All of the fruit that he had taken away fell out.' [SiT, PS 030]

adunghet osomar banghini bangkethom do... halatumke
adūng-hét   osō-mār   bàng-hiní   bàng-kethòm   dō...   hála-tūm=ke
near-INTENS   child-PL   CLF:HUM:PL-two   CLF:HUM:PL-three   exist   that-PL=TOP

juirekraksi do
jùi-rek~rāk-si   dō
play-silently~DIST.PL-NF:RL exist
'Nearby, there were two, three children, they were playing silently.' [SiT, PS 031]

tennis <a> kapathu abol lapenke bet
[tennis   ke-pathú   a-ból   lapèn=ke   bét
tennis(<Eng)   NMLZ-play   POSS-ball(<Eng)   and.then=TOP   bat(<Eng)

otdong inut oso abangke... lapenke <la>
ót-dòng   e-nūt   osō   abàng=ke]...   lapèn=ke   <là>
touch-attached   one-CLF:HUM:SG   child   NPDL =TOP   and.then=TOP   this

kachingkoidup amonit <a> aphan
[ke-chingkoí-dùp   a-monít   a-phān]
NMLZ-fall.down.HUM-IDEOPHONE   POSS-man   POSS-NSUBJ

<la> <thesere aphatang heihai thesere along>
<là>   <theseré   a-phatáng   héihái   theseré   a-lòng>
this   fruits   POSS-kd.basket   different.kinds.of   fruits   POSS-LOC

aphatang along thesere thapdunlo rapdunlo, laphan
a-phatáng   a-lòng   theseré   thàp-dūn-lò   ráp-dùn-lò   là-phān
POSS-kd.basket POSS-LOC   fruits   put.inside-JOIN-RL   help-JOIN-RL   this-NSUBJ
'(There's) one child who's holding a ball to play tennis and a bat, and then for (the benefit of) the person who had fallen down, they put with (lit., joining) him the fruit in the basket, they helped him.' [SiT, PS 032]

<raptang'et aphike> rapdun'et aphike <a> la saikel
<ráp-táng-ét   aphī=ke>   ráp-dùn-ét   aphī=ke   [là   saikél
help-PFV-PRF   after=TOP   help-JOIN-PRF   after=TOP   this   bicycle(<Eng)

kevek abang puthot chevekponthulo lapenke
ke-vèk   abàng]   puthōt   che-vēk-pōn-thū-lo   lapèn=ke
NMLZ-steer   NPDL   next/again   RR-steer-away-again-RL   and.then=TOP

inut oso abangke la aphrang along kedo <a> arlong
[e-nūt   osō   abàng=ke]   [là   aphráng   a-lòng   ke-dō   arlōng]
one-CLF:HUM:SG   child NPDL=TOP   this   first   POSS-LOC   NMLZ-exist   stone

terekpiphitlo...] penke padamlo
terék-pī-phìt-lò...   pèn=ke   pa-dàm-lò
move-BEN/MAL-away-RL   and.then=TOP   CAUS-go-RL
'After helping, the bicycle rider again got on his way, and then one child, the one who was in front, he moved the stone away for him, and then they (the children) let him (the bicycle boy) go away.' [SiT, PS 033]

latum bangkethomke amethang atovar chedamlo,
[[là-tūm   bàng-kethòm=ke]   a-metháng   a-továr   che-dām-lò]
this-PL   CLF:HUM:PL-three=TOP   POSS-self   POSS-road   RR-go-RL

lapenke saikel ingdoiponbomsi,
[lapèn=ke   saikél   ingdōi-pōn-bōm-si
and.then=TOP   bicycle(<Eng)   push-away-CONT-NF:RL

la aphrang kevang abang, dambomlo
[là   aphráng   ke-vàng   abàng]   dàm-bōm-lò]
this   first   NMLZ-come   NPDL   go-CONT-RL
'The three of them went their own way, and then pushing the bicycle, the one who first came (i.e. the one with the bicycle), he kept going.' [SiT, PS 034]

damchot aphi.... phutup kitirok theklongloklo hala
dàm-chót   aphī....   phutūp   ke-tí-ròk   thèklōng-lòk-lò   [hála
go-a.bit   after   hat   NMLZ-leave.behind-COMPL   see-just-RL   that

bol ke'otdong a'oso abang
ból	ke-ót-dòng	a-osō	abàng]
ball(<Eng)	NMLZ-touch-attached	POSS-child	NPDL

'And then, after going just a bit, he saw the hat that had been left behind, that boy that was holding the ball.' [SiT, PS 035]

pen pasi'idunvotsi phutup humra aphi
pèn	pasi'í-dùn-vòt-si	phutūp	hūm-rà	aphī
and.then	whistle-JOIN-INTENS-NF:RL	hat	pick.up-NF:IRR	behind

anat chevangthulo
a-nát	che-vàng-thū-lò
POSS-direction	RR-come-again-RL

'And then, he whistled (for the boy), picked up the hat and brought it back.' [SiT, PS 036]

hala saikel kangdoipon abangta <a> chingtonkoklo
hála	saikél	ke-ingdōi-pōn	abàng=tā	chingtòn-kòk-lò
that	bicycle(<Eng)	NMLZ-push-away	NPDL=ADD	stop.for.awhile-firmly-RL

'That bicycle pushing person also stopped for awhile.' [SiT, PS 037]

lapenke aphutup pidetlo laphan
lapèn=ke	a-phutūp	pī-dèt-lò	là-phān
and.then=TOP	POSS-hat	give-PFV-RL	this-NSUBJ

'And then, he gave the hat, to this one.' [SiT, PS 038]

lapenke la phutup <kapa..> kipidunthu apot, laphan
lapèn=ke	[là	phutūp	ke-pī-dūn-thū	apōt]	là-phān
and.then=TOP	this	hat	NMLZ-give-JOIN-again	because	this-NSUBJ

aning ingsamsi, thesere pumni tekanglo
a-nīng	ingsām-si	theseré	púm-ní	tekáng-lò
POSS-mind	be.cold-NF:RL	fruits	CLF:round-two	leave.for-RL

'And then, because he returned the hat, he (the bicycle boy) was grateful to him and gave him two pieces of fruit.' [SiT, PS 039]

an laso a'oso abang thesere pumni hala ajirpo
án	[lasō	a-osō	abàng]	[theseré	púm-ní]	[hála	a-jirpò
and.then	this	POSS-child	NPDL	fruits	CLF:round-two	that	POSS-friend

banghini aphan chepaklangdamlo
bàng-hiní	a-phān]	che-pa-klàng-dām-lò
CLF:HUM:PL-two	POSS-NSUBJ	RR-CAUS-appear-GO-RL

'And then, this child went to show the two pieces of fruit to those two friends.' [SiT, PS 040]

chepaklangdampen... latum kedamthu pangchengló
che-pe-klàng-dām-pen...   là-tūm   ke-dàm-thū   pangchèng-lò
RR-CAUS-appear-GO-NF:with this-PL NMLZ-go-again start-RL
'After he went to show them, they again started walking.' [SiT, PS 041]

anke ajabok along kethapthot
ánke   [a-jabók   a-lòng   ke-thàp-thòt
and.then POSS-pocket(<Asm) POSS-LOC NMLZ-put.inside-into.opening

akriket abet ensi juiponbomlo
a-kriket   a-bet   ēn-si   jùi-pòn-bōm-lò
POSS-cricket(<Eng) POSS-bat(<Eng) take-NF:RL play-on.the.way-CONT-RL
'And then, the cricket bat that he had put into his pocket he takes again and keeps playing while going away.' [SiT, PS 042]

penke hala thesere <a> kelikdam amonit abangta nangsunlo
pèn=ke   hála theseré ke-lík-dàm   a-monít   abàng=tā   nang=sūn-lò
and.then=TOP that fruits NMLZ-pluck-GO POSS-man NPDL=also CIS=descend-RL
'And then, the man who had gone to pick fruits, on the other hand, has come down.' [SiT, PS 043]

lapenke... phatang along thesere thaplelo... bonta isi
lapèn=ke...   phatáng   a-lòng   theseré   thàp-lè-lò...   bóntā   isī
and.then=TOP kd.basket POSS-LOC fruits put.inside-again-RL but one

aphatang along thesere chetheklongledetlo
a-phatáng   a-lòng   theseré   che-thēklòng-Cē-dèt-lò
POSS-kd.basket POSS-LOC fruits RR-see-NEG-PFV-RL
'And then, he again put more fruit in the baskets, but in one basket he didn't see any fruit.' [SiT, PS 044]

anke laso a'osomar atum nangke'otkrei
ánke   [[lasō a-osō-mār   a-tūm]   nang=ke-ót-krèi
and.then this POSS-child-PL POSS-PL CIS=NMLZ-touch-DISTR.PL

atheseresi langdunveretlo... anke inut
a-theseré=si]   làng-dūn-verèt-lò...   ánke   e-nūt
POSS-fruits=FOC:RL see-JOIN-INTENS-RL and.then one-CLF:HUM:SG

abangke juiponbom thengponbomlang
abàng=ke   jùi-pōn-bōm   thèng-pōn-bōm-làng
NPDL=TOP play-on.the.way-CONT beat.w/sth.solid-on.the.way-CONT-still
'And then, (the old man) keeps watching intently the fruit that these children are each holding, and then one (of them) keeps playing, keeps beating (the ball) still.' [SiT, PS 045]

anke la chelangdundinglo <latum aphansi
ánke   là   che-lāng-dūn-dìng-lò   là-tūm   a-phān=si
and.then this   RR-see-JOIN-steadily-RL   this-PL   POSS-NSUBJ=FOC:RL

<chonghupon> kanghupon>, "latumtong
cho-inghū-pòn   ke-inghū-pōn   là-tūm-tōng
AUTO.BEN/MAL-steal-take.away   NMLZ-steal-take.away   this-PL-INDIR.ITROG

kepon'etma? Lajo!" pu <sontong> lapusonsi
ke-pòn-èt=ma   là-jò   pu   <són-tōng>   làpusón=si
NMLZ-take.away-all:S/O=Q this-see! QUOT   like.this-instead.of like.this=FOC:RL

kamatha
ke-mathà
NMLZ-think

'And then he kept watching them for a long time, "Could they have taken them all away? Look at that!", like this he was thinking.' [SiT, PS 046]

amat jutletlo
amāt   jūt-lèt-lò
and.then   finish-PFV3-RL

'And then, (the story) is finished.' [SiT, PS 047]

Appendix D

Metadata

Table 120: Metadata of texts representing the main corpus for this grammar.

Speakers	Recording	Recording full name	Genre[a]	Date	Format[b]	Equipment[c]	hh:mm:ss	# words
CST	HM	Hingchong Musoso	FS	100331	A/V	M2,A2,V	00:10:43	1,140
CST	RO	Rengsopen Onso	FS	100331	A/V	M2,A2,V	00:06:08	649
HI	BPh	Bokolapo Phinu aBiha Choklem	FS	100402	A/V	M2,A2,V	00:03:04	226
HK, SiT	TR	Teke Rongker	FS	100410	A/V	M2,A2,V	00:11:59	1,516
KaR, BT	SWK	Status of Women in Karbi Society	I/C	111123	A/V	M4,V	00:12:19	1,128
KK	CC	Crying Child	N	100401	A/V	M2,A2,V	00:03:41	338
KK	BMS	Bamonpo lapen Methan Sibongpo	FS	100401	A/V	M2,A2,V	00:12:52	1,317
KsT	PSu	Pindeng Sumpot	PT	100402	A/V	M2,A2,V	00:01:42	131
KTa	TCS	Terang Clan Story	FS	090202	A	M1,A1	00:09:45	1,006
PI	BPR	Bamboo Pork Recipe	PT	090123	A	M1,A1	00:01:49	118
RBT	ChM	Chonghokaloso lapen Misorongpo	FS	100401	A/V	M2,A2,V	00:05:57	733
SeT	MTN	Monit Thinlangno	FS	100401	A/V	M2,A2,V	00:06:05	710
SH	CSM	Chomangkan Story Mother	PN	090226	A	M1,A1	00:08:38	827
SiH	KH	Kangmoi aHan	PT	100402	A/V	M2,A2,V	00:03:13	291
SiH	CW	Cleaning and Washing	PT	100402	A/V	M2,A2,V	00:03:53	371
SiT	HF	Trip to Hornbill Festival	PN	111206	A	A2	00:08:43	852
SiT	PS	Pear Story	OEN	121205	A	M5, A2	00:05:52	502

Table 120 (continued)

Speakers	Recording	Recording full name	Genre[a]	Date	Format[b]	Equipment[c]	hh:mm:ss	# words
Speakers	Recording	Recording full name	Genre	Date	Format	Equipment	hh:mm:ss	# words
WR	BCS	Bey Clan Story	FS	111013	A	A2	00:05:15	630
						TOTAL	02:01:38	12,485

[a] Genre abbreviations – PT: Procedural Text; FS: Folk Story; PN: Personal Narrative; N: Narrative; I/C: Inteview/Conversation; OEN: on-line elicited narrative
[b] Format abbreviations – A: .wav; V: .mts.
[c] Equipment abbreviations – M1 (Microphone1): Audio Technica AT3032; M2 (Microphone2): AT813a; M3 (Microphone3): Audio Technica AT8010; M4 (Microphone4): Audio-Technica AT831b; M5 (Microphone5): Shure SM10A; A1 (Audio recorder1): Marantz PMD 660 audio recorder; A2 (Audio recorder2): Zoom H4n digital audio recorder; V: Video recorder Sony Vixia HF S10.

Table 121: Brief descriptions of texts that have formed the main corpus for this grammar.

Recording full name	Topic
Hingchong Musoso	Folk story about two girl twins (*hingchong musoso*) that are born to the human wife of a king, who also has a second wife who is a witch; the witch is jealous and abandons the girls, who are subsequently brought up by tigers; after having grown up, they return to their father's kingdom and tell their story; the father learns the truth, the witch dies, and the reunited family lives happily ever after
Rengsopen Onso	Folk story about step-parenthood: the mother of two children (with the names *Rengso* and *Onso*; note *-sō* 'diminutive' suffix, §7.4.2) dies and the father marries again; the new stepmother is evil and mistreats her step-children, whereupon the father does not know what to do and both abandons his children in the jungle and kills his wife
Bokolapo Phinu aBiha Choklem	Folk story about a common fool character, who does stupid things (*bokolapo*); in this story, he wants to go to the market but by switching sides of the basket he is carrying also accidentally switches the direction in which he is walking; he ends up walking back to his own house without realizing it
Teke Rongker	Folk story about an orphan who encounters a tiger; by using a container with a mirror on top, he manages to convince the tiger that he (the orphan) has caught a large tiger in that container; the tiger is scared and the orphan ends up managing to steal gold from the tigers' *Rongker* (= the name of a festival in Karbi traditional culture) due to his trick with the mirror container
Status of Women in Karbi Society	Interview/conversation about the status of women in Karbi society; the interviewer is a man, the interviewee is a woman; the interviewee points out the ways in which women have traditionally played a very important role in Karbi society

Table 121 (continued)

Recording full name	Topic
Crying Child	Narration about the (traditional) everyday situation of a mother having a baby to take care of while having to perform other chores such as getting firewood and cooking (not considered a true folk story by language consultants)
Bamonpo lapen Methan Sibongpo	Folk story about an elderly couple with a dog; the wife dies and the dog takes the husband to *Chom arong* (i.e., the village of the dead); the wife does not want to leave, but the husband forces her; upon return to their village, soon somebody else in the village dies, and the wife has to die and go back to *Chom arong* with the other person
Pindeng Sumpot	Procedural text / non-fictional narration about traditional clothing items, weaving, and applying colors
Terang Clan Story	Folk story about the origin of the division into Terang subclans starting with two Terang brothers, the younger one, *Dili* and the older one, *Rongchetcho* (also referred to as Rongchercho); the older one causes a lot of hardship for the younger one, finally, the younger one, *Dili*, takes a vow to officially form separate subclans (with various societal implications)
Bamboo Pork Recipe	Procedural text about the recipe for pork with fermented bamboo shoots
Chonghokaloso lapen Misorongpo	Folk story about a chain reaction of events that sets off when a frog blocks the road and sits down on an ant that in return bites the frog; from there on, one animal suffers from being disturbed or hurt by another animal, and as a consequence accidentally disturbs or hurts another animal, and so on.
Monit Thinlangno	Folk story about a couple, in which the husband tricks his wife in order to get her to give him meat to eat; in the end, the wife leaves the husband
Chomangkan Story Mother	Personal narrative about a trip to the *Chomangkan* festival, narrated by the mother of the family that took the trip
Kangmoi aHan	Procedural text about cooking alkaline food by burning *jhum* fields and using the ashes
Cleaning and Washing	Procedural text / non-fictional narration about the important status of cleanliness in Karbi culture
Trip to Hornbill Festival	Personal narrative about a trip to the Hornbill festival in Nagaland
Pear Story	On-line narration / commentary of the Pear Story
Bey Clan Story	Folk story about the origin of the division into Bey subclans; *Bey Ki'ik* and *Bey Ke'et* have a falling out over changing marriage plans as a result of the grandmother's advice; members of the *Bey Ronghang* clan are not allowed to grind rice for rice beer, because in mythological times, the *Bey Ronghang* women kept grinding rice beer without doing anything else, even forgetting to breast-feed their children, which subsequently died from starvation

Table 122: Metadata of speakers of texts that have formed the main corpus for this grammar.

Speaker initials	Full name	Gender	From (near)	Living in	Other languages spoken, (if in brackets: only a little bit)	Dialect area	Age
BT	Bhudeswar Timung	M	Bamuni Karbi gaon		Assamese, English, Hindi		39
CST	Chandra Sing Teron	M			(Assamese)	Amri	~60
HI	Hem'ari Ingjai	M	Pharkong Abi		(Assamese)		~40
HK	Harsing Kro	M	Borkok (Boythalangso)		(Assamese)	Amri	~60
KaR	Kare Rongpipi	F	Ran Rongki Habe Arong		Assamese, Hindi		48
KK	Kache Kropi	F	Balijuri (Nowgong)		(Assamese)	Socheng Dhenta	~60
KsT	Kasang Teronpi	F	Dingso Terang (Dengaon)		Assamese		45
KTa	Kahan Terangpi	F		Diphu	Assamese		~75
PI	Puspa Engtipi	F	Diphu		Assamese		~50
RBT	Rongbang Teron	M	Ujandongka (Dongkamoka)		(Assamese)	Rongkhang	~50
SeT	Seng Tisso	M	Ujandongka (Dongkamoka)		(Assamese)	Rongkhang	~60
SH	Sashikola Hansepi	F	NC Hills	Diphu	Assamese, (English)	Amri	~50
SiH	Sika Hansepi	F	Men Terang (Dengaon)		(Assamese)		~45
SiT	Sikari Tisso	M	Bhoksong	Diphu	Assamese, English, Hindi, Bengali, Tiwa	Amri	52
WR	Welisbon Ronghipi	F	Umswai Model		Assamese, Tiwa	Amri	~40

Appendix E

Glossary

This glossary contains the morphemes that occur in the corpus that this grammar is based on. For each Karbi root it provides an indication of its part of speech category and an English gloss. Question marks indicate the lack of available data to accurately determine the part of speech of a particular item.

Prefixes and suffixes are categorized based on whether they occur on nominal or verbal roots. The list of part of speech and morpheme type labels used in the glossary is given in Table 123. Grammatical morphemes are glossed with the same abbreviations used throughout this grammar.

Table 123: Word classes and grammatical morpheme types indicated in the glossary.

Word class / Morpheme type	
adj	adjective
adv	adverb
clf	classifier
coord	coordinator
interj	interjection
n	noun
n.bound	bound noun[171]
num	numeral
pref	prefix
pref.n	nominal prefix
pref.v	verbal prefix
pro	pro-form
procltc	proclitic
ptcl	particle
rn	relator noun
subord	subordinator
suff	suffix
suff.n	nominal suffix

---

[171] Bound noun roots have been identified from among the list of noun roots on a preliminary basis. A more detailed investigation into the whole list of noun roots to find all bound noon roots is yet to be conducted.

Table 123 (continued)

Word class / Morpheme type	
suff.v	verbal suffix
suff.v.der	derivational verbal suffix
suff.v.infl	inflectional verbal suffix
v	verb
v.cop	copula

In two cases, the indication "(poet)" indicates that these words are from the song language. In the gloss 'fall.down:HUM' for the verb *chingkói*, the abbreviation 'HUM' stands for 'human' and means that this verb only refers to events of falling down in the case of humans.

Another type of gloss starts with 'EE' to refer to items used as the second element in elaborate expressions. For example, *rèt* is glossed as 'EE:nàm' because it occurs in the elaborate expression formation with *nàm* 'buy'.

Borrowings are indicated where known or assumed. Only those words are listed that are deemed to be instances of real borrowings rather than cases of *ad hoc* code switching.

Names are provided following the main glossary.

A

a	*interj.* AFF.	alang-	*pref.n.* 3.
a-	*pref.n.* POSS.	alàng	*pro.* 3.
abàng	*ptcl.* NPDL.	alíng	*subord.* INDEF.
abangphú	*n?* each one.	alohí	*n.* guest.
achár	*adv.* far away.	alōm	*n.* time.
achítchít	*adj.* tiny.	alōm	*?* approximately.
adakvám	*n.* second child.	alón	*n.* elegance.
adūng	*adv.* near.	amāt	*coord.* and then.
ái	*interj.* how strange!	amāt	*pro.* self.
ainá	*n.* mirror(<Ind).	àn	*n.* rice.
ajahák	*adj.* some.	=án(set)	*ptcl.* that much.
aját	*ptcl.* GENEX.	=án(set)	*ptcl.* all.
ajátnōn	*adv.* anyway.	-án	*suff.n.* up to.
ajerjēr	*adj.* small.	anérlo	*n.* midday.
akehái	*n.* honorable person:address.	angsé	*ptcl.* only.
akehoì	*n.* powerful person.	angsé	*v.* be naked.
akelé	*adv.* more.	anijé	*pro.* REFL(<Asm).
akò	*subord.* when.	ánke	*coord.* and then.
akò	*subord.* before.	ánlo	*coord.* and then.
akó	*adv.* on the other hand(<Asm).	anpár	*?* besides.
akó	*adv.* again(<Asm).	ansām	*n.* cold rice.

ánsi	coord. after that.	arlōng	n. stone.
ánte	coord. OK then.	árlosō	n. woman.
aphráng	adv. first.	arlù	v. weed.
apōtlo	ptcl. should.	arlū	v. climb.
arbàk	v. hold embraced.	armē	n. tail.
arbùng	n. bamboo pole in middle of roof.	arnàm	n. god.
archè	v. EE:ingkrùng.	arnè	v. invite.
archó	v. honor.	arnì	n. sun.
ardèp	v. slap.	arnì	n. day.
ardí	n. weight.	arnì	n. EE:arnàm.
ardīk	v. be heavy.	arnū	v. fry.
ardīk	v. peep.	aróng	v. be happy.
ardóm	v. pray.	arphang	v. put on shoulder.
ardòn	v. ride.	arphè	n. bamboo poles on sides of roof.
áré	interj. SURPRISE(<Asm).	arphèk	n. broom.
-arèt	suff.v.der. INTENS.	arphèk	v. EE:arkòk.
arjàng	n. immature bamboo.	arpū	n. responsibility.
arjāng	v. be light.	arsīk	v. be deep.
arjàp	v. stand.	arsō	v. sharpen.
arjè	n. appearance.	artá	n. age.
arjè	v. separate.	arthàng	v. carry.
arjū	v. ask.	artìng	v. spin(intrans).
arjū	v. hear.	arú	ptcl. and/again(<Asm).
arkè	v. scratch.	arvè	n. rain.
arklì	v. perform worship.	arvēng	n. feather.
arkòk	v. clean.	arvī	adv. left.
arlān	n. dam base.	arvó	n. leaf.
arlèng	n. slope.	ar'ē	adv. right.
arlèng	v. be steep.	ar'ì	v. crave.
arlēng	n. person.	asàp	n. little bit.
arlò	n. EE:ingjìr.	asón	? like.
arlò	n. woman.	athēma	coord. because.
-arlō	rn. inside.	avē	v.cop. not exist.
arlòk	n. foot of hill.		

B

bá	interj. how bad!	bàk	v. distribute.
bá	ptcl. or(<Asm).	-bāk	suff.num. approximately.
bá	ptcl. I mean(<Asm).	bām	v. embrace.
bā	v. carry on back.	bamón	n. wise person(<Ind).
bahák	n. share(<Asm).	bán	n. slave.
baharí	adj. very big(<Ind).	bàng	clf. CLF:HUM:PL.
baherá	adv. away from here(<Asm).	bàng	n. somebody.
baheré	n. beyond(<Asm).	-bàng	n.bound. body.
bài	v. console.	bàngphì	n. lady.
bái	interj. how mean!	bàngphù	n. each one.
bají	ptcl. o'clock(<Asm).	báp	v. press down.

bár	v. start.	-bó	n.bound. leftovers.
barī	n. garden(<Asm).	bō	n. fruit inside.
bariká	n. OFFICER.	boché	v. create.
barithè	n. god.	bói	v. be miserable.
barsō	n. peeing.	bojár	n. market(<Asm).
básápī	n. wife of headman.	bók	v. load.
bàt	v. put on elevated place.	bók	v. serve small items.
bè	v. run away.	bokán	n. EE:botór.
-bè	n.bound. handle.	-bōm	suff.v.der. CONT.
bé	n. habit.	bon	ptcl. possibly.
behá	n. trade.	bōn	v. be attached.
bèng	v. lock.	bonái	v. make(<Asm).
bēng	clf. CLF:half.	bondí	n. captivity(<Ind).
bēng	n. piece.	bondòk	n. EE:bondī.
bér	v. press down.	bòng	n. gourd.
besí	adv. more(<Asm).	bòng	n. bottle.
bí	v. keep.	-bòng	suff.v.der. nicely arranged.
bī	n. goat.	-bōng	n.bound. younger sibling.
bī	v. be small.	bongkrūi	n. leopard.
bidái	v. say goodbye(<Asm).	bonglāng	n. gourd.
bidí	n. cleverness(<Asm).	bónsetā	coord. but.
-bìn	suff.v.der. unintentionally.	bóntā	coord. but.
-binóng	suff.n. real.	-bòp	suff.v.der. RES:death.
bipót	n. difficulty(<Asm).	bòr	n. wrapped bundle.
birī	n. garden.	-bòr	suff.v.der. appearing small:S.
bírík	n. chili.	-bòr	suff.v.der. INTENS.
birtá	n. news(<Khs).	bor'á	v. EE:bor'í.
bisár	n. case(<Asm).	bor'í	suff.v.der. with great effort.
bisát	v. believe(<Asm).	botór	n. climate(<Asm).
bisīr	v. funnel for filtering ashes.	bú	n. bundle.
biskút	n. baked snack(<Eng).	bú	v. plait.
biyá-barú	v. equalize(<Asm).	bū	n. bamboo container type.
=bo	ptcl. ITROG ASSUM.	bū	v. carry on back.
=bo	ptcl. because.	-bùp	suff.v.der. RES:gone.

C

-Cē	suff.v.der. NEG.	che-	pref.v. RR.
chainōng	n. cow.	-chè	suff.v.der. unstable.
chàm	v. wash.	chē	ptcl. I mean (correction word).
chām	v. be wet.	chehē	n. crab.
chàn	v. flourish.	chehók	v. show happiness.
cháp	v. pile up.	chèk	n. bamboo.
charbàk	v. hold embraced.	-chèk	suff.v.der. firmly.
charhè	v. mourn.	cheláng	v. intermingle.
charí	v. rule.	chelòng	n. buffalo.
charlì	v. study.	chenáng	v. match.
charnàp	v. EE:chirú.	chenék	v. torture.

chèng	v. begin.	chō	v. accept responsibility.
-chéng	suff.v.der. for first time.	chō	v. spend.
chēng	n. drum.	chobēi	v. lie.
chěng	v. be narrow inbetween.	choboché	v. settle down.
chēr	v. break off.	chòi	n. shirt.
cherók	v. be alert.	chòk	v. wash clothes.
cherŏp	v? (be)twin.	chòk	v. beat w/hands.
chérsō	n. splinter.	-chòk	suff.v.der. disappearing.
chèt	n. small piece.	chók	v. be fine.
-chèt	suff.v.der. a bit.	chòkàng	n. axe(kd).
chethè	n. life.	-chòm	suff.v.der. together few close people.
chethók	v. fall out.		
chethōk	n. neck.	-chòm	suff.v.der. a little.
chetòng	v. meet.	chomāt	v. taste.
chidūn	v. resemble.	chomathā	v. think with bad consequences.
chiklō	n. moon.	chón	v. jump.
chilí	n. seed.	-chón	suff.v.der. very quickly.
chimī	n. claw.	-chòng	suff.v.der. slightly high.
chingchói	v. wear.	chōng	n. shield.
chinghīp	v. warm oneself with fire.	chonghō	n. frog.
chingjòr	n. shovel.	chonghói	n. reason.
chingkhán	v. be busy.	chopān	v. graze.
chingkì	v. bend.	chòr	v. cut.
chingkói	v. fall down:HUM.	-chòr	suff.v.der. RES:away.
chinglé	v. provide liquor ceremonially.	chór	clf. CLF:pair.
chinglú	v. take bath.	-chór	n.bound. spouse.
chingrúm	v. collect.	chōr'ī	v. crave to eat.
chingthàng	v. get stuck.	chosonsé	v. EE:choboché.
chingthí	v. wash head/hair.	-chot	suff.v.der. very.
chingtòn	v. stop for awhile.	-chòt	suff.v.der. only.
chiní	v. know.	-chót	suff.v.der. a bit.
chirú	v. cry.	chotái	n. place before house.
chirùi	v. return.	chové	v. graze.
-chìt	suff.v.der. finally.	chú	adv? long ago.
chithùr	v. drag.	chū	n. hair.
-chitìm	n.bound. half.	chū	v. suck.
chitím	n. mosquito.	chujēng	n. single hair.
cho-	pref.v. AUTO BEN/MAL.	chungkrèng	v. be thin.
-chò	suff.v.der. everything neg 1/2.		
chō	v. eat.		

D

dā	v. EE:dō.	-dàk	suff.v.der. RES:split.
dáh	interj. (let's)go!	-dàk	suff.v.der. sudden.
daitô	n. responsibility(<Asm).	-dàk	n.bound. road inbetween.
dàk	v. be spread out.	dāk	adv. here.
dàk	v. tear(intrans).	dàm	v. go.

dán	v. be able.	dō	v.cop. exist.
dán	v. get trapped.	dō	v. stay.
dán	v. fight.	dohái	n. oath(<Ind).
dàng	v. put on stove.	dòk	v. be sweet.
-dàng	suff.v.der. bright.	dolohí	n. EE:alohí.
dáng	v. start.	dolóng	n. bridge(<Asm).
dāng	v. block.	dòm	v. lie(animal).
dannoksō	n? danger.	dón	clf. CLF:family.
-dàp	suff.v.der. early.	dón	n. bridge/ladder.
-dàp	n.bound. morning.	dón	v. place ladder/bridge.
dappráng	n. dawn.	dōn	n. relative.
-dàppràng	suff.v.der. very early.	dondolón	n. ladder.
-dè	n.bound. tongue.	dondón	n. ladder.
déi	ptcl. OK?	-dòng	suff.v.der. O:small.
dèng	v. receive.	dòr	v. be enough.
déng	n. responsibility.	dorbár	n. big meeting(<Ind).
-dèr	suff.v.der. IDEOPHONE.	dorsón	type(<Asm).
dér	v. be late.	-dùk	suff.v.der. INTENS.
-dèt	suff.v.infl. PFV.	dúk	n. hardship(<Asm).
dét	n. country(<Ind).	dúk	v. be poor(<Asm).
dī	ptcl. Q tag.	-dūk	n.bound. dust.
díh	interj. leave me!	dùm	n. plains fishermen community.
dího	interj. leave me!	dumá	n. tobacco.
dihú	n. time.	dùn	v. join.
-dím	n.bound. reason.	-dūn	suff.v.der. JOIN.
-dím	n.bound. place.	-dùng	suff.v.der. exceedingly.
dín	n. day(<Asm).	dúng	v. pour.
-dìng	suff.v.der. steadily.	-dùp	suff.v.der. falling sound from high solid obj.
dīng	v. be long.		
dìnghakják	adj. odd.	-dùr	suff.v.der. fall down bigger than expected.
dìp	v. cover.		

E

e	ptcl. EXPRS.	èr	v. be red.
e-	pref.n. 1INCL POSS.	erí	v. let loose(<Asm).
e-	num. one.	èt	v. make hole.
è	v. plant.	èt	v. be yellow.
ékdóm	interj. EXCLAM(<Asm).	-èt	suff.v.der. all:S/O.
eli-	pref.n. 1INCL POSS HON.	-èt	suff.v.der. RES:yellow.
ēn	v. take.	-ét	suff.v.der. PRF.

G

gáonburá	n. village headman(<Asm).	garí	n. car(<Asm).

H

há	? over there(<Pnr).	hemthūr	n. house foundation site.
habē	n. headman.	hemthur-langnō	n. cremation ground.
habekóng	n. main headman.	hemtūn	n. good family.
habít	n. jungle.	hem'arī	n. oldest son.
haché	v. be born.	-henló	suff.v.infl. RL:EMPH.
hài	v. dare.	henō	v. bad.
hài	v. have tobacco taste.	hen'ūp	n. bamboo shoot.
-hái	suff.n. HON.	-hér	suff.v.der. high up.
háiháihái	interj. my goodness!	herāng	n. trap hole.
haihúi	adj. different kinds of.	-hèt	suff.v.der. firmly.
hák	n. finely woven bamboo basket.	-hét	suff.v.der. very near.
-hák	suff.v.der. suddenly.	hī	n. dung.
hák-chilí	n. basket with paddy seeds.	hijūk	v. shake sth big.
hakó	n? that time.	hìm	n. biscuit.
háladāk	adv. there.	hín	adv? this side.
halapú	adv. that side.	hiní	num. two.
hálasō	pro. that.	hipī	n. brinjal.
-hàm	suff.v.der. large:S/O.	hír	v. descend.
hamphāng	n. society.	hisáp	n. account(<Asm).
hán	n. prepared vegetables.	hithí	n. market(<Asm).
hàng	v. ask.	hi'ipī	n. witch.
-hàng	suff.v.der. quite.	hoʷ	interj. here you go.
háng	v. call.	ho	ptcl. EMPH:INTERACT.
hāng	v. want.	hodái	adv. always(<Asm).
hanmì	n. food taken with liquor.	hodák	adv. there.
hanmoī	n. ingmoi curry.	-hòi	suff.v.der. little bit.
hansò	n. ginger.	-hōi	n.bound. boundary.
-hàp	suff.v.der. everything neg 2/2.	-hoihōi	suff.v.der. slightly.
harái	adv. EE:parái.	-hòk	suff.v.der. dried up.
-harchī	n.bound. image.	hók	v. approve.
harēn	n. EE:habē.	-hōk	n.bound. truth.
harlūng	n. bowl.	hokum	n. will.
he	interj. hey!	hóm	v. fix by tying.
=he	ptcl. AFTERTHOUGHT.	homán	v. be equal(<Asm).
hedī	ptcl. Q.TAG	homói	n. time(<Asm).
hèk	v. remove cover.	hón	v. look after.
-hèk	suff.v.der. small.	hòng	clf. CLF:long cylindrical.
-hekhāk	suff.v.der. small:DISTR PL.	hòng	n. outside.
helō	v. be far.	hōng	v. make hole in tree.
-hēm	n.bound. house.	hong-chetāi	n. compound.
hēmarīpī	n. wife of eldest son.	hongkūp	n. entrance area Karbi house.
hēmbāng	n. extended family.		
hemepī	n. widow.	hongvàng	n. big hole in tree.
hēmphī	n. house owner FEM HON.	honjèng	n. thread.
hēmphū	n. house owner male HON.	-hōp	suff.v.der. fully agree.
-hempī	suff. intensifying.	hoptá	n. week(<Asm).
hēmtāp	n. tree house.	hòr	v. serve food.

hōr	n. liquor.	hùm	clf. CLF:house.
hormú	n. thing.	hūm	v. pick up.
horón	v. curse.	humrí	v. visit friends/relatives.
hortár	n. EE:hormú.	hùng	v. chase around.
hortón	n. EE:hormú.	hùt	v. dig.
hót	v. fix.	hút	v. interrogate.
hú	adv. over there.	hūt	n. time.
-hùi	suff.v.der. quite.	-hūt	rn. during.

I

ì	v. lie down.	ingkrūng	n. strainer.
ī	v. wear.	inglóng	n. hill.
-ī	suff.v.der. INSTR.	ingmōi	v. cook with alkali.
ìk	n. older brother.	-ingmūm	n.bound. beard.
ìk	v. be black.	ingnām	n. forest.
ìk	v. finish up(intrans).	ingnáng	v. get caught.
-īk	suff.v.der. FRML.	ingnàr	n. elephant.
-ingbòng	rn. middle.	ingnēk	v. laugh.
ingchìn	n. iron.	ingnì	v. EE:ingnēk.
ingchìr	v. be hungry.	ingnì	v. sit.
ingdàk	v. burst open.	-ingním	n.bound. smell.
ingdát	v. make a living.	-ingnò	rn. in front.
-ingdén	n.bound. general direction.	ingpen	coord. and then.
ingdēng	n. level.	-ingpìp	n.bound. foam.
-ingdēng	n.bound. border/mark.	ingplòng	v. run away animal.
ingdī	v. break long obj.	ingplùm	n. sprouts.
ingdōi	v. push.	ingpú	v. open(trans).
ingdūk	v. be immature.	ingrèng	v. call(small animals).
inghàn	n. mud.	ingrí	v. get addicted.
inghò	n. mouth.	ingròng	v. roar.
inghói	v. do.	ingsàk	v. EE:ingtāng.
inghōn	v. love.	ingsām	v. be cold.
inghòng	v. wait.	ingsìr	v. separate.
inghór	v. carry load.	ingsīr	v. filter.
inghōr	n. carrying load.	-ingsóng	rn. high up.
inghū	v. steal.	ingsū	n. thorn.
ingjàng	v. look proper.	-ingtán	rn. outside.
ingjàr	v. fly.	ingtāng	v. be strong.
ingjínsō	v. have pity.	ingthàk	v. itch.
ingjìr	n. clan sister.	ingthàng	v. be dawn.
ingjír	v. dissolve.	ingthēk	n. sign.
ingjòng	v. move.	-ingthíp	n.bound. unbroken rice.
-ingkāng	n.bound. circumference.	ingthìr	v. be clean.
ingkī	v. talk.	ingthirjìr	v. be clean.
ingki'ān	n. silkworm leaf.	ingthōng	v. be deaf.
ingkòi	num. twenty.	-ingthòr	n.bound. hole.
ingkrùng	v. strain.	ingthùm	v. go and bring.

ingthùr	v. wake up(trans).	ingvài	v. choose.
ingtí	n. salt.	ingvùi	v. stir.
ingtòn	v. conclude.	ing'í	n. sweat.
ingtòng	n. big bamboo basket roughly woven.	ing'īt	v. be thirsty.
		ing'òm	v. keep in mouth.
ingtū	v. be fat animals.	-ing'òm	n.bound. cheek.
ingtùi	v. be high.	ing'ùi	n. new jhum field.
ingtúng	v. desire.	isī	adj. whole.
ingtúng	v. EE:boché.	isī	num. one.

J

já	v. lead.	-jò	suff.v.der. many continuously:S.
jabók	n. pocket(<Asm).	jó	n. night.
jáho	interj. look there!	-jō	rn. amidst.
jāi	n. EE:rīt.	jòi	v. be for free/in vain.
jàilò	n. EE:rītlō.	-jòi	suff.v.der. quietly.
jakát	n. place(<Asm).	joiné	n. reason(<Ind).
jambili-athōn	n. cultural item(kd)..	jòk	v. drop into container.
jamboróng	n. bag.	jòk	v. get untied.
jáng	v. fall.	-jōk	rn. because.
jāng	v. hang down.	joklū	v. be foolish.
jāng	v. fit.	jōn	clf. CLF:animals.
jangrē	n. orphan.	-jōn	n.bound. height.
jangrengsō	n. orphan.	jòng	v. point.
jangresō	n. single parent child.	-jōng	suff. just.
jàngthù	n. oil.	jonghé	ptcl? as much as.
jàr	v. be upright.	jóngsi	subord. if.
jár	v. EE:chàn.	jontú	n. animal(<Asm).
ját	n. type(<Ind).	jòr	v. sell.
je	ptcl. QUOT.	-jòr	n.bound. slice of meat.
jék	v. know dos and donts.	-jōr	n.bound. value.
jèng	v. spin.	jubát	n. EE:jutáng.
-jèng	suff.v.der. for long time(sound).	jùi	v. play.
-jí	suff.v.infl. IRR2.	-jùi	suff.v.der. away.
jimán	ptcl? as much(<Asm).	juja'ē	n. cradle.
jintāk	n. bamboo strip.	júk	n. era(<Asm).
jìr	n. period of time.	jùn	v. drink.
jīr	v. climb like creeper.	jūt	v. finish.
jīrpō	n. friend.	jutáng	n. custom.
jò	interj. see!		

K

kadókavē	n. all.	kái	adv. always.
kài	v. set fire.	kái	n. time(<Asm).

kák	v. part.	klàng	v. appear.
kakót	n. paper(<Asm).	klàr	v. shine.
kalàng	interj. yes.	klém	v. do.
kalī	v.cop. NEG EQU COP.	klém	v. tremble.
kàm	v. step.	klèng	n. old one.
kám	n. work.	-klìp	suff.v.der. quietly.
kām	clf. CLF:step.	klīp	v. subside.
kamái	n. EE:kūr.	kló	v. fall.
kán	v. dance.	-klùi	suff.v.der. quite.
-káng	suff.v.der. just.	-klùng	suff.v.der. for long time.
kángburá	n. village head man(<Asm).	-klùng	suff.v.der. echoing sound.
kangthú	v. bounce.	ko	ITR.
káp	v. cross water.	ko	? buddy:ADDR.
kàr	v. burn.	kodāk	pro. where.
kardóm	interj. GREETING.	kòi	v. rub.
karlē	n. squirrel.	kōi	v. accuse.
kasú	n. plate.	kòk	v. tie.
kàt	v. run:HUM.	-kòk	suff.v.der. firmly.
=ke	ptcl. TOP.	-kòk	suff.v.der. absolutely required.
ke-	pref.v. NMLZ.	kokkedakjo	?. onomatopoeia:hens.
kēk	v. be not straight.	kolìk	v. be cunning.
=kema	that's why.	kolosón	pro. how.
kenē	ptcl. HESIT.	kóm	v. be less(<Asm).
kèng	v. be straight.	komantú	pro. when.
-kèng	n.bound. foot.	komāt	pro. who.
kengkèng	adv. all the way.	kōn	v. use up.
kengrī	n. base of tree.	konát	pro. where.
kēp	num. ten.	-kòng	suff.v.der. continuously.
kèr	n. bad omen.	kongsìn	n. shovel(kd).
kerahí	n. pan(<Asm).	kongtolōng	n. wheel.
kethòm	num. three.	kopái	n. luck.
khái	v. grow.	kopí	pro. what.
khají	n. small food.	kopichíng	pro. what possibly.
khalí	adv. all(<Asm).	kopīsi	pro. why.
khalùn	n. big basket(kd).	kopù	pro. how.
kháng	v. keep.	kopú	pro. where.
khangjáng	v. do irreversibly.	kopùlo	interj. what will happen?
khangrá	n. basket for firewood.	kòr	v. bite.
khèi	n. community.	korpī	n. sister in law.
khitirí	n. main people in charge.	-korpihái	n.bound. sister in law:R.
khobór	n. news(<Ind).	kortè	n. same gender sibling.
khóng	n. tribe.	kortetè	n. 2 siblings of same gender.
-khràm	suff.v.der. with loud noise.	kosón	pro. how.
kilīk	v. tickle.	ko'án	pro. how much.
kìm	v. build.	-kràk	suff.v.der. up to top.
kimó	v. commemorate.	kràng	n. EE:úm.
-kìng	suff.v.der. small weight:O.	-kràng	suff.v.der. loosely.
kīp	v. pour out.	kré-	num. -teen.
kirlá	v. turn over.	-krèi	suff.v.der. DIST PL.

krèng	v. be dry.	kú	v. crow.
krēp	v. fall over.	kulát	n. shop(<Asm).
krì	clf. CLF:line.	kúmbór	n. blanket(<Ind).
krì	n. EE:jòr.	-kùng	rn. at side of.
-krì	suff.v.der. follow closely.	kūp	v. cover.
krōi	v. agree.	kúr	n. clan(<Khs).
króng	clf. CLF:road.	kurjà	n. muslim.
-krùng	suff.v.der. very difficult.	kutéi	? all(<Asm).
kú	n. spade.		

L

là	pro. this.	=le	ptcl. FOC:IRR.
ladāk	adv. here.	lè	v. reach.
lahái	pro. these.	-lè	suff.v.der. again.
laháihúi	pro. these:DISTR.	lēm	v. play with toys.
lahé	interj. that way?	-lemdet	suff.v.der. repeatedly.
laheihei	pro. these.	lèng	v. split bamboo.
làk	v. be tired.	lèng	v. go long distance.
-làm	suff.v.der. RES:paste.like.	léng	v. be fat:HUM.
lám	n. word.	lengpūm	n. pestle.
lám	n. matter.	lepù-ánte	subord. when.
lám	n. language.	-lèt	suff.v.der. PFV3.
lamchōng	n. EE:lammét.	lì	v. flow.
lammét	n. literature.	-lì	suff.n. HON.
lamthē	n. matter.	lík	v. pluck.
laná	v. take care.	-lìng	suff.v.der. sth small hanging.
làng	v. see.	-lìng	rn. at bottom of.
làng	v. read.	lìt	v. exceed.
-làng	suff.v.infl. still.	=lo	ptcl. FOC.
lāng	n. water.	-lò	suff.v.infl. RL.
lānghē	n. washing place.	-lò	n.bound. male animal.
langkesō	n. tea.	ló	v. send.
langpōng	n. small bamboo container.	ló	v. let loose.
langrōi	n. river.	lō	n. banana leaf.
làngselét	v. hate.	lobōng	n. plantain.
-làp	suff.v.der. completely.	lòk	v. be white.
lapèn	coord. and.	-lòk	suff. just.
lapèn	coord. and then.	-lòk	suff.v.der. happen to.
lapú	adv. this side.	-lòk	suff.v.der. not main action.
lapú	adv. on the other hand.	=lók	ptcl. only.
làpusón	adv. like this.	-lók	suff.v.der. right then.
làr	v. switch.	-lokòt	rn. along with(<Asm).
lasì	coord. therefore.	lòkphlèp	v. be pale.
lasō	pro. this.	lòk'hù	v. be pale.
lasón	adv. that way.	-lonāng	suff.v.infl. HORT:EMPH.
lat	n. EE:króng.	lòng	clf. CLF:place.

-lòng	suff.v.der. RES:round.	-lòt	suff.v.der. INTENS.
-lòng	rn. LOC.	lothā	n. EE:lothē.
lóng	v. get.	lothē	n. banana.
-lōng	suff.v.der. get to.	lují	n. mirror.
longdāng	n. crevice.	luksón	v. lose(<Asm).
longkòi	n. grasshopper.	lúm	n. hill top(<Khs).
longkōi	n. pebble.	-lùn	suff.v.der. big:AO.
longkū	n. cave.	lún	n. song.
longlē	n. earth.	lún	v. sing.
longrī	n. subdistrict.	lūt	v. enter.
longtār	n. rock.		

M

m	interj. AFF.	meme	maybe.
ma	ptcl. I mean.	méme	n. dignitaries.
=ma	ptcl. Q.	-mémè	suff.v.der. -able.
-maháng	n.bound. face.	mèn	v. be ready to eat.
mai	interj. how bad!	-mén	n.bound. name.
mán	v. become/happen.	mená	pro. self.
mandú	n. field hut.	menā	adv. EE:menē.
mané	ptcl. HESIT(<Asm).	menē	ptcl. maybe.
-màng	rn. EE:-tèng.	ménmèn	adv. suddenly.
māng	n. dream.	methān	n. dog.
manghū	v. get confused.	-metháng	pro. self.
mánke	coord. and then.	mēthūr	n. fire with high flames.
manthū	n. dried fish.	mh'	interj. no.
mantú	pro. when.	mí	n. buttocks.
-mār	suff. PL.	mí	v. EE:mán.
marēk	ptcl. unexpectedly.	mī	v. be new.
marí	v. lock(<Asm).	milumbōng	n. buttocks.
marjèng	v. be thin.	mindár	n. world(<Pnr).
marjòng	n. big basket(kd).	mír	n. flower.
marlí	suff. PL:ADDR.	misò	n. ant.
maró	n. courtyard.	mò	n. strip of field.
masì	? the only one.	mó	n. inheritance.
māt	coord. and then.	mó	? because.
màtè	ptcl. otherwise.	mó	n. while.
mathà	v. think.	mó	DISAGREEING.
=mati	ptcl. CG.	mó	n? future.
mē	n. fire.	mō	v. hesitate.
mē	v. be good.	-mòi	n.bound. back.
mehīp	n. fireplace.	mòidāi	n. backrest.
méi	n. assembly.	-mōk	n.bound. breast.
mèk	n. wound.	mòng	v. smoke.
-mék	suff.v.der. in advance.	monít	n. man.
-mēk	n.bound. eye.	monór	n. EE:monít.
mekkrī	n. tear.	motíyár	n. POST.

motór	n. vehicle(<Eng).	mùng	n. EE:sòn.
-movē	suff.v.der. nothing to.	-munpī	n.bound. daughter-in-law.
-mū	suff.v.der. CPR.	múnthí	v. think deeply.
-mū	n.bound. younger sibling.	musosō	n. 2 siblings of diff gender.
múi	n. EE:prán(<Ind).	mutē	(postposition?). compared to.
mulúk	n. people(<Ind).	muthē	coord. but(<Asm).
mumāng	n. appearance(poet).		

N

nahōk	n. not truth.	nèp	v. catch.
nahōk	adv. anywhere.	nerkēp	num. eight.
-nài	suff.v.der. big solid:O.	nì	clf. CLF:day.
naidūng	n. border between field and jungle.	-ní	num. two.
-nàk	suff.v.der. in vain.	nihàng	? east.
nàm	v. buy.	ním	n. custom.
nám	v. be true.	nīng	n. mind.
nāmdūr	n. EE:nampī.	ningjé	v. speak.
nāmpī	n. big forest.	ningkán	n. year.
nang=	procltc. 1/2:NSUBJ.	nīngkē	ptcl. even.
nang=	procltc. CIS.	ninglák	n. EE:ningrī.
nang-	pref.n. 2 POSS.	ningrī	n. worry.
nàng	pro. 2.	ningvē	n. evening.
-nàng	suff.v.infl. HORT:CON.	ninōktòk	v. become gravy.
náng	v. need.	nióm	n. procedure(<Asm).
-nāng	suff.v.infl. HORT.	-nò	n.bound. ear.
nangli-	pref.n. 2 POSS HON.	-nō	suff.v.der. bad to.
-nangtā	suff.v. if alternatively.	-nōi	suff.v.infl. INF COND IMP.
=nàt	ptcl. only.	nòk	n. sword.
nát	n. direction.	-nòk	suff.v.der. EE:-nèk.
nátthū	n. direction.	nók	n. sugar cane.
ne=	procltc. 1EXCL:NSUBJ.	nón	adv. now.
ne-	pref.n. 1EXCL POSS.	-nōn	suff.v.infl. COND IMP.
nè	pro. 1EXCL.	nōng	v. loosen soil.
-nē	suff.n. INDEF.	nopàk	n. dao.
-néi	suff.v.der. superlative.	nothōng	adj. deaf.
-nèk	suff.v.der. doing bad unnecessarily.	nún	v. place container.
nempō	n. sesame.	-nùng	n.bound. back.
nemprù	v. have sweet smell.	nūt	clf. CLF:HUM:SG.

O

o	ptcl. VOC.	òi	v. take away sth spread out.
-ò	suff.v.der. much.	ói	v. be sad.
ó	v. leave.	ōi	interj. yes.
oi	ptcl. addr between equal women.	ōk	n. meat.

okarjāng	n. girl.	orá	v. take care.
óm	clf. CLF:mouthful.	osō	n. child.
óng	v.cop. exist much.	osopī	n. lady.
-óng	suff.v.der. too much.	ót	v. touch.
ōng	n. maternal uncle.	ovè	n. generation.
opeija	interj. my goodness!		

P

pachermát	v. test if taste is good.	penāk	? actually.
padāp	adv. this morning.	-pēnān	n.bound. husband.
-pāi	n.bound. sb's turn.	penáng	adj. a lot.
pajirmī	v. elaborate.	penáng	v. make fun.
pàk	clf. CLF:flat.	penānsō	n. couple.
paká	? very good(<Ind).	penàp	adv. tomorrow.
pān	v. clear vegetation.	-pèt	suff.v.der. all.
pangbár	v. compare.	-pèt	suff.v.der. RES:cut off.
pangchèng	v. start.	-phái	n.bound. number.
pangdòn	v. even out.	phàk	n. pig.
pangrèng	v. rear.	-phàk	suff.v.der. almost completely.
pangrì	v. reconcile.	-phān	rn. NSUBJ.
pangrúm	v. collect.	-phàng	n.bound. shoulder.
pangthàng	n. dawn.	pharlá	n. outside part Karbi house.
pang'è	v. dress up.	pharman	share.
páp	n. fault(<Ind).	pharó	num. hundred.
pár	v. cross(<Asm).	phatáng	n. basket(kd).
-pár	rn. beyond.	-phēk	n.bound. intestines.
-pār	suff.v.der. very.	phelāng	n. thatch.
parái	adv. this side of the river.	pheló	n. cotton.
parē	v. use tool.	phelō	n. alkali.
parkám	v. be half bad.	pheré	v. fear.
parók-jàngphòng	n. pineapple.	-phī	n.bound. grandmother.
pasi'í	v. whistle.	phí	v. give birth.
-paténg	? step.	phī	v. roast.
pathē	v. pretend.	-phī	n.bound. backside.
pathú	v. play.	-phī	rn. after.
patì	v. lay eggs.	phihái	n. grandmother:POL.
patīp	v. mix.	phinū	n. banana.
patú	v. hide.	-phìt	suff.v.der. right away.
pe-	pref.v. CAUS.	-phìt	suff.v.der. RES:away.
pe-	pref.n. VBLZ.	phi'īng	v. pass urine.
pé	n. cloth.	phlàk	v. split.
-pēi	n.bound. mother.	-phlák	n.bound. split off pieces.
pèk	v. give way.	-phlì	suff.v.der. for awhile.
=pen	ptcl. from.	phlī	num. four.
=pen	ptcl. with.	phlòng	v. burn.
-pen	suff.v.der. NF:with.	-phlòt	suff.v.der. becoming lose.

-phlùng	suff.v.der. spreading.	pinsō	n. married man.
phlúng	v. chase away.	pinthí	v. EE:pinchóng.
-phlùp	suff.v.der. sd falling and scattering.	-pinú	n.bound. mothers younger sister.
-phlùt	suff.v.der. miss/fail.	pirdá	n. place of worship.
-phlùt	suff.v.der. hastily.	pirthé	n. world(<Khs).
-phlùt	suff.v.der. suddenly	-pisàr	n.bound. mothers older sister.
big A/O.		-pīsō	n.bound. wife.
phō	num. five.	plàng	clf. CLF:small flat.
phō	v. reach.	pláng	v. be rich.
phói	clf. CLF:times.	plāng	v. become.
phojō	v. EE:arklì.	plāng	v. be able.
pholòng	n. grasshopper.	plēng	v. be full.
phòng	n. wild jackfruit.	-pò	suff.v.der. IRR1.
phóng	clf. CLF:times.	-pò	n.bound. ingredient.
-phráng	rn. in front of.	-pō	suff.n. male.
-phràt	suff.v.der. sd beating.	-pō	suff.n. AUGMENT.
phrín	v. throw in fire.	-pō	n.bound. father.
-phròk	suff.v.der. bulging out.	pohùi	n. pillow.
-phròng	suff.v.der. PL:S/A.	-pōk	n.bound. stomach.
-phrú	suff.v.der. EE:-tháp.	pòn	v. take away.
-phù	n.bound. grandfather.	-pōn	suff.v.der. in passing.
-phú	n.bound. head.	-pōn	suff.v.der. away.
phū	? grandfather:VOC.	pongrēp	n. outside wall area.
phuhaí	n. grandfather:POL.	-pór	n.bound. time.
phūlē	n. pot.	porhí	v. read(<Asm).
phùr	v. dig.	porí	v. fall(<Asm).
phurùi	n. yam.	pōt	n. thing.
phutūp	n. hat.	pōt	n. reason.
phu'īk	n. earthen pot.	-pōt	rn. because.
pí	pro. what.	-prán	n.bound. life(<Ind).
pī	v. give.	prāng	v. wake up.
pī	n. animal.	pràp	v. be quick.
pī	v. cut.	-prè	suff.v.der. scattered.
-pī	suff.n. AUGMENT.	prék	v. be different.
-pī	suff.n. INTENS.	-prèt	suff.v.der. acting on inflated obj.
-pī	suff.n. female.	pu	ptcl. QUOT.
-pī	suff.v.der. BEN/MAL.	pù	v. say.
-pī	n.bound. female/mother.	pù	ptcl. like this.
pibā	n. baby carrying cloth.	pùlotángtē	subord. if.
-pìk	suff.v.der. very.	pulote	subord. if.
pilolō	n. female and male animal.	púm	clf. CLF:round.
-pín	suff.v.infl. never.	pùmamāt	adv. just like that.
pinchóng	v. create(<Khs).	pún	v. measure.
pindéng	n. dress and ornaments(<Khs).	pún	n. EE:páp(<Asm).
pinì	adv. today.	punōn	? say/e g .
pinī	n. tradt fem waist cloth.	-punú	n.bound. uncle.
piníng	adv. this year.	pùr	v. open unfold.
pinkhát	v. advise(<Khs).		

-pùr	suff.v.der. move over.	pusetamē	ptcl. likewise.
pūr	v. uproot.	pusetamē	subord. even though.
purá	? all(<Ind).	puthōt	adv. again.
purthīmī	n. earth(<Asm).	puthōt	adj. next.

R

rà	and.	rihō	n. fruit of creeper.
-rà	suff.v.der. NF:IRR.	rík	v. be scattered.
-rài	suff.v.der. solid obj breaking.	rikāng	n. creeper.
-rài	suff.v.der. sideways.	-rìm	n.bound. EE:rō.
-rài	rn. at side of.	rīm	v. keep in order.
-ràk	suff.v.der. RES:little wound.	rinchithó	n. cloth(kd).
rák	v. tear.	-rìng	suff.v.der. slightly.
rakóm	n. EE:ním.	rìnràn	v. be between life and death.
ràm	n. old jhum field.	-rintí	suff.v.der. equally:PL:S/A.
-ràn	suff.v.der. delicate/about to break.	rīp	v. hold onto.
		-rirí	suff.v.der. slightly.
rán	v. set up thread.	rísanghó	n. companion.
ràng	n. EE:rū.	risō	n. unmarried man.
-ràng	suff.v.der. about to.	rīt	n. field.
ràp	v. stick.	ritlō	n. inhabited field.
-ràp	suff.v.der. together same.	rō	v. hit.
ráp	v. help.	-rō	n.bound. branch.
ráp	n. EE:dón.	robàk	n. big branch.
-rāp	suff.v.der. together.	ròi	v. sew.
rát	n. public(<Asm).	-ròi	suff.v.der. solid obj.
rè	v. be sharp.	rói	n. stall.
-rè	suff.v.der. little.	-ròk	suff.v.der. completed.
rechó	n. king.	ròn	v. distribute.
-rèk	suff.v.der. delayed.	rón	n. fight.
-rèk	suff.v.der. silently.	rōn	n. custom.
rék	v. ask for.	ròng	n. village.
-rèn	suff.v.der. in a row.	-ròng	suff.v.der. instead.
rèng	v. be alive.	róng	v. borrow.
-rèng	n.bound. skin.	-róng	n.bound. color(<Asm).
-rèp	suff.v.der. each:S/A.	rōng	n. plant.
-rēp	n.bound. side.	rongrò	? around the village.
-repī	n.bound. bone.	rongsopī	n. town.
rèt	v. cut by slowly removing.	róng'ajé	n. festival.
rèt	v. EE:nàm.	rosún	n. garlic(<Asm).
rét	v. stalk.	ròt	v. cut.
rì	v. search.	-ròt	suff.v.der. RES:wet.
-rí	n.bound. hand.	-rù	suff.v.der. quite.
rī	n. EE:pé.	rú	v. serve.
-rī	suff.v.infl. PROH.	rū	n. leftover bones after burning.

-rùi	suff.v.der. many:S/O.	rùp	n. EE:ròng.
-rùk	suff.v.der. away:PL.	-rùp	n.bound. EE:chór.
-rúm	rn. below.	rúp	n. silver.
rùng	v. lift.		

S

sá	n. tea(<Ind).	-sén	suff.v.der. INTENS.
sabí	n. key(<Asm).	sèng	n. condiments.
sabón	n. soap(<Asm).	-sèr	suff.v.der. unexpectedly(uttering).
sadú	n. EE:samé.		
-sài	suff.v.der. no obstruction or discrimination.	sér	n. gold(<Khs).
		serhéserhé	adv. in a hurry.
sái	n. labor.	setā	subord. but.
saidá	v. EE:orá.	setamē	? nevertheless.
saidé	ptcl. all over.	=si	ptcl. FOC:RL.
saikél	n. bicycle(<Eng).	-si	suff.v.infl. NF:RL.
sakōr	n. servant(<Asm).	sí	v. catch fish by picking up.
sala	interj. damn you!	-sí	suff.v. SPLT.
samé	n. path.	sík	v. prepare.
Samí	n? Mrs(ADDR).	siksāk	v. be difficult.
samphrí	n. sun(poet).	sikún	adj? neat and clean(<Asm).
sán	? five(<Pnr).	sìm	v. EE:nōng.
-sàng	suff.v.der. black.	-sināng	suff.v.infl. HORT:CON.
sáng	v. take rest.	singjám	v. have a cold.
sāng	n. raw rice.	singnām	n. head strap.
sanghó	n. clan name.	sintí	v. pray(<Asm).
sangphēr	n. flattened rice.	-sìr	suff.v.der. sd fast spinning.
sāngtēt	n. rice for journey.	sirí-sabún	n. Shree soap(<Asm).
sáp	adj? neat and clean(<Asm).	sirkēp	num. nine.
sáp	v. beat w/sth flexible.	sirkút	n. room.
saphá	v. be clean(<Asm).	skúl	n. school(<Eng).
sàr	v. be old.	sò	v. hurt.
sàr	n. village headman.	sò	v. be hot.
sàrburá	n. old man.	-sō	suff.n. DIM.
sarióphale	? around(<Asm).	-sō	suff.n. DEM.
sarnūng	n. roof.	-sō	suff.v.der. INTENS.
sarpī	n. old woman.	sodíng	? all along.
sarpīburì	n. old woman.	sòk	v. get water.
sàrthè	n. village headman.	sōk	n. paddy.
sát	n. proof.	solangdō	n. four chieftains(<Khs).
sè	n. disease.	sòm	v. put in ground.
-sè	n.bound. voice.	sōmē	n. EE:pīsō.
sé	v. keep diet.	sòn	clf. CLF:thing.
sēk	clf. CLF:section.	sòn	n. thing.
sè-kasadí	n. precelebration rituals.	sóp	? all(<Ind).
semé	n. vow(<Khs).	sopinsō	n. men:COLL.

sòr	n. people.	-sū	n.bound. grandchild.
sorsá	v. criticize.	-sū	n.bound. EE:sō.
sosē	? more.	sùi	v. turn.
-sót	suff.v.der. be required.	sumpót	n. EE:pindéng.
sovài	v. EE:archó.	sūn	v. descend.
sovái	v. be loose.	sùng	v. be difficult.
sō'arlō	n. women:COLL.	surí	num. thousand.
sō'arlosō	n. women:COLL.		

T

=tā	ptcl. ADD.	tepī	n. elder brother's wife.
tahài	ptcl. DUBIT.	tepō	n. brother in law.
-tài	suff.v.der. for a moment.	tèr	v. be dirty.
takirí	n. spindle(<Asm).	terék	v. move.
taló	n. sea.	teròi	v. walk with effort.
-tām	suff.v.der. impossible.	tèt	v. exit.
=tamē	ptcl. any.	tevàr	v. turn around.
-tàn	suff.v.der. very big.	-thā	suff.v.infl. CON IMP.
-tàng	ptcl. REP.	thaī	n. arrow.
táng	n. EE:rōn.	-thài	suff.v.der. all.
táng	v. LV.	thái	n. place(<Asm).
-táng	suff.v.der. PFV2.	thái	v. serve.
tāng	v. finish.	-thái	suff.v.der. all:S/O.
tànghò	ptcl. REP.	thàk	v. answer.
tángká	n. money.	thàk	v. weave.
tangtè	ptcl. TOP.	-thàk	rn. on top.
tángtē	subord. if.	thák	v. divide.
tàr	n. bamboo mat.	thák	v. EE:dō(<Asm).
tār	n. nest.	thakthāk	? same.
tarík	n. date(<Asm).	thàn	v. cut.
tarkòng	n. mat for sitting.	thán	v. tell.
tè	v. let dry by sun.	thanbangpī	n. fem teacher.
tè	n. elder sister.	tháng	n. anything.
tè	coord. and then/therefore.	thangbàk	? as if.
-tē	suff.v. COND.	thàp	v. put inside.
tebonsitā	coord. but.	thàp	n. cake for rice beer.
téi	v. apply.	-tháp	suff.v.der. mindlessly.
tekáng	v. leave for.	tharmīt	n. turmeric.
-tekáng	suff.v.der. leaving.	tharún	v. rock.
tekè	n. tiger.	tharvē	n. mango.
teló	v. EE:ingdát.	thàt	v. slaughter.
telòng	n. boat.	thè	v. be big.
temá	n. tobacco container(<Asm).	thē	n. reason.
temó	n. story.	thē	clf. CLF:word.
tèng	v. build dam.	-thē	n.bound. fruit.
-tèng	rn. according to.	théi	n. EE:méi.
tengnè	v. forget.	thèk	v. know how.

thèk	*ptcl.* this much.	thù	*v.* be tasty.
thèk	*v.* see.	thú	*v.* cut.
thék	*v.* put wood in fire.	thú	*v.* collect nest material.
theklōng	*v.* see.	-thú	*n.bound.* fat.
-thektík	*suff.v.* as much V as it can be.	thū	*v.* rot.
thekumbōng	*n.* EE:theseré.	-thū	*suff.v.der.* again.
thèng	*v.* beat w/sth solid.	thùi	*v.* wrap big size by rolling.
thēng	*n.* firewood.	thùr	*v.* get up.
thengphráng	*n.* broom plant.	tì	*ptcl.* definitely.
thengphráng	*n.* EE:thengpī.	tì	*v.* peel.
thengpī	*n.* tree/wood.	tí	*v.* get rid off.
thengrō	*n.* EE:thengtāk.	tibùk	*n.* earthen pot.
thengtāk	*n.* splinter.	tikì	*v.* cultivate.
thēp	*v.* dry up.	tilí	*v.* decline.
thepài	*n.* cliff.	timí	*n.* EE:tomó.
thepō	*?* huge.	timùr	*v.* root.
thér	*v.* threaten.	tín	*n.* tin(<Eng).
therāk	*v.* be ashamed.	-tín	*suff.n.* each.
therēng	*n.* EE:thepài.	tīn	*v.* mistake.
theseré	*n.* fruits.	titī	*ptcl.* habitually.
the'āng	*v.* be bright.	tò	*interj.* OK.
thì	*v.* die.	tó	*v.* gather suddenly.
thī	*v.* be short.	todáp	*adv.* this morning.
thijōk	*n.* deer.	tòk	*v.* pound.
thík	*v.* be okay(<Asm).	tòk	*v.* write.
thík	*adv.* right then.	tokklìng	*v.* pound until tight.
thìnì	*v.* be almost dead.	tòng	*v.* meet.
-thìp	*suff.v.der.* firmly.	tōng	*v.* collide.
thīp	*v.* beat drum.	-tōng	*suff.n.* instead of.
thír	*v.* be firmly fixed/ unvariable(<Asm).	-tōng	*suff.n.* INDIR ITRG.
		tòt	*v.* squat.
thirík	*v.* startle.	-tòt	*suff.v.der.* heavy going back and forth.
thó	*v.* make opening.		
thói	*n.* plains.	-tōt	*suff.v.der.* unnecessarily.
thōk	*v.* empty out.	továr	*n.* road.
thòn	*v.* drop.	-tū	*suff.v.infl.* UNCOND IMP.
thongkūp	*n.* tobacco container.	-tùk	*suff.v.der.* sd of stepping.
thòr	*v.* kindle.	tūk	*v.* dig.
-thòr	*suff.v.der.* up to the end.	tùm	*v.* hold sth.
thór	*v.* be many.	-tūm	*n.bound.* PL.
thōr	*v.* be sour.	tumì	*adv.* yesterday.
-thòt	*suff.v.der.* into opening.	tún	*v.* cook.
-thót	*suff.v.der.* exactly.	tùr	*v.* catch fish with net.
thrōk	*num.* six.	túr	*v.* kick.
thrōk	*num.* ten.	tūr	*n.* brightness.
thrōksí	*num.* seven.		

U

ulái	v. take out(<Asm).	ùn	v. get along.
-úm	n.bound. cage.	ùn	v. be able.
ùn	n. EE:àn.		

V

-vàk	suff.v.der. RES:open.	-vèt	suff.v.der. nicely.
-vám	n.bound. waist.	-vét	suff. only.
vàn	v. bring.	vì	v. do.
-ván	n.bound. share.	ví	v. herd.
vàng	v. come.	vī	n. blood.
-vàng	suff.v.der. PL.	-víng	suff.v.der. INTENS.
-váng	suff.n. every.	-vìr	suff.v.der. gently.
vankòk	n. tradt fem belt.	vír	v. lose.
vár	v. throw away.	-vír	suff.v.der. EE:-sō.
-varèt	suff.v.der. INTENS.	võ	n. chicken.
varsāi	n. way.	vói	v. return.
vé	v. pluck.	vōsō	n. EE:võtèk.
vèk	v. swim.	-vòt	suff.v.der. IDEOPHONE:be fast.
vèk	v. steer.	võtèk	n. wild bird.
-vék	suff.v.der. definitely.	võterāng	n. hornbill.
vēk	v. hang.	vùr	v. drop in.
-vèn	suff.v.der. curled up:S.		
vēn	v. wipe.		

Clan names

Bēy
Kropī
Ronghāng
Rongphàr
Rongpī
Teràng
Terón
Timùng
Tissō
Ónsō
Rasinjá
Ratul
Rengbonghōm
Réngsō
Ròngbàng
Rongchechó
Sàmprì
Sangvāi
Séng

Personal names

Birēn
Bokolā
Borsíng
Dilí
Kaché
Karé

Karbi place names

Amrī	n. AREA.
Bóithalangsō	n. TOWN.
Chinthóng	n. AREA.
Chóm	n. PLACE.
Koplī	n. RIVER.
Langpi	n. RIVER.

Rongkháng	n. AREA.
Sarthe Rongphar	n. VILLAGE.
Sochēng	n. VILLAGE.
Sochēng Dhentá	n. TOWN.
Ujándongká	n. VILLAGE.

Names of tribes

Chománg	n. Khasi.
Karbì	n. PN.
Kechè	n. EE:Chománg.

Names of festivals, ceremonies, celebrations

chingnáng	v. dance(kd).
chōjūn	n. celebration(kd).
chokú	n. EE:chojūn.
Chomangkán	n. celebration(kd).
kasadí	n. celebration(kd).
Ròngkèr	n/v. festival(kd).
ròng-ketòng	n. ceremony(kd).

Names of animals and plants

chonghōkalósō	n. frog(kd).
chosòt	n. vegetable(kd).
hanthàr	n. vegetable(kd).
ingrī	n. grass(kd).
jamír	n. grain(kd).
karlēsibóng	n. squirrel(kd).
methān-sibóngpō	n. dog(kd).
misòrongpō	n. ant(kd).
nòngnòng	n. creeper(kd).
pàk	n. tree(kd).
phàkbeléngpī	n. pig(kd).
plimplām	n. Dillenia indica.
sibū	n. indigo plant(<Khs).
sílukā	n. Terminalia chebula Retz(<Asm).
sūhō	n. thorny plant(kd).
tihà	n. root spice(kd).
võ'arbí	n. bird(kd).
vo'arkók	n. bird(kd).
vo'arkókpō	n. plant(kd).

Other names

Hingchòng	n. constellation(kd).
pinpō	n. officer(kd).

Bibliography

Austin, Peter K. 2006. "Data and Language Documentation." In *Essentials of Language Documentation*, edited by Jost Gippert, Nikolaus P. Himmelmann, and Ulrike Mosel, 87–112. Berlin: Mouton de Gruyter.

Austin, Peter K., and Julia Sallabank, eds. 2011. *The Cambridge Handbook of Endangered Languages*. Leiden: Cambridge University Press.

Balawan, Fr. Michael. 1978. *A Mikir-English Dictionary with Some Tit-Bits of Mikir Grammar*. Shillong: Khasi Jaintia Presbyterian Press.

Bauman, James. 1976. "An Issue in the Subgrouping of the Tibeto-Burman Languages: Lepcha and Mikir." Paper presented at the 9th International Conference on Sino-Tibetan Languages and Linguistics, October 22–24, Copenhagen.

Benedict, Paul K. 1972. *Sino-Tibetan: A Conspectus*. New York: Cambridge University Press.

Bey, Chitro Kumar. 2010. *Karbi Alam Ketok Kapacheton: Isi-Hini Aron*. Amlapatty, Diphu, Karbi Anglong, Assam, India: Hiddhinath Rongpi.

Bickel, Balthasar. 1999. "Nominalization and Focus Constructions in Some Kiranti Languages." In *Topics in Nepalese Linguistics*, edited by Yogendra P. Yadava and Warren W. Glover, 271–96. Kathmandu: Royal Nepal Academy.

Bickel, Balthasar. 2001. "On the Syntax of Agreement in Tibeto-Burman." *Studies in Language* 24 (3): 583–610.

Bickel, Balthasar. 2010. "Grammatical Relations Typology." In *The Oxford Handbook of Language Typology*, edited by J. J. Song, 399–444. Oxford: Oxford University Press.

Boersma, Paul, and David Weenink. 2013. *Praat: Doing Phonetics by Computer* (version 5.3.59). http://www.praat.org/.

Bradley, David. 2002. "The Subgrouping of Tibeto-Burman." In *Medieval Tibeto-Burman Languages*, edited by Christian I. Beckwith, 1:73–112. Leiden: Brill.

Burling, Robbins. 1983. "The Sal Languages." *Linguistics of the Tibeto-Burman Area* 7 (2): 1–32.

Burling, Robbins. 2003. "The Tibeto-Burman Languages of Northeastern India." In *The Sino-Tibetan Languages*, edited by Graham Thurgood and Randy J. LaPolla, 169–91. London: Routledge.

Burling, Robbins. 2004. *The Language of the Modhupur Mandi (Garo)*. Vol. 1. New Delhi: Bibliophile South Asia.

Burling, Robbins. 2007. "The Lingua Franca Cycle: Implications for Language Shift, Language Change, and Language Classification." *Anthropological Linguistics* 49 (3/4): 207–34.

Burling, Robbins. 2013. "The 'sixth' Vowel in the Boro-Garo Languages." In *North East Indian Linguistics*, 5:271–82. New Delhi: Foundation / Cambridge University Press India.

Bybee, Joan L. 1998. "'Irrealis' as a Grammatical Category." *Anthropological Linguistics* 40 (2): 257–71.

Bybee, Joan L., Revere D. Perkins, and William Pagliuca. 1994. *The Evolution of Grammar: Tense, Aspect, and Modality in the Languages of the World*. Chicago: University of Chicago Press.

Casad, Eugene. 1984. "Cora." In *Southern Uto-Aztecan Grammatical Sketches*, edited by Ronald W. Langacker, 4:151–459.Studies in Uto-Aztecan Grammar. Arlington, TX: Summer Institute of Linguistics and University of Texas, Arlington.

Census of India. 2001. "Census of India – Statement 1." 2001. http://censusindia.gov.in/Census_Data_2001/Census_Data_Online/Language/Statement1.htm.

Chafe, Wallace L. 1980. *The Pear Stories: Cognitive, Cultural, and Linguistic Aspects of Narrative Production*. Norwood, NJ: Ablex.

Chafe, Wallace L. 1995. "The Realis-Irrealis Distinction in Caddo, the Northern Iroquoian Languages, and English." In *Modality in Grammar and Discourse*, edited by Joan L. Bybee and Suzanne Fleischman, 349–65. Amsterdam/Philadelphia: John Benjamins.

Chelliah, Shobhana Lakshmi. 1997. *A Grammar of Meithei*. Berlin: Mouton de Gruyter.
Chiru, Awan. 2019. "Chiru Verb Agreement." *Himalayan Linguistics* 18 (1): 78–90.
Comrie, Bernard. 1978. "Ergativity." In *Syntactic Typology: Studies in the Phenomenology of Language*, edited by Winfred P. Lehmann, 329–94. Austin, TX: University of Texas Press.
Coupe, Alexander R. 2014. "Tone Sandhi and Vowel Harmony Patterns in Chang Negation." Paper presented at the 24th Annual Meeting of the Southeast Asian Linguistics Society (SEALS), Yangon, Myanmar.
Cristofaro, Sonia. 2012. "Descriptive Notions vs. Grammatical Categories: Unrealized States of Affairs and 'Irrealis.'" *Language Sciences* 34 (2): 131–46.
Croft, William. 2001. *Radical Construction Grammar: Syntactic Theory in Typological Perspective*. Oxford; New York: Oxford University Press.
Cysouw, Michael. 2003. *The Paradigmatic Structure of Person Marking*. Oxford: Oxford University Press.
Daladier, Anne. 2014. *A Corpus of War, Lyngam and Pnar*. Paris: Pangloss. https://lacito.vjf.cnrs.fr/pangloss/languages/War_en.php.
De Vries, Lourens. 2005. "Towards a Typology of Tailhead Linkage in Papuan Languages." *Studies in Language* 29 (2): 363–84.
Deb, Debajit, and Kh. Dhiren Singha. 2014. "Negation in Rongmei Naga." In *North East Indian Linguistics*, edited by Gwendolyn Hyslop, Linda Konnerth, and Stephen Morey, 6:95–104. Canberra, Australian National University: Asia-Pacific Linguistics Open Access.
DeLancey, Scott. 1997. "Grammaticalization and the Gradience of Categories." *Essays on Language Function and Language Type*, 51–69.
DeLancey, Scott. 2001. "Lectures on Functional Syntax." presented at the LSA Summer Institute, UC Santa Barbara. http://darkwing.uoregon.edu/~delancey/sb/fs.html.
DeLancey, Scott. 2010. "Towards a History of Verb Agreement in Tibeto-Burman." *Himalayan Linguistics* 9 (1): 1–39.
DeLancey, Scott. 2011a. "Finite Structures from Clausal Nominalization in Tibeto-Burman." In *Nominalization in Asian Languages: Diachronic and Typological Perspectives*, edited by Foong Ha Yap, Karen Grunow-Hårsta, and Janick Wrona, 343–59. Amsterdam/Philadelphia: John Benjamins.
DeLancey, Scott. 2011b. "On the Origins of Sinitic." In *Proceedings of the 23rd North American Conference on Chinese Linguistics (NACCL-23)*, edited by Zhuo Jing-Schmidt, 1:51–64. Eugene, OR: University of Oregon.
DeLancey, Scott. 2012. "On the Origins of Bodo-Garo." In *North East Indian Linguistics*, 4:3–20. New Delhi: Foundation / Cambridge University Press India.
DeLancey, Scott. 2013. "Creolization in the Divergence of Tibeto-Burman." In *Trans-Himalayan Linguistics: Historical and Descriptive Linguistics of the Himalayan Area*, edited by Nathan Hill and Thomas Owen-Smith, 41–70. Berlin: Mouton de Gruyter.
DeLancey, Scott. 2014. "Second Person Verb Forms in Tibeto-Burman." *Linguistics of the Tibeto-Burman Area* 37 (1): 3–33.
DeLancey, Scott, Krishna Boro, Prafulla Basumatary, and Bihung Brahma. in preparation. *Boro Grammar*.
Demeke, Girma A., and Ronny Meyer. 2008. "The Enclitic-Mm in Amharic: Reassessment of a Multifunctional Morpheme." *Linguistics* 46 (3): 607–28.
Diffloth, Gérard. 2008. "Shafer's 'Parallels' between Khasi and Sino-Tibetan." In *North East Indian Linguistics Volume 1*, 93–104. New Delhi: Foundation / Cambridge University Press India.
Dixon, Robert M. W. 1977. "Where Have All the Adjectives Gone?" *Studies in Language* 1 (1): 19–80.
Dixon, Robert M. W. 1979. "Ergativity." *Language* 55 (1): 59–138.
Dixon, Robert M. W. 2004. "Adjective Classes in Typological Perspective." In *Adjective Classes: A Cross-Linguistic Typology*, 1–49. Explorations in Linguistic Typology 1. Oxford, UK; New York, NY, USA: Oxford University Press.

Driem, George van. 1991. "Tangut Verbal Agreement and the Patient Category in Tibeto-Burman." *Bulletin of the School of Oriental and African Studies* 54 (3): 520–33.

Dwyer, Arienne M. 2006. "Ethics and Practicalities of Cooperative Fieldwork and Analysis." In *Essentials of Language Documentation*, edited by Jost Gippert, Nikolaus P. Himmelmann, and Ulrike Mosel, 31–66. Berlin: Mouton de Gruyter.

Enfield, Nick J. 2003. *Linguistic Epidemiology: Semantics and Grammar of Language Contact in Mainland Southeast Asia*. Asian Linguistics Series. London, New York: Routledge.

Evans, Nicholas. 2007. "Insubordination and Its Uses." In *Finiteness: Theoretical and Empirical Foundations*, edited by Irina Nikolaeva, 366–431. Oxford; New York: Oxford University Press.

Genetti, Carol. 1986. "The Development of Subordinators from Postpositions in Bodic Languages." In *Proceedings of the Annual Meeting of the Berkeley Linguistics Society*, 12:387–400. Berkeley, CA: University of California, Berkeley.

Genetti, Carol. 1991. "From Postposition to Subordinator in Newari." In *Approaches to Grammaticalization*, edited by Elizabeth Closs Traugott and Bernd Heine, 2:227–55. Amsterdam: John Benjamins Publishing Company.

Genetti, Carol. 2011. "The Tapestry of Dolakha Newar: Chaining, Embedding, and the Complexity of Sentences." *Linguistic Typology* 15 (1): 5–24.

Genetti, Carol, Ellen Bartee, Alec Coupe, Kristine Hildebrandt, and You-Jing Lin. 2008. "Syntactic Aspects of Nominalization in Five Tibeto-Burman Languages of the Himalayan Area." *Linguistics of the Tibeto-Burman Area* 31 (2): 97–143.

Georg, Stefan. 1996. *Marphatan Thakali*. LINCOM Studies in Asian Linguistics 02. Munich/Newcastle: Lincom Europa.

Gippert, Jost, Nikolaus P. Himmelmann, and Ulrike Mosel, eds. 2006. *Essentials of Language Documentation*. Berlin: Mouton de Gruyter.

Givón, Talmy. 2001a. *Syntax: An Introduction*. 2nd edition. Vol. 2. Amsterdam/Philadelphia: John Benjamins.

Givón, Talmy. 2001b. *Syntax: An Introduction*. 2nd edition. Vol. 1. Amsterdam/Philadelphia: John Benjamins.

Goddard, Cliff. 2005. *The Languages of East and Southeast Asia: An Introduction*. Oxford: Oxford University Press.

Grierson, George Abraham. 1904. *Linguistic Survey of India*. Vol. 3, parts 1-3, Tibeto-Burman family. Calcutta: Superintendent of Government Printing, India. http://www.joao-roiz.jp/LSI/search.

Grüßner, Karl-Heinz. not dated. "Karbi Dictionary." Tübingen.

Grüßner, Karl-Heinz. 1978. *Arleng Alam, Die Sprache der Mikir: Grammatik und Texte*. Beiträge zur Südasienforschung 39. Wiesbaden: Franz Steiner Verlag.

Guillaume, Antoine. 2011. "Subordinate Clauses, Switch-Reference, and Tail-Head Linkage in Cavineña Narratives." In *Subordination in Native South-American Languages*, 97:109–39. Typological Studies in Language. Amsterdam/Philadelphia: John Benjamins.

Guillaume, Antoine. 2013. "Reconstructing the Category of 'Associated Motion' in Tacanan Languages (Amazonian Bolivia and Peru)." In *Historical Linguistics 2011: Selected Papers from the 20th International Conference on Historical Linguistics, Osaka, 25–30 July 2011*, edited by Ritsuko Kikusawa and Lawrence A. Reid, 326:129–51. Current Issues in Linguistic Theory. Amsterdam/Philadelphia: John Benjamins Publishing.

Haiman, John. 1978. "Conditionals Are Topics." *Language* 54 (3): 564–89.

Harris, Alice C., and Lyle Campbell. 1995. *Historical Syntax in Cross-Linguistic Perspective*. Cambridge: Cambridge University Press.

Haspelmath, Martin. 2004. "Coordinating Constructions: An Overview." In *Coordinating Constructions*, edited by Martin Haspelmath, 3–39. Amsterdam/Philadelphia: John Benjamins.

Haspelmath, Martin. 2005. "Nominal and Verbal Conjunction." In *The World Atlas of Language Structures*, edited by Martin Haspelmath, Matthew S. Dryer, David Gil, and Bernard Comrie, 262–65. Oxford: Oxford University Press.

Heine, Bernd, and Tania Kuteva. 2002. *World Lexicon of Grammaticalization*. Cambridge: Cambridge University Press.

Heine, Bernd, and Mechthild Reh. 1984. *Grammaticalization and Reanalysis in African Languages*. Hamburg: Buske.

Henderson, Eugénie J.A. 1965. *Tiddim Chin: A Descriptive Analysis of Two Texts*. Vol. 15. London Oriental Series. London: Oxford University Press.

Herring, Susan C. 1991. "Nominalization, Relativization, and Attribution in Lotha, Angami, and Burmese." *Linguistics of the Tibeto-Burman Area* 14 (1): 55–72.

Himmelmann, Nikolaus P. 1998. "Documentary and Descriptive Linguistics." *Linguistics* 36 (1): 161–95.

Himmelmann, Nikolaus P. 2006a. "Language Documentation: What Is It and What Is It Good For?" In *Essentials of Language Documentation*, edited by Jost Gippert, Nikolaus P. Himmelmann, and Ulrike Mosel, 1–30. Berlin: Mouton de Gruyter.

Himmelmann, Nikolaus P. 2006b. "The Challenge of Segmenting Spoken Language." In *Essentials of Language Documentation*, edited by Jost Gippert, Nikolaus P. Himmelmann, and Ulrike Mosel, 253–74. Berlin: Mouton de Gruyter.

Hockett, Charles F. 1967. "The Quantification of Functional Load." *Word*, no. 23: 320–39.

Holm, John A. 1988. *Pidgins and Creoles: Theory and Structure*. Vol. 1. Cambridge: Cambridge University Press.

Hutton, John H. 1921. *The Angami Nagas – With Some Notes on Neighboring Tribes*. London: Macmillan.

Hyslop, Gwendolyn. 2011. "A Grammar of Kurtoep." Ph.D. dissertation, Eugene, OR: University of Oregon.

Hyslop, Gwendolyn. 2013. "The Kurtöp -Si Construction: Converbs, Clause-Chains and Verb Serialization." In *Functional-Historical Approaches to Explanation: In Honor of Scott DeLancey*. Vol. 103. Typological Studies in Language. Amsterdam: John Benjamins.

Israel, Michael. 2011. *The Grammar of Polarity : Pragmatics, Sensitivity, and the Logic of Scales*. Cambridge, U.K.; New York: Cambridge University Press.

Jacques, Guillaume. 2019. "The Labial Causative in Trans-Himalayan." *Journal of the Southeast Asian Linguistics Society* 12 (1): 1–11.

Jakobson, Roman. 1931. "Prinzipien der historischen Phonologie." *Travaux du Cercle Linguistique de Prague*, no. 4: 246–67.

Jenny, Matthias. 2012. "The Far West of Southeast Asia – 'give' and 'Get' in the Languages of Myanmar." Paper presented at the Mainland Southeast Asia – state of the art, November 29 – December 1, 2012, MPI Leipzig.

Jeyapaul, Vethamuthu Yesunesiah. 1987. *Karbi Grammar*. CIIL Grammar Series 15. Mysore, India: Central Institute of Indian Languages.

Johnson, Heidi. 2004. "Language Documentation and Archiving, or How to Build a Better Corpus." In *Language Documentation and Description*, edited by Peter K. Austin, 2:140–53. London: Hans Rausing Endangered Languages Project.

Joseph, U.V. 2009. "The Numeral 'one' in Khasi and Karbi." In *North East Indian Linguistics*, 2:149–61. New Delhi: Foundation / Cambridge University Press India.

Joseph, U.V., and Robbins Burling. 2006. *The Comparative Phonology of the Boro-Garo Languages*. Manasagangotri, Mysore: Central Institute of Indian Languages.

Joseph, U.V., and Linda Konnerth. 2015. "Using Eastern Indo-Aryan Borrowings in Tiwa to Help Model the Contact Scenarios: A Case Study in Loanword Phonology." In *Language and Culture* in *Northeast India and Beyond*, edited by Mark W. Post, Stephen Morey, and Scott DeLancey, 140–61. Canberra: Australian National University, Asia-Pacific Linguistics Open Access.

Kansakar, Tej R., Yogendra P. Yadava, Krishna Prasad Chalise, Balaram Prasain, Dubi Nanda Dhakal, and Krishna Paudel. 2011. *A Grammar of Baram*. Linguistic and Ethnographic Documentatation of the Baram Language, Central Department of Linguistics, Tribhuvan University.

Kaplan, Jeff. 1984. "Obligatory Too in English." *Language*, 510–18.

Kay, Sardoka Perrin. 1904. *An English-Mikir Vocabulary with Assamese Equivalents – to Which Have Been Added a Few Mikir Phrases*. Shillong: The Assam Secretariat Printing Office.

Kemmer, Suzanne. 1993. *The Middle Voice*. Amsterdam/Philadelphia: John Benjamins.

King, Deborah. 2009. "Structural and Pragmatic Functions of Kuki-Chin Verbal Stem Alternations." *Journal of the Southeast Asian Linguistics Society* 1: 141–57.

King, Deborah. 2010. "Voice And Valence-Altering Operations In Falam Chin: A Role And Reference Grammar Approach." Ph.D. dissertation, University of Texas at Arlington.

Konnerth, Linda. 2008. "Adverbial Subordination in Burmese." Unpublished manuscript. University of Oregon, Eugene, OR.

Konnerth, Linda. 2009. "The Nominalizing Prefix *gV- in Tibeto-Burman." M.A. thesis, Eugene, OR: University of Oregon.

Konnerth, Linda. 2011. "Functions of Nominalization in Karbi." In *North East Indian Linguistics*, edited by Gwendolyn Hyslop, Stephen Morey, and Mark W. Post, 3:120–34. New Delhi: Foundation / Cambridge University Press India.

Konnerth, Linda. 2012. "The Nominalizing Velar Prefix* GV-in Tibeto-Burman Languages of Northeast India." In *North East Indian Linguistics*, edited by Gwendolyn Hyslop, Stephen Morey, and Mark W. Post. Vol. 4. New Delhi: Foundation / Cambridge University Press India.

Konnerth, Linda. 2014a. "A Grammar of Karbi." Ph.D. dissertation, Eugene, OR: University of Oregon.

Konnerth, Linda. 2014b. "Additive Focus and Additional Functions of Karbi (Tibeto-Burman) =tā." In *Proceedings of the 38th Annual Meeting of the Berkeley Linguistics Society*, edited by Kayla Carpenter, Oana David, Florian Lionnet, Christine Sheil, Tammy Stark, and Vivian Wauters, 206–22. Berkeley, CA: eLanguage (Linguistic Society of America).

Konnerth, Linda. 2015. "A New Type of Convergence at the Deictic Center: Second Person and Cislocative in Karbi (Tibeto-Burman)." *Studies in Language* 39 (1): 24–45.

Konnerth, Linda. 2016. "The Proto-Tibeto-Burman Nominalizing Prefix *gV-." *Linguistics of the Tibeto-Burman Area* 39 (1).

Konnerth, Linda. 2018. "The Historical Phonology of Monsang (Northwestern South-Central/'Kuki-Chin'): A Case of Reduction in Phonological Complexity." *Himalayan Linguistics* 17 (1).

Konnerth, Linda, and Amos Teo. 2014. "Acoustic-Statistical and Perceptual Investigations of Karbi Tones: A Peculiar Case of Incomplete Neutralisation of F0." In *North East Indian Linguistics*, edited by Gwendolyn Hyslop, Linda Konnerth, Stephen Morey, and Priyankoo Sarmah, 6:13–37. Canberra, Australian National University: Asia-Pacific Linguistics Open Access.

Konnerth, Linda, and Chikari Tisso. 2018. "Karbi Texts: A Fully Glossed Corpus of Different Genres." *Himalayan Linguistics Archive* 17 (2): 117–472.

Konnerth, Linda, and Chikari Tisso. 2019. *Karbi Texts: Original Recordings of a Corpus of Different Genres*. London: SOAS, Endangered Languages Archive. http://elar.soas.ac.uk/deposit/0577.

Kortmann, Bernd. 1996. *Adverbial Subordination: A Typology and History of Adverbial Subordinators Based on European Languages*. Empirical Approaches to Language Typology 18. Berlin: Mouton de Gruyter.

Kouwenberg, N. J. C. 2009. "Ventive, Dative and Allative in Old Babylonian." *Zeitschrift Für Assyriologie Und Vorderasiatische Archäologie* 92 (2): 200–240.

Kouwenberg, Silvia, and Pieter Muysken. 1995. "Papiamento." In *Pidgins and Creoles: An Introduction*, edited by Jacques Arends, Pieter Muysken, and Norval Smith, 15:205–18. Creole Language Library. Amsterdam/Philadelphia: John Benjamins.

Krifka, Manfred. 1998. "Additive Particles under Stress." In *Proceedings of SALT*, edited by D. Strolovitch and A. Lawson, 8:111–28. Ithaca, NY: CLC Publications.

Krishan, Shree. 1980. *Thadou: A Grammatical Sketch*. Calcutta: Anthropological Survey of India, Government of India.

Kro, Bidor Sing, ed. 2009. *Akimi Karbi Lamthe Amarjong*. Second edition. Rongmongve, Diphu, Karbi Anglong, Assam, India: Kangthir Book House and Publisher (Bidya Sing Rongpi).

Kuolie, D. 2006. *Structural Description of Tenyidie: A Tibeto-Burman Language of Nagaland*. Kohima, Nagaland: Ura Academy Publication Division.

LaPolla, Randy J. 2008. "Nominalization in Rawang." *Linguistics of the Tibeto-Burman Area* 31 (2): 45–65.

Lewis, Paul M., Gary F. Simons, and Charles D. Fennig, eds. 2013. *Ethnologue: Languages of the World*. Seventeenth edition. Dallas, Texas: SIL International. http://www.ethnologue.com.

Li, Charles N., and Sandra A. Thompson. 1981. *Mandarin Chinese: A Functional Reference Grammar*. Berkeley and Los Angeles, CA: University of California Press.

Longacre, Robert E. 1968. *Discourse, Paragraph, and Sentence Structure in Selected Philippine Languages*. Vol. 1. Summer Institute of Linguistics Santa Ana, CA.

Mariae, Fr. John. 2007. *Karbi Self-Taught*. Second edition. Diphu, Karbi Anglong, Assam, India: Don Bosco Catholic Literature Committee.

Mathesius, Vilem. 1929. "La Structure Phonologique Du Lexique Du Tchèque Moderne." *Travaux Du Cercle Linguistique de Prague*, no. 1: 67–84.

Matić, Dejan, and Daniel Wedgwood. 2013. "The Meanings of Focus: The Significance of an Interpretation-Based Category in Cross-Linguistic Analysis." *Journal of Linguistics* 49 (1): 127–63.

Matisoff, James A. 1972. "Lahu Nominalization, Relativization, and Genitivization." In *Syntax and Semantics*, edited by John Kimball, 1:237–57. New York: Seminar Press.

Matisoff, James A. 1973. *The Grammar of Lahu*. Vol. 75. Berkeley, CA: University of California Press.

Matisoff, James A. 1986. "Hearts and Minds in South-East Asian Languages and English: An Essay in the Comparative Lexical Semantics of Psycho-Collocations." *Cahiers de Linguistique Asie Orientale* 15 (1): 5–57.

Matisoff, James A. 1992. "The Mother of All Morphemes: Augmentatives and Diminutives in Areal and Universal Perspective." In *Papers from the First Annual Meeting of the Southeast Asian Linguistics Society*, edited by Martha Ratliff and Eric Schiller, 293–349. Tempe: Arizona State University, Program for Southeast Asian Studies.

Matisoff, James A. 2003. *Handbook of Proto-Tibeto-Burman: System and Philosophy of Sino-Tibetan Reconstruction*. Berkeley, CA: University of California Press.

Mauri, Caterina. 2017. "Building and Interpreting Ad Hoc Categories: A Linguistic Analysis." In *Formal Models in the Study of Language*, edited by J. Blochowiak, C. Grisot, S. Durrleman, and C. Laenzlinger, 297–326. Berlin: Springer.

Mauri, Caterina, and Andrea Sansò. 2012. "What Do Languages Encode When They Encode Reality Status?" *Language Sciences* 34 (2): 99–106.

McWhorter, John H. 2007. *Language Interrupted: Signs of Non-Native Acquisition in Standard Language Grammars*. Oxford: Oxford University Press.

Mithun, Marianne. 1995. "On the Relativity of Irreality." In *Modality in Grammar and Discourse*, edited by Joan L. Bybee and Suzanne Fleischman, 367–88. Amsterdam/Philadelphia: John Benjamins.

Mithun, Marianne. 1996. "New Directions in Referentiality." In *Studies in Anaphora*, edited by Barbara Fox, 33:413–35. Typological Studies in Language. Amsterdam/Philadelphia: John Benjamins.

Moseley, Christopher, ed. 2010. *Atlas of the World's Languages in Danger*. 3rd edition. Paris: UNESCO Publishing. http://www.unesco.org/culture/en/endangeredlanguages/atlas.
Nathan, David. 2011. "Digital Archiving." In *The Cambridge Handbook of Endangered Languages*, edited by Peter Austin and Julia Sallabank, 255–73. Leiden: Cambridge University Press.
Noonan, Michael. 1997. "Versatile Nominalizations." In *Essays on Language Function and Language Type. In Honor of T. Givón*, edited by Joan L. Bybee, John Haiman, and Sandra A. Thompson, 373–94. Amsterdam/Philadelphia: John Benjamins.
Noonan, Michael. 2006. "Direct Speech as a Rhetorical Style in Chantyal." *Himalayan Linguistics Journal*, no. 6: 1–32.
Noonan, Michael. 2011. "Aspects of the Historical Development of Nominalizers in the Tamangic Languages." In *Nominalization in Asian Languages: Diachronic and Typological Perspectives*, edited by Foong Ha Yap, Karen Grunow-Hårsta, and Janick Wrona, 195–213. Amsterdam/Philadelphia: John Benjamins.
Ohala, John J. 2010. "The Relation between Phonetics and Phonology." In *The Handbook of Phonetic Sciences*, edited by W. J. Hardcastle, J. Laver, and F. E. Gibbon, 2nd ed., 653–77. Oxford: Wiley-Blackwell. http://books.google.com/books?id=Zp8xc_kZKWEC.
Öpengin, Ergin. 2013. "Topicalisation in Central Kurdish: Additive Enclitic and Other Means." Paper presented at the Information Structure in Spoken Language Corpora (ISSLaC), Bielefeld, Germany.
Overstreet, Maryann. 1999. *Whales, Candlelight, and Stuff like That: General Extenders in English Discourse*. Oxford: Oxford University Press.
Ozerov, Pavel. 2015. "The System of Information Packaging in Burmese." Ph.D. dissertation, Melbourne: La Trobe University.
Ozerov, Pavel, and Henriëtte Daudey. 2017. "Copy-Verb Constructions in Tibeto-Burman and Beyond." *Linguistic Typology* 21 (1): 53–99. https://doi.org/10.1515/lingty-2017-0002.
Peterson, David A. 2003. "Hakha Lai." In *The Sino-Tibetan Languages*, edited by Graham Thurgood and LaPolla, Randy J., 409–26. RoutledgeCurzon.
Peterson, David A. 2010. "Khumi Elaborate Expressions." *Himalayan Linguistics* 9 (1): 81–100.
Peterson, David A., and Kenneth VanBik. 2004. "Coordination in Hakha Lai (Tibeto-Burman)." In *Coordinating Constructions*, edited by Martin Haspelmath, 58:333–56. Typological Studies in Language. Amsterdam/Philadelphia: John Benjamins.
Phangcho, Morningkeey. 2012. "A Brief Study of Kinship Terminology." In *Karbi Studies*, 2nd ed., 1:21–26. Guwahati, Assam, India: Assam Book Hive.
Plaisier, Heleen. 2007. *A Grammar of Lepcha*. Leiden: Brill.
Post, Mark W. 2007. "A Grammar of Galo." Ph.D. dissertation, Melbourne: La Trobe University, Research Centre for Linguistic Typology.
Post, Mark W. 2009. "Predicate Derivations in the Tani Languages: Root, Suffix, Both or Neither?" In *North East Indian Linguistics*, 2:175–97. New Delhi: Foundation / Cambridge University Press India.
Post, Mark W., and Robbins Burling. 2017. "The Tibeto-Burman Languages of Northeast India." In *The Sino-Tibetan Languages*, edited by Randy J. LaPolla and Graham Thurgood, Second edition, 213–42. Abingdon, New York: Routledge.
Putten, Saskia van. 2011. "Marked Topics and Contrast in Avatime." Paper presented at the Information structure and spoken language: cross-linguistic comparative studies, Boulder, CO.
Ring, Hiram. 2015. "A Grammar of Pnar." Ph.D. dissertation, Singapore: Nanyang Technological University.
Robinson, William. 1849. "Notes on the Languages Spoken by the Various Tribes Inhabiting the Valley of Assam and Its Mountain Confines. Part II." *Journal of the Asiatic Society of Bengal*, no. 18: 310–49.

Schultze-Berndt, Eva. 2006. "Linguistic Annotation." In *Essentials of Language Documentation*, edited by Jost Gippert, Nikolaus P. Himmelmann, and Ulrike Mosel, 213–51. Berlin: Mouton de Gruyter.

Scott, James C. 2009. *The Art of Not Being Governed: An Anarchist History of Upland Southeast Asia*. New Haven: Yale University Press.

Shafer, Robert. 1952. "Études Sur l'austroasien." *Bulletin de La Société de Linguistique de Paris* 48 (1): 111–58.

Shafer, Robert. 1966. *Introduction to Sino-Tibetan*. Wiesbaden: Harrassowitz.

Sharma, H. Surmangol, and N. Gopendro Singh. 2008. "Pronominal Markers in Purum and Manipuri." Paper presented at the 3rd annual meeting of the North East Indian Linguistics Society, Guwahati, Assam, India.

Simons, Gary F., and Charles D. Fennig, eds. 2017. *Ethnologue: Languages of the World*. Twentieth edition. Dallas, Texas: SIL International. http://www.ethnologue.com.

So-Hartmann, Helga. 2009. *A Descriptive Grammar of Daai Chin*. STEDT Monograph Series 7. Berkeley, CA: University of California Press.

So-Hartmann, Helga. 2013. "Valence-Changing Prefixes in Kuki-Chin." Paper presented at the International Conference on Sino-Tibetan Languages and Linguistics, Dartmouth College, Hanover, NH.

Solnit, David B. 1995. "Parallelism in Kayah Li Discourse: Elaborate Expressions and Beyond." In *Proceedings of the Annual Meeting of the Berkeley Linguistics Society: Special Session on Discourse in Southeast Asian Languages*. Vol. 21. Berkeley, CA: Berkeley Linguistics Society.

Stack, Edward, and Sir Charles Lyall. 1908. *The Mikirs*. London: David Nutt.

Starosta, Stanley. 1985. "Relator Nouns as a Source of Case Inflection." *Oceanic Linguistics Special Publications*, no. 20: 111–33.

Stern, Theodore. 1984. "Sizang (Siyin) Chin Texts." *Linguistics of the Tibeto-Burman Area* 8 (1): 43–58.

Stewart, R. 1855. "Notes on Northern Cachar." *Journal of the Asiatic Society of Bengal*, no. 24: 656–75.

Sun, Jackson TS. 1993. "The Linguistic Position of Tani (Mirish) in Tibeto-Burman: A Lexical Assessment." *Linguistics of the Tibeto-Burman Area* 16 (2): 143–88.

Surendran, Dinoj, and Partha Niyogi. 2006. "Quantifying the Functional Load of Phonemic Oppositions, Distinctive Features, and Suprasegmentals." *Amsterdam Studies in the Theory and History of Linguistic Science Series* 4 279: 43.

Taro, Sarklim, ed. 2010. *Karbi-English Dictionary*. Guwahati, Assam, India: Assam Institute of Research for Tribals and Scheduled Castes.

Terang, Rongbong. 1974. *Karbi Lamtasam [A Mikir-English-Assamese Dictionary]*. Calcutta: Sadhana Press (Debdas Nath).

Teron, Dharamsing. 2011. *Karbi Studies: Reclaiming the Ancestors' Voices*. Vol. 2. Guwahati, Assam, India: Assam Book Hive.

Teron, Dharamsing, ed. 2012. *Karbi Studies: Memories, Myths, Metaphors*. Second edition. Vol. 1. Guwahati, Assam, India: Assam Book Hive.

Teron, Longkam. 2005a. *Karbi Lamtasam*. Second edition. Rontheang, Diphu, Karbi Anglong, Assam, India: Karbi Lammet Amei.

Teron, Longkam. 2005b. *Sar-Lamthe*. Second edition. Rontheang, Diphu, Karbi Anglong, Assam, India: Karbi Lammet Amei.

Teron, Longkam. 2006. *Karbi Lambeng*. Rontheang, Diphu, Karbi Anglong, Assam, India: Karbi Lammet Amei.

Teron, Longkam, ed. 2008. *Karbi Lamlir Achili*. Second edition. Diphu, Karbi Anglong, Assam, India: Longkam Teron.

Teron, Manik, and Rajendra Tumung, eds. 2007. *Karbi Lamarjong*. Diphu, Karbi Anglong, Assam, India: Kamrup Karbi Lammet Amei (Longki Phangcho).
Thompson, Sandra A. 1988. "A Discourse Approach to the Cross-Linguistic Category 'Adjective.'" In *Explaining Language Universals*, edited by John A. Hawkins, 167–85. Oxford, UK; New York, NY, USA: Blackwell.
Thurgood, Graham. 1983. "Morphological Innovation and Subgrouping: Some Tibeto-Burman Notes." In *Proceedings of the Annual Meeting of the Berkeley Linguistics Society*, 9: 257–65. Berkeley, CA: Berkeley Linguistics Society.
Tomlin, Russell S. 1995. "Focal Attention, Voice, and Word Order: An Experimental, Cross-Linguistic Study." In *Word Order in Discourse*, edited by Pamela A. Downing and Michael Noonan, 517–54. Amsterdam/Philadelphia: John Benjamins.
Tosco, Mauro. 2010. "Why Contrast Matters: Information Structure in Gawwada (East Cushitic)." In *The Expression of Information Structure: A Documentation of Its Diversity across Africa*, edited by Ines Fiedler and Anne Schwarz, 91:315–48. Typological Studies in Language. Amsterdam/Philadelphia: John Benjamins.
VanBik, Kenneth. 2009. *Proto-Kuki-Chin: A Reconstructed Ancestor of the Kuki-Chin Languages*. STEDT Monograph Series 8. Berkeley, CA: University of California Press.
Walker, George David. 1925. *A Dictionary of the Mikir Language*. Shillong: Assam Government Press.
Wolfenden, Stuart Norris. 1929. *Outlines of Tibeto-Burman Linguistic Morphology*. London: Royal Asiatic Society.
Wood, Daniel C. 2008. "An Initial Reconstruction of Proto-Boro-Garo." M.A. thesis, Eugene, OR: University of Oregon.
Woodbury, Anthony C. 2011. "Language Documentation." In *The Cambridge Handbook of Endangered Languages*, edited by Peter Austin and Julia Sallabank, 159–86. Leiden : Cambridge University Press.
Yap, Foong Ha, Karen Grunow-Hårsta, and Janick Wrona, eds. 2011. *Nominalization in Asian Languages: Diachronic and Typological Perspectives*. Amsterdam/Philadelphia: John Benjamins.

Index Karbi grammar

ablative 132, 209, 312–315, 416, 444, 445, 459–460
absolutive 428
ad-hoc category marking. *See* general extender
additive
– bisyndetic coordination 318
– discourse (information structure) 320
– exhaustive 319
– intensifier 320
– scalar additive 318–319
– simple additive 317
– universal quantification 319
addressing words 71, 72, 85, 579, 580
adjectives. *See* property-concept term
adverbial clauses
– causal 378, 379
– comparison 380
– concessive 517–518
– conditional 516–517
– posteriority 376
– purpose 379, 383, 517
– similarity (*see* comparison)
– simultaneity 377–379
– simultaneous (*see* simultaneity)
– temporal anteriority 373
adverbial construction
– causative 339–340
– nominalization 340–341
– non-final 341
adverbial suffixes. *See* predicate derivations
affective 423, 425
affirmative 71, 72, 471, 495
afterthought 27, 431, 560, 572–574
Aimol 183
alignment 413, 429
allative 133
allophony 53, 61
andative. *See* translocative
Angami Naga. *See* Tenyidie
applicative 239, 240, 460
approximants 53, 60
argument structure
– bivalent 404, 405, 413, 481
– monovalent 404–405, 413, 423
– O-high 361, 403–405, 413, 446, 450–451
– O-low 361, 368, 403, 405, 446–447
– trivalent 406–413, 447, 450–452, 455, 481

Arleng 1, 29, 114, 135
aspectual (constructions)
– aspectual-pragmatic (contexts of realis marking) 254, 255
– completive 244–245
– continuative 243
– durative 246
– exhaustive perfective 252–254
– experiential 223, 252–254
– habitual 25, 249–250, 266–267
– imperfective 393–396
– iterative 250–251
– perfect 243
– perfective 244–245
– progressive 344–345
– reduplication 85–87, 173, 192–195, 226, 249–251
– 'still' 82, 210, 223–224, 275–276
Assam 1, 2, 4, 9, 18, 23, 24, 49, 50, 502
Assamese 12, 14, 16, 25, 28–30, 31, 33, 34, 47, 53, 55, 65, 128, 354, 583, 584–587
associated motion 206, 208–209, 211, 230, 234, 235, 237, 246
associative plural 297–298
assumption marking 260–261
attributive prefix. *See* possessive prefix
augmentative 13, 114, 186–190
Austroasiatic 1, 12–14, 16, 22, 215
auto-benefactive/malefactive 48, 72, 73, 88–89, 92, 94–96, 163, 197–200, 215, 219–220

background 208, 235, 246, 523–524, 547, 576–577
benefactive 199, 220, 327–328, 339, 453
benefactive/malefactive 19, 48, 72, 73, 88–89, 92, 94–96, 163, 197–200, 215, 219–221, 228, 229, 239–240, 427
Bengali 12, 14, 65
Bodo 11
Bodo-Garo 11, 17, 168, 214
Bokolapo 202, 286, 287, 325, 435, 473, 476, 477
Boro-Garo. *See* Bodo-Garo
borrowings 8, 11–13, 23, 47, 52, 53, 55, 56, 65, 74, 75, 114, 546, 627
Brahmaputra 2, 9, 18

case marking. *See* role marking
causative 13, 19, 26, 32, 48, 91–94, 107, 109, 185, 197–200, 214, 338–341, 423, 502, 504
change of state (marking) 185, 255, 257–260, 261
Chinthong 25, 26
Chiru 13
Chomangkan 255, 256, 293, 296, 350, 399, 525
Chom Arong 245, 467, 624
Christian(ity) 3, 23, 28, 49, 56
cislocative 11, 19, 198, 200–213
classification. *See* phylogenetic classification
classifiers
– argument classification (on the verb) 241
– anaphoric use 308
– human classifier, singular 125
– human classifier, plural 121, 125
– mensural classifiers 122–124, 305
– non-classifier (construction) 117, 306
– not fully grammaticalized 117, 119, 121–124, 305–306
– self-referential 117, 124–125, 127, 305
– sortal classifiers 117, 119–122
– typical classifier construction 117, 119–122, 304–305
clause-chaining 272–273, 373, 429, 507, 527
clause union 324, 325, 399
clause types 356, 373, 388, 474, 486–531. *See also* irrealis clause types; non-declarative speech acts; non-nominalized subordinate clause types
clitics
– enclitics 62, 72, 73, 77, 83
– phonological shape 83–84
– proclitics 84, 196, 198, 203
clusters, onset 48, 51, 53, 59, 60, 87
cognate objects 353–355
collective 148, 451, 546, 549
comitative. *See* role marking
common ground (marker) 72, 560, 570, 577–578
comparative (degree) 105–107, 203, 233, 422–423
complement clauses
– as S argument 356, 360, 366, 367, 370, 372, 386, 434
– complement-taking verbs 244, 324, 325, 327, 368, 370, 373, 512, 513
– complementation scale 324–338, 368

– complementizer 325, 399, 512, 514–515, 517, 524, 560
– conditional 274, 449, 478, 516–517, 523
– indefinite (*see* indirect questions)
– indirect questions 159–160, 272, 275, 512–514, 526
– irrealis (marking) 265–271, 381
– manipulation 373
– modality 373
– nominalization 368–373
– noun phrase delimiter 372
– perception-cognition-utterance 372
– purpose 517
– quotative 325, 514–515, 517, 560
– quotative complementizer 325, 512, 515, 517, 560
– topic 514
– verb juxtaposition 512–513
compounding 80, 179–181, 188, 196, 278
conative 109, 497, 499–502, 505, 506
conditional 82, 99, 270–272, 274, 371, 422, 449, 478, 516–517, 523
conjunction
– coordinating 517
– concessive 319, 518, 551
consonants
– onset 48–53, 87
– coda 34, 55, 59, 61, 83
– marginal 52–53
– borrowed 55
constituent order 479–482
consultants 2, 7, 12, 25–27, 32, 45, 68, 154, 183, 220, 263, 265, 273, 291, 378, 385, 417, 546
contact 11–23, 28, 49, 52, 65, 129, 175, 502
coordination 177, 278–280, 292, 313, 318, 429, 455, 486, 527–530, 532–534
coordination, bisyndetic 318
copula
– copula constructions 384–388, 417–420
– equational, negative 102, 167–168, 251, 322, 392–393, 475, 556–557
– existential/locative 163–168, 257, 261, 316, 344, 345, 365, 384–388, 395, 403, 417–423, 533
copy verb construction
– additive 310
– assertive 551–553
– focus (irrealis) 554–555

- intensifier 320, 553, 554, 556–558
- perseverance 555–556
- question particle (*see* perseverance)
- topic 551–553

core vs. oblique roles 19, 449
co-relative construction 155, 160, 360, 388, 391
corpus 38–39, 42–43, 622–625
correction word 12, 532, 584–587
"creoloid" 16–19, 22

Daai Chin 166–168, 518
data
- access 39, 41
- annotation 45–47
- archive 39
- collaboration 8, 36, 37
- collection 5, 36, 37, 39–44
- genres 40, 42–43, 441
- presentation 47
- recording 32, 38–45, 66, 69

day ordinals 171
declarative 109, 273, 384, 401, 403–423, 471, 486, 489, 553–554, 566–567
demonstrative 20, 81, 132, 138, 149, 151, 154–156, 160–161, 182, 183, 263, 277, 282–283, 288–292, 308, 316, 355, 357–358, 391, 437, 479, 536
deontic clauses 496, 497, 522
derivational affixes 197–198
desiderative 266, 270–271, 524–525, 558, 561, 562
dialects
- Amri 26, 41, 55, 93, 579
- Hills Karbi 25–27, 55
- Plains Karbi 2, 7, 23–26, 29, 54, 61
- Rongkhang 23, 26–27, 41, 55

differential marking 412, 461–462
Dimasa 57, 214
diminutive 76, 78, 106, 155, 186, 189–190
diphthongs (vs. glide coda analysis) 60–61
Diphu 8, 9, 26–27, 29, 40, 41, 43, 49, 69, 208, 255, 297, 425, 427
directional (marking) 206
direct speech 470, 476, 506, 514, 515, 537, 538, 553, 560
disagreement 87, 506, 556–557
discourse
- discourse connectors 132, 156, 170, 264, 465, 473, 532, 536–537, 584

- discourse marker 72, 83, 464, 560
- discourse section marker 537–539
- discourse structure (marking) 444–485

distributive 100, 192–195, 222
dual 192–193
dubitative 558, 560, 564–565

echo word formation. *See* elaborate expressions
elaborate expressions
- compounding 181
- form 543–547
- functions 549–550
- parallelism 547–549

emphatic marking 555
endangerment (language) 1, 28–31
English language (contact) 12, 28–30, 53, 55, 65, 128
enumeration constructions 117, 127–129, 277, 278, 303–312
exclamation (exclamative) 12, 64, 253, 481, 486, 560, 571, 572, 583
exclusive 95, 149–151, 184, 203, 419, 435, 476, 514

female 13, 14, 147, 187–189, 193
Fish Film 253
focus
- additive 224, 293, 317–320
- realis 11, 191, 262–264, 390–393, 464, 471–474, 477, 520, 585
- restrictive 287, 320, 464, 472, 482–485
- irrealis 390, 392, 440, 464, 471, 474–478, 519–523, 560, 571, 572

formality marking 579–582
free variation (phonological) 49, 54
frozen prefixes 65, 93, 148, 149, 168–170, 181
future
- immediate 266
- indefinite 265, 295

Galo 242, 331, 375, 416, 534, 584
general extender 194, 319, 355, 539–543, 550
gender 89, 114, 136, 155, 179, 186–190
genre 5, 40, 42–43, 441–443, 532
'good-bye' expression 497
grammaticalization 19, 20, 82, 102, 119, 144–146, 179, 182, 214, 224, 230, 277, 287, 291, 316, 340, 374, 476, 483
greeting 243

habitual. *See* aspectual constructions
hesitation word 58, 584–586
honorific 83, 100, 101, 149, 150, 181, 184, 191, 579–582
hortative 80, 82, 109, 486, 502–507, 519–521, 566–567, 568, 584
hypoarticulated speech 48, 81–82

iambic pattern 80
imperatives
– conative imperative 109, 497, 499–502, 506, 567
– conditioned imperative 81, 109, 499, 501
– informal conditioned imperative 81, 498–499, 501, 502
– prohibitive 109, 168, 497–502
– unconditioned imperative 500–501
inclusive 9, 149, 203, 204, 419, 435
incorporation 182, 230, 347–349, 351, 352, 355
indefinite
– indefinite (or vague) amount 308–310
– indefinite article (numeral 'one') 119, 307, 310–311
– indirect questions (*see* interrogatives)
– future 265
– negative indefinite construction 159, 161, 162, 319
– pronouns 159, 311, 319, 322, 468, 540
Indic. *See* Indo-Aryan
indirect question 159–160, 272, 275, 512–514, 526, 529
indirect request 580
indirect speech 325, 515
Indo-Aryan 12–16, 22, 48, 52–53, 65, 114, 123, 128, 188
information/discourse structure 46, 317, 401, 429, 433, 434, 440–441, 444–485, 550, 555
instrumental 19, 21, 239–241, 312–315, 348, 363, 444–445, 449, 459–460
insubordination 159, 271, 486, 523–526, 561, 574
intensifier 173, 226, 229, 231, 232, 270, 320, 384, 479, 541, 549, 553–558
intention 266, 372, 381, 383, 524
interactive emphatic 555, 560, 569–570
interjection 12, 55, 58, 71–72, 85, 99, 101, 321, 495, 506, 537, 582–584
interrogatives

– content questions 99, 159, 182, 388–391, 472, 477, 486–489, 495
– disjunctive interrogatives 486, 487, 489, 493–495
– polar interrogatives 486, 487, 489–492
– pronouns (*see* pronouns)
– tag question 486, 496, 574, 576, 577
– indirect questions 159–160, 272, 275, 512–514, 526, 529
intransitivity 169
irrealis
– complement clauses 371–372, 383, 399, 512–515
– deontic 270, 329–331, 474, 496–497, 504, 522
– desiderative 270–271, 524–525, 558, 561–562
– epistemic reading 99, 269–270
– focus markers 11, 191, 254, 264, 287, 320, 346, 389–393, 471, 472, 474, 475, 479, 482–486, 518–523, 560, 571
– future 224, 265, 266, 269
– habitual 25, 99, 249–250, 266–267, 271, 565, 566
– hypothetical and counterfactual 267–269
– irrealis1 265, 266, 271, 522, 558
– irrealis2 21, 223–224, 265–271, 329–331, 364, 379, 381–384, 525, 561
– purpose 371–372
– suffixes 99–101, 223, 224, 253, 255, 270
– non-final (markers) 507–510, 518–523
irrealis clause types 474, 486, 518–523

jussive 502, 504–505

Karbi
– culture 3–8, 40
– ethnolinguistic profile 16–18
– people 1–9, 303, 387
– villages 14, 25
Karbi Anglong 1, 2, 4, 8–9, 14, 23, 24, 26, 28–32, 41, 50, 55, 56, 69, 93, 255, 303, 494, 552, 579
Karbi Lammet Amei 2, 9, 24, 33, 37, 41, 42, 68, 95, 143
Khasi 1, 2, 8, 12–16, 18, 37, 48, 65, 119, 154
kingdom system 12
Kiranti 80, 183
Kuki-Chin 10, 13, 38, 166, 187, 213–214, 219, 393, 474, 518 (*See also* South-Central)

Lepcha 183, 243
lexical suffixes. *See* predicate derivations
lexicalization 76, 82, 224
lexicon 11, 12, 22, 33, 97, 149
light verbs 352–353
locative NP marking 461

Mandarin Chinese 493
Meghalaya 2, 4, 12, 18, 24, 25, 40, 50
Meitei 10, 11, 13, 14, 154, 168, 174, 175, 183, 187, 243, 474
middle (voice) 169, 199, 218, 219
"Mikir" 2, 8, 10, 11, 16, 18
modals
– ability
  – physical 335–336
  – skillful 334–335
– deontic 329–331, 522
– morphosyntactic tests 97, 163, 324, 326–329
– non-control 331–338
modifier 20, 98, 110, 112–116, 149, 154, 155, 157, 159, 182–184, 186–190, 277–303, 316, 345, 356, 358–360, 397, 430, 482
mood
– irrealis1 265, 266, 271, 522, 558
– irrealis2 21, 223, 224, 265–267, 269–271, 330, 364, 379, 381, 383, 522, 525, 561
– realis 254
morphophonology 48, 67, 102, 214, 215, 218, 291, 324, 329
motion construction 321, 346–347, 403, 406, 412–416
motion verb 206–209, 212, 213, 217, 236, 242, 343, 414, 416, 428, 448, 457–458, 508

"Naga" 11, 154, 166, 167, 214, 287, 303, 385, 502, 552
Nagaland 18, 303, 340
narrative style 5, 27, 560, 574, 578–579
negation 87, 99–101, 167, 168, 225, 226, 251, 321–323, 334, 375, 381, 392, 504, 519, 521–522, 529, 558
nominalization
– adverbial clauses 356, 372, 373, 375, 379, 381, 383, 399, 454, 507, 516–518
– complement clauses 371–372
– derivational nominalization 356–358
– diachronic nominalization 38, 356, 360, 384, 388–397, 474
– focus 388–393
– imperfective 393–396
– inconsistent occurrence (of nominalizer) 356, 389, 397–400
– main clauses 384–397
– nominalized clauses 381–384
– relative clauses 364–365
nominal predicates 98, 99, 101, 102, 254, 262–264, 321–323, 370, 466, 493
non-final
– adverbial constructions 338, 341–343
– irrealis 272–273, 507–510, 518–523
– progressive construction 344–345
– realis 272–273, 507–510
non-obligatoriness (of grammatical markers) 17, 19–22, 400
non-subject 11, 19, 22, 34, 198, 200–213, 220, 239, 240, 288, 371, 373, 379, 403–406, 409, 410, 413, 416, 421–423, 425–428, 438, 444, 446, 450–455, 458, 460, 461, 463, 464, 476, 504
nouns
– body/kinship terms 169
– bound 146–147, 418–420
– collective 148
– compounds 74, 181, 189
– frozen prefixes 65, 93, 148, 149, 168–170, 181
– incorporation 347–349
noun phrase delimiter 84, 122, 155, 280–281, 287, 312, 357, 371, 372, 380, 381, 399, 401–443
numerals
– bound 121, 122, 127, 304, 305
– *see also* enumeration constructions
– independent 121, 123, 127, 128, 171, 175, 303
– 'one' numeral constructions
  – indefinite article (*see* indefinite)
  – indefinite pronoun (*see* indefinite)
  – whole 174–176
  – same 174–176

oblique 19, 21, 130, 151, 240, 360, 362, 401–405, 430, 444, 445, 449, 453, 458, 461, 466
off-glide 57, 58
onomatopoeia 185

Orpheus 245
orthography 1, 31, 33, 34, 45, 53, 67
palatal glide coda 60–61
parallelism 160–161, 366, 528, 529, 532–534, 547–549, 551
particles 558–579
pear story 40, 43, 610–621
perfect. *See* aspectual constructions
perfective. *See* aspectual constructions
person
– first person 95, 149–151, 184, 198, 201–206, 212–213, 427, 474, 505
– person indexation (*see* speech act participant cross-referencing (non-subject))
– second person 152, 198, 200–206, 419, 502
– third person 22, 83, 150–152, 155, 182–183, 202, 504
personification 125–127
phylogenetic classification 9
plural 37, 121, 125–126, 150–151, 179, 191–195, 239, 249–251, 277, 286–288, 297–298, 427, 435, 463, 505
Pnar 12–16, 154
possessive construction
– diachronic significance 182, 277, 287–288
– head nouns 278–281, 288–291, 365, 437–438
– possessive prefix 82, 83, 91, 130, 146, 149–151, 180, 181, 184–185, 191, 297, 580
postposition 401, 458, 466, 507
predicate derivations
– argument plurality 250–251
– argument structure changing 242
– argument structure highlighting 239–241
– aspect/aktionsart 230, 242–246
– associated motion 208–209, 234–237
– benefactive/malefactive 88–89, 95–96, 198, 219–221, 239–240, 425–427
– comparative degree 233
– degree or extent 225, 228, 231–233
– direction 206–208, 234–237
– discontinuous 227–228
– formal 248–249
– habitual 249–250
– ideophonic 231
– instrumental/comitative 239, 241, 423
– intensification 173, 249, 251
– iterative 250–251
– manner 230–233

– negative 251–252
– origins 229–230
– path 234–237
– productivity 228–229
– quantification 232–233
– reduplication 225–227, 249–251
– result 233–234
– scope of negation 225–227
– structural properties 225, 326–328
– superlative 191–192
predicate
– nominal predicate 98, 99, 101, 102, 254, 262, 263, 321, 322, 370, 466, 493
– non-verbal predicate 99, 321
– verbal predicate 99, 254, 262, 321–323, 384, 385, 494
prefixes
– derivational 183, 197
– frozen 65, 93, 148, 168–170, 181
– nominal 181–186
– verbal 19
primary object 201–204
procedural text 43, 247, 266–267, 271, 516
prohibitive 497–502
pronouns
– derived indefinite 100, 291, 294–296, 322, 468
– interrogative 149, 156–160, 264, 291, 294–296, 390, 391, 487, 514
– personal 122, 149–151, 155, 297
– reflexive/reciprocal 19, 88–89, 93–96, 151–154, 198–199, 215–219
property concept terms
– comparative 233, 422–423
– marginal types 111–115
– modifier 298–312
– post-head 299–303
– pre-head 299–303
– superlative 191–192, 233
prosody
– prosodic emphasis 539, 557–559
– prosodically marked subordination 510–512
– prosodic tone changes 70–72
Proto-Bodo-Garo 120
Proto-Tani 166
Proto-Tibeto-Burman 50, 61, 80, 149, 150, 166, 167, 168–170, 175, 183, 215, 243, 356
psycho-collocations 349–352

purpose clauses 271, 455, 517, 524, 525, 561
Purum 13, 213
quantifiers 39, 232, 482, 483
question particle 487–489, 494, 555–556
question tag 496, 576–578
quotative
– complement clauses 325, 514–515, 524–526
– desiderative clauses 524–525
– main clauses 384–397, 486–507, 524–525, 574–577
– purpose clauses 517

realis 76–77, 168, 252, 254–271, 471–474, 477, 516
reciprocal. *See* reflexive/reciprocal
reduplication
– adverbs 85, 192, 251
– noun stems
  – distributive 192–195, 222
  – dual 192–193
  – plural 193–195
– phonological form 231
– prosodic emphasis 539, 557–559
– quasi-reduplication 85, 87, 544, 546, 556
– verb stems
  – argument plurality 250–251
  – habitual 25, 99, 249–250, 266–267, 271
  – intensification 105–108, 173, 251
  – iterative 249–251
  – quasi-reduplicative negative suffix 85–87, 102, 108, 165
– vowel change 48, 85–87, 249, 556
referential properties
– animate 119, 123, 129
– human 129, 186, 187, 191, 403, 408–417, 446, 461
– inanimate 129, 155, 193, 298, 406, 411, 451
– non-human 403, 410, 412, 414–416, 446, 461
reflexive/reciprocal 11, 19, 88–89, 93–96, 151–154, 198, 199, 215–219, 462
relator nouns
– adverbs 145–146
– causal 141–142
– locational 131, 139–141
– locational/temporal 131, 139–141
– locative 133–135, 173
– subordinators 102, 141, 144–145
– temporal 139–141, 171–173
relativization

– A 361
– circumstantial (interpretation) 303
– externally-headed 360–365
– headless 392
– inherent (interpretation) 372, 383
– instrumental 363
– internally-headed 366–368
– locative 362–363
– O 362, 368
– possessors 364
– post-head 365–368
– pre-head 360–365
– S 360–365
religion 3, 53
reportative 560–563
resyllabification 34, 59, 60
Ri-Bhoi 24, 25, 50
restrictive focus 287, 320, 464, 472, 482–485
role marking
– unmarked 445–450
– 'non-subject' 450–455
– 'locative' 448, 455–458
– semantically marked
  – agent 458
  – comitative 458–460
  – goal 460
  – instrument 459–460
  – source 458

script 7, 29, 33, 34
semantic roles. *See* role marking
sesquisyllabic 77–78, 80, 82, 96
singular 13, 37, 118, 127, 149, 289, 435
Sino-Tibetan. *See* Tibeto-Burman
sociolect 23, 32, 49
South-Central 7, 11. *See also* 'Kuki-Chin'
Southeast Asia 7, 230, 308, 493
speech act participant cross-referencing (non-subject) 200–213
stress 80–81
subordinators 144–145, 176–178
superlative 105–107, 191–192, 233
syllables
– resyllabification 34, 59, 60
– sesquisyllables 83
– syllable boundary 33, 34
– syllable types 59, 61

tail-head linkage 510, 532, 534–536

Tamangic 167, 273, 345
Tangkhul 10, 166
Tenyidie 166, 339
Tibeto-Burman 1, 9–14, 16, 19, 61, 80, 144, 150, 161, 166, 167, 175, 183, 204, 213, 356, 393, 487, 518, 534
tone
– compounds 75–76
– glottalization 34, 62, 72, 76, 77, 80, 83
– grammatical functions 78–80
– identifying tones 67, 76–77
– low contrastiveness 68
– low functional load 67–72
– mid versus high tones 69–70
– production-perception mismatch 70
– prosody 70–72
– representation 77–78
– stopped syllables 62, 64, 67, 77
– interaction between stress and tone 80
– syllable types 76–77
– tone change 19, 48, 63, 67, 70–72, 77, 88–91, 95, 96
– toneless 73, 74
– tone sandhi 72–73
– tongue twister 66
topic
– assertive copy verb construction 551, 552
– conditional 274, 516–517
– framing function of adverbs 170
– (marking) complement clauses 275, 512–515
– (marking) main clauses 523–525, 574–577
– possessor 420–422
– subordinate clauses 381–384
– topic enclitic 170
– topic functions 465, 467
– topic-switch 464, 468–471, 537
transitivity 19, 169
translocative 236, 347

universal quantification

– pro-adverbs 150, 157–160, 162–163
– pronouns 161–162, 391
variation
– allomorphic variation 92
– allophony 53, 61, 174
– argument structure 238–242, 423–427
– dialectal variation 23, 25, 203, 205
– free variation 49, 54
– lexemes 23, 25, 27–28
– marginal vowels 57–59
– palatal 51, 53, 60–61
– prefix vowels 92–95
– restrictive focus 472, 481–485
– rhotic 51, 53, 59, 60
venitive. See cislocative
verbs
– action verbs 231, 232, 255–257
– elaborate expressions 181, 196, 337, 533, 541, 543–550
– prototypical verbs 103, 106, 107, 110, 116, 214, 298–299, 342–343
– stative verbs 255, 258, 260, 262
– verbal negation 87, 167, 251, 322–323
– verbal predicates 254, 262, 323, 385, 493, 494
– verbhood 104, 108–109
– verb stem 197–198
verbalizer 185–186, 214
vocative 147, 570–571
vowel change 85–87, 556
vowel insertion 53

universal quantification
– pro-adverbs 149, 156–159, 161–162
– pronouns 149–161, 184, 191, 203, 205, 264, 294–296, 391, 431–432, 580

zero anaphora 152, 402, 425, 429–433, 531

Author index

Benedict, Paul K. 169, 170, 243
Bickel, Balthasar 356, 405, 427
Burling, Robbins 9, 10, 57, 493

Chelliah, Shobhana Lakshmi 183
Croft, William 115–116

DeLancey, Scott 16–18, 49, 124, 356

Grüßner, Karl-Heinz 1, 2, 12, 31–32, 34, 38, 45, 48–50, 53, 61–63, 65, 66, 74, 75, 78–80, 88, 89, 92, 93, 106, 110, 117, 119, 123, 127, 129, 147, 148, 155, 169, 170, 175, 176, 183, 185, 186, 214, 219, 220, 224, 263, 341, 359, 393, 498, 501, 504, 555, 556, 564, 582

Joseph, U. V. 12–14, 28, 40, 119, 175

Kro, Bidor Sing 33, 40, 41, 187, 255

Lyall, Sir Charles 11, 16, 31

Matisoff, James A. 50, 60, 61, 80, 166, 170, 214, 349, 546

Ozerov, Pavel 550

Peterson, David A. 7, 549
Phangcho, Morningkeey 5, 40, 147
Post, Mark W. 224, 331

Scott, James C. 7, 49
Stack, Edward 16, 31

Teron, Longkam 4, 8, 24–26, 28, 31, 33
Tumung, Rajendra 24, 25, 33

www.ingramcontent.com/pod-product-compliance
Lightning Source LLC
Chambersburg PA
CBHW060255240426
43661CB00060B/2800